UNIVERSAL
DICTIONARY

LANGENSCHEIDT

DIZIONARIO
UNIVERSALE

GW00370605

INSIGHT
TRAVEL DICTIONARY
Italian

Italian-English
English-Italian

APA PUBLICATIONS
Part of the Langenscheidt Publishing Group

L

Contents
Indice

Abbreviations

Abbreviazioni

The tilde (~, when the initial letter changes: ⌒) stands for the catchword at the beginning of the entry or the part of it preceding the vertical bar (|).

Examples:

abdicate|; ~ion = abdication.

china; ⌒ = China.

Easter; ⌒n = eastern.

La tilde (~, quando l'iniziale cambia: ⌒) sostituisce la voce guida intera, oppure la parte che precede la riga verticale (|).

Esempi:

abdicate|; ~ion = abdication.

china; ⌒ = China.

Easter; ⌒n = eastern.

a, adj adjective, *aggettivo*
abbr abbreviation, *abbreviazione*
adv adverb, *avverbio*
aer aeronautics, *aeronautica*
agr agriculture, *agricoltura*
Am American English, *inglese americano*
anat anatomy, *anatomia*
aut automobilism, *automobilismo*
biol biology, *biologia*
bot botany, *botanica*
Brit British English, *inglese britannico*
cf confer, *confronta*
chem chemistry, *chimica*
com, comm commercial, *commerciale*
conj conjunction, *congiunzione*

eccl ecclesiastic, *ecclesiastico*
elec electricity, *elettricità*
etc et cetera, and so on, *eccetera*
f feminine, *femminile*
fam familiar, *familiare*
fig figurative, *figurato*
for forensic, law, *legge*
gast gastronomy, *gastronomia*
geog geography, *geografia*
gram grammar, *grammatica*
interj interjection, *interiezione*
irr irregular, *irregolare*
m masculine, *maschile*
mat mathematics, *matematica*
mech mechanics, *meccanica*
med medical, *medicina*
mil military, *militare*

mus music, *musica*

naut nautical, *nautico*

o.s. oneself, *sé (stesso)*

paint painting, *pittura*

phot photography, *fotografia*

pl plural, *plurale*

poet poetic, *poetico*

pol politics, *politico*

pp past participle, *participio passato*

prp preposition, *preposizione*

pron pers personal pronoun, *pronome personale*

pron poss possessive pronoun, *pronome possessivo*

qc, q.c something, *qualcosa*

qu, q.u someone, *qualcuno*

rail railway, *ferrovia*

s substantive, *sostantivo*

Scot Scottish *scozzese*

sg singular, *singolare*

s.o. someone, *qualcuno*

s.th. something, *qualcosa*

surg surgery, *chirurgia*

tel telephone, *telefono*

thea theatre, *teatro*

v/d defective verb, *verbo difettivo*

v/i intransitive verb, *verbo intransitivo*

v/r reflexive verb, *verbo riflessivo*

v/t transitive verb, *verbo transitivo*

Pronuncia delle parole inglesi

Guide to pronunciation of English words

Vocali e dittonghi

[a:]	*a* molto lunga, più che in *mare*: *far* [fa:], *father* ['fa:ðə]
[ʌ]	*a* molto breve, più che in *paradiso*: *mother* ['mʌðə], *butter* ['bʌtə]
[æ]	*e* molto aperta e lunga, più che in *testa*: *man* [mæn], *fat* [fæt]
[ɛə]	dittongo composto di una *e* molto aperta e lunga e [ə]: *care* [kɛə], *there* [ðɛə]
[ai]	dittongo composto di [a:] e [i]: *time* [taim], *my* [mai]
[au]	dittongo composto di [a:] e [u]: *cloud* [klaud], *how* [hau]
[e]	*e* aperta e breve, più che in *bello*: *get* [get], *said* [sed]
[ei]	dittongo composto di una *e* lunga, seguita da un leggero suono di *i*: *name* [neim], *day* [dei]
[ə]	suono atono simile alla *e* nell'articolo francese *le*: *about* [ə'baut], *silent* ['sailənt]
[ə:]	forma più prolungata del suono anteriore: *her* [hə:], *bird* [bə:d]
[i]	suono molto breve tra la *i* di *fitto* e la *e* di *fetta*: *stick* [stik], *city* ['siti]
[i:]	*i* molto lunga, più che in *vino*: *need* [ni:d], *tea* [ti:]
[iə]	dittongo composto di [i] e [ə]: *here* [hiə], *fear* [fiə]
[ɔ]	suono molto aperto tra la *o* di *lotta* e la *a* di *latte*: *not* [nɔt], *wash* [wɔʃ]
[ɔ:]	*o* aperta e lunga, piu che in *noto*: *law* [lɔ:], *ball* [bɔ:l]
[uə]	dittongo composto di [u] e [ə]: *poor* [puə], *sure* [ʃuə]

o di [ɔ] e [i]:
    ɘʏ [bɔi]
    posto di una *o* lunga, seguita da un
    ʹʌo di *u*:
    ʹʃ, *bone* [boun]
    ʌolto breve tralla *u* di *tutto* e la *o* di *rotto*:
    ʹɔuk], *put* [put]
    ʌiga, più che in *fiume*:
    ʹo [fjuː], *fruit* [fruːt]

Consonanti

Le consonanti si pronunciano nella maggior parte dei casi quasi come in italiano. Le doppie si pronunciano come se fossero semplici.

[b]	come la *b* in *burro*:
	bag [bæg], *cab* [kæb]
[d]	come la *d* in *dare*:
	dear [diə], *ladder* ['lædə]
[f]	come la *f* in *forte*:
	fall [fɔːl], *laugh* [lɑːf], *coffee* ['kɔfi]
[g]	come la *g* in *gatto*:
	give [giv], *stagger* ['stægə]
[h]	suono aspirato simile a quello della *c* di *casa* dei fiorentini:
	whole [houl], *ahead* [ə'hed]
[j]	come la *i* in *ieri*:
	yes [jes], *use* [juːs], *few* [fjuː]
[k]	come la *c* in *casa*:
	come [kʌm], *back* [bæk]
[l]	come la *l* in *lungo*:
	land [lænd], *call* [kɔːl]
[m]	come la *m* in *madre*:
	mean [miːn], *summer* ['sʌmə]
[n]	come la *n* in *no*:
	night [nait], *can* [kæn]
[p]	come la *p* in *pane*:
	pot [pɔt], *top* [tɔp]

[r]	una *r* gutturale che si pronuncia soltanto quando precede una vocale:
	right [rait], *carol* ['kærəl]
[s]	*s* aspra come in *sono*:
	cycle ['saikl], *sun* [sʌn], *listen* ['lisn]
[t]	come la *t* in *torre*:
	take [teik], *letter* ['letə]
[v]	come la *v* in *valore*:
	vain [vein], *cover* ['kʌvə], *of* [ɔv]
[w]	come la *u* in *uomo*:
	wait [weit], *quaint* [kweint]
[z]	*s* dolce come in *rosa*:
	rose [rouz], *disease* [di'zi:z]
[ŋ]	come la *n* in *banca*:
	bring [briŋ], *singer* ['siŋə]
[ʃ]	come *sce* in *scena*:
	she [ʃi:], *machine* [mə'ʃi:n]
[tʃ]	come *ce* in *cento*:
	chair [tʃɛə], *rich* [ritʃ]
[dʒ]	come *ge* in *gente*:
	join [dʒɔin], *range* [reindʒ]
[ʒ]	suono sonoro corrispondente di [ʃ] che non esiste in italiano:
	leisure ['leʒə], *usual* ['ju:ʒuəl]
[θ]	non esiste in italiano:
	think [θiŋk], *oath* [ouθ]
[ð]	non esiste in italiano:
	the [ðə], *lather* ['lɑ:ðə]
'	il segno dell'accento viene sempre collocato prima della sillaba accentata, es. *ability* [ə'biliti]

Trascrizione fonetica dei suffissi

Ecco la trascrizione fonetica dei suffissi che per economia di spazio tralasceremo di indicare nelle singole voci del dizionario:

-ability [-əbiliti]
-able [-əbl]
-age [-idʒ]
-al [-(ə)l]
-ally [-(ə)li]
-an [-(ə)n]
-ance [-(ə)ns]
-ancy [-ənsi]
-ant [-ənt]
-ar [-ə]
-ary [-(ə)ri]
-ation [eiʃ(ə)n]
-cious [-ʃəs]
-cy [-si]
-dom [-dəm]
-ed [-d; -t; -id]
-edness [-dnis; -tnis; -idnis]
-ee [-i:]
-en [-n]
-ence [-(ə)ns]
-ent [-(ə)nt]
-er [-ə]
-ery [-əri]
-ess [-is]
-fication [-fikeiʃ(ə)n]
-ial [-(ə)l]
-ian [-(jə)n]
-ible [-əbl]
-ic(s) [-ik(s)]
-ical [-ik(ə)l]

-ily [-ili]
-iness [-inis]
-ing [-iŋ]
-ish [-iʃ]
-ism [-iz(ə)m]
-ist [-ist]
-istic [-istik]
-ite [-ait]
-ity [-iti]
-ive [-iv]
-ization [-aizeiʃ(ə)n]
-ize [-aiz]
-izing [-aiziŋ]
-less [-lis]
-ly [-li]
-ment(s) [-mənt(s)]
-ness [-nis]
-oid [-ɔid]
-oidic [-ɔidik]
-or [-ə]
-ous [-əs]
-ry [-ri]
-ship [-ʃip]
-(s)sion [-ʃ(ə)n]
-sive [-siv]
-ties [-tiz]
-tion [-ʃ(ə)n]
-tious [-ʃəs]
-trous [-trəs]
-try [-tri]
-y [-i]

The Italian alphabet and its equivalent English pronunciation

L'alfabeto italiano e la pronuncia inglese equivalente

a	**ma**re	as in f**a**ther but shorter
b	**ba**bbo	as in English
c	**c**erto	before *e* and *i* as *ch* in **ch**urch;
	canto	before *a, o, u* almost as in **c**ake
d	**d**ado	as in English
e		has two sounds:
	b**e**llo	open as in b**e**d
	n**e**ve	there's no equivalent in English; the open stressed *e* is indicated by a grave accent: *è*
f	**f**orte	as in English
g	**g**elo	before *e* and *i* as in **g**eneral;
	gatto	before *a, o, u* as in **g**ate
h	**h**anno	not pronounced
i	v**i**no	as in mach**i**ne
l	**l**ana	as in English
m	**m**adre	as in English
n	**n**on	as in English
o		has two sounds:
	l**o**tta	open as in p**o**t
	n**o**me	closed, almost as in **o**rder; the open stressed *o* is indicated by a grave accent: *ò*
p	**p**ane	as in English
r	**r**otto	produced with the tongue against the upper teeth
s		has two sounds:
	sole	unvoiced as in ca**s**e
	ro**s**a	voiced as in chee**s**e
t	**t**utto	as in English
u	fi**u**me	as *oo* in c**oo**l but shorter

v	**venire**	as in English
z		has two sounds:
	pre**zz**o	unvoiced as *ts* in ha**ts**
	me**zz**o	voiced as *ds* in mai**ds**
j	⎫	these letters do not
k	⎪	belong to the Italian
w	⎬	alphabet and are
x	⎪	found only in foreign
y	⎭	words

Grouped consonants

ch employed only before *e* and *i* to retain the hard sound of *c*, e.g. *che, chi, chiamare*

gh similarly employed to retain the hard *g* before *e* and *i*, e.g. *luoghi, laghi*

gl before *i* resembling English *lli* in bi**lli**ards, e.g. *gli, biglietto*

gn resemble the English *ni* in o**ni**on, e.g. *ogni, compagno*

qu has the value of the English *qu* in **qu**ick, e.g. *qui, quelli*

A

a [ei, ə] un, una, uno

aback [əˈbæk]: **be taken ~** rimanere sconcertato

abandon [əˈbændən] *v/t* abbandonare; **~ment** abbandono *m*

abashed [əˈbæʃt] confuso

abate [əˈbeit] *v/t* (*anger, pain*) calmarsi; (*waters*) ritirarsi

abb|ess [ˈæbis] (ab)badessa *f*; **~ey** [ˈ~i] abbazia *f*; **~ot** [ˈ~ət] abate *m*

abbreviat|e [əˈbriːvieit] *v/t* abbreviare; **~ion** abbreviazione *f*

abdicate [ˈæbdikeit] *v/i* abdicare

abdomen [ˈæbdəmen] addome *m*

abduct [æbˈdʌkt] *v/t* rapire

abeyance [əˈbeiəns]: **in ~** in sospeso

abhor [əbˈhɔː] *v/t* aborrire; **~rence** [ˈ~rəns] orrore *m*; **~rent** odioso; ripugnante

abide [əˈbaid] *v/t*, *v/i*, *irr* attenere; sopportare

ability [əˈbiliti] abilità *f*

abject [ˈæbdʒekt] abietto

abjure [əbˈdʒuə] *v/t* abiurare; ripudiare

able [eibl] capace abile; **be ~ to** essere capace di

abnormal [æbˈnɔːməl] anormale

aboard [əˈbɔːd] a bordo; **all ~** tutti a bordo

aboli|sh [əˈbɔliʃ] *v/t* abolire; **~tion** [æbouˈliʃən] abolizione *f*

A-bomb [ˈeibɔm] bomba *f* atomica

abominable [əˈbɔminəbl] abominevole

abortion [əˈbɔːʃən] aborto *m*

abound [əˈbaund] *v/i* abbondare

about [əˈbaut] *prp* intorno a; vicino a; pressappoco; all'incirca; intorno; **be ~ to** stare per

above [əˈbʌv] sopra, al di sopra; **~ all** soprattutto

abreast [əˈbrest] allineati; **walk ~** camminare sottobraccio con qu.; **be ~ of** essere al corrente

abridge [əˈbridʒ] *v/t* abbreviare

abrupt [əˈbrʌpt] brusco

abscess [ˈæbsis] ascesso *m*

absence [ˈæbsəns] assenza *f*

absent [ˈæbsənt] *a* assente; [æbˈsent] *v/r* assentarsi; **~minded** distratto

absolute [ˈæbsəluːt] assoluto

absolve [əbˈzɔlv] *v/t* assolvere

absor|b [əbˈsɔːb] v/t assorbire; **~ption** assorbimento m

abstain [əbˈstein] v/i astenersi da; **total ~er** astemio m

abstinence [ˈæbstinəns] astinenza f

abstract [ˈæbstrækt] a astratto; s riassunto m; **in the ~** in teoria; [ʌˈstrækt] v/t astrarre; riassumere; **~ed** [ʌˈstræktid] distratto

absurd [əbˈsəːd] assurdo; **~ity** assurdità f

abundan|ce [əˈbʌndəns] abbondanza f; **~t** abbondante

abus|e [əˈbjuːs] s abuso m; [ʌz] v/t abusare di; **~ive** abusivo

abyss [əˈbis] abisso m

academ|ic [ækəˈdemik] accademico; **~y** [əˈkædəmi] accademia f

accelerat|e [əkˈseləreit] v/t accelerare; **~ion** [ʌˈreiʃən] accelerazione f; **~or** acceleratore m

accent [ˈæksənt] accento m; **~uate** [ækˈsentjueit] v/t accentuare; **~uation** accentuazione f

accept [əkˈsept] v/t accettare; **~ance** accettazione f

access [ˈækses] accesso m; **~ible** [əkˈsesəbl] accessibile

accessory [əkˈsesəri] s, a accessorio (m)

accident [ˈæksidənt] incidente m; **by ~** per caso; **~ insurance** assicurazione f

contro gli infortuni; **~al** per caso

acclimatize [əˈklaimətaiz] v/t acclimatare; v/r acclimatarsi

accomodat|e [əˈkɔmədeit] v/t accomodare; conciliare; obbligare; alloggiare; **~ing** compiacente; **~ion** alloggio m; **~ seating** posti m/pl a sedere

accompan|iment [əˈkʌmpənimənt] accompagnamento m; **~y** v/t accompagnare

accomplice [əˈkɔmplis] complice m

accomplish [əˈkɔmpliʃ] v/t compiere; completare; finire; **~ed** perfetto; colto; **~ment** talento m; compimento m

accord [əˈkɔːd] s accordo m; consenso m; v/t accordare; concedere; **~ing to** conforme a

accordeon [əˈkɔːdjən] fisarmonica f

account [əˈkaunt] conto m; resoconto m; racconto m; **on ~ of** per ragione di; **on my ~** per conto mio; **on no ~** per nessuna ragione, in nessun caso; **~ for** rendere conto di; spiegare; **take into ~** prendere in considerazione; **~ant** ragioniere m; contabile m; **current ~** conto m corrente

accredit [əˈkredit] v/t accreditare

accrue [əˈkruː] v/i provenire, derivare, accumularsi

accumulate [ə'kju:mjuleit] v/t accumulare

accura|cy ['ækjurəsi] accuratezza f, precisione f; **~te** ['~it] accurato, preciso

accusation [ækju(:)'zeiʃən] accusa f; **~e** [ə'kju:z] v/t accusare; **~er** accusatore m

accustom [ə'kʌstəm] v/t abituare; **become ~ed to** v/r abituarsi a

ace [eis] asso m

acetic [ə'si:tik] **acid** acido m acetico; **~ylene** [ə'setili:n] acetilene m

ache [eik] s dolore m; v/i far male, dolere

achieve [ə'tʃi:v] v/t compiere; condurre a termine; raggiungere; ottenere; **~ment** compimento m; realizzazione f; successo m; raggiungimento m

acid ['æsid] acido m

acknowledg|e [ək'nɔlidʒ] v/t riconoscere, ammettere; **~ receipt** accusare ricevuta; **~ment** riconoscimento m, ammissione f

acme ['ækmi] acme f

acne ['ækni] acne f

acorn ['eikɔ:n] ghianda f

acoustics [ə'ku:stiks] pl acustica f

acquaint [ə'kweint] v/t far sapere, far conoscere; **be ~ed with** conoscere; **~ance** conoscenza f

acqui|re [ə'kwaiə] v/t acquistare; **~sition** [ˌækwi-'ziʃən] acquisto m

acquit [ə'kwit] v/t assolvere; **~tal** assoluzione f

acre ['eikə] acro m (4047 metri quadrati)

acrobat ['ækrəbæt] acrobata m, f; **~ics** pl acrobazie f/pl

across [ə'krɔs] attraverso; **go ~, come ~** v/t attraversare; **come ~** v/t capitare

act [ækt] s atto m; v/t agire; thea recitare; **~ing** thea recitazione f; **~ion** azione f

activ|e ['æktiv] attivo; **~ity** [æk'tiviti] attività f

act|or ['æktə] attore m; **~ress** attrice f

actual ['æktʃuəl] effettivo, vero

acute [ə'kju:t] acuto

adapt [ə'dæpt] v/t adattare; **~er** riduttore m

add [æd] v/t aggiungere; addizionare; **~ up** far la somma, sommare

adder ['ædə] vipera f

addict ['ædikt] tossicomane m

addition [ə'diʃən] aggiunta f; addizione f; **in ~ to** inoltre

address [ə'dres] s indirizzo m; v/t indirizzare; **~ o.s. to** rivolgersi a; **~ee** [ædre'si:] destinatario m

adequate ['ædikwit] adeguato, sufficiente

adhere [əd'hiə] v/i aderire; **~nt** aderente

adhesive [əd'hi:siv] adesivo; **~ tape, ~ plaster** cerotto m

adieu [ə'dju:] addio

adjacent [ə'dʒeisənt] adiacente

adjective ['ædʒiktiv] aggettivo *m*

adjoin [ə'dʒɔin] *v/t* essere adiacente a

adjourn [ə'dʒəːn] *v/t* rimandare, rinviare

adjunct ['ædʒʌŋkt] accessorio

adjure [ə'dʒuə] *v/t* scongiurare

adjust [ə'dʒʌst] *v/t* aggiustare

administ|er [əd'ministə] *v/t* amministrare; **~ration** amministrazione *f*; **~rative** [~trətiv] amministrativo; **~rator** amministratore *m*

admirable ['ædmərəbl] ammirevole

admiral ['ædmərəl] ammiraglio *m*

admir|ation [ædmə'reiʃən] ammirazione *f*; **~e** [əd'maiə] *v/t* ammirare

admiss|ible [əd'misəbl] ammissibile; **~ion** ammissione *f*; **~ion (ticket)** (biglietto *m* d') ingresso *m*

admit [əd'mit] *v/t* ammettere; confessare; **~tance** ammissione *f*; **no ~tance** vietato l'ingresso

admonish [əd'mɔniʃ] *v/t* ammonire

adolescence [ˌædou'lesəns] adolescenza *f*

adopt [ə'dɔpt] *v/t* adottare; **~ion** adozione *f*

ador|able [ə'dɔːrəbl] adorabile; **~ation** [ædɔː'reiʃən] adorazione *f*; **~e** [ə'dɔː] *v/t* adorare

adorn [ə'dɔːn] *v/t* adornare

adroit [ə'drɔit] destro; abile

adult [ə'dʌlt] *a, s* adulto (*m*)

adulter|ate [ə'dʌltəreit] *v/t* adulterare; sofisticare; **~er** adultero(a) *m* (*f*); **~y** adulterio *m*

advance [əd'vɑːns] *s* avanzamento *m*; progresso *m*; *v/i* avanzare; progredire; **in ~** in anticipo

advantage [əd'vɑːntidʒ] vantaggio *m*; **take ~ of** approfittare di; **~ous** [ædvən'teidʒəs] vantaggioso

advent ['ædvent] avvento *m*

adventur|e [əd'ventʃə] avventura *f*; **~er** avventuriero *m*; **~ous** avventuroso

adverb ['ædvəːb] avverbio *m*

advers|ary ['ædvəsəri] avversario *m*; **~e** [~'əːs] avverso

advertis|e ['ædvətaiz] *v/t* fare pubblicità; mettere una inserzione sul giornale; **~ement** [əd'vəːtismənt] reclame *f*; avviso *m* pubblicitario; inserzione *f*; **~ing** réclame *f*; pubblicità *f*; **~ing film** film *m* pubblicitario

advice [əd'vais] consiglio *m*

advis|able [əd'vaizəbl] consigliabile; **~e** *v/t* consigliare

advocate ['ædvəkeit] *s* sostenitore *m*; *for* avvocato *m*; *v/t* sostenere; difendere

aerial ['ɛəriəl] *a* aereo; *s* antenna *f*

aero|drome ['ɛərədroum] aerodromo *m*; **~nautics** [ˌ~'nɔːtiks] aeronautica *f*;

~plane aeroplano *m*

aesthetic [i:s'θetik] estetico; **~s** *pl* estetica *f*

affable ['æfəbl] affabile

affair [ə'fεə] affare *m*, faccenda *f*

affect [ə'fekt] *v/t* riguardare, interessare; colpire; ripercuotere su; commuovere; **~ed** affettato; commosso; **~ion** affetto *m*; infezione *f*; **~ionate** [ι'] affettuoso

affinity [ə'finiti] affinità *f*

affirm [ə'fə:m] *v/t* affermare; **~ation** [ˌæfə'meiʃən] affermazione *f*; **~ative** [ə'fə:mətiv] affermativo

afflict [ə'flikt] *v/t* affliggere di; **~ion** afflizione *f*

affluen|ce ['æfluəns] affluenza *f*; **~t** affluente *m*

afford [ə'fɔ:d] *v/t* fornire; permettersi; **I can't ~** it non me lo posso permettere

affront [ə'frʌnt] *s* affraggio *m*; *v/t* affrontare; oltraggiare

afraid [ə'freid] impaurito; **be ~** avere paura

Africa ['æfrikə] Africa *f*; **~n** *s, a* africano

after ['ɑːftə] *prp, adv* dopo; *conj* dopo che; **~noon** pomeriggio *m*; **~wards** dopo

again [ə'gen] di nuovo; **now and ~** ogni tanto; **~ and ~** ripetutamente

against contro

age [eidʒ] *s* età *f*; *v/t, v/i* invecchiare; **of ~** maggiorenne; **under ~** minorenne; **~d** anziano

agen|cy ['eidʒənsi] agenzia *f*; **~t** agente *m*, rappresentante *m*

aggrandize ['ægrəndaiz] *v/t* ingrandire

aggravat|e ['ægrəveit] *v/t* aggravare; esasperare

aggregat|e ['ægrigeit] *v/t* aggregare

aggress|ion [ə'greʃən] aggressione *f*; **~ive** aggressivo: **~or** aggressore

agile ['ædʒail] agile

agitat|e ['ædʒiteit] *v/t* agitare; **~ion** agitazione *f*; **~or** agitatore *m*

ago [ə'gou] fa; **a year ~** un anno fa; **long ~** molto tempo fa

agon|izing ['ægənaiziŋ] angoscioso; **~y** angoscia *f*

agree [ə'gri:] *v/i* essere d'accordo; andare d'accordo; **~able** piacevole; simpatico; **~ment** accordo *m*

agricultur|al [ˌægri'kʌltʃərəl] agricolo; **~e** agricoltura *f*; (*faculty*) agraria *f*; **~(al)ist** agricoltore *m*

ague ['eigju:] febbre *f* intermittente

ahead [ə'hed] avanti; **straight ~** diritto avanti

aid [eid] *s* aiuto *m*; *v/t* aiutare; **first ~** pronto soccorso *m*

ailing ['eiliŋ] sofferente

aim [eim] *s* mira *f*; scopo *m*; *v/i* mirare; **~less** senza scopo

air [εə] aria *f*; **in the open ~** all'aria aperta; **~-bed** materasso *m* pneumatico; ~ **-conditioning** condizionamento *m* dell'aria; ~ **craft**, ~ **liner**, **plane** aeroplano *m*; ~ **force** Aeronautica *f* militare; ~ **line** linea *f* aerea; **mail** posta *f* aerea; **port** aeroporto *m*; ~ **pressure** pressione *f* dell'aria; **be ~sick** sentir nausea; ~ **-tight** ermetico; ~ **traffic** traffico *m* aereo

airy ['ɛəri] arioso

aisle [ail] *church:* navata *f*; passaggio *m*

ajar [ə'dʒɑ:] socchiuso

akin [ə'kin] affine; simile

alarm [ə'lɑ:m] *s* allarme *m*; *v/t* allarmare; **clock** sveglia *f*

albino [æl'bi:nou] albino *m*

alcohol ['ælkəhɔl] alcool *m*; **ic** alcoolico

alder ['ɔ:ldə] ontano *m*

ale [eil] birra *f*

alert [ə'lə:t] attento; **be on the** ~ essere all'erta

alibi ['ælibai] alibi *m*

alien ['eiljən] *s, a* straniero (*m*); ~ **to** contrario a

alight [ə'lait] *v/i* atterrare; scendere

alike [ə'laik] simile

alimony ['æliməni] alimenti *m/pl*

alive [ə'laiv] vivente; vivo

all [ɔ:l] tutto, *pl* tutti; ♀ **Fools' Day** 1 Aprile; ~ **right** va bene; ♀ **Saints' Day** 1 Novembre; ♀ **Souls' Day** 2 Novembre; ~ **at once** tutt'a un tratto; ~ **of**

us noi tutti; **not at** ~ niente affatto

allege [ə'ledʒ] *v/t* allegare

allegorical [æle'gɔrikl] allegorico; **orical** allegorico

alleviate [ə'li:vieit] *v/t* alleviare

alley ['æli] vicolo *m*

alli|ance [ə'laiəns] alleanza *f*; ~**ed** alleato

allocate ['æləkeit] *v/t* assegnare

allot [ə'lɔt] *v/t* assegnare; ~**ment** lotto *m*

allow [ə'lau] *v/t* permettere; concedere

allowance [ə'lauəns] rendita *f*; permesso *m*; riduzione *f*; **family ~s** *pl* assegni *m/pl* familiari

alloy ['æloi] lega *f*

allu|de [ə'lu:d] *v/i* alludere; **sion** allusione *f*

allure [ə'ljuə] *v/t* attirare

ally [ə'lai] *s* alleato *m*; *v/i* allearsi con

almighty [ɔ:l'maiti] onnipotente

almond ['ɑ:mənd] mandorla *f*

almost ['ɔ:lmoust] quasi

alms [ɑ:mz] *pl* elemosina *f*

aloft [ə'lɔft] in alto

alone [ə'loun] solo; **let** (*or* **leave**) ~ lasciare stare; **let** ~ tanto meno

along [ə'lɔŋ] *prp* lungo; *adv* lungo; avanti

aloof [ə'lu:f] distante

aloud [ə'laud] ad alta voce

alphabet ['ælfəbit] alfabeto *m*

Alp|ine ['ælpain] alpino; **~s** *pl* Alpi *f/pl*

already [ɔːl'redi] già

also ['ɔːlsəu] anche

altar ['ɔːltə] altare *m*

alter ['ɔːltə] *v/t* cambiare; modificare; **~ation** cambiamento *m*; modifica *f*

alternat|e ['ɔːltəneit] alternativo; **~ing current** corrente *f* alternata; **~ive** alternativa *f*

although [ɔːl'ðou] sebbene, benché

altitude ['æltitjuːd] altitudine *f*

altogether [ɔːltə'geðə] completamente; nell'insieme

always ['ɔːlweiz] sempre

am [æm]: **I ~** (io) sono

amalgamate [ə'mælgəmeit] *v/t* amalgamare; *v/i* amalgamarsi

amass [ə'mæs] *v/t* ammassare

amateur ['æmətə:] dilettante *m*

amaz|e [ə'meiz] *v/t* stupire; **~ement** stupore *m*; meraviglia *f*; **~ing** stupefacente

ambassador [æm'bæsədə] ambasciatore *m*

amber ['æmbə] ambra *f*

ambigu|ity [ˌæmbi'gjuiti] ambiguità *f*; **~ous** ambiguo

ambition [æm'biʃən] ambizione *f*; **~ous** ambizioso

ambulance ['æmbjuləns] ambulanza *f*

ambush ['æmbuʃ] imbosca-ta *f*; **to fall into an ~** cadere in un'imboscata

amen ['ɑː'men] amen *m*

amend [ə'mend] *v/t* emendare; correggere; **~ment** emendamento *m*; **~s** *pl*: **to make ~s** riparare a

America [ə'merikə] America *f*; **~n** *s*, *a* americano (*m*); **~nize** *v/t* americanizzare

amiable ['eimjəbl] cordiale

amicable ['æmikəbl] amichevole

amid(st) [ə'mid(st)] in mezzo a; tra

amiss [ə'mis]: **what's ~?** c'è che non va?; **take ~** aversene a male

ammunition [æmju'niʃən] munizioni *f/pl* di guerra

amnesty ['æmnisti] amnistia *f*

among(st) [ə'mʌŋ(st)] tra, fra

amount [ə'maunt] *s* somma *f*; quantità *f*; *v/i* ammontare

amperage [æm'pɛəridʒ] amperaggio *m*

ample ['æmpl] ampio; **~ify** *v/t* amplificare

amputat|e ['æmpjuteit] *v/t* amputare; **~ion** amputazione *f*

amulet ['æmjulit] amuleto *m*

amuse [ə'mjuːz] *v/t* divertire; *v/r* divertirsi; **~ment** divertimento *m*

an [æn, ən] un, una, uno

an(a)esthetic [ænis'θetik] anestetico *m*

analog|ous [ə'næləgəs] analogo; **~y** [~dʒi] analogia *f*

analy|se, *Am* **~ze** ['ænəlaiz]
v/t analizzare; **~sis** [ə'næləsis] analisi *f*

anatomy [ə'nætəmi] anatomia *f*

ancest|or ['ænsistə] antenato *m*; **~ry** discendenza *f*

anchor ['æŋkə] *s* ancora *f*; *v/t, v/i* ancorare

anchovy ['æntʃəvi] acciuga *f*

ancient ['einʃənt] antico *m*

and [ænd, ənd] e; **~ so on** e così via

anew [ə'nju:] di nuovo

angel ['eindʒəl] angelo *m*

anger ['æŋgə] ira *f*; rabbia *f*

angina [æn'dʒainə] angina *f*

angle ['æŋgl] *s* angolo *m*; *v/i* pescare *(all'amo)*

Anglican ['æŋglikən] *s, a* anglicano *(m)*

Anglo-Saxon ['æŋgləu-'sæksən] *s, a* anglosassone *(m)*

angry ['æŋgri] arrabbiato; **get ~** arrabbiarsi

anguish ['æŋgwiʃ] angoscia *f*

angular ['æŋgjulə] angoloso

animal ['æniməl] animale *m*

animat|e ['ænimeit] *v/t* animare; **~ed cartoon** disegno *m* animato; **~ion** animazione *f*

animosity [æni'mositi] animosità *f*

anise ['ænis] anice *m*

ankle ['æŋkl] caviglia *f*

annex ['æneks] annesso *m*

annihilate [ə'naiəleit] *v/t* annientare

anniversary [æni'və:səri]

anniversario *m*

annotat|e ['ænəteit] *v/t* annotare; **~ion** annotazione *f*

announce [ə'nauns] *v/t* annunciare; **~ment** annuncio *m*

annoy [ə'nɔi] *v/t* seccare, dare fastidio; **~ance** seccatura *f*, fastidio *m*

annual ['ænjuəl] annuale

annul [ə'nʌl] *v/t* annullare; **~ment** annullamento *m*

anodyne ['ænəudain] analgesico *m*

anomalous [ə'nɔmələs] anomalo

anonymous [ə'nɔniməs] anonimo

another [ə'nʌðə] un altro, un'altra; **one ~** l'un l'altro

answer ['ɑ:nsə] *s* risposta *f*; *v/t* rispondere

ant [ænt] formica *f*

antagonist [æn'tægənist] antagonista *m*, *f*

antarctic [ænt'ɑ:ktik] antartico

antelope ['æntiloup] antilope *f*

anthem ['ænθəm] antifona *f*; **(national) ~** inno *m* (nazionale)

anti ['ænti] anti-; **~biotic** [‚æntibai'ɔtik] *s, a* antibiotico *(m)*

anticipat|e [æn'tisipeit] *v/t* anticipare; **~ion** anticipazione *f*

anti|dote ['æntidout] antidoto *m*; **~freeze** [‚~'fri:z] anticongelante *m*

antipath|etic [‚æntipə'θetik]

antipatico; **~y** [æn'tipeθi]- antipatia *f*

antiqu|ary ['æntikwəri] antiquario *m*; **~e** [æn'tiːk] antico; **~ity** [æn'tikwiti] antichità *f*

antiseptic [ænti'septik] antisettico

antlers ['æntləz] *pl* corna *f/pl*

anvil ['ænvil] incudine *f*

anxi|ety [æŋ'zaiəti] ansietà *f*; **~ous** ansioso (**for, about** di, per)

any ['eni] qualche; **not ~ longer** non più; **~body** chiunque; qualcuno; **~how** in ogni modo; **~thing** qualsiasi cosa; **~where** in qualsiasi posto

apart [ə'pɑːt] da parte; **~ment** stanza *f*; **~ments** *pl* stanze *f/pl*; alloggio *m*; **furnished ~ments** stanze *f/pl* ammobiliate

ape [eip] scimmia *f*

aperitive [ə'peritiv] aperitivo *m*

apiece [ə'piːs] l'uno; cadauno

apolog|ize [ə'pɔlədʒaiz] *v/i* scusarsi; **~y** scusa *f*

apoplexy ['æpəpleksi] apoplessia *f*

apostle [ə'pɔsl] apostolo *m*

apostrophe [ə'pɔstrəfi] apostrofe *f*

appal [ə'pɔːl] *v/t* spaventare

apparatus [æpə'reitəs] apparecchio *m*; *med* apparato *m*

apparent [ə'pærənt] mani-

festo; evidente

appeal [ə'piːl] *s* (*for*) appello *m*; attrattiva *f*; *v/i* rivolgersi a; attirare; **Court of ~** Corte *f* di appello; **~ing** supplicante

appear [ə'piə] *v/t* apparire; sembrare; **~ance** apparizione *f*; aspetto *m*; **~ances** *pl* apparenze *f/pl*

appease [ə'piːz] *v/t* placare; **~ment** placamento *m*

append [ə'pend] *v/t* appendere; **~icitis** appendicite *f*; (**vermiform**) **~ix** intestino *m* cieco

appet|ite ['æpitait] appetito *m*; **~izing** appetitoso

applaud [ə'plɔːd] *v/t* applaudire; **~se** [~z] applauso *m*

apple ['æpl] mela *f*; **~pie** torta *f* di mele

appliance [ə'plaiəns] strumento *m*; apparecchio *m*

applica|nt ['æplikənt] aspirante *m*; richiedente *m*; **~tion** applicazione *f*; domanda *f*

apply [ə'plai] *v/t* applicare; **~ o.s. to** rivolgersi a; **~ for** fare domanda per (di)

appoint [ə'pɔint] *v/t* nominare; **~ment** nomina *f*; appuntamento *m*

apportion [ə'pɔːʃən] *v/t* ripartire

appreciat|e [ə'priːʃieit] *v/t* apprezzare; **~ion** apprezzamento *m*

apprehen|d [æpri'hend] *v/t* afferrare; arrestare; **~sion** apprensione f; **~sive** apprensivo; timoroso

apprentice [ə'prentis] apprendista m, f; **~ship** tirocinio m

approach [ə'prəutʃ] s avvicinamento m; accesso m; v/t avvicinare, avvicinarsi

appropriate [ə'prəupriit] a adatto; v/t appropriarsi; **~ion** appropriazione f

approval [ə'pru:vəl] approvazione f; **on ~al** comm in prova; **~e** v/t approvare

approximate [ə'prɔksimit] approssimato

apricot ['eiprikɔt] albicocco m

April ['eipril] aprile m

apron ['eiprən] grembiule m

apt [æpt] adatto; appropriato

aquarium [ə'kwɛəriəm] acquario m

aquatic [ə'kwætik] acquatico; **~ sports** pl sport m nautico

aqueduct ['ækwidʌkt] acquedotto m

aquiline ['ækwilain] aquilino

Arab ['ærəb] s, a arabo (m); **~ia** [ə'reibjə] Arabia f; **~ian** s, a arabo (m); **~ic** s, a arabo (m)

arbitrary ['a:bitrəri] arbitrario

arbour ['a:bə] pergolato m

arc [a:k] arco m

arcade [a:'keid] portici m/pl; galleria f

arch [a:tʃ] arco m; volta f

arch(a)eolog|ist [ˌa:ki'ɔlədʒist] archeologo m; **~y** archeologia f

archaic [a:'keiik] arcaico

arch|angel ['a:keindʒəl] arcangelo m; **~bishop** arcivescovo m

archer ['a:tʃə] arciere m; **~y** tiro m dell'arco

architect ['a:kitekt] architetto m; **~ure** architettura f

archives ['a:kaivz] pl archivio m

arctic ['a:ktik] artico

ard|ent ['a:dənt] ardente; zelante; **~our** zelo m

are [a:]: **we, you, they ~** siamo, siete, sono

area ['ɛəriə] area f

Argentine ['a:dʒəntain] s Argentina f; s, a argentino (m)

argue ['a:gju:] v/t, v/i discutere; **~ment** discussione f

arid ['ærid] arido; **~ity** aridità f

arise [ə'raiz] v/i alzarsi; sorgere

arithmetic [ə'riθmətik] aritmetica f

ark [a:k] arca f

arm [a:m] s braccio m; arma f; v/t armare; **~ament** ['a:məmənt] armamento m; **~chair** poltrona f; **~ful** bracciata f

armistice ['a:mistis] armistizio m

armo(u)r ['a:mə] armatura f

armpit ['a:mpit] ascella f

arms pl armi f/pl

army ['a:mi] esercito m

around [ə'raund] intorno a; *adv* intorno

arouse [ə'rauz] *v/t* svegliare

arrange [ə'reindʒ] *v/t* disporre; mettere in ordine; fissare; **~ment** disposizione *f*; ordine *m*; progetto *m*

arrears [ə'riəz] *pl* arretrati *m/pl*

arrest [ə'rest] *s* arresto *m*; *v/t* arrestare; fermarsi

arriv|al [ə'raivəl] arrivo *m*; **~e** *v/i* arrivare

arrow ['ærou] freccia *f*

arsenic ['ɑːsnik] arsenico *m*

art [ɑːt] arte *f*; **fine ~s** *pl* belle arti *f/pl*

arteriosclerosis [ɑː'tiəriousklə'rousis] arteriosclerosi *f*

artery ['ɑːtəri] arteria *f*

artful ['ɑːtful] astuto

artichoke ['ɑːtitʃouk] carciofo *m*

article [ɑː'tikl] articolo *m*

articulat|e [ɑː'tikjuleit] *v/t* articolare

artificial [ɑːti'fiʃəl] artificiale

artillery [ɑː'tiləri] artiglieria *f*

artisan [ˌɑːti'zæn] artigiano *m*

artist ['ɑːtist] artista *m*, *f*; **~ic** [ɑː'tistik] artistico

artless senza artifizio; ingenuo

as [æz, əz]: (*time*) mentre; (*reason*) siccome; **~ big** (*così*) grande quanto; **~ far ~ possible** il più possibile; **~ far as I know** a quanto

sappia; **~ to** in quanto a; **~ an interpreter** come interprete; **~ you like** come vuoi; **so ~** in modo da

ascen|d [ə'send] *v/t*, *v/i* salire; **~sion** ascensione *f*; **~t** salita *f*

ascertain [ˌæsə'tein] *v/t* constatare; **~ment** costatazione *f*

ascribe [əs'kraib] *v/t* attribuire

aseptic [æ'septik] asettico

ash [æʃ] cenere *f*; **~es** [ˈæʃiz] *pl* ceneri *f/pl*; **~-tray** portacenere *m*; ♀ **Wednesday** mercoledi *m* delle ceneri

ashamed [ə'ʃeimd]: **be ~ of** vergognarsi *f*

ashore [ə'ʃɔː] a terra

Asia ['eiʃə] Asia *f*; **~n** *s*, asiatico (*m*); **~tic** [ˌeiʃi'ætik] *s*, asiatico (*m*)

aside [ə'said] da parte

ask [ɑːsk] *v/t* chiedere; domandare; **~ after s.o.** chiedere notizie di q.u.; **~ a favour** chiedere un favore; **~ for** chiedere di q.u.; chiedere di vedere q.u.; **to ~ forgiveness** chiedere perdono; **~ a question** fare una domanda

asleep [ə'sliːp] addormentato; **fall ~** addormentarsi

asparagus [əs'pærəgəs] asparago *m*

aspect ['æspekt] aspetto *m*

aspir|ant [əs'pairənt] *s*, *a* aspirante (*m*); **~e** [əs'paiə] *v/i* aspirare

aspirin ['æspirin] aspirina *f*

ass [æs] asino *m*

assail [əˈseil] *v/t* assalire; aggredire; **~ant** aggressore *m*

assassin [əˈsæsin] assassino *m*; **~ate** [~eit] *v/t* assassinare

assault [əˈsɔːlt] *s* assalto *m*; *v/t* assalire; aggredire

assemble [əˈsembl] *v/t* riunire; *v/i* riunirsi; **~y** assemblea *f*; *mech* montaggio *m*; **~y line** catena *f* di montaggio

assent [əˈsent] *s* consenso *m*; *v/i* acconsentire

assert [əˈsəːt] *v/t* rivendicare; affermare

assess [əˈses] *v/t* fissare; **~ment** valutazione *f* (dell'imponibile)

assets [ˈæsets] *pl com* attivo *m*; **personal** ~ beni *m/pl* mobili; **real** ~ beni *m/pl* immobili

assign [əˈsain] *v/t* assegnare; **~ment** assegnamento *m*; incarico *m*

assimilate [əˈsimileit] *v/t*, *v/i* assimilare

assist [əˈsist] *v/t* aiutare; assistere; **~ance** aiuto *m*; assistenza *f*; **~ant** assistente *m*

assizes [əˈsaiziz] *pl* corte *f* di assisi

associate [əˈsouʃieit] *s* socio *m*; *v/t* associare; *v/i* associarsi; **~ion** associazione *f*

assorted [əˈsɔːtid] assortito

assume [əˈsjuːm] *v/t* assumere; **~ption** [əˈsʌmpʃən] assunzione *f*; *eccl* Ascensione *f*

assur|ance [əˈʃuərəns] assicurazione *f*; **~e** *v/t* assicurare

asthma [ˈæsmə] asma *m*

astir [əˈstəː] in movimento; in agitazione

astonish [əsˈtɔniʃ] *v/t* stupire; **~ed** stupito; **~ing** sorprendente; **~ment** stupore *m*

astound [əsˈtaund] *v/t* sbalordire

astray [əsˈtrei] sviato

astringent [əsˈtrindʒənt] astringente

astrology [əsˈtrɔlədʒi] astrologia *f*

astronaut [ˈæstrənɔːt] astronauta *m*

asunder [əˈsʌndə] separatamente; a pezzi

asylum [əˈsailəm] manicomio *m*; **seek** ~ cercare rifugio

at [æt, ət] a; **~ church** in chiesa; **~ first** all'inizio; **~ home** a casa; **~ John's** a casa di Giovanni, da Giovanni; **~ last** infine; **~ once** subito; **~ six** alle sei

atheist [ˈeiθiist] ateo *m*

athlet|e [ˈæθliːt] atleta *m*, *f*; **~ic** [~ˈletik] atletico; **~ics** *pl* atletica *f*

Atlantic [ətˈlæntik] atlantico; **~ Ocean** oceano Atlantico

atlas [ˈætləs] atlante *m*

atmosphere [ˈætməsfiə] atmosfera *f*

atom [ˈætəm] atomo *m*; **~ic** [əˈtɔmik] atomico; **~ic bomb** bomba *f* atomica

~ic pile reattore *m* nucleare

atomize ['ætəmaiz] *v/t* (*liquids*) nebulizzare

atone [ə'toun]: **~ for s.th.** espiare q.c.

atrocious [ə'trouʃəs] atroce; **~ty** atrocità *f*

attach [ə'tætʃ] *v/t* attaccare; **~ment** attaccamento *m*

attack [ə'tæk] *s* attacco *m*; *v/t* attaccare

attempt [ə'tempt] *s* tentativo *m*; *v/t* tentare

attend [ə'tend] *v/t* frequentare; assistere a; *v/i* fare attenzione a; provvedere a; **~ance** *med* assistenza *f*; i presenti *m/pl*; **~ant** adetto *m*

attention [ə'tenʃən] attenzione *f*; **pay ~** fare attenzione

attentive attento *m*

attest [ə'test] *v/t* attestare; certificare

attic ['ætik] soffitta *f*

attitude ['ætitju:d] atteggiamento *m*; **~ of mind** disposizione *f* di mente

attorney [ə'tə:ni] procuratore *m*; avvocato *m* (*del Ministero*)

attract [ə'trækt] *v/t* attirare; **~ion** attrazione *f*; **~iveness** fascino *m*

attribut|e ['ætribju:t] *s* attributo *m*; [ə'tribju:t] *v/t* attribuire

auction ['ɔ:kʃən] asta *f*; **by ~** all'asta; **~eer** banditore *m*

audacious [ɔ:'deiʃəs] audace

audible ['ɔ:dəbl] udibile

audience ['ɔ:djəns] udienza *f*; pubblico *m*

audit ['ɔ:dit] verifica(zione) *f*

augment [ɔ:g'ment] *v/t* aumentare

August ['ɔ:gəst] agosto *m*

aunt [ɑ:nt] zia *f*

au pair girl [ou'pɛə,gə:l] ragazza *f* alla pari

auspicious [ɔ:s'piʃəs] di buon auspicio

auster|e [ɔs'tiə] austero; **~ity** [~'teriti] austerità *f*

Australia [ɔ(:)s'treiljə] Australia *f*; **~n** *a, s* australiano (*m*)

Austria ['ɔstriə] Austria *f*; **~n** *a, s* austriaco (*m*)

authentic [ɔ:'θentik] autentico

author ['ɔ:θə] autore *m*; **~ess** autrice *f*; **~itative** autorevole; autoritario; **~ity** autorità *f*; **~ities** *pl* autorità *f/pl*; **~ize** *v/t* autorizzare

autobiography [,ɔ:toubai'ɔgrəfi] autobiografia *f*

autograph ['ɔ:təgrɑ:f] autografo *m*

automatic [,ɔ:tə'mætik] automatico

automobile [,ɔ:təmou'bi:l, 'ɔ:təmoubi:l] automobile *f*

autonomy [ɔ:'tɔnəmi] autonomia *f*

autumn ['ɔ:təm] autunno *m*

auxiliary [ɔ:g'ziljəri] ausiliare

avail [ə'veil] *v/t* servire; **be of no ~** non servire a nulla;

~able disponibile

avalanche ['ævəla:nʃ] valanga f

avaric|e ['ævəris] avarizia f; **~ious** [~'riʃəs] avaro

avenge [ə'vendʒ] v/t vendicare

avenue ['ævinju:] viale m

average ['ævəridʒ] s media f; a medio; **on an ~** in media

avers|e [ə'və:s] contrario a; **~ion** avversione f

avert [ə'və:t] v/t (eyes, thought) distogliere; (danger) allontanare

aviary ['eiviəri] uccelliera f

aviation [eivi'eiʃən] aviazione f; **~or** [~'eitə] aviatore m

avoid [ə'void] v/t evitare

avow [ə'vau] v/t confessare; ammettere; **~al** confessione f

await [ə'weit] v/t aspettare

awake [ə'weik] a sveglio; v/t svegliare; v/i svegliarsi; **~n** v/t risvegliare; v/i risvegliarsi

award [ə'wɔ:d] s giudizio m; v/t aggiudicare; conferire

aware [ə'wɛə] consapevole; **be ~ of** rendersi conto di

away [ə'wei] via; lontano

aw|e [ɔ:] soggezione f; **~ful** terribile; spaventoso

awhile [ə'wail] per qualche tempo

awkward ['ɔ:kwəd] goffo

awning ['ɔniŋ] tenda f

awry [ə'rai] di traverso

ax(e) [æks] ascia f [storto (**axis** ['æksis], pl **axes** asse f

axle ['æksl] asse f (su cui girano le ruote)

azure ['eiʒə, 'æʒə] azzurro

B

babble ['bæbl] v/t balbettare; rivelare (un segreto)

babe [beib] bimbo m

baboon [bə'bu:n] babbuino m

baby ['beibi] bimbo m; **~ carriage** carrozzella f; **~hood** prima infanzia f

bachelor ['bætʃələ] scapolo m; **~ of Arts** laureato m in lettere

back [bæk] s dorso m; schiena f; schienale m; retro m; a arretrato; posteriore; adv indietro; **look ~** guardare indietro; **put ~** rimettere;

send ~ rimandare; v/t aiutare; spalleggiare; **~ a horse** puntare su un cavallo

back|bone spina f dorsale; **~fire** accensione f difettosa; **~ground** sfondo m; (family) ambiente f; **~hand** rovescio m; **~ing** appoggio m; **~stairs** pl retroscale f; **~ward** a arretrato; tardivo; riluttante; **~ward(s)** adv (all')indietro; al rovescio; **~ wheel** ruota f posteriore

bacon ['beikən] pancetta f; lardo m

bacterium [bæk'tɪərɪəm], pl **-a** [-ɪə] batterio m

bad [bæd] cattivo; **that's too ~** che peccato!; **-ly** male; **-ly wounded** gravemente ferito

badge [bædʒ] distintivo m

badger ['bædʒə] tasso m

badminton ['bædmɪntən] volano m

baffle ['bæfl] v/t impedire; rendere perplesso

bag [bæg] sacco m; borsa f; **-gage** bagaglio m; **-gy** largo; **-pipes** pl cornamusa f

bail [beɪl] cauzione f; **go ~ for** essere garante di

bait [beɪt] esca f

bake [beɪk] v/t cuocere in forno; **-r** fornaio m; **-ry** panetteria f

balance ['bæləns] bilancio m; equilibrio m; armonia f; comm differenza f; saldo m; v/t bilanciare, equilibrare; compensare; v/i bilanciarsi; v/r mettersi in equilibrio

balcony ['bælkənɪ] balcone m; thea galleria f

bald [bɔːld] calvo

bale [beɪl] balla f

balk [bɔːk] s trave f; v/t (hinder) impedire; (refuse to move) essere ritroso

ball [bɔːl] palla f; pallone m; ballo m; **-ad** ['bæləd] ballata f; **-ast** ['bæləst] zavorra; **-et** ['bæleɪ] balletto m; **-oon** [bə'luːn] pallone m; **-ot** ['bælət] ballottaggio m; **~ point pen** matita f a sfera

balm [bɑːm] balsamo m

balustrade [bæləs'treɪd] balaustrata f

bamboo [bæm'buː] bambù m

ban [bæn] s proibizione f; v/t proibire

banana [bə'nɑːnə] banana f

band [bænd] nastro m; banda f; **-age** ['bændɪdʒ] s fascia f; v/t fasciare; **-sman** musicante m; **-stand** palco m della banda musicale

bang [bæŋ] s colpo m forte; v/t sbattere; interj pum!

banish ['bænɪʃ] esiliare; **-ment** esilio m

banisters ['bænɪstəz] pl ringhiera f

bank [bæŋk] (of river) riva f, sponda f

bank banca f; **~ account** conto m in banca; **-bill** cambiale f; **-er** banchiere m; bancario m; **-ing** operazioni f/pl bancarie; **-note** banconota f

bankrupt ['bæŋkrʌpt] fallito; **-cy** fallimento m; bancarotta f

banner ['bænə] stendardo m

banns [bænz] pl pubblicazioni f/pl di matrimonio

banquet ['bæŋkwɪt] banchetto m

banter ['bæntə] s scherzi m/pl; v/i scherzare

baptism ['bæptɪzəm] battesimo m; **-ize** [-'taɪz] v/t battezzare

bar [bɑː] s sbarra f; bar m; v/t sbarrare

barbarian [bɑːˈbɛəriən] barbaro *m*; **~ous** [ˈ~bərəs] barbaro

barbed [bɑːbd]: ~ **wire** filo *m* spinato

barber [ˈbɑːbə] barbiere *m*; **at the ~'s** dal parrucchiere

bare [bɛə] *a* nudo; desolato; *v/t* denudare; scoprire; **~foot** scalzo; **~headed** a capo scoperto; **~ly** appena

bargain [ˈbɑːgin] *s* affare *m*; occasione *f*; *v/i* contrattare

barge [bɑːdʒ] chiatta *f*; barcone *m*

bark [bɑːk] *s* scorza *f*; *v/i* abbaiare

barley [ˈbɑːli] orzo *m*

barn [bɑːn] granaio *m*

barometer [bəˈrɔmitə] barometro *m*

baron [ˈbærən] barone *m*

barracks [ˈbærəks] *pl* caserma *f*

barrel [ˈbærəl] barile *m*; (*of a gun*) canna *f*; **~organ** organino *m*

barren [ˈbærən] sterile; arido

barricade [bæriˈkeid] *s* barricata *f*; *v/i* barricare; **~ier** [ˈbæriə] barriera *f*; ostacolo *m*

barrister [ˈbæristə] penalista *m*

barrow [ˈbærou] carriola *f*

barter [ˈbɑːtə] *s* baratto *m*; *v/t* barattare

base [beis] *s* base *f*; *a* basso, meschino; *v/t* basare; **~ball** pallacanestro *m*; **~ment** sottosuolo *m*

bashful [ˈbæʃful] timido

basic [ˈbeisik] fondamentale

basin [ˈbeisn] catinella *f*; **wash-~** lavandino *m*

basis [ˈbeisis], *pl* **bases** [ˈbeisiːz] base *f*

bask [bɑːsk] *v/i* godersi (*il sole*)

basket [ˈbɑːskit] cesta *f*; cestino *m*

bas-relief [ˈbæsriˌliːf] basso rilievo *m*

bass[1] [beis] basso *m*

bass[2] [bæs], *pl unchanged* pesce *m* persico

bastard [ˈbæstəd] bastardo *m*

bat [bæt] pipistrello *m*; bastone *m* (*per il giuoco del cricket*)

bath [bɑːθ] bagno *m*

bathe [beið] bagno *m* (*nel mare*); **go for a ~** fare il bagno

bathing [ˈbeiðiŋ] balneare; **~cap** cuffia *f* da bagno; **~costume**, **~suit** costume *m* da bagno; **~trunks** mutandine *f/pl* da bagno

bath|**robe** vestaglia *f*; **~room** stanza *f* da bagno; **~tub** vasca *f* da bagno

baton [ˈbætən] bacchetta *f*

batter [ˈbætə] *gast s* pasta *f*; *v/t*, *v/i* battere; **~y** batteria *f*, pila *f*

battle [ˈbætl] *s* battaglia *f*; *v/i* lottare; **~field** campo *m* di battaglia

bawl [bɔːl] *v/t* gridare

bay [bei] *s* baia *f*; *bot* alloro *m*; *v/i* abbaiare

bazaar [bə'za:] bazar *m*

be: to ~ *v/i* essere

beach [bi:tʃ] spiaggia *f*; lido *m*

beacon ['bi:kən] faro *m*

bead [bi:d] corallo *m*

beak [bi:k] becco *m*

beam [bi:m] *s* trave *f*; fascio *m* di luce; *v/i* raggiare

bean [bi:n] fava *f*

bear [beə] *s zool* orso *m*

bear *v/t* portare; sopportare; generare

beard [biəd] barba *f*; **~ed** barbuto

bear|er ['beərə] portatore *m*, portatrice *f*; **~ing** portamento *m*

beast [bi:st] bestia *f*; **~ly** *coll* brutto; orribile

beat [bi:t] *s* battito *m*; *v/t* battere

beauti|ful ['bju:təful] bello; **~ify** ['~ifai] *v/t* abbellire; **~y** bellezza *f*; **~y parlo(ur)** salone *m* di bellezza

beaver ['bi:və] castoro *m*

because [bi'kɔz] *conj* perchè; ~ **of** *prp* per, per ragione di

beck cenno *m*; **~on** *v/t* far cenno a

become [bi'kʌm] *v/i* divenire; **~ing** grazioso

bed [bed] letto *m*; strato *m*; **go to** ~ andare a letto; ~ **clothes** *pl* coperte *f/pl*; **~ridden** allettato; **~room** camera *f* da letto; **at the ~side of** al capezzale di; **~time** ora *f* d'andare a letto

bee [bi:] ape *f*

beech [bi:tʃ] faggio *m*

beef [bi:f] manzo *m*; **~steak** bistecca *f*; ~ **tea** brodo *m* di carne

bee|hive alveare *m*; **~keeper** apicultore *m*

beer [biə] birra *f*

beet [bi:t] bietola *f*

beetle ['bi:tl] scarafaggio *m*

befall [bi'fɔ:l], *irr* **fall** *v/i* accadere

before [bi'fɔ:] *adv* prima, avanti; *prp* prima di, avanti a; *conj* prima che; **~hand** in precedenza

beg [beg] *v/t* implorare, pregare; *v/i* mendicare; **~gar** ['begə] mendicante *m*

begin [bi'gin] *v/t* cominciare, iniziare; **~ner** principiante *m*; **~ning** inizio *m*, principio *m*

behalf [bi'ha:f]: **on ~ of** da parte di; **in ~ of** a favore di

behav|e [bi'heiv] *v/t* comportarsi; **~io(u)r** [~jə] comportamento *m*, condotta *f*

behind [bi'haind] indietro

being [bi:iŋ] essere *m*; esistenza *f*

belated [bi'leitid] tardivo

belfry ['belfri] campanile *m*

Belgi|an ['beldʒən] *s, a* belga (*m, f*); **~um** il Belgio *m*

belie|f [bi'li:f] credenza *f*; fede *f*; **~vable** credibile; **~ve** [~v] *v/t* credere; **~ver** credente, *m, f*

bell [bel] (*church*) campana *f*; (*house*) campanello *m*; **ring the ~** suonare (il campanello)

bellow

bellow ['bəlou] *v/t, v/i* gridare; **~s** ['~z] *pl* soffietto *m*

belly ['beli] ventre *m*

belong [bi'lɔŋ] *v/i* appartenere a; **~ings** *pl* effetti *m/pl*

beloved [bi'lʌvd] amato; diletto

below [bi'lou] *prp* sotto (a), al di sotto di; *adv* (al di sotto

belt [belt] cintura *f*

bench [bentʃ] panca *f*, sedile *m*; *for* tribunale *m*

bend [bend] *s* curva *f*; *v/t* curvare; piegare; *v/i* curvarsi; piegarsi

beneath [bi'ni:θ] *cf* below

bene|diction [beni'dikʃən] benedizione *f*; **~factor** ['~fæktə] benefattore *m*; **~ficial** [~'fiʃəl] benefico, utile, vantaggioso; **~fit** ['~fit] *s* beneficio *m*; profitto *m*; vantaggio *m*; *v/t* far bene; *v/i* trarre vantaggio; **~volence** benevolenza *f*

benign [bi'nain] benigno; **~ity** [bi'nigniti] benignità *f*

bent [bent] *s* inclinazione *f*; *a* piegato; curvo

benzine ['benzi:n] benzina *f*

beque|ath [bi'kwi:ð] *v/t* legare, lasciare in eredità; **~st** [bi'kwest] lascito *m*

bereave [bi'ri:v] *v/t* orbare

beret ['berei] berretto *m* basco

berry ['beri] bacca *f*, *v/i*

berth [bə:θ] cuccetta *f*; *naut* posto *m* d'ancoraggio (*di una nave*)

beside [bi'said] accanto a; **~** *adv* inoltre; *prep* eccetto

besiege [bi'si:dʒ] *v/t* assediare

best [best] ottimo; **~ man** testimonio *m* dello sposo; **~ wishes** tanti auguri *m/pl*; **do one's ~** fare del proprio meglio; **at ~** tutt'al più

bestow [bi'stou] *v/t* regalare; depositare

bet [bet] *s* scommessa *f*; *v/i* scommettere

betake: ~ o.s. *v/r* recarsi a

betray [bi'trei] *v/t* tradire; **~al** tradimento *m*; **~er** traditore *m*

better ['betə] *a* migliore; *adv* meglio; *v/t* migliorare; *s* scommettitore *m*; **so much the ~** tanto meglio; **he is ~** sta meglio

between [bi'twi:n] tra, fra

beverage ['bevəridʒ] bevanda *f*

beware [bi'wɛə] *v/i* stare attento; **~ of the dog!** cane *m* mordace!

bewilder [bi'wildə] *v/t* sgomentare; **~ment** sgomento *m*

bewitch [bi'witʃ] *v/t* stregare

beyond [bi'jɔnd] *prp* al di là di, oltre a; *adv* al di là, oltre

bias ['baiəs] parzialità *f*; pregiudizio *m*

bib [bib] bavaglino *m*

Bible ['baibl] Bibbia *f*; **~ical** ['biblikəl] biblico

bicker *v/i* contrastarsi, litigare

blight

bicycle ['baisikl] *s* bicicletta
f; *v/i* andare in bicicletta
bid [bid] *v/t* ordinare; offrire; ~ **farewell** dare l'addio
bier [biə] *s* bara *f*
big [big] grande; grosso; importante
bike [baik] *fam* bicicletta *f*
bil|e [bail] bile *f*; **~ious** bilioso
bill [bil] becco *m*; conto *m*;
progetto *m* di legge; cambiale *f*; fattura *f*; **~board**
Am cartello *m* pubblicitario; ~ **of** fare menù *m*
billiards ['biljədz] *pl* biliardo *m*
billion ['biljən] bilione *m*
bin [bin] bidone *m*
bind [baind] *v/t, irr* legare; **~ing** *s* rilegatura *f*; *a* impegnativo
binoculars [bi'nɔkjuləz, bai'~] *pl* binocolo *m*
biography [bai'ɔgrəfi] biografia *f*
biology [bai'ɔlədʒi] biologia *f*
birch [bə:tʃ] betulla *f*
bird [bə:d] uccello *m*; ~ **of prey** uccello *m* di rapina;
~'s-eye view vista *f* a volo di uccello
birth [bə:θ] parto *m*; nascita *f*; **~control** controllo *m*
delle nascite; **~day** compleanno *m*
biscuit ['biskit] biscotto *m*
bishop ['biʃəp] vescovo *m*;
(*chess*) alfiere *m*
bit [bit] pezzo *m*; **a ~ of** un po' di

bitch [bitʃ] cagna *f*
bite [bait] *s* morso *m*; morsicatura *f*; *v/t, v/i* mordere
bitter ['bitə] amaro
black [blæk] *a* nero; *v/t* annerire; **~berry** mora *f*;
~bird merlo *m*; **~board** lavagna *f*; **~ eye** occhio *m*
pesto; **~mail** *s* ricatto *m*;
~mail *v/t* ricattare; **~smith**
fabbro *m* ferraio
bladder ['blædə] vescica *f*
blade [bleid] *knife* lama *f*;
grass foglia *f*
blam|e [bleim] *s* biasimo *m*;
v/t biasimare; **~eless** senza
colpa
blank [blæŋk] lacuna *f*; spazio *m* vuoto; **~cheque** assegno *m* in bianco
blanket ['blæŋkit] coperta *f*
di lana
blasphemy ['blæsfimi] bestemmia *f*
blast [blɑ:st] *s* soffio *m* di
vento; esplosione *f*; *v/i* soffiare
blaze [bleiz] *s* fiamma *f*; *v/i*
fiammeggiare
bleach [bli:tʃ] *v/t* imbiancare
bleak [bli:k] desolato
bleed [bli:d] *v/t* sanguinare
blemish ['blemiʃ] *s* macchia
f; *v/t* macchiare
blend [blend] *s* miscela *f*;
v/t, v/i mescolare
bless [bles] *v/t* benedire; **~ed**
['~id] benedetto; **~ing** benedizione *f*
blight [blait] golpe *f*; *fig* piaga *f*

blind

blind [blaind] cieco; ~ **alley** vicolo *m* cieco; ~**fold** *v/t* bendare gli occhi; ~**ness** cecità *f*

blink [blink] *v/t* ammiccare

bliss [blis] beatitudine *f*; ~**ful** beato

blister [blistə] bolla *f*

blizzard ['blizəd] tormenta *f* di neve

bloat|ed ['bloutid] gonfio; ~**er** aringa *f* affumicata

block [blɔk] *s* ceppo *m*; blocco *m*; *v/t* bloccare

blockade [blɔ'keid] blocco *m*

blond [blɔnd] biondo; ~**e** biondina *f*

blood [blʌd] sangue *m*; ~ **plasma** plasma *m* del sangue; ~ **poisoning** avvelenamento *m* del sangue; ~ **pressure** pressione *f* del sangue; ~**shot** infiammato; ~**vessel** vaso *m* sanguigno; ~**y** insanguinato

bloom [blu:m] *s* fiore *m*; *v/i* florire

blossom ['blɔsəm] *s* floritura *f*; *v/i* sbocciare

blot [blɔt] *s* macchia *f*; *v/t* macchiare; ~ **out** scancellare

blotter, blotting-paper carta *f* assorbente

blouse [blauz] blusa *f*; camicetta *f*

blow [blou] *s* colpo *m*; *v/t* soffiare; ~ **up** fare saltare

blue [blu:] azzurro; **have the ~s** essere giù di morale; ~**bell** campanula *f*

bluff [blʌf] brusco

bluish ['blu(:)iʃ] azzurrognolo

blunder ['blʌndə] gaffe *f*; svista *f*

blunt [blʌnt] (*not sharp*) che non taglia; (*lost its point*) spuntato; (*of a person*) ottuso, franco; ~**ly** chiaro e tondo

blush [blʌʃ] *s* rossore *m*; *v/i* arrossire

boar [bɔ:] cinghiale *m*

board [bɔ:d] asse *f*; comitato *m*; **full ~** pensione *f* completa; **on ~** a bordo; ℬ **of Trade** Ministero *m* del Commercio; ~**er** pensionante *m*; ~**ing-house** pensione *f*; ~**ing-school** collegio *m*

boast [boust] *s* vanteria *f*; *v/i* vantarsi

boat [bout] barca *f*; nave *f*; vaporetto *m*

bob [bɔb] *v/t* tagliare corti (*i capelli*); ~**bed hair** capelli *m/pl* alla maschietta

bobby ['bɔbi] *Brit fam* poliziotto *m*

bob-sleigh ['bɔb-] bob *m*

bodice ['bɔdis] busto *m*

bodily ['bɔdili] corporale, corporeo

body ['bɔdi] corpo *m*; parte *f* centrale; (*of a car*) carrozzeria *f*; ~**guard** guardia *f* del corpo

bog [bɔg] palude *f*

boil [bɔil] *s* foruncolo *m*; *v/i* bollire; ~**er** caldaia *f*

boisterous ['bɔistərəs] (*wind*) violento; (*behaviour*) chias-

box-office

soso, esuberante

bold [bould] audace; ardito

bolster ['boulstə] s cuscino m; v/t sostenere

bolt [boult] s paletto m; spranga f; v/t sprangare; v/i filare

bomb [bɔm] s bomba f; v/t bombardare

bond [bɔnd] legame m; contratto m; (financial) titolo m; **~age** schiavitù f

bone [boun] osso m; spina f

bonfire ['bɔnfaiə] falò m

bonnet ['bɔnit] cuffia f

bonny ['bɔni] carino

bonus ['bounəs] gratifica f

bony ['bouni] ossuto

book [buk] s libro m; v/t registrare; prenotare; **~ing-office** biglietteria f; **~keeper** contabile m; **~keeping** contabilità f; **~let** opuscolo m; **~maker** allibratore m; **~seller** libraio m; **~shop** libreria f

boom [bu:m] s rialzo m improvviso; com prosperità f

boor [buə] zoticone m

boot [bu:t] stivale m; **~blacking** lustrascarpe m

booth [bu:ð] tenda f

booty ['bu:ti] bottino m

border ['bɔ:də] s bordo m; confine m; v/t bordare

bor|e [bɔ:] s foro m; noia f; seccatore m; v/t forare; seccare; **~edom** noia f; **~ing** noioso

borrow ['bɔrou] v/t prendere in prestito

bosom ['buzəm] petto m; seno m

boss [bɔs] padrone m; principale m

botany ['bɔtəni] botanica f

botch [bɔtʃ] v/t rabberciare

both [bouθ] entrambi, ambedue; **~ ... and** e ... e; tanto ... quanto

bother ['bɔðə] s fastidio m; v/t dare fastidio; v/i preoccuparsi

bottle ['bɔtl] s bottiglia f; v/t imbottigliare

bottom ['bɔtəm] fondo m; **at the ~** in fondo

bough [bau] ramo m

bounce [bauns] s balzo m; v/i balzare

bound [baund] s salto m; limite; a legato; obbligato; **~ for** diretto per; **~ary** confine m; **~less** senza limite, sconfinato

bouquet [bu(:)'kei] mazzo m di fiori

bout [baut] sport: assalto m; med accesso m

bow [bau] s inchino m; arco m; nodo m; fiocco m; v/i inchinarsi

bowels ['bauəlz] pl intestino m

bowl [boul] s scodella f; ciotola f; boccia f; v/t, v/i giocare alle bocce

box [bɔks] scatola f; cassa f; (at the theatre) palco m; **~er** pugilatore m; **~ing** pugilato m; **~ing match** incontro m di pugilato; **~office** biglietteria f

boy

boy [bɔi] ragazzo *m*

boycott ['bɔikət] *v/t* boicottare

boy|friend ragazzo *m*; fidanzato *m*; **~hood** infanzia *f*; **~ish** giovanile; **~ scout** esploratore *m*

bra [braː] *fam* reggipetto *m*

brace [breis] *s* sostegno *m*; *v/t* rinforzare; **~let** ['breislit] braccialetto *m*; **~s** *pl* bretelle *f/pl*

bracket ['brækit] parentesi *f*

brag [bræg] *v/i* vantarsi di; **~gart** [~ət] millantatore *m*

braid [breid] *s* treccia *f* di capelli; cordoncino *m*; *v/t* intrecciare

brain [brein] cervello *m*, intelletto *m*; **~y** intelligente

brake [breik] *s* freno *m*; *v/t* frenare

bramble ['bræmbl] rovo *m*

branch [braːntʃ] ramo *m*, succursale *f*; **~out** diramare

brand [brænd] *s* tizzone *m*, *comm* marca *f*; *v/t* marcare; **~ new** nuovo di zecca

brandy ['brændi] acquavite *f*, cognac *m*

brass [braːs] ottone *m*; (*in the orchestra*) gli ottoni *m/pl*; **~ plate** targa *f* di ottone

brassière ['bræsiə] reggipetto *m*

brave [breiv] *a* coraggioso; *v/t* sfidare; **~ry** coraggio *m*

brawl [brɔːl] rissa *f*

brawny [brɔni] muscoloso

Brazil [brə'zil] il Brasile *m*; **~ian** *s*, *a* brasiliano (*m*)

breach [briːtʃ] infrazione *f*; violazione *f*; **~ of peace** attentato *m* contro l'ordine pubblico; (*between friends*) rottura *f*; (*in wall*) fenditura *f*

bread [bred] pane *m*

breadth [bredθ] larghezza *f*

break [breik] *s.* rottura *f*; frattura *f*; *v/t* rompere; **~ away** *v/t* staccare; *v/i* staccarsi da; **~down** guasto *m*; esaurimento *m* nervoso; **~down service** servizio *m* rimorchio; **~ down** *v/t* abbattere; *v/i* (*into tears*) scoppiare in lagrime; **~ open** sfondare; **~ up** (*of a crowd*) disperdere; (*health*) rovinarsi

breakfast ['brekfəst] *s* (prima) colazione *f*; *v/t* fare colazione

breast [brest] petto *m*; **~ stroke** nuotata *f* a rana

breath [breθ] respiro *m*; fiato *m*; **~e** [briːð] *v/t*, *v/i* respirare; **~ing** respiro; **~less** senza fiato; **take ~** riprendere fiato

breath [breθ] respiro *m*; fiato *m*; **~e** [briːð] *v/t*, *v/i* respirare; **~ing** respiro; **~less** senza fiato; **take ~** riprendere fiato

breeches ['britʃiz] *pl* brache *f/pl*

breed [briːd] *s* razza *f*; *v/t*, *v/i* irr generare; (*animals*) allevare; **~ing** (*persons*) educazione *f*; (*animals*) allevamento *m*

bubble

breeze [briːz] brezza *f*; venticello *m*

brevity ['breviti] brevità *f*

brew [bruː] *v/t* fare la birra; **~ery** fabbrica *f* di birra

bribe [braib] *v/t* corrompere; **~ery** corruzione *f*

brick [brik] mattone *m*; **~layer** muratore *m*; **~works** *pl* fornaci *f/pl*

brid|al ['braidl] nuziale; **~e** sposa *f*; **~egroom** sposo *m*, **~esmaid** damigella *f* d'onore

bridge [bridʒ] ponte *m*

bridle ['braidl] *s* briglia *f*; *v/t* imbrigliare

brief [briːf] breve; **~case** cartella *f*

brigade [bri'geid] brigata *f*; **fire~** pompieri *m/pl*

bright [brait] luminoso; (*light*) forte; (*colour, person*) vivace; (*sun*) splendente; *v/t, v/i* illuminare

brillian|cy ['briljənsi] splendore *m*; **~t** splendente

brim [brim] (*cup*) orlo *m*; (*hat*) ala *f*, falda *f*

bring [briŋ] *v/t, v/i* portare; **~ about** cagionare; causare; **~ in** introdurre; **~ up** educare

brink [briŋk] orlo *m*

brisk [brisk] attivo; svelto

bristle ['brisl] *s* setola *f*; *v/i* raddrizzarsi; *fig* arrabbiarsi

Brit|ain ['britən] (Gran) Bretagna *f*; **~ish** ['britiʃ] britannico

brittle ['britl] fragile

broach [broutʃ] *v/t* intavola-

re (*una discussione*)

broad [brɔːd] largo; **~cast** *s* trasmissione *f*; *v/t* trasmettere; **~casting station** stazione *f* trasmittente; **~en** *v/t, v/i* allargare; **~minded** aperto; spregiudicato

brochure [brou'ʃuə] fascicolo *m*

broil [brɔil] *v/t* arrostire

broke [brouk] *fam* senza soldi

broker ['broukə] sensale *m*

bronchitis [brɔŋ'kaitis] bronchite *f*

bronze [brɔnz] bronzo *m*

brooch [broutʃ] spilla *f*

brood [bruːd] *s* covata *f*; *v/i* covare

brook [bruk] ruscello *m*

broom [bruːm] scopa *f*; *bot* ginestra *f*; **~stick** manico *m* di scopa

broth [brɔθ] brodo *m*

brothel ['brɔθəl] bordello *m*

brother ['brʌðə] fratello *m*; **~hood** fratellanza *f*; **~-in-law** cognato *m*; **~ly** fraterno

brow [brau] fronte *f*

brown [braun] marrone; **~ paper** carta *f* da imballaggio

bruise [bruːz] *s* livido *m*; *v/t* ammaccare

brush [brʌʃ] *s* spazzola *f*; pennello *m*; *v/t* spazzolare

Brussels sprouts ['brʌsl 'sprauts] *pl* cavolini *m/pl* di Brusselle

brutal ['bruːtl] brutale; **~ity** [~'tæliti] brutalità *f*

bubble ['bʌbl] bolla *f*

2*

buck

buck [bʌk] maschio; *Am* dollaro *m*

bucket ['bʌkit] secchia *f*

buckle ['bʌkl] *s* fibbia *f*; *v/t* affibbiare

buckskin pelle *f* di daino

bud [bʌd] *s* bocciolo *m*; *v/i* germogliare

budget ['bʌdʒit] bilancio *m*

buffalo ['bʌfəlou] bufalo *m*

buffer ['bʌfə] *chem* tampone *m*; (*train*) respingente *m*; ~ **state** stato *m* cuscinetto

buffet ['bʌfit] banco *m*; caffè *m*; schiaffo *m*

bug [bʌg] cimice *f*

build [bild] *v/t*, irr. costruire; ~**er** costruttore *m*; ~**ing** costruzione *f*

bulb [bʌlb] *bot* bulbo *m*; *elec* lampadina *f*

Bulgaria [bʌl'gɛəriə] Bulgaria *f*; ~**n** *s*, *a* bulgaro (*m*)

bulge [bʌldʒ] *s* rigonfiamento *m*; protuberanza *f*; *v/i* rigonfiare

bulk [bʌlk] mole *f*; massa *f*; ~**y** ingombrante

bull [bul] toro *m*; (*of some animals*) maschio *m*

bullet ['bulit] pallottola *f*

bulletin ['bulitin] bollettino *m*

bullion ['buljən] oro *m* e argento *m* in lingotti

bull's-eye occhio *m* di bue; centro *m* del bersaglio

bully ['buli] *s* prepotente *m*, tiranno *m*; *v/t* tiranneggiare

bum [bʌm] *fam* vagabondo *m*

bumble-bee ['bʌmbl-] calabrone *m*

bump [bʌmp] *s* scossa *f*; *v/t* scuotere; urtare; ~ **into** urtarsi contro; *fig* incontrare (*per caso*)

bumper *aut* paraurti *m/pl*

bun [bʌn] brioscia *f*

bunch [bʌntʃ] mazzo *m*; ~ **of grapes** grappolo *m*

bundle ['bʌndl] fascio *m*

bungalow ['bʌngəlou] bungalò *m*; casetta *f* a un piano

bungle ['bʌngl] *v/t*, *v/i* abborracciare

bunion ['bʌnjən] infiammazione *f* del pollice del piede

buoy [bɔi] boa *f*

burden ['bə:dn] *s* peso *m*; *v/t* caricare

bureau ['bjuərou] ufficio *m*

burglar ['bə:glə] ladro *m*; scassinatore *m*; ~**y** furto *m* con scasso

burial ['beriəl] sepoltura *f*; funerali *m/pl*; ~**ground** cimitero *m*

burly ['bə:li] robusto

burn [bə:n] *s* bruciatura *f*; *v/t*, *v/i* bruciare; ~**ing** in fiamme

burst [bə:st] *s* scoppio *m*; *v/t*, irr fare scoppiare; *v/i* scoppiare

bury ['beri] *v/t* seppellire

bus [bʌs] autobus *m*; ~ **line** autolinea *f*; ~ **stop** fermata *f*

bush [buʃ] cespuglio *m*; ~**y** folto

business ['biznis] affare *m*; affari *m/pl*; ~ **hours** *pl* ora *f* d'ufficio; ~**like** capace; ~**man** uomo *m* d'affari

bust [bʌst] busto m

bustle [ˈbʌsl] s agitazione f; v/i agitarsi

busy [ˈbizi] a occupato; affaccendato; **~body** ficcanaso m

but [bʌt] conj ma; però; prp eccetto; solamente; **I cannot ~** non posso fare a meno; **the last ~ one** penultimo m; **~ for** senza; **~ that** se non; **~ then** d'altra parte

butcher [ˈbutʃə] macellaio m; **~'s** macelleria f

butt [bʌt] zimbello m; (of gun) calcio m

butter [ˈbʌtə] burro m; **~cup** ranuncolo m; **~fly** farfalla f

buttocks [ˈbʌtəks] pl natiche f/pl

button [ˈbʌtn] s bottone m; v/t abbottonare; **~hole** occhiello m

buttress [ˈbʌtris] contrafforte m

buxom [ˈbʌksəm] grassoccio m

buy [bai] irr comprare; **~er** compratore m; **~ing and selling** compravendita f

buzz [bʌz] s ronzio m; v/i ronzare

by [bai] prp (at) a; (through) per; da; **~ day** di giorno; **~ far** di gran lungo; **~o.s.** (da) solo; **~ law** per legge; **~ twos** a due a due; **~ the way** a proposito; **day ~ day** giorno per giorno; **go ~** passare davanti; **go ~ car (train)** andare in macchina (treno); adv vicino (a); **~ and ~** a poco a poco; **bye-bye** [ˈbaiˈbai] cf **good-bye**; **~gone** passato; **~pass** circonvallazione f; **~product** prodotto m secondario; **~stander** astante m; **~street** stradetta f

C

cab [kæb] vettura f di piazza

cabbage [ˈkæbidʒ] cavolo m

cabin [ˈkæbin] cabina f; **~et** [~it] (furniture) stipo; pol gabinetto m; Consiglio m (dei Ministri); **~et-maker** stipettaio m

cable [ˈkeibl] cavo m; **~car** funicolare f

cab|man tassista m, f; **~stand** posteggio m

cackle [ˈkækl] v/i chiocciare

cact|us [ˈkæktəs], pl **~uses** [~siz], **~i** [~ai] cacto m

café [ˈkæfei] caffè m

caffeine [ˈkæfiːn] coffeina f

cage [keidʒ] gabbia f

cake [keik] torta f; pasta f; dolce m

calamity [kælˈæmiti] calamità f

calcula|ble [ˈkælkjuləbl] calcolabile; **~te** v/t calcolare; **~tion** calcolo m

calendar [ˈkælində] calendario m

calf [kɑːf], pl **calves** [~vz] vitello m; anat polpaccio m

cali|bre, Am **~er** [ˈkælibə] calibro m

call [kɔːl] s chiamata f; (breve) visita f; v/t chiamare; **~ for** far venire; **~ on** far visita; **~ s.o. names** insultare; **~box** cabina f telefonica; **~ing** vocazione f

callous [ˈkæləs] (of persons) insensibile

calm [kɑːm] s calma m; v/t calmare; **~ down** v/i calmarsi

calorie [ˈkæləri] caloria f

cambric [ˈkeimbrik] batista f

camel [ˈkæməl] cammello m

camera [ˈkæmərə] macchina f fotografica; **~man** cameraman m

camomile [ˈkæməmail] camomilla f

camouflage [ˈkæmuflɑːʒ] s camuffamento m; v/t camuffare

camp [kæmp] s campo m; v/i accampare; **~stool** sedia f pieghevole

camp|aign [ˌ~ˈpein] campagna f; **~ing (-ground)** [ˈkæmpiŋ] campeggio m

campus [ˈkæmpəs] città f universitaria

can [kæn]: v/d **I can** posso; **you ~** puoi etc; s scatola f di latta

Canad|a [ˈkænədə] Canada m; **~ian** [kəˈneidjən] s, a canadese (m, f)

canal [kəˈnæl] canale m; **~ize** [ˈkænəlaiz] v/t canalizzare

canary [kəˈnɛəri] canarino m

cancel [ˈkænsəl] v/t cancellare; annullare

cancer [ˈkænsə] cancro m

candid [ˈkændid] candido; **~ate** [ˈkændideit] candidato m

cand|ied [ˈkændid] candito; **~ies** pl Am caramelle f/pl

candle [ˈkændl] candela f; **~stick** bugia f

candy [ˈkændi] Am cf **~ies**

cane [kein] canna f; bastone m da passeggio

cann|ed [kænd] in scatola; **~ery** Am stabilimento m di conserve alimentari

cannon [ˈkænən] cannone m

cannot [ˈkænət] non potere

canoe [kəˈnuː] canotto m

canopy [ˈkænəpi] baldacchino m

cant [kænt] ipocrisia f

can't cf **cannot**

canteen [kænˈtiːn] mensa f

canvas [ˈkænvəs] tela f; **~s** v/t sollecitare

cap [kæp] berretto m; cuffia f; tappo m

capab|ility [keipəˈbiliti] capacità f; **~le** (of) capace (di)

capacity [kəˈpæsiti] capacità f

cape [keip] mantella f; geog capo m

caper [ˈkeipə] cappero m; **~s:** **cut ~s** fare capriole

capital [ˈkæpitl] s capitale f; a eccellente; principale; **~ letter** maiuscolo m; **~ism** capitalismo m; **~ punishment** pena f di morte

capitulate [kəˈpitjuleit] v/t

capitolare

capricious [kə'priʃəs] capriccioso

capsize [kæp'saiz] v/t capovolgere

capsule ['kæpsju:l] capsula f

captain ['kæptin] capitano m, comandante m

caption ['kæpʃən] titolo m; didascalia f

captiv|ate ['kæptiveit] v/t affascinare; **~e** s, a prigioniero; (m); **~ity** [~'tiviti] prigionia f

capture ['kæptʃə] s cattura f; v/t catturare

car [ka:] automobile f; macchina f; (railway) vagone m

caramel ['kærəməl] caramella f

carat ['kærət] carato m

caravan ['kærəvæn] carovana f, rimorchio m da campeggio

carbo|hydrate [ˌka:bou'haidreit] idrato m di carbonio; **~n** ['ka:bən] carbonio m; **~n dioxide** anidride f carbonica; **~n paper** carta f carbone

carburet(t)or, ~ter ['ka:bjuretə] carburatore m

carca|se, ~ss ['ka:kəs] carcassa f

card [ka:d] carta f (da giuoco); biglietto m; **~board** cartone m

cardigan ['ka:digən] golf m

cardinal ['ka:dinl] s, a cardinale (m)

care [kεə] s cura f; v/i importarsi; **I don't ~** non m'importa; **~ of** presso; **take ~** stare attento; **~ for** voler bene; piacere

career [kə'riə] carriera f

care|ful accurato; attento; **~less** trascurato

caress [kə'res] carezza f; v/t accarezzare

caretaker custode m, f

cargo ['ka:gou] carico m

caricature [kærikə'tjuə] caricatura f

caries ['kεəri:z] carie f

carnation [ka:'neiʃən] garofano m

carnival ['ka:nivəl] carnevale m

carol ['kærəl] canto m (di Natale)

carp [ka:p] carpa f

car-park parcheggio m per automobili

carpenter ['ka:pintə] falegname m

carpet ['ka:pit] tappeto m

carriage ['kæridʒ] carrozza f; portamento m; **~ free** franco di porto; **~ paid** franco a domicilio; **~-way** carreggiata f

carrier ['kæriə] corriere m, imprenditore m di trasporti; **~-pigeon** piccione m viaggiatore

carrot ['kærət] carota f

carry ['kæri] v/t portare; **~ on** v/t continuare; **~ out** v/t effettuare

cart [ka:t] carretto m; **~er** carrettiere m

carton ['ka:tən] scatola f di cartone

cartoon [kɑːˈtuːn] cartone *m* animato; (*newspaper*) vignetta *f*

cartridge [ˈkɑːtridʒ] cartuccia *f*

carv|e [kɑːv] *v/t* intagliare; **~er** scultore *m*; **~ing** intaglio *m*; scultura *f*

cascade [kæsˈkeid] cascata *f*

case [keis] astuccio *m*; custodia *f*; cassa *f*; caso *m*; causa *f*; **in ~** per caso; caso mai; **in any ~** in ogni modo

cash [kæʃ] *s* denaro *m* liquido; contanti *m/pl*; **~ down** in contanti; **~ on delivery** contro assegno; **~ payment** pagamento *m* in contanti; *v/t* incassare; riscuotere; **~ier** cassiere *m*

casing [ˈkeisiŋ] copertura *f*

cask [kɑːsk] botte *f*; barile *m*

cast [kɑːst] *s* getto *m*; *v/t* gettare; **be ~ down** essere giù di morale

castanets [ˌkæstəˈnets] *pl* nacchere *f/pl*

castaway [ˈkɑːstəwei] naufrago *m*

caste [kɑːst] casta *f*

cast-iron ferro *m* fuso; ghisa *f*

castle [ˈkɑːsl] castello *m*

castor [ˈkɑːstə] **oil** olio *m* di ricino

casual [ˈkæʒjuəl] casuale; **~ty** disgrazia *f*; ferito *m*

cat [kæt] gatto *m*, gatta *f*

catalog(ue) [ˈkætələɡ] catalogo *m*

catarrh [kəˈtɑː] catarro *m*

catastrophe [kəˈtæstrəfi]

catastrofe *f*

catch [kætʃ] *s* presa *f*; cattura *f*; pesca *f*; trappola *f*; *v/t* prendere; catturare; pescare; **~ (a) cold** infreddarsi; **~ it** buscarsela; **~ing** contagioso

caterpillar [ˈkætəpilə] bruco *m*

cathedral [kəˈθiːdrəl] cattedrale *f*; duomo *m*

Catholic [ˈkæθəlik] *a*, *s* cattolico (*m*)

cattle [ˈkætl] bestiame *m*

cauliflower [ˈkɔliflauə] cavolfiore *m*

cause [kɔːz] *s* causa *f*; *v/t* causare; **~way** passerella *f*

cauterize [ˈkɔːtəraiz] *v/t* cauterizzare

caution [ˈkɔːʃən] *s* cautela *f*; ammonizione *f*; *v/t* ammonire; **~ous** cauto; prudente

cavalry [ˈkævəlri] cavalleria *f*

cave [keiv] cava *f*; **~rn** [ˈkævən] caverna *f*

cavity [ˈkæviti] cavità *f*

caw [kɔː] *v/t* gracchiare

cease [siːs] *v/i* cessare; **~less** incessante

cedar [ˈsiːdə] cedro *m*

cede [siːd] *v/t* cedere; *v/i* rendersi

ceiling [ˈsiːliŋ] soffitto *m*

celebr|ate [ˈselibreit] *v/t* celebrare; **~ated** rinomato; **~ation** celebrazione *f*; **~ity** [siˈlebriti] celebrità *f*

celery [ˈseləri] sedano *m*

celibacy [ˈselibəsi] celibato *m*

cell [sel] cella *f*; *biol* cellula *f*; **~ar** [selə] cantina *f*; **~ulose** ['seljulo:s] cellulosa *f*

Celt [kelt] celta *m*; **~ic** celtico

cement [si'ment] *s* cemento *m*; *v/t* cementare

cemetery ['semitri] cimitero *m*

cens|or ['sensə] censore *m*; **~orship** censura *f*; **~ure** ['senʃə] *s* censura *f*; biasimo *m*; *v/t* censurare

census ['sensəs] censimento *m*

cent [sent] centesimo *m* di dollaro; **per ~** per cento

centen|ary [sen'ti:nəri], **~nial** [sen'tenjəl] *a,s* centenario (*m*)

centi|metre, *Am* **~meter** ['sentimi:tə] centimetro *m*

central ['sentrəl] centrale; **~al heating** riscaldamento *m* centrale; **~re**, *Am* **~er** ['sentə] centro *m*; **~re-forward** centro-attacco *m*

century ['sentʃuri] secolo *m*

ceramics [si'ræmiks] *pl* ceramica *f*

cereal ['siəriəl] cereale *m*

cerebral ['seribrəl] cerebrale

ceremon|ial [seri'mounjəl] *s, a* cerimoniale (*m*); **~y** ['~məni] cerimonia *f*

certain ['sə:tn] certo; **~ty** certezza *f*

certif|icate [sə'tifikit] certificato *m*; **~y** ['sə:tifai] *v/t* certificare

chaffinch ['tʃæfintʃ] fringuello *m*

chain [tʃein] *s* catena *f*; *v/t* incatenare; **~ reaction** reazione *f* a catena

chair [tʃɛə] sedia *f*; **~man** presidente *m*

chalk [tʃɔ:k] gesso *m*

challenge ['tʃælindʒ] *s* sfida *f*; *v/t* sfidare; obiettare

chamber ['tʃeimbə] camera *f*; **~maid** cameriera *f*; **♀ of Commerce** camera *f* di commercio

chameleon [kə'mi:ljən] camaleonte *m*

chamois ['ʃæmwa:] camoscio *m*

champagne [ʃæm'pein] sciampagna *m*

champion ['tʃæmpjən] campione *m*; **~ship** campionato *m*

chance [tʃɑ:ns] caso *m*; possibilità *f*; **by ~** per caso

chancellor ['tʃɑ:nsələ] cancelliere *m*

chandelier [ʃændi'liə] lampadario *m*

change [tʃeindʒ] *s* cambiamento *m*; (*money*) spiccioli *m/pl*; *v/t* cambiare; **~able** mutevole; **~ one's mind** cambiar idea

channel ['tʃænl] canale *m*; **the (English)** ♀ la Manica *f*

chant [tʃɑ:nt] canto *m*

chap [tʃæp] *s* (*man*) tipo *m*; (*of the skin*) screpola *f*; *v/t* screpolare

chap|el ['tʃæpəl] cappella *f*; **~lain** ['~lin] cappellano *m*

chapter ['tʃæptə] capitolo *m*

character ['kæriktə] carattere *m*; *thea* parte *f*; **~istic** caratteristico; **~ize** *v/t* caratterizzare

charcoal [ˈtʃɑːkoul] carbone *m* di legno

charge [tʃɑːdʒ] *s* carica *f*; incarico *m*; prezzo *m*; accusa *f*; *v/t* caricare; incaricare; mettere a un certo prezzo; addebitare; accusare; **~s** *pl* spese *f/pl*; **in ~ of** incaricato di

charit|able [ˈtʃæritəbl] caritatevole; **~y** [ˈtʃæriti] carità *f*

charm [tʃɑːm] *s* fascino *m*; *v/t* affascinare; **~ing** affascinante

chart [tʃɑːt] carta *f*; grafico *m*

charter [ˈtʃɑːtə] *s* carta *f*; *v/t* noleggiare

charwoman [ˈtʃɑːwumən] donna *f* delle pulizie

chase [tʃeis] *s* caccia *f*; rincorso *m*; *v/t* cacciare; rincorrere

chasm [ˈkæzəm] abisso *m*

chast|e [tʃeist] casto; puro; **~ity** [ˈtʃæstiti] castità *f*

chat [tʃæt] *s* chiacchierata *f*; *v/i* chiacchierare; **~ter** *s* chiacchiera *f*; *v/i* ciarlare; **~terbox** ciarlone *m*

chauffeur [ˈʃoufə] autista *m*

cheap [tʃiːp] a basso prezzo, a buon prezzo; **~en** *v/t* abbassare; *v/i* abbassare di prezzo

cheat [tʃiːt] *v/t*, *v/i* truffare; frodare; ingannare

check [tʃek] *s* controllo *m*; ostacolo *m*; scontrino *m*; as-

segno *m*; *v/t* controllare; arrestare; reprimere; **~ed** a quadretti; **~mate** scacco matto *m*; **~room** *Am* guardaroba *m*

cheek [tʃiːk] guancia *f*; **~y** impertinente

cheer [tʃiə] *s* grido *m* di acclamazione; *v/t* acclamare; **~ up** *v/i* rianimarsi; farsi coraggio; **~ up!** su!; coraggio!; **~ful** allegro; **~less** triste

cheese [tʃiːz] formaggio *m*

chef [ʃef] cuoco *m*

chemical [ˈkemikəl] chimico; **~s** *pl* prodotti *m/pl* chimici

chemist [ˈkemist] chimico *m*; farmacista *m*; **~ry** chimica *f*; **~'s shop** drogheria *f*; farmacia *f*

cheque [tʃek] assegno *m* (bancario); **~-book** libretto *m* di assegni

cherish [ˈtʃeriʃ] *v/t* curare con affetto; tenere caro

cherry [ˈtʃeri] ciliegia *f*; **~tree** ciliegio *m*

chess [tʃes] scacchi *m/pl*; **~board** scacchiera *f*; **~man** scacco *m*

chest [tʃest] cassa *f*; torace *m*

chestnut [ˈtʃesnʌt] castagna *f*; **~tree** castagno *m*

chew [tʃuː] *v/t* masticare; **~ingum** gomma *f* americana

chicken [ˈtʃikin] pulcino *m*; *gast* pollo *m*; **~pox** varicella *f*

chief [tʃiːf] a principale; *s*

capo *m*

chilblain ['tʃilblein] gelone *m*

child [tʃaild], *pl* **~ren** ['tʃildrən] bambino(a), figlio(a) *m* (*f*); **~birth** parto *m*; **~hood** infanzia *f*; **~ish** infantile, puerile

chill [tʃil] *s* fresco *m*; colpo *m* di freddo; *v/t* raffreddare; **~y** (*weather*) fresco; (*person*) freddoloso

chime [tʃaim] *s* rintocco *m*; *v/i* (*bell*) suonare

chimney ['tʃimni] camino *m*; **~sweep** spazzacamino *m*

chin [tʃin] mento *m*

chin|a ['tʃainə] porcellana *f*; **2a** Cina *f*; **2ese** *a*, *s* cinese (*m,f*)

chip [tʃip] *s* scheggia *f*; *v/t* scheggiare; *v/i* scheggiarsi

chirp [tʃə:p] *v/i* cinguettare

chisel ['tʃizl] *s* cesello *m*, scalpello *m*; *v/t* cesellare

chivalr|ous ['ʃivəlrəs] cavalleresco; **~y** cavalleria *f*

chive [tʃaiv] cipollina *f*

chlor|ine ['klɔːriːn] cloro *m*; **~oform** ['klɔrəfɔːm] cloroformio *m*

chocolate ['tʃɔkəlit] cioccolata *f*; cioccolatino *m*

choice [tʃɔis] *a* scelto; prelibato; squisito; *s* scelta *f*

choir ['kwaiə] coro *m*

choke [tʃouk] *v/t* soffocare; affogare; *v/i* soffocarsi; affogarsi

choose [tʃuːz] *v/t* scegliere

chop [tʃɔp] *s* costoletta *f* (di maiale o di agnello); *v/t* tagliare; tagliuzzare; **~sticks** *pl* bacchette *f/pl*

chord [kɔːd] corda *f*; *mus* accordo *m*

chorus ['kɔːrəs] coro *m*

Christ [kraist] Cristo *m*; **2en** ['krisn] *v/t* battezzare; **~endom** ['krisndəm] cristianità *f*; **~ening** battesimo *m*; **~ian** ['kristjən] cristiano(a) *m* (*f*); **~ianity** [ˌkristi'æniti] cristianesimo *m*; **~mas** Natale *m*; **~mas Day** Natale; **~mas Eve** vigilia *f* di Natale; **Merry ~mas!** Buon Natale!

chromium ['kroumjəm] cromio *m*

chronic ['krɔnik] cronico

chron|icle ['krɔnikl] cronaca *f*; **~ological** [ˌkrɔnə'lɔdʒikəl] cronologico

chubby ['tʃʌbi] grassetto

chuckle ['tʃʌkl] *v/t* ridere sotto voce

chum [tʃʌm] *fam* compagno(a) *m* (*f*)

chunk [tʃʌŋk] grosso pezzo *m*

church [tʃəːtʃ] chiesa *f*; **2 of England** chiesa *f* anglicana; **~ services** *pl* funzioni *f/pl*; **~yard** cimitero *m*

cider ['saidə] sidro *m*

cigar [si'gɑː] sigaro *m*; **~ette** [sigə'ret] sigaretta *f*

Cinderella [ˌsində'relə] Cenerentola *f*

cine-camera ['sini-] macchina *f* da presa; **~ma** ['sinəmə] cinema *m*

cipher

cipher ['saifə] zero *m*; cifra *f*

circle ['sə:kl] *s* cerchio *m*; circolo *m*; *v/t* circondare; *v/i* girare intorno

circuit ['sə:kit] circuito *m*; **~ short** corto circuito *m*

circula|r ['sə:kjulə] *a* circolare; **~r letter** circolare *f*; **~te** *v/i* circolare; **~tion** circolazione *f*; (*of a newspaper*) tiratura *f*

circum|ference [sə'kʌmfərəns] circonferenza *f*; **~scribe** [~skraib] *v/t* circoscrivere

circumstance circostanza*f*; condizione *f*

circus ['sə:kəs] circo *m*

cistern ['sistən] cisterna *f*; serbatoio

cite [sait] *v/t* citare

cit|izen ['sitizn] cittadino(a) *m* (*f*); **~izenship** cittadinanza *f*; **~y** ['siti] città *f*; **little ~y** cittadina *f*; **~y guide** pianta *f* della città

civ|ic ['sivik] civico; **~il** ['sivl] civile; educato; gentile; **~il service** amministrazione *f* dello Stato; **~ilian** [si'viljən] *a, s* borghese (*m,f*); **~ility** cortesia *f*; **~ilization** civiltà *f*; **~ilize** *v/t* incivilire

claim [kleim] *s* pretesa *f*; reclamo *m*; *v/t* pretendere; reclamare

clam|orous ['klæmərəs] clamoroso; **~o(u)r** *s* clamore *m*; rumore *m*; *v/i* vociferare

clamp [klæmp] grappa *f*

clan [klæn] tribù *f*; clan *m*

clap [klæp] *s* colpo *m*; applauso *m*; *v/i* applaudire, battere le mani

claret ['klærət] claretto *m*

clari|fy ['klærifai] *v/t* chiarire; **~ty** chiarezza *f*

clash [klæʃ] *s* contrasto *m*; *v/i* contrastarsi

clasp [klɑ:sp] *s* gancio *m*; abbraccio *m*; *v/t, v/i* agganciare; stringere; abbracciare; **~knife** temperino *m*

class [klɑ:s] *s* classe *f*; (*social*) ceto *m*; *v/t* classificare

classic ['klæsik] *a, s* classico (*m*)

class|ification [ˌklæsifi'keiʃən] classificazione *f*; **~ify** ['~fai] *v/t* classificare

class room aula *f*

clause [klɔ:z] clausola *f*

claw [klɔ:] *s* artiglio *m*; *v/t* graffiare

clay [klei] argilla *f*; creta *f*

class-mate compagno *m* di classe; **~room** aula *f*

clause [klɔ:z] clausola *f*

claw [klɔ:] *s* artiglio *m*; *v/t* graffiare

clay [klei] argilla *f*; creta *f*

clean [kli:n] pulito; *v/t* pulire; **~cut** *Am* netto; **~er's** (*shop*) tintoria *f*; **~ing, ~ness** pulizia *f*; **~se** [klenz] *v/t* pulire

clear [kliə] *a* chiaro; libero; *v/t* chiarire; liberare; (*weather*) schiarirsi; **~ance** liquidazione *f*

clef [klef] *mus* chiave *f*

clemency ['klemənsi] clemenza *f*

clergy ['klə:dʒi] clero *m*; **~man** ecclesiastico *m*

clerk [klɑ:k] impiegato *m* d'ufficio; commesso *m*; chierico *m*

clever ['klevə] abile; bravo; intelligente

client ['klaiənt] cliente *m*

cliff [klif] scogliera *f*

climate ['klaimit] clima *m*

climax ['klaimæks] punto *m* culminante

climb [klaim] *s* salita *f*; *v/t* salire

clinch [klintʃ] *v/t*, *v/i* afferrare; confermare; avvinghiare

cling [kliŋ] *irr*, *v/i*, *irr* aderire a; attaccarsi a

clinic ['klinik] clinica *f*

clink [kliŋk] *v/t* far tintinnare

clip [klip] *s* fermaglio *m*; gancio *m*; taglio *m*; tosatura *f*; *v/t* tagliare; tosare

clique [kli:k] cricca *m*

cloak [klouk] mantello *m*; **~room** guardaroba *f*

clock [klɔk] orologio *m* da muro

clog [klɔg] zoccolo *m*

close [klous] *s* conclusione *f*; fine *f*; *v/t* chiudere; concludere; finire; **~ to** *prp* vicino a

closet ['klɔzit] *Am* armadio *m*; gabinetto *m*

cloth [klɔθ] stoffa *f*; tessuto *m*; tovaglia *f*; **~e** [klouð] *v/t* vestire

clothes [klouðz] *pl* vestiti *m/pl*, abiti *m/pl*; **~brush**

spazzola *f* per vestiti; **hanger** gruccia *f*; **~pin**, **~peg** fermabiancheria *m*

clothing vestiti *m/pl*

cloud [klaud] *s* nuvola *f*; *v/i* rannuvolarsi; **~y** nuvoloso

clove [klouv] chiodo *m* di garofano

clover ['klouvə] trifoglio *m*

clown [klaun] pagliaccio *m*

club [klʌb] mazzo *m*; circolo *m*

clue [klu:] indizio *m*

clumsy ['klʌmzi] goffo

clutch [klʌtʃ] *s* stretta *f*; *aut* frizione *f*; *v/t* afferrare; aggrapparsi a

coach [koutʃ] *s* carrozza *f*; corriera *f*; ripetitore *m*; allenatore *m*; *v/t* dare ripetizioni; allenare

coal [koul] carbone *m*; **~mine**, **~pit** miniera *f* di carbone

coarse [kɔ:s] rozzo; ruvido; grossolano

coast [koust] *s* costa *f*; *v/i* costeggiare; **~guard** milizia *f* guardacoste

coat [kout] cappotto *m*; giacca *f*; paltò *m*; **~ of arms** stemma *m*; **~ing** rivestimento *m*

coax [kouks] *v/t* invogliare

cobra ['koubrə] cobra *m*

cobweb ['kɔbweb] ragnatela *f*

cock [kɔk] gallo *m*; maschio *m* (*di uccelli*); **~chafer** maggiolino *m*; **~pit** carlinga *f*; **~tail** cocktail *m*; **~y** presuntuoso

cocoa ['koukou] cacao *m*

coconut ['koukənʌt] noce *f* di cocco

cocoon [kə'ku:n] bozzolo *m*

cod [kɔd] merluzzo *m*; **~liver oil** olio *m* di fegato di merluzzo

coddle ['kɔdl] *v/t* vezzeggiare

code [koud] codice *m*; cifrario *m*

coffee ['kɔfi] caffè *m*; **~bean** chicco *m* di caffè; **~mill** macchinetta *f* da caffè; **~pot** caffettiera *f*

coffin ['kɔfin] bara *f*

cog [kɔg] *mech* dente *f*; **~wheel** ruota *f* dentata

coherent [kou'hiərənt] coerente

coiffure [kwɑ:'fjuə] pettinatura *f*

coil [kɔil] *s* rotolo *m* (di corda); spira *f* (di serpe); *elec* bobina *f*; *v/t* arrotolare

coin [kɔin] *s* moneta *f*; *v/t* coniare; *fig* inventare

coincide [ˌkouin'said] *v/i* coincidere; **~nce** [kou'insidəns] coincidenza *f*

cold [kould] *a* freddo *m*, insensibile; **it is ~** fa freddo; **feel ~** aver freddo; *s* freddo *m*; raffreddore *m*; **~ness** freddezza *f*

colic ['kɔlik] colica *f*

collaborat|e [kə'læbəreit] *v/i* collaborare; **~ion** collaborazione *f*

collapse [kə'læps] *s* collasso *m*; crollo *m*; *v/t* avere un collasso; crollare

collar ['kɔlə] colletto *m*; **~bone** clavicola *f*

colleague ['kɔli:g] collega *m*

collect [kə'lekt] *s* colletta *f*; *v/t* fare collezione; mettere insieme; radunare; **~ion** collezione *f*; raccolta *f*; **~ive** collettivo

college [kɔlidʒ] collegio *m* universitario; istituto *m* superiore

collide [kə'laid] *v/i* scontrarsi

colliery [kɔljəri] miniera *f* di carbone

collision [kə'liʒən] scontro *m*

colloqu|ial [kə'loukwiəl] familiare; **~y** colloquio *m*

colon ['koulən] *gram* due punti *m/pl*

colonel ['kə:nl] colonnello *m*

colonial [kə'lounjəl] coloniale

colony ['kɔləni] colonia *f*

colo(u)r ['kʌlə] *s* colore *m*; colorito *m*; tinta *f*; *v/t* colorire; *v/i* colorirsi; **~ bar** discriminazione *f* razziale; **~blind** daltonico; **~ed** di colore; **~ed man** uomo *m* di colore; negro *m*; **~less** incolore; senza colore; **~print** fotografia *f* a colori

column ['kɔləm] colonna *f*; rubrica *f* (di un giornale)

comb [koum] *s* pettine *m*; *v/t* pettinare

combat ['kɔmbæt] *s* lotta *f*; *v/t* combattere; lottare contro

combin|ation [ˌkɔmbi'neiʃən] combinazione *f*;

[kəm'bain] v/t combinare; v/i combinarsi

combust|ible [kəm'bʌstəbl] combustibile; **~ion** [~st∫ən] combustione f

come [kʌm] irr venire; **~ about** accadere; **~ across** incontrare; **~ back** ritornare; **~ down** (di)scendere; **~ in** entrare; **~ off** scendere; verificarsi; **~ on!** su!; avanti; **~ up** salire

comed|ian [kə'mi:djən] comico m; **~y** ['kɔmidi] commedia f

comfort ['kʌmfət] conforto m; consolazione f; v/t confortare; consolare; **~able** comodo

comic|(al) ['kɔmik(əl)] comico; buffo; **~ strips** pl fumetti m/pl

comma ['kɔmə] virgola f

command [kə'mɑ:nd] s ordine f; comando m; padronanza f; v/t ordinare; comandare; **~er-in-chief** comandante m in capo; **~ment** comandamento m

commemorate [kə'meməreit] v/t commemorare

commence [kə'mens] v/t, v/i cominciare; iniziare

commend [kə'mend] v/t raccomandare

comment ['kɔment] s commento m; v/i commentare; **~ary** commento m; **~ator** cronista m, f

commerce ['kɔmə(:)s] commercio m; **~ial** commerciale

commission [kə'mi∫ən] s commissione f; v/t incaricare; **~er** commissario m

commit [kə'mit] v/t commettere; consegnare affidare; **~ oneself (to)** v/i compromettersi; **~ment** impegno m

committee [kə'miti] comitato m

commodity [kə'mɔditi] genere m di prima necessità; merce f; comodità f

common ['kɔmən] comune; pubblico; volgare; **in ~** in comune; **~ market** Mercato m Comune Europeo; **~ sense** buon senso m; **~place** s luogo comune m; a banale; **~wealth** repubblica f

commotion [kə'mou∫ən] agitazione f

commun|al ['kɔmjunl] comunale; pubblico; **~icate** [kə'mju:nikeit] v/t comunicare; comunicazione f; avviso m; **~icative** comunicativo; **~ion** comunione f

commun|ism ['kɔmjunizəm] comunismo m; **~ist** comunista m, f

community [kə'mju:niti] comunità f

commut|ation [ˌkɔmju'tei∫ən] commutazione f; **~ ticket** Am biglietto m d'abbonamento; **~e** [kə'mju:t] v/t commutare; viaggiare regolarmente

compact ['kɔmpækt] compatto

companion [kəm'pænjən] compagno(a) m (f); **~ship** compagnia f; cameratismo m

company ['kʌmpəni] compagnia f

compar|able ['kɔmpərəbl] paragonabile; **~ative** [kəm'pærətiv] comparativo; **~e** [kəm'pɛə] v/t paragonare; v/i sostenere il paragone; **~ison** [~'pærisn] paragone m

compartment [kəm'pɑːtmənt] scompartimento m

compass ['kʌmpəs] s bussola f; v/t circondare; **(pair of) ~es** pl compasso m

compassion [kəm'pæʃən] compassione f

compatible [kəm'pætəbl] compatibile

compatriot [kəm'pætriət] compatriota m

compel [kəm'pel] v/t costringere

compensat|e ['kɔmpenseit] v/t compensare; v/i compensarsi; **~ion** compensazione f; compenso m

compère ['kɔmpɛə] presentatore m

compet|e [kəm'piːt] v/i concorrere; **~ence** ['kɔmpitəns] competenza f; capacità f; **~ent** competente; capace; **~ition** [kɔmpi'tiʃən] concorrenza f; **~itor** [kəm'petitə] concorrente m.f

compile v/t compilare

complacent [kəm'pleisnt]

contento di se stesso

complain [kəm'plein] v/i lagnarsi; reclamare; **~t** lagnanza f; med malattia f

complete [kəm'pliːt] a completo; intero; perfetto; v/t completare; finire

complex ['kɔmpleks] a, s complesso (m)

complexion [kəm'plekʃən] carnagione f

complicat|e ['kɔmplikeit] v/t complicare; **~ion** complicazione f

compliment ['kɔmplimənt] s complimento m; **~s** pl saluti m/pl; v/t congratularsi con; **~ary** di omaggio; **~ary ticket** biglietto m di omaggio

comply (with) [kəm'plai] v/i acconsentire

component [kəm'pounənt] a, s componente (m)

compos|e [kəm'pouz] v/t comporre; **~e oneself** v/i calmarsi; **~ed** calmo; composto; **~er** compositore m; **~ition** composizione f; **~ure** [kəm'pouʒə] compostezza f; calma f

compote ['kɔmpot] conserva f

compound ['kɔmpaund] s composto m; v/t comporre

comprehen|d [kɔmpri'hend] v/t comprendere; includere; **~sible** comprensibile; **~sion** comprensione f; **~sive** comprensivo

compress [kəm'pres] v/t comprimere; condensare

comprise [kəm'praiz] v/t comprendere; includere

compromise ['komprəmaiz] s compromesso m; v/t, v/i accomodarsi; compromettere

compulsion [kəm'pʌlʃən] costrizione f; **.ory** obbligatorio

compunction [kəm'pʌŋkʃən] rimorsi m/pl

compute [kəm'pju:t] v/t computare; **.er** calcolatore m elettronico: computer m

comrade ['komrid] compagno m

conceal [kən'si:l] v/t nascondere

concede [kən'si:d] v/t concedere

conceit [kən'si:t] presunzione f; **.ed** presuntuoso

conceivable concepibile; **.e** v/t concepire

concentrate ['konsəntreit] v/t concentrare; v/i concentrarsi

concept ['konsept] concetto m; **.ion** [kən'sepʃən] concezione f

concern [kən'sə:n] s ansietà f; faccenda f; azienda f; ditta f; v/t concernere; riguardare; preoccupare; **.ed** interessato; preoccupato

concert ['konsət] s concerto m; v/t concertare

concession [kən'seʃən] concessione f

conciliate [kən'silieit] v/t conciliare; **.ion** [kənsili'eiʃən] conciliazione f

concise [kən'sais] conciso

conclude [kən'klu:d] v/t concludere; terminare; **.sion** conclusione f; termine m

concord ['konkɔ:d] armonia f; mus accordo m

concrete ['konkri:t] a concreto; s cemento m

concur [kən'kə:] v/i concorrere; accordarsi

concussion (of the brain) [kən'kʌʃən] commozione f cerebrale

condemn [kən'dem] v/t condannare; **.ation** condanna f

condense [kən'dens] v/t condensare; v/i condensarsi; **.r** condensatore m

condescend [kondi'send] v/i (ac)condiscendere; degnarsi

condition [kən'diʃən] s condizione f; v/t condizionare; stipulare; **.al**, s condizionale (m)

condole [kən'doul] v/i fare le condoglianze; **.nce** condoglianza f

conduct ['kondʌkt] s condotta f; direzione f; [kən'dʌkt] v/t condurre; dirigere; **.or** [kən'dʌktə] mus direttore m d'orchestra; (on a bus) fattorino m; elec conduttore m

cone [koun] cono m

confection [kən'fekʃən] confetto m; (dress) confezione f; **.er** pasticciere m;

~ery pasticceria f
confedera|cy [kən'fedərəsi] confederazione f; **~te** [~it] alleato
confer [kən'fəː] v/i conferire; **~ence** ['kɔnfərəns] conferenza f
confess [kən'fes] v/t confessare; **~ion** confessione f
confid|ant [ˌkɔnfi'dænt] confidente m; **~e** [kən'faid] v/t confidare; **~ence** confidenza f; fiducia f; **~ent** fiducioso; **~ential** [~'denʃəl] confidenziale
confine [kən'fain] v/t rinchiudere; **~ment** reclusione f; med parto m
confirm [kən'fəːm] v/t confermare; rettificare; cresimare; **~ation** conferma f; cresima f
confiscate ['kɔnfiskeit] v/t confiscare
conflict ['kɔnflikt] s conflitto m; [kən'flikt] v/i contradirsi; **~ing** contraddittorio; opposto
conform [kən'fɔːm] v/i conformare; **~ity** conformità f
confound [kən'faund] v/t confondere; **~ it!** fam maledetto
confront [kən'frʌnt] v/t affrontare; confrontare
confus|e [kən'fjuːz] v/t confondere; **~ion** confusione f
congeal [kən'dʒiːl] v/t congelare
congestion [kən'dʒestʃən] congestione f
congratulat|e [kən'grætju-

leit] v/t congratularsi con; **~ion** congratulazione f; rallegramento m
congregat|e ['kɔŋgrigeit] v/i congregare; congregare; **~ion** (church) fedeli m/pl
congress ['kɔŋgres] congresso m
conjecture [kən'dʒektʃə] s congettura f; v/t congetturare
conjugal ['kɔndʒugəl] coniugale
conjugat|e ['kɔndʒugeit] v/t coniugare; **~ion** coniugazione f
conjunction [kən'dʒʌŋkʃən] congiunzione f
conjunctivitis [ˌkɔndʒʌŋkti'vaitis] congiuntivite f
conjure [kən'dʒuə] v/t scongiurare; ['kʌndʒə] v/i fare incanti; **~r** mago m
connect [kə'nekt] v/t legare; collegare; associare; connettere; v/i legarsi; collegarsi; associarsi; connettersi; **~ion** legame m; collegamento m; parente m
connexion [kə'nekʃən] cf **connection**
conque|r ['kɔŋkə] v/t conquistare; vincere; **~ror** conquistatore m; **~st** conquista f
conscien|ce ['kɔnʃəns] coscienza f; **~tious** [~i'ənʃəs] coscienzioso
conscious ['kɔnʃəs] cosciente; **~ness** coscienza f
consecrat|e ['kɔnsikreit] v/t consacrare; dedicare; **~ion**

consacrazione f; dedica f

consecutive [kən'sekjutiv] consecutivo

consent [kən'sent] s consenso m; v/i acconsentire

consequen|ce ['kɔnsikwəns] conseguenza f; **~t** conseguente; **~tly** in conseguenza

conserv|ation [kɔnsə'veiʃən] conservazione f; **~ative** [kən'sə:vətiv] a, s conservatore m; **~atory** mus conservatorio m; **~e** v/t conservare; s conserva f

consider [kən'sidə] v/t considerare; **~able** considerevole; **~ate** [~rit] riguardoso; **~ation** considerazione f

consign [kən'sain] v/t consegnare; **~ee** destinatario m; **~ment** consegna f; partita f

consist [kən'sist] v/i consistere; **~ence**, **~ency** consistenza f; **~ent** costante

consol|ation [kɔnsə'leiʃən] consolazione f; **~e** [kən'soul] v/t consolare

consolidate [kən'sɔlideit] v/t. consolidare

consonant ['kɔnsənənt] consonante f

conspicuous [kən'spikjuəs] cospicuo

conspir|acy [kən'spirəsi] s congiura f; v/i cospirare; **~ator** congiurato m; **~e** [~'spaiə] v/i congiurare

constant ['kɔnstənt] costante

consternation [kɔnstə(:)-'neiʃən] costernazione f

constipation [kɔnsti'peiʃən] stitichezza f

constituen|cy [kən'stitjuənsi] votanti m/pl; collegio m elettorale; **~t** s membro m di un collegio elettorale; a costituente

constitute ['kɔnstitju:t] v/t costituire; **~ion** med costituzione f; fisico m; pol costituzione f

constrain [kən'strein] v/t costringere; **~t** costrizione f

constrict [kən'strikt] v/t comprimere; contrarre

construct [kən'strʌkt] v/t costruire; **~ion** costruzione f; **~ive** costruttivo

consul ['kɔnsəl] console m; **~ate** [~julit] consolato m; **~ship** consolato m

consult [kən'sʌlt] v/t consultare; **~ation** [kɔnsəl'teiʃən] consultazione f; consulto m; **~ing hours** pl ora f d'ufficio; orario m per le visite

consum|e [kən'sju:m] v/t consumare; v/i consumarsi; **~er** consumatore m; **~mate** [kən'sʌmit] consumato; ['kɔnsəmeit] v/t consumare; **~ption** [kən'sʌmpʃən] consumo m; med tisi f

contact ['kɔntækt] s contatto m; v/t mettersi in rapporto con; **~ lenses** pl lenti f/pl a contatto

contagious [kən'teidʒəs] contagioso

contain [kən'tein] v/t contenenere; **~er** recipiente *m*; involucro *m*

contaminate [kən'tæmineit] *v/t* contaminare

contemplate ['kɔntempleit] *v/t* contemplare; **~ion** contemplazione *f*

contemporary [kən'tempərəri] *a, s* contemporaneo (*m*)

contempt [kən'tempt] disprezzo *m*; **~uous** sprezzante

contend [kən'tend] *v/t* sostenere; affermare; *v/i* contendere

content [kən'tent] *a* contento; soddisfatto; *s* ['kɔntent] contento *m*; contentezza *f*; *v/t* accontentare, soddisfare

contents ['kɔntents] *pl* contenuto *m*

contest ['kɔntest] *s* gara *f*; *v/t* contendere

context ['kɔntekst] contesto *m*

continent ['kɔntinənt] continente *m*

contingency [kən'tindʒənsi] contingenza *f*

continual [kən'tinjuəl] continuo; **~ation** continuazione *f*; seguito *m*; **~e** *v/t* continuare; proseguire; **~ity** continuità *f*; **~ous** continuo

contort [kən'tɔːt] *v/t* contorcere

contour ['kɔntuə] contorno *m*

contraband ['kɔntrəbænd] contrabbando *m*

contraceptive [ˌkɔntrə'septiv] *a, s* anticoncezionale (*m*)

contract ['kɔntrækt] *s* contratto *m*; [kən'trækt] *v/t* contrarre; contrattare; **~ion** contrazione *f*; abbreviazione *f*; **~or** imprenditore *m*

contradict [kɔntrə'dikt] *v/t* contraddire; **~ion** contraddizione *f*; **~ory** contraddittorio

contrary ['kɔntrəri] *a, s* contrario (*m*); opposto (*m*); **on the ~** al contrario

contrast ['kɔntrɑːst] contrasto *m*; [kən'trɑːst] *v/t* confrontare; *v/i* contrastare

contribute [kən'tribju(ː)t] *v/t* contribuire; *v/i* collaborare; **~ion** contributo *m*; collaborazione *f*; **~or** [kən'tribjutə] collaboratore *m*; donatore *m*

contrite ['kɔntrait] contrito

contrivance [kən'traivəns] apparecchio *m*; **~e** *v/t* trovare il modo di

control [kən'troul] *s* controllo *m*; direzione *f*; dominio *m*; freno *m*; *v/t* controllare; dirigere; dominare; **~ler** controllore *m*

controversial [ˌkɔntrə'vəːʃəl] controverso; **~y** ['~.vəːsi] controversia *f*

contuse [kən'tjuːz] *v/t* contundere

convalescence [ˌkɔnvə'lesns] convalescenza *f*; **~t** convalescente *m, f*

convene [kən'viːn] *v/t* con-

vocare; **.ience** comodità *f*;
public **.ièe** gabinetto *m*
pubblico; **.ient** comodo

convent ['kɔnvənt] convento
m

convention convenzione *f*;
assemblea *f*; **.al** convenzionale

convers|ation [ˌkɔnvə'sei-
ʃən] conversazione *f*; **.e**
[kən'vɜːs] *v/i* conversare;
a, *s* converso (*m*);
(*m*)

conver|sion [kən'vɜːʃən]
conversione *f*; **.t** *s* convertito *m*; *v/t* convertire; **.tible**
trasformabile; convertibile

convey [kən'vei] *v/t* portare;
trasportare; esprimere;
trasmettere; **.ance** mezzo
m di trasporto; **.or belt**
nastro *m* scorrevole

convict ['kɔnvikt] ergastolano *m*; [kən'vikt] *v/t* dichiarare colpevole; **.ion** convinzione *f*

convince [kən'vins] *v/t* convincere

convoy ['kɔnvɔi] convoglio
m

convulsion [kən'vʌlʃən]
convulsione *f*

cook [kuk] *s* cuoco(a) *m* (*f*);
v/t, *v/i* cuocere; cucinare;
.er fornello *m*; **.ery** arte *f*
culinaria; **.ie**, *v/* biscotto *m*

cool [kuːl] *s* fresco *m*; *a* fresco; *fig* calmo; indifferente;
v/t raffreddare; *v/i* raffreddarsi; **~ down** *v/t* calmare;
v/i calmarsi

co-op [kou'ɔp] *fam* cf **co-**
operative society

co(-)operat|e [kou'ɔpəreit]
v/i cooperare; **.ion** cooperazione *f*; **.ive** cooperativo;
.ive society cooperativa *f*;
.or collaboratore *m*

co(-)ordinate [kou'ɔːdineit]
v/t coordinare; *s* mat coordinata *f*

cop [kɔp] *fam* poliziotto *m*

cope [koup]: **~ with** *v/i* far
fronte a; lottare contro

copious ['koupjəs] copioso

copper ['kɔpə] rame *m*

copy ['kɔpi] *s* copia *f*; esemplare *m*; edizione *f*; *v/t* copiare; imitare; **.right** diritti *m/pl* d'autore

coral ['kɔrəl] corallo *m*

cord [kɔːd] corda *f*

cordial ['kɔːdjəl] cordiale;
.ity cordialità *f*

corduroy ['kɔdjurɔi] velluto
m a coste

core [kɔː] *s* nucleo *m*; centro
m; (*fruit*) torsolo *m*

cork [kɔːk] sughero *m*; tappo
m; **.screw** cavatappi *m*

corn [kɔːn] grano *m*; callo *m*
(*del piede*)

corner ['kɔːnə] angolo *m*;
svolta *f*

cornet ['kɔːnit] cornetta *f*

coronation [ˌkɔrə'neiʃən]
incoronazione *f*

coroner ['kɔrənə] magistrato
m inquirente

corpora|l ['kɔːpərəl] *s* caporale *m*; *a* corporale; corporeo; **.tion** corporazione *f*;
ente *m* autonomo

corpse [kɔːps] cadavere *m*

correct [kə'rekt] v/t correggere; _.ion_ correzione f

correspond [kɔris'pɔnd] v/i corrispondere; _.ence_ corrispondenza f; _.ent_ corrispondente m, f

corridor ['kɔridɔ:] corridoio m

corroborate [kə'rɔbəreit] v/t corroborare

corro|de [kə'roud] v/t corrodere; v/i corrodersi; _.sion_ [~ʒən] corrosione f

corrugate ['kɔrugeit] v/t corrugare; _.d iron_ lamiera f ondulata

corrupt [kə'rʌpt] v/t corrompere; v/i corrompersi; a corrotto; _.ion_ corruzione f

corset ['kɔ:sit] busto m

cosmetic [kɔz'metik] cosmetica f; _.ian_ [~ə'tiʃən] estetista f

cosm|onaut ['kɔzmənɔ:t] cosmonauta m, f; _.os_ cosmo m

cost [kɔst] s costo m; prezzo m; v/i, irr costare; _.ly_ costoso; _.s_ pl spese f/pl

costume ['kɔstju:m] costume m; completo m; **bathing ~** costume m da bagno

cosy ['kouzi] accogliente; piacevole

cottage ['kɔtidʒ] casetta f

cotton ['kɔtn] s cotone m; a di cotone; **~ wool** cotone m idrofilo

couch [kautʃ] divano m

cough [kɔf] s tosse f; v/i tossire

council ['kaunsl] concilio m; consiglio m; _.lor_ consigliere m

counsel ['kaunsəl] consiglio m; parere m; avvocato m; _.lor_ consigliere m

count [kaunt] s conto m; calcolo m; (noble) conte m; v/t, v/i contare; **~ on** contare su

countenance ['kauntinəns] (espressione f del) viso m

counter ['kauntə] s banco m; v/t opporsi a; adv contrario a

counter|act [,kauntə'rækt] v/t neutralizzare; _.balance_ contrappeso m; _.clockwise_ sinistroso; _.espionage_ controspionaggio m; _.feit_ ['~fit] falso m; _.part_ riscontro m

countess ['kauntis] contessa f

countless ['kauntlis] illimitato; innumerevole

country ['kʌntri] campagna f; paese m; patria f; **~man** compatriota m, f; contadino m; **~seat** casa f di campagna; **~town** città f di provincia

county ['kaunti] contea f

coup|le ['kʌpl] s coppia f; paio m; v/t accoppiare; v/i accoppiarsi; **~ing** mec attacco m

coupon ['ku:pɔn] cedola f

courage ['kʌridʒ] coraggio m; _.ous_ [kə'reidʒəs] coraggioso

courier ['kuriə] corriere m; messaggero m

course [kɔ:s] corso m; direzione f; portata f (in un pranzo); (sport) pista f; in due ~ in tempo utile; **matter of** ~ cosa f ovvia

court [kɔ:t] s corte f; tribunale m; v/t corteggiare; **~eous** ['kɔ:tjəs] cortese; **~esy** ['kɔ:tisi] cortesia f; **~ier** cortigiano m; **~martial** corte f marziale; **~room** aula f di udienza; **~ship** corte f; **~yard** cortile m

cousin ['kʌzn] cugino(a) m (f)

cover ['kʌvə] s coperta f; copertina f; riparo m; v/t coprire; **~ing** copertura f

covet ['kʌvit] v/t invidiare; **~ous** invidioso; bramoso

cow [kau] vacca f; femmina f (di elefante ecc); **~ard** codardo m; **~boy** vaccaro m

cower ['kauə] v/i rannicchiarsi

cow-hide vacchetta f

coxswain ['kɔkswein] timoniere m

coy [kɔi] timido

crab [kræb] granchio m

crack [kræk] s spaccatura f; v/t spaccare; v/i spaccarsi; **~er** petardo m; Am biscotto m; **~up** incidente m

cradle ['kreidl] culla f

craft [krɑ:ft] abilità f; arte f; furberia f; barchetta f; **~sman** artigiano m; **~smanship** artigianato m; **~y** furbo

crag [kræg] picco m

cramp [kræmp] s crampo m; v/t impacciare

crane [krein] s gru f; v/t, v/i allungare il collo

crank [kræŋk] manovella f; **~ up** avviare (il motore) a mano; **~y** eccentrico

crash [kræʃ] s fracasso m; comm crollo m; v/i collare; precipitare (di aeroplano); **~helmet** casco m

crate [kreit] gabbia f da imballaggio

crater ['kreitə] cratere m

crave [kreiv] v/t bramare

crawl [krɔ:l] v/i trascinarsi

crayon ['kreiən] matita f

crazy (about) ['kreizi] pazzo (di)

creak [kri:k] v/i cigolare; scricchiolare

cream [kri:m] crema f; (del latte) panna f; **~y** cremoso

crease [kri:s] s grinza f; piega f (del pantalone); v/t sgualcire; v/i sgualcirsi

create [kri(:)'eit] v/t creare; **~ion** creazione f; creato m; **~or** creatore m; **~ure** ['kri:tʃə] creatura f

credentials [kri'denʃəlz] credenziali f/pl

credible ['kredəbl] credibile

credit ['kredit] s credito m; **~ card** tessera f assegno; v/t credere

creed [kri:d] credo m; fede f

creek [kri:k] fiumicino m

creep [kri:p] v/i, irr arrampicarsi; strisciare; **~er** bot rampicante m

cremate [kri'meit] *v/t* cremare

crescent ['kresnt] quarto *m* di luna

cress [kres] crescione *m*

crest [krest] cresta *f*; criniera *f*; cima *f*; **~fallen** abbattuto

crevasse [kri'væs] crepaccio *m*

crevice ['krevis] fessura *f*; crepaccio *m*

crew [kru:] equipaggio *m*

crib [krib] presepio *m*; culla *f* (*di bambino*)

cricket ['krikit] grillo *m*; cricket *m*

crim|e [kraim] reato *m*; delitto *m*; **~inal** ['kriminl] *a*, *s* criminale (*m*,*f*); delinquente (*m*)

crimson ['krimzn] cremisi *m*

cripple ['kripl] *s* zoppo *m*; invalido *m*; mutilato *m*; *v/t* mutilare

crisis ['kraisis], *pl* **es** [*'*~iz] crisi *f*

crisp [krisp] crespo; croccante

criterion [krai'tiəriən], *pl* **ria** [*~*riə] criterio *m*

critic ['kritik] critico *m*; **al** critico, *m*; **ism** ['~sizəm] critica *f*; **ize** *v/t* criticare

croak [krouk] *v/i* gracidare

crochet ['krouʃei] *v/t*, *v/i* lavorare all'uncinetto

crockery ['krɔkəri] vasellame *m*

crocodile ['krɔkədail] coccodrillo *m*

crocus ['kroukəs], *pl* **es** [*~*iz] croco *m*

crook [kruk] malvivente *m*; **ed** *v/t* storto

crop [krɔp] *s* raccolto *m*; *v/t* tagliare corto; **~ up** *v/i* venire fuori

cross [krɔs] *s* croce *f*; *biol* incrocio *m*; *v/t* attraversare; contrariare; *a* nervoso; **~eyed** strabico; *v/t* out scancellare; **~examination** interrogatorio *m* in contraddittorio; **~roads** *pl* crocevia *f*; **~word puzzle** parole *f*/*pl* incrociate

crouch [krautʃ] *v/i* accucciarsi

crow [krou] *s* corvo *m*; cornacchia *f*; *v/i* cantare; **~bar** leva *f*; piede *m* di porco

crowd [kraud] *s* folla *f*; massa *f*; *v/t* affollare; *v/i* affollarsi; **ed** affollato

crwon [kraun] *s* corona *f*; *v/t* incoronare; **~ prince** principe *m* ereditario

crucial ['kru:ʃəl] cruciale; decisivo

crucif|ix ['kru:sifiks] crocifisso *m*; **~y** ['~fai] *v/t* crocifiggere

crude [kru:d] rozzo; volgare; primitivo

cruel [kruəl] crudele; **~ty** crudeltà *f*

cruet ['kru:it] ampollina *f*

cruise [kru:z] croceria *f*

crumb [krʌm] briciola *f*; **~le** ['~bl] *v/t* sbriciolare; *v/i* sbriciolarsi

crumple ['krʌmpl] *v/t* sgualcire; *v/i* sgualcirsi

crunch [krʌntʃ] v/t schiacciare rumorosamente

crusade [kruːˈseid] crociata f

crush [krʌʃ] v/t schiacciare; sgualcire

crust [krʌst] crosta f

crutch [krʌtʃ] stampella f

cry [krai] s grido m; pianto m; v/t gridare; piangere

crypt [kript] cripta f

crystal [ˈkristl] s cristallo m; a di cristallo

cube [kjuːb] cubo m; ~ **root** radice f cubica

cuckoo [ˈkuku] cuculo m

cucumber [ˈkjuːkəmbə] cetriolo m

cuddle [ˈkʌdl] v/t abbracciare; coccolare

cue [kjuː] battuta f

cuff [kʌf] polsino m; ~**links** pl gemelli m/pl

cuisine [kwiˈziːn] cucina f

culminate [ˈkʌlmineit] v/i culminare

culprit [ˈkʌlprit] colpevole m

cult [kʌlt] culto m; ~**ivate** [ˈ.iveit] v/t coltivare; ~**ural** [ˈkʌltʃərəl] culturale; ~**ure** [ˈ.tʃə] cultura f; ~**ured** colto

cunning [ˈkʌniŋ] s astuzia f; a astuto

cup [kʌp] tazza f; coppa f; ~**board** armadio m

curdle [ˈkəːdl] v/i accagliarsi

cure [kjuə] s cura f; rimedio m; v/t guarire

curfew [ˈkəːfjuː] coprifuoco m

curio|sity [ˌkjuəriˈɒsiti] curiosità f; ~**us** curioso

curl [kəːl] s ricciolo m; v/t arricciare; v/i arricciarsi; ~**y** riccioluto

currant [ˈkʌrənt] ribes m

curren|cy [ˈkʌrənsi] moneta f circolante; **foreign** ~**cy** valuta f estera; ~**t** a, s corrente (f)

curriculum [kəˈrikjuləm], pl ~**a** [ˈ.ə] curricolo m

curse [kəːs] s maledizione f; v/t, v/i maledire

curt [kəːt] brusco

curtail [kəːˈteil] v/t diminuire; ridurre; impedire

curtain [ˈkəːtn] tenda f; thea sipario m

curts(e)y [ˈkəːtsi] s riverenza f; v/i fare una riverenza

curve [kəːv] s curva f; v/t curvare; v/i curvarsi

cushion [ˈkuʃən] cuscino m

custard [ˈkʌstəd] crema f

custody [ˈkʌstədi] custodia f; arresto m

custom [ˈkʌstəm] costume m; abitudine f; ~**ary** consueto; ~**er** cliente m; ~**s** pl dogana f; ~**s officer** doganiere m

cut [kʌt] s taglio m; riduzione f; v/t, v/i irr tagliare; ~ **down** (tree) abbattere; (price) ridurre

cute [kjuːt] astuto; Am attraente; bellino

cutlery [ˈkʌtləri] posate f/pl

cutlet [ˈkʌtlit] costoletta f

cutter [ˈkʌtə] tagliatore m; (boat) cottro m

cutthroat ['kʌtθrout] assassino *m*

cutting trincea *f*; ritaglio *m*

cycl|e ['saikl] *s* bicicletta *f*; ciclo *m*; *v/i* andare in bicicletta; **~ist** ciclista *m*

cylinder ['silində] cilindro *m*

cynical ['sinikəl] cinico

cypress ['saipris] cipresso *m*

cyst [sist] ciste *f*

Czech [tʃek] *a*, *s* ceco (*m*); **~oslovak** *a*, *s* cecoslovacco (*m*)

D

dachshund ['dækshund] bassotto *m*

dad [dæd], **~dy** ['~i] papà *m*; babbo *m*

daffodil ['dæfədil] narciso *m*

daft [dɑːft] sciocco; scemo

dagger ['dægə] daga *f*; pugnale *m*

daily ['deili] *s* quotidiano *m*; *a* giornaliero; quotidiano

dairy ['dɛəri] latteria *f*; **~man** lattaio *m*; **~ product** latticinio *m*

daisy ['deizi] margherita *f*

dam [dæm] *s* diga *f*; argine *m*; *v/t* arginare

damage ['dæmidʒ] *s* danno *m*; perdita *f*; *v/t* danneggiare; *v/i* danneggiarsi

damn [dæm] *v/t* dannare; maledire; **~ it!** maledetto!; **I don't care a ~** non me ne importa niente

damp [dæmp] *a* umido; *s* umidità *f*; *v/t* inumidire

dance [dɑːns] *s* danza *f*; ballo *m*; *v/t*, *v/i* danzare; ballare; **~er** ballerino(a) *m* (*f*); **~ing** ballo *m*

dandelion ['dændilaiən] radicchiella *f*

Dane [dein] danese *m*, *f*

danger ['deindʒə] pericolo *m*; **~ous** pericoloso

dangle ['dæŋgl] *v/t* dondolare; *v/i* dondolarsi

Danish ['deiniʃ] danese

dar|e [dɛə] *s* sfida *f*; *v/t* sfidare; *v/i* osare; **~ing** *s* audacia *f*; *a* audace

dark [dɑːk] *a* oscuro; buio; tenebroso; *s* buio *m*; oscurità *f*; **~en** *v/t* oscurare; *v/i* oscurarsi; **~ness** oscurità *f*; buio *m*

darling ['dɑːliŋ] *s* tesoro *m*; amore *m*; *a* delizioso; incantevole

darn [dɑːn] *s* rammento *m*; *v/t* rammentare

dart [dɑːt] *s* dardo *m*; *v/t* dardeggiare; *v/i* balzare; lanciarsi

dash [dæʃ] *s* scatto *m*; (*pen*) tratto *m*; *v/i* lanciarsi; **~board** cruscotto *m*

data ['deitə] *pl* dati *m/pl*

date [deit] *s* bot dattero *m*; data *f*; *v/t*, *v/i* datare; **up to ~** aggiornato; moderno; **out of ~** antiquato

daughter ['dɔːtə] figlia *f*; **~in-law** nuora *f*

daunt [dɔːnt] *v/t* scoraggiare

dawn [dɔ:n] *s* alba *f*; *v/i* albeggiare

day [dei] giorno *m*; giornata *f*; di *m*; **all ~ long** tutto il santo giorno; **by ~** di giorno; **every other ~** ogni due giorni; **in the ~s of** ai tempi di; all'epoca di; **the ~ after tomorrow** dopodomani; **the ~ before yesterday** l'altro ieri; **~break** alba *f*; **~dream** fantasticheria *f*; **~light-saving time** ora *f* d'estate

daze [deiz] *s* stordimento *m*; *v/t* stordire

dazzle ['dæzl] *v/t* abbagliare

dead [ded] morto; **the ~** i morti *m/pl*; **~en** *v/t* ammortire; smorzare; **~end** vicolo *m* cieco; **~line** limite *m*; **~lock** punto *m* morto; **~ly** mortale

deaf [def] sordo; **~en** *v/t* assordare; **~-mute** *a*, *s* sordomuto (*m*)

deal [di:l] *s* affare *m*; trattativa *f*; distribuzione *f* (*di carte*); **a good ~** abbastanza; *v/t* distribuire; **~ in** *v/i* trattare in; **~er** commerciante *m*

dean [di:n] decano *m*

dear [diə] caro; **~ me!** Dio mio!

death [deθ] morte *f*; **~rate** mortalità *f*

debase [di'beis] *v/t* abbassare

debate *s* dibattito *m*; discussione *f*; *v/t*, *v/i* dibattere; discutere

debauch [di'bɔ:tʃ] *s* orgia *f*; *v/t* pervertire

debit ['debit] *comm s* debito *m*; *v/t* addebitare

debris ['deibri:] detriti *m/pl*

debt [det] debito *m*; **~or** debitore *m*

decade ['dekeid] decade *f*; decennio *m*

decaden|ce ['dekədəns] decadenza *f*; **~t** decadente

decapitate [di'kæpiteit] *v/t* decapitare

decay [di'kei] *s* decomposizione *f*; decadenza *f*; *v/i* decomporsi; decadere

decease [di'si:s] *s* morte *f*; *v/i* decedere; morire

deceit [di'si:t] inganno *m*; frode *f*; **~ful** falso; **~ve** *v/t* ingannare

December [di'sembə] dicembre *m*

decen|cy ['di:snsi] decenza *f*; decoro *m*; **~t** decente, decoroso

deception [di'sepʃən] inganno *m*; **~ive** ingannevole

decide [di'said] *v/t*, *v/i* decidere

decimal ['desiməl] decimale *f*

decipher [di'saifə] *v/t* decifrare

decis|ion [di'siʒən] decisione *f*; **~ve** [di'saisiv] decisivo

deck [dek] ponte *m*; **~-chair** sdraia *f*

declaim [di'kleim] *v/i* declamare

declar|ation [deklə'reiʃən] declarazione *f*; **~e** [di'klɛə *v/t* dichiarare; *v/i* dichiararsi

decl|ension [di'klenʃən] declinazione *f*; **~ine** [di'klain] *s* declino *m*; ribasso *m* (*di prezzo*); consunzione *f*; *v/t gram* declinare; rifiutare; *v/i* declinarsi; rifiutarsi

decode ['di:'koud] *v/t* decifrare

decompos|e [ˌdi:kəm'pouz] *v/t* decomporre; *v/i* decomporsi

decor|ate ['dekəreit] *v/t* decorare; ornare; **~ation** decorazione *f*; ornamento *m*; **~um** decoro *m*

decrease ['di:kri:s] *s* diminuzione *f*; *v/t, v/i* diminuire

decree [di'kri:] *s* decreto *m*; *v/t* decretare

decrepit [di'krepit] decrepito

dedicat|e ['dedikeit] *v/t* dedicare; **~ion** dedicazione *f*; (*of a book*) dedica *f*

deduce [di'dju:s] *v/t* dedurre; desumere

deduct [di'dʌkt] *v/t* dedurre; sottrarre; **~ion** deduzione *f*

deed [di:d] atto *m*

deep [di:p] profondo; **~en** *v/t* approfondire; *v/i* approfondirsi; **~ness** profondità *f*

deer [diə] cervo *m*; daino *m*; **~skin** pelle *f* di daino

deface [di'feis] *v/t* sfigurare

defame [di'feim] *v/t* diffamare; calunniare

defeat [di'fi:t] *s* sconfitta *f*; *v/t* sconfiggere

defect [di'fekt] difetto *m*; **~ive** difettoso; **mentally ~ive** deficiente; anormale

defen|ce, *Am* **~se** [di'fens] difesa *f*; protezione *f*; **~celess** indifeso; **~d** *v/t* difendere; **~dant** *for* accusato *m*; **~der** difensore *m*

defer [di'fə:] *v/t* differire; rimandare; **~ence** deferenza *f*

defiance [di'faiəns] sfida *f*

deficien|cy [di'fiʃənsi] deficienza *f*; **~t** deficiente; difettoso

deficit ['defisit] disavanzo *m*

defin|e [di'fain] *v/t* definire; **~ite** ['definit] definito; sicuro; **~ition** definizione *f*; **~itive** [di'finitiv] definitivo

deflate [di'fleit] *v/t* deflazionare; sgonfiare

deform [di'fɔ:m] *v/t* deformare; sformare

defraud [di'frɔ:d] *v/t* defraudare

defrost [di'frɔst] *v/t* togliere il ghiaccio a; (*refrigerator*) sbrinare

deft [deft] destro; abile

defy [di'fai] *v/t* sfidare

degenerate [di'dʒenərit] *v/i* degenerare

degrade [di'greid] *v/t* degradare

degree [di'gri:] grado *m*; laurea *f*

dejected [di'dʒektid] abbattuto

delay [di'lei] *s* ritardo *m*; *v/t* ritardare; *v/i* tardare; **without ~** immediatamente

delegate ['deligit] s delegato m; ['deligeit] v/t delegare; **~ion** [~'geiʃən] delegazione f

deliberate [di'libəreit] v/t, v/i deliberare; [~it] a deliberato; premeditato

delicacy ['delikəsi] delicatezza f; (food) leccornia f; **~te** [~it] delicato

delicious [di'liʃəs] delizioso

delight [di'lait] s gioia f; incanto m; v/t piacere molto; **~ful** delizioso

delinquency [di'liŋkwənsi] delinquenza f; **~t** delinquente m

deliver [di'livə] v/t liberare; distribuire (posta); pronunciare (un discorso); sgravare (una partoriente); **~y** liberazione f; distribuzione f; parto m

delude [di'lu:d] v/t deludere; ingannare

deluge ['delju:dʒ] diluvio m

delusion [di'lu:ʒən] delusione f; inganno m; allucinazione f

demand [di'mɑ:nd] s richiesta f; esigenza f; v/t richiedere; esigere; **in ~** richiesto

democracy [di'mɔkrəsi] democrazia f; **~t** ['deməkræt] democratico m; **~tic** [~'krætik] democratico

demolish [di'mɔliʃ] v/t demolire

demon ['di:mən] demonio m

demonstrate ['demənstreit] v/t dimostrare; **~ion**

dimostrazione f; **~ive** [di'mɔnstrətiv] dimostrativo

demoralize [di'mɔrəlaiz] v/t demoralizzare

den [den] tana f

denial [di'naiəl] diniego m; rifiuto m

denomination [dinɔmi'neiʃən] denominazione f; confessione f

denote [di'nout] v/t denotare; indicare

denounce [di'nauns] v/t denunciare

dense [dens] denso; ottuso

dent [dent] s intaccatura f; v/t intaccare

dental ['dentl] dentale; **~al surgeon, ~ist** dentista m, f; **~ure** dentiera f; **~istry** odontoiatria f

deny [di'nai] v/t negare; rifiutare

depart [di'pɑ:t] v/i partire; **~ment** riparto m; **~ment store** grande magazzino m; **~ure** partenza f

depend (**on**) [di'pend] v/i dipendere (da); **~ence** dipendenza f; **~ent** s, a dipendente (m)

deplorable [di'plɔ:rəbl] deplorabile; **~e** v/t deplorare

depopulate [di:'pɔpjuleit] v/t spopolare

deport [di'pɔ:t] v/t deportare

depose [di'pouz] v/t deporre; **~it** [di'pozit] s deposito m; sedimento m; v/t depositare; **~ition** deposizione f; testimonianza f; **~itor** depositante *m*; correntista *m,f*

depot ['depou] deposito *m*

depraved [di'preivd] depravato

depreciate [di'pri:fieit] *v/t* screditare; deprezzare

depress [di'pres] *v/t* deprimere; **~ion** depressione *f*

deprive [di'praiv] *v/t* privare

depth [depθ] profondità *f*; fondo *m*

deputation [ˌdepju'teiʃən] deputazione *f*; delegazione *f*; **~y** delegato *m*; deputato *m*

derail [di'reil] *v/t* deragliare

deride [di'raid] *v/t* deridere

derive [di'raiv] *v/t, v/i* derivare

descend [di'sent] *v/t, v/i* scendere; **~dant** discendente *m*; **~t** discesa *f*

describe [dis'kraib] *v/t* descrivere; **~ption** descrizione *f*

desert ['dəzət] *a, s* deserto (*m*); [di'zə:t] *v/t, v/i* disertare; abbandonare

deserve [di'zə:v] *v/t, v/i* meritare

design [di'zain] *s* disegno *m*; *v/t* disegnare

designate ['dezigneit] *v/t* designare

designer [di'zainə] disegnatore *m*

desirable [di'zaiərəbl] desiderabile; **~e** *s* desiderio *m*; *v/t* desiderare; **~ous** desideroso

desk [desk] scrivania *f*; banco *m* (*di scuola*)

desolate ['desəleit] desolato; **~ion** desolazione *f*

despair [dis'peə] *s* disperazione *f*; *v/i* disperare; disperarsi; **in ~** disperato

despatch *s* spedizione *f*; dispaccio *m*; prontezza *f*; *v/t* spedire

desperate ['despərit] disperato

despise [dis'paiz] *v/t* disprezzare

despite of [dis'pait] *prp* malgrado; nonostante

despond [dis'pond] *v/i* scoraggiarsi

dessert [di'zə:t] dolci e frutta (*serviti alla fine del pranzo*)

destination [desti'neiʃən] destinazione *f*; **~e** ['~in] *v/t* destinare; **~y** destino *m*; sorte *f*

destitute ['destitju:t] bisognoso

destroy [dis'trɔi] *v/t* distruggere; **~uction** distruzione *f*

detach [di'tætʃ] *v/t* staccare

detail ['di:teil] dettaglio *m*; **in ~** dettagliatamente

detain [di'tein] *v/t* trattenere

detect [di'tekt] *v/t* scoprire; scorgere; **~ive** agente *m* (*di polizia*); **~ive story** romanzo *m* poliziesco

detention [di'tenʃən] detenzione *f*

deter [di'tə:] *v/t* impedire; **~gent** detergente *m*

deteriorate [di'tiəriəreit] *v/t*

deteriorare; v/i deteriorarsi

determin|ation [ditə:mi-'neiʃən] determinazione f; **~e** (di'tə:min) v/t determinare; decidere; v/i decidersi

deterrent [di'terənt] misura f d'intimidazione f

detest [di'test] v/t detestare; **~able** detestabile

detonate ['detouneit] v/t, v/i detonare

detour ['deituə] deviazione f

detriment ['detriment] detrimento m

devalu|ation [,di:vælju'eiʃən] svalutazione f; **~e** ['~'vælju:] v/t svalutare

devastate ['devəsteit] v/t devastare

develop [di'veləp] v/t sviluppare; v/i svilupparsi; **~ment** sviluppo m

deviate ['di:vieit] v/t deviare

device [di'vais] congegno m; espediente m

devil ['devl] diavolo m; demonio m

devise [di'vaiz] v/t escogitare

devoid [di'vɔid]: **~ of** privo di

devote [di'vout] v/t dedicare; **~ion** devozione f

devour [di'vauə] v/t divorare

devout [di'vaut] devoto

dew [dju:] rugiada f

dexter|ity [deks'teriti] destrezza f; **~ous** ['~rəs] destro; abile

diagnose ['daiəgnouz] v/t

diagnosticare; **~is** [,daiəg-'nousis], pl **~es** [~siːz] diagnosi f

dial ['daiəl] s quadrante m; v/t tel fare il numero

dialect ['daiəlekt] dialetto m

dialog(ue) ['daiəlɔg] dialogo m

diameter [dai'æmitə] diametro m

diamond ['daiəmənd] diamante m; **~s** pl (cards) quadri m/pl

diaper ['daiəpə] Am pannolino m

diaphram ['daiəfræm] diaframma m

diarrh(o)ea [daiə'riə] diarrea f

diary ['daiəri] diario m

dict|ate [dik'teit] v/t, v/i dettare; **~ion** dizione f; **~ionary** vocabolario m

die [dai] v/i morire; **~ out** scomparire

die [dai] dado m, pl **dice** [dais] dadi m/pl.

diet ['daiət] s dieta f; regime m; v/i essere a dieta

differ ['difə] v/i differire; **~ence** differenza f; **~ent** differente

difficult ['difikəlt] difficile; **~y** difficoltà f

diffident ['difidənt] timido

diffuse [di'fju:z] a diffuso; v/t diffondere; **~ion** diffusione f

dig [dig] v/t, irr vangare; scavare

digest [dai'dʒest, di'~] v/t digerire; assimilare; **~ion** [di-

ˈdʒestʃən] digestione *f*

digni|fied [ˈdignifaid] digni-
toso; **~ty** dignità *f*

digress [daiˈgres] *v/i* fare digres-
sioni

digs [digz] *pl fam* alloggio *m*;
stanza *f* (*in affitto*)

dike [daik] diga *f*

dilapidated [diˈlæpideitid]
dilapidato

dilate [daiˈleit] *v/t* dilatare

diligen|ce [ˈdilidʒəns] dili-
genza *f*; **~t** diligente

dilute [daiˈljuːt] *v/t* diluire

dim [dim] oscuro; indistinto; fioco; vago; (*of a person*)
tonto

dime [daim] *Am* pezzo *m* da
dieci centesimi (*di dollaro*)

dimension [diˈmenʃən] dimensione *f*

diminish [diˈminiʃ] *v/t, v/i*
diminuire

dimple [ˈdimpl] fossetta *f*

din [din] frastuono *m*

din|e [dain] *v/i* pranzare;
~ing-car vagone *m* ristorante; **~ingroom** sala *f* da
pranzo; **~ner** vagone *m* ristorante

dinner [ˈdinə] pranzo *m*; **~**
party tavolata *f*

dip [dip] *v/t* immergere; tuffare

diphtheria [difˈθiəriə] difterite *f*

diploma [diˈploumə] diploma *m*; **~cy** diplomazia *f*; **~t**
[ˈ~mæt] diplomatico *m*;
~tic [~ˈmætik] diplomatico

dipper [ˈdipə] escavatore *m*

direct [diˈrekt] *a* diretto *v/t*

dirigere; **~ current** corrente *f* continua; **~ion** direzione *f*; **~ions** *pl* istru-
zioni *f/pl*; **~or** direttore *m*;
consigliere *m*; **~ managing
~or** consigliere *m* delegato;
~(telephone) ~ory elenco *m*
(telefonico)

dirt [dəːt] sudiciume *m*;
sporcizia *f*; **~y** sudicio;
sporco

disabled [disˈeibld] invalido

disadvantage [disədˈvɑːn-
tidʒ] svantaggio *m*; **~ous**
[ˌdisædvɑːnˈteidʒəs] svan-
taggioso

disagree [disəˈgriː] *v/i* non
essere d'accordo; non andare d'accordo; dissentire;
~able sgradevole; antipatico; **~ment** disaccordo *m*

disappear [disəˈpiə] *v/i*
scomparire; **~ance** scom-
parsa *f*; sparizione *f*

disappoint [disəˈpoint] *v/t*
deludere; **~ment** delusione
f

disapprov|al [disəˈpruːvəl]
disapprovazione *f*; **~e** *v/t*,
v/i disapprovare

disarm [disˈɑːm] *v/t, v/i* di-
sarmare; **~ament** disarmo
m

disarrange [ˌdisəˈreindʒ]
v/t mettere in disordine;
disorganizzare

disast|er [diˈzɑːstə] disastro
m; **~rous** disastroso

disbelie|f [ˌdisbiˈliːf] incre-
dulità *f*; **~ve** *v/t* non credere
a

disc [disc] disco *m*

discard [dis'kɑ:d] v/t scartare

discern [di'sə:n] v/t discernere

discharge [dis'tʃɑ:dʒ] s scarico m; sparo m (di arma); emissione f (di liquido); licenziamento m; v/t sparare; emettere; licenziare; compiere (un dovere); v/i scaricarsi

disciple [di'saipl] discepolo m

discipline ['disiplin] disciplina f

disclaim [dis'kleim] v/t negare

disclose [dis'klouz] v/t rivelare; scoprire

discolo(u)r [dis'kʌlə] v/t scolorire; v/i scolorirsi

discomfort [dis'kʌmfət] disagio m

disconcert [,diskən'sə:t] v/t sconcertare

disconnect [,diskə'nekt] v/t staccare

disconsolate [dis'kɔnsəlit] sconsolato

discontent [,diskən'tent] scontentezza f

discontinue [,diskən'tinju:] v/t sospendere; v/i interrompersi

discord ['diskɔ:d] discordia f; mus disarmonia f; dissonanza f; **~ance** [-'kɔ:dəns] discordanza f; disaccordo m

discotheque ['discoutek] discoteca f

discount ['diskaunt] s sconto m; **give a ~** fare uno sconto

discourage [dis'kʌridʒ] v/t scoraggiare; dissuadere

discover [dis'kʌvə] v/t scoprire; **~y** scoperta f

discredit [dis'kredit] s discredito m; v/t screditare

discreet [-'kri:t] discreto

discret|e ['dis'kri:t] distinto; separato; **~ion** [dis'kreʃən] discrezione f

discriminate [dis'krimineit] v/t discriminare; **~ion** discussione f

discuss [dis'kʌs] discutere; **~ion** discussione f

disdain [dis'dein] s disdegno m; v/t disdegnare; **~ful** sdegnoso

disease [di'zi:z] malattia f; **~d** malato

disembark [disim'bɑ:k] v/t, v/i sbarcare

disengage ['disin'geidʒ] v/t disimpegnare; liberare

disentangle ['disin'tæŋgl] v/t districare

disfavo(u)r [dis'feivə] disfavore m

disfigure [dis'figə] v/t deformare

disgrace [dis'greis] vergogna f; **~ful** vergognoso

disguise [dis'gaiz] s maschera f; travestimento m; v/t mascherare; travestire

disgust [dis'gʌst] s disgusto m; v/t disgustare; **~ing** disgustoso

dish [diʃ] piatto m; **~-cloth** strofinaccio m

dishearten [dis'hɑ:tn] v/t scoraggiare

dishonest [dis'ɔnist] diso-
nesto

dishono(u)r [dis'ɔnə] s diso-
nore m; v/t disonorare;
comm protestare (una
cambiale)

dish-washer lavastoviglie
m, f

disillusion [disi'lu:ʒən] delusione f

disinclined ['disin'klaind]:
feel **.ed to** non avere voglia
di

disinfect [disin'fekt] v/t dis-
infettare; **.ant** disinfettan-
te m

disinherit ['disin'herit] v/t
diseredare

disintegrate [dis'intigreit]
v/t disintegrare

disinterested [dis'intristid]
disinteressato

disjointed [dis'dʒɔintid]
sconnesso

disk cf **disc**

dislike [dis'laik] s antipatia f;
avversione f; v/t avere antipatia per; non piacere

dislocat|e v/t dislocare; slo-
gare

disloyal [dis'lɔiəl] sleale

dismal ['dizməl] triste

dismantle [dis'mæntl] v/t
smontare

dismay [dis'mei] costernazione f

dismember [dis'membə]
v/t smembrare

dismiss [dis'mis] v/t mandare via; licenziare; scac-
ciare; **.al** licenziamento m

dismount [dis'maunt] v/i
scendere

disobedien|ce [disə'bi:-
djəns] disobbedienza f; **.t**
disobbediente

disobey ['disə'bei] v/t disobbedire

disorder [dis'ɔ:də] disordine
m; confusione f

disorganize [dis'ɔ:gənaiz]
v/t disorganizzare

disown [dis'oun] v/t ripudiare

disparage [dis'pæridʒ] v/t
sprezzare

disparity [dis'pæriti] dispa-
rità f

dispassionate [dis'pæʃənit]
spassionato

dispatch [dis'pætʃ] cf **despatch**

dispel [dis'pel] v/t dissipare

dispens|ation [¸dispen'sei-
ʃən] dispensa f; **.e** v/t dispensare; distribuire; **.e
with** fare a meno di

disperse [dis'pə:s] v/t disperdere; v/i disperdersi

displace [dis'pleis] v/t spostare; **.d: .d person** profugo m

display [dis'plei] s esibizio-
ne f; mostra f; v/t esibire;
mettere in mostra

displease [dis'pli:z] v/t dispiacere; non piacere; **.ure**
dispiacere m

dispos|al [dis'pouzəl] dispo-
sizione f; **.e** v/t disporre;
.ition disposizione f; carattere m

disproportionate [dispra-
'pɔ:ʃnit] sproporzionato

dispute [dis'pju:t] s disputa

f; controversia *f*; *v/t, v/i* disputare

disqualif|ication [dis₁kwɔlifi'keiʃən] squalifica *f*; **~y** [~'kwɔlifai] *v/t* squalificare

disregard [₁disri'ga:d] *v/t* non dare retta

disreputable [dis'repjutəbl] di cattiva reputazione; malfamato

dissatisf|action ['dis₁sætis'fækʃən] malcontento *m*; **~ied: be ~ied** essere scontento

dissen|sion [di'senʃən] dissenso *m*; **~t** *s* dissenso *m*; *v/i* dissentire

dissimilar ['di'similə] dissimile

dissipate ['disipeit] *v/t* dissipare; *v/i* dissiparsi

dissociate [di'souʃieit] *v/t* dissociare

dissol|ute ['disəlu:t] dissoluto; **~ve** [di'zɔlv] *v/t* dissolvere; *v/i* dissolversi

dissonance ['disənəns] dissonanza *f*

dissua|de [di'sweid] *v/t* dissuadere; **~sion** dissuasione *f*

distan|ce ['distəns] distanza *f*; **~t** distante

distaste ['dis'teist] ripugnanza *f*; **~ful** ripugnante

distemper [dis'tempə] (*on a wall*) intonaco *m*; (*dogs*) cimurro *m*

distend [dis'tend] *v/t* dilatare

distil [dis'til] *v/t* distillare; **~lation** distillazione *f*

distinct [dis'tiŋkt] distinto; nitido; **~ion** distinzione *f*; nitidezza *f*

distinguish [dis'tiŋgwiʃ] *v/t* distinguere; **~ed** illustre

distort [dis'tɔ:t] *v/t* deformare

distract [dis'trækt] *v/t* distrarre; **~ed** sconvolto; **~ion** distrazione *f*

distress [dis'tres] *s* dolore *m*; *v/t* addolorare; **~ed** addolorato; **~ing** doloroso

distribut|e [dis'tribju(:)t] *v/t* distribuire; **~ion** [~'bju:ʃən] distribuzione *f*

district ['distrikt] zona *f*

distrust [dis'trʌst] *s* diffidenza *f*; *v/t* diffidare di; **~ful** diffidente

disturb [dis'tə:b] *v/t* disturbare; **~ance** disturbo *m*; **~er** perturbatore *m*

disuse [dis'ju:s] disuso *m*

ditch [ditʃ] fossa *f*

dive [daiv] tuffo *m*; *v/i* tuffarsi; **~r** tuffatore *m*

diverge [dai'və:dʒ] *v/i* divergere; **~nce** divergenza *f*

diver|se [dai'və:s] diverso; **~sion** diversione *f*; deviazione *f*; **~t** *v/t* divertire; deviare

divid|e [di'vaid] *v/t* dividere; *v/i* dividersi

divin|e [di'vain] divino; **~ity** [di'viniti] divinità *f*

divis|ible [di'vizəbl] divisibile; **~ion** divisione *f*

divorce [di'vɔ:s] *s* divorzio *m*; *v/t* divorziare; *v/i* divorziarsi

dizz|iness ['dizinis] vertigine *f*; **∼y** vertiginoso; **feel ∼y, get ∼y** avere le vertigini

do *v/t* fare; eseguire; *fam* imbrogliare; **∼ away with** sopprimere; abolire; **how ∼ you ...?** come sta?; **that will ∼** basta cosi; **∼ without** fare a meno di

docile ['dousail] docile

dock [dɔk] *s* bacino *m* con chiusa; **∼yard** scalo *m* marittimo

doctor ['dɔktə] *s* dottore *m*; medico *m*; *v/t* medicare; falsificare

document ['dɔkjumənt] *s* documento *m*; **∼ary** [∼-'mentəri] documentario *m*

dodge [dɔdʒ] *s* trucco *m*; *v/t* scansare

doe [dou] cerva *f*

dog [dɔg] cane *m*; **∼ged** ['∼id] tenace

dogma ['dɔgmə] dogma *m*

doings [du(:)iŋz] *pl fam* ciò che la gente fa, combina, briga

dole [doul] *fam* sussidio *m* di disoccupazione

doll [dɔl] bambola *f*

dollar ['dɔlə] dollaro *m*

dolorous ['dɔlərəs] doloroso

dolphin ['dɔlfin] delfino *m*

dome [doum] cupola *f*

domestic [dou'mestik] domestico; casalingo; **∼ate** *v/t* addomesticare

domicile ['dɔmisail] domicilio *m*

domin|ate ['dɔmineit] *v/t* dominare; **∼ation** domi-

nio *m*; tirannia *f*; **∼eer** [∼'niə] *v/i* tiranneggiare

domino ['dɔminou], *pl* **∼es** [∼'nouz] domino *m*

dona|te [dou'neit] *v/t* donare; **∼tion** donazione *f*

done [dʌn] fatto; (*food*) cotto

donkey ['dɔŋki] asino *m*; somaro *m*

doom [du:m] destino *m* (*funesto*); **∼sday** il Giudizio Universale

door [dɔ:] porta *f*; **∼keeper,** *Am* **∼man** portinaio *m*; **∼step** gradino *m* della porta

dope [doup] *s* narcotico *m*; *v/t* eccitare con stupefacenti

dormant ['dɔ:mənt] addormentato; inattivo

dormitory ['dɔ:mitri] dormitorio *m*

dose [dous] *s* dose *f*; *v/t* dosare

dot [dɔt] punto *m*; puntino *m*

dote [dout]: **∼ (up)on** *v/i* adorare

double ['dʌbl] *a* doppio; *s* doppio *m*; duplicato *m*; (*film*) controfigura *f*; *v/t* raddoppiare; *v/i* raddoppiarsi; **∼breasted** a doppio petto; **∼cross** *v/t* ingannare; **∼dealing** duplicità *f*; **∼meaning** *s* ambiguità *f*; *a* ambiguo

doubt [daut] *s* dubbio *m*; *v/t, v/i* dubitare; **∼ful** dubbioso; **∼less** senza dubbio

dough [dou] pasta *f*; impasto *m*; **∼nut** bombolone *m*

dove [dʌv] colombo *m*;

~tailed a coda di rondine

down [daun] *adv* giù; *prp* giù per; s landa *f*; peluria *f*; **~cast** abbattuto; **~fall** rovina *f*; **~pour** diluvio *m*; **~stairs: go stairs** scendere le scale; andare al piano di sotto

dowry ['dauəri] dote *f*

doze [douz] *s* sonnellino *m*; *v/i* sonnecchiare

dozen ['dʌzn] dozzina *f*

drab [dræb] *a* smorto; squallido

draft [drɑːft] bozza *f*; brutta copia *f*; tratta *f*; **~sman** disegnatore *m*

drag [dræg] *v/t* trascinare; dragare

dragon ['drægən] dragone *m*; **~fly** libellula *f*

drain [drein] s fogna *f*; tubo *m* di scarico; *v/t* scolare; prosciugare; **~age** prosciugamento *m*

drama ['drɑːmə] dramma *m*; **~tic** [drə'mætik] drammatico; **~tist** ['dræmətist] drammaturgo *m*; **~tize** *v/t* drammatizzare

drape [dreip] *v/t* coprire; drappeggiare

drastic ['dræstik] drastico

draught, Am draft [drɑːft] corrente *f* d'aria; **~s** *pl* dama *f* (*game*)

draw [drɔː] *s* attrazione *f*; (*football*) pareggio *m*; *v/t* tirare; estrarre; attrarre; tirare a sorte; (*football*) pareggiare; (*money*) riscuotere; **~ out** tirare

fuori; **~ up** redigere

draw|back inconveniente *m*; **~bridge** ponte *m* levatoio; **~er** cassetto *m*; **~ing** disegno *m*; sorteggio *m*; **~ing-room** salotto *m*

dread [dred] *s* terrore *m*; *v/t* avere il terrore di; temere; **~ful** terribile; spaventoso

dream [driːm] *s* sogno *m*; *v/t, v/i, irr* sognare

dreary ['driəri] triste; melanconico

dregs [dregz] *pl* fondi *m/pl*

drench [drentʃ] *v/t* inzuppare

dress [dres] *s* vestito *m*; abito *m*; *v/t* vestire; medicare; *v/i* vestirsi; **~er** credenza *f* (*di cucina*); **~ing** condimento *m*; *med* bende *f/pl*; **~ing-gown** vestaglia *f*; **~maker** sarta *f*; **~ rehearsal** prova *f* generale

drift [drift] *s* corrente *f*; deriva *f*; proposito *m*; *v/i* andare alla deriva; lasciarsi andare; **~wood** legno *m* flottante

drill [dril] *s* trapano *m*; esercizi *m/pl*; *v/t* perforare; fare esercitare; *v/i* fare esercizi

drink [drink] *s* bevanda *f*; *v/t, v/i, irr* bere

drip [drip] *s* goccia *f*; *v/i* gocciolare

driv|e [draiv] *s* passeggiata *f* in carrozza; viale *m* carrozzabile; *v/t, irr* condurre; guidare; *v/i* andare in carrozza; andare in macchina; **~er** autista *m*; **~ing licence**

patente *f*; **~ing school** scuola *f* (di) guida; **~ing-wheel** volante *m*

drizzle ['drizl] *s* pioggerella *f*; *v/i* piovigginare

drone [droun] fuco *m*

droop [dru:p] *v/i* languire

drop [drɔp] *s* goccia *f*; *v/t* fare cadere; *v/i* cadere; **~per** contagocce *m*

drown [draun] *v/t* affogare; annegare; *v/i* affogarsi; annegarsi

drowsy ['drauzi] sonnolento

drudge [drʌdʒ] *v/i* affaticarsi

drug [drʌg] *s* droga *f*; *v/t* drogare; **~ addict** tossicomane *m*, *f*; **~gist** farmacista *m*, *f*; droghiere *m*; **~store** *Am* farmacia *f*

drum [drʌm] *s* tamburo *m*; (*of an ear*) timpano *m*; *v/i* tamburellare

drunk [drʌŋk] ubriaco; **~ard** ubriacone *m*; **~en** ubriaco

dry [drai] *a* asciutto; arido; secco; *v/t* asciugare; seccare; **~-clean** *v/t* lavare a secco; **~ dock** bacino *m* di carenaggio *f*; **~-goods** *pl Am* stoffe *f/pl*; tessuti *m/pl*; **~ness** aridità *f*; siccità *f*

dubious ['dju:bjəs] dubbio

dual ['dju(:)əl] duale

duchess ['dʌtʃis] duchessa *f*

duck [dʌk] anitra *f*

due [dju:] *a* dovuto; debito; *s* tassa *f*; **be ~ to** dovere

duel ['dju(:)əl] duello *m*

duke [dju:k] duca *m*

dull [dʌl] noioso; monotono; (*colour*) smorto; (*sound*) sordo; **~ness** noia *f*

duly ['dju:li] debitamente

dumb [dʌm] muto; **~found** *v/t* stupefare

dummy ['dʌmi] *a* imitato; falso; *s* manichino *m*

dump [dʌmp] *v/t* scaricare

dune [dju:n] duna *f*

dung [dʌŋ] letame *m*

dungeon ['dʌndʒən] prigione *f* sotterranea

dupe [dju:p] *v/t* ingannare

duplicate ['dju:plikit] *a*, *s* duplicato (*m*); [-'keit] *v/t* duplicare

dura|ble ['djuərəbl] duraturo; **~tion** durata *f*

during ['djuəriŋ] durante

dusk [dʌsk] crepuscolo *m*

dust [dʌst] *s* polvere *f*; *v/t* spolverare; **~bin** bidone *m*; **~er** cencio *m* (*per la polvere*); **~pan** pattumiera *f*; **~y** polveroso

Dutch [dʌtʃ] *s*, *a* olandese (*m,f*); **the ~** *pl* gli olandesi *m/pl*; **~ cheese** formaggio *m* olandese; **~man** olandese *m*; **~woman** olandese *f*

duty ['dju:ti] dovere *m*; imposta *f*; **be on ~** essere di servizio; **~y-free** esente da tasse

dwarf [dwɔ:f] nano *m*

dwell [dwel] *v/i*, *irr* abitare; dimorare; **~er** abitante *m*; **~ing** abitazione *f*; dimora *f*

dwindle ['dwindl] *v/i* diminuire

dye [dai] *s* tintura *f*; *v/t*

tingere; v/i tingersi; **~r's:
~r's and cleaner's** tintoria f
dying ['daiiŋ] moribondo
dynamic [dai'næmik] dinamico; **~s** pl dinamica f

dynamite ['dainəmait] dinamite f; **~o** dinamo f
dysentery ['disntri] dissenteria f
dyspepsia [dis'pepsiə] dispepsia f

E

each [i:tʃ] a ogni; ciascuno; pron ognuno; **~ other** l'un l'altro
eager ['i:gə] ansioso; desideroso; **~ness** ansietà f
eagle ['i:gl] aquila f
ear [iə] bot spiga f; anat orecchio m; **~drum** timpano m
earl [ə:l] conte m
early ['ə:li] a mattutino; mattiniero; adv presto; di buon ora
earn [ə:n] v/t guadagnare; **~ings** pl guadagni m/pl
earnest ['ə:nist] serio; **in ~** seriamente; sul serio
earnings ['ə:niŋz] pl guadagni m/pl
ear|-phone cuffia f; **~ring** orecchino m
earth [ə:θ] terra f; **~en** di terra; **~enware** vasellame m di terracotta; **~quake** terremoto m; **~worm** lombrico m
ease [i:z] s agio m; facilità f; v/t sollevare; calmare
easel ['i:zl] cavalletto m
east [i:st] est m; oriente m; **Near ~** Vicino Oriente; **Middle ~** Medio Oriente
Easter ['i:stə] Pasqua f; **~-week** settimana f santa

eastern ['i:stən] orientale
eastward(s) ['i:stwəd(z)] verso est
easy ['i:zi] facile; comodo
eat [i:t] v/t, irr mangiare; **~ up** consumare; divorare
ebb(-tide) ['eb('taid)] bassa marea f
ebony ['ebəni] ebano m
eccentric [ik'sentrik] a, s eccentrico (m)
ecclesiastic [ikli:zi'æstik] ecclesiastico
echo ['ekou] eco m
eclipse [i'klips] eclissi f
econom|ic [i:kə'nɔmik], **~ical** economo; **~ics** pl economia f; scienze f/pl economiche; **~ist** [i'kɔnəmist] economista m; **~ize** v/t, v/i economizzare; **~y** economia f
edge [edʒ] s bordo m; filo m (tagliente); v/t bordare; **~ing** bordo m
edible ['edibl] mangiabile
edif|ice ['edifis] edificio m; **~y** v/t edificare
edit ['edit] v/t editare; dirigere; redigere; **~ion** [i'diʃən] edizione f; **~or** ['edita] direttore m; **~orial** [edi'tɔ:riəl] a editoriale; s articolo

m di fondo

educate ['edju(:)keit] *v/t* istruire; **~ion** istruzione *f*

eel [i:l] anguilla *f*

efface [i'feis] *v/t* scancellare

effect [i'fekt] *s* effetto *m*; conseguenza *f*; risultato *m*; *v/t* effettuare; **~ive** effettivo; efficace; **~s** *pl* effetti *m/pl*; beni *m/pl*

effeminate [i'feminit] effeminato

effervescent [efə'vesnt] effervescente

efficien|cy [i'fiʃənsi] efficienza *f*; **~t** efficace

effort ['efət] sforzo *m*

effusive [i'fju:siv] espansivo

egg [eg] uovo *m*; **~cup** portauovo *m*; **~plant** melanzana *f*; **~shell** guscio *m* d'uovo

egoism ['egouizəm] egoismo *m*

Egypt ['i:dʒipt] Egitto *m*; **~ian** [i'dʒipʃən] *a, s* egiziano (*m*)

either ['aiðə, *Am* 'i:ðə] l'uno o l'altro; (*with negative verb*) nessuno; **~ ... or ~** o; sia ... che; **not ... ~** neanche

eject [i(:)'dʒekt] *v/t* cacciare fuori; emettere

elaborate [i'læbərit] *a* elaborato; complicato; [~eit] *v/t* elaborare

elapse [i'læps] *v/i* passare

elastic [i'læstik] *a, s* elastico (*m*)

elate [i'leit] *v/t* esaltare

elbow ['elbou] gomito *m*; *v/i* spingere a gomitate

elde|r ['eldə] *a, s* maggiore (*m*); *bot* sambuco *m*; **~rly** anziano; **~st** ['~ist] *a, s* maggiore (*m*) (*di tutti*)

elect [i'lekt] *a* eletto; scelto; *v/t* eleggere; **~ion** elezione *f*; **~or** elettore *m*; **~orate** elettorato *m*; votanti *m/pl*

electr|ic [i'lektrik] elettrico; **~ical** elettrico; **~ician** [~'triʃən] elettricista *m*; **~icity** elettricità *f*; **~ocute** [i'lektrəkjut] *v/t* fulminare

elegan|ce ['eligəns] eleganza *f*; **~t** elegante

element ['elimənt] elemento *m*; componente *m*; **~ary** elementare

elephant ['elifənt] elefante *m*

elevat|e ['eliveit] *v/t* elevare; **~ion** elevazione *f*; **~or** montacarichi *m*; *Am* ascensore *m*

eligible ['elidʒəbl] eleggibile

eliminat|e [i'limineit] *v/t* eliminare; **~ion** eliminazione *f*

elk [elk] alce *m*

ellipse [i'lips] ellissi *f*

elm [elm] olmo *m*

elope [i'loup] *v/i* fuggire

eloquen|ce [e'ləkwəns] eloquenza *f*; **~t** eloquente

else [els] altro; **nothing ~** niente altro; **somebody ~** qualcun'altro; **something ~** qualche altra cosa; **~ where** in qualche altro posto; da qualche altra parte

elu|de [i'lu:d] *v/t* eludere; **~sive** elusivo

emaciated [i'meiʃieitid] emaciato

emanate ['eməneit] v/i emanare

emancipat|e [i'mænsipeit] v/t emancipare; **~ion** emancipazione f

embalm [im'bɑːm] v/t imbalsamare

embankment [im'bæŋkmənt] argine m; diga f

embargo [em'bɑːgou], pl **~es** [~ouz] embargo m

embark [im'bɑːk] v/t imbarcare; v/i imbarcarsi; ~ **upon something** mettersi a; lanciarsi a; **~ation** [embɑː'keiʃən] imbarcazione f

embarrass [im'bærəs] v/t imbarazzare; **~ing** imbarazzante; **~ment** imbarazzo m

embassy ['embəsi] ambasciata f

embellish [im'beliʃ] v/t abbellire

embers ['embəz] f/pl ceneri f/pl ardenti

embezzle [im'bezl] v/t appropriarsi (con frode)

embitter [im'bitə] v/t amareggiare

emblem ['embləm] emblema m

embody [im'bɔdi] v/t incarnare; incorporare

embolism ['embəlizəm] embolia f

embrace [im'breis] s abbraccio m; v/t abbracciare

embroider [im'brɔidə] v/t ricamare; **~y** ricamo m

emerald ['emərəld] smeraldo m

emerge [i'məːdʒ] v/i emergere

emergency [i'məːdʒənsi] emergenza f; ~ **brake** freno m di emergenza; ~ **call** numero m telefonico di soccorso; ~ **exit** uscita f di sicurezza; ~ **landing** aer atterraggio m di fortuna

emery ['eməri] smeriglio m; **~paper** carta f smerigliata

emigra|nt ['emigrənt] emigrante m; **~te** [~eit] v/i emigrare; **~tion** emigrazione f

eminent ['eminənt] eminente

emi|ssion [i'miʃən] emissione f; **~t** v/t emettere

emotion [i'mouʃən] emozione f; **~al** emotivo

emperor ['empərə] imperatore m

empha|sis ['emfəsis] enfasi f; **~ize** mettere in rilievo

empire ['empaiə] impero m

employ [im'plɔi] v/t impiegare; adoperare; **~ee** [emplɔi'iː] impiegato m; **~er** datore m di lavoro; padrone m; **~ment** impiego m; occupazione f; **~ment exchange** ufficio m di collocamento

empress ['empris] imperatrice f

empt|iness ['emptinis] vuoto m; **~y** vuoto

enable [i'neibl] v/t dare la possibilità; permettere

enact [i'nækt] v/t mettere in

atto

enamel [i'næml] *s* smalto *m*; *v/t* smaltare

enchant [in't∫ɑːnt] *v/t* incantare

encircle [in'sɔːkl] *v/t* circondare

enclos|e [in'klouz] *v/t* rinchiudere; **~ure** [~ʒə] *s* recinto *m*

encounter [in'kauntə] *s* incontro *m*; *v/t* incontrare

encourag|e [in'karidʒ] *v/t* incoraggiare; **~ement** incoraggiamento *m*

end [end] *s* fine *f*; termine *m*; *v/t, v/i* finire; terminare; **in the ~** in fin dei conti

endanger [in'deindʒə] *v/t* mettere in pericolo

endear [in'diə] *v/t* rendere caro

endeavo(u)r [in'devə] *s* sforzo *m*; *v/i* sforzarsi

ending ['endiŋ] fine *f*; conclusione *f*; *gram* desinenza *f*; **~less** interminabile

endorse [in'dɔːs] *comm v/t* girare; firmare (*cheques*)

endow [in'dau] *v/t* dotare; **~ed with** dotato di

endur|ance [in'djuərəns] sopportazione *f*; **~e** *v/t* sopportare

enemy ['enimi] *a, s* nemico (*m*)

energ|etic [ˌenə'dʒetik] energico; **~y** ['enədʒi] energia *f*

enforce [in'fɔːs] *v/t* mettere in vigore

enfranchise [in'frænt∫aiz]

v/t affrancare

engage [in'geidʒ] *v/t* occupare; assumere (*in servizio*); **~d** occupato; impegnato; fidanzato; **~ment** impegno *m*; fidanzamento *m*

engine ['endʒin] motore *m*; macchina *f*; **~-driver** macchinista *m*; **~er** [endʒi'niə] ingegnere *m*; **~ering** ingegneria *f*

England ['iŋglənd] Inghilterra *f*

English *a* inglese; (*language*) inglese *m*; **the ~** *pl* gli inglesi; **~man** inglese *m*; **~woman** inglese *f*

engrav|e [in'greiv] *v/t* incidere; **~ing** incisione *f*

engross [in'grous] *v/t* assorbire

enigma [i'nigmə] enimma *m*

enjoy [in'dʒɔi] *v/t* godere; **~ o.s.** *v/r* divertirsi; **~able** piacevole

enlarge [in'lɑːdʒ] *v/t* estendere; ingrandire; **~ment** ingrandimento *m*

enlighten [in'laitn] *v/t* illuminare

enlist [in'list] *v/t* arrolare; *v/i* arrolarsi

enliven [in'laivn] *v/t* ravvivare

enmity ['enmiti] inimicizia *f*

enormous [i'nɔːməs] enorme

enough [i'nʌf] abbastanza

enquire [in'kwaiə] *cf* **inquire**

enrage [in'reidʒ] *v/t* rendere furioso

enrapture [in'ræptʃə] v/t entusiasmare

enrich [in'ritʃ] v/t arricchire

enrol [in'roul] v/t iscrivere; v/i iscriversi; **~ment** iscrizione f; registrazione f

ensign ['ensain] insegna f; bandiera f

enslave [in'sleiv] v/t fare schiavo

ensue [in'sju:] v/i risultare

ensure [in'ʃuə] v/t assicurare

entangle [in'tæŋgl] v/t imbrogliare

enter ['entə] v/t entrare in; comm registrare

enterpris|e ['entəpraiz] impresa f; **~ing** intraprendente

entertain [entə'tein] v/t intrattenere; divertire; ricevere (ospiti); **~ing** divertente; **~ment** trattenimento m; divertimento m

enthusias|m [in'θju:ziæzəm] entusiasmo m; **~t** entusiasta m, f; **~tic** [~'æstik] entusiastico; entusiasmato

entice [in'tais] v/t attrarre; allettare

entire [in'taiə] intero

entitle [in'taitl] v/t autorizzare; dare il diritto; **be ~d to** avere il diritto a

entity ['entiti] entità f

entrails ['entreilz] pl viscere f/pl

entrance ['entrəns] entrata f; ingresso m; **~fee** prezzo m d'ingresso

entreat [in'tri:t] v/t supplicare

entrust [in'trʌst] v/t affidare

entry ['entri] ingresso m; entrata f

enumerate [i'nju:məreit] v/t enumerare

envelop [in'veləp] v/t avvolgere; **~e** ['envəloup] busta f

envi|able ['enviəbl] invidiabile; **~ous** invidioso

environment [in'vaiərəment] ambiente m; **~al pollution** inquinamento m dell'ambiente

environs ['environz, in'vaiərənz] pl dintorni m/pl

envisage [in'vizidʒ] v/t contemplare

envoy ['envoi] inviato m

envy ['envi] s invidia f; v/t invidiare

epidemic (disease) [epi'demik] epidemia f

epidermis [epi'də:mis] epidermide f

epilep|sy ['epilepsi] epilessia f; **~tic** [,epi'leptik] epilettico

episode ['episoud] episodio m

epoch ['i:pɔk] epoca f

equal ['i:kwəl] a, s uguale; **~ity** [i(:)'kwɔliti] uguaglianza f; **~ize** v/t uguagliare

equanimity [ekwə'nimiti] equanimità f

equation [i'kweiʒən] equazione f

equator [i'kweitə] equatore m

equilibrium [,i:kwi'libriəm] equilibrio m

equip [i'kwip] *v/t* equipaggiare; attrezzare; **~ment** attrezzatura *f*

equivalent [i'kwivələnt] equivalente

era ['iərə] epoca *f*

eradicate [i'rædikeit] *v/t* sradicare

erase [i'reiz] *v/t* scancellare

erect [i'rekt] *a* eretto; ritto; *v/t* erigere; innalzare; **~ion** erezione *f*; elevazione *f*

erosion [i'rouʒən] erosione *f*

erotic [i'reiz] erotico

err [əː] *v/i* errare; sbagliare

errand ['erənd] commissione *f*; **~boy** fattorino *m*; garzone *m*

errant ['erənt] errante

err|oneous [i'rounjəs] erroneo; **~or** ['erə] errore *m*; sbaglio *m*

erupt [i'rʌpt] *v/i* eruttare

escalator ['eskəleitə] scala *f* mobile

escape [is'keip] *v/t* sfuggire a; evitare; *v/i* sfuggire; scappare; *s* fuga *f*

escort ['eskɔːt] *s* scorta *f*; accompagnatore *m*; [is'kɔːt] *v/t* scortare; accompagnare

especial [is'peʃəl] speciale; **~ly** specialmente; soprattutto

espionage [espiə'nɑːʒ] spionaggio *m*

essay ['esei] saggio *m*; tema *m* (*scolastico*); **~ist** saggista *m*

essen|ce ['esns] essenza *f*; **~tial** [i'senʃəl] essenziale

establish [is'tæbliʃ] *v/t* sta-

bilire; istituire; fondare; **~ment** stabilimento *m*; istituzione *f*; istituto *m*; casa *f* commerciale

estate [is'teit] proprietà *f*; tenuta *f*; **~ car** giardinetta *f*; **real ~** beni *m/pl* immobili

esteem [is'tiːm] *s* stima *f*; *v/t* stimare

estima|te ['estimeit] *s* preventivo *m*; *v/t* valutare; **~ion** valutazione *f*; stima *f*

estrange [is'treindʒ] *v/t* alienare

estuary ['estjuəri] estuario *m*

etcetera [it'setrə, et~] eccetera

etern|al [i(ː)'təːnl] eterno; **~ity** eternità *f*

ether ['iːθə] etere *m*

ethics ['eθiks] *pl* etica *f*

Ethiopia [iːθi'oupjə] Etiopia *f*

eucalyptus [juːkə'liptəs] eucalipto *m*

Europe ['juərəp] Europa *f*; **~an** [juərə'pi(ː)ən] *a, s* europeo (*m*)

evacuate [i'vækjueit] *v/t* evacuare; sfollare; sgombrare

evade [i'veid] *v/t* evitare; sottrarsi a

evaluate [i'væljueit] *v/t* valutare

evangelical [iːvæn'dʒelikəl] evangelico

evaporate [i'væpəreit] *v/t* evaporare; *v/i* evaporarsi

evasion [i'veiʒən] evasione *f*; sotterfugio *m*

eve [iːv] vigilia *f*

even ['iːvən] *a* piano, liscio; uguale, pari; fermo; *adv* anche; perfino; ~ **though** anche se; **not** ~ neanche; *v/t* appianare; livellare; aggiustare

evening ['iːvniŋ] sera *f*; **good** ~ buona sera; ~ **dress** abito *m* da sera

event [i'vent] avvenimento *m*; **at all** ~**s** in tutti i casi; ~**ful** memorabile; movimentato; ~**ual** eventuale; ~**ually** finalmente

ever ['evə] mai; sempre; **for** ~; ~**green** sempreverde; per sempre; ~ **since** da quando

every ['evri] ogni; tutti; ~ **other day** ogni due giorni; ~**body**, ~**one** ognuno; tutti; ~**day** quotidiano; ~**thing** tutto; ~**where** da tutte le parti

eviden|ce ['evidəns] evidenza *f*; testimonianza *f*; **give** ~**ce** testimoniare; ~**t** evidente; chiaro

evil ['iːvl] *s* male *m*; *a* cattivo

evince [i'vins] *v/t* manifestare

evoke [i'vouk] *v/t* evocare

evolution [iːvə'luːʃən] evoluzione *f*; svolgimento *m*

evolve [i'vɔlv] *v/t* evolvere; *v/i* evolversi

ewe [juː] pecora *f*

exact [ig'zækt] *a* esatto; preciso; *v/t* esigere; ~**ly** esattamente; ~**ness** esattezza *f*

exaggerat|e [ig'zædʒəreit]

v/t esagerare; ~**ion** esagerazione *f*

exalt [ig'zɔːlt] *v/t* esaltare; ~**ation** esaltazione *f*

examin|ation [igˌzæmi'neiʃən] esame *m*; ~**e** *v/t* esaminare

example [ig'zaːmpl] esempio *m*; **for** ~ per esempio

exasperate [ig'zaːspəreit] *v/t* esasperare

excavate ['ekskəveit] *v/t* scavare

exceed [ik'siːd] *v/t* eccedere; superare

excellen|ce ['eksələns] eccellenza *f*; ~**t** eccellente; ottimo

except [ik'sept] *prp* eccetto; salvo; ~ **for** all'infuori di; *v/t* eccettuare; *v/i* obbiettare; meno; ~**ion** eccezione *f*; ~**ional** eccezionale

excerpt ['eksəpt, ik'səːpt] estratto *m*

excess [ik'ses] eccesso *m*; ~ **fare** supplemento *m*; ~**ive** eccessivo

exchange [iks'tʃeindʒ] *s* cambio *m*; Borsa *f*; centrale *f* (telefonica); *v/t* scambiare; ~ **rate** cambio *m*

Exchequer [iks'tʃekə]: **Chancellor of the** ~ Cancelliere *m* dello Scacchiere; Ministro *m* delle Finanze

excit|e [ik'sait] *v/t* eccitare; agitare; ~**ement** eccitazione *f*; agitazione *f*; ~**ing** emozionante; avvincente

exclaim [iks'kleim] *v/t*, *v/i* esclamare; ~**mation** esclamazione f; **∼mation mark** punto m esclamativo

exclu|de [iks'klu:d] v/t escludere; **∼sion** esclusione f; **∼sive** esclusivo

excommunicate [ˌekskə-'mju:nikeit] v/t scomunicare

excursion [iks'kə:ʃən] s gita f

excuse [iks'kju:z] s scusa f; v/t scusare; **∼ me** scusi signore!

execut|e ['eksikju:t] v/t eseguire; giustiziare; **∼ion** esecuzione f; **∼ive** [ig'zekjutiv] s potere m esecutivo; a esecutivo

exemplary [ig'zempləri] esemplare

exempt [ig'zempt] a esente; v/t esentare

exercise ['eksəsaiz] s esercizio m; v/t esercitare; **∼ book** libro m scolastico

exert [ig'zə:t] v/t esercitare; **∼ o.s.** v/r sforzarsi; **∼ion** sforzo m

exhale [eks'heil] v/t esalare

exhaust [ig'zɔ:st] scarico m; **∼ pipe** tubo m di scarico; v/t esaurire; **∼ion** esaurimento m

exhibit [ig'zibit] s oggetto m in esposizione; v/t esibire; **∼ion** [eksi'biʃən] esposizione f

exhort [ig'zɔ:t] v/t esortare

exigence [ek'sidʒənsi, 'eksidʒənsi] esigenza f

exile ['eksail] s esilio m; v/t esiliare

exist [ig'zist] v/i esistere;

∼ence esistenza f; **∼ent, ∼ing** esistente

exit ['eksit] uscita f

exorbitant [ig'zɔ:bitənt] esorbitante

exotic [eg'zɔtik] esotico

expan|d [iks'pænd] v/t espandere; sviluppare; v/i espandersi; svilupparsi; **∼se** distesa f; **∼sion** espansione f; sviluppo m; **∼sive** espansivo

expect [iks'pekt] v/t aspettare; aspettarsi; **∼ance, ∼ation** aspettativa f; **∼ant mother** donna f incinta

expedient [iks'pi:djənt] espediente m

expedition [ekspi'diʃən] spedizione f

expel [iks'pel] v/t espellere

expen|d [iks'pend] v/t espendere; consumare; **∼diture** spesa f; **∼se** spesa f; **∼sive** costoso

experience [iks'piəriəns] s esperienza f; v/t provare; sentire; **∼d** esperto

experiment [iks'perimənt] s esperimento m; v/i sperimentare

expert ['ekspə:t] a esperto; s esperto m; perito m

expir|ation [ˌekspaiə'reiʃən] espirazione f; morte f; comm scadenza f; **∼e** [iks-'paiə] v/i espirare; morire; comm scadere

expla|in [iks'plein] v/t spiegare; **∼nation** spiegazione f

explicit [iks'plisit] esplicito

explode [iks'ploud] v/t fare esplodere; v/i esplodere

exploit [iks'ploit] s prodezza f; v/t sfruttare

explor|ation [eksplɔ:'reiʃən] esplorazione f; **~e** v/t esplorare; **~er** esploratore m

explos|ion [iks'plouʒən] esplosione f; **~ive** esplosivo

export ['ekspɔ:t] s esportazione f; [eks'pɔ:t] v/t esportare; **~ation** esportazione f; **~er** esportatore m

expose [iks'pouz] v/t esporre; smascherare; **~ition** [ekspou'ziʃən] esposizione f; **~ure** esposizione f; smascheramento m; **~ure meter** esposimetro m

express [iks'pres] s espresso m; **~ train** rapido m; a apposito; espresso; v/t esprimere; **~ion** espressione f; **~ive** espressivo

expropriate [eks'prouprieit] v/t espropriare

expulsion [iks'pʌlʃən] espulsione f

exquisite ['ekskwisit] a squisito

extant [eks'tænt] esistente

exten|d [iks'tend] v/t estendere; prolungare; allargare; v/i estendersi; prolungarsi; allargarsi; **~sion** estensione f; prolungamento m; allargamento m; **~sive** esteso; distesa f; **to a certain ~** fino a un certo punto

exterior [eks'tiəriə] s esterno m; a esteriore; esterno

exterminate [eks'tə:mineit] v/t sterminare

external [eks'tə:nl] esterno

extin|ct [iks'tiŋkt] estinto; **~guish** [iks'tiŋwiʃ] v/t estinguere

extirpate ['ekstə:peit] v/t estirpare

extort [iks'tɔ:t] v/t estorcere

extra ['ekstrə] a extra; straordinario; addizionale; s supplemento m; aggiunta f; adv extra; in più

extract ['ekstrækt] estratto m; [iks'trækt] v/t estrarre; **~ion** estrazione f

extradite ['ekstrədait] v/t estradare

extraordinary [iks'trɔ:dnri] straordinario

extravagan|ce [iks'trævigəns] stravaganza f; **~t** stravagante

extrem|e [iks'tri:m] a estremo; s estremo m; estremità f; **~ist** estremista m, f; **~ity** [~'tremiti] estremità f

exuberant [ig'zju:bərənt] esuberante

exult [ig'zʌlt] v/i esultare; **~ant** esultante

eye [ai] occhio m; **keep an ~ on** tenere d'occhio; v/t adocchiare; **~ball** globo m dell'occhio; **~brow** sopracciglio m; **~glasses** pl occhiali m/pl; **~lash** ciglio m; **~let** occhiello m; **~lid** palpebra f; **~shot** vista f; **~sight** vista f; **~witness** testimone m oculare

F

fable [ˈfeibl] favola *f*

fabric [ˈfæbric] tessuto *m*; **.ate** [ˈ.eit] *v/t* inventare; fabbricare

fabulous [ˈfæbjuləs] favoloso

façade [fəˈsɑːd] facciata *f*

face [feis] *s* faccia *f*; viso *m*; **.e to .e** faccia a faccia; *v/t* fare fronte a; affrontare; essere di fronte a; **.ing** di fronte a

facili|tate [fəˈsiliteit] *v/t* facilitare; **.ity** facilità *f*

fact [fækt] fatto *m*; **in .** infatti

factor [ˈfæktə] fattore *m*; elemento *m*; **.y** fabbrica *f*

faculty [ˈfækəlti] facoltà *f*

fade [feid] *v/i* (*colour*) sbiadire; (*flowers*) appassire; (*light*) spegnersi; (*memory*) scancellarsi; (*sound*) perdersi

fail [feil] *v/t* abbandonare; essere bocciato (*a un esame*); *v/i* fallire; mancare; **.ure** [ˈ.jə] fallimento *m*; bocciatura *f* (*a un esame*)

faint [feint] *a* debole; (*colour*) pallido; *v/i* svenire

fair [fɛə] *a* biondo; giusto; discreto; bello; buono; *s* fiera *f*; **. play** giuoco *m* leale; **.ly** piuttosto; **.ness** giustizia *f*

fairy [ˈfɛəri] fata *f*; **.tale** fiaba *f*

faith [feiθ] fede *f*; fiducia *f*; **.ful** fedele; **Yours .fully** con profonda stima

fake [feik] *s* imitazione *f*; *v/t* imitare; falsificare

falcon [ˈfɔːlkən] falcone *m*

fall [fɔːl] *s* caduta *f*; abbassamento *m*; ribasso *m*; *v/i* cadere; abbassarsi; **. asleep** addormentarsi; **. due** comm scadere; **. ill** ammalarsi; **. in love with** innamorarsi di; **. (up)on** attaccare

fallacious [fəˈleiʃəs] fallace

false [fɔːls] falso; **.hood** bugia *f*

falsify [ˈfɔːlsifai] *v/t* falsificare

falter [ˈfɔːltə] *v/i* vacillare

fame [feim] fama *f*

famil|iar [fəˈmiljə] familiare; **.iarity** [.iˈæriti] familiarità *f*; **.y** [ˈfæmili] famiglia *f*; **.y name** cognome *m*; **.y tree** albero *m* genealogico

fami|ne [ˈfæmin] carestia *f*; **.shed** affamato; morto di fame

famous [ˈfeiməs] famoso; celebre

fan [fæn] *s* ventaglio *m*; ventilatore *m*; (*slang*) tifoso *m*; *v/t* sventolare; ventilare

fanatic [fəˈnætik] *a*, *s* fanatico (*m*)

fanci|ful [ˈfænsiful] fantasioso; **.y** *s* fantasia *f*; capriccio *m*; *a* (di) fantasia; **.y dress** maschera *f*

fang [fæŋ] zanna *f*

fantas|tic [fænˈtæstik] fantastico; **~y** ['fæntəsi] fantasia *f*

far [fɑː] lontano; **as ~ as** fino a; **by ~** di molto; **di gran lungo; ~ better** molto migliore; **how ~?** fin dove?; *adv* molto meglio; **~off** lontano; **so ~** finora; **~reaching** di grande portata; **so ~** finora

farce [fɑːs] farsa *f*

fare [feə] cibo *m*; tariffa *f*; **~well** addio *m*

farm [fɑːm] *s* podere *m*; fattoria *f*; *v/t* coltivare; **~er** agricoltore *m*; **~hand** bracciante *m*; **~house** casa *f* colonica; **~ing** coltivazione *f*

far-sighted lungimirante

farth|er più lontano; **~est** il più lontano

fascinat|e ['fæsineit] *v/t* affascinare; **~ing** affascinante; **~ion** fascino *m*

fashion ['fæʃən] *s* moda *f*; **~able** di moda

fast [fɑːst] *a*, *s* veloce; leggero; *adv* velocemente; fermamente; *s* digiuno *m*; *v/i* digiunare

fasten ['fɑːsn] *v/t* attaccare; fissare; **~er** chiusura *f*; fermatura *f*

fat [fæt] *a*, *s* grasso (*m*)

fat|al ['feitl] fatale; **~e** destino *m*; sorte *f*

father ['fɑːðə] padre *m*; **~hood** paternità *f*; **~-in-law** suocero *m*; **~land** patria *f*; **~less** orfano di padre; **~ly** paterno

fatigue [fə'tiːg] *s* fatica *f*; *v/t*

affaticare

fatten ['fætn] *v/t* ingrassare

fatuous ['fætjuəs] fatuo

faucet ['fɔːsit] *Am* rubinetto *m*

fault [fɔːlt] colpa *f*; difetto *m*; **~less** perfetto; **~y** difettoso

favo(u)r ['feivə] *s* favore *m*; *v/t* favorire; **~able** favorevole; **~ite** ['~rit] *a*, *s* preferito (*m*)

fear [fiə] paura *f*; timore *m*; *v/t* temere; avere paura di; **~ful** pauroso; terribile

feasible ['fiːzəbl] possibile

feast [fiːst] *s* festa *f* (religiosa); banchetto *m*; *v/t* festeggiare; banchettare

feat [fiːt] prodezza *f*

feather ['feðə] piuma *f*; penna *f*; **~weight** peso *m* piuma

feature ['fiːtʃə] *geog* configurazione *f*; caratteristica *f*; **~s** *pl* fattezze *f/pl*; lineamenti *m/pl*

February ['februəri] febbraio *m*

fecund ['fiːkənd] fecondo

federa|l ['fedərəl] federale; **~tion** federazione *f*; confederazione *f*

fee [fiː] onorario *m*; quota *f*; tassa *f*

feeble ['fiːbl] debole

feed [fiːd] *s* nutrimento *m*; *v/t* nutrire; dare da mangiare; *v/i* nutrirsi; **be fed up with** essere stufo di; **~ing** nutrizione *f*; **~ing-bottle** poppatoio *m*

feel

feel [fi:l] *v/t, irr* sentire; toccare; provare; *v/i* sentirsi; **~ well** stare bene; **~ing** sentimento *m*; sensazione *f*

feign [fein] *v/t* fingere

felicitate [fi'lisiteit] *v/t* congratularsi con

fell [fel] *v/t* abbattere

fellow ['felou] *s* tipo *m*; compagno *m*; individuo *m*; socio *m*; **~citizen** concittadino *m*

felt [felt] feltro *m*

female ['fi:meil] *s* femmina *f*; *a* femminile

feminine ['feminin] femminile

fen [fen] pantano *m*

fence [fens] *s* recinto *m*; steccato *m*; *v/t* chiudere con recinto; *v/i* schermire; **~ing** scherma *f*

fend [fend] *v/t* parare; **~er** *Am* parafango *m*

ferment ['fə:ment] *s* fermento *m*; *v/t* far fermentare; *v/i* fermentare; **~ation** fermentazione *f*

fern [fə:n] felce *f*

ferocity [fə'rɔsiti] ferocità *f*

ferry ['feri] *s* traghetto *m*; *v/t* traghettare

fertile ['fə:tail] fertile; **~ity** [~'tiliti] fertilità *f*; **~ize** ['~ilaiz] *v/t* fertilizzare

fervent ['fə:vənt] fervente

fester ['festə] *v/i* suppurare

festival ['festəvl] *a mus* festival *m*; *a* festivo; **~ities** [~'tivi- tiz] *pl* festa *f*

festoon [fes'tu:n] festone *m*; ghirlanda *f*

fetch [fetʃ] *v/t* andare a prendere; *v/i* vendersi per

fête [feit] festa *f*

fetish ['fetiʃ] feticcio *m*

fetters ['fetəz] ceppi *m/pl*

feudal ['fju:dl] feudale

fever ['fi:və] febbre *f*; **~ish** febbrile

few [fju:] *a, pochi(e)* (*m/pl, f/pl*); **a ~** alcuni(e)

fiancé [fi'ɑ:nsei] fidanzato *m*; **~e** fidanzata *f*

fib [fib] (piccola) bugia *f*

fibre, *Am* **~er** ['faibə] fibra *f*; **~rous** fibroso

fickle ['fikl] incostante

fiction ['fikʃən] finzione *f*; romanzi *m/pl*; **~tious** [~'ti- ʃəs] fittizio

fiddle ['fidl] *s* violino *m*; *v/i* suonare il violino; giuocare con; **~sticks** *pl* sciocchezze *f/pl*

fidelity [fi'deliti] fedeltà *f*

fidget ['fidʒit] *v/i* agitarsi

field [fi:ld] campo *m*; prato *m*; **~glasses** *pl* binocolo *m*

fiend [fi:nd] demonio *m*

fierce [fiəs] feroce

fiery ['faiəri] focoso

fife [faif] piffero *m*

fig [fig] fico *m*

fight [fait] *s* lotta *f*; litigio *m*; *v/t, vir* combattere; lottare; litigare

figurative ['figjurətiv] figurativo

figure ['figə] *s* figura *f*; cifra *f*; *v/t* raffigurare; *v/i* fare calcoli; figurare; **~skating** pattinaggio *m* artistico

file [fail] *s* lima *f*; *mil* fila *f*;

fist

schedario *m*; *v/t* limare; classificare; archiviare

filigree ['filigri:] filigrana *f*

fill [fil] *v/t* riempire; occupare; otturare (*un dente*); ~ **in**, ~ **up** riempire; completare; *v/i* riempirsi

fillet ['filit] filetto *m*; fetta *f* (*di pesce*)

filling (*of tooth*) otturazione *f*; ~ **station** *Am* stazione *f* di servizio

filly ['fili] puledra *f*

film [film] *s* pellicola *f*; film *m*; patina *f*; *v/t* filmare; girare una pellicola

filter ['filtə] *s* filtro *m*; *v/t* filtrare

filth [filθ] sudiciume *m*; ~**y** sudicio

fin [fin] pinna *f*

final ['fainl] *s* finale *m*; *a* finale; ultimo; ~**ity** [fai-'næliti] finalità *f*

finance [fai'næns] *s* finanza *f*; *v/t* finanziare; ~**ial** [~ʃəl] finanziario; ~**ier** finanziere *m*; ~**ing** finanziamento *m*

finch [fintʃ] fringuello *m*

find [faind] *v/t*, *irr* trovare; incontrare; ~ **out** scoprire; *s* scoperta *f*; ~**ings** *pl* conclusioni *f/pl*; *med, for* reperto *m*

fine [fain] *a* fine; bello; **it is ~ weather** fa bel tempo; **that is ~** va benissimo; *s* multa *f*; *v/t* multare

finger ['fiŋgə] *s* dito *m*; *pl* dita *f/pl*; **little ~** mignolo *m*; ~**nail** unghia *f*; ~**prints** *pl* impronte *f/pl* digitali

finish ['finiʃ] *s* fine *f*; termine *m*; rifinitura *f*; *v/t* finire; rifinire

finite ['fainait] finito

Fin|land ['finlənd] Finlandia *f*; ~**n** [fin] finlandese *m*, *f*; ~**nish** *a, s* finlandese (*m*,*f*)

fir [fə:] abete *m*

fire ['faiə] *s* fuoco *m*; incendio *m*; **on ~** in fiamme; **set on ~** incendiare; *v/t fam* licenziare; *v/i* sparare; ~**arms** *pl* armi *f/pl* da fuoco; ~**escape** scala *f* di sicurezza; ~**extinguisher** estintore *m*; ~**insurance** assicurazione *f* contro gli incendi; ~**man** pompiere *m*; fuochista *m*; ~**place** camino *m*; ~**proof** incombustibile; ~**side** camino *m*; ~**works** *pl* fuochi *m/pl* d'artificio

firm [fə:m] *a* fermo; deciso; *s* ditta *f*; ~**ness** fermezza *f*

first [fə:st] primo; ~ **aid** primo soccorso *m*; ~**class** ottimo; ~**hand** di prima mano; ~**ly** in primo luogo; ~ **night** *thea* la prima *f*; ~**rate** di prima classe

firth [fə:θ] estuario *m*

fiscal ['fiskəl] fiscale

fish [fiʃ] *pl* ~**es** [~iz] *s* pesce *m*; *v/t, v/i* pescare; ~**bone** spina *f* di pesce; ~**erman** pescatore *m*; ~**ing rod** canna *f* da pesca; ~**ing tackle** attrezzi *m/pl* da pesca; ~**monger's** pescheria *f*

fissure ['fiʃə] fessura *f*

fist [fist] pugno *m*

fit 84

fit *a* adatto; conveniente; in forma; *v/t* andare bene; *s* attacco *m*; colpo *m*; **~ on** applicare; **~ out** attrezzare; **~ness** opportunità *f*; buona salute *f*; **~ting** *a* adatto; conveniente; *s* prova *f*; **~tings** *pl* accessori *m/pl*

fix [fiks] difficoltà *f*; *v/t* fissare; **~ up** combinare; **~tures** *pl* infissi *m/pl*

flabbergast ['flæbəga:st] *v/t* sbalordire

flabby ['flæbi] floscio

flag [flæg] bandiera *f*; **lower the ~** abbassare la bandiera; **hoist the ~** innalzare la bandiera

flagrant ['fleigrənt] flagrante

flake [fleik] scaglia *f*; fiocco *m* (di neve)

flamboyant [flæm'bɔiənt] fiammeggiante

flame [fleim] *s* fiamma *f*; *v/i* fiammeggiare

flank [flæŋk] *s* fianco *m*; *v/t* fiancheggiare

flannel ['flænl] flanella *f*

flap [flæp] *v/t* battere; *s* battito *m*

flare [fleə] *v/i* fiammeggiare; brillare

flash [flæʃ] *s* lampo *m*; baleno *m*; *v/i* brillare; **~light** lampada *f* elettrica

flask [flɑ:sk] fiasco *m*

flat [flæt] *a* piatto; piano; monotono; *s mus* bémolle *m*; appartamento *m*; **~ of the hand** palma *f*; **~ten** *v/t* appiattire; *v/i* appiattirsi

flatter ['flætə] *v/t* lusingare; **~y** lusinga *f*

flavo(u)r ['fleivə] sapore *m*; gusto *m*; *v/t* dare il sapore di

flaw [flɔ:] difetto *m*; **~less** perfetto; senza difetti

flax [flæks] lino *m*; **~en** biondo

flea [fli:] pulce *f*

flee [fli:] *v/i, v/t, irr* fuggire

fleece [fli:s] *s* vello *m*; lana *f*; *v/t* tosare; *fam* pelare

fleet [fli:t] flotta *f*; **~ing** veloce

Fleming ['flemiŋ] fiammingo *m*; **~sh** *a, s* fiammingo (*m*)

flesh [fleʃ] carne *f* viva; **~y** carnoso

flexible [fl'eksəbl] flessibile

flick [flik] colpetto *m*

flicker ['flikə] *s* tremolio *m*; *v/i* vacillare

flight [flait] fuga *f*; volo *m*; **~ of stairs** rampa *f* di scale

flimsy ['flimzi] inconsistente

flinch [flintʃ] *v/i* indietreggiare; smuoversi

fling [fliŋ] *v/t, irr* gettare; lanciare

flint [flint] pietra *f* focaia

flippant ['flipənt] leggero; poco serio

flirt [flɔ:t] *s* civetta *f*; *v/i* civettare; flirtare; **~ation** flirt *m*

float [flout] *v/i* galleggiare; *v/t* far galleggiare

flock [flɔk] gregge *f* (di pecore); stormo *m* (di uccelli); branco *m* (di animali); *v/i*

flog [flɔg] *v/t* fristare

flood [flʌd] *s* inondazione *f*; *fig* abbondanza *f*; *v/t* inondare; **~-gates** *pl* cateratta *f*

floor [flɔː] *s* pavimento *m*; piano *m*; *v/t* pavimentare; *fig* atterrare; **take the ~** prendere la parola; **~-lamp** lampada *f* a stelo; **~-walker** ispettore *m* di magazzino

flop [flɔp] *s* fiasco *m*; *v/i* far fiasco

florist ['flɔrist] fioraio *m*

flounder ['flaundə] passera *f*

flour ['flauə] farina *f*

flourish ['flʌriʃ] *v/t* agitare; *v/i* fiorire; prosperare

flow [flou] *s* corrente *f*; flusso *m*; *v/i* scorrere; fluire

flower ['flauə] *s* fiore *m*, *v/i* fiorire; **~-bed** aiuola *f*; **~-vase** vaso *m* da fiori; **~-show** mostra *f* di fiori

fluctuate ['flʌktjueit] *v/i* fluttuare

flu [fluː] *cf* influenza

flue [fluː] canna *f* fumaria

fluent ['flu(ː)ənt] corrente; scorrevole

fluff [flʌf] peluria *f*

fluid ['flu(ː)id] *a*, *s* liquido (*m*)

flunk [flʌŋk] *v/i* Am bocciare

flurry ['flʌri] raffica *f* (*di vento*); agitazione *f*

flush [flʌʃ] *s* rossore *m*; *v/t* sciacquare; *v/i* arrossire

fluster ['flʌstə] *s* agitazione *f*; *v/t* innervosire

flute [fluːt] flauto *m*

flutter ['flʌtə] *s* svolazzamento *m*; agitazione *f*; (*slang*) speculazione *f*; *v/t* agitare; *v/i* svolazzare; agitarsi

flux [flʌks] flusso *m*

fly [flai] *s* mosca *f*; *v/i*, *irr* volare; rigare; **~ing squad** pronto intervento *m*; **~ing time** durata *f* di volo

foal [foul] puledro *m*

foam [foum] *s* schiuma *f*; spuma *f*; *v/i* schiumare; spumeggiare; **~y** schiumeggiante; spumeggiante

focus ['foukəs] fuoco *m*; *v/t* mettere a fuoco

fodder ['fɔdə] foraggio *m*

foetus ['fiːtəs] feto *m*

fog [fɔg] nebbia *f*; **~gy** nebbioso

foil [fɔil] *s* lamina *f*; *v/t* far fallire

fold [fould] *s* piega *f*; ovile *m*; *v/t* piegare; incrociare (*le braccia*); **~ing bed** branda *f*

foliage ['fouliidʒ] fogliame *m*

folk [fouk] gente *f*

follow ['fɔlou] *v/t*, *v/i* seguire; **~er** seguace *m*; **~ing** seguente

folly ['fɔli] follia *f*

fond [fɔnd] affezionato; appassionato; **be ~ of** essere affezionato a; **~le** *v/t* accarezzare

food [fuːd] cibo *m*; alimento *m*; **~stuffs** *pl* commestibili *m*/*pl*

fool [fuːl] sciocco(a) *m* (*f*);

make a ~ of o.s. rendersi ridicolo; *v/t* ingannare; *v/i* fare lo sciocco; **~ish** sciocco; **~ishness** sciocchezza *f*; **~proof** assolutamente sicuro; **~scap** carta *f* protocollo

foot [fut], *pl* **feet** [fi:t] piede *m*; zampa *f* (*di animali*); **on** ~ a piedi; **put one's** ~ **in it** fare una gaffe; **~ball** calcio *m*; **~lights** *pl* luci *f/pl* della ribalta; **~print** orma *f*; impronta *f* del piede; **be ~sore** aver male ai piedi; **~step** passo *m*

for [fɔ:, fə] *prp* per; per ragione di; *conj* perché

forbear [fɔ:'bɛə] *v/i*, *irr* guardarsi da; trattenersi da

forbid [fə'bid] *v/t*, *irr* proibire; vietare

force [fɔ:s] *s* forza *f*; potere *m*; *v/t* forzare; **~armed** ~a *pl* forze *f/pl* armate; **come into** ~ entrare in vigore; **~ful** energico

forceps ['fɔ:seps] *pl* forcipe *m*

forcible ['fɔ:səbl] forzato; potente

ford [fɔ:d] guado *m*

fore [fɔ:] *s* davanti *m*; *a* anteriore; **~arm** avambraccio *m*; **~cast** *v/t* prevedere; *s* previsione *f*; **weather ~cast** previsioni *f/pl* del tempo; **~fathers** *pl* antenati *m/pl*; **~finger** indice *m*; **~front** avanguardia *f*; **~going** precedente; **~ground** primo piano *m*; **~head** ['fɔrid] fronte *f*

foreign ['fɔrin] straniero; ~ **currency** moneta *f* estera; ~ **er** straniero *m*; ~ **exchange** moneta *f* estera; ♀ **Office** Ministero *m* degli Affari Esteri (*in Inghilterra*)

fore|leg gamba *f* anteriore; **~man** capo *m* operaio; **~most** primo; **~see** *v/t* prevedere; **~sight** previsione *f*

forest ['fɔrist] foresta *f*

fore|stall *v/t* prevenire; anticipare; **~taste** *v/t* pregustare; **~tell** *v/t* predire

forever [fə'revə] per sempre

foreword prefazione *f*

forfeit ['fɔ:fit] pegno *m*

forge [fɔ:dʒ] *v/t* falsificare; **~ry** falsificazione *f*; firma *f* falsa

forget [fə'get] *v/t*, *irr* dimenticare; **~ful** dimentico; **~me-not** non ti scordar di me *m*

forgive [fə'giv] *v/t*, *irr* perdonare; **~ness** perdono *m*

forgo [fɔ:'gou] *v/t*, *irr* rinunciare a

fork [fɔ:k] forchetta *f*; forca *f*; biforcazione *f*; *v/i* biforcarsi

forlorn [fə'lɔ:n] abbandonato

form [fɔ:m] *s* forma *f*; modulo *m*; banco *m*; modello *m*; *v/t* formare

formal ['fɔ:məl] formale; **~ity** [~'mæliti] formalità *f*

formation [fɔ:'meiʃən] formazione *f*

former ['fɔ:mə] *a* precedentete; **the ~** il primo; quegli; **~ly** prima; nel passato

formidable [ˈfɔːmidəbl] formidabile

formula [ˈfɔːmjulə] formula f; **~te** v/t formulare

forsake [fəˈseik] v/t, irr abbandonare

fort [fɔːt] fortezza f

forth [fɔːθ] (in) avanti; fuori; **and so ~** eccetera; **~coming** prossimo; **~with** immediatamente

fortify [ˈfɔːtifai] v/t fortificare

fortitude [ˈfɔːtitjuːd] fortezza f (d'animo)

fortnight [ˈfɔːtnait] quindici giorni; **~ly** quindicinale

fortress [ˈfɔːtris] fortezza f

fortuitous [fɔːˈtju(ː)itəs] fortuito

fortunate [ˈfɔːtʃnit] fortunato

fortune [ˈfɔːtʃən] fortuna f; sorte f

forum [ˈfɔːrəm] foro m

forward [ˈfɔːwəd] a precoce; adv (in) avanti; in poi; v/t far proseguire; spedire

foster [ˈfɔstə] v/t nutrire; **~child** figlio m adottivo; **~mother** madre f adottiva

foul [faul] a sudicio; osceno; v/t sporcare

found [faund] v/t fondare; **~ation** fondazione f; **~er** fondatore m; **~ling** trovatello m

foundry [ˈfaundri] fonderia f

fountain [ˈfauntin] fontana

f; fonte f; **~pen** penna f stilografica

four [fɔː]: **on all ~s** a quattro zampe; **~footed** quadrupede

fowl [faul] pollame m

fox [fɔks] volpe f

fraction [ˈfrækʃən] frazione f; **~ure** [ˈfræktʃə] s frattura f; v/t fratturare; v/i fratturarsi

fragile [ˈfrædʒail] fragile; delicato

fragment [ˈfrægmənt] frammento m

fragrance [ˈfreigrəns] fragranza f; **~t** fragrante

frail [freil] delicato; fragile

frame [freim] s cornice f; struttura f; telaio m; v/t incorniciare; **~work** ossatura f; cornice f

franc [fræŋk] franco m

France [frɑːns] Francia f

franchise [ˈfræntʃaiz] diritto m di voto

frank [fræŋk] franco; **~ly** francamente

frankfurter [ˈfræŋkfətə] salsiccia f

frantic [ˈfræntik] fuori di sè; frenetico

fraternal [frəˈtəːnl] fraterno; **~ity** fraternità f

fraud [frɔːd] frode f; **~ulent** fraudolento

freak [friːk] fenomeno m; uomo m strambo; eccentrico m

freckle [ˈfrekl] lentiggine f

free [friː]: libero; gratuito; **~ on board** franco a bordo; **~**

trade libero scambio *m; v/t* liberare; **~dom** libertà *f*; **~mason** massone *m*; **~ticket** biglietto *m* gratuito; **~way** *Am* strada *f* di grande comunicazione

freez|e [fri:z] *v/t, irr* gelare; congelare; *v/i* gelarsi; congelarsi; **~er** frigorifero *m*; **~ing-point** punto *m* di congelamento

freight [freit] nolo *m*

French [frentʃ] *a, s* francese (*m, f*); **the ~** *pl* i francesi; **~window** balcone *m*; **~woman** francese *f*

frequen|cy ['fri:kwənsi] frequenza *f*; **~t** frequente

fresh [freʃ] fresco; nuovo; **~air** aria *f* pura; **~water** acqua *f* dolce; **~man** matricola *f*; **~ness** freschezza *f*

fret [fret] *v/i* innervosirsi; **~ful** nervoso

friar ['fraiə] frate *m*

friction ['frikʃən] frizione *f*; attrito *m*

Friday ['fraidi] venerdì *m*

fridge [fridʒ] *fam* frigorifero *m*

fried [fraid] fritto; cotto

friend [frend] amico(a) *m* (*f*); **boy~** fidanzato *m*; **girl~** fidanzata *f*; **~ly** amichevole; **~ship** amicizia *f*

fright [frait] spavento *m*; **~en** *v/t* spaventare; **~ful** spaventoso; terribile

frigid ['fridʒid] frigido

frill [fril] gala *f*

fringe [frindʒ] frangia *f*; bordo *m*

frisky [friski] allegro

frivolous ['frivələs] frivolo

fro [frou]: **to and ~** avanti e indietro

frock [frɔk] vestito *m*; tonaca *f*

frog [frɔg] rana *f*

frolic [frɔlik] *v/i* far capriole

from [frɔm, frəm] da; fin da; **~ ... to** da ... a

front [frʌnt] *s* davanti *m*; facciata *f*; *a* anteriore; **in ~ (of)** davanti (a); **~ier** ['~iə] frontiera *f*; **~ page** frontespizio *m*; **~ seat** sedile *m* anteriore; **~-wheel drive** trasmissione *f* sulle ruote anteriori

frost [frɔst] gelo *m*; **~y** gelido

froth [frɔθ] schiuma *f*; spuma *f*

frown [fraun] *s* aggrottamento *m* delle ciglia; *v/i* aggrottare le ciglia

frozen [frouzn] gelato; congelato

frugal ['fru:gəl] frugale

fruit [fru:t] frutto *m*; frutta *f*; prodotto *m*; **dried ~** frutta secca; **preserved ~** frutta conservata

fruit|ful fruttuoso; **~less** infruttuoso

frustrate [frʌs'treit] *v/t* frustrare

fry [frai] *v/t, v/i* friggere; **~ing-pan** padella *f*

fuel [fjuəl] combustibile *m*

fugitive ['fju:dʒitiv] *a, s* fuggitivo (*m*)

fulfil [ful'fil] *v/t* compiere; eseguire

full [ful] pieno; completo; ~
board pensione *f* completa; ~ **stop** punto *m*

fumble [fʌmbl] *v/i* frugare

fume [fju:m] *s* fumo *m*; vapore *m*; *v/i* fumare; emettere vapore; essere arrabbiato

fun [fʌn] divertimento *m*; sva-
go *m*; **for ... in ~** per scherzo

function [fʌŋkʃən] funzio-
ne *f*; **~ary** funzionario *m*

fund [fʌnd] fondo *m*

fundamental   [ˌfʌndə-
'mentl] fondamentale

funeral ['fju:nərəl] funerale
m

fung|us ['fʌŋgəs],   *pl* **~i**
['fʌŋgai] fungo *m*

funicular [fju:'nikjulə] funicolare *f*

funnel ['fʌnl] imbuto *m*; ciminiera *f* (*di nave, macchina
a vapore*)

funny ['fʌni] divertente;
buffo; strano

fur [fə:] pelliccia *f*; ~ **coat**
pelliccia *f*

furious ['fjuəriəs] furioso

furnace ['fə:nis] fornace *f*;
caldaia *f* (*del termosifone*)

furni|sh ['fə:niʃ] *v/t* fornire;
ammobiliare; **~ture** mobili
m/pl

furrow ['fʌrou] solco *m*; ruga *f*

furth|er ['fə:ðə] *a* ulteriore;
adv oltre; più lontano; *v/t*
promuovere; favorire; **~er-
more** inoltre; **~est** il più
lontano (*di tutti*)

furtive ['fə:tiv] furtivo

fury ['fjuəri] furia *f*

fuse [fju:z] *s* fusibile *m*; spo-
letta *f*; *v/t* fulminare; fondere; *v/i* fulminarsi

fusion ['fju:ʒən] fusione *f*

fuss [fʌs] *s* agitazione *f*; storie *f/pl*; *v/i* agitarsi; fare
storie; **~y** pignolo; difficile

futile ['fju:tail] futile

future ['fju:tʃə] *a* venturo;
futuro; *s* futuro *m*; avvenire
m

fuzzy ['fʌzi] confuso

G

gab [gæb] chiacchiere *f/pl*

gabardine ['gæbədi:n] ga-
bardina *f*

gadfly ['gædflai] tafano *m*

gadget ['gædʒit] aggeggio *m*

gag [gæg] *s* bavaglio *m*; *v/t*
imbavagliare

gage [geidʒ] pegno *m*

gai|ety ['geiəti] allegria *f*; **~ly**
allegramente

gain [gein] *s* (*money*) guada-

gno *m*; (*weight*) aumento *m*;
v/t guadagnare; aumentare; (*watch*) andare avanti

gait [geit] andatura *f*

gale [geil] bufera *f* di
vento

gall [gɔ:l] bile *f*; fiele *f*

gallant ['gælənt] *a* valoroso;
galante

gall-bladder cistifellea *f*;
vescica *f* biliare

gallery ['gæləri] galleria f; *thea* loggione m

galley ['gæli] galea f

gallon ['gælən] gallone m (litri 4,543)

gallop ['gæləp] s galoppo m; v/i galoppare

gallows ['gælouz] pl forca f

gall-stone calcolo m biliare

galore [gə'lɔ:] a bizzeffe

gambl|e ['gæmbl] v/t, v/i giuocare; **~er** giuocatore m; **~ing** giuoco m d'azzardo

gambol ['gæmbəl] salto m

game [geim] giuoco m; partita f; **~keeper** guardacaccia m

gander ['gændə] papero m

gang [gæŋ] banda f; squadra f

gangrene ['gæŋgri:n] cancrena f

gangster ['gæŋstə] gangster m

gangway ['gæŋwei] passerella f

gaol [dʒeil] prigione f; carcere m; **~er** carceriere m

gap [gæp] fenditura f; breccia f; lacuna f

gape [geip] v/i stare con la bocca aperta

garage ['gæra:dʒ] autorimessa f

garbage ['gɑ:bidʒ] rifiuti m/pl

garden ['gɑ:dn] giardino m; **~er** giardiniere m

gargle ['gɑ:gl] s gargarismo m; v/i fare gargarismi

garland ['gɑ:lənd] ghirlanda f

garlic ['gɑ:lik] aglio m

garment ['gɑ:mənt] indumento m; articolo m di vestiario

garnish ['gɑ:niʃ] v/t guarnire

garret ['gærət] soffitta f

garrison ['gærisn] guarnigione f

garrulous ['gæruləs] loquace

garter ['gɑ:tə] giarrettiera f

gas [gæs] s gas m; Am benzina f; v/t asfissiare

gash [gæʃ] squarcio m

gasket ['gæskit] guarnizione f

gas-mask maschera f antigas

gasoline ['gæsəli:n] Am benzina f

gasp [gɑ:sp] v/i boccheggiare

gas|station Am posto m di rifornimento; **~stove** fornello m a gas

gastritis [gæs'traitis] gastrite f

gastronomy [gæs'trɔnəmi] gastronomia f

gas-works pl officine f/pl del gas

gate [geit] porta f; cancello m

gather ['gæðə] v/t raccogliere; riunire; capire; v/i riunirsi; **~ing** riunione f

gaudy ['gɔ:di] sfarzoso

gauge [geidʒ] s calibro m; scartamento m; misura f; indicatore m; v/t misurare; calibrare

gaunt [gɔ:nt] sparuto; macilento

giddy

gauze [gɔːz] garza f

gawky [ˈgɔːki] goffo

gay [gei] allegro

gaze [geiz] s sguardo m fisso; v/i guardare fisso

gear [giə] equipaggiamento m; mec ingranaggio m; **in ~** ingranato; in azione; **out of ~** non ingranato; guasto; **~ change** cambio m delle marce; **~ lever** leva f del cambio

gem [dʒem] gioiello m; gemma f

gender [ˈdʒendə] genero m

general [ˈdʒenərəl] a generale; s generale m; **~ize** v/t, v/i generalizzare

generate [ˈdʒenəreit] v/t generare; **~ion** generazione f; **~or** generatore m

genero|sity [ˌdʒenəˈrɔsiti] generosità f; **~us** generoso

genial [ˈdʒiːnjəl] geniale

genital [ˈdʒenitl] genitale; **~s** pl genitali m/pl

genitive [ˈdʒenitiv] genitivo m

genius [ˈdʒiːnjəs] genio m

gentle [ˈdʒentl] dolce; ben nato; **~man** gentiluomo m; signore m; **~manlike** cavalleresco; **~ness** mitezza f; **~woman** gentildonna f; signora f

genuine [ˈdʒenjuin] genuino; autentico

geography [dʒiˈɔgrəfi] geografia f

geology [dʒiˈɔlədʒi] geologia f

geometry [dʒiˈɔmitri] geometria f

geranium [dʒiˈreinjəm] geranio m

germ [dʒəːm] germe m

German [ˈdʒəːmən] s, a tedesco (m); **~y** Germania f

germinate [ˈdʒəːmineit] v/i germinare

gerund [ˈdʒerənd] gerundio m

gest|iculate [dʒesˈtikjuleit] v/i gesticolare; **~ure** [ˈdʒestʃə] gesto m

get [get] v/t, v/i irr ottenere; comprare; ricevere; guadagnare; prendere; v/i arrivare; raggiungere; diventare; **~ about** andare in giro; viaggiare; **~ away** scappare; **~ back** v/i tornare; v/t recuperare; **~ lost** perdersi; **~ on** procedere; **~ on with** andare avanti; andare d'accordo con; **~ out** scendere; interj fuori di qui; **~ ready** prepararsi; **~ up** alzarsi; **have got** avere; tenere; **I have got to** ho da; devo

geyser [ˈgaizə] scaldabagno m

ghastly [ˈgɑːstli] orribile

gherkin [ˈgəːkin] cetriolino m

ghost [goust] fantasma m; spettro m; **Holy 2 Spirito m** Santo; **give up the ~** morire; **~ly** spettrale

giant [ˈdʒaiənt] gigante m

gibbon [ˈgibən] gibone m

giblets [ˈdʒiblits] pl rigaglie f/pl

giddy [ˈgidi] vertiginoso;

feel ~ avere le vertigini

gift [gift] regalo m; dono m; talento m; **~ed with** dotato di

gigantic [dʒaiˈgæntik] gigantesco

giggle [ˈgigl] s risata f sciocca; v/i ridere scioccamente

gild [gild] v/t, irr dorare

gill [gil] branchia f

gilt-edged securities pl titoli m/pl sicuri

gin [dʒin] gin m

ginger [ˈdʒindʒə] zenzero m

gipsy [ˈdʒipsi] zingaro(a) m (f)

giraffe [dʒiˈrɑːf] giraffa f

gird [gəːd] v/t, irr cingere; **~le** cintura f; panciera f

girl [gəːl] ragazza f; ~ **guide** esploratrice f; **~ish** da ragazza

girth [gəːθ] circonferenza f

gist [dʒist] sostanza f; contenuto m essenziale

give [giv] v/t, irr dare; regalare; ~ **back** restituire; ~ **in** cedere; ~ **out** distribuire; ~ **up** rinunciare a; ~ **o.s. up** v/r arrendersi; ~ **name** nome m di battesimo; ~**n to** dedito a

glacier [ˈglæsjə] ghiacciaio m

glad [glæd] contento; lieto; **~ly** volentieri

glamo(u)r [ˈglæmə] fascino m; **~ous** affascinante

glance [glɑːns] s occhiata f; sguardo m; v/i, v/t dare un'occhiata; gettare uno sguardo; ~ **over a book** sfogliare un libro

gland [glænd] ghiandola f

glare [glɛə] s bagliore m; sguardo m feroce; v/t risplendere; guardare ferocemente

glass [glɑːs] a di vetro; di cristallo; s vetro m; bicchiere m; cristallo m; specchio m; barometro m; (**a pair of**) **~es** pl occhiali m/pl; **stained** ~ vetro m colorato; **~ware** cristallerie f/pl; **~works** pl vetreria f

glaucoma [glɔːˈkoumə] glaucoma m

glaz|e [gleiz] s vernice f; smalto m; v/t verniciare; smaltare; fornire di vetri; **~ier** vetraio m

gleam [gliːm] s barlume m; v/i brillare; **~ing** brillante

glee [gliː] giubilo m

glib [glib] pronto di lingua

glide [glaid] v/i scivolare; planare; **~r** aliante m

glimmer [ˈglimə] s luce f fioca; v/i mandare una luce fioca

glimpse [glimps] s sguardo m; v/i intravedere

glint [glint] s luccichio m; v/i luccicare

glisten [ˈglisn] v/i luccicare

glitter [ˈglitə] s luccichio m; v/i luccicare

gloat [glout] (**over**) v/i gioire di

globe [gloub] mappamondo m

gloom [gluːm] oscurità f; tristezza f; **~y** oscuro; triste

glor|ify [ˈglɔːrifai] v/t glorifi-

goodwill

care; **~ious** glorioso; **~y** gloria *f*

gloss [glɔːs] *s* lucidezza

glossary ['glɔsəri] glossario *m*

glove [glʌv] guanto *m*

glow [glou] *s* incandescenza *f*; ardore *m*; splendore *m*; *v/i* ardere; essere incandescente; **~ing** ardente; incandescente; entusiasta; **~worm** lucciola *f*

glue [gluː] *s* colla *f*; *v/t* incollare

glum [glʌm] triste; di mal umore

glut [glʌt] *s* saturazione *f*; sazietà *f*; *v/t* saturare; saziare; **~ton** ghiottone *m*; ingordigia *f*; golosità *f*; **~tony** golosità *f*

gnarled [nɑːld] nodoso

gnash [næʃ] *v/t* digrignare (*i denti*)

gnat [næt] moscerino *m*

gnaw [nɔː] *v/t* rodere; rosicchiare

go [gou] *v/i, irr* andare; camminare; funzionare; **~ ahead** andare avanti; **~ away** andare via; **~ back** tornare; **~ by** passare; **~ for** andare a prendere; attaccare; **~ home** andare a casa; **~ in for** iscriversi a; dedicarsi a; **~ off** allontanare; andare a male; **~ on** continuare; proseguire; **~ out** uscire; spegnersi; **~ through** passare per; **~ up** salire; **~ without** fare a meno; **~s** *f sm* spirito *m*; energia *f*; **on the ~** in attività

goad [goud] *s* pungolo *m*; *v/t* pungolare

goal [goul] metà *f*; porta *f* (*nel calcio*); rete *f* (*nel calcio*); **~keeper** portiere *m*

goat [gout] capra *f*

go-between mediatore *m*

goblet ['gɔblit] coppa *f*

goblin ['gɔblin] folletto *m*

God [gɔd] Dio *m*

god|child figlioccio(a) *m* (*f*); **~dess** dea *f*; **~father** padrino *m*; **~less** ateo; empio; **~ly** devoto; pio; **~mother** madrina *f*; **~parents** *pl* padrini *m/pl*

goggles ['gɔglz] *pl* occhiali *m/pl* di protezione

going ['gouin]: **be ~ to** stare per

goitre ['gɔitə] gozzo *m*

gold [gould] oro *m*; **~en** d'oro; **~fish** pesce *m* rosso; **~smith** orefice *m*

golf [gɔlf] golf *m*; **~-course** campo *m* da golf; **~er** giocatore *m* di golf

gone [gɔn] andato; perduto; passato; morto

good [gud] *s* bene *m*; *a* buono; **as ~ as** (tanto) buono quanto; **a ~ deal** parecchio; **~ afternoon** buona sera; **~bye** arrivederci; **~-for-nothing** buono a niente *m*; ♀ **Friday** Venerdì *m* Santo; **it's no ~** non vale niente; è inutile; **~-looking** bello; **~ luck!** buona fortuna!; **~ morning** buon giorno; **~ness** bontà *f*; **~will** buona volontà *f*

goods

goods pl merce f; ~ **train** treno m merci

goose [gu:s], pl **geese** [gi:s] oca f

gooseberry ['guzbəri] uva f spina; ~**flesh** ['gu:s-] pelle f d'oca

gorge [gɔːdʒ] geog gola f; ~**ous** splendido; sfarzoso

gorilla [gə'rilə] gorilla m

gospel ['gɔspəl] vangelo m

gossip ['gɔsip] s pettegolezzi m/pl; pettego(a) m (f); v/i pettegolare

gothic ['gɔθik] gotico

gourd [guəd] zucca f

gout [gaut] gotta f

govern ['gʌvən] v/t governare; dominare; ~**ess** istitutrice f; ~**ing board** consiglio m amministrativo; ~**ment** governo m

gown [gaun] vestito m; toga f

grab [græb] v/t acchiappare

grace [greis] s grazia f; favore m; v/t favorire; ~**ful** aggraziato

gracious ['greiʃəs] condiscendente; **good** ~! caspita!

grad|e [greid] s grado m; v/t classificare; ~**e crossing** Am passaggio m a livello; ~**ient** ['greidjənt] pendenza f; ~**ual** ['grædʒuəl] graduale; ~**ually** adv a poco a poco; ~**uate** ['-djueit] v/t graduare; v/i (university) laurearsi

graft [grɑːft] s innesto m; v/t innestare

grain [grein] grano m

grammar ['græmə] gram-

matica f; ~**ian** grammatico m; ~**school** scuola f media

gram [græm] cf **gramme**

gramme [græm] grammo m

gramophone ['græməfoun] grammofono m

grand [grænd] in grande; illustre; magnifico; ~**daughter** nipote f; ~**eur** ['-ndʒə] splendore m; ~**father** nonno m; ~**iose** grandioso; ~**mother** nonna f; ~**pa** ['-npɑ:] fam nonno m; ~**son** nipote m; ~**stand** tribuna f

granite ['grænit] granito m

granny ['græni] fam nonna f

grant [grɑːnt] s concessione f; borsa f di studio; v/t concedere; **take for** ~**ed** essere sicuro; dare per fatto

granulate ['grænjuleit] v/t granulare

grape [greip] uva f; chicco m d'uva; ~**fruit** pompelmo m

graphic ['græfik] grafico

grasp [grɑːsp] v/t afferrare; s presa f; stretta f; comprensione f; ~**ing** avido; avaro

grass [grɑːs] erba f; ~**hopper** cavalletta f

grate [greit] s grata f; griglia f; v/t grattugiare

grateful ['greitful] grato; riconoscente; ~**ness** gratitudine f

grating ['greitiŋ] s grata f; inferriata f; a irritante

gratis ['greitis] a gratuito; adv gratis

gratuit|ous [grə'tju(:)itəs]

gratuito; **~y** gratificazione *f*
grave [greiv] *a* grave; serio; *s* tomba *f*
gravel ['grævəl] ghiaia *f*
graveyard camposanto *m*
gravitation [grævi'teiʃən] gravitazione *f*
gravity ['~ti] gravità *f*; serietà *f*
gravy ['greivi] sugo *m* di carne
gray [grei] *Am* grigio
graz|e [greiz] *s* abrasione *f*; *v/t* sfiorare; escoriare; *v/i* pascolare; **~ing** pascolo *m*
greas|e [gri:s] *s* grasso *m*; lubrificante *m*; unto *m*; *v/t* ungere; lubrificare; **~y** grasso; unto; untuoso
great [greit] grande; **a ~ deal** molto; **a ~ many** molti(e); **~est** massimo; **~grandfather** bisnonno *m*; **~grandmother** bisnonna *f*; **~ly** molto; **~ness** grandezza *f*
Grecian ['gri:ʃən] greco
greed [gri:d] golosità *f*; avidità *f*; **~y** goloso; avido
Greek [gri:k] *a, s* greco (*m*)
green [gri:n] *a* verde; *s* verde *m*; **~grocer** ortolano *m*; **~house** serra *f*; **~s** *pl* verdura *f*
greet [gri:t] *v/t* salutare; **~ing** saluto *m*
grenade [gri'neid] granata *f*
grey [grei] grigio; **~hound** levriere *m*
grid [grid] rete *f*
grie|f [gri:f] dolore *m*; **~vance** lagnanza *f*; **~ve** *v/t*

affliggere; *v/i* essere addolorato; soffrire
grill [gril] *s* griglia *f*; *v/t* fare alla griglia
grim [grim] torvo; fosco
grimace [gri'meis] smorfia *f*
grim|e [graim] sudiciume *m*; **~y** sudicio
grin [grin] *s* sogghigno *m*; *v/i* sogghignare
grind [graind] *v/t, irr* macinare; digrignare (*i denti*); *v/i* sgobbare; **~stone** macina *f*
grip [grip] *s* stretta *f*; presa *f*; *v/t* afferrare
gripes [graips] *pl* colica *f*
grisly ['grizli] spaventoso; orribile
gristle ['grisl] cartilagine *f*
grit [grit] sabbia *f*
grizzled ['grizld] grigio
groan [groun] *s* gemito *m*; *v/i* gemere
grocer ['grousə] negoziante *m* di generi alimentari; droghiere *m*; **~'s ~y** negozio *m* di generi alimentari; (**shop**) drogheria *f*
grog [grɔg] grog *m*; **~gy** debole; intontito
groin [grɔin] inguine *m*
groom [grum] *s* mozzo *m* (*di stalla*); *v/t* strigliare
groove [gru:v] *s* solco *m*; *v/t* solcare
grope [group] *v/t, v/i* andare a tentoni
gross [grous] grossolano; volgare; *comm* lordo; **~ weight** peso *m* lordo
grotesque [grou'tesk] grot-

tesco

ground [graund] s suolo m; terreno m; terra f; motivo m; base f; v/t basare; fondare; v/i incagliarsi; **~floor** pianterreno m; **~hog** marmotta f; **~less** infondato; **~nut** arachide f; **~work** fondamento m; base f

group [gru:p] s gruppo m; v/t raggruppare; v/i raggrupparsi

grove [grouv] boschetto m

grow [grou] v/t, irr coltivare; v/i crescere; svilupparsi; diventare; **~ dark** oscurarsi; farsi buio; **~less** diminuire; **~ up** crescere; **~er** coltivatore m; **~ing** a crescente; s coltivazione f

growl [graul] s borbottio m; v/i borbottare

grown-up adulto m

growth [grouθ] crescita f; sviluppo m; med tumore m

grub [grʌb] larva f; **~by** sudicio

grudge [grʌdʒ] s rancore m; risentimento m; v/t dare malvolentieri

gruel [gruəl] pappa f

gruesome ['gru:səm] macabro; orribile

gruff [grʌf] aspro; sgarbato

grumble ['grʌmbl] v/i borbottare; brontolare; **~r** brontolone m

grunt [grʌnt] v/i grugnire

guarantee [ˌgærən'ti:] s garanzia f; v/t garantire; **~or**

[~'tɔ:] mallevadore m; **~y** ['~ti] garanzia f

guard [gɑːd] s guardia f; mil sentinella f; **on one's ~** in guardia; v/t, v/i proteggere; custodire; **~ian** guardiano m; tutore m

guess [ges] s supposizione f; congettura f; v/t, v/i indovinare; supporre

guest [gest] ospite m, f; cliente m, f; **~house** pensione f

guid|ance ['gaidəns] guida f; **~e** s guida f; v/t guidare; **~ebook** guida f

guild [gild] arte f; corporazione f

guile [gail] astuzia f

guillotine [ˌgilə'ti:n] ghigliottina f

guilt [gilt] colpa f; colpevolezza f; **~less** innocente; **~y** colpevole

guinea ['gini] ghinea f; **~ pig** porcellino m d'India

guise [gaiz] apparenza f; foggia f

guitar [gi'tɑː] chitarra f

gulf [gʌlf] golfo m

gull [gʌl] gabbiano m

gull|et ['gʌlit] esofago m; gola f; **~y** burrone m

gulp [gʌlp] v/t trangugiare

gum [gʌm] s somma f; gengiva f; v/t ingommare

gun [gʌn] fucile m; cannone m; pistola f; **~powder** polvere f da sparo; **~smith** armaiolo m

gurgle ['gə:gl] s gorgoglio m; v/t gorgogliare

gush [gʌʃ] s zampillo m; fam effusioni f/pl; v/i zampillare; fare effusioni

gust [gʌst] raffica f

gusto ['gʌstou] gusto m; entusiasmo m

guts [gʌts] pl intestino m; minugia f; **have ~s** avere coraggio

gutter ['gʌtə] cunetta f; grondaia f

guy [gai] spauracchio m; Am uomo m; tipo m

gym [dʒim], **gymnas|ium** [~'neizjəm] palestra f; **~tics** [~'næstiks] pl ginnastica f

gyn(a)ecolog|ist [ˌgaini'kɔlədʒist] ginecologo m; **~y** ginecologia f

gypsy ['dʒipsi] zingaro(a) m (f)

H

haberdashery ['hæbədæʃə] merceria f

habit ['hæbit] abitudine f; costume m; abitabile

habitual [hə'bitjuəl] abituale

hack [hæk] cavallo m di nolo; **~neyed** comune; **~saw** sega f per metalli

haddock ['hædək] merluzzo m

h(a)emorrhage ['heməridʒ] emorragia f

hag [hæg] strega f

haggard ['hægəd] magro; sparuto

hail [heil] s grandine f; grido m; saluto m; v/i grandinare; v/t chiamare

hair [hεə] pelo m; capelli m/pl; **~brush** spazzola f per capelli; **~cut** taglio m di capelli; **~dresser** parrucchiere m per signora; **~drier** asciugatore m per capelli; **~pin** forcina f; **~raising** orripilante; **~y** peloso

half [hɑːlf] s mezzo m; metà f; a mezzo; adv a metà; **~an hour** mezz'ora f; **~back** (sport) secondo m; **~baked** immaturo; **~breed** mesticcio m; **~brother** fratellastro m; **~moon** mezza luna f; **~witted** scemo; **~yearly** semestrale

halibut ['hælibət] pianuzza f

hall [hɔːl] ingresso m; sala f; salone m

hallo! [hə'lou] ciao!

hallowed ['hæloud] santificato

hallucination [həˌluːsi'neiʃən] allucinazione f

halo ['heilou] aureola f

halt [hɔːlt] s fermata f; v/t fermare; v/i fermarsi

halter ['hɔːltə] capestro m

halve [hɑːv] v/t dividere in due parti uguali; dimezzare

ham [hæm] prosciutto m

hamlet ['hæmlit] piccolo villaggio m

hammer ['hæmə] s martello m; v/t martellare

hammock ['hæmək] amaca f

hamper ['hæmpə] cesta *f*; *v/t* impedire; ostacolare

hamster ['hæmstə] criceto *m*

hand [hænd] *s* mano *f*; lancetta *f* (*dell'orologio*); calligrafia *f*; **at** ~ disponibile; **on the one** ~ da una parte; **on the other** ~ dall'altra parte; **on the right** ~ a destra; **second** ~ di seconda mano; *v/t* porgere; ~ **in**, ~ **over** consegnare; ~**bag** borsa *f* a mano; ~**book** manuale *m*; ~**cuffs** *pl* manette *f/pl*; ~**ful** manata *f*; pugno *m*

handi|cap ['hændikæp] *s* impedimento *m*; svantaggio *m*; *v/t* mettere a svantaggio; ~**craft** lavoro *m* a mano; artigianato *m*

handkerchief ['hæŋkətʃif] fazzoletto *m*

handle ['hændl] *s* manico *m*; maniglia *f*; *v/t* maneggiare; ~ **bar** manubrio *m*

hand|-luggage bagaglio *m* a mano; ~**made** fatto a mano; ~**rail** mancorrente *m*; ~**shake** stretta *f* di mano; ~**some** bello; ~**work** lavoro *m* a mano; ~**writing** calligrafia *f*; ~**y** comodo

hang [hæŋ] *v/t*, *v/r* appendere; attaccare; impiccare (*un criminale*); *v/i* pendere; essere sospeso

hangar ['hæŋə] aviorimessa *f*

hanger ['hæŋə], **coat** ~ gruccia *f*

hang|ings ['hæŋiŋz] *pl* tappezzeria *f*; ~**man** boia *m*; ~**over** conseguenze *f/pl* (di ubriachezza)

hank [hæŋk] matassa *f*

haphazard ['hæp'hæzəd] *a* a casaccio

happen ['hæpən] *v/i* succedere; accadere; trovarsi; ~**ing** avvenimento *m*

happ|ily ['hæpili] felicemente; ~**iness** felicità *f*; ~**y** felice; ~**y-go-luck** spensierato

harass ['hærəs] *v/t* tormentare

harbo(u)r ['ha:bə] *s* porto *m*; *fig* rifugio *m*; *v/t* accogliere; albergare; *fig* nutrire

hard [ha:d] duro; difficile; severo; ~**boiled egg** uovo *m* sodo; ~ **up** a corto di quattrini; ~**en** *v/t* indurire; *v/i* indurirsi; ~**headed** pratico; ~**hearted** duro; insensibile; ~**ly** appena; ~**ever** quasi mai; ~**ness** durezza *f*; ~**ship** sacrificio *m*; ~**ware** ferramenta *f/pl*; ~**y** robusto

hare [hɛə] lepre *f*; ~**bell** campanula *f*; ~**brained** scervellato; ~**lip** labbro *m* leporino

harem ['hɛərəm] arem *m*

haricot ['hærikou] fagiolino *m*

hark! [ha:k] ascoltate!

harlequin ['ha:likwin] Arlecchino *m*

harm [ha:m] *s* danno *m*; *v/t* danneggiare; ~**ful** dannoso; ~**less** innocuo

harmon|ious [haːˈmounjəs] armonioso; **~y** [ˈhaːməni] armonia f

harness [ˈhaːnis] bardatura f; finimenti m/pl; v/t bardare; fig utilizzare

harp [haːp] s arpa f; **~ on** v/i insistere; **~ist** arpista m, f

harpoon [haːˈpuːn] s fiocina f; v/t fiocinare

harpsichord [ˈhaːpsikɔːd] clavicembalo m

harrow [ˈhærou] v/t fig straziare; s erpice m

harsh [haːʃ] aspro; severo

harvest [ˈhaːvist] s raccolto m; v/t raccogliere; **combine ~er** mietitrebbia f

hash [hæʃ] s ragù m; fig pasticcio m; v/t pasticciare; **make a ~** fare un pasticcio

hast|e [heist] s fretta f; **~en** v/i affrettarsi; **~y** frettoloso

hat [hæt] cappello m

hatch [hætʃ] s covata f; v/t covare; v/i schiudersi; (ideas) maturarsi

hatchet [ˈhætʃit] accetta f

hat|e [heit] s odio m; v/t odiare; **~eful** odioso; **~red** odio m

haughti|ness [ˈhɔːtinis] superbia f; **~y** altero; superbo

haul [hɔːl] s retata f (di pesci); fig guadagno m; v/t tirare; trascinare

haunch [hɔːntʃ] anca f

haunt [hɔːnt] s ritrovo m; v/t frequentare; ossessionare

have [hæv, həv] v/t, irr avere; **I had rather** prefe-

rirei; **~ got** fam avere; **~ to** dovere

haven [ˈheivn] porto m; rifugio m

havoc [ˈhævək] distruzione f; devastazione f

hawk [hɔːk] falco m; **~er** venditore m ambulante

hawthorn [ˈhɔːθɔːn] biancospino m

hay [hei] fieno m; **~ fever** asma m del fieno; **~loft** fienile m

hazard [ˈhæzəd] s azzardo m; v/t azzardare

haz|e [heiz] nebbia f; **~y** nebbioso

H-bomb [ˈeitʃbɔm] bomba f H; bomba f all'idrogeno

he pron egli; **~ who** quello che; chi

head [hed] s testa f; capo m; v/t intestare; v/i dirigersi; **~ache** mal m di testa; **~gear** acconciatura f del capo; **~ing** titolo m; **~lights** pl fari m/pl; **~line** titolo m; **~master** direttore m; **~ mistress** direttrice f; **~ office** sede f centrale; **~quarters** pl quartieri m/pl generali; **~strong** testardo; **~way** progressi m/pl

heal [hiːl] v/t guarire; sanare

health [helθ] s salute f; **~y** sano

heap [hiːp] s mucchio m; cumulo m; v/t ammucchiare; accumulare

hear [hiə] v/t, irr sentire; **~er** ascoltatore m; **~ing** udito m; ascolto m; udienza f; **with-**

in ~ing a portata di voce; ~say diceria f

hearse [hə:s] carro m funebre

heart [hɑːt] cuore m; at ~ in fondo; by ~ a memoria; ~breaking straziante; ~burn bruciore m di stomaco; ~en v/t rincorare; ~y cordiale

hearth [hɑːθ] focolare m

heat [hiːt] s caldo m; calore m; v/t riscaldare; v/i riscaldarsi; ~er stufa f

heathen ['hiːðən] a, s pagano (m)

heather ['heðə] erica f

heating ['hiːtiŋ] riscaldamento m

heave [hiːv] v/t, irr alzare; sollevare; ~ a sigh sospirare

heaven ['hevn] cielo m; paradiso m; ~ly divino; celeste

heav|iness ['hevinis] pesantezza f; ~y pesante; ~y current corrente f elettrica ad alta tensione; ~y-handed maldestro; ~yweight peso m massimo

Hebrew ['hiːbruː] a, s ebraico (m) ebreo (m)

hectic ['hektik] febbrile; agitato

hedge [hedʒ] s siepe f; v/i essere evasivo; ~hog riccio m

heed [hiːd] s attenzione f; v/t fare attenzione; ~less disattento

heel [hiːl] tallone m; tacco m (della scarpa); take to one's ~s fuggire

hefty ['hefti] forte; robusto

heifer ['hefə] giovenca f

height [hait] altezza f; fig colmo m; culmine m; ~en v/t aumentare

heinous ['heinəs] orribile; atroce

heir [ɛə] erede m; ~dom eredità f; ~ess ereditaria f

helicopter ['helikɔptə] elicottero m

hell [hel] inferno m; ~ish infernale

hello ['he'lou] interj buon giorno; (telephone) pronto

helm [helm] timone m

helmet ['helmit] casco m

help [help] s aiuto m; soccorso m; v/t aiutare; soccorrere; I can't ~ laughing non posso fare a meno di ridere; ~ful servizievole; utile; ~ing porzione f; ~less impotente

hem [hem] s orlo m; v/t orlare; fare l'orlo a

hemisphere ['hemisfiə] emisfero m

hemlock ['hemlɔk] cicuta f

hemp [hemp] canapa f

hemstitch ['hemstitʃ] orlo m a giorno

hen [hen] gallina f

hence [hens] adv da qui; quindi; perciò; ~forth d'ora in poi

hen|-coop ['henkuːp] pollaio m; ~pecked dominato dalla moglie

hepatitis [ˌhepə'taitis] epatite f

her [hə:] adj poss suo, sua (di

lei); suoi; sue *(di lei)*; *pron pers* lei, la, le

herald ['herəld] *s* araldo *m*; *v/t* annunciare; **~ry** araldica *f*

herb [həːb] erba *f*; **sweet ~s** *pl* erbe *f/pl* aromatiche

herd [həːd] branco *m*; gregge *f*; mandria *f*; *v/t* riunire in greggi; *v/i* formare greggi; **~sman** mandriano *m*

here [hiə] *adv* qui; **~ you are** eccoti; **~'s to you** alla sua salute; **look ~** guardate qui; **over ~** per di qui; **~after** in seguito

hereditary [hi'reditəri] ereditario

here|in qui dentro; **~of** di questo

heresy ['herəsi] eresia *f*

heritage ['heritidʒ] eredità *f*

hermit ['həːmit] eremito *m*

hernia ['həːnjə] ernia *f*

hero ['hiərou] eroe *m*; protagonista *m*; **~ic** [hi'rouik] eroico; **~ine** ['herouin] eroina *f*; protagonista *f*; **~ism** eroismo *m*

heron ['herən] airone *m*

herring ['heriŋ] aringa *f*

hers [həːz] *pron poss* suo, sua; il suo, la sua; suoi, sue; i suoi, le sue; **~elf** sè stessa; lei stessa

hesita|te ['heziteit] *v/i* esitare; **~tion** esitazione *f*

hew [hjuː] *v/t, irr* abbattere *(alberi)*; spaccare *(pietra)*

hi! [hai] *Am* ciao

hibernate ['haibəneit] *v/i* svernare

hiccup ['hikʌp] singhiozzo *m*

hide [haid] *v/t* nascondere; *v/i* nascondersi; *s* pelle *f*

hideous ['hidiəs] orribile; mostruoso

hiding-place nascondiglio *m*

hierarchy ['haiərɑːki] gerarchia *f*

high [hai] alto; elevato; caro, **be ~** essere alticcio; **it is ~ time** sarebbe proprio ora; **~brow** intellettuale; **~ness** altezza *f*; **~ pressure** alta pressione *f*; **~school** scuola *f* media; **~spirited** vivace; **~ tide** alta marea *f*; **~way** *Am* strada *f* maestra; **~way code** codice *m* stradale

hijack ['haidʒæk] *v/t* rapire

hike [haik] *v/i* fare una gita *(a piedi)*; *s* gita *f*; **~r** viandante *m*

hilarious [hi'lɛəriəs] allegrissimo

hill [hil] colle *m*; collina *f*; **~y** collinoso

hilt [hilt] elsa *f*; impugnatura *f*

him [him] *pron pers* lui, lo, gli; **~self** sè stesso; lui stesso

hind [haind] *s* daina *f*; cerva *f*; *a* posteriore

hinder ['hində] *v/t* impedire; ostacolare

hindmost ['haindmoust] ultimo

hindrance ['hindrəns] impedimento *m*; ostacolo *m*

hinge [hindʒ] cardine *m*; ganghero *m*

hint [hint] *s* allusione *f*; accenno *m*; *v/t* alludere; accennare

hinterland ['hintəlænd] retroterra *f*

hip [hip] anca *f*; fianco *m*

hippopotamus [hipə'pɔtəməs] ippopotamo *m*

hire [haiə] *s* nolo *m*; *v/t* noleggiare; affittare; ~**ling** mercenario *m*; ~**purchase** vendita *f* a rate

his *adj poss* suo, sua *(di lui)*; suoi, sue *(di lui)*; *pron poss* suo, sua; il suo, la sua; suoi, sue; i suoi, le sue

hiss [his] *s* fischio *m*; sibilo *m*; *v/t*, *v/i* fischiare; sibilare

histor|ian [his'tɔriən] storico *m*; ~**ic**, ~**ical** storico *m*; ~**y** ['ˌɔri] storia *f*

hit [hit] *s* colpo *m*; successo *m*; *v/t* colpire; picchiare; ~**and-run-driving** latitanza *f* del conducente; ~ **the nail on the head** dire proprio giusto

hitch [hitʃ] *s* scossa *f*; *v/t* agganciare; ~**hike** fare l'autostop

hither ['hiðə] qui; qua; ~**to** finora

hive [haiv] alveare *m*

hoard [hɔːd] *s* provvisione *f*; *v/t* ammassare; accumulare; ~**ing** impalcatura *f*

hoarfrost ['hɔː'frɔst] brina *f*

hoarse [hɔːs] rauco

hoax [houks] *s* inganno *m*; *v/t* ingannare

hobble ['hɔbl] *v/i* zoppicare

hobby ['hɔbi] passione *f*; passatempo *m* preferito; ~**horse** cavallo *m* a dondolo; passione *f*

hobgoblin ['hɔgɔblin] folletto *m*

hobo ['houbou] vagabondo *m*

hocus-pocus ['houkəs'poukəs] sciocchezze *f/pl*

hoe [hou] *s* zappa *f*; *v/t* zappare

hog [hɔg] porco *m*; maiale *m*

hoist [hɔist] *s* montacarico *m*; *v/t* innalzare; sollevare

hold [hould] *s* presa *f*, *fig* dominio *m*; *v/t*, *irr* tenere; ~ **back** ritenere; ~ **off** tenere lontano; ~ **out** resistere; ~ **up** tenere in alto; reggere; trattenere; ~**ing** tenuta *f*; ~ **up** assalto *m* a mano armata; congestionamento *m*

hole [houl] buco *m*

holiday ['hɔlədi, ~dei] festa *f*; ~**s** *pl* vacanze *f/pl*

hollow ['hɔlou] *a* incavato; *s* incavo *m*; *v/t* scavare

holly ['hɔli] agrifoglio *m*

holy ['houli] santo; 2 **Ghost** Spirito *m* Santo; 2 **Thursday** Giovedì *m* Santo

homage ['hɔmidʒ]: **pay** ~ fare omaggio

home [houm] casa *f*; **at** ~ in casa; ~**less** senza tetto; ~**ly** casalingo; semplice; ~ **market** mercato *m* nazionale; 2 **Office** Ministero *m* degli Interni (*in Inghilter-ra*); ♀ **Secretary** Ministro *m* degli Interni (*in Inghilterra*); **~sick: feel ~sick** avere la nostalgia; **~ town** città *f* natale; **~ward(s)** a casa, verso casa

homicide ['hɔmisaid] omicidio *m*

homosexual *a*, *s* ['hɔmou-'seksjuəl] omosessuale (*m*)

honest ['ɔnist] onesto; **~y** onestà *f*

honey ['hʌni] miele *m*; **~comb** favo *m*; **~moon** luna *f* di miele; **~suckle** caprifoglio *m*

hono(u)r ['ɔnə] *s* onore *m*; onoranza *f*; (*title*) eccellenza *f*; *v/t* onorare; *comm* accettare; pagare; **~able** onorevole

hood [hud] cappuccio *m*; mantice *m* (*di carrozza, carrozzina*); **~wink** *v/t* ingannare

hoodlum ['hu:dləm] teppista *m*

hoof [hu:f], *pl* **~s, hooves** zoccolo *m*

hook [huk] *s* gancio *m*; uncino *m*; amo *m*; **by ~ or by crook** per dritto o per traverso; in un modo o in un altro; *v/t* agganciare

hoop [hu:p] cerchio *m* (*di legno o di metallo*)

hooping cough ['hu:piŋkɔf] tosse *f* canina

hoot [hu:t] *v/i* gridare; (*train*) fischiare; (*car*) suonare

hop [hɔp] *s* salto *m*; *v/i* saltare

hope [houp] *s* speranza *f*; *v/t, v/i* sperare; **~ful** speranzoso; ottimista; **~less** senza speranza; disperato

horizon [hə'raizn] orizzonte *m*; **~tal** [hɔri'zɔntl] orizzontale

horn [hɔːn] corno *m*

hornet ['hɔːnit] calabrone *m*

horny ['hɔːni] calloso

horoscope ['hɔrəskoup] oroscopo *m*

horr|ible ['hɔrəbl] orribile; **~id** odioso; **~ify** [~ifai] *v/t* far inorridire; **~or** orrore *m*

horse [hɔːs] cavallo *m*; cavalleria *f*; **on ~back** a cavallo; **~hair** crine *m* di cavallo; **~man** cavaliere *m*; **~power** cavallo *m* vapore; **~race** corsa *f* di cavalli; **~radish** rafano *m*; **~shoe** ferro *m* di cavallo; **~whip** frustino *m*

horticulture ['hɔːtikʌltʃə] orticultura *f*

hose [houz] pompa *f*, **~** *pl* calze *f/pl*; **~iery** maglieria *f*

hospi|table ['hɔspitəbl] ospitale; **~tal** ospedale *m*; **~tality** ospitalità *f*

host [houst] ospite *m*; moltitudine *f*

hostage ['hɔstidʒ] ostaggio *m*

hostel ['hɔstəl] casa *f* dello studente; **youth ~** albergo *m* della gioventù

hostess ['houstis] padrona *f* di casa

hostile ['hɔstail] ostile; **~ity**

[~'tiliti] ostilità f

hot [hɔt] caldo; *fig* ardente; **~ dog** salsiccia f con panino; **~ get ~** riscaldarsi; **it is ~** fa caldo; **~-blooded** di sangue caldo; **~water-bottle** bottiglia f d'acqua calda

hotel [hou'tel] albergo m

hot-headed impulsivo; **~house** serra f; **~ springs** pl acque f/pl termali; **~water-bottle** bottiglia f d'acqua calda

hound [haund] cane m da caccia; levriero m

hour ['auə] ora f; **~ly** adv ora

house [haus] s casa f; *teat* sala f; ♀ **of Commons** Camera f dei Comuni; Camera f dei Deputati (in Inghilterra); ♀ **of Lords** Senato m (in Inghilterra); ♀s pl of **Parliament** Parlamento m (in Inghilterra); v/t alloggiare; **~keeper** governante f; **~maid** cameriera f; **~wife** massaia f; **~work** lavoro m domestico; faccende f/pl di casa

how [hau] adv come; (exlamatory) come; quanto; **~ far?** quant'è lontano?; **~ long?** quanto tempo?; **~ much?** quanto(a)?; **~ many?** quanto(e)?; **~ do you do?, ~ are you?** come sta?; **know-how** cognizione f di causa

however conj comunque; tuttavia; adv per quanto ... che sia

howl [haul] s grido m; v/i gridare; urlare

hub [hʌb] mozzo m (di ruota); *fig* punto m centrale

hubbub ['hʌbʌb] tumulto m; vociare m

huckle ['hʌkl] anca f, fianco m

huddle ['hʌdl] v/i ammucchiarsi; accoccolarsi

hue [hju:] colore m; tinta f

hug [hʌg] abbraccio m forte; v/t abbracciare

huge [hju:dʒ] enorme; immenso

hull [hʌl] scafo m

hullabaloo [hʌləbə'lu:] chiasso m

hullo [hʌ'lou] interj (telephone) pronto

hum [hʌm] s ronzio m; v/t canticchiare (a labbre chiuse); v/i ronzare

human ['hju:mən] umano; **~e** [~'mein] umano; **~itarian** [~mæni'tɛəriən] umanitario; **~ity** [~'mæniti] umanità f

humble ['hʌmbl] umile; **~ness** umiltà f

humbug ['hʌmbʌg] sciocchezze f/pl; (person) impostore m

humdrum ['hʌmdrʌm] monotono

humid ['hju:mid] umido; **~ity** [~ju(:)'miditi] umidità f

humiliate [hju(:)'milieit] v/t umiliare; umano **~ation** umiliazione f; **~ty** umiltà f

humming-bird ['hʌmiŋbəd] colibrì m

humorous ['hju:mərəs] umoristico; spiritoso

humo(u)r ['hju:mə] s umore m; umorismo m; v/t prendere per il verso buono

hump [hʌmp] gobba f

hunch [hʌntʃ] gobba f; fam idea f; **~back** gobbo m

hundredweight ['hʌndrədweit] quintale m

Hungar|ian [hʌŋ'gɛəriən] a, s ungherese (m, f); **~y** Ungheria f

hung|er ['hʌŋgə] s fame f; v/i bramare; **~ry** affamato m; **be ~ry** avere fame

hunk [hʌŋk] tozzo m

hunt [hʌnt] s caccia f; v/t, v/i cacciare; **~er** cacciatore m; **~ing** caccia f

hurdle ['hɜːdl] graticcio m; siepe f mobile

hurl [hɜːl] v/t scagliare

hurra|h!, ~y [hurei] evviva!

hurricane ['hʌrikən] uragano m

hurry ['hʌri] s fretta f; **be in a ~** avere fretta; v/t affrettare; v/i affrettarsi; **~ up!** sbrigati!

hurt [hɜːt] s danno m; ferita f; v/t, v/i, irr far male a

husband ['hʌzbənd] marito m; sposo m

hush [hʌʃ] s silenzio m; v/t far star zitto; interj zitto!; silenzio!; **~ up** mettere a tacere

husk [hʌsk] buccia f; **~y** rauco; forte

hustle ['hʌsl] v/t spingere; v/i affaccendarsi

hut [hʌt] capanna f

hutch [hʌtʃ] capanna f; gabbia f (per conigli)

hyacinth ['haiəsinθ] giacinto m

hybrid ['haibrid] a, s ibrido (m)

hydrant ['haidrənt] idrante m

hydraulic [hai'drɔ:lik] idraulico

hydro|carbon ['haidrou-] idrocarburo m; **~chloric** cloridrico; **~gen** idrogeno m; **~gen bomb** bomba f all'idrogeno; **~plane** idrovolante m; **~therapy** idroterapeutica f

hyena [hai'i:nə] iena f

hygien|e ['haidʒi:n] igiene f; **~ic** [hai'dʒi:nik] igienico

hymn [him] inno m

hyphen ['haifən] trattino m

hypnotize ['hipnətaiz] v/t ipnotizzare

hypocri|sy [hi'pɔkrəsi] ipocrisia f; **~te** ['-] ipocrita m, f; **~tical** [hipou'kritikəl] ipocrito

hypothe|sis [hai'pɔθisis] ipotesi f; **~tical** ipotetico

hysteri|a [his'tiəriə] isteria f; isterismo m; **~cal** isterico; **~cs** pl accesso m d'isterismo

I

I [ai] io
ice [ais] ghiaccio *m*; **~-cream** gelato *m*
Iceland ['aislənd] Islanda *f*; **~er** islandese *m*, *f*; **~ic** islandese
ice-skate pattino *m*
ic|icle ['aisikl] ghiacciolo *m*; **~ing** smaltatura *f* di zucchero; **~y** gelato; gelido; di ghiaccio
idea [ai'diə] idea *f*; **~l** *a*, *s* ideale (*m*); **~lize** *v/t* idealizzare
identi|cal [ai'dentikəl] identico; **~fication** [~fi'keiʃən] identificazione *f*; **~ifation papers** *pl* documenti *m/pl*; **~fy** *v/t* identificare; **~ty** identità *f*; **~ty card** carta d'identità
idiom ['idiəm] idioma *m*; modo *m* di dire
idle ['aidl] *s* ozioso; vano; *v/i* oziare; **~ness** ozio *m*
idol ['aidl] idolo *m*; **~ize** *v/t* deificare; idolatrare
if [if] se; **as ~** come se; **~ not** se non
ignit|e [ig'nait] *v/t* accendere; **~ion** [ig'niʃən] ignizione *f*; combustione *f*
ignoble [ig'noubl] ignobile
ignor|ance ['ignərəns] ignoranza *f*; **~e** [ig'nɔ:] *v/t* trascurare
ill [il] *a* malato; *adv* male; *s* male *m*; **fall ~** ammalarsi; **~-advised** imprudente
illegal [i'li:gəl] illegale
illiterate [i'litərit] *a*, *s* inalfabeto (*m*)
ill|-tempered di brutto carattere; **~-timed** inopportuno; **~-treated** maltrattato
illuminat|e [i'lju:mineit] *v/t* illuminare; **~ion** illuminazione *f*
illus|ion [i'lu:ʒən] illusione *f*; **~ory** illusorio
illustrat|e ['iləstreit] *v/t* illustrare; **~ion** illustrazione *f*; **~ive** illustrativo
illustrious [i'lʌstriəs] illustre
ill will cattiva volontà *f*
imag|e ['imidʒ] immagine *f*; **~ination** [i,mædʒi'neiʃən] immaginazione *f*; fantasia *f*; **~ine** [i'mædʒin] *v/t* immaginare
imbecile ['imbisi:l] imbecile
imitate ['imiteit] *v/t* imitare
immeasurable [i'meʒərəbl] immensurabile
immediate [i'mi:djət] immediato
immature [,imə'tjuə] immaturo
immense [i'mens] immenso
immerse [i'mə:s] *v/t* immergere
immigra|nt ['imigrənt] *a*, *s* immigrante (*m*, *f*); **~tion** immigrazione *f*
im|minent ['iminənt] imminente; **~mobile** [i'moubail] immobile; **~moderate** immoderato; **~modest** immodesto; impudico;

~moral immorale; **~mortal** [i'mɔːtl] immortale; **~mune** immune

impact ['impækt] urto m; impressione f

impair [im'peə] v/t danneggiare; menomare

impart [im'paːt] v/t impartire; comunicare

impatient [im'peiʃənt] impaziente

imped|e [im'piːd] v/t impedire; ostacolare; **~iment** impedimento m

impending [im'pendiŋ] imminente

imperative [im'perativ] a imperioso; imperativo; s imperativo m

imperfect [im'pəːfikt] a, s imperfetto (m)

imperial [im'piəriəl] imperiale

im|peril [im'peril] v/t mettere in pericolo; **~permeable** impermeabile; **~personal** impersonale

imperishable [im'periʃəbl] non deperibile

impetuous [im'petjuəs] impetuoso

impet|us ['impitəs], pl **~es** [~iz] impeto m

implement ['implimənt] strumento m

implicat|e ['implikeit] v/t implicare; **~ion** implicazione f

implicit [im'plisit] implicito

implore [im'plɔː] v/t supplicare

imply [im'plai] v/t implicare; insinuare

impolite [,impə'lait] scortese; **~ness** scortesia f

import [im'pɔːt] v/t importare; ['impɔːt] s importazione f; **~ance** [~'pɔːtəns] importanza f; **~ant** importante; **~ation** importazione f

importune [im'pɔːtjuːn] v/t importunare

impos|e [im'pouz] v/t imporre; **~e upon** approfittare; **~ing** imponente

impossible [im'pɔsibl] impossibile

impostor [im'pɔstə] impostore m

impotent ['impətənt] impotente

impoverish [im'pɔveriʃ] v/t impoverire

impregnate ['impregneit] v/t impregnare; ingravidare

impresario [,impre'saːriou] impresario m

impress [im'pres] v/t impressionare; imprimere; **~ion** impressione f; **~ive** impressionante

imprint [im'print] s impronta f; v/t imprimere; stampare

imprison [im'prizn] v/t imprigionare; **~ment** imprigionamento m

improper [im'prɔpə] scorretto; sconveniente

improve [im'pruːv] v/t, v/i migliorare; **~ment** miglioramento m

improvise ['imprəvaiz] v/t, v/i improvvisare

impudent ['impjudənt] sfacciato

impuls|e ['impʌls] impulso m; **~ive** [im'pʌlsiv] impulsivo

impunity [im'pju:niti] impunito

impure [im'pjuə] impuro

in [in] prp in; a; entro; adv dentro; in casa; **~ 1979** nel 1979; **~ my opinion** secondo me; **~ the morning** di mattina; **~ time** a tempo; **~ order** in regola; **~ print** stampato

in|accessible [inæk'sesəbl] inaccessibile; **~accurate** inesatto; **~active** inattivo; **~appropriate** inadatto; **~attentive** disattento; distratto

inborn ['inbɔːn] innato

incapable incapace

incapacit|ate [inkə'pæsiteit] v/t incapacitare; **~y** incapacità f

incarcerate [in'kɑːsəreit] v/t incarcerare

incarnate [in'kɑːnit] v/t incarnare

incense ['insens] s incenso m; [in'sens] v/t incensare; fig far arrabbiare

incentive [in'sentiv] incentivo m

incessant [in'sesənt] incessante

incest ['insest] incesto m

inch [intʃ] pollice m (2,54 cm)

inciden|ce ['insidəns] incidenza f; **~t** s incidente m; a incidente; inerente; **~tal** fortuito; **~tally** a proposito

incise [in'saiz] v/t incidere

incite [in'sait] v/t incitare; **~ment** incitamento m

incline [in'klain] s pendio m; v/t,v/i pendere; **~d** propenso

inclu|de [in'kluːd] v/t comprendere; **~ding** compreso; **~sion** inclusione f; **~sive terms** pl prezzo m globale

incom|e ['inkʌm] rendita f; reddito m; entrata f; **~e-tax** imposta f sul reddito; **~ing** in arrivo

inconceivable [inkən'siːvəbl] inconcepibile

inconsiderate irriguardoso; incurante

inconsistent incoerente

inconstant incostante

inconvenien|ce s inconveniente m; v/t disturbare; scomodare; **~t** scomodo

incorporate [in'kɔːpəreit] v/t incorporare

incredible incredibile

increase [in'kriːs] s aumento m; v/t aumentare; v/i aumentarsi

incriminat|e [in'krimineit] v/t incriminare

incubator ['inkjubeitə] incubatrice f

incur [in'kəː] v/t incorrere; **~ debts** contrarre un debito

indebted [in'detid] indebitato

indecen|cy [in'di:snsi] indecenza f; **~t** indecente

indecisive [indi'saisiv] indeciso

indeed [in'di:d] infatti; effettivamente; **~?** veramente?; davvero?

indefatigable [indi'fætigəbl] instancabile

indefinite [in'definit] indefinito

indelicate [in'delikeit] indelicato

indemni|fy [in'demnifai] v/t indennizzare; **~ty** indennità f

indent [in'dent] v/t dentellare

independen|ce indipendenza f; **~t** indipendente

indescribable [indis'kraibəbl] indescrivibile

indeterminate indeterminato; indefinito

index ['indeks] indice m

India ['indjə] India f; **~rubber** gomma f per cancellare; **~n** a, s indiano (m); **(Red) ~** pellirossa m; **~n summer** estate f di San Martino

indicate ['indikeit] v/t indicare; **~ion** indicazione f; **~ive** indicativo; **~or** indicatore m

indict [in'dait] v/t accusare; **~ment** accusa f

indifferen|ce indifferenza f; **~t** indifferente

indigent ['indidʒənt] indigente

indigesti|ble [indi'dʒestəbl] indigesto; **~on** indigestione f

indign|ant [in'dignənt] indignato; **~ation** indignazione f

indirect [in'dairekt] indiretto

indiscre|et [indis'kri:t] indiscreto; **~tion** indiscrezione f

indiscriminate [indis'kriminit] che non fa discriminazioni; generale

indispensable [indis'pensəbl] indispensabile

indispos|ed [indis'pouzd] indisposto; **~ition** indisposizione f

in|disputable ['indis'pju:təbl] indiscutibile; **~distinct** confuso

individual [indi'vidjuəl] a individuale; s individuo m

indolen|ce ['indələns] indolenza f; **~t** indolente

indoor ['indɔ:] interno; interiore; in casa; **~s** [in'dɔz] in casa

indorse [in'dɔ:s] cf **endorse**

induce [in'dju:s] v/t indurre; **~tion** [in'dakʃən] induzione f

indulge [in'dʌldʒ] v/t assecondare; v/i indulgere; abbandonarsi a; **~nce** indulgenza f; **~nt** indulgente

industr|ial [in'dʌstriəl] industriale; **~ialize** v/t industrializzare; **~ious** [-iəs] industrioso; **~y** ['indəstri] industria f

in|effective [ini'fektiv] inef-
ficace; **~efficient** [-'fiʃənt]
inefficiente

inept [i'nept] inetto

inequality [ini'kwɒliti] inu-
guaglianza f; disuguaglian-
za f

inert [i'nɔːt] inerte; **~ia** [‿ʃiə]
inerzia f

in|evitable [in'evitəbl] inevi-
tabile; **~exhaustible** [-ig-
z'ɔːstəbl] inesauribile;
~expensive [-iks'pænsiv]
poco costoso; di poco
prezzo; **~experienced**
[-iks'piəriənsd] inesperto;
~expressible [-iks'pres-
səbl] inesprimibile

infam|ous ['infəməs] infa-
me; **~y** infamia f

infan|cy ['infənsi] infanzia f;
~t bimbo(a) m (f); **~tile** ['in-
fəntail] infantile

infect [in'fekt] v/t infettare;
contagiare; **~ion** infezione
f; **~ious** contagioso

infer [in'fɔː] v/t inferire;
~ence ['infərəns] deduzione
f

inferior [in'fiəriə] s, a inferiore (m); **~ity** [‿'ɒriti] infe-
riorità f

infernal [in'fɔːnl] infernale

infidelity infedeltà f

infiltrate ['infiltreit] v/t in-
filtrare

infinit|e ['infinit] infinito;
~y [in'finiti] infinità f

infirm [in'fɔːm] infermo

inflammable [in'flæməbl]
infiammabile

inflat|e [in'fleit] v/t, v/i gon-

fiare; **~ion** gonfiamento;
(financial) inflazione f

inflect [in'flekt] v/t inflet-
tere

inflexible [in'fleksəbl] inflessibile

inflict [in'flikt] v/t infligge-
re; **~ion** inflizione f

influen|ce ['influəns] s in-
fluenza f; v/t influenzare;
~tial [‿'enʃəl] influente

influenza [influ'enzə] influenza f

influx ['inflʌks] afflusso m

inform [in'fɔːm] v/t infor-
mare; **~ against** denunciare; **~al** informale; **~ation**
[infə'meiʃən] informazione
f; **~ation office** ufficio m
informazioni; **~er** informa-
tore m; denunciante

infuriate [in'fjuərieit] v/t
infuriare

infuse [in'fjuːz] v/t infon-
dere

ingen|ious [in'dʒiːnjəs] in-
gegnoso; **~uity** [‿i'nju(ː)iti]
ingegnosità f

ingot ['iŋɡɒt] lingotto m

ingredient [in'ɡriːdjənt] ingrediente m

inhabit [in'hæbit] v/t abitare; **~ant** abitante m, f

inhale [in'heil] v/t inalare

inherent [in'hiərənt] ine-
rente

inherit [in'herit] v/t eredi-
tare; **~ance** eredità f

initial [i'niʃəl] a, s iniziale (f)

inject [in'dʒekt] v/t iniettare; **~ion** iniezione f

injur|e ['indʒə] v/t ferire;

~ious [in'dʒuəriəs] ingiurioso; **~y** ['~əri] ferita f

injustice [in'dʒʌstis] ingiustizia f

ink [iŋk] inchiostro m

inkling ['iŋkliŋ] nozione f vaga; accenno m vago

inland ['inlənd] a s interno; adv nell'interno; verso l'interno

inmate ['inmeit] inquilino m; ricoverato m

inmost ['inmoust] intimo; profondo

inn [in] albergo m; locanda f

inner ['inə] interiore; interno

innocen|ce ['inəsns] innocenza f; **~t** innocente

innovation [inou'veiʃən] innovazione f

inquest ['inkwest] inchiesta f

inquir|e [in'kwaiə] v/t domandare; v/i indagare; informarsi; **~y** indagine f

inquisit|ion [inkwi'ʒiʃən] inquisizione f; **~ive** [in'kwizitiv] curioso

insan|e [in'sein] pazzo; folle; **~ity** [in'sæniti] pazzia f; follia f

inscri|be [in'skraib] v/t iscrivere; **~ption** [~ipʃən] iscrizione f

insect ['insekt] insetto m

insert [in'sə:t] v/t inserire

inside [in'said] a interiore; interno; s interno m; adv nell'interno; **~ out** al rovescio; rivoltato

insight ['insait] penetrazione f

insincere insincero

insist [in'sist] v/i insistere

in|solent ['insələnt] insolente; **~soluble** ['~sɔljubl] insolubile

insomnia [in'sɔmniə] insonnia f

insomuch [insou'mʌtʃ] fino al punto; tanto

inspect [in'spekt] v/t ispezionare; **~ion** ispezione f; **~or** ispettore m

inspir|ation [inspə'reiʃən] ispirazione f; **~e** [in'spaiə] v/t ispirare

instal(l) [in'stɔ:l] v/t installare; **~ation** installazione f; impianto m; **~ment** puntata f; rata f; **~ment payment** pagamento m a rate

instan|ce ['instəns] istanza f; esempio m; **for ~ce** per esempio; **~t** istante m; **~tly** immediatamente

instead [in'sted] adv invece; **~ of** prp invece di; al posto di

instinct ['instinkt] istinto m; **~ive** [in'stinktiv] istintivo

institu|te ['institju:t] s istituto m; v/t istituire; **~ion** istituzione f

instruct [in'strʌkt] v/t istruire; **~ion** istruzione f; **~ive** istruttivo

instrument ['instrumənt] strumento m

insufferable insopportabile

insulate ['insjuleit] v/t isolare

insurance [in'ʃuərəns] assicurazione f; **~ company** compagnia f d'assicurazioni

insure [in'ʃuə] v/t assicurare

insurrection [insə'rekʃən] insurrezione f

intact [in'tækt] intatto

integrate ['intigreit] v/t integrare; v/i integrarsi

intellect ['intilekt] intelletto m; **~ual** [‿'lektjuəl] intellettuale

intelligen|ce [in'telidʒəns] intelligenza f; informazione f; **~t** intelligente

intend [in'tend] v/t intendere; avere intenzione di

intens|e [in'tens] intenso; **~ity** intensità f; **~ive** intensivo

intent [in'tent] intento; **~ion** intenzione f

inter [in'tə:] v/t seppellire

intercede [intə(:)'si:d] v/i intercedere

interchange [intə'tʃeindʒ] s scambio m; v/t scambiare; v/i scambiarsi

intercourse ['intə(:)kɔ:s] rapporto m; rapporti m/pl sessuali

interdict [intə(:)'dikt] v/t interdire; proibire

interest ['intrist] s interesse m; v/t interessare; **~ing** interessante

interfer|e [intə'fiə] v/i intromettersi; intervenire; **~e with** ostacolare; **~ence** in-

tromissione f

interior [in'tiəriə] a interiore; interno; s interiore m

intermediary [intə(:)'mi:djəri] a, s intermediario (m)

inter|mingle v/t inframmischiare; v/i inframmischiarsi; **~mission** intervallo m

intern ['intə:n] Am medico m assistente

interpret [in'tə:prit] v/t, v/i interpretare; **~er** interprete m, f

inter|rupt [intə'rʌpt] v/t interrompere; **~sect** v/t secare; v/i incrociarsi

interval ['intəvəl] intervallo m

interven|e [,intə(:)'vi:n] v/i intervenire; **~tion** [‿'venʃən] intervento m

interview ['intəvju:] s intervista f; colloquio m; v/t intervistare

intestines [in'testinz] pl intestino m

intima|cy ['intiməsi] intimità f; **~te** a intimo; v/t annunciare; comunicare

into ['intu, 'intə] in

intolerant [in'tɔlərənt] intollerante

intoxicat|e [in'tɔksikeit] v/t ubriacare; med intossicare

intricate ['intrikit] intricato

intrigue [in'tri:g] s intrigo m; trama f; v/i intrigare

introduc|e [intrə'dju:s] v/t presentare; introdurre; **~tion** [‿'dʌkʃən] presentazione f; introduzione f

intrude [in'tru:d] *v/i* intromettersi

intuition [intju(:)'iʃən] intuizione *f*

inundation [inʌn'deiʃən] inondazione *f*

invade [in'veid] *v/t* invadere

invalid [in'vӕli(:)d] *a, s* malato (*m*); [in'vælid] invalido

invaluable [in'væljuəbl] inestimabile

invent [in'vent] *v/t* inventare; **~ion** invenzione *f*

inver|se [in'vəːs] inverso; **~t** *v/t* invertire; **~ted com·mas** *pl* virgolette *f/pl*

invest [in'vest] *v/t* investire; **~ment** investimento *m*

invit|ation [invi'teiʃən] invito *m*; **~e** [in'vait] *v/t* invitare

invoice ['invɔis] fattura *f*

involve [in'vɔlv] *v/t* coinvolgere; significare

inward ['inwəd] interno; intimo; **~(s)** verso l'interno

iodine ['aiədi:n] iodio *m*

irascible [i'ræsibl] irascibile

Ireland ['aiələnd] Irlanda *f*

Irish ['aiəriʃ] *a, s* irlandese (*m, f*); **~man** irlandese *m*

irk [əːk] *v/t* infastidire

iron ['aiən] *s* ferro *m*; ferro da stiro; *a* di ferro; ferreo; *v/t* stirare

ironic(al) [ai'rɔnik(əl)] ironico

irregular irregolare

irrelevant non pertinente

irrespective of senza tenere conto di

irrigat|e ['irigeit] *v/t* irrigare; **~ion** irrigazione *f*

island ['ailənd] isola *f*

isolat|e ['aisəleit] *v/t* isolare; **~ion** isolazione *f*

issue ['iʃu:] *s* problema *m*; esito *f*; discendenza *f*; emissione *f*; pubblicazione *f*; *v/t* emettere; pubblicare; *v/i* uscire; emergere; risultare

it *pron pers* esso, essa; lo, la; *impers* ~ **is hot** fa caldo; **who is ~?** chi è

Italian [i'tæljən] *a, s* italiano (*m*)

italic [i'tælik] corsivo

itch [itʃ] prurito *m*; *v/i* prudere

item ['aitəm] articolo *m*; voce *f*; numero *m* (*di rivista*)

itinerary [ai'tinərəri] itinerario *m*

its [its] *pron poss* suo, sua; il suo, la sua; **~elf** [it'self] sè; sè stesso; **by ~elf** sè da sè

ivory ['aivəri] ivorio *m*

ivy ['aivi] edera *f*

J

jab [dʒæb] *v/t, v/i* pugnalare

jack [dʒæk] *mec* binda *f*; cricco *m*; fante *m* (*a carte*)

jackal ['dʒækɔ:l] sciacallo *m*

jackass ['dʒækæs] asino *m*

jacket ['dʒækit] giacca *f*

jack|-knife coltello *m* a serramanico; **~ of all trades**

jade

uomo *m* di tutti i mestieri

jade [dʒeid] giada *f*

jagged [dʒægid] dentellato; frastagliato

jaguar [dʒəgjuə] giaguaro *m*

jail [dʒeil] carcere *m*; prigione *f*

jam [dʒæm] *s* marmellata *f*; blocco *m* (*stradale*); *v/t* incastrare; *v/i* incastrarsi

janitor ['dʒænitə] bidello *m*

January ['dʒænjuəri] gennaio *m*

Japan [dʒə'pæn] Giappone *m*; **~ese** [dʒæpə'ni:z] *a*, *s* giapponese (*m*, *f*)

jar [dʒɑ:] *s* barattolo *m*; scossa *f*; *v/t* stonare; scuotere

jargon ['dʒɑ:gən] gergo *m*

jasmin(e) ['dʒæsmin] gelsomino *m*

jaundice ['dʒɔ:ndis] itterizia *f*

javelin ['dʒævlin] giavellotto *m*

jaw [dʒɔ:] mascella *f*

jealous ['dʒeləs] geloso

jeer [dʒiə] *s* derisione *f*; *v/t*, *v/i* deridere

jelly ['dʒeli] gelatina *f*; **~ fish** medusa *f*

jeopardize ['dʒepədaiz] *v/t* mettere in pericolo

jerk [dʒə:k] *s* scatto *m*; *v/t* strappare; *v/i* muoversi a scatti

jersey ['dʒə:zi] maglia *f*

jest [dʒest] *s* scherzo *m*; *v/i* scherzare

Jesuit ['dʒezjuit] gesuita *m*

Jesus ['dʒi:zəs] Gesù

jet [dʒet] getto *m*; aeroplano

m a reazione; **~ engine** motore *m* a reazione

jetty ['dʒeti] molo *m*

Jew [dʒu:] ebreo *m*

jewel ['dʒu:əl] gioiello *m*; **~(l)er** gioielliere *m*; **~lery** gioielli *m/pl*

Jew|ess ['dʒu(:)is] ebrea *f*; **~ish** ebreo; ebraico

jiffy ['dʒifi] *Am fam* istante *m*

jig [dʒig] giga *f*

jingle ['dʒiŋgl] *s* tintinnio *m*; *v/t* tintinnare

job [dʒɔb] impiego *m*; lavoro *m*; posto *m*

jockey ['dʒɔki] fantino *m*

jog [dʒɔg] *s* urto *m*; *v/t* urtare

join [dʒɔin] *v/t* unire; raggiungere; *v/i* unirsi; associarsi; **~er** falegname *m*

joint [dʒɔint] *s* articolazione *f*; giuntura *f*; pezzo *m* di carne (*macellata*); *fam* locale *m*; *a* unito; collettivo; **~ stock company** società *f* anonima

joke [dʒɔuk] *s* scherzo *m*; barzelletta *f*; *v/i* scherzare

jolly ['dʒɔli] *a* allegro; *adv fam* molto

jolt [dʒɔult] *s* scossa *f*; sobbalzo *m*; *v/t*, *v/i* scuotere

jostle ['dʒɔsl] *v/t* spingere

journal ['dʒə:nl] giornale *m*; diario *m*; **~ist** giornalista *m*

journey ['dʒə:ni] *s* viaggio *m*; *v/i* viaggiare; **~man** operaio *m* esperto

joy [dʒɔi] ellegria *f*; **~ful** allegro

jubil|ant ['dʒu:bilənt] giubilante; **~ee** giubileo *m*

judg|e [dʒʌdʒ] *s* giudice *m*; *v/t* giudicare; **~ment** giudizio *m*

judicious [dʒu(:)'diʃəs] giudizioso

jug [dʒʌg] brocca *f*; anfora *f*

juggle ['dʒʌgl] *v/i* fare giochi di destrezza; raggirare; **~r** prestigiatore *m*

Jugoslav ['ju:gou'slɑ:v] *a*, *s* iugoslavo (*m*); **~ia** Iugoslavia *f*

juic|e [dʒu:s] sugo *m* (*di carne*); succo *m* (*di frutta*); **~y** succoso

juke-box ['dʒu:k-] music-box *m*

July [dʒu(:)'lai] luglio *m*

jumble ['dʒʌmbl] *s* confusione *f*, mescolanza *f*; *v/t* confondere; mescolare

jump [dʒʌmp] *s* salto *m*; balzo *m*; *v/i* saltare; balzare; **~y** nervoso

junction ['dʒʌŋkʃən] unione *f*; nodo *m* ferroviario

June [dʒu:n] giugno *m*

jungle ['dʒʌŋgl] giungla *f*

junior ['dʒu:njə] *s* giovane *m*; subalterno *m*; *a* più giovane; di grado inferiore

junk [dʒʌŋk] robaccia *f*

juri|sdiction giurisdizione *f*; **~sprudence** giurisprudenza *f*; **~st** giurista *m*, *f*

juror ['dʒuərə] giurato *m*

jury ['dʒuəri] giuria *f*

just [dʒʌst] *a* giusto; *adv* esattamente; giustamente; appena; in questo momento

justice ['dʒʌstis] giustizia *f*

justif|ication [dʒʌstifi'keiʃən] giustificazione *f*; **~y** ['dʒʌstifai] *v/t* giustificare

jut dʒʌt *v/i* sporgere

juvenile ['dʒu:vinail] giovanile; **~ court** tribunale *m* dei minorenni

K

kale, kail [keil] cavolo *m*

kangaroo [,kæŋgə'ru:] canguro *m*

keel [ki:l] chiglia *f*

keen [ki:n] acuto; entusiasta

keep [ki:p] *v/t* tenere; mantenere; conservare; trattenere; osservare; festeggiare; *v/i* mantenersi; conservarsi; continuare; **~ in mind** tener presente; **~ on** continuare; proseguire; seguitare; **~ talking** continuare a parlare; **~ to** tenersi a; **~**

books tenere i libri; fare la contabilità; **~er** custode *m*, *f*; **~ing** custodia *f*; **~sake** ricordo *m*

kennel ['kenl] canile *m*

kerb [kə:b] bordo *m* del marciapiede

kernel ['kə:nl] gheriglio *m*; *fig* nocciolo *m*

kettle ['ketl] bollitore *m*; **~drum** timpano *m*

key [ki:] chiave *f*; *mus* chiave *f*; tasto *m*; *mec* chiavetta *f*; tasto *m* (*della macchina da* *scrivere*); **~board** tastiera *f*; **~hole** buco *m* della serratura; **~ring** anello *m* portachiavi

kick [kik] *s* calcio *m*; *v/t, v/i* dare calci

kid [kid] capretto *m*; *fam* bambino(a) *m* (*f*); *v/t fam* prendere in giro

kidnap [ˈkidnæp] *v/t* rapire; **~per** rapitore *m*; **~ping** rapimento *m*

kidney [ˈkidni] rene *m*; rognone *m*

kill [kil] *v/t* uccidere; ammazzare; **~ing** *fam* buffo

kilo|gram(me) [ˈkilougræm] chilogramma *m*; **~metre** [ˈkilou] chilometro *m*; **~watt** kilowatt *m*

kilt [kilt] gonnellina *f* scozzese

kimono [kiˈmounou] chimono *m*

kin [kin] parentela *f*

kind [kaind] *a* gentile; buono; **~ regards** *pl* cordiali saluti *m/pl*; *s* genere *m*; specie *f*; tipo *m*

kindergarten [ˈkindəgɑːtn] giardino *m* d'infanzia

kindle [ˈkindl] *v/t* accendere; *v/i* ardere

kind|ly [ˈkaindli] gentile; **~ness** gentilezza *f*

kindred [ˈkindrid] *s* parenti *m/pl*; parentela *f*; *a* affine

king [kin] re *m*; **~dom** reame *m*; **~fisher** martin *m* pescatore

kiosk [kiˈɔsk] chiosco *m*

kiss [kis] *s* bacio *m*; *v/t* baciare

kit [kit] gattuccio *m*; **~bag** sacco *m* a spalla

kitchen [ˈkitʃin] cucina *f*; **~garden** orto *m*

kite [kait] aquilone *m*

kitten [ˈkitn] gattino *m*

knack [næk] facoltà *f*

knapsack [ˈnæpsæk] zaino *m*

knead [niːd] *v/t* impastare

knee [niː] ginocchio *m*; **~l (down)** *v/i, irr* inginocchiarsi

knickerbockers [ˈnikəbɔkəz] *pl* calzoni *m/pl* alla zuava

knickers [ˈnikəz] *pl* mutande *f/pl* da donna

knife [naif], *pl* **knives** [~vz] *s* coltello *m*; *v/t* accoltellare

knight [nait] cavaliere *m*

knit [nit] *v/t, irr* fare a maglia; *v/i* lavorare a maglia; fare la calza; **~ting-needle** ferro *m* da calza; **~wear** maglieria *f*

knob [nɔb] bottone *m*; pomo *m*; bernoccolo *m*

knock [nɔk] colpo *m*; *v/t* bussare; **~ down** rovesciare; investire; **~ out** mettere fuori combattimento

knot [nɔt] *s* nodo *m*; gruppo *m*; *naut* miglio *m* marino; *v/t* annodare; **~ty** nodoso; *fig* difficile

know [nou] *v/t, v/i, irr* sapere; conoscere; **~ing** abile; accordo; **~ledge** conoscenze *f/pl* sapere; **how to ~** sapere; **to my ~ledge** per quanto sappia io; a quel che

lantern

so; **without my ⌐ledge** a mia insaputa; **make ⌐n** far sapere; far conoscere; **well-**

⌐n ben conosciuto
knuckle ['nʌkl] nocca f
Koran [kɔ'rɑːn] Corano m

L

label ['leibl] s etichetta f; v/t mettere un'etichetta; fig classificare

laboratory [lə'bɔrətəri] laboratorio m

laborious [lə'bɔːriəs] laborioso

labor union ['leibə] Am sindacato m (operaio)

labo(u)r ['leibə] s fatica f; lavoro m faticoso; mano f d'opera; doglie f/pl del parto; 2 **Party** Partito m Laborista; **hard ⌐** lavori m/pl forzati; v/i affaticarsi; **⌐er: (farm) ⌐er** bracciante m; **(manual) ⌐er** operaio m

labyrinth ['læbərinθ] labirinto m

lace [leis] s pizzo m; merletto m; v/t allacciare

lacquer ['lækə] lacca f

lad [læd] giovane m; ragazzo m

ladder ['lædə] s scala f (a piuoli); smagliatura f (di calze)

Ladies pl Signore f/pl; **⌐and Gentlemen** Signore e Signori

ladle ['leidl] ramaiolo m

lady ['leidi] signora f; **⌐doctor** dottoressa f; **⌐like** elegante; ben educato

lag [læg] v/i rimanere indietro

lagoon [lə'guːn] laguna f

lair [lɛə] covo m; tana f

lake [leik] lago m

lamb [læm] agnello m

lame [leim] zoppo; v/t zoppicare

lament [lə'ment] s lamento m; v/t lamentare; v/i lamentarsi; **⌐able** deplorevole

lamp [læmp] lampada f; **⌐shade** paralume m

lance [lɑːns] s lancia f; v/t surg tagliare col bisturi

land [lænd] s terra f; terreno m; suolo m; paese m; **by ⌐** per terra; v/i sbarcare; terrare; **⌐holder** proprietario m di terra; **⌐ing** sbarco m; atterraggio m; **⌐lady** ['lændleidi] padrona f di casa; **⌐lord** padrone m di casa; **⌐mark** punto m di riferimento; **⌐scape** passaggio m; **⌐slide** frana f

lane [lein] viottolo m

language ['læŋgwidʒ] lingua f; linguaggio m

languid ['læŋgwid] languido; **⌐ish** v/i languire; **⌐or** languore m

lank [læŋk] magro; **⌐ hair** capelli m/pl lisci

lantern ['læntən] lanterna f

lap [læp] grembo *m*; **~el** [lə-ˈpel] risvolta *f*

lapse [læps] periodo *m* di tempo

larceny [ˈlɑːsəni] furto *m*

lard [lɑːd] strutto *m*; **~er** dispensa *f*

large [lɑːdʒ] grande; ampio; grosso; **at ~** latitante; **~ly** in gran parte

lark [lɑːk] allodola *f*; *fam* scherzo *m*

larva [ˈlɑːvə] larva *f*

laryn|gitis [ˌlærinˈdʒaitis] laringite *f*; **~x** laringe *f*

lascivious [ləˈsiviəs] lascivo

lash [læʃ] ciglio *m*; sferza *f*; *v/t* sferzare

lass [læs] ragazza *f*

lasso [læˈsuː] laccio *m*

last [lɑːst] *a* ultimo; passato; finale; **~ but one** penultimo; **~ night** stanotte; ieri sera; **~ week** la settimana scorsa; *adv* in ultimo; finalmente; **at ~** alla fine; *v/i* durare; **~ing** duraturo; **~ly** in ultimo; **~ name** nome *m* di famiglia

latch [lætʃ] saliscendi *m*; **~key** chiavetta *f*

late [leit] *a* in ritardo; recente; ultimo; *adv* tardi; **it is ~** è tardi; **I am ~** sono in ritardo; **~ly** ultimamente; recentemente; **~r on** più tardi; **~st** il più tardi (*di tutti*); il più recente (*di tutti*)

lath [lɑːθ] listello *m*

lathe [leið] tornio *m*

lather [ˈlɑːðə] schiuma *f*

Latin [ˈlætin] *s, a* latino (*m*)

latitude [ˈlætitjuːd] latitudine *f*

latter [ˈlætə] *pron* questi; ultimo; secondo; *a* ultimo; secondo

lattice [ˈlætis] grata *f*

laudable [ˈlɔːdəbl] lodevole

laugh [lɑːf] *s* risata *f*; *v/i* ridere; **~ter** risata *f*

launch [lɔːntʃ] *s* lancia *f*; *v/t* lanciare; varare; **~ing** varo *m*

laund|erette [lɔːndəˈret] lavanderia *f* con autoservizio; **~ress** lavandaia *f*; **~ry** lavanderia *f*

laurel [ˈlɔrəl] lauro *m*

lavatory [ˈlævətəri] gabinetto *m*

lavender [ˈlævində] lavanda *f*

lavish [ˈlæviʃ] prodigo; *v/t* prodigare

law [lɔː] legge *f*; diritto *m*; **by ~** per legge; **civil ~** diritto civile; **criminal ~** diritto penale; **~court** tribunale *m*; **~ful** legale; legittimo; **~less** illegale; illegittimo

lawn [lɔːn] prato *m*

law|suit [ˈlɔːsjuːt] causa *f*; **~yer** [ˈlɔːjə] avvocato *m*

lax [læks] trascurato; **~ative** *a, s* lassativo (*m*); purgante *m*

lay [lei] *v/t, irr* porre; collocare; **~ down** deporre; **~ out** stendere

layer [ˈleiə] strato *m*

layman [ˈleimən] laico *m*

lazy [ˈleizi] pigro

lead[1] [liːd] *s* guida *f*; guinzaglio m; *elec* filo m; *v/t, irr* guidare; condurre

lead[2] [led] piombo m; mina f (*del lapis*); **~en** di piombo

leader ['li:də] capo m

leaf [li:f], *pl* **leaves** [~vz] foglia f; **~let** foglietto m

league [li:g] lega f

leak [li:k] *s* fuga f; perdita f; *v/i* perdere; *naut* far acqua; **~age** perdita f; **~y** difettoso

lean [li:n] *a* magro; scarno; *v/i, s* appoggiarsi; **~ out** sporgersi

leap [li:p] *s* salto m; balzo m; *v/i* saltare; balzare; **~year** anno m bisestile

learn [lə:n] *v/t, v/i, irr* imparare; **~ed** dotto; erudito; **~ing** sapere m; cultura f; istruzione f

lease [li:s] *s* contratto m d'affitto; *v/t* affittare

leash [li:ʃ] guinzaglio m

least [li:st] *s* il meno; il minimo; *a* minimo; *adv* minimamente; **at ~** almeno

leather ['leðə] cuoio m; pelle f

leave [li:v] *s* permesso m; congedo m; licenza f; *v/i, irr* partire; *v/t* lasciare; abbandonare

lecture ['lektʃə] *s* conferenza f; lezione f (*universitaria*); *v/i* fare una conferenza; fare la lezione; **~r** conferenziere m; docente m universitario

ledge [ledʒ] ripiano m

leech [li:tʃ] sanguisuga f

leek [li:k] porro m

leer [liə] *s* occhiata f lasciva; *v/i* dare un'occhiata lasciva

left [left] *s* sinistra f; *a* sinistro; **to the ~** a sinistra; *adv* sinistra; **~-handed** mancino; **~-luggage office** deposito m bagagli; **~overs** *pl* resti *m/pl*; rimanenze *f/pl*

leg [leg] gamba f; (*animal*) zampa f; (*furniture*) piede m; **pull s.o.'s ~** prendere in giro

legacy ['legəsi] lascito m

legal ['li:gəl] legale; legittimo; **~ize** *v/t* legalizzare; legittimare

legation [li'geiʃən] legazione f

legend ['ledʒənd] leggenda f; **~ary** leggendario

legible ['ledʒəbl] leggibile

legion ['li:dʒən] legione f

legislat|ion [ledʒis'leiʃən] legislazione f; **~ive** ['~ətiv] legislativo; **~or** legislatore m

legitimate [li'dʒitimit] legittimo

leisure ['leʒə] tempo m libero; **~ly** senza fretta

lemon ['lemən] limone m; **~ade** [~'neid] limonata f; **~ juice** succo m di limone; **~ squash** limonata f

lend [lend] *v/t, irr* prestare; **~ing library** biblioteca f circolante

length [leŋθ] lunghezza f; **at ~** a lungo; **~en** *v/t* allungare; *v/i* allungarsi; **~wise** ['~waiz] per il lungo

lenient ['li:njənt] indulgente

lens [lenz] lente f

Lent [lent] quaresima f
lentil ['lentil] lenticchia f
leopard ['lepəd] leopardo m
leprosy ['leprəsi] lebbra f
less [les] meno; **grow ~** diminuire; **more or ~** più o meno; **~en** v/t diminuire; attenuare; **~er** minore
lesson ['lesn] lezione f
lest [lest] per paura che
let [let] v/t, irr lasciare; permettere; affittare; **~ down** abbassare; abbandonare; **~ in** far entrare; **~ off** esentare; sparare; lasciare in libertà; lasciare senza punizione; **~ out** far uscire
lethal ['li:θəl] letale
lethargy ['leθədʒi] letargia f
letter ['letə] lettera f; **registered ~** lettera raccomandata; **~box** cassetta f postale
lettuce ['letis] lattuga f
leuc(a)emia [lju(:)'ki:miə] leucemia f
level ['levl] livello m; **~ crossing** passaggio m a livello; v/t livellare; spianare
lever ['li:və] leva f
levity ['leviti] levità f
levy ['levi] s imposta f; v/t imporre; arrolare
lewd [lu:d] lascivo
liability [laiə'biliti] responsabilità f; pl comm passività f; **~le** ['laiəbl] responsabile; soggetto a; tenuto a
liaison [li(:)'eizən] relazione f
liar ['laiə] bugiardo(a) m (f)
libel ['laibəl] s diffamazione f; v/t diffamare

liberal ['libərəl] s, a liberale (m)
liberate ['libəreit] v/t liberare; **~ion** liberazione f
liberty ['libəti] libertà f; **be at ~** essere libero
librarian [lai'brɛəriən] bibliotecario m; **~y** ['laibrəri] biblioteca f
Libya ['libiə] Libia f; **~n** a, s libico (m)
lice [lais] (pl de louse) pidocchi m/pl
licence, Am **~se** ['laisəns] licenza f; permesso m; patente f; v/t autorizzare; permettere; **~tious** [lai'senʃəs] licenzioso
lick [lik] s leccata f; v/t leccare
lid [lid] coperchio m; anat palpebra f
lie[1] [lai] s bugia f; menzogna f; v/i mentire
lie[2] [lai] v/i, irr essere sdraiato; giacere; essere situato; **~ down** sdraiarsi
lieutenant [lef'tenənt] luogotenente m
life [laif], pl **lives** [~vz] vita f; **~belt** cintura f di salvataggio m; **~boat** barca f di salvataggio; **~buoy** salvagente m; **~ insurance** assicurazione f sulla vita; **~jacket** giubbotto m di salvataggio; **~less** senza vita
lift [lift] s ascensore m; montacarichi m; passaggio m (in macchina); v/t alzare; sollevare; v/i dissiparsi
ligature ['ligətʃuə] legatura f

light [lait] s luce f; giorno m; a leggero; chiaro; v/t ~ (**up**) accendere; illuminare; v/i accendersi; **~en** alleggerire; **~er** accendisigaro m; **~house** faro m; **~ing** illuminazione f; **~ning** ['laitnin] lampo m; **~ning-conductor** parafulmine m

like [laik] a simile; adv come; s simile m; v/t piacere; amare; avere simpatia; **feel** ~ aver voglia di; **I ~ tea** mi piace il te; **~lihood** probabilità f; **~ly** probabile; **~ness** somiglianza f; **~wise** similmente

liking ['laikin] simpatia f

lilac ['lailək] lilla m

lily ['lili] giglio m

limb [lim] membro m

lime [laim] calce f; bot tiglio m; **~light** luce f della ribalta

limit ['limit] s limite m; v/t limitare

limp [limp] a floscio; debole; v/i zoppicare

line [lain] s linea f; ruga f; comm ramo m; v/t rigare; foderare; v/i ~ **up** allinearsi

linen ['linin] lino m; biancheria f

liner ['lainə] transatlantico m

linger ['lingə] v/i indugiare

lingerie ['læːnʒəri:] lingeria f

linguist ['lingwist] linguista m, f

lining ['lainin] fodera f

link [link] s legame m; v/t collegare

links [links] pl campo m da golf

lion ['laiən] leone m; **~ess** leonessa f

lip [lip] labbro m; **~stick** rossetto m

liqueur [li'kjuə] liquore m

liquid ['likwid] a, s liquido (m); **~ate** v/t liquidare

liquorice ['likəris] liquorizia f

lisp [lisp] v/i balbettare

list [list] s lista f; elenco m; v/t elencare

listen ['lisn] v/i ascoltare

listless ['listlis] indifferente; svogliato

literal ['litərəl] letterale

literary ['litərəri] letterario; **~ture** ['~ritʃə] letteratura f

lithe ['laið] flessibile

lit|**re**, Am **~er** ['liːtə] litro m

litter ['litə] s lettiga f; figliata f (di animali); rifiuti m/pl; **~basket**, **~bin** secchio m della spazzatura

little ['litl] a piccolo; poco; ~ **finger** mignolo m; s poco m; adv poco

live [laiv] a vivo; vivente; [liv] v/i vivere; abitare; **~lihood** ['laivlihud] sussistenza f; **~ly** ['laivli] vivace

liver ['livə] fegato m

livestock ['laivstɔk] bestiame m

livid ['livid] livido; furioso

living ['livin] a vivo; vivente; s vita f; **~room** soggiorno m

lizard ['lizəd] lucertola f

load [loud] *s* carica *f*; *v/t* caricare

loaf [louf], *pl* **loaves** [~vz] pagnotta *f*; pane *m*; *v/i* oziare; **~er** bighellone *m*

loam [loum] terriccio *m*

loan [loun] *s* prestito *m*; *v/t* prestare; **on ~** in prestito

loath [louθ] restio; **~e** [louð] *v/t* detestare; **~some** ripugnante

lobby ['lɔbi] ingresso *m*; corridoio *m*

lobe [loub] lobo *m*

lobster ['lɔbstə] aragosta *f*

loca|l ['loukəl] locale; **~lity** [~'kæliti] località *f*; **~lize** *v/t* localizzare; **~te** [lou'keit] *v/t* individuare; **be ~ted** trovarsi; **~tion** situazione *f*

loch [lɔk] *Scot* lago *m*

lock [lɔk] *s* serratura *f*; chiusa *f*; *v/t* chiudere a chiave

locomotive ['loukə'moutiv] locomotiva *f*

locust ['loukəst] locusta *f*

lodg|e [lɔdʒ] casetta *f*; portineria *f*; *v/t*, *v/i* alloggiare; **~er** pensionante *m*; **~ings** *pl* stanze *f/pl* in affitto

loft [lɔft] abbaino *m*; solaio *m*; **~y** alto; altero

log [lɔg] ceppo *m*; tronco *m*; **~-book**) *naut* diario *m* di bordo

loggerhead ['lɔgəhed]: **at ~s with** in urto con

loggia ['lɔdʒə] loggia *f*

logic ['lɔdʒik] logica *f*; **~al** logico

loin [lɔin] lombo *m*

loiter ['lɔitə] *v/i* indugiare

London ['lʌndən] Londra *f*; **~er** londinese *m*, *f*

lone|liness ['lounlinis] solitudine *f*; **~ly**, **~some** solitario; solo

long [lɔŋ] *a* lungo; *adv* a lungo; **in the ~ run** alla lunga; **as ~ as** finché; **~ ago** molto tempo fa; **all day ~** tutto il giorno; **how ~?** per quanto tempo?; **no ~er** non più; **~ since** da molto tempo; **~ for** *v/i* bramare; desiderare (*fortemente*)

long-distance call telefonata *f* interurbana

longing desiderio *m* (*forte*)

look [luk] *s* sguardo *m*; aspetto *m*; espressione *f*; *v/i* guardare; sembrare; **~ after** curare; occuparsi di; **~ at** guardare; **~ for** cercare; **~ bad** star male; sembrare brutto; **~ into** investigare; **~ out** take care; badare; **~ over** riguardare; **~ing-glass** specchio *m*

loom [lu:m] telaio *m*

loop [lu:p] laccio *m*; **~hole** scappatoia *f*

loose [lu:s] sciolto; **~n** *v/t* sciogliere

loot [lu:t] bottino *m*; *v/t* saccheggiare

lord [lɔ:d] signore *m*; **♀ Mayor** Sindaco *m* di Londra; **♀'s Prayer** paternostro *m*

lorry ['lɔri] camion *m*; autotreno *m*

los|e [lu:z] *v/t*, *irr* perdere; **~s** [lɔs] perdita *f*; **be at a ~s**

non sapere che fare; **~t** perduto; **get ~t** perdersi

lost-property office ufficio *m* oggetti smarriti

lot [lɔt] destino *m*; sorte *f*; quantità *f*; **a ~ of, ~s of** molto

lotion [ˈlouʃən] lozione *f*

lottery [ˈlɔtəri] lotteria *f*

lotus [ˈloutəs] loto *m*

loud [laud] alto; forte; vistoso; **~ly** ad alta voce; **~ speaker** altoparlante *m*

lounge [laundʒ] salotto *m*

louse [laus], *pl* **lice** [lais] pidocchio *m*

lout [laut] zoticone *m*

love [lʌv] *s* amore *m*; *v/t* amare; voler bene; **fall in ~** innamorarsi; **make ~** far l'amore; **~affair** amori *m/pl*; **~r** amante *m/f*; **~ly** bello; **~story** romanzo *m* d'amore

loving [ˈlʌviŋ] affettuoso

low [lou] *a* basso; *v/i* muggire; **~er** a più basso; inferiore; *v/t* abbassare; **~lands** terra *f* bassa; **~ly** umile; **~tide, ~water** marea *f* bassa

loyal [ˈlɔiəl] leale; **~ty** lealtà *f*

lozenge [ˈlɔzindʒ] losanga *f*; pasticca *f*

lubricant [ˈluːbrikənt] *a, s* lubrificante (*m*); **~te** *v/t* lubrificare

lucid [ˈluːsid] lucido

luck [lʌk] sorte *f*; fortuna *f*; **~y** fortunato; **bad ~** sfortuna *f*; **good ~** buona fortuna

lucrative [ˈluːkrətiv] lucrativo

ludicrous [ˈluːdikrəs] ridicolo; assurdo

lug [lʌg] *v/t* reascinare

luggage [ˈlʌgidʒ] bagagli *m/pl*; **~carrier** facchino *m*; **~ (delivery) office** ufficio *m* dei bagagli; **~ticket** scontrino *m* dei bagagli; **~van** bagagliaio *m*

lukewarm [ˈluːkwɔːm] tepido; *fig* indifferente

lull [lʌl] *s* momento *m* di calma; *v/t* cullare; addormentare; **~aby** [ˈ~əbai] ninnananna *f*

lumbago [lʌmˈbeigou] lombaggine *f*

lumber [ˈlʌmbə] legname *m*

luminous [ˈluːminəs] luminoso

lump [lʌmp] *s* massa *f*; pezzo *m*; gonfiore *m*; zolletta *f* (*di zucchero*); **~sum** somma *f* globale

luna|cy [ˈl(j)uːnəsi] pazzia *f*; follia *f*; **~r** lunare; **~tic** [ˈluːnətik] *a, s* pazzo (*m*); **~tic asylum** manicomio *m*

lunch [lʌntʃ] (seconda) colazione *f*

lung [lʌŋ] polmone *m*

lurch [ləːtʃ] *v/i* traballare

lure [ljuə] *s* attrattiva *f*; inganno *m*; *v/t* attrarre

luscious [ˈlʌʃəs] saporoso

lust [lʌst] sensualità *f*; lussuria *f*

lusty [ˈlʌsti] robusto

Lutheran [ˈluːθərən] *a, s* luterano (*m*)

luxur|ious [lʌgˈzjuəriəs] lussuoso; **~y** [ˈlʌkʃəri] lusso *m*

lying   124

lying falso
lymph [limf] linfa *f*
lynch [lintʃ] *v/t* linciare

lynx [liŋks] lince *f*
lyric [ˈlirik] *a* lirico; *s* poema
m lirico

M

macaroni [ˌmækəˈrouni]
pasta *f* asciutta; maccheroni
m/pl
machine [məˈʃiːn] macchina *f*; **~-gun** mitragliatrice *f*;
sewing-~ macchina da cucire
mackerel [ˈmækrəl] sgombro *m*
mack [mæk] *fam for* **mackintosh** [ˈ~intɒʃ] impermeabile *m*
mad [mæd] pazzo; folle; **be
~ about** andare pazzo per;
go ~ impazzire
madam [ˈmædəm] signora *f*
made [meid] fatto; fabbricato; **~ up** fittizio; truccato
madhouse manicomio *m*
magazine [mægəˈziːn] rivista *f*
magic [ˈmædʒik] *a* magico; *s* magia *f*; **~ian** [məˈdʒiʃən] mago *m*
magistrate [ˈmædʒistreit] magistrato *m*
magnet [ˈmægnit] calamita *f*; **~ic** magnetico
magnify [ˈmægnifai] *v/t* ampliare; esagerare
magnitude [ˈmægnitjuːd] grandezza *f*
mahogany [məˈhɒgəni] mogano *m*
maid [meid] cameriera *f*;
old ~ zitella *f*

mail [meil] *s* corrispondenza *f*; *v/t* mandare per posta; **~
box** buca *f* per lettere; **~
man** postino *m*
maim [meim] *v/t* mutilare
main [mein] principale; essenziale; **~land** continente *m*
main|tain [meinˈtein] *v/t* mantenere; sostenere; **~te-
nance** [ˈmeintənəns] mantenimento *m*; manutenzione *f*
maize [meiz] granturco *m*
majest|ic [məˈdʒestik] maestoso; **~y** [ˈmædʒisti] maestà *f*; maestosità *f*
major [ˈmeidʒə] *s* maggiore *m*; *a* maggiore; più importante; **~ road** strada *f* principale
majority [məˈdʒɒriti] maggioranza *f*; età *f* maggiore
make [meik] *s* marca *f*; fattura *f*; fabbricazione *f*; *v/t*, *irr* fare; produrre; **~ fun of** prendere in giro; **~ good** riparare; **~ known** far sapere; far conoscere; **~ the best of** approfittare; **~ out** stendere; capire; **~ up** formare; comporre; truccarsi; **~ up
for** compensare; **~ up one's
mind** decidersi; **~ it up** far pace; **~r** creatore *m*; **~shift** espediente *m*; **~-up** trucco *m*

mark

malady ['mælədi] malattia *f*
malaria [mə'lɛəriə] malaria *f*

male [meil] *s* maschio *m*; *a* maschile

male|diction [mæli'dikʃən] maledizione *f*; ~**factor** malfattore *m*; ~**volent** [mə'levələnt] malevolo

malic|e ['mælis] malignità *f*; ~**ious** [mə'liʃəs] maligno

malignant [mə'lignənt] maligno

malnutrition ['mælnju(:)-'triʃən] cattiva nutrizione *f*

malt [mɔ:lt] malto *m*

mammal ['mæməl] mammifero *m*

man [mæn], *pl* **men** [men] uomo *m*

manage ['mænidʒ] *v/t* dirigere; amministrare; *v/i* riuscire; ~**ment** direzione *f*; amministrazione *f*; gestione *f*; ~**r** direttore *m*; amministratore *m*; gestore *m*; impresario *m*

mandate ['mændeit] mandato *m*

mane [mein] criniera *f*

maneuver [mə'nu:və] *Am* for manoeuvre

manger ['meindʒə] mangiatoia *f*

mangle ['mæŋgl] *s* mangano *m*; *v/t* maganare

mania ['meinjə] mania *f*

manifest ['mænifest] *a* manifesto; chiaro; *v/t* manifestare

manifold ['mænifould] molteplice

manipulate [mə'nipjuleit] *v/t* manipolare

man|kind [mæn'kaind] genere *m* umano; ~**ly** virile

manner ['mænə] maniera *f*; modo *m*; ~**s** *pl* maniere *f/pl*

manoeuvre [mə'nu:və] *s* manovra *f*; *v/t*, *v/i* manovrare

manslaughter ['mæn'slɔ:tə] omicidio *m*

mansion ['mænʃən] palazzo *m*

mantelpiece ['mæntlpi:s] mensola *f* di caminetto

manual ['mænjuəl] *a*, *s* manuale (*m*)

manufacture [,mænju'fæktʃə] *s* fabbricazione *f*; *v/t* fabbricare

manure [mə'njuə] concime *m*; *v/t* concimare

manuscript ['mænjuskript] manoscritto *m*

many ['meni] molti(e); **a great** ~ moltissimi(e)

map [mæp] carta *f*

maple ['meipl] acero *m*

marble ['mɑ:bl] marmo *m*

March [mɑ:tʃ] marzo *m*

mare [mɛə] giumenta *f*

margarine [,mɑ:dʒə'ri:n] margarina *f*

margin ['mɑ:dʒin] margine *m*; bordo *m*

marine [mə'ri:n] *a* marino; marittimo; *s* marina *f*

marionette [,mæriə'net] pupazzo *m*

maritime ['mæritaim] marittimo

mark [mɑ:k] *s* segno *m*;

marca *f*; voto *m* (*scolastico*; *v/t* segnare; marcare; correggere (*compiti*); **~ed** segnato

market ['mɑ:kit] *s* mercato *m*; *v/t* piazzare sul mercato

marmalade ['mɑ:məleid] marmellata *f* di arance

marquis ['mɑ:kwis] marchese *m*

marri|age ['mærid3] *s* matrimonio *m*; **~age certificate**, **~age lines** *pl* fede *f* di matrimonio; **~ed** sposato(a); **get ~ed** sposarsi

marrow ['mærou] midolla *f*; zucchino *m*

marry ['mæri] *v/t* sposare; sposarsi con; *v/i* sposarsi

marsh [mɑ:ʃ] palude *f*

marshal ['mɑ:ʃəl] maresciallo *m*

martial ['mɑ:ʃəl] marziale

martyr ['mɑ:tə] martire *m*

marvel ['mɑ:vəl] *s* meraviglia *f*; *v/t* meravigliarsi; **~(l)ous** meraviglioso

mascot ['mæskət] portafortuna *m*

masculine ['mæskjulin] maschile

mash [mæʃ] *v/t* schiacciare; **~ed potatoes** *pl* purè *m* di patate

mask [mɑ:sk] maschera *f*

mason ['meisn] muratore *m*; massone *m*; **~ry** massoneria *f*

mass [mæs] massa *f*; (*church*) messa *f*

massage ['mæsɑ:3] *s* massaggio *m*; *v/t* fare massaggi a

massive ['mæsiv] massiccio

mast [mɑ:st] albero *m*

master ['mɑ:stə] *s* padrone *m*; maestro *m*; *v/t* impadronirsi di; **~key** comunella *f*; **~ly** autorevole; **~piece** capolavoro *m*

mat [mæt] stoia *f*

match [mætʃ] fiammifero *m*; partita *f*; uguale *m*; *v/t* assortire; **~ing** assortito

mate [meit] *s* compagno *m*; *naut* secondo *m*; *v/t* accoppiare

material [mə'tiəriəl] *s* materiale *m*; tessuto *m*; *a* materiale

matern|al [mə'tə:nl] materno; **~ity** maternità *f*

mathematic|ian [mæθimə'tiʃən] matematico *m*; **~s** [~'mætiks] *pl* matematica *f*

maths [mæθs] *fam* for **mathematics**

matriculate [mə'trikjuleit] *v/t, v/i* immatricolare

matron ['meitrən] matrona *f*; caposala *f* (*in un ospedale*)

matter ['mætə] *s* cosa *f*; faccenda *f*; **what's the ~?** che cosa c'è?; **it doesn't ~** non importa; *v/i* importare; **a ~ of fact** fatto *m*

mattress ['mætris] materasso *m*

matur|e [mə'tjuə] *a* maturo; *comm* scaduto; *v/i* maturare; *comm* scadere; **~ity** maturità *f*; *comm* scadenza *f*

Maundy Thursday ['mɔ:ndi] giovedì *m* santo

May [mei] maggio *m*

may [mei] *v/d* potere; **~ I come in?** posso entrare?; **~be** forse

mayonnaise [ˌmeiəˈneiz] maionese *f*

mayor [mɛə] sindaco *m*

maze [meiz] labirinto *m*

me [mi(ː)] *pron* me; mi; **it's ~** sono io; **he told ~** me disse

meadow [ˈmedou] prato *m*

meagre, *Am* **~er** [ˈmiːgə] magro; scarno; povero

meal [miːl] pasto *m*; farina *f*

mean [miːn] *s* medio; meschino; *v/t, irr* significare; voler dire; **~s** *pl* mezzi *m/pl*; **by no ~s** in nessun modo; per niente; **by ~s of** per mezzo di

meaning significato *m*; **~less** senza senso

mean|time, **~while** frattempo

measles [ˈmiːzlz] *sg* morbillo *m*

measure [ˈmeʒə] *s* misura *f*; *v/t* misurare; **~ment** misura *f*

meat [miːt] carne *f*

mechani|c [miˈkænik] meccanico *m*; **~cal** meccanico; **~cs** *pl* meccanica *f*; **~sm** [ˈmekənizəm] meccanismo *m*; **~ze** *v/t* meccanizzare

medal [ˈmedl] medaglia *f*

meddle [ˈmedl] *v/i* intromettere

mediate [ˈmiːdieit] *v/t, v/i* mediare; **~ion** mediazione *f*

medic|al [ˈmedikəl] medico; **~ine** [ˈmedsin] medicina *f*

medieval [ˌmediˈiːvəl] medioevale

meditat|e [ˈmediteit] *v/t, v/i* meditare; **~ion** meditazione *f*

Mediterranean [meditəˈreinjən] **(Sea)** (Mar *m*) mediterraneo

medium [ˈmiːdjəm] *a* medio; *s* mezzo *m*

meek [miːk] remissivo

meet [miːt] *v/t, irr* incontrare; far fronte; **~ing** riunione *f*; incontro *m*

melancholy [ˈmelənkəli] malinconia *f*

mellow [ˈmelou] maturo; tenere

melon [ˈmelən] mellone *m*

melt [melt] *v/t* fondere; sciogliere; *v/i* fondersi; sciogliersi

member [ˈmembə] membro *m*; socio *m*; **~ship** affiliati *m/pl*

memory [ˈmeməri] memoria *f*; ricordo *m*

men [men] *pl* of **man**

menace [ˈmenəs] *s* minaccia *f*; *v/t, v/i* minacciare

mend [mend] *v/t* accomodare; rammendare; riparare

menstruation [ˌmenstruˈeiʃən] mestruazione *f*; regole *f/pl*

mental [ˈmentl] mentale; **~ home** manicomio *m*

mention [ˈmenʃən] *s* accenno *m*; *v/t* accennare; **don't ~ it!** prego!, non c'è di che!

menu [ˈmenjuː] lista *f*

merchan|dise [ˈmɔːtʃəndaiz] merce f; **~t** commerciante m

merci|ful ['mɔ:siful] misericordioso; **~less** senza pietà

mercury ['mɔ:kjuri] mercurio m

mercy ['mɔ:si] misericordia f; pietà f

mere [miə] semplice

merge [mɔ:dʒ] v/t fondere; v/i fondersi

merit ['merit] s merito m; v/t meritare

merr|iment ['meriment] allegria f; **~y** allegro; **~y-go-round** carosello m

mess [mes] pasticcio m; confusione f; **make a ~** fare un pasticcio

mess|age ['mesidʒ] messaggio m; **~enger** [mesindʒə] messaggero m

metal ['metl] s metallo m; a di metallo; **~lic** [mi'tælik] metallico

meter ['mi:tə] contatore m (del gas, della luce)

method ['meθəd] metodo m

met|re, Am **~er** ['mi:tə] metro m

metropolitan [metrə'pɔlitən] metropolitano

mew [mju:] v/i miagolare

Mexic|an ['meksikn] a, s messicano m; **~o** Messico m

mice [mais] pl of **mouse**

microphone ['maikrəfoun] microfono m

middle ['midl] a medio; di mezzo; s mezzo m; **2 Ages** medioevo m; **~ class** ceto m

medio; classe f media

midnight mezzanotte f

midwife levatrice f

might [mait] s potere m; **~y** potente

migra|te [mai'greit] v/i migrare; **~tion** migrazione f

mild [maild] mite; dolce

mile [mail] miglio m

military ['militəri] militare

milk [milk] s latte m; v/t mungere; **~man** lattaio m

mill [mil] molino m; fabbrica f

milliner ['milinə] modista f

million ['miljən] milione m; **~aire** [~'nɛə] miliardario m

mimic ['mimik] v/t imitare

mince [mins] s carne f tritata; v/t tritare

mind [maind] s mente f; spirito m; **bear in ~** tenere presente; **change one's ~** cambiare idea; v/t badare a; v/i dispiacersi; **do you ~?** ti dispiace?; **never ~** non importa

mine¹ [main] pron poss mio, mia, miei, mie; il mio, la mia, i miei, le mie

mine² [mein] s miniera f; mina f; v/t, v/i minare; **~r** minatore m

mineral ['minərəl] minerale m

mingle ['miŋgl] v/t mescolare

miniature ['minjətʃə] miniatura f

minimum ['miniməm] a, s minimo (m)

minist|er ['ministə] ministro m; pastore m; **~ry** ministero m

mink [miŋk] visone m

minor ['mainə] a minore; s
minorenne m; **.ity** [ˌ-'nɔriti]
minoranza f; (age) minorità
f

minster ['minstə] duomo m

minstrel ['minstrəl] trovatore m

mint [mint] bot menta f;
zecca f

minus ['mainəs] prp meno

minute [mai'nju:t] a minuto; ['minit] s minuto m; **.s** pl verbale m

miracle ['mirəkl] miracolo m; **.ulous** miracoloso

mirror ['mirə] specchio m

mirth [mə:θ] allegria f

misadventure disgrazia f

misapply v/t applicare sbagliatamente

misapprehend v/t fraintendere; **.sion** malinteso m

misbehave v/i comportarsi male

miscarriage aborto m; **.y** v/i abortire

mischief ['mistʃif] birichinata f; **.vous** birichino

misdeed malefatto m

miser ['maizə] avaro

miser|able ['mizərəbl] misero; **.y** miseria f

mishap ['mishæp] contrattempo m; incidente m

mislay v/t, irr (**lay**) smarrire

mislead v/t, irr (**lead**) sviare; ingannare

mismanage v/t amministrare male; **.ment** cattiva amministrazione f

misprint [mis'print] errore m di stampa

misrule malgoverno m; v/t governare male

Miss [mis] s signorina f

miss [mis] v/t perdere; sentire la mancanza di; v/i mancare

missile ['misail] missile m

mission ['miʃən] missione f

mist [mist] nebbia f

mistake [mis'teik] s sbaglio m; v/t fraintendere; **by .** per sbaglio; **make a .** fare uno sbaglio

Mister ['mistə] signore m

mistletoe ['misltou] vischio m

mistress ['mistris] padrona f; (school) maestra f; signora f; amante f

mistrust [mis'trʌst] s sfiducia f; v/t diffidare di

misty ['misti] nebbioso

misunderstand v/t, irr (**stand**) fraintendere; **.ing** malinteso m

misuse ['mis'ju:z] s abuso m; maltrattamento m; v/t abusare; maltrattare

mix [miks] v/t mescolare; v/i mescolarsi; **.ture** miscela f; miscuglio m

moan [moun] s gemito m; v/i gemere

mob [mɔb] folla f

mobile ['moubail] mobile m

mock [mɔk] a falso; finto; imitato; v/t deridere; **.ery** derisione f

mode [moud] (way) modo m; (fashion) moda f

model

model ['mɔdl] *a* modello; *s* modello *m*; modella *f*

moderate ['mɔdərit] *a* moderato; *v/t* moderare

modern ['mɔdən] moderno

modest ['mɔdist] modesto; **~y** modestia *f*

modify ['mɔdifai] *v/t* modificare

moist [mɔist] umido

molar ['moulə]: **~ teeth** *pl* molari *m/pl*

molest [mou'lest] *v/t* molestare

moment ['moumənt] momento *m*; **~ary** momentaneo

monarch ['mɔnək] monarca *m*; **~y** monarchia *f*

monastery ['mɔnəstəri] monastero *m*

Monday ['mʌndi] lunedì *m*

monetary ['mʌnitəri] monetario

money ['mʌni] denaro *m*; **~ order** vaglia *m* postale

monk [mʌŋk] monaco *m*

monkey ['mʌŋki] scimmia *f*

monopolize [mə'nɔpəlaiz] *v/t* monopolizzare

monotonous [mə'nɔtənəs] monotono

monst|er ['mɔnstə] *s* mostro *m*; *a* enorme; **~rous** mostruoso

month [mʌnθ] mese *m*; **~ly** mensile

monument ['mɔnjumənt] monumento *m*

mood [mu:d] umore *m*; capriccio *m*; **~y** di malumore; capriccioso

moon [mu:n] luna *f*; **~light** luce *f* della luna; **~shine** chiaro *m* di luna

moor [muə] *s* brughiera *f*; *v/t* ormeggiare

mop [mɔp] straccio *m*; *v/t* pulire

moral ['mɔrəl] *a, s* morale (*m*); **~ity** moralità *f*; **~ize** *v/t, v/i* moralizzare; **~s** *pl* morale *f*

morbid ['mɔːbid] morboso

more [mɔː] *a* più; *adv* più; di più; **~ and ~** sempre più; **once ~** ancora una volta; **~over** inoltre

morning ['mɔːniŋ] mattina *f*; **good ~** buon giorno; **tomorrow ~** domani mattina; *a* mattutino

morose [mə'rous] non socievole; sgarbato

morph|ia ['mɔːfjə], **~ine** ['mɔːfiːn] morfina *f*

mortal ['mɔːtl] *a, s* mortale (*m*); **~ity** [mɔː'tæliti] mortalità *f*

mortgage ['mɔgidʒ] *s* ipoteca *f*; *v/t* ipotecare

mortician [mɔː'tiʃən] *Am* imprenditore *m* di pompe funebri

mortuary ['mɔːtjuəri] camera *f* mortuaria

mosaic [mou'zeiik] mosaico *m*

Moslem ['mɔzləm] *cf* **Muslim**

mosque [mɔsk] moschea *f*

mosquito [mɔs'kiːtou] zanzara *f*; **~net** zanzariera *f*

moss [mɔs] muschio *m*

most [moust] *a* la maggior parte; *adv* il più; **at** (**the**) ~ al più; **~ly** per lo più

moth [moθ] tarma *f*

mother ['mʌðə] madre *f*; **~country** patria *f*; **~hood** maternità *f*; **~-in-law** suocera *f*; **~ly** materno; **~of-pearl** madreperla *f*; **~ tongue** lingua *f* materna

motif [mou'ti:f] motivo *m*

motion ['mouʃən] movimento *m*; **~less** immobile; **~ picture** pellicola *f*

motive ['moutiv] *s* motivo *m*; *a* motore

motor ['moutə] *a*, *s* motore (*m*); **~bicycle, ~bike** motocicletta *f*; **~boat** motoscafo *m*; **~car** automobile *f*; macchina *f*; **~cycle** motocicletta *f*; **~ist** automobilista *m*; **~ize** *v/t* motorizzare; **~ road** autostrada *f*

mould [mould] *s* muffa *f*; forma *f*; *v/t* modellare; formare

mound [maund] montagnola *f*

mount [maunt] *s* monte *m*; *v/t* salire

mountain ['mauntin] montagna *f*; **~eer** [~'niə] alpinista *m*; **~ range** catena *f* di montagne

mourn [mɔ:n] *v/t*, *v/i* piangere; **~ful** afflitto; lugubre; **~ing** lutto *m*

mouse [maus], *pl* **mice** [mais] topo *m*

moustache [məs'tɑ:ʃ] baffi *m/pl*

mouth [mauθ], *pl* **~s** [mauðz] bocca *f*; sbocco *m*; **~ful** boccata *f*; boccone *m*; **~piece** bocchino *m*; portavoce *m*

mov|e [mu:v] *s* mossa *f*; *v/t* muovere; *v/i* muoversi; **~ment** movimento *m*; **~ies** ['mu:viz] *pl* cinema *m*; **~ing** commovente

much [mʌtʃ] molto; **as ~ as** tanto quanto; **so ~ the better** tanto meglio; **too ~** troppo; **very ~** moltissimo

muck [mʌk] sudiciume *m*

mucus ['mju:kəs] *biol* muco *m*

mud [mʌd] fango *m*

muddle ['mʌdl] *s* confusione *f*; imbroglio *m*; *v/t* imbrogliare

mud|dy ['mʌdi] fangoso; **~guard** parafango *m*

muff [mʌf] manicotto *m*

muffle ['mʌfl] *v/t* attutire

mug [mʌg] coppa *f*

mulberry ['mʌlbəri] moro *m*

mule [mju:l] mulo *m*

multi|ple ['mʌltipl], *s*, *a* multiplo (*m*); **~plication table** [~pli'keiʃən] abbaco *m*; tavola *f* pitagorica; **~ply** ['~plai]; *v/t* moltiplicare; **~tude** moltitudine *f*

mumble ['mʌmbl] *v/t*, *v/i* borbottare

mummy ['mʌmi] mummia *f*

mumps [mʌmps] *pl* orecchioni *m/pl*

munch [mʌntʃ] *v/t* masticare

municipal [mju(:)'nisipəl] municipale; **~ity** [~'pæliti] municipalità f

munition [mju(:)'niʃən], pl munizioni f/pl

murder ['mɔ:də] s assassinio m; v/t assassinare; **~er** s assassino m

murmur ['mɔ:mə] s mormorio m; v/t mormorare

musc|le ['mʌsl] muscolo m; **~ular** ['~kjulə] muscoloso

muse [mju:z] v/t, v/i meditare

museum [mju(:)'ziəm] museo m

mushroom ['mʌʃrum] fungo m

music ['mju:zik] musica f; **~al** a musicale; s film m musicale; **~al comedy** operetta f; **~hall** varietà f; **~ian** musicista m, f

musket ['mʌskit] moschetto m; **~eer** moschettiere m

Muslim ['muslim] a, s mussulmano (m)

must[1] [mʌst] v/d dovere; avere a; **I ~ write** devo scrivere; **it ~ be late** deve essere tardi

must[2] [mʌst] s muffa f

mustache ['mʌstæʃ] Am baffi m/pl

mustard ['mʌstəd] senape f; mostarda f

muster ['mʌstə] v/t radunare

musty ['mʌsti] ammuffito

mute [mju:t] a muto; s muto(a) m(f)

mutilate ['mju:tileit] v/t mutilare

mutin|ous ['mju:tinəs] sedizioso; ribelle; **~y** ammutinamento m

mutter [mʌtə] v/t, v/i borbottare

mutton ['mʌtn] carne f di montone

mutual ['mju:tʃuəl] reciproco

muzzle ['mʌzl] museruola f

my [mai] a poss mio, mia, miei, mie

myrtle ['mɔ:tl] mirto m

myself [mai'self] me stesso

myst|erious [mis'tiəriəs] misterioso; **~ery** ['~təri] mistero m; **~ify** ['mistifai] v/t mistificare

N

nag [næg] v/t trovare da ridire su tutto

nail [neil] s chiodo m; v/t inchiodare

naïve [na:'i:v] ingenuo

naked ['neikid] nudo

name [neim] s nome m; v/t nominare; **~less** senza nome; **what is your ~?** Qual è il suo nome?

nanny ['næni] bambinaia f

nap [næp] pisolino m; pelo m

nape [neip] nuca f

napkin ['næpkin] tovagliolo m

narcosis [na:'kousis] narcosi f

narcotic [nɑː'kɔtik] *a*, *s* narcotico (*m*)

narrat|e [næ'reit] *v/t* narrare; **∼ion** narrazione *f*

narrow ['nærou] *a* stretto; ristretto; *v/t* restringere; *v/i* restringersi

nasty ['nɑːsti] brutto

nation ['neiʃən] nazione *f*; **∼al** ['næʃənl] nazionale; **∼ality** [∼'næliti] nazionalità *f*

native ['neitiv] *a* nativo; indigeno; *s* indigeno *m*; **∼ language** lingua *f* madre

natural ['nætʃrəl] naturale

nature ['neitʃə] natura *f*

naught [nɔːt] zero *m*

naughty ['nɔːti] birichino

nausea ['nɔːsjə] nausea *f*; **∼ting** [∼ieitiŋ] ripugnante

nave [neiv] navata *f*

navel ['neivəl] ombelico *m*

navy ['neivi] marina *f*

near [niə] *a* vicino; vicino; *prp* vicino a; *v/i* avvicinarsi; **∼ly** quasi; **∼ness** prossimità *f*; **∼sighted** miope

neat [niːt] ordinato

necessary ['nesisəri] necessario

necessit|ate [ni'sesiteit] *v/t* richiedere; **∼y** necessità *f*

neck [nek] collo *m*; **∼lace** ['∼lis] collana *f*; **∼tie** cravatta *f*

need [niːd] *s* bisogno *m*; *v/t*, *v/i* avere bisogno di; **he ∼ not come** non è necessario che venga

needle ['niːdl] ago *m*

negati|on [ni'geiʃən] negazione *f*; **∼ve** [ˈnegətiv] *s* negativo *m*; *a* negativo

neglect [niɡ'lekt] *s* trascuratezza *f*; *v/t* trascurare

negligible ['neɡlidʒəbl] trascurabile

negotiat|e [ni'gouʃieit] *v/t* negoziare; contrattare; **∼ion** trattative *f/pl*

negr|ess ['niːgris] negra *f*; **∼o** [ˈ∼ou], *pl* **∼oes** negro *m*

neighbo(u)r ['neibə] vicino(a) *m* (*f*); **∼hood** vicinanza *f*; **∼ing** vicino

neither ['neiðə, *Am* 'niːðə] *a*, *pron* nessuno (dei due); *conj* nè; neppure; **∼ ... nor** nè ... nè

nephew ['nevju(ː)] nipote *m*

nerv|e [nəːv] nervo *m*; **∼ous** nervoso; **∼ousness** nervosità *f*

nest [nest] nido *m*

net [net] rete *f*

Netherlands ['neðələndz] *pl* Paesi *m/pl* Bassi

nettle ['netl] ortica *f*

network ['netwəːk] rete *f*

neurosis [njuə'rousis] nevrosi *f*

neuter ['njuːtə] *a*, *s* neutro (*m*); **∼ral** *a*, *s* neutro (*m*); **∼ral gear** *aut* marcia *f* folle

never ['nevə] mai; non ... mai; **∼theless** nonostante

new [njuː] nuovo; fresco; **∼born** neonato; *s* [njuːz] *pl* notizie *f/pl*; **∼s-boy** giornalaio *m*; **∼spaper** giornale *m*; **∼sreel** attualità *f/pl*; notiziario m; ♀ **Year's Day** il primo dell'anno

next [nekst] a prossimo; ~ **door** accanto; ~ **month** il mese prossimo; ~ **time** la volta prossima

nibble ['nibl] v/t, v/i rosicchiare

nice [nais] simpatico; bello; carino

nickname ['nikneim] soprannome m

nicotine ['nikəti:n] nicotina f

niece [ni:s] nipote f

niggardly ['nigədli] taccagno

night [nait] notte f; **at ~** di notte; **last ~** stanotte; ieri sera; **tomorrow ~** domani sera; **~gown** camicia f da notte; **~ingale** rosignolo m

nip [nip] s pizzicotto m; v/t pizzicare

nipple ['nipl] capezzolo m

no [nou] adv no; non; a nessuno; **it's ~ good** non serve; ~ **matter** non importa; ~ **one** nessuno

noble ['noubl] nobile m

nobody ['noubədi] nessuno

nod [nɔd] s cenno m; v/i fare cenno

noise [nɔiz] rumore m; **~less** silenzioso; **~y** rumoroso

nominal ['nɔminl] nominale; **~te** ['~eit] v/t nominare; **~tion** nomina f

non-|alcoholic analcolico; **~descript** indefinito

none [nʌn] nessuno

non-existent inesistente

nonsense ['nɔnsəns] sciocchezze f/pl

non-|smoker non fumatori m/pl; **~stop** senza fermate

noodle ['nu:dl]: **~s** pl tagliatelle f/pl

noon [nu:n] mezzogiorno m

nor [nɔ:] né; neppure

north [nɔ:θ] s nord m; a del nord; settentrionale; adv al nord; **~erly, ~ern** del nord; **~wards** al nord; verso il nord

Norway ['nɔ:wei] Norvegia f; **~egian** [nɔ:'wi:dʒən] a, s norvegese (m, f)

nostrils ['nɔstrils] narici f/pl

not [nɔt] non; ~ **at all** per niente; ~ **yet** non ancora

notary ['noutəri] notaio m

note [nout] s nota f; biglietto m; appunto m; v/t notare; **~book** agenda f; quaderno m; **~paper** carta f da scrivere; **~worthy** notevole

nothing ['nʌθiŋ] niente; nulla; **for ~** gratis

notice ['noutis] s avviso m; attenzione f; v/t notare; avvertire; **give ~** preavvisare; dare gli otto giorni

notion ['nouʃən] nozione f; opinione f; idea f

notwithstanding [nɔtwiθ-'stændiŋ] nonostante

nougat ['nu:gɑ:] torrone m

noun [naun] nome m; sostantivo m

nourish ['nʌriʃ] v/t nutrire; **~ing** nutriente; **~ment** nutrimento m

novel ['nɔvəl] *a* nuovo; *s* romanzo *m*; **~ty** novità *f*
November [nou'vembə] novembre *m*
now [nau] ora; **~ and then** ogni tanto
nowhere ['nouweə] da nessuna parte
nucle|ar ['nju:kliə] nucleare; **~us** ['nju:kliəs] nucleo *m*
nud|e [nju:d] nudo
nuisance ['nju:sns] fastidio *m*
null [nʌl] nullo; **~ify** *v/t* annullare
numb [nʌm] intorpidito

number ['nʌmbə] *s* numero *m*; *v/t* numerare
numer|al ['nju:mərəl] *s* numero *m*; *a* numerale; **~ous** numeroso
nun [nʌn] monaca *f*; **~nery** convento *m* (di monache)
nurs|e [nə:s] *s* infermiera *f*; bambinaia *f*; **~ing** cura *f*; **~ery** stanza *f* dei bambini; **~ery school** giardino *m* d'infanzia
nut [nʌt] noce *f*; *mech* dado *m*; **~crackers** schiaccianoci *m*

O

oak [ouk] quercia *f*
oar [ɔ:] *s* remo *m*; *v/t* remare
oat [out]: **~s** *pl* avena *f*
oath [ouθ] giuramento *m*; bestemmia *f*
oatmeal giocchi *m/pl* d'avena
obdurate ['ɔbdjurit] ostinato
obedien|ce [ə'bi:djəns] ubbidienza *f*; **~t** ubbidiente
obey [ə'bei] *v/t* ubbidire
obituary [ə'bitjuəri] necrologia *f*
object ['ɔbdʒikt] oggetto *m*; *gram* complimento *m*; *v/t* obiettare; *v/i* opporsi; **~ion** obiezione *f*; **~ive** *a, s* obiettivo (*m*)
obligat|ion [ɔbli'geiʃən] obbligo *m*; **~ory** [ə'bligətəri] obbligatorio
oblige [ə'blaidʒ] *v/t* obbli-

gare; costringere
oblique [ə'bli:k] obliquo
obliterate [ə'blitəreit] *v/t* cancellare; spegnere
oblivious [ə'bliviəs] dimentico
oblong ['ɔblɔŋ] oblungo
obnoxious [ɔb'nɔkʃəs] odioso
obscene [ɔb'si:n] osceno
obscure [ɔb'skjuə] *a* oscuro; *v/t* oscurare
observan|ce [ab'zɔ:vəns] osservanza *f*; **~t** osservante
observ|ation [ɔbzə(:)- 'veiʃən] osservazione *f*; **~atory** osservatorio *m*; **~e** *v/t* osservare; **~er** osservatore *m*
obsess [əb'ses] *v/t* ossessionare; **~ion** ossessione *f*
obsolete ['ɔbsəli:t] caduto in disuso

obstacle [ˈɔbstəkl] ostacolo m

obstetric|ian [ˌɔbsteˈtriʃən] ostetrico m; **~s** pl ostetricia f

obstina|cy [ˈɔbstinəsi] ostinazione f; **~te** ostinato

obstruct [əbˈstrʌkt] v/t ostacolare

obtain [əbˈtein] v/t ottenere

obvious [ˈɔbviəs] ovvio

occasion [əˈkeiʒən] occasione f; **~al** raro; **~ally** di quando in quando

Occident [ˈɔksidənt] occidente m

occult [ɔˈkʌlt] occulto

occupant [ˈɔkjupənt] inquilino m; occupante m

occupa|tion [ˌɔkjuˈpeiʃən] occupazione f; impiego m; **~y** [ˈ~pai] v/t occupare

occur [əˈkəː] v/i accadere; **~rence** [əˈkʌrəns] avvenimento m

ocean [ˈouʃən] oceano m; **~ liner** transatlantico m

o'clock [əˈklɔk]: **it is two ~** sono le due

October [ɔkˈtoubə] ottobre m

ocul|ar [ˈɔkjulə] oculare; **~ist** oculista m, f

odd [ɔd] strano; dispari; strano; **thirty ~** trenta e tanto; **~s and ends** pl oggetti m/pl disparati

odo(u)r [ˈoudə] odore m

of [ɔv, əv] prp di, a, da, per; **~ silk** di seta; **a friend ~ mine** un mio amico; **~ late** ultimamente; **~ course** naturalmente

off [ɔf] prp via da; lontano da; adv via; lontano; **take ~** v/t togliere; v/i decollare (dell'aeroplano)

offen|ce, Am **~se** [əˈfens] offesa f; reato m; **~d** v/t offendere; v/i trasgredire; **~sive** s offensiva f; a offensivo

offer [ˈɔfə] s offerta f; proposta f; v/t offrire; v/i offrirsi; **~ing** offerta f

office [ˈɔfis] ufficio m; **~r** ufficiale m

official [əˈfiʃəl] a ufficiale; s funzionario m

offspring [ˈɔ(ː)fspriŋ] progenie f

often [ˈɔfn] spesso

oil [ɔil] s olio m; petrolio m; v/t ungere; **~cloth** tela f cerata; **~painting** pittura a olio; **~y** oleoso; untuoso

ointment [ˈɔintmənt] unguento m; pomata f

okay [ouˈkei] okay; va bene

old [ould] vecchio; anziano; antico; **~ age** vecchiaia f; **~fashioned** passato di moda; all'antica; **2 Testament** Antico Testamento m; **~ town** città f vecchia

olive [ˈɔliv] oliva f

Olympic games [ouˈlimpik] pl olimpiadi f/pl

omelet(te) [ˈɔmlit] frittata f

omen [ˈoumen] augurio m; presagio m

ominous [ˈɔminəs] minaccioso

omi|ssion [əˈmiʃən] omissione f; **~t** v/t omettere

omnipotent [ɔmˈnipətənt]

onnipotente

on [ɔn] *prp* su; sopra; ~ **account** of a causa di; ~ **Monday** il lunedì; ~ **foot** a piedi; ~ **horseback** a cavallo; ~ **purpose** apposta; *adv* avanti; addosso; **go** ~! avanti!; **come** ~! andiamo!; **and so** ~ e così via

once [wʌns] una volta; **at** ~ subito; ~ **more** ancora una volta

one [wʌn] *a* un, uno(a); unico; *pron* uno m; una f; un tale m; ~ **hundred** cento; **it is** ~ è l'una; ~ **by** ~ uno a uno; ~ **self** sè; sè stesso ~ **sided** unilaterale; ~ **way** (*street*) a senso unico

onion ['ʌnjən] cipolla f

only ['ounli] *a* unico; solo; solamente; *conj* solo che

onward ['ɔnwəd] avanti; ~ **s** in avanti

open ['oupən] *a* aperto; libero; *v/t* aprire; *v/i* aprirsi; ~ **ing** apertura f; inaugurazione f

opera ['ɔpərə] opera f; ~ **glasses** *pl* binocolo m da teatro

operate ['ɔpəreit] *v/t* operare; ~ **ion** [ˌɔpə'reiʃən] operazione f; ~ **or** ['ɔpəreitə] operatore m

opinion [ə'pinjən] opinione f

opponent [ə'pounənt] antagonista m; avversario m

opportun|e ['ɔpətjuːn] opportuno; ~ **ity** [ˌɔpə'tjuːniti]

occasione f

oppos|e [ə'pouz] *v/t* opporre; opporsi a; ~ **ed** contrario; opporsi a; ~ **ing** contrario; opposto; ~ **ite** ['ɔpəzit] *s* opposto m; *a* contrario; opposto; *prp* di fronte; ~ **ition** [ɔpə'ziʃən] opposizione f

oppress [ə'pres] *v/t* opprimere; ~ **ion** oppressione f; ~ **ive** oppressivo

optic|al ['ɔptikəl] ottico; ~ **ian** [ɔp'tiʃən] ottico m; ~ **s** *pl* ottica f

optional ['ɔpʃənl] facoltativo

opulent ['ɔpjulənt] opulento

opus ['ɔpəs, 'oupəs] opera f

or [ɔː] o; oppure

oral ['ɔːrəl] orale

orange ['ɔrindʒ] arancia f; ~ **ade** [ˌ'eid] aranciata f

orator ['ɔrətə] oratore m

orchard ['ɔːtʃəd] frutteto m

orchestra ['ɔːkistrə] orchestra f

orchid ['ɔːkid] orchidea f

ordain [ɔː'dein] *v/t* ordinare

ordeal [ɔː'diːl] prova f dura

order ['ɔːdə] *s* ordine m; **put in** ~ mettere in ordine; **out of** ~ guasto; **in** ~ **to** per (*e infinito*); **in** ~ **that** affinchè; *v/t* ordinare; ~ **ly** ordinato

ordinary ['ɔːdnri] comune; solito

ore [ɔː] minerale m

organ ['ɔːgən] organo m

organic [ɔː'gænik] organico; ~ **sm** ['ɔːgənizm] organismo m

organiz|**ation** [ˌɔːgənai'zei-

[ən] organizzazione f; **~e** [ˈ~aiz] v/t organizzare

orgy [ˈɔːdʒi] orgia f

Orient [ˈɔːriənt] Oriente m; **~al** orientale

orientation [ˌɔːrienˈteiʃən] orientazione f

origin [ˈɔridʒin] origine m; **~al** [əˈridʒənl] s, a originale (m); **~ality** [əridʒiˈnæliti] originalità f; **~ate** [əˈridʒineit] v/i avere origine

orna|ment [ˈɔːnəmənt] s ornamento m; v/t adornare; **~te** [ɔːˈneit] ornato

orphan [ˈɔːfən] orfano(a) m (f); **~age** orfanotrofio m

oscillate [ˈɔsileit] v/i oscillare

ostrich [ˈɔstritʃ] struzzo m

other [ˈʌðə] a, pron altro, altra, altri, altre; **the ~ day** recentemente; **~wise** [ˈ~waiz] altrimenti

ought [ɔːt] v/d: **I ~** dovrei; **he ~ to write** dovrebbe scrivere

ounce [auns] oncia f

our [ˈauə] a nostro(a, i, e); **~s** il nostro, la nostra, i nostri, le nostre; **~selves** noi stessi

oust [aust] v/t soppiantare

out [aut] adv fuori; prp fuori di; **go ~** uscire; **way ~** uscita f; **~ of danger** fuori pericolo; **~burst** esplosione f; **~come** risultato m; **~doors** all'aperto; **~fit** corredo m; equipaggiamento m; **~law** fuorilegge m; **~lay** spesa f; **~let** uscita f; **~live** v/t sopravvivere a;

~look prospettiva f; **~put** produzione f; **~rage** s oltraggio m; v/t oltraggiare; **~rageous** scandaloso; **~side** a, s esterno (m); adv fuori; prp fuori di; **~skirts** pl periferia f; **~spoken** franco; sincero; **~standing** preminente; comm in sospeso; **~ward** esterno; esterno; **~wit** v/t superare (in furberia)

oval [ˈouvəl] a, s ovale (m)

oven [ˈʌvn] forno m

over [ˈouvə] prp sopra; **~ again** di nuovo; **~ and ~** ripetutamente

over|all [ˈouvərɔːl] grembiule m; tuta f; **~board** in mare; **~burden** v/t sovraccaricare; **~coat** cappotto m; **~come** v/t, irr superare; vincere; **~do** v/t esagerare; **~due** scaduto; **~flow** v/t inondare; v/i straripare; **~head costs** pl spese f/pl generali; **~hear** v/t, irr udire per caso; **~joyed** contentissimo; **~load** v/t sovraccaricare; **~look** v/t dominare; passare sopra; **~night** durante la notte; **~seas** d'oltremare; **~sight** svista f; **~state** v/t esagerare; **~strain** tensione f eccessiva; **~take** v/t, irr raggiungere; sorpassare; **~throw** v/t rovesciare; **~time** straordinario m

overture [ˈouvətjuə] preludio m

over|turn v/t capovolgere;

~weight peso *m* eccessivo;
~whelm *v/t* sopraffare;
~work *v/i* lavorare troppo
owe [ou] *v/t* dovere
owing ['ouin] **to** dovuto a
owl [aul] civetta *f*; gufo *m*
own [oun] *v/t* possedere; *a.*
proprio; **~er** proprietario *m*
ox [ɔks], *pl* **~en** ['ɔ·ən]
bue *m*
ox|ide ['ɔksaid] ossido *m*;
~ygen ['ɔksidʒən] ossigeno
m
oyster ['ɔistə] ostrica *f*

P

pace [peis] passo *m*
pacif|ic [pə'sifik] pacifico;
~ist pacifista *m*, *f*; **~y**
['pæsifai] *v/t* pacificare
pack [pæk] *s*, balla *f*; sacco *m*
(*di bugie*); banda *f* (*di ladri*);
mazzo *m* (*di carte*); *v/t* im-
ballare; *v/i* fare le valigie
pack|age ['pækidʒ] collo *m*;
balla *f*; **~et** pacchetto *m*
pact [pækt] patto *m*
pad [pæd] tampone *m*; cuscinetto *m*; **~ding** imbottitura *f*; **~lock** lucchetto *m*
pagan ['peigən] *a*, *s* pagano
(*m*)
page [peidʒ] *s* pagina *f*; *v/t*
impaginare
pageant ['pædʒənt] corteo *m*
(*storico*)
pain [pein] *s* dolore *m*; pena
f; *v/t* affliggere; soffrire;
~ful doloroso; **~less** indo-
lore
paint [peint] *s* pittura *f*;
dipingere; *v/t* dipingersi;
~er pittore *m*; **~ing** pittura
f; quadro *m*
pair [pɛə] *s* paio *m*; **~ of**
scissors forbici *f/pl*; **~ of**
scales bilancia *f*; **~ of**
glasses occhiali *m/pl*; **~ of**

trousers pantaloni *m/pl*; **~**
of shoes paio *m* di scarpe;
v/t accoppiare
palace ['pælis] palazzo *m*;
reggia *f*
palate ['pælit] palato *m*
pale [peil] pallido; **grow ~**
impallidire
palm [pɑːm] palmo *m* (*della
mano*); palma *f*
palpitat|e ['pælpiteit] *v/i*
palpitare; **~ion** palpitazione
f
paltry ['pɔːltri] meschino
pamphlet ['pæmflit] opuscolo *m*
pan [pæn] tegame *m*; padella
f; **~cake** frittella *f*
pane [pein] vetro *m*
panel ['pænl] pannello *m*
pang [pæŋ] dolore *m* acuto
panic ['pænik] *s* panico *m*;
v/t perdere la testa
pant [pænt] *v/i* affannare
panther ['pænθə] pantera *f*
panties ['pæntiz] *pl fam* mutandine *f/pl*
pantry ['pæntri] dispensa *f*
pants [pænts] *pl* calzoni
m/pl; mutande *f/pl*
papa [pə'pɑː] papà *m*
paper ['peipə] carta *f*; gior-

nale m; **~back** libro m tascabile; **~ money** carta f moneta

par [pɑ:] pari f; **be on a ~ with** essere alla pari di

parachute [ˈpærəʃuːt] paracadute m; **~ist** paracadutista m

parade [pəˈreid] s sfilata f; v/i sfilare

paradise [ˈpærədais] paradiso m

paradox [ˈpærədɔks] paradosso m

paragraph [ˈpærəgrɑːf] paragrafo m

parallel [ˈpærəlel] a, s parallelo (m)

paraly|se, Am **~ze** [ˈpærəlaiz] v/t paralizzare; **~sis** [pəˈrælisis] paralisi f

paramount [ˈpærəmaunt] supremo

parasite [ˈpærəsait] parassita m

parasol [ˌpærəˈsɔl] parasole m

parcel [ˈpɑːsl] s pacco m; v/t fare un pacco

parch [pɑːtʃ] v/t inaridire; **~ment** pergamena f

pardon [ˈpɑːdn] s perdono m; v/t perdonare; **I beg your ~** scusi; **~able** perdonabile

pare [peə] v/t sbucciare

parent [ˈpeərənt] padre m; madre f; **~s** pl genitori m/pl

parenthe|sis [pəˈrenθisis], pl **~ses** [~siːz] parentesi f

parish [ˈpærif] parrocchia f; **~ priest** parroco m

park [pɑːk] s parco m; v/t parcheggiare; **~ing** parcheggio m

parliament [ˈpɑːləmənt] parlamento m; **Member of ~** Brit deputato m

parlo(u)r [ˈpɑːlə] salotto m

parrot [ˈpærət] pappagallo m

parsley [ˈpɑːsli] prezzemolo m

parsimony [ˈpɑːsiməni] parsimonia f

parson [ˈpɑːsn] parroco m (anglicano)

part [pɑːt] s parte f; **take ~** partecipare; v/t separare; v/i separarsi; **~ with** disfarsi di

partake [pɑːˈteik] v/i partecipare

partial [ˈpɑːʃəl] parziale; **~ity** [~ʃiˈæliti] parzialità f

participate [pɑːˈtisipeit] v/i partecipare

particular [pəˈtikjulə] a particolare; speciale; s particolare m; (**personal**) **~s** pl particolari m/pl

parting [ˈpɑːtiŋ] (hair) riga f

partisan [ˌpɑːtiˈzæn] a, s partigiano (m)

partition [pɑːˈtiʃən] divisione f; parete f divisoria

partly [ˈpɑːtli] in parte

partner [ˈpɑːtnə] socio(a) m (f); **~ship** società f

partridge [ˈpɑːtridʒ] pernice f

party [ˈpɑːti] partito m; festa f; ricevimento m

pass [pɑːs] s passo m; passaggio *m*; *v/t* passare; approvare (*una legge*); **~age** ['pæsidʒ] passaggio *m*; corridoio *m*; brano *m*; **~enger** ['pæsindʒə] passeggero *m*; **~er-by** ['pɑːsə'bai] passante *m*

passion ['pæʃən] passione *f*; **~ate** appassionato

passive ['pæsiv] passivo

pass|port ['pɑːspɔːt] passaporto *m*; **~word** parola *f* d'ordine

past [pɑːst] *a*, *s* passato *m*; *prp* oltre; dopo; *adv* oltre; **half ~ six** le sei e mezzo; **~ hope** senza speranza

paste [peist] pasta *f*; colla *f*; *v/t* incollare; **~board** cartone *m*

pastime ['pɑːstaim] passatempo *m*

pastry ['peistri] pasta *f* frolla; pasticceria *f*

pasture ['pɑːstʃə] *s* pascolo *m*; *v/i* pascolare

pat [pæt] *s* colpetto *m*; *v/t* dare colpetti (*con la mano*)

patch [pætʃ] *s* toppa *f*; *v/t* rattoppare; **~work** raffazzonamento *m*

patent ['peitənt, *Am* 'pætənt] *a* brevettato; *s* brevetto *m*; *v/t* far brevettare; **~ leather** pelle *f* lucida

patern|al [pə'təːnl] paterno; **~ity** paternità *f*

path [pɑːθ], *pl* **~s** [pɑːðz] sentiero *m*

pathetic [pə'θetik] patetico; commovente

patien|ce ['peiʃəns] pazienza

f; **~t a** paziente; *s* ammalato *m*

patriot ['peitriət] *a*, *s* patriota (*m*, *f*)

patrol [pə'troul] *s* pattuglia *f*; *v/t* pattugliare

patron ['peitrən] *s* patrono *m*; **~age** ['pætrənidʒ] patronato *m*; **~ize** ['pætrənaiz] *v/t* frequentare; *comm* favorire

pattern ['pætən] modello *m*; campione *m*

paunch [pɔːntʃ] pancia *f*

pauper ['pɔːpə] povero *m*

pause [pɔːz] *s* pausa *f*; *v/i* fermarsi

pave [peiv] *v/t* pavimentare; **~ment** marciapiede *m*

pavilion [pə'viljən] padiglione *m*

paw [pɔː] zampa *f*

pawn [pɔːn] *s* pegno *m*; *v/t* impegnare; **~shop** monte *m* di pietà

pay [pei] *s* paga *f*; *v/t* pagare; **~ back** rimborsare; **~ cash** pagare in contanti; **~ in advance** pagare in anticipo; **~ a visit** fare una visita; **~able** pagabile; **~ment** pagamento *m*

pea [piː] pisello *m*

peace [piːs] pace *f*; **~ful** pacifico

peach [piːtʃ] pesca *f*

peacock ['piːkɔk] pavone *m*

peak [piːk] cima *f*; culmine *m*

peal [piːl] *s* scampanio *m*; *v/i* scampanare; risuonare

peanut ['piːnʌt] arachide *f*

pear [pɛə] pera *f*

pearl [pə:l] perla *f*

peasant ['pezənt] contadino *m*

pebble ['pebl] sassolino *m*

peck [pek] *v/t* beccare

peculiar [pi'kju:ljə] strano; **~ity** [~li'æriti] peculiarità *f*

pedal ['pedl] *s* pedale *m*; *v/t* pedalare

pedant ['pedənt] pedante *m*

peddler ['pedlə] *cf* pedlar

pedestrian [pi'destriən] pedone *m*; **~ crossing** passaggio *m* pedonale

pedigree ['pedigri:] albero *m* genealogico

pedlar ['pedlə] venditore *m* ambulante

peel [pi:l] *v/t* sbucciare; *s* buccia *f*

peep [pi:p] *v/i* far capolino

peer [piə] *s* pari *m*; *v/t* guardare da presso

peevish ['pi:viʃ] nervoso; innervosito

peg [peg] piuolo *m*

pelican ['pelikən] pelicano *m*

pelvis ['pelvis] *anat* pelvi *f*

pen [pen] penna *f*

penalty ['penlti] pena *f*

penance ['penəns] penitenza *f*

pence [pens] *pl of* **penny**

pencil ['pensil] matita *f*; **~-sharpener** temperalapis *m*

pendant ['pendənt] *s*, *a* pendente (*m*); **~ing** *a* pendente; sospeso; *prp* durante

pendulum ['pendjuləm] pendolo *m*

penetrate ['penitreit] *v/t* penetrare

penguin ['peŋgwin] pinguino *m*

penicillin [ˌpeni'silin] penicillina *f*

peninsula [pi'ninsjulə] penisola *f*

penitent ['penitənt] penitente

penknife ['penaif] temperino *m*

penniless ['penilis] senza soldi

penny ['peni], *pl* **pence** [pens] soldo *m*

pension ['penʃən] *s* pensione *f*; *v/t* pensionare; **~er** pensionato *m*

pensive ['pensiv] pensoso

penthouse ['penthaus] appartamento *m* in soffitta

people ['pi:pl] popolo *m*; gente *f*

pepper ['pepə] pepe *m*; **~mint** menta *f*

per [pə:] per

perambulator ['præmbjuleitə] carrozzina *f* (*per bambini*)

perceive [pə'si:v] *v/t* accorgersi di

percent, **~age** [pə'sent] percentuale *f*

per|ception percezione *f*

perch [pə:tʃ] *v/i* appollaiarsi; posarsi

percussion [pə'kʌʃən] percussione *f*

peremptory [pə'remptəri] perentorio

perfect ['pə:fikt] *a* perfetto; *s gram* passato *m* prossimo; *v/t* perfezionare; **~ion** perfezione f

perforation [ˌpəːfəˈreiʃən] perforazione f

perform [pəˈfɔːm] v/t eseguire; *thea* rappresentare; **~ance** esecuzione f; rappresentazione f

perfume [ˈpəːfjuːm] s profumo m; v/t profumare

perhaps [pəˈhæps, præps] forse

peril [ˈperil] pericolo m; **~ous** pericoloso

period [ˈpiəriəd] periodo m; punto m

perish [ˈperiʃ] v/i perire; **~able** deperibile

perm, ~anent [pəːm] permanente; **~anent wave** permanente f

permi|ssion [pəˈmiʃən] permesso m, **~t** v/t permettere; s permesso m

perpetual [pəˈpetʃuəl] perpetuo

perplex [pəˈpleks] v/t rendere perplesso

persecu|te [ˈpəːsikjuːt] v/t perseguitare; **~ion** persecuzione f; **~or** persecutore m

persevere [ˌpəːsiˈviə] v/i perseverare

Persian [ˈpəːʃən] a, s persiano (m)

persist [pəˈsist] v/i persistere; **~ence** persistenza f; **~ent** persistente

person [ˈpəːsn] persona f; **~age** personaggio m; **~al** personale; **~ality** [ˌpəːsəˈnæliti] personalità f; **~ify** [ˌsəˈ-

nifai] v/t personificare; **~nel** [ˌsəˈnel] personale m

perspective [pəˈspektiv] prospettiva f

perspir|ation [ˌpəːspəˈreiʃən] traspirazione f; sudore m; **~e** [pəsˈpaiə] v/i traspirare; sudare

persua|de [pəˈsweid] v/t persuadere; **~sion** [ˌsˈʒən] persuasione f; **~sive** persuasivo

perturb [pəˈtəːb] v/t perturbare

perus|al [pəˈruːzəl] lettura f; **~e** v/t leggere attentamente

pervade [pəːˈveid] v/t permeare

perver|se [pəˈvəːs] perverso; ostinato; **~sion** perversione f; corruzione f

pessimis|m [ˈpesimizəm] pessimismo m; **~t** pessimista m, f

pest [pest] peste f; **~er** v/t infastidire; tormentare

pet [pet] animale m domestico; beniamino m

petal [ˈpetl] petalo m

petition [piˈtiʃən] petizione f

petrify [ˈpetrifai] v/t petrificare

petrol [ˈpetrəl] benzina f; **~ station** posto m di rifornimento

petticoat [ˈpetikout] sottoveste f

petty [ˈpeti] meschino; insignificante

pew [pjuː] banco m di chiesa

pharmac|ist [ˈfaːməsist] farmacista m (laureato in

farmacia); **~y** farmacia f (facoltà)

pheasant ['feznt] fagiano m

phenomenal [fi'nɔminl] fe-
nomenale

philolog|ist [fi'lɔlədʒist] fi-
lologista m; **~y** filologia f

philosoph|er [fi'lɔsəfə] filo-
sofo m; **~ic, ~ical** filosofico;
~y filosofia f

phone [foun] fam for
telephone

photo ['foutou] fam for
~graph ['~təgra:f] fotografia f; **take ~s** fare foto-
grafie

photograph|er [fə'tɔgrəfə]
fotografo m; **~y** fotografia f

phrase [freiz] frase f

physic|al ['fizikl] fisico;
~ian [fi'ziʃən] medico m;
~ist ['~sis] fisico m; **~s** sg
fisica f

physique [fi'zi:k] fisico m

pian|ist ['piænist, 'piənist]
pianista m, f; **~o** ['pjænou,
'pja:nou] pianoforte m

pick [pik] s piccone m; scelta
f; v/t scegliere; cogliere; **~
up** raccogliere

picket ['pikit] picchetto m

pickle ['pikl]: **~s** pl sottaceti
m/pl; v/t mettere sotto
aceto

pickpocket borsaiuolo m

picnic ['piknik] merenda f
(in campagna)

picture ['piktʃə] quadro m;
~gallery pinacoteca f; **~
postcard** cartolina f illu-
strata; **~sque** [~'resk] pitto-
resco

pie [pai] torta f; pasticcio m

piece [pi:s] pezzo m; **~ of
advice** consiglio m; **~ of
furniture** mobile m

pier [piə] molo m; pilone m

pierce [piəs] v/t forare; penetrare

piety ['paiəti] pietà f

pig [pig] maiale m; porco m

pigeon ['pidʒin] piccione m;
~hole casella f

pig|sty porcile m; **~tail** trec-
cia f

pike [paik] luccio m

pile [pail] s mucchio m; v/t
ammucchiare; **~ up** am-
mucchiarsi

pilgrim ['pilgrim] pellegri-
no m; **~age** pellegrinaggio m

pill [pil] pillola f

pillar ['pilə] pilastro m; colonna f; fig sostegno m

pillow ['pilou] cuscino m

pilot ['pailət] s pilota m; v/t
pilotare

pimple ['pimpl] foruncolo
m

pin [pin] s spillo m; v/t attaccare con lo spillo

pincers ['pinsəz] pl pinze
f/pl; tenaglie f/pl

pinch [pintʃ] s pizzico m; v/t
pizzicare

pine [pain] s pino m; v/i
struggersi; **~apple** ananas
m

pink [piŋk] a rosa

pinnacle ['pinəkl] pinnacolo
m; fig culmine m

pint [paint] pinta f

pioneer [paiə'niə] pioniere
m

pliers

pious ['paɪəs] pio

pipe [paɪp] tubo m; canna f (dell'organo); pipa f (per fumare)

pirate ['paɪərit] pirata m

pistol ['pistl] pistola f

piston ['pistən] mech pistone m; stantuffo m

pit [pit] pozzo m; thea platea f

pitch [pitʃ] s pece f; grado m; tono m; v/t lanciare; ~ **dark** buio pesto

piteous ['pitiəs] pietoso

pitfall trappola f

piti|ful ['pitiful] pietoso; **~less** spietato

pity ['piti] s pietà f; v/t compatire; **what a** ~ che peccato!

pivot ['pivət] s pernio m; v/i girare su pernio

placard ['plækɑːd] manifesto m; affisso m

place [pleis] s posto m; luogo m; **in** ~ **of** al posto di; **take** ~ avere luogo; v/t mettere

placid ['plæsid] placido

plague [pleig] s peste f; pestilenza f; v/t tormentare

plain [plein] a piatto; chiaro; semplice; s pianura f

plaint|iff ['pleintif] querelante m; **~ive** lamentoso

plait [plæt, Am pleit] treccia f (di capelli)

plan [plæn] s progetto m; v/t progettare

plane [plein] s piano a; s platano m; aeroplano m

planet ['plænit] pianeta m

plank [plæŋk] asse f; tavola f

plant [plɑːnt] s pianta f; impianto m; v/t piantare; **~ation** [plænˈteiʃən] piantagione f

plaque [plɑːk] placca f

plaster ['plɑːstə] s gesso m; cerotto m; intonaco m; v/t intonacare

plastic ['plæstik] plastico; **~s** pl plastica f

plate [pleit] s piatto m; targa f; tavola f; dentiera f

platform ['plætfɔːm] piattaforma f

platinum ['plætinəm] platino m

play [plei] s giuoco m; thea commedia f; v/t giuocare; thea rappresentare; (instrument) suonare; **~er** (game) giocatore m; (instrument) sonatore m; **~ful** scherzoso; **~ground** campo m per ricreazione; **~mate** compagno m di giochi; **~wright** drammaturgo m

plead [pliːd] v/t difendere (una causa); addurre; v/i supplicare

pleas|ant ['pleznt] piacevole; simpatico; **~e** [pliːz] v/t piacere a; **~ed** contento; **~ure** ['pleʒə] piacere m

pleat [pliːt] s piega f; v/t piegare

pledge [pledʒ] s pegno m; v/t impegnare

plent|iful ['plentiful] abbondante; **~y** abbondanza f

pliable ['plaiəbl] flessibile

pliers ['plaiəz] pl pinzette f/pl

plight [plait] difficoltà f

plot [plɔt] s cospirazione f; trama f (di commedia, libro); pezzo m (di terreno); v/t cospirare

plough, *Am* **plow** [plau] s aratro m; v/t arare

pluck [plʌk] s coraggio m; v/t cogliere; spenare (un pollo)

plug [plʌg] s tappo m; spina f; presa f; v/t tappare

plum [plʌm] susina f; prugna f

plumage ['plu:midʒ] piumaggio m

plump [plʌmp] grassoccio

plunder ['plʌndə] s bottino m; v/t saccheggiare

plunge [plʌndʒ] s tuffo m; immersione f; v/t tuffare; immergere

plural ['pluərəl] a, s plurale (m)

plus [plʌs] più

ply [plai] s piega f; v/t assalire; v/i andare e venire

pneumonia [nju(:)'mounjə] polmonite f

poach [poutʃ] v/t cuocere in camicia (di uova); cacciare di frodo; **~er** cacciatore m di frodo

pocket ['pɔkit] s tasca f; v/t intascare; **~book** portafoglio m

poem ['pouim] poesia f

poet ['pouit] poeta m; **~ry** ['~itri] poesia f

poignant ['pɔinənt] commuovente

point [pɔint] punto m; punta f; **on the ~ of** sul punto di;

come to the ~ venire al sodo; **see the ~** capire; **~ed** appuntato; **~less** inutile; **~ out** far notare

poise [pɔiz] s equilibrio m; v/t equilibrare

poison ['pɔizn] s veleno m; v/t avvelenare; **~ous** velenoso

poke [pouk] v/t attizzare (il fuoco); dare colpi

Poland ['poulənd] Polonia f

polar ['poulə] polare; **~ bear** orso m bianco

Pole [poul] polacco(a) m (f)

pole [poul] palo m; *elec* polo m

polemic [pɔ'lemik] polemico

police [pə'li:s] polizia f; **~man** poliziotto m; guardia f; vigile m urbano; **~ station** commissariato m

policy ['pɔlisi] politica f; polizza f (di assicurazioni)

polio ['pouliou], **~myelitis** ['pouliou,maiə'laitis] poliomielite f

Polish ['pouliʃ] polacco

polish ['pɔliʃ] v/t lucidare; verniciare; s lucido m; vernice f

polite [pə'lait] cortese; **~ness** cortesia f

political [pə'litikəl] politico; **~ian** [pɔli'tiʃən] politico m; **~s** ['pɔlitiks] pl politica f

poll [poul] lista f elettorale; elezione f; scrutinio m

pollut|e [pə'lu:t] v/t contaminare; **~ion** contaminazione f

pomp [pomp] pompa *f*; **~ous** pomposo

pond [pond] laghetto *m*

ponder ['pondə] *v/t* meditare; **~ous** ponderoso

pontiff ['pontif] pontefice *m*

pony ['pouni] cavallino *m*

poodle ['pu:dl] barboncino *m*

pool [pu:l] laghetto *m*

poor [puə] povero

pop [pop] scoppio *m*

pope [poup] papa *m*

poplar ['poplə] pioppo *m*

poppy ['popi] papavero *m*

popular ['popjulə] popolare; **~arity** [~'læriti] popolarità *f*; **~ate** ['~eit] *v/t* popolare; **~ation** popolazione *f*

porcelain ['po:slin, -lein] porcellana *f*

porch [po:tʃ] portico *m*; veranda *f*

pore [po:] poro *m*

pork [po:k] carne *f* di maiale

pornography [po:'nogrəfi] pornografia *f*

porridge ['porid3] papa *f* d'avena

port [po:t] porto *m*

portable ['po:təbl] portatile *m*

porter ['po:tə] facchino *m*; portiere *m*

portfolio [po:t'fouljou] cartella *f*; portafoglio *m* (*ministeriale*)

porthole [pothoul] oblò *m*

portion ['po:ʃən] porzione *f*

portly ['po:tli] corpulento

Portugal ['po:tjugəl] il Portogallo

portrait ['po:trit] ritratto *m*

Portuguese [,po:tju'gi:z] *a*, *s* portoghese (*m*, *f*)

pose [pouz] *s* posa *f*; *v/t* porre; *v/i* posare

position [pə'ziʃən] posizione *f*

positive ['pozətiv] *a*, *s* positivo (*m*)

possess [pə'zes] *v/t* possedere; **~ion** possesso *m*

possibility [posə'biliti] possibilità *f*; **~le** ['posəbl] possibile; **~ly** possibilmente

post [poust] *s* posto *m*; posta *f*; palo *m*; *v/t* imbucare; mandare; spedire; **~age** affrancatura *f*; **~age stamp** francobollo *m*; **~card** cartolina *f* postale; **~er** manifesto *m*

poste restante ['poust're-stã:nt] fermo posta

postpone [poust'poun] *v/t* rimandare

posture ['postʃə] atteggiamento *m*

pot [pot] pentola *f*

potato [pə'teitou], *pl* **~es** patata *f*

potent ['poutənt] potente

pottery ['potəri] stoviglie *f/pl*

pouch [pautʃ] borsa *f*

poultice ['poultis] cataplasma *m*

poultry ['poultri] pollame *m*

pounce [pauns] *v/t* chiappare

pound [paund] *s* libbra *f*; **~ sterling** sterlina *f*; *v/t* pestare

pour [pɔ:] v/t versare; v/i riversarsi

poverty ['pɔvəti] povertà f

powder ['paudə] polvere f

power ['pauə] potere m; potenza f; **~ful** potente; **~less** impotente; **~plant, ~station** centrale f elettrica

practicable ['præktikəbl] praticabile; **~ce** [~tis] pratica f; esercizio m; **~se** v/t esercitare; praticare; v/i esercitarsi

prairie ['prɛəri] prateria f

praise [preiz] s lode f; v/t lodare

pram [præm] fam carrozzina f

prank [præŋk] burla f

pray [prei] v/t pregare; **~er** [prɛə] preghiera f

preach [pri:tʃ] v/t, v/i predicare; **~er** predicatore m

precede [pri(:)'si:d] v/t precedere; **~ent** ['presidənt] precedente m

precept ['pri:sept] precetto m

precious ['preʃəs] prezioso

precipice ['presipis] precipizio m; **~tate** [pri'sipiteit] v/t, v/i precipitare; **~tation** [~'teiʃən] precipitazione f; **~tous** precipitoso

precise [pri'sais] preciso; **~on** [~'siʒən] precisione f

precocious [pri'kouʃəs] precoc...

predecessor ['pri:disesə] predecessore m

predicament [pri'dikəmənt] difficoltà f

predict [pri'dikt] v/t predire

predisposition ['pri:dispə'ziʃən] predisposizione f

predominant [pri'dominənt] predominante; **~te** v/i predominare

preface ['prefis] prefazione f; eccl prefazio m

prefect ['pri:fekt] prefetto m

prefer [pri'fə:] v/t preferire; **~able** ['prefərəbl] preferibile; **~ence** ['prefərəns] preferenza f

prefix ['pri:fiks] prefisso m

pregnancy ['pregnənsi] gravidanza f; **~t** incinta

prejudice ['predʒudis] s pregiudizio m; v/t pregiudicare

preliminary [pri'liminəri] preliminare

premeditate [pri(:)'mediteit] v/t, v/i premeditare

premier ['premjə] primo ministro m

premise ['premis] premessa f; **~s** pl locale m

premium ['pri:mjəm] premio m

preoccupation [pri(:)ɔkju'peiʃən] preoccupazione f; **~y** [~'ɔkjupai] v/t preoccupare

preparation [prepə'reiʃən] preparazione f; preparativo m; preparato m; **~e** [pri'pɛə] v/t preparare

preposition [prepə'ziʃən] preposizione f

preposterous [pri'pɔstərəs] assurdo

Presbyterian [ˌprezbiˈtiə-
riən] a, s. presbiteriano (m)
prescri|be [prisˈkraib] v/t
prescrivere; ordinare;
~ption [ˌˈkripʃən] ricetta f
medica
presence [ˈprezns] presenza
f
present[1] [ˈpreznt] s regalo
m; presente m; a presente;
attuale; **at ~** attualmente;
be ~ at assistere a
present[2] [priˈzent] v/t pre-
sentare; regalare
present|ation [prezenˈtei-
ʃən] presentazione f; **~ly**
[ˈprezntli] tra un poco
preserv|ation [prezə(ː)ˈvei-
ʃən] conservazione f; **~e**
[priˈzəːv] v/t conservare;
preservare; **~es** pl conserve
f/pl
preside [priˈzaid] v/t presie-
dere; **~ncy** [ˈprezidənsi]
presidenza f; **~nt** presidente m
press [pres] s stampa f; v/t
premere; comprimere; in-
sistere; **~ure** [ˈˌʃə] pressione f
prestige [presˈtiːʒ] prestigio
m
presume [priˈzjuːm] v/t
presumere
presumpt|ion [priˈzʌmp-
ʃən] presunzione f; **~uous**
presuntuoso
preten|ce, Am **~se** [priˈtens]
finzione f; **~d** v/t fingere;
~sion pretesa f
pretext [ˈpriːtekst] pretesto
m

pretty [ˈpriti] a carino; adv
fam abbastanza
prevail [priˈveil] v/i prevalere; **~ on** indurre
prevent [priˈvent] v/t impedire; **~ion** misura f preven-
tiva
previous [ˈpriːvjəs] precedente
prey [prei] preda f
price [prais] s prezzo m; v/t
valutare; **~less** inestimabile; **~-list** listino m dei prezzi
prick [prik] s puntura f; v/t
punzecchiare; **~ one's ears**
drizzare gli orecchi
pride [praid] orgoglio m
priest [priːst] sacerdote m
primary [ˈpraiməri] prima-
rio; **~ school** scuola f elementare
prime [praim] primo; principale
cipale
primitive [ˈprimitiv] primitivo
prince [prins] principe m;
~ss [ˌˈses] principessa f
principal [ˈprinsəpəl] a
principale;; s principale
m; capo m; **~ity** [ˌprinsi-
ˈpæliti] principato m
principle [ˈprinsəpl] principio m
print [print] s stampa f; impronta f; tessuto m stampato; v/t stampare; **in ~** stampato; **~ed matter** stampe
f/pl; **~ing-works** pl tipo-
grafia f
prior [ˈpraiə] a. anteceden-
te; s priore m; **~ity** [ˌˈɔriti]
priorità f

prison ['prizn] prigione *f*; carcere *m*; **~er** prigioniero *m*

privacy ['praivəsi, 'pri-] intimità *f*; solitudine *f*

private ['praivit] privato

privation [prai'veiʃən] privazione *f*

privilege ['privilidʒ] privilegio *m*; **~d** privilegiato

prize [praiz] *s* premio *m*; *v/t* valutare

probability [probə'biliti] probabilità *f*; **~le** ['~əbl] probabile

probation [prə'beiʃən] prova *f*

probe [proub] *v/t* sondare; *s* sonda *f*

problem ['probləm] problema *m*

procedure [prə'si:dʒə] procedura *f*

proceed [prə'si:d] *v/i* procedere; **~ings** *pl* procedimento *m*; **~s** ['prousi:dz] *pl* ricavo *m*

process ['prouses] processo *m*; **~ion** [prə'seʃən] processione *f*; corteo *m* funebre

proclaim [prə'kleim] *v/t* proclamare; **~mation** [prɔklə'meiʃən] proclamazione *f*

procure [prə'kjuə] *v/t* procurare

prodigal ['prɔdigəl] prodigo

prodigious [prə'didʒəs] prodigioso; **~y** ['prɔdidʒi] prodigio *m*

produce [prə'dju:s] *s* prodotto *m*; *v/t* produrre; **~r**

produttore *m*; regista *m* (*di teatro, e di cinema*)

product ['prɔdəkt] prodotto *m*

profane [prə'fein] profano

profess [prə'fes] *v/t* professare; esercitare; **~ion** professione *f*; professionale; **~ional** professionale; **~or** professore *m*

proficiency [prə'fiʃənsi] conoscenza *f*; **~t** esperto

profile ['proufail] profilo *m*

profit ['prɔfit] *s* profitto *m*; **~ and loss** guadagno e perdita; *v/t* giovare; **~ by** approfittare; **~able** vantaggioso

profound [prə'faund] profondo

profusion [prə'fju:ʒən] profusione *f*

prognosis [prɔg'nousis], *pl* **~es** [~si:z] prognosi *f*

program(me) ['prougræm] programma *m*

progress *s* progresso *m*; [~'gres] *v/i* fare progressi; **~ive** [prə'gresiv] progressivo

prohibit [prə'hibit] *v/t* proibire; **~ion** [proui'biʃən] proibizione *f*

project ['prɔdʒekt] *s* progetto *m*; [prə'dʒekt] *v/t* progettare; *v/i* sporgere; **~ile** proiettile *m*; **~ion** proiezione *f*; **~or** proiettore *m*

prologue, *Am* **~log** ['prouləg] prologo *m*

prolong [prou'lɔŋ] *v/t* prolungare

promenade [prɔmi'nɑ:d]

passeggiata f; lungomare m

prominent ['prɔminənt] prominente

promise ['prɔmis] s promessa f; v/t promettere

promot|e [prə'mout] v/t promuovere; **~ion** promozione f

prompt [prɔmpt] a pronto; v/t incitare; suggerire; **~er** suggeritore m

prone [proun] prostrato; propenso

pronoun ['prounaun] pronome m

pron|ounce [prə'nauns] v/t pronunciare; **~unciation** [~nʌnsi'eiʃən] pronuncia f

proof [pru:f] prova f; bozze f/pl (di stampe)

prop [prɔp] s appoggio m; sostegno m; v/t appoggiare, sostenere

propaganda [ˌprɔpə-'gændə] propaganda f

propagate ['prɔpəgeit] v/t propagare

propel [prə'pel] v/t spingere

propensity [prə'pensiti] propensione f

proper ['prɔpə] proprio; vero; **~ty** proprietà f

prophe|cy ['prɔfisi] profezia f; **~sy** [~'ai] v/t profetizzare; **~t** profeta m

propitious [prə'piʃəs] propizio

proportion [prə'pɔ:ʃən] proporzione f; **out of ~** sproporzionato

propos|al [prə'pouzəl] proposta f; proposta f di matri-

monio; **~e** v/t proporre; v/i fare una proposta di matrimonio; **~ition** [prɔpə'ziʃən] proposizione f; proposta f

propriet|ary [prə'praiətəri] brevettato; **~or, ~ress** proprietario(a) m (f)

propulsion [prə'pʌlʃən] propulsione f

prose [prouz] prosa f

prosecut|e ['prɔsikju:t] v/i intentare giudizio; **~ion** [ˌprɔsi'kju:ʃən] processo m

prospect ['prɔspekt] prospettiva f

prospectus [prəs'pektəs] opusculo m

prosper ['prɔspə] v/i prosperare; **~ity** [~'periti] prosperità f; **~ous** ['~pərəs] prospero

prostitut|e ['prɔstitju:t] s prostituta f; v/t prostituire; **~ion** [ˌprɔsti'tju:ʃən] prostituzione f

prostrat|e [prɔs'treit] a prostrato; v/t prostrare

protect [prə'tekt] v/t proteggere; **~ion** protezione f; **~ive** protettivo

protest ['proutest] s protesta f; v/i protestare

Protestant ['prɔtistənt] a, s protestante (m, f); **~ism** protestantesimo m

protract [prə'trækt] v/t protrarre

protrude [prə'tru:d] v/i sporgere

proud [praud] orgoglioso; superbo

prove [pru:v] v/t provare;

v/i risultare

proverb ['prɒvə:b] proverbio *m*; **~ial** [prə'və:bjəl] proverbiale

provide [prə'vaid] *v/t* provvedere; **~d (that)** purché

providence ['prɒvidəns] provvidenza *f*

province ['prɒvins] provincia *f*; **~ial** [prə'vinʃəl] provinciale

provision [prə'viʒən] provvista *f*

provocation [prɒvə'keiʃən] provocazione *f*; **~ke** [prə'vouk] *v/t* provocare

proxy ['prɒksi] procura *f*

prude [pru:d] puritana *f*

prudence ['pru:dəns] prudenza *f*; **~t** prudente

prune [pru:n] *s* prugna *f* secca; *v/t* potare

psalm [sɑ:m] salmo *m*

pseudo ['sju:dou] pseudo; **~nym** pseudonimo *m*

psychiatrist [sai'kaiətrist] psichiatra *m, f*; **~y** psichiatria *f*

psychic ['saikik] psichico; **~ological** [ˌsaikə'lɒdʒikəl] psicologico; **~ologist** [~'kɒlədʒist] psicologo *m*; **~ology** [~'kɒlədʒi] psicologia *f*

pub [pʌb] *fam* osteria *f*

puberty ['pju:bəti] pubertà *f*

public ['pʌblik] *a, s* pubblico; **~ house** bar *m*; **~ity** [~'lisiti] pubblicità *f*

publish ['pʌbliʃ] *v/t* pubblicare; **~ing house** casa *f* editrice

pudding ['pudiŋ] budino *m*

puddle ['pʌdl] pozzanghera *f*

puff [pʌf] *s* soffio *m*; *v/t* soffiare

pull [pul] *v/t* tirare

pulley ['puli] puleggia *f*

pull-over ['pulvə] golf *m*; pullover *m*

pulp [pʌlp] polpa *f*

pulsate [pʌl'seit] *v/i* pulsare; **~e** polso *m*

pulverize ['pʌlvəraiz] *v/t* polverizzare

pump [pʌmp] *s* pompa *f*; *v/t* pompare

pumpkin ['pʌmpkin] zucca *f*

punch [pʌntʃ] *s* pugno *m*; *v/t* dare un pugno a

Punch [pʌntʃ] burattino *m*; **~ and Judy show** ['dʒu:di] teatro *m* di burattini

punctual ['pʌŋktjuəl] puntuale

punctuation [ˌpʌŋktju'eiʃən] punteggiatura *f*

puncture ['pʌŋktʃə] foratura *f*

pungent ['pʌndʒənt] pungente

punish ['pʌniʃ] *v/t* punire; **~ment** punizione *f*; castigo *m* (solaro *m*)

pupil ['pju:pl] alunno *m, f*

puppet ['pʌpit] burattino *m*

puppy ['pʌpi] cucciolo *m*

purchase ['pə:tʃəs] *s* acquisto *m*; *v/t* acquistare; comprare

pure [pjuə] puro

purgative ['pə:gətiv] *a, s*

purgante (*m*)

purg|atory [ˈpəːgətəri] purgatorio *m*; **.e** [pəːdʒ] *s* purga *f*; *v/t* purgare

purify [ˈpjuərifai] *v/t* purificare

Puritan [ˈpjuəritən] *a*, *s* puritano (*m*)

purple [ˈpəːpl] *s* porpora *f*; *a* porporeo

purport [ˈpəːpət] significato *m*

purpose [ˈpəːpəs] *s* scopo *m*; proposito *m*; *v/t* proporsi; **on ~** apposta

purr [pəː] *v/i* far le fusa

purse [pəːs] *s* portamonete *m*

pursu|e [pəˈsjuː] *v/t* inseguire; continuare; *v/i* proseguire; **.it** [ˈsjuːt] inseguimento *m*; occupazione *f*

pus [pʌs] pus *m*

push [puʃ] *s* spinta *f*; *v/t* spingere

puss [pus], **.y(-cat)** gatto *m*

put [put] *v/t*, *irr* mettere; **~ back** rimettere; **~ down** deporre; **~ in** inserire; **~ off** rimandare; **~ on** mettersi; indossare; **~ out** spegnere; **~ up** ospitare; **~ up with** sopportare

putr|efy [ˈpjuːtrifai] *v/t* putrefare; *v/i* putrefarsi; **.id** putrido

puzzle [ˈpʌzl] rompicapo *m*; problema *m*; *v/i* essere perplesso; **(cross-word) ~** cruciverba *m*

pyjamas [pəˈdʒɑːməz] *pl* pigiama *m*

pylon [ˈpailən] pilone *m*

pyramid [ˈpirəmid] piramide *f*

Q

quack [kwæk] *v/i* schiamazzare

quadrangle [ˈkwɔdræŋgl] quadrangolo *m*

quadruped [ˈkwɔdruped] quadrupede *m*; **.le** quadruplo

quaint [kweint] strano

quake [kweik] *v/i* tremare

qualif|ication [ˌkwɔlifiˈkeiʃən] requisito *m*; titolo *m*; **.ied** [ˈ.faid] idoneo; **.y** *v/t* qualificare; *v/i* essere idoneo

quality [ˈkwɔliti] qualità *f*

qualm [kwaːm] nausea *f*; *fig* scrupolo *m*

quantity [ˈkwɔntiti] quantità *f*

quarantine [ˈkwɔrəntiːn] quarantena *f*

quarrel [ˈkwɔrəl] *s* litigio *m*; *v/i* litigare; **.some** litigioso

quarry [ˈkwɔri] cava *f*

quarter [ˈkwɔːtə] quarto *m*; quartiere *m*; trimestre *m*; **a ~ (of an hour)** un quarto (d'ora); **.ly** trimestrale

quartet(te) [kwɔːˈtet] quartetto *m*

quaver [ˈkweivə] *v/i* tremolare

quay [kiː] banchina *f*

queen [kwiːn] regina *f*

queer [kwiə] strano

quell [kwel] *v/t* reprimere

quench [kwentʃ] *v/t* spegnere; calmare

querulous [ˈkwerələs] querulo

query [ˈkwiəri] *s* domanda *f*; *v/t* mettere in dubbio; interrogare

question [ˈkwestʃən] *s* domanda *f*; questione *f*; **ask a ~** fare una domanda; *v/t* interrogare; mettere in dubbio; **~able** in questione; dubbioso; **~mark** punto *m* interrogativo; **~naire** [ˌ~stiəˈnɛə] questionario *m*

queue [kjuː] *s* coda *f*; **~ (up)** *v/i* far la coda

quick [kwik] veloce; rapido; **~en** *v/t* affrettare; **~ness** velocità *f*; rapidità *f*

quiet [ˈkwaiət] *a* tranquillo; quieto; silenzioso; *s* tranquillità *f*; quiete *f*

quilt [kwilt] coltrone *m*

quinine [kwiˈniːn, *Am* ˈkwainain] chinino *m*

quit [kwit] *v/t* lasciare; smettere

quite [kwait] completamente; abbastanza

quiver [ˈkwivə] *v/i* tremare

quiz [kwiz] *s* esame *m*; *v/t* esaminare

quota [ˈkwoutə] quota *f*

quot|ation [kwouˈteiʃən] citazione *f*; *comm* quotazione *f*; **~ation marks** *pl* virgolette *f/pl*; **~e** [kwout] *v/t* citare; *comm* quotare

quotient [ˈkwouʃənt] quoziente *m*

R

rabbi [ˈræbai] rabbino *m*

rabbit [ˈræbit] coniglio *m*

rabble [ˈræbl] ciurmaglia *f*

race [reis] *s* razza *f*; corsa *f* (*di cavalli*); **~course** ippodromo *m*; **~horse** cavallo *m* da corsa

rack [ræk] *s* rete *f*; tortura *f*; *v/t* torturare

racket [ˈrækit] racchetta *f*

racoon [rəˈkuːn] procione *m* lavatore

radar [ˈreidə] radiotelemetro *m*

radian|ce [ˈreidjəns] splendore *m*; **~t** risplendente

radi|ate [ˈreidieit] *v/t* irradiare; **~o** radio *f*; **~o station** stazione *f* radio

radioactive radioattivo

radish [ˈrædiʃ] ravanello *m*

raffle [ˈræfl] lotteria *f*

raft [rɑːft] zattera *f*

rag [ræg] cencio *m*; straccio *m*

rage [reidʒ] s rabbia f; v/i infuriare; essere furibondo

raid [reid] s incursione f; v/t assalire

rail [reil] sbarra f; inferriata f; rotaia f (del treno); **~ing(s)** pl inferriata f

railway ferrovia f; **~ guide** orario m ferroviario

rain [rein] s pioggia f; v/i piovere; **~bow** arcobaleno m; **~coat** impermeabile m; **~y** piovoso

raise [reiz] v/t alzare; allevare; **~ one's voice** alzare la voce

raisin ['reizn] uva f passa

rake [reik] s rastrello m

rally ['ræli] s riunione f; v/t riunire; v/i riunirsi

ram [ræm] montone m

ramble ['ræmbl] v/i vagare; divagare

rampart ['ræmpɑːt] bastione m

ranch [rɑːntʃ, Am ræntʃ] azienda f

random ['rændəm] caso m; casaccio m; **at ~** a casaccio

range [reindʒ] s estensione f; fila f; serie f; catena f (di montagne); assortimento m; cucina f economica; v/t disporre; v/i estendersi; andare

rank [ræŋk] s fila f; grado m; rango m; v/t classificare; a esuberante; flagrante

ransack ['rænsæk] v/t frugare; saccheggiare

ransom ['rænsəm] s ricatto m; v/t ricattare

rap [ræp] s colpo m; picchio m; v/t colpire; picchiare

rapacious [rə'peiʃəs] rapace

rape [reip] s ratto m; v/t rapire; violare

rapid ['ræpid] rapido; **~ity** [rə'piditi] rapidità f

rapt [ræpt] rapito; estasiato; **~ure** estasi f

rare [rɛə] raro

rascal ['rɑːskəl] mascalzone m

rash [ræʃ] a imprudente; s sfogo m; eruzione f

raspberry ['rɑːzbəri] lampone m

rat [ræt] topo m; **I smell a ~** qualche gatto ci cova sotto

rate [reit] s tasso m; velocità f; **at any ~** in ogni caso; **~ of exchange** cambio m; v/t valutare; calcolare

rather [ˈrɑːðə] abbastanza; piuttosto; **I would ~, I had ~** preferirei

ratify ['rætifai] v/t ratificare

ratio ['reiʃiou] proporzione f

ration ['ræʃən] s razione f; v/t razionare

rational ['ræʃənl] razionale; **~ize** ['~nəlaiz] v/t razionalizzare

rattle ['rætl] s sonaglio m; rumore m secco; v/i fare rumori secchi; v/t fig innervosire; **~ snake** serpente m a sonagli

ravage ['rævidʒ] v/t devastare

rave [reiv] v/i delirare

raven ['reivn] corvo m; **~ous** ['rævənəs] vorace; affamato

ravine [rə'vi:n] burrone *m*

raving ['reiviŋ] delirante

ravish ['ræviʃ] *v/t* estasiare

raw [rɔ:] crudo; grezzo; ~ **flesh** carne *f* viva; ~ **material** materia *f* prima; ~ **silk** seta *f* cruda

ray [rei] raggio *m*

razor ['reizə] rasoio *m*

reach [ri:tʃ] *s* distesa *f*; portata *f*; *v/t* raggiungere; *v/i* estendersi

react [ri(:)'ækt] *v/i* reagire; **~ion** reazione *f*; **~ionary** [~ʃnəri] reazionario *m*; **~or** reattore *m*

read [ri:d] *v/t, irr* leggere; **~ aloud** leggere ad alta voce; **~er** lettore *m*

readiness prontezza *f*

reading ['ri:diŋ] lettura *f*

readjust ['ri:ə'dʒʌst] *v/t* raggiustare

ready ['redi] pronto; **~ made** confezionato

reaffirm ['ri:ə'fə:m] *v/t* riaffermare

real [riəl] reale; vero; ~ **estate**, ~ **property** beni *m/pl* immobili; **~ism** realismo *m*; **~ist** realista *m, f*; **~istic** realistico; **~ity** [ri(:)'æliti] realtà *m*; **~ize** *v/t* rendersi conto; realizzare; **~ly** veramente

realm [relm] reame *m*; regno *m*

reap [ri:p] *v/t* mietere; **~er** mietitore *m*

rear [riə] *a* posteriore; *s* parte *f* posteriore; *v/t* allevare; educare; sollevare; *v/i* (ca-

valli) impennarsi; **~guard** retroguardia *f*; **~lamp**, **~light** riflettore *m* posteriore

rearmament [ri(:)'ɑ:məmənt] riarmo *m*

rear-view mirror specchio *m* retrovisore

reason ['ri:zn] *s* ragione *f*; *v/i* ragionare; **~able** ragionevole; **~ing** ragionamento *m*

reassure [ri:ə'ʃuə] *v/t* rassicurare

rebate ['ri:beit] sconto *m*; restituzione *f*

rebel [rebl] *a, s* ribelle (*m*); *v/i* ribellarsi; **~lion** [~'beljən] ribellione *f*

re-book ['ri:'buk] *v/t* cambiare la prenotazione

rebound [ri'baund] *v/i* rimbalzare

rebuff [ri'baf] *v/t* respingere

rebuke [ri'bju:k] *v/t* rimproverare

recall [ri'kɔ:l] *v/t* rievocare; ricordare

recapture ['ri:'kæptʃə] *v/t* riprendere; catturare di nuovo

recast ['ri:'kɑ:st] *v/t* rifare

recede [ri'si:d] *v/i* recedere

receipt [ri'si:t] ricevuta *f*

receive [ri'si:v] *v/t* ricevere; **~r** ricevitore *m*

recent ['ri:snt] recente

reception [ri'sepʃən] ricevimento *m*; accoglienza *f*

recess [ri'ses] nicchia *f*

recipe ['resipi] ricetta *f*

recipient [ri'sipiənt] recipiente *m*

reciprocal [ri'siprəkəl] reciproco

recital [ri'saitl] racconto m; mus audizione f; recital m; ~e v/t recitare; raccontare

reckless ['reklis] temerario

reckon ['rekən] v/t contare; pensare

reclaim [ri'kleim] v/t reclamare

recline [ri'klain] v/i sdraiarsi

recognition [rekəg'niʃən] riconoscimento m; ~ze v/t riconoscere

recoil [ri'kɔil] v/i indietreggiare

recollect [rekə'lekt] v/t ricordare; ~ion ricordo m

recommend [rekə'mend] v/t raccomandare; ~ation [rekəmen'deiʃən] raccomandazione f

recompense ['rekəmpens] s ricompensa f; v/t ricompensare

reconcile ['rekənsail] v/t conciliare; ~iation [rekənsili-'eiʃən] riconciliazione f

reconsider ['ri:kən'sidə] v/t riconsiderare

reconstruct ['ri:kən'strʌkt] v/t ricostruire

record ['rekɔ:d] s registro m; disco m; primato m; ricordo m; [ri'kɔ:d] v/t registrare; incidere; ~er registratore m; ~-player giradischi m

recourse [ri'kɔ:s] ricorso m

recover [ri'kʌvə] v/t recuperare; v/i rimettersi; ~y guarigione f; ricupero m

recreation [rekri'eiʃən] ri-

creazione f; riposo m

recruit [ri'kru:t] s recluta f; v/t reclutare

rectangle ['rektæŋgl] rettangolo m

rectify ['rektifai] v/t rettificare

rector ['rektə] rettore m; parroco m

recuperate [ri'kju:pəreit] v/t recuperare; v/i rimettersi

recur [ri'kə:] v/i ricorrere; ritornare; ripetersi; ~rence [ri'kʌrəns] ricorrenza f; ritorno m; ripetizione f

red [red] rosso m; ℑ Cross Croce f Rossa; ~den v/i arrossire; ~dish rossiccio

redeem [ri'di:m] v/t redimere; ~er redentore m; ~mption [ri'dempʃən] redenzione f

red-handed in flagrante; ℑ **Indian** indiano m

redouble [ri'dʌbl] v/i raddoppiarsi

reduce [ri'dju:s] v/t ridurre; ~tion [ri'dʌkʃən] riduzione f

redundant [ri'dʌndənt] sovrabbondante

reed [ri:d] canna f

reef [ri:f] scoglio m; scogliera f

reek [ri:k] v/i fumare; odorare male; ~ of odorare di

re-establish [ri:-] v/t ristabilire

refer [ri'fə:] v/t riferire; v/i riferirsi a; ~ee [refə'ri:] arbitro m; ~ence ['refrəns] referenza f; riferimento m; allusione f; ~ence book opera f di consultazione

refill ['ri:fil] s ricambio m; v/t riempire

refine [ri'fain] v/t raffinare; v/i raffinarsi; **~ment** raffinatezza f; **~ry** raffineria f

reflect [ri'flekt] v/t riflettere; **~ion** riflesso m; riflessione f

reflex ['ri:fleks] riflesso m

reform [ri'fɔ:m] s riforma f; v/t riformare; **~ation** [refə'meiʃən] riforma f

refract [ri'frækt] v/t rifrangere; **~ion** rifrazione f; **~ory** refrattario

refrain [ri'frein] s ritornello m; v/i trattenersi

refresh [ri'freʃ] v/t rinfrescare; **~ment** rinfresco m

refrigerator [ri'fridʒəreitə] frigorifero m

refuge ['refju:dʒ] s rifugio m; **~e** [ˌrefju(:)'dʒi:] profugo m

refund [ri:'fʌnd] s rimborso m; v/t rimborsare

refus|al [ri'fju:zəl] rifiuto m; **~e** v/t rifiutare; ['refju:s] s rifiuti m/pl

refute [ri'fju:t] v/t confutare

regain [ri'gein] v/t recuperare

regard [ri'gɑ:d] s considerazione f; **with ~ to**, **~ing** riguardo a; **~less of** ciò nonostante; senza tenere in considerazione; **kind ~s** pl cordiali saluti m/pl

regenerate [ri:'dʒenəreit] v/t rigenerare

regent ['ri:dʒənt] reggente m

regime [rei'ʒi:m] regime m

regiment ['redʒimənt] s reggimento m; v/t reggimentare

region ['ri:dʒən] regione f; **~al** regionale

regist|er ['redʒistə] s registro m; v/t registrare; iscrivere; **~ration** [ˌredʒis'treiʃən] registrazione f

regret [ri'gret] s dispiacere m; rammarico m; v/t rammaricarsi di; v/i dispiacersi; **~table** spiacevole

regula|r ['regjulə] regolare; **~rity** [ˌ~'læriti] regolarità f; **~te** ['regjuleit] v/t regolare; **~tion** regolamento m

rehears|al [ri'hə:səl] prova f; **~e** v/t, v/i provare

reign [rein] v/i regnare; s regno m

rein [rein] redine m/pl

reindeer ['reindiə] renna f

reinforce [ri:in'fɔ:s] v/t rinforzare

reissue ['ri:'isju:, -'iʃju:] v/t ristampare

reject [ri'dʒekt] v/t respingere; scartare; s scarto m

rejoice [ri'dʒɔis] v/i far festa

relapse [ri'læps] s med ricaduta f; v/i ricadere

relat|e [ri'leit] v/t raccontare; riguardare; v/i riferirsi a; **~ed** affine; connesso; **~ion** [ri'leiʃən] relazione f; rapporto m; parente m; **~ionship** rapporto m; parentela f; **~ive** [ˈrelətiv] a relativo; s parente m

relax [ri'læks] v/t rilassare; v/i rilassarsi

relay ['ri:'lei] v/t ritrasmettere

release [ri'li:s] s liberazione f; v/t liberare

relent [ri'lent] v/i ritornare su una decisione; lasciarsi intenerire

relevant ['relivənt] pertinente

reliable [ri'laiəbl] fidato

relic ['relik] reliquia f

relief [ri'li:f] sollievo m; assistenza f; cambio m; soccorso m

relieve [ri'li:v] v/t sollevare

religion [ri'lidʒən] religione f; **~us** religioso

relinquish [ri'liŋkwiʃ] v/t abbandonare

relish ['reliʃ] s gusto m; piacere m; v/t gustare; piacere

reluctance [ri'lʌktəns] riluttanza f; **~t** riluttante

rely [ri'lai]: **~(up)on** v/i contare su

remain [ri'mein] v/i rimanere; **~der** resto m

remand [ri'mɑ:nd] v/t rimandare in carcere

remark [ri'mɑ:k] s osservazione f; v/t, v/i osservare; **~able** notevole

remedy ['remidi] s rimedio m; v/t rimediare

remember [ri'membə] v/t ricordarsi di; **~rance** ricordo m

remind [ri'maind] v/t ricordare

reminiscence [‚remi'nisnt] reminiscenza f

remiss [ri'mis] negligente

remit [ri'mit] v/t rimettere; **~tance** rimessa f

remnant ['remnənt] resto m; scampolo m

remodel ['ri:'mɔdl] v/t rimodellare

remonstrate ['remənstreit] v/i protestare

remorse [ri'mɔ:s] rimorso m; **~less** spietato

remote [ri'mout] remoto; lontano

removal [ri'mu:vəl] trasloco m; **~e** v/t togliere; v/i sgomberare

remunerate [ri'mju:nəreit] v/t rimunerare

renaissance [rə'neisəns] rinascimento m

render ['rendə] v/t rendere; fare

renew [ri'nju:] v/t rinnovare; **~al** rinnovamento m

renounce [ri'nauns] v/t rinunciare a

renown [ri'naun] fama f; **~ed** famoso

rent [rent] s affitto m; v/t affittare

reopen ['ri:'oupən] v/t riaprire; **~ing** riapertura f

repair [ri'pɛə] v/t riparare

reparation [repə'reiʃən] riparazione f

repay [ri:'pei] v/t, irr rimborsare; restituire

repeat [ri'pi:t] v/t ripetere

repel [ri'pel] v/t respingere; **~lent** ripellente

repent [ri'pent] v/t pentirsi di; **~ance** pentimento m; **~ant** pentito

repetition [repi'tiʃən] ripetizione *f*

replace [ri'pleis] *v/t* sostituire; **~ment** sostituzione *f*

replenish [ri'pleniʃ] *v/t* riempire di nuovo

reply [ri'plai] *v/t* risposta *f*; *v/i* rispondere

report [ri'pɔːt] *s* rapporto *m*; resoconto *m*; *v/t* riferire; denunziare; **~er** giornalista *m, f*

repose [ri'pouz] *s* riposo *m*; *v/i* riposare

reprehend [,repri'hend] *v/t* riprendere

represent [,repri'zent] *v/t* rappresentare; **~ation** rappresentazione *f*; **~ative** *a* rappresentativo; *s* rappresentante *m*

repress [ri'pres] *v/t* reprimere; **~ion** repressione *f*

reprieve [ri'priːv] *s* sospensione *f*; *v/t* sospendere

reprimand ['reprimɑːnd] *s* rimprovero *m*; *v/t* rimproverare

reprint ['riː'print] *s* ristampa *f*; *v/t* ristampare

reprisal [ri'praizəl] rappresaglia *f*

reproach [ri'proutʃ] *s* rimprovero *m*; *v/t* rimproverare

reproduc|e [riːprə'djuːs] *v/t* riprodurre; *v/i* riprodursi; **~tion** [-'dʌkʃən] riproduzione *f*

repro|of [ri'pruːf] rimprovero *m*; **~ve** [ri'pruːv] *v/t* rimproverare

reptile ['reptail] rettile *m*

republic [ri'pʌblik] repubblica *f*; **~an** *a*, *s* repubblicano (*m*)

repudiate [ri'pjuːdieit] *v/t* ripudiare

repugnan|ce [ri'pʌgnəns] ripugnanza *f*; **~t** ripugnante

repuls|e [ri'pʌls] *v/t* respingere; **~ion** ripugnanza *f*; **~ive** ripugnante

reput|able ['repjutəbl] rispettabile; **~ation** riputazione *f*; **~e** [ri'pjuːt] *s* fama *f*

request [ri'kwest] *s* richiesta *f*; domanda *f*; **by ~, on ~** a richiesta; *v/t* richiedere

requi|re [ri'kwaiə] *v/t* avere bisogno di; **~rement** necessità *f*; requisiti *m/pl*; **~site** ['rekwizit] *a* necessario; *s* requisito *m*

rescue ['reskjuː] *v/t* salvare; *s* salvamento *m*

research [ri'sɜːtʃ] *s* ricerca *f*; **~ work** ricerche *f/pl*; **~ worker** ricercatore *m*

resembl|ance [ri'zembləns] rassomiglianza *f*; **~e** *v/t* rassomigliare

resent [ri'zent] *v/t* risentirsi di; **~ful** risentito; **~ment** risentimento *m*

reserv|ation [rezə'veiʃən] riserva *f*; posto *m* prenotato; **~e** [ri'zəːv] *s* riserbo *m*; *v/t* riservare; prenotare

reservoir ['rezəvwɑː] serbatoio *m*

reside [ri'zaid] *v/i* risiedere; **~nce** ['rezidəns] residenza *f*; **~nce permit** permesso *m* di soggiorno; **~nt** a residente; *s* abitante *m*

residue ['rezidju:] residuo *m*

resign [ri'zain] *v/i* dimettersi; **~ation** [rezig'neiʃən] dimissioni *f/pl*

resin ['rezin] resina *f*

resist [ri'zist] *v/t, v/i* resistere; **~ance** resistenza *f*; **~ant** resistente

resolut|e ['rezəlu:t] risoluto; deciso; **~ion** risoluzione *f*; risolutezza *f*

resolve [ri'zɔlv] *v/t* risolvere; decidere; *v/i* decidersi

resonan|ce ['reznəns] risonanza *f*; **~t** risonante

resort [ri'zɔːt] *s* ricorso *m*; espediente *m*; luogo *m* di villeggiatura; **~ to** ricorrere a

resound [ri'zaund] *v/i* risuonare

resource [ri'sɔːs] risorsa *f*; **~ful** pieno di risorse

respect [ris'pekt] *s* rispetto *m*; **in every ~** sotto tutti i punti di vista; *v/t* rispettare; **~able** rispettabile; **~ful** rispettoso; **yours ~fully** con la più profonda stima; **~ive** rispettivo; **~s** *pl* ossequi *m/pl*

respir|ation [ˌrespi'reiʃən] respirazione *f*; **~e** [ris'paiə] *v/t, v/i* respirare

respite ['respait] respiro *m*; tregua *f*

resplendent [ris'plendənt] risplendente

respon|d [ris'pɔnd] *v/i* rispondere; **~se** risposta *f*; responso *m*; **~sibility** [risˌpɔnsi'biliti] responsabilità *f*; **~sible** responsabile

rest [ris'pɔnd] *s* riposo *m*; resto *m*; *v/t* appoggiare; *v/i* riposarsi

restaurant ['restrɔŋ, 'restərɔŋ] ristorante *m*; trattoria *f*

rest|ful riposante; **~less** agitato

restor|ation [ˌrestə'reiʃən] restauro *m*; restaurazione *f*; **~e** [ris'tɔː] *v/t* restaurare; restituire

restrain [ris'trein] *v/t* trattenere; frenare; **~t** freno *m*; controllo *m*

restrict [ris'trikt] *v/t* restringere; limitare; **~ion** restrizione *f*

result [ri'zʌlt] *s* risultato *m*; *v/i* risultare

resume [ri'zjuːm] *v/t* riprendere

resurrection [rezə'rekʃən] risurrezione *f*

retail ['riːteil] *s* vendita *f* a dettaglio; [riː'teil] *v/t* vendere a dettaglio; **~er** venditore *m* a dettaglio

retain [ri'tein] *v/t* ritenere; trattenere

retaliate [ri'tælieit] *v/i* rendere

retard [ri'tɑːd] *v/t* ritardare

retention [ri'tenʃən] ritenimento *m*

reticent ['retisənt] reticente

retir|e [ri'taiə] *v/i* ritirare; andare in pensione; andare a riposo; **~ed** in pensione; a riposo; **~ement** riposo *m*

retort [ri'tɔːt] *s* risposta *f*; *v/t* rispondere

retrace [ri'treis] *v/t* rintracciare

retract [ri'trækt] *v/t* ritrarre

retreat [ri'triːt] *s* ritiro *m*; ritirata *f*; *v/i* ritirarsi

retribution [retri'bjuːʃən] retribuzione *f*

return [ri'təːn] *s* ritorno *m*; **by ~ of post** a giro di posta; *v/t* restituire; rimandare; *v/i* (ri)tornare; **~ ticket** biglietto *m* di andata e ritorno

reuni|on [ˈriːˈjuːnjən] riunione *f*; **~te** [ˈriːjuˈnait] *v/t* riunire; *v/i* riunirsi

reveal [ri'viːl] *v/t* rivelare

revel [ˈrevl] *s* baldoria *f*; *v/i* far baldoria

revelation [ˌreviˈleiʃən] rivelazione *f*; **~s** apocalisse *f*

revenge [ri'vendʒ] *s* vendetta *f*; *v/t* vendicare; **~ful** vendicativo

revenue [ˈrevinjuː] entrata *f*; reddito *m*

revere [ri'viə] *v/t* riverire; venerare; **~nce** [ˈrevərəns] riverenza *f*; **~nd** reverendo

reverse [ri'vəːs] *s* rovescio *m*; contrario *m*; *v/t* capovolgere; *a* contrario; opposto; **~egear** retromarcia *f*; **~ible** rivoltabile

revert [ri'vəːt] *v/i* ritornare

review [ri'vjuː] *s* rivista *f*; recensione *f*; *v/t* passare in rivista; recensire; **~er** critico *m*

revis|e [ri'vaiz] *v/t* rivedere; correggere; **~ion** [~ˈviʒən] revisione *f*; correzione *f*

reviv|al [ri'vaivəl] risveglio *m*; rinascita *f*; **~e** *v/t* far rivivere; ridare vita; *v/i* riprendere vita; riprendere i sensi

revoke [ri'vouk] *v/t* revocare

revolt [ri'voult] *s* rivolta *f*; *v/i* ribellarsi

revolution [revəˈluːʃən] rivoluzione *f*; **~ary** *a, s* rivoluzionario (*m*); **~ize** *v/t* rivoluzionare

revolve [ri'volv] *v/i* girare; **~r** rivoltella *f*

reward [ri'wɔːd] *s* ricompensa *f*; *v/t* ricompensare

rheumat|ic [ruːˈmætik] reumatico; **~ism** [ˈruːmətizm] reumatismo *m*

rhubarb [ˈruːbɑːb] rabarbero *m*

rhyme [raim] *s* rima *f*; *v/i* rimare

rhythm [ˈriðəm] ritmo *m*; **~ic, ~ical** ritmico

rib [rib] costola *f*; stecca *f* (*dell'ombrello*)

ribbon [ˈribən] nastro *m*

rice [rais] riso *m*

rich [ritʃ] ricco; **~es** [ˈ~iz] *pl*, **~ness** ricchezza *f*

ricket|s [ˈrikits] *pl* rachitismo *m*; **~y** rachitico

rid [rid] *v/t, irr* liberare; **get ~ of** liberarsi di

riddle [ˈridl] indovinello *m*; enigma *m*

rid|e [raid] *s* cavalcata *f*; passeggiata *f* (*in bicicletta, in* *macchina*); *v/i*, *irr* cavalcare; andare in bicicletta; andare in macchina; **~er** cavaliere *m*

ridge [ridʒ] cresta *f*

ridicul|e ['ridikju:l] *s* ridicolo *m*; *v/t* mettere in ridicolo; **~ous** [~'dikjuləs] ridicolo

riding ['raidiŋ] equitazione *f*

rifle ['raifl] fucile *m*

rift [rift] spaccatura *f*, *fig* dissenso *m*

right [rait] *s* destra *f*; bene *m*; giusto *m*; *a* destro; diretto; corretto; **all ~** va bene; **~ angle** angolo *m* retto; **be ~** avere ragione; **put ~, set ~** mettere in ordine; **on the ~, to the ~** a destra; **~eous** retto; giusto; **~ of way** precedenza *f*

rigid ['ridʒid] rigido

rig|orous ['rigərəs] rigoroso; **~o(u)r** rigore *m*

rim [rim] bordo *m*

rind [raind] buccia *f*

ring [riŋ] *s* cerchio *m*; anello *m*; recinto *m*; arena *f* (*pugilato*); pista *f* (*corse*); suonata *f* (*campanello*); *v/t* suonare (*campanello*); **~ up** telefonare

ringlet ['riŋlit] ricciolo *m*

rink [riŋk] pista *f* (*di pattinaggio*)

rinse [rins] *v/t* sciacquare

riot ['raiət] *s* tumulto *m*; *v/i* tumultuare

rip [rip] *s* strappo *m*; *v/t* strappare

ripe [raip] maturo; **~n** *v/i*,

v/i maturare; **~ness** maturità *f*

ripple ['ripl] *s* increspatura *f*; *v/i* incresparsi

rise [raiz] *s* salita *f*; aumento *m*; origine *f*; *v/i* salire; sorgere; alzarsi

risk [risk] *s* rischio *m*; *v/t* rischiare

rit|e [rait] rito *m*; **funeral ~es** *pl* riti *m/pl* funebri

rival ['raivəl] *a* rivale; *s* rivale *m*; concorrente *m*; *v/t* concorrere con; **~ry** rivalità *f*; concorrenza *f*

river ['rivə] fiume *m*

road [roud] strada *f*; via *f*; **~ map** carta *f* stradale; **~ sign** cartello *m* stradale

roam [roum] *v/i* vagare

roar [rɔ:] *s* ruggito *m*; *v/i* ruggire

roast [roust] *a*, *s* arrosto *m*; *v/t* arrostire

rob [rɔb] *v/t* derubare; **~ber** ladro *m*; **~bery** furto *m*

robe [roub] toga *f*; tunica *f*

robin ['rɔbin] pettirosso *m*

robot ['roubət] robot *m*

robust [rou'bʌst] robusto, vigoroso

rock [rɔk] roccia *f*; *v/t* cullare; dondolare; *v/i* dondolarsi; **~er** sedia *f* a dondolo

rocket ['rɔkit] razzo *m*

rocking-chair sedia *f* a dondolo

rocky ['rɔki] roccioso

rod [rɔd] bacchetta *f*; verga *f*; canna *f* (*da pesca*)

roe [rou] cerva *f*

rogue

rogu|e [roug] furfante *m*;
~ish birichino

role, rôle [roul] parte *f*; ruolo *m*

roll [roul] *s* rotolo *m*; panino *m*; *v/t* rotolare; avvolgere; *v/i* rotolarsi; ~er rullo *m*; cilindro *m*; ~er-skates *pl* pattini *m/pl* a rotelle

Roman ['roumən] *a, s* romano (*m*)

romance [rou'mæns] romanzo *m* cavalleresco; *mus* romanza *f*

Romanesque [ˌroumə'nesk] di stile romano

romantic [rou'mæntik] romantico

roof [ru:f] tetto *m*

rook [ruk] cornacchia *f*

room [rum] stanza *f*; camera *f*; posto *m*; ~-mate compagno(a) *m(f)* di stanza; ~y spazioso

roost [ru:st] pertica *f*; ~er gallo *m*

root [ru:t] radice *f*; origine *m*; ~ out *v/t* sradicare

rope [roup] corda *f*

rosary ['rouzəri] rosario *m*

ros|e [rouz] rosa *f*; ~e-bush rosaio *m*; ~emary rosmarino *m*; ~y roseo

rot [rɔt] *s* putrefazione *f*; marciume *m*; decadenza *f*; *v/i* imputridire; marcire; decadere

rota|ry ['routəri] rotario *m*; ~tion [rou'teiʃn] rotazione *f*

rotten ['rɔtn] putrido; marcio

rouge [ru:ʒ] rossetto *m*

rough [rʌf] ruvido; rozzo; agitato (*del mare*)

round [raund] *a* tondo; rotondo; *s* tondo *m*; giro *m*; cerchio *m*; *prp* intorno a; *adv* intorno; in giro; all the year ~ tutto l'anno; *v/t* arrotondare; girare; ~ off *v/t* completare

rouse [rauz] *v/t* destare; svegliare

route [ru:t] itinerario *m*; percorso *m*

routine [ru:'ti:n] abitudini *f/pl* fisse; pratica *f*

rove [rouv] *v/i* vagabondare

row [rou] *s* fila *f*; passeggiata *f* in barca (*a remi*); *v/t* remare

row [rau] chiasso *m*

royal ['rɔiəl] reale

rub [rʌb] *v/t* strofinare

rubber ['rʌbə] cacciù *m*; gomma *f*; ~-boots *pl* stivali *m/pl* di gomma

rubbish ['rʌbiʃ] rifiuti *m/pl*; *fam* sciocchezze *f/pl*

rubble ['rʌbl] rottami *m/pl* di mattoni o di sassi

ruby ['ru:bi] rubino *m*

rucksack ['ruksæk] sacco *m* da montagna

rudder ['rʌdə] timone *m*

ruddy ['rʌdi] rubicondo

rude [ru:d] scortese; sgarbato

ruffian ['rʌfjən] malfattore *m*

ruffle ['rʌfl] increspatura *f*; *v/t* increspare

rug [rʌg] coperta *f*; tappetino m; **~ged** ruvido; aspro

ruin ['ru:in] s rovina f; v/t rovinare

rul|e [ru:l] s regola f; regolamento m; **as a ~e** generalmente; v/t governare; regolare; **~er** governatore m; riga f (per tracciare linee)

rum [rʌm] rum m

rumble ['rʌmbl] v/i rumoreggiare

ruminant ['ru:minənt] ruminante m/pl

rummage ['rʌmidʒ] v/t, v/i frugare

rumo(u)r ['ru:mə] voce f; **it is ~ed** si dice

run [rʌn] s corsa f, serie f; **in the long ~** alla lunga; v/t, irr far correre; gestire; v/i correre; scorrere; essere in visione (di un film); **~**

across incontrare; **~ away** fuggire; **~ into** investire; **~ out of** essere a corto di; **~ over** investire; **~ning** corridore m

runway ['rʌnwei] pista f

rupture ['rʌptʃə] rottura f; ernia f

rural ['ruərəl] rurale

rush [rʌʃ] s bot giunco m; precipizio m; afflusso m; v/t precipitare; v/i precipitarsi; **~ hours** pl ore f/pl di punta

Russia ['rʌʃə] Russia f; **~n** a, s russo (m)

rust [rʌst] s ruggine f; v/i arrugginirsi

rustic ['rʌstik] rustico

rustle ['rʌsl] s fruscio m; v/i frusciare

rusty ['rʌsti] arrugginito

S

Sabbath ['sæbəθ] giorno m di riposo

sable ['seibl] zibellino m

sabotage ['sæbətɑ:ʒ] sabotaggio m

sack [sæk] s sacco m; saccheggio m; **give the ~** licenziare; v/t saccheggiare

sacrament ['sækrəmənt] sacramento m

sacred ['seikrid] sacro

sacrifice ['sækrifais] s sacrificio m; v/t sacrificare

sacrilege ['sækrilidʒ] sacrilegio m

sad [sæd] triste; **~den** v/t

intristire

saddle ['sædl] sella f

sadness ['sædnis] tristezza f

safe [seif] a sicuro; salvo; s cassaforte f; **~ and sound** sano e salvo; **~guard** s salvaguardia f; v/t salvaguardare; **~ty** sicurezza f; salvezza f; **~ty-belt** cintura f di sicurezza; **~ty-pin** spillo m di sicurezza; **~ty-valve** valvola f di sicurezza

sag [sæg] v/i pendere; piegarsi; cadere

sagacious [sə'geiʃəs] sagace

said [sed] detto

sail

sail [seil] *s* vela *f*; passeggiata *f* in barca (*a vela*); *v/t* navigare; **~ing-boat** barca *f* a vela; **~or** marinaio *m*

saint [seint] *s* santo(a) *m* (*f*); *a* santo; San (*davanti nomi maschili che non iniziano con st, o z, o vocale*); **All ♀'s Day** Tutti i Santi

sake [seik]: **for the ~ of peace** per amor di pace; per motivi di pace; **for God's ~** per l'amor di Dio

salad ['sæləd] insalata *f*; **~ bowl** insalatiera *f*

salary ['sæləri] stipendio *m*

sale [seil] vendita *f*; **on ~** in vendita; **~sman** venditore *m*; commesso *m* (*di negozio*)

saliva [sə'laivə] saliva *f*

sallow ['sæləu] olivastro

salmon ['sæmən] salmone *m*

salon ['sælɔn] salone *m*

saloon [sə'luːn] sala *f* grande; *Am* birreria *f*

salt [sɔːlt] sale *m*; *v/t* salare; **~y** salato

salute [sə'luːt] *s* saluto *m*; *v/t* salutare

salvation [sæl'veiʃən] redenzione *f*; ♀ **Army** Esercito *m* della Salvezza

salve [sɑːv] unguento *m*

same [seim] stesso; medesimo

sample ['sɑːmpl] *s* campione *m*; *v/t* provare; **~-book** campionario *m*

sanatorium [sænə'tɔːriəm] sanatorio *m*

sanctify ['sæŋktifai] *v/t* santificare

sanction ['sæŋkʃən] *s* sanzione *f*; *v/t* autorizzare

sanctuary ['sæŋktjuəri] santuario *m*

sand [sænd] sabbia *f*

sandal ['sændl] sandalo *m*

sandpaper carta *f* vetrata

sandwich ['sænwidʒ] panino *m* ripieno; tartina *f*

sandy ['sændi] sabbioso

sane [sein] sano

sanguinary ['sæŋgwinəri] sanguinario

sanita|ry ['sænitəri] sanitario; igienico; **~ry napkin; ~ry towel** assorbente *m* igienico; **~tion** igiene *f*

sanity ['sæniti] sanità *f*

Santa Claus [sæntə'klɔːz] babbo *m* Natale

sap [sæp] *s* linfa *f*; *v/t* minare

sapphire ['sæfaiə] zaffiro *m*

sarcas|m ['sɑːkæzəm] sarcasmo *m*; **~tic** [sɑː'kæstik] sarcastico

sardine [sɑː'diːn] sardina *f*

Sardinia Sardegna *f*; **~n** *a*, *s* sardo (*m*)

Satan ['seitən] Satano *m*

satchel ['sætʃəl] cartella *f*

satellite ['sætəlait] satellite *m*

satir|e ['sætaiə] satira *f*; **~ical** [sə'tirikəl] satirico

satisf|action [sætis'fækʃən] soddisfazione *f*; **~actory** soddisfacente; **~y** ['~fai] *v/t* soddisfare

Saturday ['sætədi] sabato *m*

sauc|e [sɔːs] salsa *f*; **~epan** casseruola *f*; **~er** piattino *m*; **~y** impertinente

saunter ['sɔ:ntə] v/i andare piano piano

sausage ['sɔsidʒ] salsiccia f

savage ['sævidʒ] a, s selvaggio (m)

save [seiv] prp salvo; eccetto; v/t salvare; economizzare; risparmiare; **~ings** pl risparmi m/pl; **~ings-bank** cassa f di risparmio

saviou(r) ['seivjə] salvatore m; redentore m

savou(r) ['seivə] s gusto m; sapore m; v/t sapere di; **~y** a saporito

saw [sɔ:] s sega f; v/t, irr segare; **~dust** segatura f

Saxon ['sæksn] a, s sassone (m, f)

say [sei] v/t, v/i, irr dire; **they ~** dicono; **I ~!** davvero!; **that is to ~** cioè; **~ing** detto m ~

scab [skæb] crosta f

scaffold ['skæfəld] patibolo m; **~ing** impalcatura f

scald [skɔ:ld] s scottatura f; v/t scottare

scale [skeil] s scala f; scaglia f (della pelle); v/t scalare; **~s** pl bilancia f

scalp [skælp] cuoio m capelluto

scandal ['skændl] scandalo m; **~ous** scandaloso

Scandinavian [skændi'neivjən] a, s scandinavo (m)

scant [skænt], **~y** scarso

scapegoat ['skeitgout] capro m espiatorio

scar [ska:] cicatrice f a tro-

vare; **~ely** appena; **~ely ever** quasi mai; **~ity** carestia f

scare [skɛə] s spavento m; v/t spaventare; **~crow** spauracchio m

scarf [ska:f], pl **~s** [~fs], **scarves** [~vz] sciarpa f

scarlet ['ska:lit] scarlatto; **~-fever** scarlattina f

scatter ['skætə] v/t, v/i spargere; sparpagliare

scene [si:n] scena f; scenata f; **~ry** scenario m; panorama m; paesaggio m

scent [sent] s profumo m; v/t profumare

sceptic ['skeptik] s, a scettico (m); **~al** scettico

schedule ['ʃedju:l], Am ['skedʒu:l] s lista f; programma m; Am orario m; v/t schedare

scheme [ski:m] s piano m; progetto m; sistema m; v/i intrigare

scholar ['skɔlə] studioso m; **~rship** borsa f di studio

school [sku:l] scuola f; istruzione f; **~master** maestro m; insegnante m; **~mate** compagno(a) m (f) di scuola; **~teacher** maestro(a) m (f); professore m; professoressa f

scien|ce ['saiəns] scienza f; **~tific** scientifico; **~tist** scienziato m

scissors ['sizəz] pl forbici f/pl

scoff [skɔf]: **~ at** v/t deridere

scold [skould] v/t rimproverare

scoop [sku:p] s cucchiaia f; ramaiuolo m; v/t travasare

scope [skoup] libertà f d'azione; campo m (d'attività)

scorch [skɔ:tʃ] v/t bruciare

score [skɔ:] s ventina f; punteggio m; spartito m; v/t segnare

scorn [skɔ:n] s disprezzo m; v/t disprezzare; **~ful** sprezzante

Scot [skɔt] scozzese m, f

Scotch [skɔtʃ], **Scottish** a, s scozzese (m, f)

Scotch|man, **~woman**, **Scotsman**, **Scotswoman** scozzese m, f

scoundrel ['skaundrəl] mascalzone m

scout [skaut] esploratore m

scowl [skaul] v/i guardare male

scramble ['skræmbl] s precipizio m; v/i precipitarsi; **~d eggs** uova f/pl strapazzate

scrap [skræp] s pezzetto m; rottame m; litigio m; v/t scartare; v/i litigare

scrape [skreip] v/t raschiare

scratch [skrætʃ] s graffio m; v/t graffiare

scream [skri:m] s strillo m; urlo m; v/i strillare; urlare

screech [skri:tʃ] s strillo m (acuto); v/i strillare

screen [skri:n] s paravento m; schermo m (cinematografico); v/t riparare; proteggere

screw [skru:] s vite f; v/t avvitare; **~driver** giravite m

scribble ['skribl] s scarabocchio m; v/t scarabocchiare

script [skript] scrittura f; copione m (di un film); **~ure** scrittura f; **the Holy ~ures** pl la Sacra Scrittura

scrub [skrʌb] v/t strofinare

scrup|le ['skru:pl] scrupolo m; **~ulous** ['~pjuləs] scrupoloso

scrutinize ['skru:tinaiz] v/t scrutinare

sculpt|or ['skʌlptə] scultore m; **~ure** scultura f

scum [skʌm] schiuma f; feccia f

scurvy ['skə:vi] scorbuto m

scythe [saið] s falce f; v/t falciare

sea [si:] mare m; **at ~** sul mare; **~gull** gabbiano m

seal [si:l] s zool foca f; sigillo m; v/t sigillare

sea level livello m del mare

sealing-wax ceralacca f

seam [si:m] cucitura f; giacimento m

seaport porto m di mare

search [sə:tʃ] s. ricerca f; v/i cercare; **~light** riflettore m

seasick: be ~ avere il mal di mare; **~ness** mal m di mare

seaside costa f; lido m

season ['si:zn] s stagione f; v/t condire; **~able** di stagione; **~ing** condimento m; **~ticket** biglietto m d'abbonamento m

seat [si:t] s posto m (a sedere); panchina f; sede f; fondello *m (del calzone); v/r ~ **o.s.** sedersi; ~**belt** cintura *f* di sicurezza

seaweed alga *f*

seclu|ded [si'klu:did] appartato; ~**sion** solitudine *f*; ritiro *m*

second ['sekənd] *a* secondo; 2~**class** di seconda classe; *s.* secondo *m*; *v/t* appoggiare; assecondare; ~**ary** secondario; ~**ary school** scuola *m* media; ~ **floor** *Am* primo piano; ~**rate** di qualità minore

secre|cy ['si:krisi] segretezza *f*; ~**t** *a, s* secreto (*m*)

secretary ['sekrətri] segretario *m*

secret|e [si'kri:t] *v/t med* secernere; ~**ion** secrezione *f*

sect [sekt] setta *f*

sect|ion ['sekʃən] sezione *f*; ~**or** ['sektə] settore *m*

secular ['sekjulə] secolare

secur|e [si'kjuə] *a* sicuro; *v/t* assicurare; ~**ity** sicurezza *f*

sedative ['sedətiv] *a, s* sedativo (*m*)

sediment ['sedimənt] sedimento *m*

seduc|e [si'dju:s] *v/t* sedurre; ~**tion** [~'dʌkʃən] seduzione *f*

see [si:] *v/t, irr* vedere; ~ **off** accompagnare; ~ **to** provvedere a

seed [si:d] seme *m*

seek [si:k] *v/t, irr* cercare

seem [si:m] *v/i* sembrare

seep [si:p] *v/i* trasudare

seesaw ['si:sɔ:] altalena *f*

segregate ['segrigeit] *v/t* segregare

seismograph ['saizməgrɑ:f] sismografo *m*

seiz|e [si:z] *v/t* afferrare; ~**ure** presa *f*; *med* attacco *m*

seldom ['seldəm] raramente

select [si'lekt] *a* scelto; *v/t* scegliere; ~**ion** selezione *f*

self [self], *pl* **selves** [~vz] *a* stesso; *s* se stesso; ~**command** padronanza *f* di se stesso; ~**confidence** fiducia *f* in se stesso; ~**contained** riservato; ~**ish** egoista; ~**made man** uomo *m* fatto da sè; ~**possessed** padrone *m* di se stesso; ~**reliant** conscio del proprio valore; ~**sacrificing** che sacrifica se stesso; ~**service** autoservizio *m*; ~**timer** *phot* autoscatto *m*

sell [sel] *v/t, irr* vendere; *v/i* vendersi; ~**er** venditore *m*; ~**ing** vendita *f*

semblance ['sembləns] apparenza *f*

semester [si'mestə] semestre *m*

semicolon ['semi'koulən] punto *m* e virgola

senate ['senit] senato *m*; ~**or** senatore *m*

send [send] *v/t, irr* mandare; spedire; ~ **back** rimandare

senior ['si:njə] maggiore di età; più anziano

sensation [sen'seiʃən] sensazione *f*; ~**al** sensazionale

sens|e [sens] *v/t* accorgersi di; *s.* senso *m*; buon senso

m; significato *m*; **~eless**
senza significato; assurdo;
~ible sensato; **~itive** sensible; **~ual** sensuale; **~uality**
sensualità *f*

sentence ['sentəns] *s* sentenza *f*; frase *f*; *v/t* condannare
sentiment ['sentimənt] sentimento *m*; **~al** [~'mentl]
sentimentale
sentry ['sentri] sentinella *f*
separate ['sepərit] *a* sepa-
rato; ['sepəreit] *v/t* separare; *v/i* separarsi; **~ion** [ˌse-
pə'reiʃən] separazione *f*
September [sap'tembə] settembre *m*
septic ['septik] settico
seque|l ['siːkwəl] seguito *m*;
~nce successione *f*; serie *f*
serenade [ˌseri'neid] sere-
nata *f*
serene [si'riːn] sereno
sergeant ['saːdʒənt] sergen-
te *m*
serial ['siəriəl] romanzo *m* a
puntate
series ['siəriːz] *pl* serie *f*
serious ['siəriəs] serio; grave
sermon [sə:mən] predica *f*
serpent ['sə:pənt] serpente
m; **~ine** serpentino
serum ['siərəm] siero *m*
serv|ant ['sə:vənt] domesti-
co(a) *m* (*f*); **~e** *v/t*, *v/i* servire; **~ice** servizio *m*
serviette [ˌsə:vi'et] tovagliolo *m*
servile ['sə:vail] servile
session ['seʃən] sessione *f*
set [set] . partita *f*; serie *f*;
servizio *m*; **hair ~** messa in

piega; *v/t, irr* disporre;
mettere; regolare; fissare; **~**
aside mettere da parte; **~**
on fire incendiare; **~ up**
stabilire; mettere su; *v/i*
tramontare (*del sole*); soli-
dificarsi; **~back** contrattempo *m*
sett|er compositore *m*; **~ing**
ambiente *m*; messa *f* in
scena
settle ['setl] *v/t* sistemare;
accomodare; stabilire;
comm saldare; pagare; *v/i*
sistemarsi; accomodarsi;
~ment sistemazione *f*; colonia *f*; *comm* saldo *m*
sever ['sevə] *v/t* separare; *v/i*
separarsi
several ['sevrəl] vari; diversi
sever|e [si'viə] severo; **~ity**
severità *f*
sew [sou] *v/t, irr* cucire
sew|age ['sju(ː)idʒ] acque
f/pl luride; **~er** fogna *f*
sewing ['souiŋ] cucito *m*; **~-**
machine macchina *f* da cucire
sex [seks] sesso *m*
sexton ['sekstən] sacrestano
m
sexual ['seksjuəl] sessuale
shabby ['ʃæbi] logoro; mal-
landato
shad|e [ʃeid] *s* ombra *f*; pa-
ralume *m*; sfumatura *f*; *v/t*
dare ombra; **~ow** ['ʃædou]
ombra *f*
shaft [ʃɑːft] asta *f*; raggio *m*
(*di luce*); pozzo *m* (*di miniera*)
shake [ʃeik] *s.* scossa *f*; *v/t*

scuotere; agitare; **~ hands with** stringere la mano a; *v/i* tremare

shall [ʃæl] *v/d* dovere; *or: future tense of verb*

shallow [ˈʃæloʊ] poco profondo; *fig* superficiale

sham [ʃæm] *a* finto; falso; *s* finzione *f*

shame [ʃeim] vergogna *f*; **what a ~!** che peccato!; **~ful** vergognoso; **~less** svergognato

shampoo [ʃæmˈpuː] shampoo *m*

shank [ʃæŋk] gamba *f*; stinco *m*; *mech* asta *f*

shape [ʃeip] *s* forma *f*; *v/t* formare; modellare; **~less** informe; **~ly** ben fatto

share [ʃɛə] *s* parte *f*; porzione *f*; *comm* azione *f*; *v/t* (con)dividere; **~holder** azionista *m*

shark [ʃɑːk] pescecane *m*

sharp [ʃɑːp] *a* acuto; affilato; vivace; penetrante; piccante; *s mus* diesis *m*; *adv* in punto; **four o'clock ~** alle quattro in punto; **~en** *v/t* affilare; aguzzare; **~ener** temperalapis *m*

shatter [ˈʃætə] *v/t* frantumare; *v/i* andare in frantumi; frantumarsi

shave [ʃeiv] *v/t*, *irr* far la barba

shawl [ʃɔːl] scialle *m*

she [ʃiː] lei, ella, essa; (*in nomi composti*) femmina; **~cat** gatta *f*; **~goat** capra *f*

sheaf [ʃiːf], *pl* **sheaves** [~vz]

fascio *m*

shear [ʃiə] *v/t*, *irr* tosare

sheath [ʃiːθ] astuccio *m*; guaino *m*

shed [ʃed] *s* capanna *f*; *v/t* togliersi

sheep [ʃiːp], *pl ~* pecora *f*; **~dog** cane *m* pastore; **~ish** vergognoso

sheer [ʃiə] puro; fine

sheet [ʃiːt] lenzuolo *m*; foglio *m* (*di carta*); lastra *f*

shelf [ʃelf], *pl* **shelves** [~vz] scaffale *m*; ripiano *m*

shell [ʃel] conchiglia *f*; guscio *m* (*dell'uovo*); proiettile *m*

shelter [ˈʃeltə] rifugio *m*; asilo *m*; riparo *m*; *v/t* riparare; *v/i* ripararsi; rifugiarsi

shepherd [ˈʃepəd] pastore *m*

shield [ʃiːld] *s* scudo *m*; protezione *f*; *v/t* proteggere

shift [ʃift] *s* cambiamento *m*; turno *m*; *v/t* cambiare; spostare

shilling [ˈʃiliŋ] scellino *m*

shin(-bone) [ˈʃin(-)] *anat* stinco *m*

shine [ʃain] *s* lustro *m*; splendore *m*; *v/i*, *irr* brillare; splendere

shingle [ˈʃiŋgl] assicella *f*

shingles [ˈʃiŋglz] *pl* fuoco *m* di Sant'Antonio; erpete *m*

ship [ʃip] *s* nave *f*; *v/t* spedire; **~load** carico *m*; **~ment** spedizione *f*; **~owner** armatore *m*; **~ping agent** spedizioniere *m* marittimo; **~ping company** compagnia *f* di navigazione; **~wreck** naufragio m; **~yard** cantiere m navale

shire [ˈʃaiə] contea f

shirk [ʃəːk] v/t, v/i evitare; sottrarsi a

shirt [ʃəːt] camicia f

shiver [ˈʃivə] s brivido m; v/i rabbrividire

shock [ʃɔk] s cozzo m; colpo m; v/t scandalizzare; **~ing** scandaloso

shoe [ʃuː] s scarpa f; ferro m (da cavallo); v/t calzare; ferrare; **~lace** laccio m; **~maker** calzolaio m; **~shop** calzoleria f

shoot [ʃuːt] bot germoglio m; tiro m; v/t, irr fucilare; germogliare; sparare; andare a caccia; **~ing** caccia f

shop [ʃɔp] negozio m; **~assistant** commesso m; **~keeper** negoziante m; **~ping** compra f; **~window** vetrina f

shore [ʃɔː] riva f; spiaggia f

short [ʃɔːt] corto; breve; basso (di statura); cut **~** interrompere; abbreviare; **run ~** essere a corto di; **~age** scarsezza f; **~circuit** corto circuito m; **~coming** difetto m; **~cut** scorciatoia f; **~en** v/t accorciare; abbreviare; short **~hand** stenografia f; **~ly** tra poco; **~s** pl pantaloni m/pl corti; **~sighted** miope; poco accorto; **~term** a breve scadenza f

shot [ʃɔt] sparo m; tiro m

shoulder [ˈʃouldə] spalla f;

~blade scapola f; **~strap** bretella f

shout [ʃaut] s grido m; v/t gridare

shove [ʃʌv] s spinta f; v/t spingere

shovel [ˈʃʌvl] pala f

show [ʃou] s mostra f; esposizione f; spettacolo m; revista f; ostentazione f; v/t, irr mostrare

shower [ˈʃauə] acquazzone m; **~bath** doccia f

shred [ʃred] s pezzetto m; v/t tagliuzzare

shrew [ʃruː] bisceccia f; **~d** perspicace

shriek [ʃriːk] s strillo m; v/t strillare

shrill [ʃril] stridulo m

shrimp [ʃrimp] gamberetto m

shrine [ʃrain] santuario m

shrink [ʃriŋk] v/i, irr restringersi

Shrove Tuesday [ˈʃrouv-ˈtjuːzdi] martedì m grasso

shrub [ʃrʌb] arbusto m; cespuglio m

shrug [ʃrʌg] s alzata f di spalle; v/t stringersi nelle spalle

shudder [ˈʃʌdə] s brivido m; v/i rabbrividire

shuffle [ˈʃʌfl] v/t mescolare (carte); v/i strascicarsi

shut [ʃʌt] v/t, irr chiudere; v/i chiudersi; **~ up!** sta zitto!; **~ter** persiana f; saracinesca f; phot otturatore m

shy [ʃai] timido; **~ness** timidezza f

sick [sik] malato; **~ of** stanco di; **be ~** essere malato, vomitare; **~en** v/i ammalare; ammalarsi

side [said] lato m; parte f; fianco m; **~ by ~** fianco a fianco; **take ~s with, ~ with** prendere la parte di; **~board** credenza f; **~dish** frammesso m; **~walk** Am marciapiede m; **~ways** di lato

siege [si:dʒ] assedio m

sieve [siv] staccio m; vaglio m

sift [sift] v/t stacciare; crivellare

sigh [sai] s sospiro m; v/i sospirare

sight [sait] vista f; spettacolo m; **by ~** di vista; **at first ~** a prima vista; **~seeing** visita f della città

sign [sain] s segno m; v/t firmare; far segno a

signal [signl] s segnale m; v/t segnalare; fare segnali

signature [signitʃə] firma f

significance [sigˈnifikəns] significato m; **~icant** significativo; **~y** [sigˈnifai] v/t significare

silence [ˈsailəns] s silenzio m; v/t far tacere; **~t** silenzioso

silk [silk] seta f; **~worm** baco m da seta

sill [sil] davanzale m

silly [ˈsili] sciocco

silver [ˈsilvə] argento m; **~wedding** nozze f/pl d'argento; **~y** aregntino

similar [ˈsimile] simile; **~ity** [~ˈlæriti] somiglianza f

simple [ˈsimpl] semplice; **~ify** [~ˈfai] v/t semplificare

simulate [ˈsimjuleit] v/t simulare

simultaneous [siməlˈteinjəs] simultaneo

sin [sin] s peccato m; v/i peccare

since [sins] adv da allora; conj da che; da quando; prp da; fino da

sincer|e [sinˈsiə] sincero; **~ity** [~ˈseriti] sincerità f

sinew [ˈsinju:] nerbo m

sing [siŋ] v/t, v/i cantare

singe [sindʒ] v/t bruciare

singer [ˈsiŋə] cantante m, f

single [ˈsiŋgl] solo; unico; singolo; **~handed** senza aiuto

singular [ˈsiŋgjulə] singolare

sinister [ˈsinistə] sinistro

sink [siŋk] s acquaio m; v/t, irr immergere; affondare

sinner [ˈsinə] peccatore m, peccatrice f

sip [sip] sorso m

sir [sə:] signore m

sirloin [ˈsə:lɔin] lombo m

sister [ˈsistə] sorella f; suora f; **~in-law** cognata f

sit [sit] v/i, irr essere seduto; **~ down** sedersi

site [sait] posto m; sito m

sitting [ˈsitiŋ] a seduto; s seduta f; udienza f; **~room** salotto m

situat|ed [ˈsitjueitid] situato; **~ion** situazione f; posizione *f*; posto *m*; impiego *m*

size [saiz] grandezza *f*; misura *f*

skat|e [skeit] *s* pattino *m*; *v/i* pattinare; **~ing-rink** pista *f* da pattinaggio

skeleton ['skelitn] scheletro *m*

skeptic [skeptik] *Am for* **sceptic**

sketch [sketʃ] *s* schizzo *m*; abbozzo *m*; *v/t* schizzare; abbozzare

ski [ski] *s* sci *m*; *v/i* sciare

skid [skid] *v/i* sbandare

skier ['skiːə] sciatore *m*

skil|ful ['skilful] abile; destro; **~l** abilità *f*; **~led** pratico; esperto; **~led worker** operaio *m* specializzato

skim [skim] *v/t* scremare; sfiorare

skin [skin] *s* pelle *f*; *v/t* pelare

skip [skip] *v/i* saltare

skirmish ['skəːmiʃ] *s* scaramuccia *f*; *v/i* scaramucciare

skirt [skəːt] *s* gonna *f*; sottana *f*; *v/t* costeggiare

skittles ['skitlz] *sg* birillo *m*

skull [skʌl] cranio *m*; teschio *m*

skunk [skʌŋk] moffetta *f*

sky [skai] cielo *m*; **~scrapper** grattacielo *m*

slab [slæb] lastra *f*

slack [slæk] *a* allentato; inattivo; **~en** *v/i* allentarsi; **~s** *pl* pantaloni *m/pl* lunghi (*da donna*); calzoni *m/pl*

slam [slæm] *v/t* sbattere

slander ['slɑːndə] *s* calun-

nia *f*; *v/t* calunniare

slang [slæŋ] gergo *m*

slant [slɑːnt] *s* pendio *m*; punto *m* di vista; *v/i* inclinarsi

slap [slæp] *s* schiaffo *m*; *v/t* schiaffeggiare

slash [slæʃ] *s* sqarcio *m*; *v/t* tagliare

slate [sleit] *s* tegola *f*; lavagnetta *f*

slaughter ['slɔːtə] *s* macello *m*; massacro *m*; *v/t* macellare; massacrare; **~house** mattatoio *m*

Slav [slɑːv, slæv] *a*, *s* slavo (*m*)

slave [sleiv] *s* schiavo(a) *m* (*f*); *v/i* lavorare come un negro; **~ry** schiavitù *f*

slay [slei] *v/t*, *irr* ammazzare

sled(ge) [sled(ʒ)] slitta *f*

sleek [sliːk] *a* liscio; *v/t* lisciare

sleep [sliːp] *s* sonno *m*; *v/t*, *v/i* dormire; **~er** cuccetta *f*; **~ing-bag** sacco *m* a pelo; **~ing-pill** sonnifero *m*; **~less** insonne; **~-walker** sonnambulo(a) *m* (*f*); **~y** assonnato

sleet [sliːt] nevischio *m*

sleeve [sliːv] manica *f*

sleigh [slei] slitta *f*

slender ['slendə] snello

slice [slais] *s* fetta *f*; *v/t* affettare

slide [slaid] *v/i*, *irr* scivolare; **~ rule** regolo *m* calcolatore

slight [slait] leggero

slim [slim] *a* sottile; magro; *v/i* dimagrire

slim|e [slaim] melma *f*; **~y** melmoso

sling [sliŋ] *s* fionda *f*; *v/t, irr* lanciare; scagliare

slip [slip] *s* svista *f*; federa *f*; sottoveste *f*; *v/i* scivolare; sbagliare; **~per** pantofola *f*; **~pery** scivoloso

slit [slit] *s* fessura *f*; *v/t, irr* tagliare

slogan ['slougən] parola *f* d'ordine; motto *m*

slope [sloup] *s* pendenza *f*; *v/i* inclinarsi

sloppy ['slɔpi] trasandato; fradiccio

slot [slɔt] buco *m*

sloth [slouθ] pigrizia *f*

slot-machine distributore *m* automatico

slovenly ['slʌvnli] trasandato; trasurato

slow [slou] lento; **~ down** *v/t, v/i* rallentare; **~ly** lentamente; adagio; piano; **~ motion** rallentatore *m*

sluice [slu:s] chiusa *f*

slums [slʌmz] quartiere *m* povero; bassofondo *m*

slush [slʌʃ] fanghiglia *f*

slut [slʌt] puttana *f*

sly [slai] astuto; furbo

smack [smæk] *s* pacca *f*; battello *m*; *v/i* schiaffeggiare

small [smɔːl] piccolo; **~ hours** *pl ore f/pl* piccole; **~pox** vaiolo *m*

smart [smɑːt] *a* elegante, sveglio; *s* bruciore *m*; *v/i* bruciare

smash [smæʃ] *s* crollo *m*;

scontro *m*; *v/t* frantumare; *v/i* frantumarsi; **~ing** (*gergo*) bellissimo

smear [smiə] *v/t* macchiare

smell [smel] *s* odore *m*; *v/i* sentire l'odore; *v/i* odorare; **nasty ~** puzzo *m*; *v/t* sentire l'odore; **~t** [smelt] *v/t* fondere

smile [smail] *s* sorriso *m*; *v/i* sorridere

smith [smiθ] fabbro *m*

smock [smɔk] camiciotto *m*; camice *m*

smok|e [smouk] *s* fumo *m*; *v/t* fumare; affumicare; *v/i* emettere fumo; **~ing-compartment** (s)compartimento *m* per fumatori; **no ~ing** proibito fumare

smooth [smu:ð] *a* liscio; *v/t* lisciare

smother ['smʌðə] *v/t* soffocare

smo(u)lder ['smouldə] *v/i* bruciare senza fiamma; *fig* covare

smudg|e [smʌdʒ] *s* macchia *f*; *v/t* macchiare

smug [smʌg] soddisfatto di sè

smuggl|e ['smʌgl] *v/t* far passare di contrabbando; *v/i* fare il contrabbando; **~er** contrabbandiere *m*; **~ing** contrabbando *m*

smut [smʌt] macchia *f*; **~ty** macchiato; *fig* osceno

snack [snæk] spuntino *m*

snail [sneil] lumaca *f*; **at a ~'s pace** a passo di tartaruga

snake [sneik] serpente *m*; serpe *f*

snap [snæp] s rumore m secco; v/t rompere con rumore secco; fig rispondere male; **~-fastener** bottone m a molla; **~shot** phot istantanea f

snare [snɛə] trappola f

snarl [snɑːl] s ringhio m; v/i ringhiare

snatch [snætʃ] v/t afferrare; strappare

sneak [sniːk] v/i fare la spia

sneer [sniə] s ghigno m; v/i sogghignare; **~ at** disprezzare

sneeze [sniːz] s starnuto m; v/i starnutire

sniff [snif] v/t annusare

snivel ['snivl] v/i piagnucolare

snore [snɔː] v/i russare

snout [snaut] muso m; grugno m

snow [snou] s neve f; v/i nevicare; **~drop** bucaneve m; **~fall** nevicata f; **~flake** fiocco m di neve; **~storm** tormenta f di neve

snuff [snʌf] tabacco m da naso

snug [snʌg] comodo; **~gle** v/i rannicchiarsi

so [sou] adv, pron così; in questo modo; **~ far** fino a questo momento; fino a questo punto; **~ long** tanto tempo; arrivederci!; **~ much** tanto; **I think ~** credo di sì; **Mr. ~and ~** Signor Tal dei Tali

soak [souk] v/t bagnare; inzuppare

soap [soup] s sapone m; v/t insaponare

soar [sɔː] v/i volare

sob [sɔb] s singhiozzo m; v/i singhiozzare

sober ['soubə] non ubriaco; sobrio; serio

soccer ['sɔkə] Am calcio m

socia|ble ['souʃəbl] socievole; **~l** sociale; **~l insurance** assicurazione f sociale; **~lism** socialismo m; **~list** a, s socialista (m, f)

society [sə'saiəti] società f

sock [sɔk] calzino m

socket ['sɔkit] orbita f

soda soda f; **~-water** seltz m

sofa ['soufə] sofà m

soft [sɔft] morbido; molle; dolce; **~ drink** bibita f non alcoolica; **~ water** acqua f dolce; **~en** v/t ammorbidire; v/i intenerirsi

soil [sɔil] s terreno m; suolo m; v/t sporcare

sojourn ['sɔdʒəːn] s soggiorno m; v/i soggiornare

soldier ['souldʒə] soldato m; militare m

sole [soul] s pianta f del piede; suola f (della scarpa); sogliola f; v/t risuolare

solemn ['sɔləm] solenne; grave

solicit [sə'lisit] v/t sollecitare; importunare; **~or** avvocato m

solid ['sɔlid] solido; **~ify** [sə'lidifai] v/t solidificare

solit|ary ['sɔlitəri] solitario; **~ude** ['~tjuːd] solitudine f

solo ['soulou] assolo; **~ist** solista m, f

solu|ble ['sɔljubl] solubile; **~tion** [sə'luːʃən] soluzione f

solve [sɔlv] v/t risolvere; **~nt** solvente

some [sʌm, səm] a un po' di; qualche; alcuno; alcuni; pron qualcuno; alcuni; **~body, ~one** qualcuno; **~body else** qualcun altro; **~how** qualche modo; **~what** piuttosto; **~where** in qualche parte

somersault ['sʌməsɔːlt] capriola f; salto m mortale

son [sʌn] figlio m; **~-in-law** genero m

song [sɔŋ] canzone f; canto m

soon [suːn] presto; tra un po'; **as ~ as** appena che; **as ~ as possible** il più presto possibile; **~er or later** presto o tardi

soothe [suːð] v/t calmare

soporific [ˌsɔpə'rifik] a, soporifico m

sorcer|er ['sɔːsərə] strega f; mago m; **~y** stregoneria f

sordid ['sɔːdid] sordido a

sore [sɔː] a dolente; **my foot is ~** mi fa male il piede

sorrow ['sɔrou] dolore m

sorry ['sɔri] dispiaciuto; spiacente; **be ~** dispiacersi

sort [sɔːt] s genere m; specie f; v/t scegliere; classificare

soul [soul] anima f; **All ~s' Day** Tutti i Santi

sound [saund] a solido; profondo; logico; v/t suonare;

med ascoltare; v/i suonare; **~proof** con isolamento acustico

soup [suːp] minestra f; brodo m; zuppa f

sour ['sauə] acerbo; acido

source [sɔːs] fonte f; origine m

south [sauθ] s sud m; a meridionale; **~ern** meridionale f; **~east** sud-est m

souvenir ['suːvəniə] ricordo m

sovereign ['sɔvrin] a, s sovrano

sow¹ [sau] scrofa f

sow² [sou] v/t, irr seminare; spargere; **~ing-machine** seminatrice f

spa|ce [speis] spazio m; **~ious** spazioso

spade [speid] vanga f; **~s** pl (a carte) picche f/pl

Spain [spein] Spagna f

span [spæn] palmo m (della mano); periodo m (di tempi); v/t abbracciare

spangle ['spæŋgl] lustrino m

Spaniard ['spænjəd] spagnolo(a) m (f)

spaniel ['spænjəl] spagnolo m

Spanish ['spæniʃ] spagnolo m

spank [spæŋk] v/t sculacciare

spanner ['spænə] chiave f inglese

spar|e [spɛə] a di ricambio; di riserva; disponibile; **~e parts** pl parti f/pl di ricambio; **~e time** tempo m libero; v/t risparmiare; **~ing** economo

spark [spɑ:k] s scintilla f; **~ingplug** candela f d'accensione; **~le** v/i scintillare

sparrow ['spærou] passero m

sparse [spɑ:s] sparso

spasm ['spæzəm] spasmo m; **~odic** [~'mɔdik] spasmodico

spatter ['spætə] s spruzzo m; v/t spruzzare

speak [spi:k] v/i, irr parlare; **~er** oratore m

spear [spiə] lancia f

special ['speʃəl] speciale; particolare; **~ity** [~i'æliti] specialità f; **~ize** v/i specializzarsi; **~ly** specialmente; soprattutto

species ['spi:ʃiːz] pl specie f

specific [spi'sifik] specifico

specimen ['spesimin] campione m; esemplare m

specta|cle ['spektəkl] spettacolo m; **~cles** pl occhiali m/pl; **~cular** [spek'tækjulə] spettacolare; **~tor** [spek'teitə] spettatore m

speculate ['spekjuleit] v/t, v/i speculare; **~ion** speculazione f

speech [spi:tʃ] discorso m; parlare m

speed [spi:d] velocità f; **at full** ~ a tutta velocità; v/t, irr sfrecciare; ~ **up** accelerare; **~ometer** tachimetro m; **~y** veloce

spell [spel] s incanto m; fascino m; v/t, v/i, irr scrivere; **~ing** ortografia f

spend [spend] v/t, irr spendere (danaro); passare (tempo)

sperm [spə:m] sperma m

spher|e [sfiə] sfera f; **~ical** ['sferikl] sferico

spic|e [spais] spezie f/pl; **~y** saporoso

spider ['spaidə] ragno m; **~'s web** ragnatela f

spike [spaik] chiodo m

spill [spil] v/t, irr rovesciare; v/i rovesciarsi

spin [spin] v/i, irr girare

spinach ['spinidʒ] spinaci m/pl

spindle ['spindl] fuso m

spine [spain] spina f dorsale

spinster ['spinstə] zittella f

spiral ['spaiərəl] spirale

spirit ['spirit] spirito m; **~s** pl alcool m; **high ~s** allegria f; **low ~s** abbattimento m; **~ed** vivace; **~ual** [~'tjuəl] spirituale

spit [spit] s spiedo m; saliva f; v/t, irr sputare

spite [spait] dispetto m; **in ~ of** malgrado; **~ful** dispettoso

spittle ['spitl] saliva f

splash [splæʃ] s schizzo m; v/t schizzare

spleen [spli:n] bile f

splend|id ['splendid] splendido; **~o(u)r** splendore m

splint [splint] med stecca f; **~er** s scheggia f; v/t scheggiare

split [split] rottura f; spaccatura f; v/t, irr spaccare

spoil [spɔil] s bottino m; v/t, irr guastare; v/i guastarsi; **~t child** bambino m viziato

spoke [spouk] raggio m

spokesman portavoce m

sponge [spʌndʒ] s spugna f; v/t sbafare

sponsor ['spɔnsə] garante m

spontaneous [spɔn'teinjəs] spontaneo

spook [spu:k] spettro m

spool [spu:l] bobina f

spoon [spu:n] cucchiaio m; **~ful** cucchiaiata f

sport [spɔ:t] sport m; **~sman**, **~swoman** sportivo(a) m (f)

spot [spɔt] luogo m; posto m; macchia f; v/t macchiare; fam vedere; individuare

spout [spaut] becco m

sprain [sprein] s storta f; v/t storcere

sprat [spræt] sardinetta f

sprawl [sprɔ:l] v/i sdraiarsi

spray [sprei] s spruzzo m; v/t spruzzare

spread [spred] s distesa f; v/t, irr stendere; v/i stendersi

sprig [sprig] rametto m

spring [spriŋ] s primavera f; fonte f (di acqua); mech molla f; salto m; v/i, irr balzare; nascere; derivare; **~board** trampolino m

sprinkle ['spriŋkl] v/t spruzzare

sprint [sprint] s corsa f; v/i correre a tutta velocità; **~er** velocista m, f

sprout [spraut] germoglio

m; **Brussels ~s** cavolini m/pl di Brusselle

spy [spai] s spia f; v/t, v/i spiare

squad [skwɔd] squadra f

squalid ['skwɔlid] squallido

squander ['skwɔndə] v/t scialcquare

square [skwɛə] a quadrato; s piazza f; quadrato m; v/t quadrare; elevare al quadrato; saldare (i conti)

squash [skwɔʃ] s spremuta f; v/t spremere; schiacciare

squat [skwɔt] v/i accucciarsi

squeak [skwi:k] s cigolio m; v/i cigolare

sqeamish ['skwi:miʃ] schizzinoso

squeeze [skwi:z] v/t spremere; strizzare

squint [skwint] s strabismo m; v/i essere strabico

squirm [skwə:m] v/i contorcersi

squirrel ['skwirəl] scoiattolo m

squirt [skwə:t] s schizzetto m; v/t schizzare

stab [stæb] s pugnalata f; v/t pugnalare

stability [stə'biliti] stabilità f; **~ilize** ['steibilaiz] v/t stabilizzare

stable[1] [steibl] stabile

stable[2] [steibl] stalla f; scuderia f

stack [stæk] pagliaio m; mucchio m; v/t ammucchiare

stadium ['steidjəm] stadio m

staff [staːf] bastone *m*; asta *f*; personale *m*

stag [stæg] cervo *m*

stage [steidʒ] *s* palcoscenico *m*; *v/t* mettere in scena

stagger ['stægə] *v/i* barcollare

stagnate ['stægneit] *v/i* stagnare

stain [stein] *s* macchia *f*; *v/t* macchiare; *v/i* macchiarsi; **~ed glass** vetro *m* colorato; **~less** immacolato; **~less steel** acciaio *m* inossidabile

stair [steə] gradino *m*; scalino *m*; **~s** *pl* scale *f/pl*

stake [steik] *s* palo *m*; rogo *m*; **be at ~** essere in giuoco; *v/t* rischiare; scommettere

stale [steil] raffermo; stantio

stalk [stɔːk] *s bot* stelo *m*; passo *m* maestoso; *v/i* andare maestosamente; *v/t* inseguire

stall [stɔːl] bancherella *f*; edicola *f*; poltrona *f* (*di teatro*)

stallion ['stæljən] stallone *m*

stalwart ['stɔːlwət] robusto

stamina ['stæminə] vigore *m*

stammer ['stæmə] *s* balbuzie *f*; *v/t*, *v/i* balbettare

stamp [stæmp] *s* francobollo *m*; timbro *m*; impronta *f*; *v/t* stampare; timbrare; *v/i* pestare i piedi

stand [stænd] *s* banco *m*; edicola *f*; sostegno *m*; piedistallo *m*; posizione *f*; *v/t*, *irr* appoggiare; resistere a;

sopportare; *v/i* stare in piedi; **~ up** alzarsi in piedi; **~ up against** ribellarsi contro; **~ for** rappresentare; **~ out** resistere

standard ['stændəd] stendardo *m*; livello *m*

standing ['stændiŋ] riputazione *f*

stand|point punto *m* di vista; **~still: be at a ~still** essere fermo

star [staː] stella *f*

starboard ['staːbəd] lato *m* destro (*della nave*)

starch [staːt] *s* amido *m*; *v/t* inamidire

stare [steə] *s* sguardo *m* fisso; *v/i* fissare; guardare fisso

stark [staːk] rigido; vero e proprio; **~ naked** nudo del tutto

starling ['staːliŋ] stornello *m*

start [staːt] *s* principio *m*; soprassalto *m*; partenza *f*; *v/t* iniziare; *v/i* trasalire; partire

start|le ['staːtl] *v/t* far trasalire; allarmare; **~ling** allarmante

starv|ation [staː'veiʃən] fame *f*; **~e** *v/i* morire di fame; *v/t* far morire di fame

state [steit] stato *m*; condizione *f*; *v/t* dichiarare; affermare; ♀ **Department** *Am* ministero *m* degli esteri; **~ly** imponente; **~ment** dichiarazione *f*; affermazione *f*; **~sman** uomo *m* di Stato

static ['stætik] statico

station ['steiʃən] stazione f; **ary** stazionario; **er** cartolaio m; **master** capo m stazione

statistics [stə'tistiks] sg statistica f; pl statastische f/pl

steal [sti:l] v/t, irr rubare

steam [sti:m] vapore m; **boat** piroscafo m

steel [sti:l] acciaio m

steep [sti:p] erto; ripodo

steeple [sti:pl] campanile m

stem [stem] s bot stelo m; stirpe f; gram radicale m

stench [stentʃ] puzzo m; fetore m

stencil ['stensl] stampino m

step [step] s passo m; scalino m; **in** entrare; **brother** fratellastro m; **father** patrigno m; **mother** matrigna f

steril|e ['sterail] sterile; **ize** ['**·**ilaiz] v/t sterilizzare

sterling ['stə:liŋ] a genuino; s sterlina f

stern [stə:n] a severo; s poppa f

stew [stju:] s stufato m; v/t cuocere a fuoco lento

steward ['stjuəd] amministratore m; cameriere m (sulla nave); **ess** cameriera f; stewardess f

stick [stik] s bastone m; v/t, irr incollare; affiggere; ficcare; v/i aderire; **er** etichetta f; **y** attaccaticcio

stiff [stif] duro; difficile; rigido; **en** v/t irrigidire; v/i irrigidirsi

stifle ['staifl] v/t soffocare

still [stil] a immobile; calmo; silenzioso; adv ancora; tuttavia; s calma f; quiete f; v/t calmare; **born** nato morto; **ness** quiete f

stimul|ant ['stimjulənt] a, s stimolante; **ate** v/t stimolare; **us** stimolo m

sting [stiŋ] s puntura f; v/t .pungere

stingy ['stindʒi] tirchio

stink [stiŋk] s puzzo m; v/i, irr puzzare

stipulate ['stipjuleit] v/t stipolare

stir [stə:] s agitazione f; movimento m; v/t agitare; girare; v/i muoversi

stirrup ['stirəp] staffa f

stitch [stitʃ] s punto m; v/t cucire

stock [stɔk] s bestiame m; stirpe f; merce f in magazzino; v/t tenere in magazzino; **breeder** allevatore m di bestiame; **broker** agente m di cambio; **exchange** borsa f; **holder** azionista m

stocking ['stɔkiŋ] calza f

stock-taking inventario m

stocky ['stɔki] tozzo

stoic ['stouik] stoico

stomach ['stʌmək] s stomaco m; v/t mandare giù; tollerare

ston|e [stoun] s pietra f; sasso m; med calcolo m; nocciolo m; v/t lapidare; **y** pietroso

stool [stu:l] sgabello m

stoop [stu:p] v/i curvarsi

stop [stɔp] s fermata f; v/t

fermare; *v/i* fermarsi;
~page arresto *m*; **~over**
fermata *f* intermedia; **~per**
tappo *m*; **~ping** sosta *f*

stor|age ['stɔ:ridʒ] magazzinaggio *m*; **~e** [stɔ:] *s* grande magazzino *m*; provvista *f*; *v/t* immagazzinare; accumulare; **~e-house** magazzino *m*

storey ['stɔ:ri] piano *m*

stork [stɔ:k] cicogna *f*

storm [stɔ:m] tempesta *f*; temporale *m*; **~y** tempestoso

story ['stɔ:ri] storia *f*; racconto *m*

stout [staut] forte; robusto; solido

stove [stouv] stufa *f*; fornello *m*

stow [stou] *v/t* stivare; **~away** passeggero *m* clandestino

straggle ['strægl] *v/i* disperdersi

straight [streit] diritto; retto; **~en** *v/t* raddrizzare; **~forward** franco

strain [strein] *s* tensione *f*; *v/i* sforzarsi; **~er** colino *m*

strait [streit] stretto *m*; **in ~s** in difficoltà; **~jacket** camicia *f* di forza

strand [strænd] riva *f*

strange [streindʒ] strano; **~r** sconosciuto *m*

strangle ['stræŋgl] *v/t* strangolare

strap [stræp] cinghia *f*

strateg|ic, ~ical [strə'ti:dʒik] strategico; **~y** ['strætidʒi]

strategia *f*

straw [strɔ:] paglia *f*; **~berry** fragola *f*

stray [strei] smarrito; randagio

streak [stri:k] *s* striscia *f*; *v/t* striare; **~y** striato

stream [stri:m] *s* corrente *f*; flume *m*; *v/i* scorrere; **~lined** aerodinamico

street [stri:t] strada *f*; **~car** *Am* tram *m*

strength [streŋθ] forza *f*; **~en** *v/t* rinforzare

strenuous ['strenjuəs] strenuo

stress [stres] *s* tensione *f*; enfasi *f*; *v/t* mettere l'accento su; mettere in rilievo

stretch [stretʃ] *s* distesa *f*; *v/t* stendere; *v/i* stendersi; allargarsi; **~er** barella *f*

strew [stru:] *v/t*, *irr* cospargere

stricken ['strikən] colpito

strict [strikt] severo

stride [straid] *s* passo *m* grande; *v/i*, *irr* andare a passi grandi

strife [straif] lotta *f*

strike [straik] *s* sciopero *m*; *v/t* colpire; suonare (*orologio*); **be on ~s** fare sciopero; *v/i*, *irr* scioperare; **~breaker** crumiro *m*; **~r** scioperante *m*

string [striŋ] *s* corda *f*; spago *m*; *v/t*, *irr* infilare

strip [strip] *s* striscia *f*; *v/t* spogliare; *v/i* spgliarsi

stripe [straip] striscia *f*; riga *f*; **~d** a strisce; a righe

strive [straiv] v/i, irr sforzarsi

stroke [strouk] colpo m; attacco m; ~ **of luck** colpo di fortuna

stroll [stroul] passeggiatina f

strong [strɔŋ] forte; robusto

structure ['strʌktʃə] struttura f

struggle ['strʌgl] s lotta f; v/i lottare

stub [stʌb] mozzicone m

stubble ['stʌbl] stoppia f

stubborn ['stʌbən] testardo

stud [stʌd] bottone m della camicia

stud|ent ['stju:dənt] studente m; studentessa f; ~io ['stju:diou] s studio m; ~ious studioso; ~y ['stʌdi] s studio m; v/t studiare

stuff [stʌf] s materia f; materiale m; tessuto m; v/t imbottire; ~ **and nonsense** sciocchezze f/pl; ~ing imbottitura f

stumble ['stʌmbl] v/i inceppare

stump [stʌmp] moncone m

stun [stʌn] stordire

stupefy ['stju:pifai] v/t stupefare

stupid ['stju:pid] stupido; ~ity stupidità f

sturdy ['stə:di] robusto

stutter ['stʌtə] v/i balbettare

sty[1] [stai] porcile m

sty[2] [stai] orzaiolo m

style [stail] stile m

subconscious ['sʌb'kɔnʃəs] a subcosciente; ~ness subcoscienza f

subdue [səb'dju:] v/t soggiogare

subject ['sʌbdʒikt] a soggetto; ~ **to** soggetto a; s soggetto m; argomento m; suddito m; v/t sottomettere; esporre; ~ion soggezione f

subjunctive [səb'dʒʌŋktiv] a, s congiuntivo (m)

sublime [sə'blaim] sublime

sunmarine ['sʌbməri:n] sommergibile m

submerge [səb'mə:dʒ] v/t sommergere

submi|ssion [səb'miʃən] sottomissione f; ~ssive remissivo; ~t v/t sottomettere

subscri|be [səb'skraib] v/i abbonarsi; ~ber abbonato m; ~ption [səb'skripʃən] abbonamento m

subsequent ['sʌbsikwənt] successivo

subsid|e [səb'said] v/i abbassare; decrescere; tacere; ~y ['sʌbsidi] sussidio m

substan|ce ['sʌbstəns] sostanza f; ~tial [səb'stænʃəl] sostanziale

substitute ['sʌbstitju:t] s sostituto m; supplente m; v/t sostituire; supplire

subtle ['sʌtl] sottile; fine

subtract [səb'trækt] sovversivo

subway ['sʌbwei] ferrovia f sotterranea; metropolitana f

succ|eed [sək'si:d] v/i riuscire a; succedere a; ~ess [sək'ses] successo m; ~essful riuscito; ~essive successi-

vo; **~essor** successore *m*
such [sʌtʃ] *a*, *pron* tale
suck [sʌk] *v/t* succhiare
sudden [ˈsʌdn] improvviso
suds [sʌdz] *pl* schiuma *f*
sue [sjuː] *v/t* citare
suède [sweid] camoscio *m*
suet [ˈsjuit] lardo
suffer [ˈsʌfə] *v/t*, *v/i* soffrire; **~er** vittima *f*; **~ing** sofferenza *f*
suffic|e [səˈfais] *v/i* bastare; **~iency** [səˈfiʃənsi] sufficienza *f*; **~ient** sufficiente
suffocate [ˈsʌfəkeit] *v/t* soffocare; *v/i* soffocarsi
sugar [ˈʃugə] *s* zucchero *m*; *v/t* zuccherare
suggest [səˈdʒest] *v/t* suggerire; **~ion** suggestione *f*; **~ive** suggestivo
suicide [ˈsjuisaid] (*person*) suicida *n*, *f*; (*act*) suicidio *m*
suit [sjuːt] *s* vestito *m*; *jur* causa *f*; *v/t* stare bene a; andare bene a; convenire a; **~able** adotto; comodo; **~case** valigia *f*
suite [swiːt] serie *f*; appartamenti *m/pl*
sulk [sʌlk] *v/i* tenere il broncio; **~y** imbronciato
sullen [ˈsʌlən] cupo; imbronciato
sulphur [ˈsʌlfə] zolfo *m*
sum [sʌm] *s* somma *f*; *v/t* sommare; **~ up** riassumere
summar|ize [ˈsʌməraiz] *v/t* riassumere; **~y** sommario *m*
summer [ˈsʌmə] estate *f*
summit [ˈsʌmit] cima *f*

summon [ˈsʌmən] *v/t* citare; convocare; chiamare; **~s** [ˈ~z], *pl* **~s(es)** [ˈ~ziz] citazione *f*; chiamata *f*
sun [sʌn] sole *m*; **~bathe** *v/i* prendere il sole; **~beam** raggio *m* di sole; **~burnt** bruciato dal sole; abbronzatura *f*
Sunday [ˈsʌndi] domenica *f*
sundries [ˈsʌndriz] *pl* generi *m/pl* diversi
sun|rise alba *f*; sorgere *m* del sole; **~set** tramonto *m*; **~shine** sole *m*; **~stroke** insolazione *f*
superb [sjuˈ(ː)pəːb] splendido
super|ficial [sjuːpəˈfiʃəl] superficiale; **~fluous** [ˈ~pəːfluəs] superfluo; **~highway** *Am* autostrada *f*
superintend *v/t* sovrintendere a; **~ent** sovrintendente *m*
supernatural soprannaturale
superstition [ˌsjuːpəˈstiʃən] superstizione *f*
supervis|e [ˈsjuːpəvaiz] *v/t* sorvegliare; **~or** sorvegliante *m*
supper [ˈsʌpə] cena *f*
supplement [ˈsʌplimənt] supplemento *m*
suppl|ier [səˈplaiə] forniture *m*; **~y** *s* provvista *f*; *v/t* fornire
support [səˈpɔːt] *s* appoggio *m*; *v/t* sostenere; appoggia-
suppos|e [səˈpouz] *v/t* sup-

porre; **~ition** [ˌsʌp-
ˈzɪʃən] supposizione f

suppress [səˈpres] v/t sopprimere

suprem|acy [sjuˈpreməsi]
supremazia f; **~e** [~ˈpriːm]
supremo

sure [ʃuə] sicuro; **make ~ of**
assicurarsi di; **~ty** garante m

surf [səːf] frangenti m/pl

surface [ˈsəːfis] superficie f

surg|eon [ˈsəːdʒən] chirurgo
m; **~ery** chirurgia f; ambu-
latorio m; **~ical** chirurgico

surly [ˈsəːli] scontroso

surmise [səˈmaiz] v/t congetturare

surmount [səːˈmaunt] v/t
surmontare

surname [ˈsəːneim] cognome m

surpass [səːˈpɑːs] v/t sorpas-
sare; superare

surplus [ˈsəːpləs] s sovrappiù m; a in sovrappiù

surprise [səˈpraiz] s sorpresa
f; v/t sorprendere

surrender [səˈrendə] s resa
f; v/t abbandonare; v/i arrendersi

surround [səˈraund] v/t circondare; **~ings** pl dintorni
m/pl

survey [ˈsəːvei] s esame m;
[səˈvei] v/t esaminare; **~or**
[səˈveiə] geometra m

surviv|al [səˈvaivəl] soprav-
vivenza f; **~e** v/t, v/i sopravvivere

susceptible [səˈseptəbl] suscettibile

suspect [[ˈsʌspekt] a sospet-

to; [səsˈpekt] v/t sospettare

suspen|d [səsˈpənd] v/t so-
spendere; **~der** giarrettiera
f; **~sion** sospensione f

suspicio|n [səsˈpiʃən] so-
spetto m; **~us** sospettoso

sustain [səsˈtein] v/t sostenere

swallow [ˈswɔlou] v/t inghiottire; s orn rondinella f

swamp [swɔmp] palude f;
~y paludoso

swan [swɔn] cigno m

swarm [swɔːm] s sciame m;
v/i sciamare

swarthy [ˈswɔːði] di carnagione scura

sway [swei] v/i oscillare

swear [swεə] v/t, v/i, irr bestemmiare;   giurare;
~word bestemmia f

sweat [swet] s sudore m; v/i,
irr sudare

Swede [swiːd] svedese m, f;
~en Svezia f; **~ish** svedese

sweep [swiːp] v/t, irr spazzare; v/i distendersi

sweet [swiːt] a dolce; s caramella f; **~heart** innamora-
to(a) m (f); tesoro

swell [swel] a elegante; v/t,
irr gonfiare; v/i gonfiarsi;
~ing gonfiore m

swerve [swəːv] v/i deviare

swift [swift] rapido; veloce;
~ness rapidità f; velocità f

swim [swim] v/i, irr nuotare; **~ming** nuoto m; **~ming
pool** piscina f

swindle [ˈswindl] s truffa f;
v/t truffare; **~r** truffatore m

swine [swain], pl ~ maiale m

swing [swiŋ] *s* altalena *f*; oscillazione *f*; *v/t*, *v/i*, *irr* dondolare

swirl [swəːl] *v/i* trubinare

Swiss [swis] *a*, *s* svizzero (*m*)

switch [switʃ] *s* interruttore *m*; *v/t* cambiare; ~ **on** accendare la luce; ~ **off** spegnere la luce; **~board** quadro *m*

Switzerland ['switsələnd] Svizzera *f*

swollen ['swoulən] gonfio *m*

sword [sɔːd] spada *f*

syllable ['siləbl] sillaba *f*

symbol ['simbəl] simbolo *m*; **~ic(al)** [~'bɔlik(əl)] simbolico

sympath|etic [ˌsimpə'θetik] comprensivo; **~y** ['simpəθi] comprensione *f*

symphony ['simfəni] sinfonia *f*

symptom ['simptəm] sintomo *m*

synonym ['sinənim] sinonimo *m*

syntax ['sintæks] sintassi *f*

synthe|sis ['sinθisis], *pl* **~ses** [~'siːz] sintesi *f*; **~tic** [~'θetik] sintetico

syringe ['sirindʒ] siringa *f*

syrup ['sirəp] sciroppo *m*

system ['sistim] sistema *m*; metodo *m*; **~atic** [ˌsistə'mætik] sistematico

T

tab [tæb] etichetta *f*

table ['teibl] tavolta *f*; **~cloth** tovaglia *f*; **~spoon** cucchiaio *m*

tablet ['tæblit] pasticca *f*; **sleeping ~** sonnifero *m*

tacit ['tæsit] tacito; **~urn** taciturno

tack [tæk] puntina *f*

tact [tækt] tatto *m*; **~ful** discreto; di tatto; **~ics** *pl* tattica *f*; **~less** indiscreto; senza tatto

tadpole ['tædpoul] girino *m*

tag [tæg] cartellino *m*

tail [teil] coda *f*

tailor ['teilə] sarto *m*

taint [teint] traccia *f*; *v/t* guastare

take [teik] *v/t*, *irr* prendere; portare; ~ **advantage of** approfittare di; ~ **charge of** incaricarsi di; ~ **off** togliere; (*aeroplane*) decollare; ~ **place** aver luogo; ~ **up** raccogliere; intraprendere

tale [teil] racconto *m*; **fairy-~** favola *f*

talent ['tælənt] talento *m*; **~ed** dotato

talk [tɔːk] *s* conversazione *f*; discorso *m*; *v/i* parlare; discorrere; **~ative** loquace

tall [tɔːl] alto; grande

tallow ['tælou] sega *f*

tame [teim] *a* addomesticato; *v/t* addomesticare; **~r** domatore *m*

tamper ['tæmpə]: ~ **with** *v/i* modificare

tan [tæn] s concia f; abbronzatura f; v/t conciare; abbronzare

tangerine [ˌtændʒəˈriːn] mandarino m

tangle [ˈtæŋɡl] s imbroglio m; v/t imbrogliare

tank [tæŋk] serbatoio m

tanner [ˈtænə] conciatore m

tantalize [ˈtæntəlaiz] v/t tormentare

tantamount [ˈtæntəmaunt] equivalente

tap [tæp] s rubinetto m; chiave f; colpetto m; v/t battere

tape [teip] nastro m; ~ **recorder** registratore m

tapestry [ˈtæpistri] arazzi m/pl; tappezzeria f

tapeworm tenia f

tar [taː] catrame m

target [ˈtaːɡit] bersaglio m; objettivo m

tariff [ˈtærif] tariffa f

tart [taːt] a acido; s torta f

task [taːsk] compito m

taste [teist] s gusto m; sapore m; v/t assaggiare; v/i avere il gusto m; sapere di; **~eful** di buon gusto; **~eless** senza gusto; **~y** saporito

tattle [ˈtætl] v/i ciarlare

tattoo [təˈtuː] tatuaggio m

tax [tæks] s tassa f, imposta f; v/t tassare; **~free** esente da tassa

taxi [ˈtæksi] tassi m; **~ driver** tassista m

tax|payer contribuente m; **~return** dichiarazione f delle imposte

tea [tiː] tè m

teach [tiːtʃ] v/t, irr insegnare; **~er** insegnante m; **~ing** insegnamento m

team [tiːm] squadra f; **~work** lavoro m collettivo

teapot teiera f

tear [tɛə] s strappo m; v/t, irr strappare

tear² [tiə] lacrima f; **~ful** lacrimoso

tea-room sala f da tè

tease [tiːz] v/t prendere in giro; cardare (lana)

teat [tiːt] tettarella f

techn|ical [ˈteknikəl] tecnico; **~ician** [~ˈniʃən] tecnico m; **~ique** [~ˈniːk] tecnica f

tedious [ˈtiːdjəs] noioso

teen|ager [ˈtiːnˌeidʒə] adolescente m, f; **~s** pl dai 13 al 19 anni

teeth [tiːθ] pl of **tooth**

teetotal|ler [tiːˈtoutlə] astemio m (completo)

telegra|m [ˈteligræm] telegramma m; **~ph** telegrafo m; **~phic** [~ˈgræfik] telegrafico; **~phy** [tiˈleɡrəfi] telegrafia f

telephone [ˈtelifoun] s telefono m; v/t, v/i telefonare; **~call** telefonata f; **~exchange** centrale m telefonica

tele|printer [ˈteliprintə] telescrivente m; **~type(writer)** telescrivente f

televis|e [ˈtelivaiz] v/t trasmettere per televisione; **~ion** televisione f; **~ion set** apparecchio m televisio

tell 188

tell [tel] v/t, v/i, irr dire; raccontare

temper ['tempə] s umore m; indole m; collera f; tempera f (metalli); **lose one's ~** predere la pazienza; v/t temperrare (metalli); **~ament** temperamento m; **~ance** temperanza f; astinenza f (completa); **~ate** temperato; **~ature** temperatura f; febbre f

tempest ['tempist] tempesta f; **~uous** [~'pestjuəs] tempio m

temporal ['tempərəl] temporale; **~ary** temporaneo

tempt [tempt] v/t tentare; **~ation** tentazione f; **~ing** alettante

tenant ['tenənt] inquilino m

tend [tend] v/i tendere; **~ency** tendenza f

tender [['tɔndə] tenero; **~ness** tenerezza f

tendon ['tendən] tendine f

tennis ['tenis] tennis m; **~court** campo m da tennis

tense [tens] a teso; s gram tempo m; **~ion** tensione f

tent [tent] tenda f

tepid ['tepid] tiepido

term [tə:m] s termine m; periodo m; limite m; trimestre m; **~s** pl condizioni f/pl; **be on good ~s with** essere in buoni rapporti con; **come to ~s** venire a un accordo

terminal ['tə:minl] terminale

terminus ['tə:minəs] capoli-

nea m; termine m

terrible ['terəbl] terrible; spaventoso

terrific [tə'rifik] tremendo; **~y** ['terifai] v/t spaventare

territory ['teritəri] territorio m

terror ['terə] terrore m; **~ism** terrorismo m; **~ist** terroroista m, f; **~ize** v/t terrorizzare

test [test] s prova f; v/t provare

testament ['testəmənt] testamento m

testify ['testifai] v/t testimoniare

testimonial [testi'mounjəl] a testimoniale; s certificato m; **~y** [~'məni] testimonianza f

text [tekst] testo m

textile ['tekstail] a tessile; s tessuto m

texture ['tekstʃə] tessitura f

than [ðæn, ðən] di; che; **more ~ ten** più di dieci; **more ~ once** più di una volta

thank [θæŋk] v/t ringraziare; **~ful** grato; **~s** pl grazie f/pl

that [ðæt, ðət], pl **those** [ðouz] a pron quello, quella; pron rel, pl **that** che, il quale, la quale; conj che

thatch [ðætʃ] tetto m di paglia

thaw [θɔ:] s disgelo m; v/i disgelarsi

the [ðə, ði] il, lo, la; pl i, gli, le

theatre, Am ~er ['θiətə] teatro m; **~rical** [θiˈætrikəl] teatrale

theft [θeft] furto m

their [ðɛə], pl adj poss il loro, la loro, i loro, le loro; **~s** pron poss il loro, la loro, i loro, le loro

them [ðɛm, ðəm] pl li, le, loro

theme [θiːm] tema m

themselves [ðəmˈselvz] sè stessi, sè stesse

then [ðen] allora; poi; quindi; dunque

theolog|ical [θiəˈlɔdʒikəl] teologico; **~y** teologia f

theor|etic(al) [θiəˈretik(əl)] teorico; **~y** [ˈ~ri] teoria f

therapeutic(al) [ˌθerəˈpjuːtik(əl)] terapeutico; **~s** pl terapeutica f

therapy [ˈθerəpi] terapia f

there [ðɛə] li; là; **~ is** c'è; **~ are** ci sono; **~ was** c'era; **~fore** quindi

thermo|meter [θəˈmɔmitə] termometro m; **~s flask** termos m

these [ðiːz] pl of **this**

thes|is [ˈθiːsis], pl **~es** [ˈ~iːz] tesi f

they [ðei] pl essi, esse, loro

thick [θik] spesso; denso; folto; fitto

thief [θiːf], pl **thieves** [~vz] ladro m

thigh [θai] coscia f

thimble [ˈθimbl] ditale m

thin [θin] magro; fine; sottile

thing [θiŋ] cosa f

think [θiŋk] v/t, v/i, irr pen-

sare; **~er** pensatore m

thirst [θəːst] sete f; **~y** assetato

this [ðis], pl **these** [ðiːz] a, pron questo, questa

thistle [ˈθisl] cardo m

thorax [ˈθɔːræks] torace m

thorn [θɔːn] spina f

thorough [ˈθʌrə] completo; approfondito; perfetto; minuzioso; **~fare** arteria f (di grande traffico); strada f principale

those [ðouz] pl of **that**

though [ðou] sebbene, benché

thought [θɔːt] pensiero m; **~ful** pensieroso; **~less** sconsiderato

thousand [ˈθauzənd] mille

thrash [θræʃ] v/t battere; bastonare

thread [θred] s filo m; v/t infilare

threat [θret] s minaccia f; **~en** v/t minacciare

three [θriː] tre; **~fold** triplice

threshold [ˈθreʃhould] soglia f

thrift [θrift] economia f; frugalità f; **~y** economo; frugale

thrill [θril] s brivido m; v/i rabbrividire; **~er** romanzo m giallo; **~ing** emozionante

thrive [θraiv] v/i, irr prosperare

throat [θrout] gola f

throb [θrɔb] v/i palpitare

throne [θroun] trono m

throng [θrɔŋ] s folla f; v/t affollare

throttle ['θrɒtl] s valvola f; v/t strangolare

through [θru:] a diretto; prp attraverso; **~out** prp in tutto; adv dappertutto; **go ~, pass ~** attraversare; **~ train** diretto m

throw [θrou] s lancio m; v/t, irr lanciare; gettare; buttare

thrust [θrʌst] s spinta f; v/t, irr cacciare

thud [θʌd] tonfo m

thumb [θʌm] pollice m

thump [θʌmp] s botta f; v/t dare pugni a

thunder ['θʌndə] s tuono m; v/i tuonare; **~bolt** fulmine m; **~storm** temporale m

Thursday ['θə:zdi] giovedì m

thus [ðʌs] così; in questo modo

thwart [θwɔ:t] v/t frustare

thy [ðai] eccl, poet tuo

thyroid gland ['θaiərɔid] tiroide f

tick [tik] fare tic-tac

ticket ['tikit] biglietto m; etichetta f; **~ office** biglietteria f

tickle ['tikl] v/t solleticare

tidy ['taidi] a ordinato; v/t mettere in ordine

tie [tai] s cravatta f; v/t legare

tier [tiə] fila f

tiger ['taigə] tigre f

tight [tait] stretto; **~en** v/t stringere; v/i stringersi

tile [tail] mattonella f; piastrella f

till¹ [til] prp fino a; conj finchè

till² v/t lavorare; coltivare

till³ cassetto m

tilt [tilt] s inclinazione f; v/t inclinare; v/i inclinarsi

timber ['timbə] legname m

time [taim] s tempo m; volta f; ora; time f divertirsi; v/t cronometrare; **~less** eterno; **~ly** opportuno; **on ~** in orario; in tempo; **~table** orario m

timid ['timid] timido; **~orous** timoroso

tin [tin] stagno m; latta f; scatola f

tinge [tindʒ] v/t sfumare; s sfumatura f

tin|ned in scatola; **~opener** apriscatole m

tint [tint] tinta f

tiny ['taini] minuscolo

tip [tip] s punta f; mancia f; v/t dare la mancia

tipsy ['tipsi] brillo

tiptoe ['tiptou] v/i andare in punta dei piedi

tire¹ ['taiə] v/t stancare; **~ed** stanco; **~esome** noioso.

tire² ['taiə] pneumàtico m

tissue ['tiʃu:] tessuto m; **~ paper** f velina

title ['taitl] titolo m

to [tu:, tu, tə] prp a; verso; **it is five minutes ~ ten** sono le dieci meno cinque; **~ and fro** avanti e indietro; **have ~** dovere

toad [toud] rospo m

toast [toust] s pane m abbrustolito; brindisi *m*; *v/t* abbrustolire; fare un brindisi a; *v/i* brindare

tobacco [tə'bækou] tabacco *m*; **~nist** tabaccaio *m*

today [tə'dei] oggi

toe [tou] dito *m* del piede

together [tə'geðə] insieme

toil [tɔil] *s* fatica *f*; *v/i* affaticare

toilet ['tɔilit] toeletta *f*; gabinetto; **~paper** carta *f* igienica

token ['toukən] segno *m*

tolera|ble ['tɔlərəbl] tollerabile; **~nce** tolleranza *f*; **~nt** tollerante

tomato [tə'mɑːtou, *Am* tə-'meitou], *pl* **~es** pomodoro *m*

tomb [tuːm] tomba *f*; **~stone** lapide *f* sepolcrale

tomcat ['tɔm'kæt] gatto *m*

tomorrow [tə'mɔrou] domani; **~ night** domani sera; **the day after ~** dopodomani

ton [tʌn] tonnellata *f*

tone [toun] tono *m*

tongs [tɔŋz] *pl* mollette *f/pl*

tongue [tʌŋ] lingua *f*

tonic ['tɔnik] tonico *m*

tonsil ['tɔnsl] tonsilla *f*; **~li-tis** [~si'laitis] tonsillite *f*

too [tuː] troppo; **~ much** troppo

tool [tuːl] arnese *m*; strumento *m*

tooth [tuːθ], *pl* **teeth** [tiːθ] dente *m*; **~ache** mal *m* di denti; **~brush** spazzolino *m* da denti; **~less** senza denti; **~paste** dentifricio *m*

top [tɔp] *s* cima *f*; **at the ~ of** in testa; **from ~ to bottom** da capo a fondo; **~ hat** cilindro *m*

topic ['tɔpik] argomento *m*; **~al** del giorno

topsy-turvy ['tɔpsi'təːvi] sottosopra

torch [tɔːtʃ] torcia *f*; lampadina *f* elettrica

torment ['tɔːment] *s* tormento *m*; *v/t* tormentare

torrent ['tɔrənt] torrente *m*

tortoise ['tɔːtəs] tartaruga *f*

torture ['tɔːtʃə] *s* tortura *f*; *v/t* torturare

toss [tɔs] *v/t* buttare in aria; buttare; *v/i* agitarsi

total ['toutl] *a, s* totale (*m*)

totalitarian [ˌtoutæli-'tɛəriən] totalitario

totter ['tɔtə] *v/i* traballare

touch [tʌtʃ] *s* tocco *m*; tatto *m*; *v/t* toccare; commuovere; **get in ~ with** mettersi in contatto con; **~ing** commuovente; **~y** permaloso; suscettibile

tough [tʌf] difficile; resistente; duro; tenace

tour [tuə] *s* giro *m*; viaggio *m*; *v/t* viaggiare; **~ist** turista *m, f*; **~ist agency, ~ist office** agenzia *f* (di) viaggi

tournament ['tuənəmənt] torneo *m*; concorso *m*

tow [tou] *v/t* rimorchiare

toward(s) [tə'wɔːd(z)] verso

towel ['tauəl] asciugamano *m*

tower ['tauə] torre *f*

town [taun] città f; ~ **hall** municipio m

tow-rope cavo m da rimorchio

toy [tɔi] giocattolo m

trace [treis] s traccia f; v/t rintracciare

track [træk] pista f; sentiero m; binario m; ~**-and-field events** pl atletica f leggera

tract|ion ['trækʃən] trazione f; ~**or** trattrice f

trade [treid] s commercio m; mestiere m; occupazione f; v/t trattare; ~ **mark** marca f di fabbrica; ~ **union** sindacato m

tradition [trə'diʃən] tradizione f; ~**al** tradizionale

traffic ['træfik] s traffico m; v/t trafficare; commerciare; ~**light(s** pl) semaforo m; ~ **regulations** pl regolamento m stradale; ~ **sign** segnale m stradale

trag|edy ['trædʒidi] tragedia f; ~**ic(al)** tragico

trail [treil] s traccia f; scia f; v/t trascinare; v/i trascinarsi; ~**er** rimorchio m; (cinema) presentazione f

train [trein] s treno m; seguito m; serie f; v/t ammaestrare; allenare; ~**er** allenatore m; ~**ing** allenamento m

trait [trei, Am treit] caratteristica f

traitor ['treitə] traditore m

tram [træm] tram m

tramp [træmp] s vagabondo m; v/i calpestare; vagabondare

trample ['træmple] v/t calpestare

trance [trɑːns] catalessi f; estasi f

tranquil ['træŋkwil] tranquillo; ~**ity** tranquillità f; ~**ize** v/t tranquillizzare

transact [træn'zækt] v/t trattare; ~**ion** transazione f

transcend [træn'send] v/i trascendere

transcri|be [træns'kraib] v/t trascrivere; ~**ption** trascrizione f

transfer ['trænsfə:] s trasferimento m; [træns'fə:] v/t trasferire

transform [træns'fɔːm] v/t trasformare; ~**ation** trasformazione f

transfusion [træns'fjuːʒən] trasfusione f

transgress [træns'gres] v/t tragredire; ~**ion** trasgressione f

transient ['trænziənt] transitorio; passeggero

transit ['trænsit] transito m; ~**ion** [~'siʒən] transizione f; ~**ory** ['trænsitəri] transitorio

translat|e [træns'leit] v/t tradurre; ~**ion** traduzione f; ~**or** traduttore m, traduttrice f

transmi|ssion [trænz'miʃən] trasmissione f; ~**t** v/t trasmettere; ~**tter** trasmettitore m

transparent [træns'pɛərənt] trasparente

transpire [træns'paiə] v/i

tropical

traspirare

transport ['trænspɔːt] *s* trasporto *m*; [træns'pɔːt] *v/t* trasportare; **~ation** *s* trasporto *m*

trap [træp] *s* trappola *f*; *v/t* prendere in trappola

trapeze [trə'piːz] trapezio *m*

trash [træʃ] robaccia *f*; sciocchezze *f/pl*

travel ['trævl] *v/i* viaggiare; *s* viaggiare *m*; **~ agency** agenzia *f* viaggi; **~(l)er** viaggiatore *m*; **~(l)er's cheque** (*Am* **check**) assegno *m* turistico; taveller cheque *m*

tray [trei] vassoio *m*

treacherous ['tretʃərəs] traditore

tread [tred] *v/i, irr* camminare; calpestare; passare

treason ['triːzn] tradimento *m*

treasure ['treʒə] *s* tesoro *m*; *v/t* tenere caro; **~er** tesoriere *m*; **~y** tesoreria *f*; **2y-Department** *Am* Ministero *m* del Tesoro

treat [triːt] *v/t* trattara; **~ise** ['~iz] trattato *m*; **~y** trattato *m*

treble ['trebl] *a* triplo; *v/t* triplicare; *v/i* triplicarsi

tree [triː] albero *m*

trefoil ['trefɔil] trifoglio *m*

tremble ['trembl] *v/i* tremare

tremendous [tri'mendəs] enorme; tremendo

tremor ['tremə] tremore *m*; fremito *m*

trench [trentʃ] trincea *f*

trend tendenza *f*

trespass ['trespəs] *s* trasgressione *f*; *v/i* trasgredire; **~er** trasgressore *m*

trial ['traiəl] prova *f*; processo *m*; **on ~** in prova

triangle ['traiæŋgl] triangolo *m*

tribe [traib] tribù *f*

tribunal [trai'bjuːnl] tribunale *m*

tributary ['tribjutəri] affluente *m*

trick [trik] *s* trucco *m*; *v/t* ingannare

trickle ['trikl] *v/i* gocciolare

trifle ['traifl] nonnulla *m*

trigger ['trigə] grilletto *m*

trim [trim] *a* ordinato; *v/t* tagliare; guarnire; **~mings** *pl* guarnizioni *f/pl*

trinket ['triŋkit] gioiello *m*

trip [trip] *s* gita *f*; *v/i* inciampare

tripe [traip] trippa *f*

triple ['tripl] *s* triplo *m*; *v/t* triplicare; **~ts** ['~its] *pl* fratelli *m/pl* trigemini

triumph ['traiəmf] *s* trionfo *m*; *v/i* trionfare

trivial ['triviəl] banale; trascurabile

troll(e)y ['trɔli] carrello *m*; carretto *m*; **~-bus** filobus *m*

trombone [trɔm'boun] tromba *f*; trombone *m*

troop [truːp] truppa *f*; banda *f*

trophy ['troufi] trofeo *m*

tropic[al] ['trɔpik(əl)] tropicale; **~s** pl paesi m/pl tropicali

trot [trɔt] s trotto m; v/i trottare

trouble [trʌbl] s disturbo m; seccatura f; guaio m; v/t disturbare; seccare; **~d** preoccupato; **~some** fastidioso; seccante

trough [trɔf] trogolo m

trousers ['trauzəz] pl pantaloni m/pl

trout [traut] trotta f

truant ['tru(:)ənt]: **play ~** marinare la scuola; far forca

truce [tru:s] tregua f

truck [trʌk] carro m; autocarro m

trudge [trʌdʒ] v/i camminare faticosamente

true [tru:] vero; **~ly** veramente; **yours ~ly** con profonda stima

trumpet ['trʌmpit] tromba f

truncheon ['trʌntʃən] bastone m

trunk [trʌŋk] tronco m; baule m; **~-call** chiamata f interurbana

trust [trʌst] s fiducia f; v/t fidarsi di; **~ee** [~'ti:] fiduciario m; **~ful** fiducioso

truth [tru:θ], pl **~s** [~ðz] verità f

try [trai] s prova f; tentativo m; v/t, v/i provare; tentare; **~ing** duro; difficile

tub [tʌb] tino m tinozza f

tube [tju:b] tubo m; fam metropolitana f

tuberculosis [tju(:)bə:kju-'lousis] tubercolosi f

tuck [tʌk] piega f

Tuesday ['tju:zdi] martedì m

tuft [tʌft] ciuffo m

tug [tʌg] v/t tirare

tulip ['tju:lip] tulipano m

tumble ['tʌmbl] v/i cadere; **~r** bicchiere m

tummy ['tʌmi] fam pancina f

tumo(u)r ['tju:mə] tumore m

tumult ['tju:mʌlt] tumulto m; **~uous** [~'mʌltjuəs] tumultuoso

tun [tʌn] tonnellata f; botte f

tuna ['tu:nə], pl **~(s)** tonno m

tune [tju:n] s motivo m; v/i armonizzare; **out of ~** scordato

tunnel ['tʌnl] galleria f

turban ['tə:bən] turbante m

Turk [tə:k] turco(a) m (f)

turkey ['tə:ki] tacchino m

Turkey ['tə:ki] Turchia f; **~ish** a, s turco (m)

turmoil ['tə:mɔil] tumulto m

turn [tə:n] s turno m; volta f; giro m; cambio m; **it is your ~** tocca a te; v/t voltare; girare; cambiare; **~ off** spegnere; **~ on** accendere; **~ out** produrre; **~ over** girare; **~ up** comparire; **~ing** svolta f; curva f

turnip ['tə:nip] rapa f

turnover giro m d'affari

turpentine ['tə:pəntain] acqua f ragia

turquoise ['tə:kwɑ:z] turchese

turtle ['tə:tl] tartaruga f

tusk [tʌsk] zanna *f*

tweezers ['twi:zəz] *pl* pinzette *f/pl*

twice [twais] due volte

twilight ['twailait] crepuscolo *m*

twin [twin] *a*, *s* gemello (*m*)

twine [twain] *s* spago *m*; *v/t* attorcigliare

twinkle ['twiŋkl] *s* scintillio *m*; *v/i* scintillare

twirl [twə:l] *v/t* girare

twist [twist] *v/t* torcere

twitter ['twitə] *v/i* cinguettare

two [tu:] due; **~fold** doppio;

~way traffic traffico *m* contrario

type [taip] *s* tipo *m*; *v/t* scrivere a macchina; **~writer** macchina *f* da scrivere

typhoid (fever) ['taifɔid] febbre *f* tifoidea

typhus ['taifəs] tifo *m*

typical ['tipikəl] tipico

typist ['taipist] dattilografo(a) *m* (*f*)

tyrann|ical [ti'rænikəl] tirannico; **~ize** ['tirənaiz] *v/t* tiranneggiare; **~y** tirannia *f*

tyrant ['taiərənt] tiranno *m*

tyre ['taiə] pneumàtico *m*

U

udder ['ʌdə] mammella *f*

ugly ['ʌgli] brutto

ulcer ['ʌlsə] ulcera *f*

ulterior [ʌl'tiəriə] ulteriore

ultimate ['ʌltimit] ultimo

umbrella [ʌm'brelə] ombrello *m*

umpire ['ʌmpaiə] *s* arbitro *m*; *v/t* fare da arbitro

unabated [ˌʌnə'beitid] non diminuito

un|able [ʌn'eibl] incapace; **~acceptable** inaccettabile; **~accountable** inspiegabile; **~accustomed** non abituato; insolito; **~affected** naturale; semplice; **~afraid** senza paura

unanimous [ju(:)'næniməs] unanime

un|approachable inaccessibile; **~armed** disarmato;

~asked non richiesto; **~assuming** modesto; **un|available** non disponibile; **~avoidable** inevitabile; **~aware** inconsapevole

un|balanced non equilibrato; **~bearable** insopportabile; **~becoming** sconveniente; **~believer** miscredente *m*

unbend *v/t* raddrizzare; **~ing** inflessibile

un|bias(s)ed imparziale; **~bind** *v/t* sciogliere; slegare; **~broken** intatto; **~button** *v/t* sbottonare

un|cared (for) trascurato; **~ceasing** incessante; **~certain** incerto; **~changeable** immutevole; **~checked** incontrollato

uncle ['ʌŋkl] zio *m*

un|comfortable scomodo; ~common raro; ~completed incompleto; ~compromising intransigente; ~conditional incondizionale; ~confirmed non confermato

unconscious inconsapevole; senza conoscenza; inconscio; ~ness incoscienza f

un|controllable incontrollabile; ~conventional spregiudicato

un|couth [ʌn'ku:θ] grazioso; ~cover v/t scoprire

unction ['ʌŋkʃən] unzione f

un|cultivated incolto; ~damaged intatto; ~deniable innegabile

under ['ʌndə] sotto; inferiore; ~age minorenne; ~way in corso

under|clothing biancheria f personale; ~done [,ʌndə'dʌn]; ~estimate v/t sottovalutare; ~go [,ʌndə'gou] subire

underground [,ʌndə'graund] a sotterraneo; ['ʌndə~] s metropolitana f

under|line v/t sottolineare; ~mine v/t minare; ~neath sotto; ~paid mal pagato; ~pass sottopassaggio m; ~rate v/t sottovalutare

undersecretary sottosegretario m

under|signed sottoscritto; ~stand v/t, v/i, irr capire; ~standing a comprensivo; s comprensione f

undertak|e v/t, irr intraprendere; ~er imprenditore m di pompe funebri; ~ing impresa f

under|value v/t sottovalutare; ~wear biancheria f personale; ~wood sottobosco m

underworld inferno m; malavita f

un|deserved immeritato; ~desirable non desiderabile; ~developed sottosviluppato

un|disputed incontestato; ~disturbed indisturbato

undo [ʌn'du:] v/t, irr disfare; ~dress v/t spogliare; v/i spogliarsi

unemploy|ed disoccupato; ~ment disoccupazione f

unequal disuguale; ~(l)ed ineguagliato

un|erring infallibile; ~even disuguale; ~expected inaspettato; ~failing immancabile; ~fair ingiusto; ~faithful infedele; ~familiar non familiare; ~fasten v/t scogliere; slacciare; ~favo(u)rable sfavorevole; ~finished incompiuto; ~fit inabile; ~fold v/t aprire; spiegare; ~foreseen imprevisto

unfortunate sfortunato; ~ly sfortunatamente

un|founded infondato; ~friendly non cordiale; ~furnished non ammobiliato; ~generous poco generoso; ~graceful senza grazia; sgraziato; **~gracious** sgarbato; **~grateful** ingrato; **~guarded** non sorvegliato; non attento

un|happy infelice; **~harmed** illeso; **~healthy** non sano; malsano; **~heard (of)** inaudito

unhinge [ʌn'hindʒ] v/t scardinare; sconvolgere

unification [ju:nifi'keiʃən] unificazione f

uniform ['ju:nifɔ:m] a uniforme; s uniforme m; divisa f

unify ['ju:nifai] v/t unificare

un|imaginable inimmaginabile; **~important** non importante; insignificante

uninhabit|able inabitabile; **~ed** inabitato

uninjured illeso

unintellig|ent non intelligente; **~ible** inintelligibile

un|intentional non intenzionale; **~interested** non interessato; disinteressato; **~interrupted** interrotto; **~invited** non invitato

union ['ju:njən] unione f; **~ist** sindacalista m, f

unique [ju:'ni:k] unico

unit ['ju:nit] unità f; **~e** [~'nait] v/t unire; unificare; v/i unirsi; **~ed** Nations Nazioni f/pl Unite; **~ed States** Stati m/pl Uniti; **~y** unità f

univers|al [ju:ni'və:səl] universale; **~e** ['~ə:s] universo m; **~ity** [~'və:siti] università f

un|just ingiusto; **~kind** cat-

tivo; **~known** sconosciuto; **~lace** v/t slacciare; **~lawful** illecito; illegale

unless [ən'les] a meno che

unlike diverso; **~ly** improbabile

un|limited illimitati; **~load** v/t scaricare; **~lock** v/t aprire (con la chiave); **~lucky** sfortunato; **~mannerly** maleducato; **~married** nubile (di donna); celibe (di uomo); non sposato

unmask v/t smascherare

un|mistakable inconfondibile; chiaro; **~natural** non naturale; **~necessary** non necessario; inutile; **~noticed, ~observed** inosservato; **~official** non ufficiale; **~opposed** incontrastato

unpack [ʌn'pæk] v/t disfare le valige

un|paid non pagato; **~paralleled** unico; senza pari; **~pardonable** imperdonabile; **~pleasant** spiacevole; **~popular** impopolare; **~practical** non pratico; **~precedented** senza precedenti; **~prejudiced** imparziale; **~prepared** impreparato; **~profitable** senza profitto; **~provided** sprovvisto; **~published** inedito; non pubblicato; **~punished** impunito; **~qualified** incompetente; **~questionable** incontestabile; **~quiet** inquieto; agitato

un|reasonable irragionevo-

le; **⟋refined** non raffinato;
⟋reliable che non dà affidamento; **⟋reserved** non riservato; senza riserve; **⟋resisting** senza resistenza; che non oppone resistenza; **⟋restrained** illimitato; sfrenato; **⟋ripe** non maturo; immaturo; **⟋rival(l)ed** impareggiabile; **⟋ruly** turbolento

un⟋safe non sicuro; pericoloso; **⟋said** non detto; **⟋satisfactory** non soddisfacente; **⟋screw** v/t svitare; **⟋scrupulous** senza scrupoli; **⟋seen** non inosservato; **⟋selfish** altruista; **⟋shrinkable** irrestringibile; **⟋skilled** inesperto; **⟋solved** insoluto; non risolto; **⟋sound** non solido; cattivo; **⟋speakable** indicibile; **⟋spoilt** non guastato; (of a child) non viziato; **⟋stable** instabile; **⟋successful** non riuscito; senza successo; **⟋suitable** inadatto; **⟋thinkable** impensabile; **⟋tidy** disordinato; **⟋tie** v/t slegare; disfare

until [ən'til] prp fino a; conj finché ... non

un⟋timely inopportuno; **⟋tiring** instancabile; **⟋touched** non toccato; **⟋tried** non provato; **⟋troubled** tranquillo; non turbato; **⟋true** falso

un⟋used non usato; **⟋varying** invariabile; **⟋veil** v/t svelare; togliere il velo a;
⟋warranted ingiustificato; **⟋well** indisposto; **⟋willing** maldisposto

up [ʌp] prp su, su per; **~ and down** su e giù; **~ to date** moderno; aggiornato; **~ to now** fino ad ora; **what's ~?** che c'è?

up⟋bringing educazione f; **⟋hill** in salita; difficile; **⟋hold** v/t, irr sostenere

up⟋holsterer [ʌp'houlstərə] tappezziere m; **⟋keep** mantenimento m

upon [ə'pɔn] su, sopra

upper ['ʌpə] superiore

up⟋right diritto; in piedi; fig onesto; **⟋roar** clamore m; chiasso m; **⟋root** v/t sradicare

upset v/t, irr rovesciare; turbare; sconvolgere

upside down sottosopra

up⟋stairs sopra; al piano di sopra; **⟋wards** in alto

uranium [ju'reinjəm] uranio m

urban ['əːbən] urbano

urchin ['əːtʃin] monello m

urge [əːdʒ] v/t spingere; s spinta f; **~nt** urgente

urin⟋ate ['juərineit] v/i orinare; **⟋e** orina f

urn [əːn] urna f

us [ʌs, əs] noi; ci

usage ['juːzidʒ] uso m

use [juːs] s uso m; impiego m; [juːz] v/t usare; adoperare; impiegare; **it is no ~** non serve; **what is the ~ of?** a che cosa serve?; **~ up** con-

sumare; **~d to** abituato a;
get ~d to abituarsi a
usher ['ʌʃə] usciere m; **~ette**
[~'ret] maschera f
usual ['ju:ʒuəl] abituale;
usuale; solito
utensil [ju(:)'tensl] utensile m

uterus ['ju:tərəs] utero m
utili|ty [ju(:)'tiliti] utilità f;
~ze v/t utilizzare
utmost ['ʌtmoust] estremo;
massimo
utter ['ʌtə] a completo; assoluto; v/t proferire

V

vaca|ncy ['veikənsi] posto m
vacante; **~nt** vacante; vuoto; libero; **~te** [və'keit] v/t
liberare; **~tion** vacanza f
vaccin|ate ['væksineit] v/t
vaccinare; **~ation** vaccina-
zione f; **~e** [~i:n] vaccino m
vacuum ['vækjuəm] vuoto
m; **~ cleaner** aspirapolvere
m
vagabond ['vægəbɔnd] a, s
vagabondo (m)
vague [veig] vago
vain [vein] vanitoso; vano;
in ~ invano
valerian [və'liəriən] valeriana f
valet ['vælit] cameriere m
valid ['vælid] valido; **~ity**
[və'liditi] validità f
valu|able ['væljuəbl] prezio-
so; di valore; **~ables** pl oggetti m/pl di valore; **~e** s
valore m; v/t valutare; tenersi; **~eless** senza valore
valve [vælv] valvola f
vampire ['væmpaiə] vampiro m
van [væn] camioncino m;
furgoncino m
vanish ['væniʃ] v/i sparire
vanity ['væniti] vanità f

vapor|ize ['veipəraiz] v/t va-
porizzare; **~ous** vaporoso
vapo(u)r ['veipə] vapore m
varia|ble ['vɛəriəbl] variabi-
le; **~nt** variante f; **~tion** va-
riazione f
varicose vein ['værikous]
varice f; **vena** f varicosa
var|ied ['vɛərid] svariato;
~iety [və'raiəti] varietà f;
~ious ['vɛəriəs] vario; diverso
varnish ['vɑ:niʃ] s vernice f;
v/t verniciare
vary ['vɛəri] v/t, v/i variare
vase [vɑ:z, Am veis, veiz] s
vaso m
vast [vɑ:st] vasto; enorme
Vatican ['vætikən] Vatica-
no m
vault [vɔ:lt] volta f; salto m
veal [vi:l] carne f di vitello
vegeta|bles ['vedʒitəblz] pl
verdure f/pl; **~rian** [vedʒi-
'tɛəriən] vegetariano m;
~tion [~'teiʃən] vegetazione
f
vehement ['vi:əmənt] vee-
mente
vehicle ['vi:ikl] veicolo m
veil [veil] s velo m; v/t velare

vein [vein] vena *f*

velocity [vi'lɔsiti] velocità *f*

velvet ['velvit] velluto *m*

venal ['vi:nl] venale

vend [vend] *v/t* vendere; **~ing machine** distributore *m* automatico

venera|ble ['venərəbl] venerabile; **~te** *v/i* venerare

venereal [vi'niəriəl] venereo

Venetian [vi'ni:ʃən] *a, s* veneziano (*m*); **~ blinds** *pl* tende *f/pl* alla veneziana

vengeance ['vendʒəns] vendetta *f*

venom ['venəm] veleno *m*; **~ous** velenoso

vent [vent] *v/t* dare sfogo a; sfogare; **~ilate** ['ventileit] *v/t* ventilare; **~ilator** ventilatore *m*

ventriloquist [ven'triləkwist] ventriloquo *m*

venture ['ventʃə] *s* ventura *f*; rischio *m*; *v/t* rischiare; *v/i* arrischiarsi

veranda(h) [və'rændə] terrazza *f* coperta

verb [və:b] verbo *m*

verdict ['və:dikt] verdetto *m*

verge [və:dʒ] bordo *m*

verify ['verifai] *v/t* verificare

versatility [,və:sə'tiliti] versatilità *f*

vers|e [və:s] verso *m*; **~ed** versato; **~ion** versione *f*

vertebra ['və:tibrə], *pl* **~æ** ['~i:] vertebra *f*

vertical ['və:tikəl] verticale

vertiginous [və:'tidʒinəs] vertiginoso

very ['veri] molto *f*; **the ~**

best l'ottimo *m*; (*selfsame*) stesso

vest [vest] maglia *f* (*di lana o di cotone*)

vestry ['vestri] sagrestia *f*

vessel ['vesl] recipiente *m*; nave *f*

vet [vet] *fam* for **veterinary**

veteran ['vetərən] veterano *m*

veterinary (**surgeon**) ['vetərinəri] *s* veterinario *m*

veto ['vi:tou], *pl* **~es** veto *m*; *v/t* vietare

vex [veks] *v/t* far arrabbiare; dispiacere

vibrate [vai'breit] *v/t, v/i* vibrare; **~ion** vibrazione *f*

vice [vais] vizio *m*

vice- (*prefix*) vice-; **~president** vicepresidente *m*

vicinity [vi'siniti] vicinanza *f*

vicious ['viʃəs] vizioso; cattivo

victim ['viktim] vittima *f*

victor ['viktə] vincitore *m*; **~ious** [vik'tɔ:riəs] vittorioso; **~y** ['viktəri] vittoria *f*

view [vju:] *s* veduta *f*; panorama *m*; **in ~ of** in vista di; *v/t* considerare; **~point** punto *m* di vista

vigil ['vidʒil] vigilia *f*; veglia *f*; **~ant** vigilante

vigo|rous ['vigərəs] vigoroso; **~(u)r** vigore *m*

vile [vail] vile

village ['vilidʒ] paese *m*

villain ['vilən] mascalzone *m*

vindicate ['vindikeit] *v/t* rivendicare

vindictive [vin'diktiv] vendicativo

vine [vain] *bot* vite *f*; **~gar** ['vinigə] aceto *m*; **~yard** ['vinjəd] vigneto *m*

vintage ['vintidʒ] vendemmia *f*

viol|ate ['vaiəleit] *v/t* violare; **~ation** violazione *f*; contravvenzione *f*; **~ence** violenza *f*; **~ent** violento

violet ['vaiəlit] *s* mammola *f*; *a* viola

violin [vaiə'lin] violino *m*

viper ['vaipə] vipera *f*

virgin ['vəːdʒin] vergine *f*; **~ity** [~'dʒiniti] verginità *f*

viril|e ['virail] virile; **~ity** [~'riliti] virilità *f*

virtu|al ['vəːtjuəl] virtuale; **~e** virtù *f*

virus ['vaiərəs] virus *m*

visa ['viːzə] visto *m*

visib|ility [vizi'biliti] visibilità *f*; **~le** visibile

vision ['viʒən] visione *f*; **~ary** visionario

visit ['vizit] *s* visita *f*; *v/t* visitare; **~or** visitatore *m*

vital ['vaitl] vitale; **~ity** [~'tæliti] vitalità *f*

vitamin ['vitəmin] vitamina *f*

vivaci|ous [vi'veiʃəs] vivace; **~ty** [~'væsiti] vivacità *f*

vivid ['vivid] vivo; vivace

vocabulary [vou'kæbjuləri] vocabolario *m*

vocation [vou'keiʃən] vocazione *f*

vogue [voug] voga *f*; moda *f*; **in ~** di moda

voice [vois] *s* voce *f*; *v/t* esprimere

void [void] nullo; privo

volcano [vɔl'keinou] vulcano *m*

volley ['vɔli] scarica *f*

volt [voult] volt *m*; **~age** voltaggio *m*

voluble ['vɔljubl] volubile

volum|e ['vɔljum] volume *m*; **~inous** [və'lju:minəs] voluminoso

volunt|ary ['vɔləntəri] volontario; **~eer** [~'tiə] volontario *m*

voluptuous [və'lʌptjuəs] voluttuoso

vomit ['vɔmit] *v/t*, *v/i* vomitare

voracious [və'reiʃəs] vorace

vot|e [vout] *s* voto *m*; *v/t*, *v/i* votare; **~er** votante *m*, *f*; **~ing** votazione *f*

vouch [vautʃ] *v/t* attestare; **~ for** rispondere di; **~er** buono *m*

vow [vau] *s* voto *m*; *v/t* far voto di; giurare

vowel ['vauəl] vocale *f*

voyage ['voiidʒ] *s* viaggio *m* (*per mare*); *v/i* viaggiare (*per mare*); navigare

vulgar ['vʌlgə] volgare; **~ity** [~'gæriti] volgarità *f*

vulnerable ['vʌlnərəbl] vulnerabile

vulture ['vʌltʃə] avvoltoio *m*

W

wad [wɔd] batuffolo *m*; **~ding** ovatta *f*

wade [weid] *v/t* passare a guado

wag [wæg] *v/t* scodinzolare

wage [weidʒ] paga *f*

wail [weil] *s* lamento *m*; *v/t* lamentarsi

waist [weist] *anat* vita *f*; **~coat** panciotto *m*; **~line** vita *f*

wait [weit] *s* attesa *f*; *v/i* aspettare; servire (*a tavola*); **~er** cameriere *m*; **~ress** cameriera *f*

wake [weik] scia *f*; *v/t*, *irr* svegliare; *v/i* svegliarsi; **~n** *v/t* svegliare; *v/i* svegliarsi

walk [wɔ:k] *s* passeggiata *f*; **go for a ~, take a ~** fare una passeggiata; *v/i* camminare; **~ing-stick** bastone *m* da passeggio

wall [wɔ:l] muro *m*; parete *f*

wallet ['wɔlit] portafoglio *m*

walnut ['wɔ:lnʌt] noce *f*

waltz [wɔ:ls] valzer *m*

wan [wɔn] pallido

wander ['wɔndə] *v/i* vagare; divagare

wane [wein] *v/i* declinare; calare (*della luna*)

want [wɔnt] *s* mancanza *f*; deficienza *f*; *v/t* volere; mancare di; *v/i* mancare

war [wɔ:d] guerra *f*; **make ~** far la guerra

ward [wɔ:d] corsia *f* (*in ospedale*); collegio *m* elettorale; pupillo *m*; **~en** custode *m*;

~er carceriere *m*; **~robe** guardaroba *m*; armadio *m*

ware|house magazzino *m*; **~s** *pl* merce *f*

warm [wɔ:m] *a* caldo; *v/t* riscaldare; *v/i* calore *m*

warn [wɔ:n] *v/t* ammonire; avvertire; **~ing** ammonimento *m*; avvertimento *m*; avviso *m*

warrant ['wɔrənt] *s* mandato *m*; *v/t* autorizzare

warrior ['wɔriə] guerriero *m*

wart [wɔ:t] verruca *f*

wash [wɔʃ] *v/t* lavare; *v/i* lavarsi; **~basin**, *Am* **~-bowl** lavabo *m*; lavandino *m*; **~er**, **~ing-machine** lavatrice *f*; **~ing** bucato *m*

wasp [wɔsp] vespa *f*

waste [weist] *s* spreco *m*; *v/t* sprecare; **~paper-basket** cestino *m* della carta straccia

watch [wɔtʃ] *s* guardia *f*; orologio *m*; **be on the ~** stare attento; *v/t* osservare; sorvegliare; guardare; **~ful** vigilante; guardare; **~man** guardiano *m*

water ['wɔ:tə] *s* acqua *f*; *v/t* inaffiare; **~colou**r acquerella *f*; **~fall** cascata *f*; **~proof** *a*, *s* impermeabile (*m*); **~y** acquoso

watt [wɔt] *elec* watt *m*

wave [weiv] *s* onda *f*; *v/t* agitare; *v/i* agitarsi

waver ['weivə] *v/i* vacillare

whatever

wax [wæks] cera *f*; ceralacca *f*

way [wei] cammino *m*; via *f*; strada *f*; modo *m*; maniera *f*; **by the ~** a proposito; **by ~ of** via; **on the ~** strada facendo; per via; **give ~** cedere; **~ back** ritorno *m*; **~ of life** tenore *m* di vita; **~ out** uscita *f*; **~ward** ['~wəd] capriccioso; ostinato

we [wi:] noi

weak [wi:k] debole; **~en** *v/t* indebolire; *v/i* indebolirsi; **~-minded** imbecille; deficiente; **~ness** debolezza *f*

wealth [welθ] ricchezza *f*; **~y** ricco

wean [wi:n] *v/t* svezzare

weapon ['wepən] arma *f*

wear [wεə] *s* uso *m*; **~ and tear** logorìo *m*; *v/t*, *irr* portare; indossare; **~ out** *v/t* consumare; *v/i* consumarsi

weary ['wiəri] *a* stanco; *v/t* stancare

weasel ['wi:zl] donnola *f*

weather ['weðə] tempo *m*; **~forecast** bollettino *m* meteorologico

weav|e [wi:v] *v/t*, *irr* tessere; **~er** tessitore *m*; **~ing** tessitura *f*

web [web] tela *f*; trama *f*

wedding ['wediŋ] nozze *f/pl*; matrimonio *m*

wedge [wedʒ] cuneo *m*

Wednesday ['wenzdi] mercoledì *m*

weed [wi:d] erbaccia *f*

week [wi:k] settimana *f*; **to-day** oggi a otto; **~day**

giorno *m* feriale; **~end** fine *f* settimana *f*; **~ly** *a, s* settimanale (*m*)

weep [wi:p] *v/t*, *v/i*, *irr* piangere; **~ing** pianto *m*; lagrime *f/pl*

weigh [wei] *v/t*, *v/i* pesare; **~t** peso *m*; **~t-lifting** sollevamento *m* pesi; **~ty** pesante

weird [wiəd] misterioso; strano

welcome ['welkəm] *a* benvenuto; gradito; *s* accoglienza *f*; *v/t* accogliere; **(you are) ~!** prego, non c'è di che

welfare ['welfεə] benessere *m*; **~ state** stato *m* assistenziale

well[1] [wel] pozzo *m*

well[2] [wel] *a* in buona salute; *adv* bene; **I am ~, I feel ~** sto bene; **very ~** molto bene; **~-known** ben conosciuto; noto; **~ then!** ebbene!; **~-off, ~-to-do** benestante

Welsh [welʃ] *a, s* gallese (*m*); **the ~** *pl* i gallesi *m/pl*

west [west] *s* occidentale; *s* occidente *m*; ovest *m*; **~ern** occidentale

wet [wet] *a* bagnato; *v/t*, *irr* bagnare

whale [weil] balena *f*

wharf [wɔ:f], *pl* **~fs** or **~ves** banchina *f*

what [wɔt] *pron* quello che; *interj* che!; *a* rel *e* interr che, quale; *pron* interr che soa; **~ever** *a* qualunque; *pron* qualunque cosa

wheat [wiːt] frumento *m*; grano *m*

wheel [wiːl] ruota *f*; volante *m* (*dell'automobile*)

when [wen] quando; **~ever** ogni volta

where [weə] dove; **~as** mentre; **~ver** dovunque

whether ['weðə] se

which [witʃ] *pron rel* che; il quale, la quale, i quali, le quali; *a interr* quale

while [wail] mentre

whim [wim] capriccio *m*

whimper ['wimpə] *v/i* piagnucolare

whine [wain] *v/i* (*del cane*) uggiolare; piagnucolare

whip [wip] *s* frusta *f*; *v/t* frustare

whirl [wɜːl] *s* turbine *m*; *v/t* turbinare

whisk [wisk] *v/t* frullare

whiskers ['wiskəz] *pl* basette *f/pl*; baffi *m/pl* (*di gatto*)

whisper ['wispə] *s* bisbiglio *m*; mormorio *m*; *v/t* bisbigliare; mormorare

whistle ['wisl] *s* fischio *m*; *v/t*, *v/i* fischiare

white [wait] bianco; **~-collar worker** impiegato *m*; **~n** *v/t* imbiancare; **~wash** intonaco *m*

Whitsuntide [‚wit'sʌntaid] Pentecoste *f/pl*

whizz [wiz] *v/i* sibilare

who [huː] *pron rel* che; il quale, la quale, i quali, le quali; *pron interr* chi; **~dun(n)it** [huː'dʌnit] gial-

lo *m*; **~ever** chiunque

whole [houl] *a* tutto; intero; intatto; totale; *s* insieme *m*; tutto *m*; totale *m*; **~sale** *comm* all'ingrosso; *fig* generale; **~some** sano; salutare

whom [huːm] *pron rel* che; il quale, la quale, i quali, le quali; *pron interr* chi

whooping-cough ['huːpiŋ-] tosse *f* canina; pertosse *f*

whore [hɔː] puttana *f*

whose [huːz] *a rel* il cui, la cui, i cui, le cui; *a e pron interr* di chi

why [wai] *adv interr* perché; *interj* come!

wicked ['wikid] malvagio; cattivo

wide [waid] largo; esteso; vasto; **~n** *v/t* allargare; *v/i* allargarsi; **~spread** diffuso

widow ['widou] vedova *f*; **~er** vedovo *m*

width [widθ] larghezza *f*

wife [waif], *pl* **wives** [~vz] moglie *f*

wig [wig] parrucca *f*

wild [waild] selvaggio; selvatico

wilful ['wilful] testardo

will [wil] volontà *f*; testamento *m*; **~ing** disposto

willow ['wilou] salice *m*

wilt [wilt] *v/i* appassire; languire

win [win] *s* vittoria *f*; *v/t*, *irr* vincere; guadagnare; *v/i* vincere

wind¹ [wind] vento *m*

wind² [waind] *v/t*, *irr* avvolgere; **~ up** caricare (*l'orologio*); concludere; *v/i* serpeggiare; **~ing stairs** scala *f* a chiocciola

window ['windou] finestra *f*; **~sill** davanzale *m*

wind|pipe trachea *f*; **~screen**, *Am* **~shield** parabrezza *m*; **~screen-wiper** tergicristallo *m*; **~y** ventoso

wine [wain] vino *m*

wing [wiŋ] ala *f*

winner ['winə] vincitore *m*

winter ['wintə] *s* inverno *m*; *a* d'inverno; invernale; *v/i* svernare; passare l'inverno

wipe [waip] *v/t* pulire; asciugare

wir|e ['waiə] *s* filo *m* (*metallico*); telegramma *m*; mettere i fili; telegrafare; **~less** radio *f*; **~less set** apparecchio *m* radio; **~y** robusto

wis|dom ['wizdəm] saggezza *f*; giudizio *m*; **~dom-tooth** dente *m* del giudizio; **~e** [waiz] saggio; giudizioso

wish [wiʃ] *s* desiderio *m*; augurio *m*; *v/t*, *v/i* desiderare; augurare

wistful ['wistful] desideroso; pensoso

wit [wit] spirito *m*

witch [witʃ] strega *f*; **~craft** stregoneria *f*

with [wið] con; insieme a

withdraw [wið'drɔ:] *v/t*, *v/i* irr ritirare; (*si*) ritirarsi

wither ['wiðə] *v/i* appassire; inaridirsi

withhold [wið'hould] *v/t*, *irr*

negare; trattenere

with|in [wið'in] dentro; entro; **~out** *prp* senza; *do* **~out** fare a meno di; *adv* fuori

withstand [wið'stænd] *v/t* resistere a

witness ['witnis] *s* testimone *m*, *f*; testimonianza *f*; *v/t* assistere a; testimoniare

witty ['witi] spiritoso

wives [waivz] *pl* of **wife**

wizard ['wizəd] stregone *m*; mago *m*

wolf [wulf], *pl* **wolves** [~vz] lupo *m*

woman ['wumən], *pl* **women** ['wimin] donna *f*

womb [wu:m] utero *m*

women ['wimin] *pl* of **woman**

wonder ['wʌndə] *s* meraviglia *f*; *v/t* meravigliarsi; domandarsi; **~ful** meraviglioso

woo [wu:] *v/t* corteggiare; far la corte a

wood [wud] bosco *m*; legno *m*; **~en** di legno

wool [wul] lana *f*; **~(l)en** di lana; **~ly** di lana; lanoso

word [wə:d] parola *f*; **~y** verboso

work [wə:k] *s* lavoro *m*; opera *f*; *v/t* lavorare; *v/i* lavorare; funzionare; **get (set) to ~** mettersi al lavoro; **~day** giorno *m* feriale; **~er** operaio *m*; **~less** senza lavoro; **~man** operaio *m*; **~ of art** opera *f* d'arte; **~s** *pl* officina *f*; **~s council** consiglio *m* di fabbrica; **~shop** laboratorio *m*; officina *f*

world [wə:ld] mondo *m*; **~ly** mondano; terreno; **~ war** guerra *f* mondiale; **~wide** mondiale

worm [wə:m] verme *m*; baco *m*

worry ['wʌri] *s* preoccupazione *f*; *v/t* preoccupare; *v/i* preoccuparsi

worse [wə:s] *a* peggiore; *adv* peggio

worship ['wə:ʃip] *s* culto *m*; adorazione *f*; *v/t* adorare

worst [wə:st] *a* il peggiore; *adv* il peggio

worsted ['wustid] pettinato *m* di lana

worth [wə:θ] *s* valore *m*; merito *m*; *a* del valore di; **be ~** valere; **~less** senza valore; **be ~while** valere la pena, convenire; **~y** degno

wound [wu:nd] *s* ferita *f*; *v/t* ferire

wrangle ['ræŋgl] *s* litigio *m*; *v/i* litigare

wrap [ræp] *v/t* avvolgere; **~per** fascia *f* (*per giornale*); copertina *f* (*di libro, staccabile*); **~ping** involucro *m*

wrath [rɔθ] collera *f*; ira *f*

wreath [ri:θ], *pl* **~s** [~ðz] ghirlanda *f*; corona *f*

wreck [rek] *s* naufragio *m*; rovina *f*; *v/t* distruggere; rovinare; *v/i* naufragare

wren [ren] scricciolo *m*

wrench [rentʃ] *v/t* strappare

wrest [rest] *v/t* strappare

wrestle ['resl] *v/t* lottare; **~ing** lotta *f* libera

wretch [retʃ] *s* disgraziato *m*; sciagurato *m*; **~ed** [~id] bruttissimo; misero malissimo

wriggle ['rigl] *v/i* contorcersi; dimenarsi

wring [riŋ] *v/t, irr* torcere; strizzare; strappare

wrinkle ['riŋkl] ruga *f*

wrist [rist] polso *m*; **~watch** orologio *m* da polso

writ [rit] mandato *m*

write [rait] *v/t, v/i, irr* scrivere; **~r** scrittore *m*

writhe [raið] *v/i* contorcersi

writing ['raitiŋ] scrittura *f*; scritto *m*; **in ~** per iscritto; **~desk** scrivania *f*; **~paper** carta *f* da scrivere

wrong [rɔŋ] *s* sbagliato; ingiusto; **be ~** sbagliarsi; avere torto; *s* torto *m*; ingiustizia *f*; *v/t* fare un torto a; **be ~** aver torto

wrought [rɔ:t] battuto (*di ferro*); lavorato; **~ up** nervoso

X, Y

Xmas ['krisməs] *cf* **Christmas**

X-ray ['eks'rei] *v/t* fare una radiografia; *s* raggio *m* X

xylophone ['zailəfoun] silofono *m*

yacht [jɔt] panfilo *m*

yard [jɑːd] (*misura*) iarda *f*; cortile *m*

yarn [jɑːn] filo *m*

yawn [jɔːn] *s* sbadiglio *m*; *v/i* sbadigliare

year [jəː] anno *m*; **~ly** annuale

yearn [jəːn] *v/i* bramare

yeast [jiːst] lievito *m*

yell [jel] *s* grido *m*; *v/t*, *v/i* gridare

yellow ['jelou] giallo

yes [jes] sì

yesterday ['jestədi] ieri; **the day before ~** ieri l'altro

yet [jet] ancora; tuttavia

yield [jiːld] *v/t* rendere; cedere; *v/i* acconsentire; cedere

yoke [jouk] *s* giogo *m*

yolk [jouk] tuorlo *m*

yonder ['jɔndə] laggiù

you [juː] tu; te; voi; Lei; lo; Loro

young [jʌŋ] giovane; **~ster** giovane *m*

your [jɔː] tuo; tua; tuoi; tue; vostro(a, i, e); Suo(a, i, e); Loro

yours [jɔːz] (il) tuo, (la) tua, (i) tuoi, (le) tue; (il) vostro, (la) vostra, (i) vostri, (le) vostre; (il) Suo, (la) Sua, (i) Suoi, (le) Sue; (il) Loro, (la) Loro, (i) Loro, (le) Loro

your|self [jɔː'self], *pl* **~selves** [~'selvz] te stesso(a); Lei stesso(a)

youth [juːθ], *pl* **~s** [~ðz] gioventù *f*; **~ful** giovanile; **~ hostel** albergo *m* per la gioventù

Yugoslav ['juːgou'slɑːv] *a*, *s* iugoslavo (*m*); **~ia** Jugoslavia *f*

Z

zeal [ziːl] zelo *m*; **~ous** ['zeləs] zelante

zebra ['ziːbrə] zebra *f*; **~crossing** passaggio *m* pedonale

zero ['ziərou] zero *m*

zest [zest] gusto *m*; entusiasmo *m*

zinc [ziŋk] zinco *m*

zip|code [zip-] *Am* numero *m* di codice postale; **~fastener**, **~per** chiusura *f* lampo

zone [zoun] zona *f*

zoo [zuː] giardino *m* zoologico

zoology [zou'ɔlədʒi] zoologia *f*

A

a *prp* to, at, in; **a Roma** in (to) Rome; **a casa** (at) home; **alle quattro** at four o'clock; *dativo* **l'ho dato ~ lui** I gave it to him

abl ate *m* abbot; **~adessa** *f* abbess

abbacchio *m* lamb

abbaglio *m* error

abbaiare *v/i* bark

abbaino *m* attic; skylight

abbaio *m* barking

abbandon are *v/t* abandon; desert; *sto dai medici* given up by the physicians; **~o** *m* abandonment; desertion

abbass amento *m* lowering; humiliation; **~are** *v/t* lower; reduce; humble; **~o** down; below

abbastanza enough; quite

abbàtt ere *v/t* knock down; fell; *aer* shoot down; *fig* depress; **~ersi** *v/r* despair

abbazia *f* abbey

abbell imento *m* embellishment; **~ire** *v/t* embellish

abbiamo we have

abbigliamento *m* clothes *pl*

abboccare *v/t* bite; fill to the brim

abbon amento *m* subscription; **biglietto** *m* **d'~amen-** to season ticket; **~arsi (a)** *v/r* subscribe to; **~ato** *m* subscriber

abbond ante abundant; plentiful; **~anza** *f* abundance

abbonire *v/t* appease

abbord aggio *m naut* boarding a ship; **~are** *v/t* approach; *naut* land; **~o** *m* approach; boarding

abbottonare *v/t* button

abbozz are *v/t* sketch; outline; **~o** *m* sketch; draft

abbracci amento, **~o** *m* embrace; hug(ging); **~are** *v/t* embrace

abbrevi amento *m* abbreviation; **~are** *v/t* abbreviate; **~azione** *f* abbreviation

abbronz are *v/t* bronze, tan, burn; **~arsi** *v/r* become sunburnt

abbrustolire *v/t* toast; (*coffee*) roast

abbuiare *v/t* darken; obscure

abdicare *v/i* abdicate

abete *m* fir-tree

abietto *m* abject

abiezione *f* abjection

àbile clever; skilful; capable

abilità *f* ability, skill; cleverness

abisso m abyss; chasm

abit|ante m, f inhabitant; dweller; resident; **~are** v/i dwell; reside; live; **~azione** f dwelling, residence

àbito m dress, gown; suit; **~ da lutto** mourning clothes; **~ da sera** evening dress; **~ da spiaggia** beach-wear

abitu|ale habitual; customary; **~are** v/t accustom; **~arsi** v/r become used (**a** to)

abitùdine f habit

abnegazione f abnegation; self-denial

abolire v/t abolish; **~zione** f abolition

abominare v/t abominate, detest

aborrire v/t abhor; loathe

abort|ire v/i miscarry; abort; **~o** m miscarriage; abortion

abrogare v/t abrogate

àbside f apse

abus|are (di) v/i abuse (of); **~ivo** abusive; **~o** m abuse

accad|èmia f academy; **~èmia di Belle Arti** school of Fine Arts; **~èmico** adj academic; m academician

accad|ere v/i happen; take place; **~uto** m event

accampamento m encampment, camping place

accanimento m tenacity

accanto beside; alongside; **~ a** beside; next to

accaparrare v/t hoard (up); corner

accappatoio m bathrobe

accarezzare v/t caress

accatt|are v/t beg for alms; **~onaggio** m begging

accel|erare v/t accelerate; **~erato** m rail ordinary train; **~eratore** m aut gas pedal; Am accelerator

accèndere v/t light; radio switch on; com open (account); fig kindle

accendisigaro m (cigarette-)lighter

accenn|are v/t, v/i point out; hint; **~o** m hint

accensione f aut ignition

accent|o m accent; **~uare** v/t accentuate; stress

accerchiare v/t encircle; surround

accert|amento m ascertainment; **~are** v/t ascertain

acceso alight

access|ibile accessible; **~o** m access; med fit

accessorio adj accessory; m accessory

accetta f hatchet

accett|àbile acceptable; **~are** v/t accept; approve

acchiapp|amosche m flycatcher; **~are** v/t catch

acciabattare v/t botch

accia|eria f steel-works pl; **~o** m steel

acciden|tale accidental; **~te** m accident; casualty; med apoplectic stroke

accingersi v/r set about

acciò, acciocché so that

acciottol|are v/t gravel; **~ato** m pavement

acciuffare *v/t* grasp

acciuga *f* anchovy

acclam|are *v/t* acclaim, cheer; **~azione** *f* acclamation

acclimare, acclimatare *v/t* acclimatize

accl|udere *v/t* enclose; **~usa** *f* enclosure; **~uso** enclosed

accoglienza *f* reception

accògliere *v/t* receive

accomodamento *m* arrangement; adjustment

accomod|are *v/t* adjust; repair; **~arsi** *v/r* take a seat; make o.s. comfortable; **si accòmodi!** sit down, please

accompagn|amento *m* accompaniment; **~are** *v/t* accompany; **~arsi** *v/r* match

acconci|are *v/t* arrange; *Am* fix; **~atura** *f* hair-do

acconsentire *v/i* agree (**a** on)

accontentare *v/t* content

acconto *m* instalment; account

accorciare *v/t* shorten; curtail

accord|are *v/t* grant; *mus* tune; **~o** *m* agreement; **èssere d'~o** agree

accòrgersi *v/r* be aware (**di** of)

accòrrere *v/i* run up

accort|ezza *f* shrewdness; **~o** shrewd; prudent

accost|amento *m* approach; **~are** *v/t* approach; (*door*) leave ajar; **~o** near (by)

accostumare *v/t* accustom

accozzaglia *f* huddle

accredit|amento *m* credit (-ing); **~are** *v/t* (ac)credit

accréscere *v/t, v/i* increase

accudire (a) *v/i* attend to, take care of

accumul|are *v/t* accumulate; **~atore** *m* accumulator

accuratezza *f* accuracy

accurato accurate

accus|a *f* accusation; **~are** *v/t* charge; **~are ricevuta** acknowledge receipt

acerb|ità *f* acerbity; **~o** sour

àcero *m* maple

acet|o *m* vinegar; **~oso** acetous

àcido *adj* sour; *m* acid

acme *f* acme

acne *f* acne

acqua *f* water; **~ potabile** drinking water; **~ santa** holy water; **~io** *m* sink; **~ragia** *f* turpentine; **~rio** *m* aquarium

acqua|ta *f* shower; **~vite** *f* brandy

acquazzone *m* heavy shower; cloud-burst

acque *f/pl* mineral (*or:* medicinal) spring

acquerello *m* water-colour

acquietare *v/t* appease

acqui|stare *v/t* acquire; **~sto** *m* purchase

acre acrid

acrèdine *f* acridity

acrobata *m, f* acrobat

acuire *v/t* sharpen; stimulate

acùleo *m* prickle; sting

acume *m* insight

acùstic|a f acoustics pl; **~o** acoustic

acutezza f acuteness; shrewdness

acuto acute, keen; (voice) shrill; mus high note

ad = a (before a vowel)

adagio gently slowly; mus adagio

adattamento m adaptation

adatt|are v/t adapt; fit; **~arsi** v/r adapt oneself; suit; **~o** fit, suitable

addaziare v/t put duty on

addebitare v/t debit; **~ di** charge with

addèbito m debit; charge

addens|amento m thickening; **~arsi** v/r thicken; crowd

addentrarsi v/r penetrate

addestr|are v/t (animal) train, break in; **~amento** m training

addetto adj assigned; employed; m attaché; **~ al rifornimento** attendant

addietro behind; (time) ago

addio good-bye, farewell; m parting

addir|ittura even; and what is more; downright; **~izzare** v/t straighten

addizion|ale additional; **~are** v/t add; **~e** f addition

addobbare v/t decorate

addolc|imento m sweetening; soothing; **~ire** v/t sweeten; soften

addolorare v/t grieve, sadden

addome m abdomen

addomesticare v/t tame; domesticate

addorment|are v/t send to sleep; **~arsi** v/r fall asleep

addossare v/t burden; lay on; fig assume

addosso on, upon (one)

addottorarsi v/r graduate (from a university)

addurre v/t bring up; adduce

adegu|are v/t equalize; level; **~ato** adequate

adémpiere, ~empire v/t accomplish, fulfil; **~empimento** m fulfilment

adenite f adenitis

ader|ente adherent; **~ire** v/i adhere; join; support (a party)

adesso now; presently

adiacente adjacent

Àdige m Adige; **Alto ~** (late) Southern Tyrol

àdito m entrance; fig access

adolescen|te adj adolescent; m, f adolescent, youth; **~za** f adolescence; youth

adombrare v/i shade

adoper|àbile usable; **~are** v/t use

ador|are v/t adore; **~azione** f worship

adorn|amento m adornment; **~are** v/t adorn, trim

adottare v/t adopt

adozione f adoption

adrenalina f adrenalin

Adriàtico m Adriatic

adul|are v/t flatter; **~atore** m flatterer; **~terio** m adultery

adulto adj adult; m adult; grown-up

adun|anza f meeting; **~are** v/t assemble

aerazione f aeration

aère|o airy; **ferrovìa** f **~a** elevated railway; **flotta** f **~a** airfleet; **posta** f **~a** air mail

aerodinàmico streamlined

aeròdromo m aerodrome

aero|nàutica f aeronautics pl; aviation; **~nave** f airship; **~plano** m airplane; **~porto** m airport

aeròstato m aer balloon

afa f sultriness

aff|àbile kind; **~abilità** f affability

affaccendarsi v/r busy oneself

affamare v/t starve out

affann|are v/t trouble; **~ato** panting; **~o** m trouble; shortness of breath; **~oso** gasping; anxious

affar|e m business; matter; **ministro** m **degli ~i èsteri** minister of foreign affairs

affascinare v/t charm; fascinate

affaticare v/t fatigue

affatto absolutely; perfectly; **~ niente** not at all

affatturare v/t bewitch; adulterate

afferm|are v/t affirm; state; **~ativo** affirmative; **~azione** f affirmation; statement

afferr|are v/t seize; grasp; **~arsi (a)** v/r cling to

affett|ato affected; sliced (meat); **~o** m affection;

love; **~uoso** affectionate

affezion|ato affectionate; fond (of); **~e** f affection

affibbiare v/t buckle

affid|amento m reliance; **~are** v/t entrust; **~arsi** v/r rely (**a** upon)

affìggere v/t affix; stick

affilare v/t whet; sharpen

affili|are v/t affiliate; **~ato** m member

affinché in order that

affine akin, kindred

affinità f affinity

affisso m bill, poster

affitt|àbile rentable; **~are** v/t let; rent; lease; **~o** m rent; lease; **dare in ~o** let, lease

affl|ìggere v/t afflict; **~izione** f affliction

afflu|ente adj affluent; m affluent, tributary; **~enza** f concourse; **~ire** v/i flow; flock

afflusso m rush; flow

affogare v/t suffocate; drown; v/i be drowned

affoll|amento m crowd; **~are** v/t crowd, throng

affondare v/t sink; v/i sink, go down

affrancare v/t enfranchise; set free; stamp (letter)

affresco m fresco

affrett|are v/t hasten; **~si** v/r hurry

affrontare v/t: **~ qu.** face s.o.

affronto m insult

affum|are, **~icare** v/t smoke, fumigate

afoso sultry

Africa f Africa

africano s/m, adj African

àgave f agave

agenda f note-book

agente m agent; broker; **~ di cambio** stockbroker; **~ di polizia, di pùbblica sicurezza** policeman; **~ investigativo** detective

agenzia f agency; **~ (di) viaggi** travel agency; **~ d'informazioni** inquiry office

agevolare v/t facilitate

agévole easy

agevolezza f facility

agganciare v/t hook; fasten

aggettivo m adjective

agghiacciare v/t freeze

aggio m premium

aggiornare v/t adjourn; v/i poet dawn

aggirare v/t encircle; fig deceive; cheat

aggiùngere v/t add

aggiun|ta f addition; **~tare** v/t join; **~to** m assistant

aggiustare v/t adjust; mend

aggranchirsi v/r get benumbed

aggrappar|e v/t grapple; **~si** v/r cling (to)

aggravare v/t aggravate; make worse

aggregare v/t aggregate

aggressi|one f aggression; **~vo** aggressive

aggrinzire v/t wrinkle; shrivel

aggruppare v/t group; assemble

agguato m ambush; **stare in ~** lie in wait

aghett|are v/t lace up; **~o** m lace

aghifòglia f conifer

aghiforme needle-shaped

agiatezza f comfort; wealth

agiato well off

àgile nimble, agile

agilità f agility

agio m comfort; leisure

agire v/i act; do

agit|are v/t agitate; shake; **~ato** agitated; troubled

aglio m garlic

agnello m lamb

ago m needle; tongue (balance)

agonia f agony; anguish

agosto m (month) August

agr|ario s/m, adj agrarian; **~icoltura** f agriculture; farming

agrifoglio m holly

agrodolce bitter-sweet

agrumi m/pl citrus fruits pl

aguzz|are v/t sharpen; **~o** sharp

ahi! ahimè! alas!

Aia f: **l'~** the Hague

airone m heron

aiuola f flower-bed

aiut|ante m assistant; mil adjutant; **~are qu** v/t help s.o.; **~o** m help; aid

aizzare v/t instigate

ala f wing

alabastro m alabaster

alacrità f alacrity; zeal

alb|a f dawn; **~eggiare** v/i dawn

alberg|are v/t lodge; harbour; **~atore** m innkeeper

albergo m hotel; **~ per la gioventù** youth hostel

àlbero m tree; naut mast; aut shaft

albicocc|a f apricot; **~o** m apricot-tree

albume m white of egg; albumen

alce m elk

àlcole m alcohol

alcòl|ici v/t alcoholic drinks pl; **~co** alcoholic

àlcool m alcohol

alcun|o anybody; somebody; **~i** a few

alfabètico alphabetical

alfabeto m alphabet

alga f sea-weed

algebra f algebra

àlias alias

àlibi m alibi

alieno alien, strange

aliment|are v/t feed; **gèneri** m/pl **~ari** food; foodstuffs pl; **~azione** f **di rete** light-mains connection; **~o** m food; **~i** m/pl alimony

àlito m breath; gentle breeze

allacciare v/t lace

allarg|amento m enlargement; **~are** v/t enlarge; widen

allarmare v/t alarm; worry

allarme m alarm, alert; fright; **corda f (segnale m) d'~** communication cord (emergency signal)

allatt|amento m nursing; breast-feeding; **~are** v/t nurse

alle|anza f alliance; **~ato** adj allied; m ally

alleg|are v/t enclose; allege; **~ato** adj enclosed; m enclosure

alleggerire v/t relieve

allegr|ia f mirth; cheerfulness; **~o** merry, cheerful

allen|amento m training; **~are** v/t coach; train; **~atore** m trainer

allent|are v/t loosen; relent; slacken; **~atura** f med hernia

allergìa f allergy

allettare v/t allure

allevare v/t breed; rear

allietare v/t cheer; amuse

allievo m pupil; scholar

alligatore m alligator

alline|amento m alignment; **~are** v/t range; line up

allòdola f lark

alloggi|are v/t lodge; v/i live, stay; **~o** m lodging

allontan|are v/t remove; **~arsi** v/r go away

allora then; **d'~ in poi** from that time on

allorché when; whenever

alloro m laurel

allucin|are v/t hallucinate; dazzle; **~azione** f hallucination

allùdere v/i allude (**a** to), hint (at)

all|ume m alum; **~umina** f alumina; **~uminio** m aluminium

allung|amento m prolongation; **~are** v/t lengthen,

prolong

allusione f allusion, hint

alluvione f flood, inundation

almeno at least

alpaca m alpaca

alpestre mountainous

Alpi: le ~ f/pl the Alps pl

alpi|nismo m mountain-climbing; **~nista** m, f mountain-climber; **~no** adj Alpine; m mil mountain-soldier

alquant|o somewhat; rather; **~i** several

alt! halt!

altalena f seesaw; swing

altare m altar

alterare v/t alter; forge; irritate

alter|ezza f pride; **~igia** f haughtiness

altern|are v/t alternate; **~ativo** alternative; **~o** alternate

altero proud; haughty

altezza f height; title: Highness

altipiano m plateau

altitùdine f altitude, height

alto high; tall; loud; **dall'~** from above; **in ~** upstairs; **l' Alta Italia** f Northern Italy

altoparlante m loud speaker

altopiano m plateau

altrettanto as much; equally

altrimenti otherwise

altro other; **~ che!** rather! **l'~ anno** last year; **ieri l'~** the day before yesterday;

senz'~ certainly; **l'un l'~** each other

altrove elsewhere

altrui of others

altura f height

alunno m pupil

alveare m beehive

alz|are v/t raise; lift; **~arsi** v/r rise, get up

amàbile amiable

amabilità f amiability; kindness

amaca f hammock

amante m, f lover; f mistress

amare v/t love; like

amar|eggiare v/t embitter; **~ezza** f bitterness; **~o** bitter

ambasciat|a f embassy; **~ore** m ambassador

ambedue both

ambiente m surroundings pl; environment

ambiguità f ambiguity

ambiguo equivocal

ambizi|one f ambition; **~oso** ambitious

ambul|ante travelling; **venditore** m **~ante** pedlar; **~anza** f ambulance; field hospital; **~atorio** adj ambulatory; m dispensary

amen|ità f amenity; **~o** pleasant

Amèrica f America

americano s/m, adj American

amic|a f lady-friend; **~hévole** friendly; **~cizia** f friendship; **~co** m friend

àmido m starch

amigdala f tonsil

ammaccatura f bruise

ammaestrare v/t train

ammal|**are** v/i, **~arsi** v/r fall ill; **~ato** adj sick; m patient

ammarare v/i land on water

ammassare v/t pile up; hoard

ammazzare v/t kill; (animals) slaughter

ammenda f fine

amméttere v/t admit; receive

amminstr|**are** v/t manage; administer; **~azione** f administration; management

ammiràbile admirable

ammiraglio m admiral

ammir|**are** v/t admire; **~a-zione** f admiration; **~évole** admirable

ammis|**sìbile** admissible; **~sione** f admission

ammobili|**amento** m furnishing; **~are** v/t furnish

ammogliare v/t give a wife to (marry)

ammoll|**are** v/t soak; soften

ammon|**imento** m warning; admonition; **~ire** v/t warn; admonish

ammont|**are** v/t heap; pile; v/i amount (**a** to); **~icchiare** v/t heap up

ammort|**amento** m amortization; **~izzare** v/t amortize; **~izzatore** m (**d'urto**) shock-absorber

ammost|**are** v/t press (grapes); **~atoio** m wine-press

ammucchiare v/t pile up

ammuffire v/i grow mouldy

ammutinamento m mutiny

ammutolire v/i become dumb

amnesia f amnesia

amnist|**ia** f amnesty; **~iare** v/t grant amnesty

amo m fish-hook; fig bait

amorale amoral

amor|**e** m love; **~eggiare** v/i flirt; **~évole** loving

amorfo shapeless

amor|**ino** m paint amoretto; **~oso** loving; amorous

amperaggio m amperage

ampi|**ezza** f breadth; **~o** ample; wide; spacious

ampli|**are**, **~ficare** v/t amplify; increase; **~ficatore** m radio: amplifier

ampoll|**a** f cruet; **~e** f/pl oil and vinegar cruet; **~iera** f cruet-stand

ampolloso bombastic

amput|**are** v/t amputate; **~azione** f amputation

anacoreta m hermit

anàgrafe f registrar's office

analfabe|**ta** s/m, f, adj illiterate; **~tismo** illiteracy

analgèsico s/m, adj med anodyne

anàlisi f analysis

analitico analytic(al)

ananasso m pineapple

anarchìa f anarchy

anàrchico adj anarchic(al); m anarchist

anatomìa f anatomy

ànatra f duck

anca f haunch; hip

anche also, too

anchilosi f anchylosis

ancona f altar-piece

ancora still; more; **non ~** not yet

àncora f anchor; **salpare l'~** weigh anchor

and|amento m progress; **~ante** current; mus andante

andare v/i go; walk; ride; **~ a cavallo** ride on horseback; **~ in bicicletta** ride a bicycle; **~ in giro** walk about; **~ in treno** go by train; **come va?** how are you?

andàrsene v/r go away

andata: sémplice ~ f single ticket; **biglietto m di ~ e ritorno** return ticket

and|ato gone; **~iamo** we go; let us go!

àndito m corridor; passage

androne m lobby

anèddoto m~anecdote

anelare v/i pant

anello m ring; **~ matrimoniale** wedding-ring

an|emía f anaemia; **~èmico** anaemic

anestesia f anesthesia

aneto m dill

anfiteatro m amphitheatre

ànfora f amphora; jar

angèlico angelic

àngelo m angel

angheria f vexation

angina f med angina

angiporto m blind alley

angolare angular

àngolo m angle; corner

angoloso angular

ang|oscia f anguish; **~osciare** v/t grieve; vex; **~oscioso** grievous

anguill|a f eel; **~aia** f eel-pond

anguria f water-melon

angustia f narrowness; fig misery, trouble

ànice m anise

ànima f soul

anim|ale adj animal; m animal; beast; **~are** v/t animate, enliven; **~arsi** v/r take courage; **~strada f ~ata** lively street

ànimo m mind; spirit; courage; **fare ~** give courage

anim|osità f animosity; **~oso** courageous; bold

ànitra f duck

annacquare v/t dilute (wine); fig water down

annaf|fiare v/t water; **~fiatoio** m watering-can

annali m/pl annals pl

annata f year; crop

annebbiare v/t blur; dim

anneg|are v/t drown; v/i get drowned

annerire v/t blacken

annes|sione f annexation; **~o** m annex

annèttere v/t annex

annichilare v/t annihilate

annid|are v/t, **~arsi** v/r nestle

anniversario m anniversary

anno m year; **capo m d'~** New Year's Day; **buon anno!** happy New Year!; **quanti anni hai?**

how old are you?

annodare v/t knot; tie

annoi|are v/t annoy; weary; **~ato** annoyed; bored

annoso old

annotare v/t note; annotate

annottare v/i grow dark

annu|ale adj yearly; m anniversary; **~ario** m yearbook; directory

annull|are v/t annul; cancel; **~amento** m annulment; cancellation

annun|ciare, ~ziare v/t announce; **~ziatore** m, **~ziatrice** f radio: announcer; **~cio, ~zio** m announcement; advertisement

ànnuo annual

annusare v/t smell; sniff (animals)

annuvolare v/t cloud; fig make gloomy

anòfele f anopheles; gnat

anònim|o anonymous; **società f ~a** joint-stock company

anormale abnormal

ansa f handle; fig pretext; 2 (the) Hanse

ansare v/i pant

ansia f, **ansietà** f anxiety; eagerness

ansioso anxious; eager

ant. = antimeridiano

antagonismo m antagonism

antàrtico antarctic

ante... before ...

ante|cedente previous; **~cèdere** v/i precede; **~cessore** m predecessor;

guerra m pre-war period; **~nato** m ancestor; **~porre** v/t place before, prefer; **~riore** anterior;(time) former, previous

antenna f antenna; aerial

anti... anti..., counter...

anti|càmera f antechamber; **~chità** f antiquity; ancient times pl; **~co** ancient; old; 2**co Testamento** Old Testament

anticipa|to in advance; **~zione** f advance

anticipo m advanced payment; **in ~** beforehand

anticongelante m antifreeze

antidoto m antidote

antifurto m safety-lock

antilope f antelope

antimeridiano before noon

anti|pasto m hors-d'œuvre; appetizer; **~patia** f antipathy; dislike; **~pàtico** disagreeable

antiqua|to antiquated; **~ria** f antiquarianism

antisettico s/m, adj antiseptic

antrace m med anthrax

antracite f anthracite

antro m cave; den

antropòfago m cannibal

anulare adj annular; m ringfinger

anzi rather; on the contrary

anzian|ità f seniority; **~o** adj aged; m senior

anzidetto above-mentioned

anzitutto first of all

apatìa f apathy

apàtico apathetic; indifferent

ape f bee

aperitivo m appetizer

aper|to adj open; m open space; **~tura** f opening

ap|iaio m beekeeper; **~iario** m beehouse; apiary

àpige m apex

apòlide adj stageless; m stateless person

apopl|essia f apoplexy; **~èttico** adj apoplectic; **colpo** m **~èttico** apoplectic fit

apostòlico apostolic

apòstolo m apostle

appacchettare v/t pack together

appaiamento m coupling

appaltare v/t contract

appannare v/i tarnish; dim

apparato m apparatus

apparecchi|are v/t prepare; lay (table); **~o** m device; set; **~o radio** wireless set; **~o a reazione** jet

appar|ente apparent; **~enza** f (outward) appearance

appariamo we appear

appar|ire v/i appear; look; **~isco** I appear; **~isce** he appears

apparso appeared

appart|amento m flat, apartment; **~enenza** f belonging; **~enere** v/i belong; pertain

appassion|arsi v/r be fond (**di** of); be sorry (**di** for); **~ato** passionate

appassire v/i fade, wither

appell|arsi v/r appeal (**a** to);

~o m roll-call; appeal

appena scarcely; hardly; just; **~ che** as soon as

appèndere v/t hang up

appen|dice f appendix; **~dicite** f appendicitis

Appennino m Apennines pl

appetito m appetite; **~so** appetizing

appianare v/t level; smooth

appiattire v/t flatten

appiccare v/t hang up; (fire) kindle; (quarrel) start

appiccic|are v/t paste; stick; fig palm off on s.o.; **~arsi** v/r stick, adhere

appiè at the foot (of)

appieno fully

appigionare v/t let, rent

appi|gliarsi v/r take hold (**a** of); **~glio** m pretext

appiombo perpendicularly

applau|dire v/t, v/i applaud; cheer; **~so** m applause

applic|àbile applicable; **~are** v/t apply; (law) enforce; **~arsi** v/r devote o.s.; **~azione** f application; fig diligence

appoggi|are v/t support; **~arsi** v/r lean; fig **~arsi** (**a qu**) depend (on s.o.); **~o** m support; fig aid; backing

apportare v/t bring; fetch

apporto m contribution

appòsito special

apposizione f apposition

apposta on purpose

appost|amento m ambush; **~are** v/t lie in wait for

ap|prèndere v/t learn; hear;

~prendista *m, f* apprentice;
~prendistato *m* apprentice
ship

appren|sione *f* apprehen-
sion; **~sivo** timid, fearful

appresso near by

appretto *m* dressing, finish

apprezz|àbile appreciable;
~amento *m* appreciation;
~are *v/t* appreciate; value

appr|odare *v/i* land; **~odo** *m*
landing-place

approfittare *v/i* profit (**di**
by)

approfondire *v/t* deepen;
fig investigate carefully

approntare *v/t* make ready

appropri|are *v/t* adjust;
~arsi *v/r* (**di**) appropriate
(s.th.); **~ato** appropriate

approssimativo approximate

approv|are *v/t* approve;
~azione *f* approval; appro-
bation

approvvigionare *v/t* supply

appunt|amento *m* appoint-
ment; date; **~are** *v/t* sharp-
en; write down; stick; **~o**
m note; *adv* just, precisely;
per l'~o exactly

appurare *v/t* ascertain

aprile *m* April

aprire *v/t* open; unlock

apriscàtole *m* tinopener

àquila *f* eagle

àrabo *adj* Arabic; *m* Arab

aràchide *f* peanut

aragosta *f* lobster

aràldica *f* heraldry

aran|ceto *m* orange-grove;

~cia *f* orange; **~ciata** *f* or-
angeade; **~cio** *m* orangetree

ar|are *v/t* plough; **~atro** *m*
plough

arazzo *m* arras; piece of tapestry

arbitr|aggio *m* arbitration;
~ario arbitrary; **~io** *m* will;
libero ~io free will

àrbitro *m* arbiter; judge;
referee

arbusto *m* shrub

arca *f* ark; **~ santa** ark of the
covenant

arcàico archaic

arcàngelo *m* archangel

arcata *f* arcade; *mus* bowing

arche|ologia *f* archaeology;
~òlogo *m* archaeologist

archetto *m* fret-saw; *mus*
bow

archi|pèndolo *m* plummet;
~tetto *m* architect; **~tettu-
ra** *f* architecture

archi|viare *v/t* file; **~ivio** *m*
archives; file

arcipèlago *m* archipelago

arci|prete *m* archpriest;
dean; **~vescovado** *m* arch-
bishopric; **~véscovo** *m*
archbishop

arc|o *m* bow; **~obaleno** *m*
rainbow; **~uata** bent, curved

ardente burning; ardent;
fiery

àrdere *v/t, v/i* burn

ardèsia *f* slate

ard|ire *v/i* dare; **~ito** bold

ardore *m* ardour

àrea *f* area

àrem *m* harem

aren|a f sand; arena; **~arsi** v/r get stranded; **~oso** sandy

argent|are v/t silver; **~iere** m silversmith

argènt|eo silvery; **~o** m silver; **~o vivo** mercury

Argentin|a f Argentine; **~o** m Argentine

argill|a f clay; **~oso** clayey

àrgine m dike; embankment

argoment|are v/i argue; infer; deduce; **~azione** f argumentation, reasoning; **~o** m subject; topic; argument

argu|to keen, witty; **~ùzia** f shrewdness; witticism

ari|a f air; mus tune; **all'~aperta** in the open air; **~compressa** compressed air

àrido dry, arid

arieggiare v/t look like; air

aringa f herring

arioso airy

àrista f roast loin of pork

aristocr|àtico adj aristocratic; m aristocrat; **~azìa** f aristocracy

aritmètica f arithmetic

Arlecchino m Harlequin

arm|a f weapon; **~a da fuoco** firearm; **~i** pl **nucleari** nuclear weapons

armadio m wardrobe

arm|amento m armament; **~are** v/t arm; **~ata** f army; fleet; **~e** f weapon; (coat of) arms pl; **~i** pl troops pl; **piazza** f **d'~i** drill ground; **~erìa** f arsenal; **~istizio** m armistice

arm|onìa f harmony; **~ònica** f **da bocca** harmonica; **~onioso** harmonious

armoraccio m horse-radish

arnese m tool

àrnica f arnica

arnione m kidney

arom|a m aroma; flavour; fragrance; **~àtico** aromatic; **~atizzare** v/t flavour

arpa f harp

arrabb|iarsi v/r get angry; **~iato** enraged; rabid (dog)

arraffare v/t snatch, seize

arrampic|arsi v/r climb; creep; **~tore** m climber

arred|are v/t furnish, equip; **~o** m outfit; **~i** pl sacri holy vessels and clothes

arrenare v/i strand

ar|rendersi v/r surrender

arrest|are v/t stop; arrest; **~arsi** v/r stop; **~o** stop; arrest

arretrato adj backward; m arrears pl

arricchire v/t enrich

arricciare v/t curl; frown; wrinkle

arridere v/i smile

arrivare v/i arrive

arrivederci!, arrivederla! good-bye

arrivista m, f social climber

arrivo m arrival

arrog|ante arrogant; **~anza** f arrogance; **~arsi** v/r arrogate

arrolamento = arruolamento

arross|are v/t redden; **~ire**

v/i blush

arr|ostire *v/t* roast; grill; **~osto** *adj* roasted; *m* roast

arrot|are *v/t* whet; grind; **~ino** *m* knife-grinder; **~olare** *v/t* roll up

arrotondare *v/t* make round

arrotolare *v/t* roll up; coil

arruffare *v/t* ruffle; entangle

arrugginirsi *v/r* rust, become rusty

arruola|mento *m* enlistment; **~re** *v/t* enlist; enroll

arruvidire *v/t* roughen

arsenale *m* arsenal; *naut* shipyard

arsiccio scorched; dry

arte *f* art; skill; craft; **~fatto** artificial; adulterated

artéfice *m* craftsman

artèria *f* artery

arteriosclerosi *f* arteriosclerosis

àrtico Arctic

articol|are *adj*, *v/t* articulate; **~re** *v/t* articulate; jointed; **~azione** *f* articulation; joint

artìcolo *m* article; **~ di fondo** editorial; **~ di prima necessità** commodity

artificiale (**~iziale**) artificial; **fuochi** *m/pl* **~iciali** fireworks *pl*

artigiano *m* artisan; craftsman

artiglier|e *m* gunner; **~ia** *f* artillery; **pezzo** *m* **d'~ia** ordnance piece

artiglio *m* claw

artista *m*, *f* artist

artìstico artistic

arto *m* limb

artrite *f* arthritis

arzillo vigorous; sparkling (wine); spry

ascella *f* arm-pit

ascendente upward

ascen|sione *f* ascent; climbing; *eccl* Ascension; **~sore** *m* lift

ascesso *m* abscess

ascia *f* axe

asciuga|capelli *m* hairdryer; **~amano** *m* towel; **carta** *f* **~ante** blotting-paper; **~are** *v/t* dry; wipe

asciutto dry

ascolt|are *v/t* listen (to); **~o** *m* listening; **dare ~o** give ear (to)

ascrìvere *v/t* ascribe; register

ascrizione *f* registration

Asia *f* Asia; **~ Minore** Asia Minor

asiàtico Asiatic

asilo *m* asylum; refuge; **~ infantile** kindergarten

asinaio *m* ass-driver

àsino *m* ass; donkey

asma *f* asthma; **~ del fieno** hay fever

asparago *m* asparagus

aspèrgere *v/t* sprinkle; strew

asper|sione *f* (be)sprinkling; **~sorio** *m* holy-water sprinkler

aspett|are *v/t* wait (for); expect; **~o** *m* aspect; look; **sala** *f* **d'~o** waiting-room

aspir|ante m applicant, candidate; **~apòlvere** m vacuum cleaner; **~are** v/t inhale; v/i: **~are a qc** aim at s.th.

aspirina f aspirin

aspr|ezza f harshness; **~o** rough, harsh; sharp

assaggiare v/t taste; assay

assai very much; very

assalire v/t attack; assault

assalto m assault; mil attack

assass|inare v/t murder; assassinate; **~ìnio** m murder; **~ino** adj murderous; m assassin

asse f board; m axis; axle

assedi|are v/t besiege; **~o** m siege

assegn|amento m allotment; allowance; **~are** v/t assign; **~azione** f assignment; **~o** m: **~o bancario** cheque; **~contro ~o** cash on delivery

assemblea f assembly; meeting

assembrare v/t assemble

assennato sensible

assente absent

assent|imento m assent; **~ire** v/i assent

assenza f absence

assenzio m absinth

asserire v/t assert

assessore m alderman; **~ municipale** town councillor

assetato thirsty; fig eager

assetto m order; arrangement

assicur|are v/t assure; fasten; insure; **~arsi** v/r se-

cure; make sure; **~ata** f money-letter; **~azione** f assurance; insurance; **~azione di responsabilità civile** third party insurance; **~azione sulla vita** life assurance

assiderare v/t chill

assiduità f assiduity

assiduo assiduous; regular

assieme together

assiepare v/t hedge

assillo m gadfly

assioma m axiom

assise f Court of Assizes

assist|ente adj assisting; m,f assistant; **~enza** f assistance; attendance; **~enza sociale** social work

assistere v/t assist, help

asso m ace

associ|are v/t associate; unite; affiliate; **~ato** m associate; partner; **~azione** f association

assoggettare v/t subject

assolare v/t expose to the sun

assoldare v/t enlist

assol|utamente adv absolutely; **~uto** absolute; unrestricted; **~uzione** f acquittal; eccl absolution

assòlvere v/t acquit; relieve; (task) perform

assomigli|anza f resemblance; **~are** v/i resemble; v/t compare; **~arsi** v/r look like

assorbire v/t absorb

assord|amento m deafening; **~are** v/t deafen; **~ire**

v/i become deaf

assort|imento m assortment; choice; **~ire** v/t assort

assottigliare v/t thin

assue|fare v/t accustom (a to); **~fazione** f habit

assùmere v/t assume;appoint s.o.

Assun|ta f Holy Virgin; Assumption Day; **2to** m task; **~zione** f Assumption

assurdo absurd

asta f rod; staff; mil spear; writing: stroke; compasses: leg; (**~ pùbblica**) auction

astèmio adj abstemious; m total abstainer

astenersi v/r **da** abstain from

asterisco m asterisk

àstero m aster

astin|ente abstinent; **~enza** f abstinence

astio m grudge; envy; **~osità** f spitefulness; **~oso** spiteful

astore m goshawk

astrale astral

astr|arre v/t abstract; **~atto** abstract; absent-minded

astringente astringent

astringere v/t compel; med render costive

astr|o m star; **~ologìa** f astrology; **~onave** f spaceship; **~onomìa** f astronomy; **~ònomo** m astronomer

astruso abstruse

astuccio m case; sheath

ast|uto astute; cunning; **~ùzia** f slyness; trick

atlante m geog atlas; **oceàno ~ico** Atlantic Ocean

atlet|a m, f athlete; **~ica** f athletics pl

atmosfera f atmosphere

atollo m atoll

atòmic|o atomic; **bomba f ~a** atomic bomb

àtomo m atom

atrio m entrance-hall; porch

atroce atrocious; dreadful

attacc|àbile assailable; **~abrighe** m quarrelsome person; **~apanni** m coathanger; **~are** v/t attach; fasten; stick; sew on; (speech) begin; mil assail

attacco m assault; med attack; elec connection; ski: binding

atteggi|amento m attitude; **~arsi** v/r assume an attitude

attèndere v/t expect; v/i look after

attendìbile reliable

attenersi v/r **a qc** conform to, stick to s.th.

attent|are v/i attempt acc; **~are alla propria vita** attempt one's own life; **~arsi** v/r dare; **~ato** m attempt; **~o** attentive

attenuare v/t attenuate; extenuate

attenzione f attention; carefulness

atterr|àggio m aer landing; descent; **~are** v/t knock down; v/i land

attesa f waiting; **in ~ di** while waiting for

attest|are v/t certify; **~ato** m

8

certificate; attestation

atticciato stout

attìguo adjoining

attillato tight fitting

àttimo *m* instant, moment

attin|ente pertaining; **~enza** *f* relation; connection

attìngere *v/t* draw; attain

attirar|e *v/t* attract; allure; **~e l'attenzione** draw attention (**su** to); **~si** *v/r* *qc* draw s.th. upon oneself

attitùdine *f* attitude

att|ività *f* activity; **~ivo** *adj* active; busy; *m gram* active

attizzare *v/t* stir

att|o *adj* apt; *m* action; deed; *thea* act; **~i** *m/pl* legal proceedings *pl*

attònito astonished

attorcigliare *v/t* twist

attore *m* actor

attorniare *v/t* surround

attorno about; around

attr|arre *v/t* attract; **~attiva** *f* attraction; charm; **~attivo** *m* attractive

attraversare *v/t* cross

attraverso across; through

attrazione *f* attraction

attrezz|are *v/t* equip; *naut* rig; **~o** *m* tool; **~i** *pl* tools *pl*; rigging

attribuire *v/t* ascribe

attributo *m* attribute

attrice *f* actress

attrupparsi *v/r* troop

attu|ale present; **~alità** *f* reality; *f/pl* current news *pl*; **~are** *v/t* carry out; realize; **~ario** *m* registrar

aud|ace bold; **~acia** *f* dar-

ing; boldness

auditòrio *m* auditory; auditorium

augur|are *v/t* wish; **~io** *m* wish

augusto august

àula *f* hall; classroom

aument|are *v/t* increase; (*price*) raise; **~o** *m* increase; rise

àureo golden

aurèola *f* halo

aurora *f* dawn

ausili|are auxiliary; **verbo** *m* **~are** auxiliary verb; **~o** *m* aid

auspicato: bene (**male**) **~** well (ill) promising

àuspice *m* protector

auster|ità *f* austerity; **~o** austere; severe

Austràlia *f* Australia

Àustria *f* Austria

austrìaco *m*, *adj* Austrian

autentic|are *v/t* certify; **~ità** *f* authenticity

autèntico authentic; genuine

autista *m*, *f* driver; chauffeur

auto *f* car

auto... self ...; **~biografia** *f* autobiography; **~bus** *m* bus; **~carro** *m* motor-lorry; **~crazia** *f* autocracy; **~grafare** *v/t* autograph; **~lìnea** *f* busline

autòma *m* automaton

automàtico automatic

auto|mezzo *m* motor-vehicle; **~mòbile** *f* automobile; car; **~mobilismo** *m* motor-

avvenenza

ing; ~**mobilista** m, f motorist; ~**motrice** f diesel train

autonomia f autonomy

autoparcheggio m parking area

autopsia f autopsy; post-mortem

autor|e m author; ~**évole** authoritative; reliable

autorimessa f garage

autor|**ità** f authority; influence; pl authorities pl; ~**itario** authoritarian; ~**izzare** v/t authorize; entitle

auto|**scafo** m motor-boat; ~**strada** f motor-road; highway; ~**treno** m lorry; truck; ~**veicolo** m motor-vehicle

autunnale autumnal

autunno m autumn; fall

av = avanti

ava f grandmother

avallare v/t guarantee

avam|**braccio** m forearm; ~**posto** m mil outpost

avana brown, beige

avanguardia f vanguard

avannotto m young fish; fig greenhorn

avanti before; forward; ~**che** sooner than; ~! come in! forward! **andare** ~ precede; be fast (watch)

avantieri the day before yesterday

avanz|**amento** m advancement; promotion; ~**are** v/i proceed; be left; v/t promote; ~**o** m remnant; surplus; ~**i** pl remains pl

avaria f damage; average;

~**iato** damaged; ~**izia** f avarice

avaro adj avaricious; m miser

Ave Maria, avemmaria f Hail Mary

avemmo we got

avena f oats pl

aver|**e** v/t have; get; obtain; m property; ~**i** m/pl possessions

aveste pl, ~**i** sg you got

avete you have (pl)

aveva he had; ~**amo** we had

avévano they had

avevate you had (pl)

avev|**li** you had (sg); ~**o** I had

avia|**tore** m aviator; ~**zione** f aviation

avidità f greediness

àvido greedy; eager

avio|**getto** m jet plane; ~**linea** f airline; ~**rimessa** f hangar; ~**trasportato** airborne

avo m grandfather

avorio m ivory

avr|**à** he will have; ~**ai** you will have (sg); ~**anno** they will have; ~**emo** we shall have; ~**ete** you will have (pl); ~**ò** I shall have

avvallamento m depression

avvampare v/i blaze up

avvantaggi|**are** v/t improve; ~**arsi** v/r: ~**arsi di qc** draw advantage from, profit by s.th.

avvedersi v/r (**di**) notice, perceive (s. th.)

avvelenare v/t poison

avven|**ente** lovely; ~**enza** f

prettiness

avven|imento *m* event; **~ire**
v/i occur; *m* future

avvent|are *v/t* hurl; **~arsi**
v/r rush (upon); **~ato** rash;
reckless; **~izio** adventitious

avvento *m* advent

avvent|ore *m* customer;
~ura *f* adventure; **~urare**
v/t venture; risk; **~uriere** *m*
adventurer; **~uroso** adven-
turous; enterprising

avverarsi *v/r* prove true

avverbi|ale adverbial; **~o** *m*
adverb

avver|sario *m* adversary;
~sione *f* aversion; **~sità** *f*
adversity; **~so** adverse; un-
favourable

avvert|enza *f* note; warn-
ing; foreword; **~imento** *m*
warning; **~ire** *v/t* warn; inform

avvezzare *v/t* accustom

avvi|are *v/t* start; introduce;
~arsi *v/r* set out; **~atore** *m*
starter

avvicinare *v/t* approach

avvil|imento *m* dejection;

~ire *v/t* debase; (*price*) depreciate; **~irsi** *v/r* degrade
oneself

avviluppare *v/t* wrap up;
entangle

avvis|are *v/t* inform; warn;
~o *m* notice; advice; announcement; warning; **a
mio ~o** in my opinion

avvitare *v/t* screw (up)

avvocato *m* lawyer; barrister; solicitor

avvòlgere *v/* wind; wrap
(up)

avvoltare *v/t* roll up

azalea *f* azalea

azienda *f* business; firm;
consiglio *m* d'**~** managing
board

azion|e *f* action; share; **~ista**
m, f shareholder

azoto *m* nitrogen; azote

azzard|are *v/t* risk; **~arsi** *v/r*
venture; **~o** *m* hazard; risk;
gioco *m* d'**~o** game of
chance

azzoppire *v/i* become lame

azzurro blue; **~ chiaro**
lightblue; **~ cupo** dark-blue

B

babbo *m* dad, daddy, pa

babbuino *m* baboon

babordo *m* larboard

bac|aio *m* silk-grower; **~ato**
worm-eaten

bacca *f* berry

baccal|à, **~aro** *m* codfish

bacc|anale *m* noisy revel;
orgy; **~ano** *m* uproar

bacchetta *f* rod; wand; (*con-
ductor's*) baton

Bacco *m* Bacchus; **per ~!** by
Jove!

bachicul|tore *m* silk-worm
breeder; **~tura** *f* silk-worm
breeding

baciamano *m* hand-kissing

baciare *v/t* kiss

barbaro

bacillo *m* bacillus

bacino *m* basin

bacio *m* kiss

baco *m* **da seta** silk-worm

badare *v/i* mind; pay attention (**a** to); look out

ba|dessa *f* abbess; **~dìa** *f* abbey

baffi *m/pl* moustaches *pl*

bagagliaio *m* luggage-van

bagaglio *m* luggage

bagliore *m* gleam

bagn|aiuola *f*, **~aiuolo** *m* bath-attendant; **~ante** *m, f* bather; **~are** *v/t* wet; moisten; sprinkle; **~ato** wet; **~ino** *m* bath-attendant, lifeguard

bagno *m* bath; **~ all'aperto** open air bath; **~ di sole** sunbathing; **~ di vapore** the Turkish baths *pl*; **~lo** *m* wet pack

baia *f geog* bay

baionetta *f* bayonet

balbettare *v/i* stammer

Balcani *m/pl* Balkan

balcone *m* balcony

balena *f* whale

balen|are *v/i* lighten; *fig* flash; **~lo** *m* continual lightning; **~o** *m* lightning

balìa *f* power

bàlia *f* nurse

balla *f* bale

ball|are *v/t, v/i* dance; **~ata** *f* ballad; **~erina** *f* ballet-girl; *orn* wagtail; **~erino** *m* dancer; **~o** *m* dance; ball; *thea* ballet

balneario bathing; **stabilimento** *m* **~** bathing establishment

balsàmico balmy

bàlsamo *m* balm

Bàltico *m* (**mare ~**) Baltic (Sea)

baluardo *m* bulwark

balz|are *v/i* spring; jump; leap (*heart*); **~o** *m* leap; bound

bambin|a *f* little girl; **~aia** *f* nurse-maid; **~o** *m* little boy

bàmbola *f* doll

bambù *m* bamboo

banalità *f* banality; platitude

banan|a *f* banana; **~o** *m* banana-tree

banc|a *f* bank; **casa** *f* **~aria** banking house; **~ario** pertaining to banks; **~arotta** *f* bankruptcy

banch|ettare *v/i* feast; **~etto** *m* banquet

banchiere *m* banker

banchina *f* pier

banco *m* bank; table; bench; counter; **~ del lotto** lottery office; **~giro** *m com* clearing; **~nota** *f* banknote

banda *f* band; gang

bandiera *f* flag; banner

band|ire *v/t* banish; **~ito** *m* bandit; outlaw; **~o** *m* banishment; exile

bar *m* bar

bara *f* bier; coffin

baracca *f* barrack; shack

barba *f* beard; **~ a punta** pointed beard; **fare la ~ a qu** shave s.o.

barbabiètola *f* beetroot

bàrbaro *adj* barbarous; *m*

barbarian
barbiere *m* barber
barca *f* boat
barcaiuola *m* boatman; **~rola** *f* barcarolle
barella *f* stretcher
barile *m* barrel
barista *m* barman; *f* barmaid
baritono *m,adj* baritone
barlume *m* glimmer, gleam
barocco *m, adj* baroque
baròmetro *m* barometer
baron|e *m* baron; **~essa** *f* baroness
barr|a *f* bar; rod; **~icare** *v/t* barricade; **~iera** *f* barrier
basare *v/t* base, ground
basco *adj* Basque; *m* Basque; beret
base *f* base; basis; foundation
bassa *f* plain
bassetta *f* whisker
bass|ezza *f* lowness; *fig* meanness; **~o** low; mean; **~a voce** in a low voice; **~o** *m* (*mus*) bass; **~ofondo** *m* slum; **~opiano** *m* lowland; **~orilievo** *m* bas-relief
bassoventre *m* abdomen
basta *adv* enough; *f* tuck; hem
bastaio *m* saddler
bastardo *adj* illegitimate; bastard; mongrel
bastare *v/i* suffice; be enough
bastimento *m* ship; vessel
bastione *m* rampart
baston|are *v/t* cane; beat; **~ata** *f* blow; **~e** *m* stick; cane

batista *f* batiste; cambric
battaglia *f* battle
battaglione *m* battalion
battell|iere *m* boatman; **~o** *m* boat; **~o a remi** rowboat; **~o pneumático** rubber boat

battente *m* (*door*) leaf; (*window*) shutter; knocker
bàtt|ere *v/t, v/i* beat; strike; knock; **~ere le mani** clap hands; **~ersela** run away
batteria *f* battery; **~a secco** dry battery
bat|tésimo *m* christening; **~tezzando** *m* child to be christened; **~tezzare** *v/t* christen
battibecco *m* squabble
batticuore *m* palpitation
battist|a *m,f* baptist; **~ero** *m* baptistry
battitoio *m* door-knocker
battuta *f* beat; *mus* bar
baule *m* trunk
bavarese *m,f, adj* Bavarian
bàvero *m* collar
Baviera *f* Bavaria
bazàr *m* bazaar
bazzotto softboiled (*egg*)
be' = **bene** well
beat|itúdine *f* beatitude; blissfulness; **~o** happy; blessed
bébé *m* baby
beccaccia *f* *orn* woodcock
becc|are *v/t* peck; **~atoio** *m* trough
becchime *m* birdsfood
becco *m* beak; burner; **~ a gas** gasburner
befana *f* old woman who

brings presents on Twelfth Night

beffa *f* mockery; **farsi ~ di qu** make a fool of s.o.

beff|ardo *adj* mocking; *m* mocker; **~arsi** *v/r* **di qu** laugh at s.o.

belare *v/i* bleat

belga *m, f, adj* Belgian

Belgio *m* Belgium

belletto *m* make-up

bellezza *f* beauty; **salone di ~** beauty parlour

bèllico, bellicoso bellicose; warlike

bellino pretty; nice

bello *adj* beautiful; *m* beauty; **bell'e fatto** it is done

beltà *f* beauty

belva *f* wild beast

belvedere *m* belvedere (= beautiful view)

benché although

bend|a *f* bandage; blindfold; headband; **~aggio** *m/pl* dressing material (*for wounds*); **~are** *v/t* bandage; blindfold

bene *adv* well; *m* good

benedetto blessed

bene|dicite *m* grace (*before meals*); **~dire** *v/t* bless; **~dizione** *f* blessing

beneducato well bred

bene|fattore *m* benefactor; **~ficenza** *f* beneficence; **~ficio** *m* benefit; (del corpo) relief of the bowels

benèfico beneficent

benemèrito well deserving

benèssere *m* well-being;

comfort

bene|stante well-to-do; **~volenza** *f* benevolence

benèvolo benevolent; kindly

beni *m/pl* goods, estate

ben|igno benign; kind; **~ino** fairly well; **~inteso** provided (that); **~one** very well; **~portante** healthy

bensì *conj* but; *adv* certainly; really

benvenuto *adj* welcome; *m* welcome; **dare il ~ a qu** welcome s.o.

benzina *f* petrol; gasoline; **serbatoio m di ~** gasoline-tank

bere *v/t* drink

berlina *f* salon-car

berlinese *adj* Berlinese; *m, f* Berliner

Berlino *f* Berlin

Berna *f* Bern

berr|etta *f* cap; **~ettaio** *m* cap-maker; **~etto** *m* cap

bersagliere *m* bersagliere; sharp-shooter

bersaglio *m* target

bestemmi|a *f* curse; blasphemy; **~are** *v/t, v/i* swear; curse; **~atore** *m* swearer

besti|a *f* beast; **~ale** beastly; brutal; **~ame** *m* cattle; livestock

béttola *f* tavern; pub

betulla *f* birch

bevanda *f* drink; beverage

bev|erino *m* trough (*bird-cage*); **~ibile** drinkable; **~itore** *m* drinker; **~uta** *f* draught

bezzi|care v/t peck; fig tease
biada f fodder; oats pl
biancastro whitish
bian|cheria f linen; **~cherìa da dosso** body-linen; **~chetto** m whitewash; cosmetic; **~chìre** v/t bleach
bianco white; **lasciare in ~** leave blank; **girata f in ~** blank endorsement
biancospino m whitethorn
biasim|àbile blamable; **~are** v/t blame; reprove
biàsimo m blame
Bibbia f Bible
bibita f drink
biblico biblical
bibliografìa f bibliography
bibliotèca f library
bicarbonato m **(di soda)** (sodium) bicarbonate
bicchiere m (drinking-)glass
bicicletta f bicycle
bidello m janitor; usher
bidone m can; tank
bieco sullen; grim
biennio m two-year period
bifor|carsi v/r branch off; **~azione** f bifurcation
biga f two-horsed chariot
bigamìa f bigamy
bigio grey
bigliett|àrio, **~inàio** m booking-clerk; ticket-collector; conductor; **~erìa** f ticket-office
biglietto m ticket; note; **~ aèreo** air ticket; **~ d'andata e ritorno** return ticket; **~ circolare** tourist ticket; **~ di visita** (visiting-) card; **~ di banca** banknote; **~ di**

prenotazione reserved seat ticket; **~ d'ingresso** platform ticket; **~ di volo** flying-ticket
bigodini mpl haircurlers
bikini m bikini
bilan|cia f scales pl; balance; **~ciare** v/t weigh; balance; **~cio** m budget; balance
bile f bile; gall
biliardo m billiards pl
bìlico m equilibrium
bilingue bilingual
bimb|a f, **o** m small child
bimensìle twice a month
bimotore m two-engined plane
binàrio m railway-track
binòccolo m binoculars pl; **~ da teatro** opera-glasses
biografìa f biography
biògrafo m biographer
biologìa f biology
biond|ino fair-haired; **~o** fair; blond
biplano m biplane
birbone m rogue; rascal
birichino m little rogue; urchin
birillo m skittle
birr|a f beer; **~erìa** f beer-house; brewery
birro m police-spy
bis! once more! encore; **chièdere un ~** call for an encore
bisbètico peevish
bisbigli|are v/t, v/i whisper; **~o** m whisper
bisc|a f gambling-house; **~aiuolo** m gambler; **~azière** m gambling-house

borghese

keeper
biscott|erìa f biscuit-shop; **~o** m biscuit; cookie
bisestile: anno m ~ leap-year
bislungo oblong
bisnipote m, f great-grand-child
bisognare v/i be necessary; **mi bisogna(no)** I need; **bisogna** (with infinitive) it is necessary; one ought (to)
bisogno m want; need; **al** ~ in case of need; **avere ~ di qc** need s.th.; **~so** needy
bisonte m bison
bistecca f beefsteak
bivio m cross-road
bizza f anger; wrath
bizz|arro odd; queer; **a ~effe** plentifully
blando bland; soft
blatta f cockroach
bleso lisping
blindato armoured; **carro** ~ m tank
blocc|are v/t block (up); **~o** m block; blockade
blu blue; **~astro** bluish
blusa f blouse
bobina f coil; bobbin
bocca f mouth; muzzle; **a ~ aperta** open-mouthed
boccetta f phial
bocchino m mouth-piece; cigar-holder; small mouth
boccia f decanter; bowl (game); bot bud; **~are** v/t reject; **èssere bocciato** flunk (exams)
bocc|oncino m choice morsel; **~one** m mouthful; **~oni** lying on one's face
boia m hangman
boicott|aggio m boycotting; **~are** v/t boycott
boliviano m, adj Bolivian
boll|are v/t stamp; fig brand; **carta** f **~ata** stamped paper
bollente boiling; hot
bollettino m bulletin
boll|icina f small bubble; **~ire** v/t, v/i boil; fig seethe
bollo m stamp
bollore m boiling (-point)
bomba f bomb; **~ all'idrògeno** hydrogen bomb, H-bomb; **~ atòmica** atom bomb
bombard|amento m bombardment; **~iere** m bomber
bòmbice m silkworm
bomboletta nebulizzante f aerosol bomb
bonànima f late; **mio padre** ~ my late father
bonario good-natured
bonificare v/t reclaim; refund
bonomìa f kindness
bonsenso m common sense
bontà f goodness
bora f north-east wind
borbottare v/t, v/i grumble; mutter
borchia f metal-work
bordello m brothel
bordo m border; edge; **a ~ di** aboard, on board (of) fig **di alto** ~ of high rank
bòreo m north wind
bor|gata f hamlet; **~ghese** adj bourgeois; **in ~ghese** in

civilian clothes; *m* middle class person; **~ghesia** *f* bourgeoisie; middle class

borgo *m* village

bòrico *m* boric (acid)

borraccia *f* water-bottle

bors|a *f* purse; briefcase; *com* stock-exchange; **~a di studio** scholarship; **~aiuolo** *m* pickpocket; **~etta** *f* purse; handbag

bos|caiuolo *m* wood-cutter; **~co** *m* wood; **~coso** woody

bòssolo *m* box-wood; dice-box; cartridge-case

botànica *f* botany

bott|a *f* blow; **~aio** *m* cooper; **~e** *f* barrel

bottega *f* shop

botteghino *m* box-office

bottiglia *f* bottle

bottiglieria *f* wine-shop

bottone *m* button; *bot* bud; **~ automàtico** press-stud

bovino bovine

bozz|a *f* sketch; **~e** *f/pl* printer's proof (sheets)

bòzzolo *m* cocoon

bracc|ialetto *m* bracelet; **~ata** *f* armful; **~o** *m* arm

braciere *m* brazier

bram|a *f* ardent desire; **~are** *v/t* long (for); **~oso** covetous; eager

branchia *f* gill

branda *f* camp bed

brano *m* passage; excerpt

Brasile *m* Brazil

brasiliano *m*, *adj* Brazilian

bravo clever; brave

bretelle *f/pl* braces *pl*

breve short; **~etto** *m* patent;

~ità *f* brevity

brezza *f* breeze

bricco *m* kettle

briciola *f* crumb; bit

brig|antaggio *m* brigandage; **~ante** *m* brigand

briglia *f* bridle

brill|ante *adj* brilliant; shining; *m* diamond; **~are** *v/i* shine; glitter

brina *f* white frost

brindare *v/i* toast

brindisi *m* toast

britànnico British

brìvido *m* shiver; chill

brizzolato spotted; slightly grey (*hair*)

brocca *f* jug; pitcher

brodo *m* broth; bouillon; **~ ristretto** consommé

bromuro *m* bromide

bronchi *m/pl* bronchi; **~chite** *f* bronchitis

brontol|are *v/i* grumble; **~one** *m* grumbler

bronz|are *v/t* bronze; **~o** *m* bronze

bruciare *v/t* burn

bruciore di stòmaco *m* heartburn

bruco *m* caterpillar

brulicare *v/i* swarm

brunire *v/t* polish; brown

bruno brown

brusco sharp; harsh

brut|alità *f* brutality; **~o** brute

brutt|ezza *f* ugliness; **~o** ugly

buc|a *f* **delle lèttere** letter-box; **~are** *v/t* pierce

bucato *m* washing; **dare in ~**

send to the wash
buccia *f* skin; peel
buco *m* hole
budell|o *m* bowel; **~a** *f/pl* bowels *pl*
budino *m* pudding
bue *m* ox; *pl* buoi
bùfalo *m* buffalo
bufera *f* storm
buffè *m* buffet; refreshment room
buff|o funny; **~one** *m* buffoon; fool
bugìa *f* lie
bugiardo *adj* lying; *m* liar
bugno *m* bee-hive
buio dark
Bulgarìa *f* Bulgaria
bùlgaro *m,adj* Bulgarian
bullett|a *f* tack; small nail; **~ino** *m* bulletin
bùngalow *m* bungalow
buongustaio *m* gourmet
buon|o *adj* good; *m* bill; coupon; **~ mercato** *m* cheapness
burattino *m* puppet
burl|a *f* trick; joke; **~arsi** *v/r* **di qu** make fun of s.o.; **~esco** comical
burocràtico bureaucratic
burrasca *f* tempest; storm
burro *m* butter
burrone *m* ravine
bussare *v/i* knock
bùssola *f* compass
busta *f* envelope
busto *m* bust; corset
buttare *v/t* throw; cast; **~ via** throw away

C

c. = corrente, centèsimo, centìmetro
cabina *f* cabin; **~ telefònica** telephone booth
cablogramma *m* cablegram
cacao *m* cocoa
cacc|ia *f* hunting; **~a-mosche** *m* fly-flap; **~are** *v/t, v/i* hunt; chase; pursue; **~atore** *m* hunter; **~avite** *m* screw-driver
cacio *m* cheese
cacto, cactus *m* cactus
cad|àvere *m* corpse; **stella** *f* **~ente** shooting star; **~enza** *f* cadence; *mus* cadenza; **~ere** *v/i* fall; **~uta** *f* fall; downfall
caffè *m* coffee; coffeehouse; **~ettiera** *f* coffeepot; percolator; **~eina** *f* caffeine
cagionare *v/t* cause
cagn|a *f* bitch; **~olino** *m* little dog; puppy
cala *f* cove; bay
Calabria *f* Calabria
calabrone *m* bumblebee; hornet
calam|aio *m* inkstand; **~aro** *m* cuttlefish; **~ità** *f* calamity; **~ita** *f* magnet; **~ago** *m* **~itato** magnetic needle
calapranzi *m* service-lift
calare *v/i* go down (*prices*); fall; ebb; *v/t* let down; strike (*sails*)
calca *f* crowd; throng

calcagno m heel

calce f lime

calciatore m football player

calcin|a f mortar; **~oso** limy

calcio m kick; *chem* calcium; **gioco il ~ del** game of football

calco m tracing; cast

calcolare v/t calculate; estimate

càlcolo m calculation; **~ biliare** gallstone

cald|aia f boiler; kettle; **~eggiare** v/t favour; **~o** *adj* warm; m warmth; heat; **ho ~o** I feel hot

caleidoscopio m kaleidoscope

calendario m calender

càlice m chalice; cup

calle m path; road; (*waterstreets in Venice*)

calligrafia f penmanship; handwriting

callo m callus; corn

callotta f small cap

calm|a f calm; tranquillity; **~o** calm; quiet; **~are** v/t calm; soothe

cal|ore m heat; warmth; **~orifero** m heating apparatus; radiator

caloria f calorie

caloscia f overshoe

calpest|are v/t trample (on); **~io** m trampling

calunni|a f calumny; **~are** v/t slander

Calvario m Calvary

calvo bald(headed)

calz|a f stocking; **far la ~** knit; **~atoio** m shoe-horn;

~atura f footwear; **~erotto** m, **~ino** m sock; **~olaio** m shoemaker; **~oleria** f shoemaker's shop; **~oni** m/pl trousers pl

cambi|ale f bill of exchange; **~amento** m change; **~are** v/t, v/i change; alter

cambiavalute m money-changer

cambio m change; exchange; rate of exchange; *mech* change-gear; **in ~ di** instead of; **~ automàtico dei dischi** automatic record changer; **~ di velocità** *aut* change of gear; gearbox

càmera f room; **~da letto** bedroom; **~ d'aria** airchamber; inner tube

camer|ata m comrade; **~iera** f house-maid; waitress; **~iere** m waiter; **~ino** m dressing-room; lavatory

camiceria f shirt-shop

camicia f shirt; chemise; **~ spottiva** sport-shirt

camino m chimney

cammello m camel

cammin|are v/i walk; **~ata** f walk; **~o** m road; way

camomilla f camomile

camoscio m chamois; shammy leather

campagna f country; campaign

campan|a f bell; **~accio** m cow-bell; **~ello** m small bell; **~ile** m bell-tower

camp|eggiare v/i camp; **~eggio** m camping (place);

caos

log-wood; **~estre** rural
campionari|o m sample-book; **fiera** f ~a sample fair
campio|nato m championship; **~ne** m sample; champion
campo m field; camp; (gun) ground; **~ di concentramento** concentration camp; **~ sportivo** sports-field; **~ di tennis** tennis court
camposanto m cemetery, churchyard
Cana|da m Canada; **2dese** m, f, adj Canadian
canal|e m canal; channel; pipe; **~izzazione** f canalization
cànapa f hemp
cànapo m cable; rope
Canarie f/pl Canary Islands
canarino m canary
cancell|are v/t efface; wipe out; erase; **~eria** f chancery; **oggetti di ~eria** stationary; **~iere** m recorder; pol chancellor; **~o** m gate
cancro m med cancer
candel|a f candle; **~a d'accensione** sparking-plug; **~abro** m chandelier; **~iere** m candlestick
candid|ato m candidate; nominee; **~atura** f candidacy
candidezza f whiteness; fig innocence
càndido white; candid
candire v/t candy
cane m dog
canestro m basket

cànfora f camphor
cangiamento m change
can|ile m (dog) kennel; **tosse f ~ina** whooping-cough
canizie f white hair
cann|a f reed; cane; (gun) barrel; **~ella** f pipe; spout; cinnamon; **~ello** m small tube; **~occhiale** m telescope; **~one** m gun; cannon
cannuccia di paglia f straw (for drinking)
canònico m canon
canoro melodious
canottiere m rower; oarsman
canotto m **pneumàtico** rubber-boat; **~smontàbile** folding boat
cant|àbile suited for singing; **~ante** m, f singer; **~are** v/t, v/i sing; chant; crow (cock); cackle (hen); **~erellare** v/t hum; **~erino** m singing bird
càntico m hymn
cantiere m shipyard
cantin|a f cellar; **~iere** m butler; wine-shop keeper
canto m song; chant; corner; side; **~ popolare** folksong; **dal ~ mio** for my part
cantoniera f corner cupboard
cantoniere m road-mender; rail line-keeper
cantore m singer; chorister
cantuccio m corner; nook
canz|onaccia f vulgar song; **~onare** v/t ridicule; **~one** f song; **~oniere** m song-book
caos m chaos

capac|e capable; able; **~ità** f ability; capacity

capanna f hut; cabin

capell|o m hair; **~uto** hairy

capezzale m bolster; pillow

cap|igliatura f hair; **~illare** capillary

capire v/t understand

capit|ale adj principal; chief; f capital (town); m capital (money); **~alismo** m capitalism; **~alista** m capitalist

capitano m captain; leader

capitare v/i arrive (by chance); happen

capitolo m chapter

capo m head; leader; chief; geog cape; **~ d'anno** New Year's Day; **~ di bestiame** head of cattle; **da ~** once more; **in ~ alla strada** at the end of the street; **~banda** m bandmaster; outlaw chief; **~cameriere** m headwaiter

capocchia f head (of pin, nail)

capo|còmico m head comedian; **~comitiva** m travel manager; **~danno** m New Year's Day; **~fàbbrica** m foreman; **~giro** m dizziness; **~lavoro** m masterpiece; **~linea** m terminus; **~mastro** m master-builder; **~mùsica** m bandmaster; **~pòpolo** m popular leader; demagogue

capo|rale m mil corporal; **~stazione** m station-master; **~treno** m conductor; **~vòlgere** v/t overturn; capsize

cappa f mantle; **~ del camino** chimney mantle

cappella f chapel

cappell|aio m hatter; **~erìa** f hatter's shop; **~iera** f hatbox; **~ino** m small hat

cappello m hat; **~ di paglia** straw hat; **~ duro** bowler; **méttersi il ~** put on one's hat; **tògliersi il ~** take off one's hat

càppero m caper

cappio m knot; loop

cappone m capon

cappotta f aut top

capp|otto m overcoat; insalata f **~uccia** butter lettuce; **~uccino** m capuchin; coffee with a little milk; **~uccio** m hood; cowl

capr|a f goat; **~aio** m goatherd; **~etto** m kid; **~iccio** m caprice; whim; **~iccioso** capricious; **~o** m he-goat

càpsula f capsule; percussion cap

carabina f carbine

carabiniere m carabineer (Italian gendarme)

caraffa f decanter

caramell|o m, **~a** f caramel, candy

carato m carat

caràttere m character; disposition; type

carbon|aia f charcoal-pit; **~aio** m charcoal-burner; **~ato** m carbonate; **~e** m coal; **àcido ~ carbònico** carbon dioxide

carburante *m* gas; fuel
carburatore *m* carburettor
carburo *m* carbide
carcer|are *v/t* imprison; **~ato** *m* prisoner
càrcere *m* prison; jail
carceriere *m* jailer
carciofo *m* artichoke
cardellino *m* goldfinch
cardìaco *med* cardiac
cardinale *m* cardinal; **nùmero ~** cardinal number; **punto ~** cardinal point
càrdine *m* hinge
cardite *f* carditis
cardo *m* thistle
caren|a *f naut* bottom; **~aggio** *m* careenage
carestia *f* dearth; famine
carezz|a *f* caress; **~are** *v/t* caress
cariato carious; decayed (tooth)
càrica *f* office; charge
caric|are *v/t* load; (*watch*) wind up; *elec* charge; **~arsi** *v/r* overburden oneself; **~atura** *f* caricature
càrico *adj* loaded; full; *m* load; cargo; burden
carie *f med* caries; decay
carino nice; dear
cariola *f* wheelbarrow
carità *f* charity; love; **per ~!** for heaven's sake!
caritatévole charitable
carlinga *f* cockpit
carminio *n* carmine
carnagione *f* complexion
carn|e *f* meat; **~e salata** corned beef; **~éfice** *m* executioner; **~evale** *m* carnival;

~oso fleshy
caro dear; expensive
carosello *m* merry-go-round
carota *f* carrot
carovana *f* caravan
carpa *f* carp
carpentiere *m* carpenter
carponi on all fours
carr|aia *f* cart-road; **~ata** *f* cartload; **~eggiata** *f* wheeltrack; **~eggio** *m* cartage; freight; **~etta** *f* cart; **~etto** *m* hand-cart; **~iera** *f* career; **~iola** *f* wheel-barrow
carro *m* car; truck; van; wagon; **~ armato** tank; **~ fùnebre** hearse
carr|ozza *f* carriage; coach; **~ozza letti** sleeping-car; **~ozza ristorante** diner; **~ozzella** *f* perambulator; cab; **~ozzeria** *f aut* body; **~ozzino** *m* side-car
carruba *f* carob
carrùcola *f* pulley
carta *f* paper; **~ carbone** carbon paper; **~ da lèttere** notepaper; **~ da parati** wall-paper; **~ d'identità** identity card; **~ igiènica** toilet paper; **~ intestata** letterhead; **~ geogràfica** map; **~ lùcida** tracing paper; **~ moneta** paper money; **~ stradale** street map; **~ sugante** blotting paper
cartapècora *f* parchment
cart|ella *f* satchel; portfolio; briefcase; **~ellino** *m* ticket; label; **~ello** *m* bill; placard;

..iera f paper-mill
cartilàgine f cartilage
cart|ina f med dose; **..occio** m paper-bag; **..olaio** m stationer; **..oleria** f stationary; **..olina** f card; **..olina illustrata** figure postcard; **..olina con risposta pagata** reply postcard; **..one** m cardboard; **..oni** m/pl animati animated cartoons pl
cartuccia f cartridge
casa f house; **~ di salute** nursing home; **a ~ mia** at (my) home; **~ di campagna** country house; **fatto in ~** homemade; **..le** m hamlet; **..linga** f housewife; **..lingo** homely; **cucina f ..linga** plain cooking
cascata f (water)fall
cascina f dairy-farm
casco m helmet
casell|a f postale post-office box; **..ante** m linesman; **..rio** m filling-cabinet; **..o** gatekeeper's house
caserma f barracks pl
casetta f per il fine settimana weekend house
casino m casino
caso m case; **per ~** by chance; **a ~** at random; **..che** if
cas|olare m (isolated) cottage; **..otto** m cabin; box
càspita by Jove!
cass|a f case; box; chest; **..a da morto** coffin; **..a di risparmio** savings bank; **..a toràcica** thorax; **..aforte** f safe; **..apanca** f chest

cassare v/t cancel; revoke
casseruola f saucepan
cass|etta f box; case; **..etta postale** letter-box; **..etto** m drawer; **..ettone** m chest of drawers
cassiere m cashier, teller
castagn|a f chestnut; **..eto** m chestnut grove; **..o** adj brown; auburn; m chestnut-tree
castello m castle; mech tower; (watch) train; **~ in aria** castle in Spain; **~ di prua** forecastle
castig|are v/t punish; chastise; **..o** m punishment
cast|ità f chastity; **..o** chaste
castoro m beaver
castr|are v/t castrate, geld; **..one** m gelding
casuale casual; accidental
casùpola f hut
catacomba f catacomb
catàlogo m catalogue
cataplasma m poultice
catapulta f catapult
catarifrangente m reflector stud; cat's eye
catarro m catarrh; cold
catast|a f pile; heap; **..o** m register of landed property
catàstrofe f catastrophe
catechismo m catechism
categoria f category; class
catena f chain; **..ccio** m bolt
cateratta f sluice; waterfall; med cataract
catètere m catheter
catinella f basin; **piove a ..e** it rains in torrents
catram|are v/t tar; **..e** m tar

càttedra f desk; chair

cattedrale f cathedral

cattiv|eria f wickedness; **~o** bad; naughty; **~mare** m **~o** rough sea

catt|olicismo m catholicism; **~òlico** m, f, adj catholic

cattura f capture; arrest

cau(c)ciù m india-rubber

causa f cause; (law)suit; **far ~** take legal action; **a ~ di** on account of

caus|ale f cuase; motive; **~are** v/t cause; bring about

cautela f caution

cauto cautious

cauzione f bail; security

cav abbr for **cavaliere**

cava f quarry; pit; **~fango** m dredger

cavalc|are v/t ride; v/i ride on horseback; **~ata** f ride; **~atore** m rider

cavalci|one (**~oni**) astride

cavaliere m horseman; knight

cavall|a f mare; **~etta** f grasshopper; **~etto** m trestle; *paint* easel

cavallo m horse; **~ da corsa** race-horse; **~ da sella** saddle-horse; **andare a ~** ride on horseback

cavallo-vapore m horsepower

cavare v/t dig; (tooth) extract

cava|stivali m boot-jack; **~tappi** m cork-screw

caverna f cave

cavezza f halter

cavia f guinea-pig

caviale m caviar

caviglia f plug; ankle

cav|ità f cavity; hole; **~o** adj holow; m cable

cavolfiore m cauliflower

càvolo m cabbage; **~ rapa** m kohlrabi; **~ cappuccio** m white cabbage

cazzuola f trowel

C/c = conto corrente

cece m chick-pea

cecità f blindness

Cecoslov|acchia f Czechoslovakia; **2acco** m, adj Czecho-Slovak

cèdere v/t cede; give up; v/i yield; give in

ced|évole yielding; **~ibile** transferable

cèdola f coupon

cedro m cedar

ceffo m snout; muzzle

celare v/t conceal

celebèrrimo cf **cèlebre**

celebr|are v/t celebrate; praise; **~azione** f celebration

cèlebre famous; celebrated

celebrità f celebrity

cèlere rapid; quick

celerità f rapidity; speed

celeste heavenly; sky-blue

celia f jest; joke; **~re** v/i joke

celibato m celibacy

cèlibe adj single; unmarried; m bachelor

cell|a f cell; **~òfane** m cellophane

cèllula f cell

celluloíde f celluloid

cèltico Celtic

cement|are *v/t* cement; *fig* strenghten; **~o** *m* cement; **~o armato** reinforced concrete

cen|a *f* supper; **~àcolo** *m* supper-room; *paint* Last-Supper; **~are** *v/i* dine; sup

cencio *m* rag; **cappello** *m* a **~** soft hat

cénere *f* ash; **le Céneri** Ash-Wednesday

cenno *m* sign; **fare ~** wave; nod

censo *m* wealth; income; **~uare** *v/t* tax; asses; **~ura** *f* censure

cent|enario *adj* centenarian; *m* centenary; **~èsimo** *adj* hundredth; *m* hundredth part; centime; **~igrado** *m* centigrade; **~ìmetro** *m* centimetre; **~inaio** *m* hundred

centr|ale *adj* central; *f* head-office; **~alino telefònico** telephone exchange; **~o** *m* centre

ceppo *m* stump; block

cera *f* wax; (boot-)polish; look; **avere buona (cattiva) ~** look well (ill); **~lacca** *f* sealing-wax

ceràmica *f* ceramics *pl*; **~ata** *f* oil-cloth

cerc|a *f* search; quest; **~are** *v/t* look for; seek; *v/i* try

cerchi|a *f* circle; sphere; **~are** *v/t* hoop; **~atura** *f* hooping; **~one** *m* rim; tyre; **~one di ricambio** spare-tyre

cereali *m/pl* cereals *pl*

cerebrale cerebral

cèreo waxen; very pale

cererìa *f* wax-factory; wax-chandler's shop

cerimònia *f* ceremony; formality

cerimoni|ale ceremonial; **~oso** ceremonious

cer|inaio *m* match-seller; **~ino** *m* (wax-)match; **~o** *m* (church-)candle; **~otto** *m* plaster; *fig* bore

cert|ezza *f* certainly; **~ificare** *v/t* certify; confirm; **~ificato** *m* certificate; **~o** certain; sure

cerùleo sky-blue

cervello *m* brain; *fig* brains

cervice *f* cervix

cervo *m* stag; deer

cespuglio *m* bush; thicket

cess|are *v/t*, *v/i* cease; **~ione** *f* cession; transfer

cesso *m* water-closet

cest|aio *m* basket-maker; **~ino** *m* small basket; waste-basket; **~o** *m* hamper; basket; tuft

ceto *m* order; rank; **~ medio** middle class

cetra *f* zither

cetriolo *m* cucumber

che who, which; what; that; **ciò ~** that which ...; *conj* that; *(after comparative)* than; **ma ~!** not at all!; **~bell'idea!** what a good idea!

checché whatever

cherubino *m* cherub

chet|are *v/t* calm; **~o** quiet

chi who; whom; **di ~?** whose?; **a ~?** to whom?

chiàcchier|a *f* chat; gossip;

far due ~e have a chat
chiacchier|are v/i chatter; ~ata f chat
chiam|are v/t call; name; tel ring up; ~arsi v/r be called; ~ata f telefònica phone-call
Chianti m Tuscan wine
chiappamosche f fly-trap
chiar|ezza f clearness; ~ificare v/t clarify; ~ire v/t make clear; ~o clear; bright; evident; m light; ~o di luna moonlight; ~o d'uovo white of an egg; ~oscuro m light and shade; ~oveggenza f clairvoyance
chiasso m noise; fare ~ fig make a sensation
chiatta f barge
chiave f key (mus); ~e inglese monkey-wrench; aut ~etta f d'accensione ignition key; ~istello m bolt
chiazzato spotted; stained
chicco m (coffee-)bean; grain; hailstone
chièdere v/t ask (di for); request
chiesa f church
chilo m kilo; fare il ~ rest a while after dinner; ~gramma m kilogram(me)
chilòmetro m kilometre
chilowatt m kilowatt
chimic|a f chemistry; ~o adj chemical; m chemist
chimono m Kimono
chin|a f slope; ~are v/t bend; bow; ~arsi v/r stoop; fig submit; ~o bent
chincaglie f/pl knick-knacks

pl
chinino m quinine
chioccia f brooding-hen; ~are v/i cluck
chiòcciola f snail; scala f a ~ winding staircase
chiodo m nail; spike
chioma f mane
chiosco m kiosk; stall
chiostro m cloister; convent
chirurg|ia f surgery; ~o m surgeon
chissà who knows; perhaps
chitarra f guitar
chiùdere v/t close; shut (up); ~ a chiave lock
chiunque whoever
chius|a f conclusion; barrier; lock (of canal); ~ura f closing (down); ~ura lampo zipper
ci pron pers us; adv here, there; to it; at it; ~ penso I think about it
C.ia = Compagnìa
ciab|atta f slipper; ~attino m cobbler
cialda f waffle
ciambella f doughnut
ciano m cornflower
ciao hallo, hi; so long!
ciarl|a f idle talk; ~e v/i gossip; ~atano m charlatan; mountebank
ciarpa f scarf
ciascuno each (one); everybody
cib|o m food; nourishment (also fig); ~i m/pl vegetariani a vegetarian diet
cicala f cicada
cicatrice f scar

cicca f cigar-butt; cigarette-end

cicerone m guide

ciclismo m cycling; **~ista** m, f cyclist; **~o** m cycle; **~one** m cyclone

cicogna f stork

cicoria f chicory

cieco adj blind; m blind man; **vicolo** m **~** blind alley

cielo m sky; heaven

cifra f figure; **~ d'affari** turnover

ciglio m eyelash

cigno m swan

cigolìo m creaking

ciliegia f cherry; **~o** m cherry-tree

cilindrata f cylinder displacement; **~dro** m cylinder; roller; top-hat

cima f top; summit; **da ~ a fondo** from top to bottom

cimentoso m perilous; risky

cimice f (bed)bug; drawing-pin

ciminiera f smoke-stack; funnel

cimitero m cemetery

Cina f China

cine abbr for cinema

cinegiornale m news reel

cinema m, **cinematografo** m cinema; movies

cinèreo ash-coloured

cinese m, f, adj Chinese

cingere v/t gird; encircle

cinghia f strap; belt; **~ale** m wild boar

cinguettare v/i chirp

cìnico adj cynical; m cynic

cinquanta fifty; **~antena-**

rio m fiftieth anniversary

cintura f belt; girdle; **~ di salvataggio** life belt; **~ di sicurezza** safety belt

ciò this; that; it; **a ~ for** this purpose

ciocco m log

cioccolata f chocolate; **~atino** m chocolate drop

cioè, ~ a dire that is to say; namely

ciottolato m cobbled pathway

ciòttolo m pebble

cipolla f onion; **~ina** f young onion; chive

cipresseto m cypress grove; **~o** m cypress

cipria f face-powder

circa about; **~o** m circus

circolare v/i circulate; adj circular; **viaggio** m **~** round trip; **biglietto** m **~** return ticket; **(lèttera) ~** f circular (letter)

circolazione f circulation; traffic

circolo m circle; club; group

circondare v/t surround, encompass

circonvallazione f circumvallation; **linea** f **di ~** roundabout tramway

circostanza f circumstance; occasion

circuire v/t surround; **~ùito** m circuit; **corto ~ùito** short circuit

cistifèllea f gall-bladder

citare v/t quote; cite; summon

città f town; city; **~ giardino**

garden city; **~ universitaria** campus; **~ vecchia** old (part of a) city

cittadin|anza f citizenship; **~o** adj civic; m citizen

ciuffo m tuft; forelock

ciurm|are v/t cheat

civett|a f owl; **~are** v/i flirt

civic|o adj civic; **~ile** m civilian; **guardia** f **~a** municipal guard

civile civil; civilized; **guerra** f **~** civil war; **stato** m **~** registrar's office

civiltà f civilization; courtesy

clacson m horn

clam|ore m clamour; **~oroso** noisy

clandestino clandestine; secret

clarinetto m clarinet

classe f class; **prima ~** first class; **~ turistica** tourist class

clàssico adj classic(al); m classic

classificare v/t classify; grade

clàusola f clause

clava f club

clavicola f collar-bone

clem|ente mild; merciful; **~enza** f clemency

clero m clergy

cliente m, f client; customer; **~ abituale** regular customer; **~la** f clientele

clim|a m climate; **stazione** f **~àtica** climatic health-resort

clinica f clinic

cloaca f sewer; drain

clòrico chloric

cloro m chlorine; **~si** f chlorosis

c. m. = corrente mese current month

coabitare v/i live together

co|aderente adherent together; **~adiuvare** v/t help

coagularsi v/r coagulate

coalizione f coalition

cobalto m cobalt

cobra m cobra

cocaina f cocaine

cocchiere m coachman; driver

cocci m/pl earthenware; **~nella** f ladybug

cocci|o m potsherd; **~uto** obstinate

cocco m coco(nut); fam darling

coccodrillo m crocodile

cocolla f cowl

cocòmero m watermelon

coda f tail; train (dress); line; **piano** m **a ~** grand piano; **fare la ~** queue up; **~rdo** adj cowardly; m coward

codesto this, that

còdice m code; **~ stradale** highway code

coercitivo coercive; compulsive

coe|rede m co-heir; **~rente** coherent; consistent; **~sistenza** f coexistence; **~sivo** cohesive

coetàneo of the same age

còfano m casket; chest; aut hood

coffa f mar top

cògliere v/t gather; catch; seize (*opportunity*)

cognàc m cognac; brandy

cogn|ata f sister-in-law; **~ato** m brother-in-law

cògnito known

cognizione f knowledge

cognome m surname; family name

coincidenza f coincidence; rail connection

coinvòlgere v/t involve

cola f strainer; sieve

colà (over) there

coll|are v/t strain; cast (*metal*); v/i drip; **~ata** f cast; lava stream

colazione f breakfast; lunch; **far ~** have breakfast (lunch)

colei she; her

coler|a m cholera; **~ina** f British cholera

còlica f colic

colla f paste; glue

collabor|are v/i collaborate; **~atore** m collaborator

coll|ana f necklace; **~are** m collar; bands pl; **~asso** m collapse

colle m hill

collega m,f colleague

collegare v/t connect; unite

colleg|iale adj collegial; **~o** m college boy; **~o** m boarding-school; college; (professional) body

còllera f anger; **andare in ~** fly into a passion

collèrico choleric

collett|a f collection; **~are** v/t collect; **~ivo** collective; joint

colletto m collar

collezion|e f collection; **~ista** m, f collector

collimare v/i coincide; agree

collina f hill

collisione f collision

collo m neck; com parcel

colloc|amento m placement; **agenzia** f **di ~amento** employment agency; **~are** v/t place; put

collòquio m conversation; talk

colloso sticky

colm|are v/t fill up; **~o** adj full up; m summit

colombo m dove

colonia f colony; settlement; **~le** colonial; **gèneri** m/pl **~li** groceries

colonn|a f column; pillar; **~ello** m colonel

color|are v/t colour; **~ato** coloured; **~e** m colour; **~ire** v/t colour; paint; **~itura** f colouring

coloro they; those

colossale colossal

colp|a f fault; guilt; **~évole** guilty; **~etto** m light blow, tap

colpire v/t strike; hit

colpo m blow; stroke; hit; shot; **~ d'aria** draught; **~ di màgano** sudden attack; **~ di sole** sun-stroke; **~ di stato** coup d'état; **~so** guilty

colta f harvest

coltell|ata f stab; **~o** m knife;

~o a serramànico jack-knife

coltiv|are v/t till; grow; fig cultivate; **~azione** f agr farming

colto learned; educated; gathered

coltr|e f coverlet; pall; **~one** m quilt

coltura f cultura; farming

colui he; him

coma m coma

comand|amento m commandment; **~ante** m commander; **~are** v/t command; **~are qc com** order s.th.; **~o** m command; order; mech drive; control

comare f godmother

comb|àttere v/i fight; v/t fight against; **~attimento** m combat

combin|àbile combinable; **~are** v/t combine; **~azione** f agreement; chance

combustibile adj combustible; m fuel

come how; as; like; ~ **me** like me; ~ **se** as if; ~ **mai** why (on earth)?

cometa f comet

còmico comic(al); **poeta** m ~ comic writer

comignolo m chimney-top; ridge

cominciare v/t, v/i start; begin

comino m cumin

comit|ato m committee; board; **~iva** f party; company

commèdia f comedy

commedi|ante m, f comedian; **~ògrafo** m playwright

commemor|are v/t commemorate; **~ativo** memorial

commensale m table companion

comment|are v/t comment; **~atore** m commentator; **~o** m comment; commentary

commerci|ale commercial; **società** f **~ale** business concern; **~ante** adj trading; m dealer; business man; merchant; **~are** v/t trade; deal; **~o** m business; **~o èstero** foreign trade

commesso m clerk; employee; ~ **viaggiatore** travelling salesman

commestibili m/pl foodstuffs pl

commèttere v/t (crime) commit; form order

commiss|ariato m **di pùblica sicurezza** police station; **~ario** m commissary; **~ione** f order; errand; committee; **~ione** f **interna** works council

commisto mixed

committente m, f customer

comm|ovente moving; **~ozione** f commotion; **~uòvere** v/t move; touch; affect

commut|are v/t commute; **~azione** f commutation; elec switching

comò m chest of drawers

comod|are v/i suit; **~ino** m bedside table; **~ità** f comfort; convenience

còmodo comfortable; well off

compaesano *m* compatriot

compagn|a *f* female companion; **∼ia** *f* company; **∼o** *m* mate; *com* partner

compar|àbile comparable; **∼are** *v/t* compare; **∼azione** *f* comparison

compare *m* godfather

comparire *v/i* appear

compart|ecipare *v/i* share (in); **∼ecipazione** *f* share; **∼imento** *m* compartment; department; **∼imento per (non) fumatori** (non) smoking compartment

compassi|one *f* pity; compassion (**di** with); **∼onévole** pityful

compasso *m* compasses *pl*

compatìbile compatible

compatriota *m, f* compatriot; *m* fellow-countryman

compatto compact

compendi|are *v/t* summarize; **∼o** *m* compendium; digest

compens|àbile compensable; **∼are** *v/t* compensate; **∼o** *m* reward; compensation; **stanza di ∼o** clearing house

comperare *cf* comprare

com|petente competent; qualified; **∼petenza** *f* competence; **∼pètere** *v/i* compete

compiac|ente obliging; **∼enza** *f* kindness; complacence; **∼ere** *v/t* please; com-

ply (with)

compiàn|gere *v/t* lament; pity; **∼to** bemoaned

còmpiere *v/t* accomplish; fulfil

compilare *v/t* compile

compi|mento *m* accomplishment; fulfilment; **∼ire** *cf* còmpiere

compit|are *v/t* spell; **∼ezza** *f* politeness; **∼o** accomplished

còmpito *m* task

compleanno *m* birthday

complementare complementary

compless|ione *f* constitution (*health*); **∼ivo** total; **∼o** *m* whole; complex

complet|are *v/t* complete; **∼o** complete; entire; full (up)

complicare *v/t* complicate

còmplice *adj* accessory; *m,f* accomplice

complim|entare *v/t* congratulate; compliment (s.o.); **∼enti** *m/pl:* **fare ∼enti** stand on ceremony

complotto *m* plot

comp|onimento *m* composition; essay; **∼orre** *v/t* compose; arrange; **∼orsi di** consist of; **∼ositore** *m* type-setter; composer

comport|àbile tolerable; **∼amento** *m* behaviour; **∼are** *v/t* bear; tolerate; **∼arsi** *v/r* behave

compos|itore *m* composer; **∼izione** *f* composition; **∼osta** *f* compote; stewed fruit; **~ostiera** f dish for compote; **~osto** composed; settled

compr|a f purchase; **~are** v/t buy; **~atore** m buyer

comprèndere v/i comprehend; realize; include

compren|sibile understandable; **~sione** f comprehension

compreso: tutto ~ everything included

compress|a f compress; tablet; **~ione** f compression

comprimere v/t compress

compromèttere v/t compromise

comprov|àbile provable; **~are** v/t prove (by evidence)

compunto repentant

comput|àbile computable; **~are** v/t compute; reckon

còmputo m computation

comunale municipal; **consiglio m ~** city council

comune common; usual; mutual; **in ~** in common

communic|are v/t communicate; inform; v/i eccl communicate; be in communication; **~azione** f communication; rail, tel connection

comunione f communion; eccl Communion

comun|ismo m communism; **~ista** m, f communist

comunità f community

comunque however; anyway

con with; by; to

cònca f tub; shell; **~vo** hollow

concèdere v/t grant; concede; allow

concentr|are v/t concentrate; **~arsi** v/r concentrate (attention); gather; **~azione** f concentration

concep|ibile conceivable; **~ire** v/t conceive

conceria f tannery

concèrnere v/t concern

concert|are v/t plan; concert; **~o** m concert

concessione f concession; grant

concetto m conception; idea

conchiglia f shell

conchiùdere cf conclùde

conci|a f tan; tanning; **~atore** m tanner

concili|are v/t reconcile; **~arsi** v/r make up; reconcile; **~azione** f (re)conciliation; eccl **~o** m council

concime m compost; manure

conciso concise

concitare v/t agitate

concittadino m fellow-citizen

conclave m conclave

conclùdere v/t close; v/i draw the conclusion; **~usione** f conclusion; **~usivo** conclusive

concomitante concomitant

concord|anza f agreement; **~are** v/t, v/i agree (upon); **~ia** f harmony; agreement

concorr|ente m competitor; candidate; **~enza** f competition

concórrere *v/i* compete; contribute (**a** to)

concorso *m* concourse; competition; tournament

concreto concrete

concubina *f* concubine

concussione *f* extortion

condanna *f* condemnation; **~ a morte** death sentence

condann|ábile condemnable; **~are** *v/t* sentence (**a** to); condemn

condensare *v/t* condense; thicken

cond|imento *m* seasoning; **~ire** *v/t* season

condiscen|dente condescendent; indulgent; **~éndere** *v/i* condescend; comply (with)

condiscépolo *m* schoolmate

condizion|ale *m, adj* conditional; **~e** *f* condition; state; **a ~e** on condition that

condoglianza *f* condolence

condolersi *v/r*: **~ con qu** condole with s.o.

cond|otta *f* conduct; behaviour; *auto:* driving; **mèdico ~otto** *m* panel doctor

conducente *m* driver

cond|urre *v/t* guide; drive; **~ursi** *v/r* behave; **~uttore** *m* leader; *rail* conductor; manager

confeder|ale confederate; **~arsi** *v/r* unite; confederate; **~ato** *m* confederate; ally; **~azione** *f* confederation

confer|enza *f* lecture; conference; **~enziere** *m* lectu-

rer; **~ire** *v/t* confer; bestow

conferm|a *f* confirmation; **~are** *v/t* confirm; **mi confermo ...** *letter:* I remain ...

confess|are *v/t* confess; admit; **~arsi** *v/r* go to confession; **~ione** *f* confession; **~o** pleading guilty; **~ore** *m* confessor

confett|are *v/t* candy; **~eria** *f* confectionary; confectioner's shop; **~i** *m/pl* candies *pl*; **~ura** *f* sweetmeat

confezionare *v/t* manufacture; make

confid|are *v/t* confide; *v/i* confide (**in** in); **~enza** *f* confidence; **~enziale** confidential

confíggere *v/t* nail; fix (*in memory*)

configurare *v/t* shape; symbolize

confin|are *v/t* confine; *v/i* border (**con** on); **~e** *m* border; boundary; **~o político** political confinement

confisca *f* confiscation; **~are** *v/t* confiscate

conflitto *m* conflict

conflu|ente *m* confluent; **~ire** *v/i* flow together

confóndere *v/t* confound; confuse: addle

conform|are *v/t* conform; **~e** conforming; **~e a** in conformity with; in accordance with

confort|àbile consolable; **~are** *v/t* comfort; encourage; **~o** *m* comfort; relief

confronto *m* comparison

conf|usione f confusion; ~uso mixed up; confounded

conged|are v/t dismiss; give leave; ~o m leave; farewell

congegno m device; contraption; gadget

congelarsi v/r congeal; freeze

congènito congenital

congestione f: ~ cerebrale congestion of the brain

congetturare v/i conjecture; surmise

con|giùngere v/t connect; ~giùngersi v/r join; ~giuntivite f conjunctivitis; ~giuntivo m subjunctive; ~giunto adj joint; m relative; ~giuntura f juncture; conjuncture; anat joint; ~giunzione f (con)junction

congiur|a f conspiracy; plot; ~are v/i plot

congratul|arsi v/r: ~arsi con qu congratulate s.o. (on); ~azione f congratulation

congregarsi v/r congregate

congresso m congress; convention

congruente congruent

coniare v/t coin; fig invent

cònico conical

conifere f/pl conifers pl

coniglio m rabbit

conio m wedge; coinage

coniug|are v/t conjugate; ~azione f conjugation

còniuge m husband; f wife; còniugi m/pl X Mr. and Mrs. X

conness|ione f connection; ~o related

connotato m feature

cono m cone

conosc|ente m,f acquaintance; ~enza f knowledge; acquaintance

conóscere v/t know; be acquainted with

conoscitore m connoisseur

conqu|ista f conquest; ~istare v/t conquer; ~istatore m conqueror

consacr|are v/t consecrate; devote; ~azione f consecration

consanguìneo adj akin; m kin(sman)

consapévole conscious; aware

conscio conscious; aware

consecutivo consecutive

consegn|a f delivery; consignment; ~a bagagli cloak-room; ~are v/t deliver; consign; hand over

consegu|ente following; ~enza f consequence; ~itare v/i result (di from)

consenso m consent

consèntire v/i consent

conserv|a f preserve(s); ~are v/t preserve; keep; ~atore m, adj conservative; ~azione f conservation; preservation

consider|àbile considerable; ~are v/t consider; ~azione f consideration; ~évole considerable

consigli|are v/t advise; counsel; ~ere m counsellor; adviser

consiglio m advice; council; board

consistenza f consistency; solidity

consistere v/i consist (**in, di** in, of)

consocio m co-partner

consol|are v/t console; comfort; **~ato** m consulate; **~azione** f solace; comfort

cònsole m consul

consolidare v/t consolidate

consommé m broth

consonante adj conforming; f gram consonant

consorte m,f consort; mate

consorzio m syndicate; trust

constare v/i: **~ di** consist of

constatare v/t ascertain

consueto customary; habitual

consuetùdine f habit

consult|are v/t consult; **~azione** f consultation

consum|are v/t consume; fig wear out; **~o** m consumption; **imposte di ~o** excise tax

consunto consumed; worn out

contàbile m accountant; book-keeper

contabilità f book-keeping

contachilòmetri m speedometer

contad|ina f peasant-woman; **~ino** adj rustic; m farmer; peasant

contagioso contagious

contamin|are v/t contaminate; pollute; **~azione** f **dell'aria** air pollution

cont|ante m cash; **pagare in ~anti** pay in cash; **~are** v/t, v/i count; **~are su** v/t count on; rely on

contatto m contact; touch

conte m count; earl

cont|eggiare v/t compute; **~eggio** m reckoning; calculation

contempl|are v/t contemplate; **~azione** f contemplation

contemporàneo adj contemporaneous; m contemporary

contèndere v/t contest; v/i contend

conten|ere v/t contain; **~ersi** v/r restrain oneself

content|are v/t satisfy; **~arsi** v/r be content (**di** with)

contento satisfied (**di** with)

contenuto m contents pl

contesa f contest; strife

contessa f countess

contestare v/t contest

contesto m context

contìguo adjacent

contin|ente adj chaste; m continent; **~enza** f continence

continu|are v/t continue; **~azione** f continuation

continuo continuous; **di ~** continuously

conto m calculation; bill; account; **rèndere ~ di** account for; **rèndersi ~ di qc** realize s.th.; **in fin dei conti** ultimately; **~ corrente** current account

contòrcere v/t distort

contorno m contour; outline; gast (side-) dish) vegetables pl

contorsione f contortion

contrabbando m smuggling

contrac|cambiare v/t return; reciprocate; **~cambio** m equivalent

contrada f region; road

contradd|ire v/t contradict; **~izione** f contradiction

contraf|fare v/t imitate; forge; **~farsi** v/r feign

contrap|peso m counterbalance; **~porre** v/t oppose

contrari|are v/t counteract; vex; **~età** f vexation; obstacle

contrario contrary; adverse; **èssere ~** be against; **al ~** on the contrary

contrar|re v/t contract; stipulate; **~si** v/r shrink

contr|astare v/t oppose; v/i be in contrast (with); **~asto** m contrast; opposition; **~attacco** m counter-attack

contratt|are v/t negotiate; bargain; **~o** m contract

contravv|veleno m antidote; **~venire** v/i infringe; **~venzione** f violation; fine

contrazione f contraction

contri|buente m/f taxpayer; **~buire** v/t contribute; **~buto** m contribution; **~buzione** f contribution; tax

contro against, versus; **~ assegno** COD

controll|are v/t control; check; v/i control; inspection; **~o** m control; inspection; **~ore** m controller

(ticket-) collector

contum|ace for defaulting; **~acia** f for default; quarantine

conturbare v/t disturb

contusione f contusion

convalesc|ente m, f, adj convalescent; **~enza** f convalescence

convalidare v/t validate; confirm

convegno m meeting

conven|évole, ~iente convenient; **~ienza** f convenience; **~ire** v/i meet; agree; suit; **~irsi** v/r be fit; be proper

convento m convent; monastery

convenzion|ale conventional; **~e** f convention

convèrgere v/i converge

convers|are v/i converse; talk; **~azione** f conversation; **~ione** f (eccl, pol) conversion

convert|ire v/t change; convert; **~irsi** be converted; **~ito** m convert

convesso convex

con|vincere v/t convince; **~vinzione** f conviction

convito m banquet; feast; **~itto** m boarding-school

convìvere v/i live together

convocare v/t convoke

convoglio m convoy; **~ fùnebre** funeral procession

convul|sione f convulsion; **~sivo** convulsive

cooper|are v/i cooperate; **~ativa** f cooperative society

coordin|are v/t coordinate; **~azione** f coordination

coperchio m lid; cover

copert|a f blanket; cover; naut deck; **~ina** f cover (of books); **~o** adj covered; fig masked; m (table) cover; **~one** m tarpaulin; auto: tyre

copia f abundance; copy; specimen; **bella ~** fair copy; **~lèttere** m letter-book; copying-press

copi|are v/t copy; transcribe; **~are qu** imitate s.o.; **lapis** m **~ativo** copying pencil; **~one** m scenario

copioso copious

coppa f cup; trophy

coppia f couple

copri|fuoco m curfew; **~re** v/t cover; **~tetto** m tilelayer

copulare v/t copulate; join

coraggio m courage; **~so** brave

corale m choral; **società** f **~** choral society

corall|aio m coral-dealer; **banco ~ifero** coral reef; **~o** m coral

corano m Koran

corazza f cuirass

corbell|aio m basket-maker; **~o** m basket

cord|a f rope; cord; string; chord; **~a vocale** vocal chord; **~aio** m rope-maker; **~ame** m cordage; naut rigging; **~ellina** f small cord; string

cordial|e hearty; **~ità** f cordiality

cordonare v/t surround; girdle

cordone m cordon; braid

Corea f Korea

coreografia f choreography

coriandoli m/pl confetti

coricarsi v/r lie down; go to bed; set (sun)

corista m, f chorus-singer; m tuning-fork

cornamusa f bagpipe

cornatura f antlers pl

còrnea f anat cornea

corn|eggiare v/t butt; **~etta** f cornet; bugle; aut hooter

cornice f frame; **~tta** f per diapositive slide frame

corniciare v/t frame

corno m horn; bump (head); corn (foot); **~ da scarpe** shoe-horn

coro m chorus

coron|a f crown; wreath; **~are** v/t crown; **~azione** f coronation

corp|etto m waistcoat; vest; **~o** m body; corps; **~orale** bodily; **~ulenza** f corpulence

corred|are v/t provide; equip (**di** with); **~o** m outfit; trousseau

corr|èggere v/t correct; **~ersi** v/r amend

correlazione f coreelation

corrente adj running; flowing; f elec current; stream; fig trend; **~ alternata** alternating current; **~ continua** direct current; **~ d'aria** draught

córrere v/i run; flow; be

current (*money*); **~ in aiuto di qu** run to s.o.'s assistance; **~ pericolo** run a risk

corr|ettivo *adj* corrective; *m* corrective agent; **~etto** correct; right; **~ezione** *f* correction

corridoio *m* corridor; passage; lobby

corr|iera *f* mail coach; **~iere** *m* courier; mail; **a volta ~iere** by return of mail

corris|pondente *m, f* correspondent; **~pondenza** *f* correspondence; **~póndere** *v/i* correspond; *v/t* allow; pay

corrivo rash; inconsiderate

corroborare *v/t* corroborate; strenghten

corródere *v/t* corrode

corrómpere *v/t* corrupt; bribe

corrugare *v/t* wrinkle; frown

corruttìbile corruptible

corruzione *f* corruption

corsa *f* run; race; **cavallo m da ~** race-horse; **di ~** running

corsaro *m* corsair

corseggiare *v/t, v/i* privateer

corsetto *m* corset

corso *m* course; trend; *com* rate; *~*, *m, adj* Corsican

corte *f* court; **~ d'assise** court of assize; Court of General Sessions

corteccia *f* bark; crust

corteggi|amento *m* courtship; **~are** *v/t* court

cort|eggio *m*, **~èo** *m* procession; attendance; suite; **~eggio**, **~èo fùnebre** funeral procession; **~ese** courteous; polite; **~esia** *f* politeness; **per ~esia** please; kindly

cortezza *f* shortness; **~ di mente** narrow-mindedness

corti|giano *m* courtier; flatterer; **~le** *m* courtyard

cortina *f* curtain

corto short; brief; *fig* shortwitted; **~ tagliar** ~ cut short; **tenersi** ~ be brief

corvino jet-black

corvo *m* raven; crow

cosa *f* matter; thing; **(che) ~?** what?; **qualche ~** something; **a che ~?** what for?; **di che ~?** of what?

coscetto *m* leg (*of lamb*)

coscia *f* thigh

coscien|te conscious; aware; attendance; **~za** *f* conscience; consciousness; **~zioso** scrupulous

coscri|tto *m* conscript; **~zione** *f* conscription; draft

così so; thus; **~ ~** not too bad

cosicché so that

cosiddetto so called

cosiffatto such

cosm|ètici *m/pl* cosmetics *pl*; **~òpoli** *f* metropolis

cospetto *m*: **al ~ di** in front of; facing

cospi|cuità *f* conspicuousness; **~ìcuo** prominent

cospir|are *v/i* conspire; **~azione** *f* plot

costa *f* rib; shore; coast

costà (over) there

costan|te constant; firm; **~za** f steadiness; firmness; perseverance

cost|are v/i cost; **~a molto** it's dear

costat|are v/t state; notice; **~azione** f statement

costeggiare v/t coast; skirt; *naut* sail along

costei she; her

costellazione f constellation

costern|are v/t dismay; **~ato** abashed; **~azione** f consternation

costì there

costiera f coast; shore

costip|ato constipated; having a cold; **~azione** f constipation

costit|uire v/t constitute; form; **~utore** m constitutor; **~uzione** f formation; *pol* constitution

costo m cost

còstola f rib

costoletta f cutlet; chop; **~ di maiale** pork chop

costoro those

costoso costly; dear; valuable

costringere v/t compel; force; constrain

costr|uire v/t build; **~uttivo** constructive; **~uttore** m constructor; **~uzione** f building; construction

costui m this

costum|anza f custom; usage; **~ato** well-mannered

costum|e m usage; habit; costume; dress; **~e da ba-**

gno bathing suit; **cattivi (buoni) ~i** pl loose (good) morals pl

cote f whetstone

cotidiano daily

cotogna f quince

coton|e m cotton; **~erie** f/pl cotton goods pl; **~ificio** m cotton-mill

cotta f surplice; *fig* infatuation

còttimo m job-work; **lavorare a ~** work by the job

cov|a f brood; **~are** v/t brood; hatch; v/i smoulder (*hatred*)

cov|ile m couch; **~o** m den; lair

covone m sheaf

crampo m cramp

cranio m skull

cràpula f excess; debauch

crapulare v/i revel

cratère m crater

crauti m/pl **acidi** sauerkraut

cravatta f (neck-) tie

creanza f breeding; manners pl

creare v/t create; appoint

crea|to m universe; **~tore** adj creating; m creator; **~tura** f creature; **~zione** f creation

credente m *eccl* believer

credenz|a f pantry; sideboard; belief; *com* credit; **~iali** f/pl credentials; **~one** m credulous person

crédere v/t, v/i believe (**in** in); think

cred|ibile credible; **~ibilità** f credibility

crédito m credit; *fig* reputa-

tion; **méttere a ~** credit
cred|itore m creditor; **~o** m faith; credo
crèdulo credulous
crema f cream; **~ caramella** custard; **~ da barba** shaving cream; **~ solare** suntan cream; **~ da scarpe** shoe polish; **~ di gelato** ice-cream; **~ per la pelle** skin cream
crem|are v/t cremate; **~atoio** m, **~atorio** m crematory; **~azione** f cremation
crèmisi m, adj crimson
crepa f crack; fissure; **~cuore** m heart-break
crep|are v/i crack; burst; die; **~atura** f crack
crepit|are v/i crackle; **~ìo** m, **crèpito** m crackling; rattling
crepùscolo m twilight
crescendo mus growing
créscere v/i grow; increase
créscita f growth
crèsima f eccl confirmation
cresimare v/t confirm
cresp|a f wrinkle; crease; **~o** adj crisp; m crape
creta f clay; **~aceo** clayey
cricch|e! bang!; **~iare** v/i crack; **~io** m crackling
cricco m lifting-jack
criminale m, f, adj criminal
crìmine m crime
criminoso criminal
crin|e m hair; **~iera** f mane; **~o** m horsehair
cripta f crypt
crisi f crisis

cristall|ino crystalline; **~izzare** v/t, v/i crystallize; **~o** m crystal; (window-)pane
cristian|a f Christian; **~èsimo** m Christianity; **~o** m, adj Christian
Cristo m Christ
criterio m criterion; sense
crìtica f criticism; critique
criticare v/t criticize
crìtico adj critical; m critic
crivell|are v/t sift; riddle; **~o** m sieve
croccante adj crisp; m almond cake
crocchett|a f meat-ball; croquette; **~o** m small hook
crocchi|are v/t tap; v/i cluck (hen)
croce f cross; **fare il segno della ~** cross o.s.; **~fisso** m crucifix; **~via** m cf **crocicchio**
croci|ata f crusade; **~ato** m crusader; **~icchio** m cross-road; rail junction; **~iera** f cruise; **~ifiggere** v/t crucify; **~ifissione** f crucifixion; **~ifisso** m crucifix
croll|are v/i collapse; v/t shake; **~o** m breakdown; crash
cromo m chrome
cromolitografìa f chromolithography
cromosoma m chromosome
cròn|aca f chronicle; review; news; **~ico** chronic
cron|ista m, f reporter; **~ologìa** f chronology; **~ològico** chronological

crosciare v/i pelt; roar

crost|**a** f crust; med scab; **~ata** f pie

crucci|**are** v/t worry; vex; **~io** m worry; vexation; **~ioso** angry

cruciale crucial

cruciverba m cross-word; puzzle

crud|**ele** cruel; **~eltà** f cruelty

crudo crude; raw; harsh

crumiro m strike-breaker; scrab

cruna f eye of a needle

crusca f bran; freckles pl

cruscotto m instrument panel; dashboard

c. s. = come sopra as above

cùbico cubic

cubiforme cubiform

cubo adj cubic; m cube

cuccagna f, **paese di ~** Utopia; fam Lubberland

cucchi|**aino** m tea-spoon; **~aio** m spoon; **~aione** m ladle

cuccia f dog's bed

cuccio m, **cùcciolo** m puppy

cucco m, **~ù** cuckoo

cucin|**a** f kitchen; **libro** m **di ~a** cookery-book; **~are** v/t cook

cuc|**ire** v/t sew; **màcchina** f **da (per) ~ire** sewing machine; **~itrice** f seamstress; **~itura** f seam

cùculo m cuckoo

cuffia f cap; bonnet; thea prompter's box; radio: headphones

cugin|**a** f, **~o** m cousin

cui (to) whom; (to) which; **di ~** whose; **il ~ nome** whose name

culinaria f cookery

cull|**a** f cradle; **~are** v/t cradle

culminare v/i culminate

cùlmine m summit; top; climax

culo m posterior

culto m worship

cult|**ore** m cultivator; **~ura** f culture; refinement; **~urale** cultural

cumul|**are** v/t (ac)cumulate; **~azione** f accumulation

cùmulo m heap; pile

cùneo m wedge

cunetta f road-ditch; gutter

cunicolo m underground passage

cuoc|**a** f, **~o** m cook

cuòcere v/t, v/i cook; bake; rost; fig vex

cuoi|**aio** m leather-seller; **~o** m leather

cuor|**e** m heart; **di (gran) ~e** (most) heartily; **stare a ~e** have a heart; **~i** m/pl playing-cards hearts

cupid|**igia** f, **~ità** f cupidity; greed

cùpido covetous; greedy

cupo dark; gloomy; sullen

cùpola f dome

cura f care; accuracy; med cure; treatment; **~ della bellezza** beauty culture; **~ del corpo** physical culture

cur|**àbile** curable; **~are** v/t take care of; med treat; **~ar-**

si v/r **di qc** mind s.th.
curia f court of justice
curios|ità f curiosity; **~o** curious; odd
curriculum m curriculum; **~ vitae** curriculum vitae
curv|a f curve; bend; **~are** v/t curve; **~arsi** bend; bow; **~o** bent; crooked

cuscinetto m **a sfere** ball bearing; **stato** m **~** buffer state
cuscino m cushion
custod|e m custodian; guardian; **~ia** f custody; case; **~ire** v/t guard; keep
cutàneo cutaneous
cute f skin

D

da from; at; to; by; since; from ...'s (house, shop); **vado dal mèdico** I am going to the doctor; **~ ieri** since yesterday; **tazza** f **~ té** teacup
dà he gives
dabbene upright
daccapo once more
dacché conj since
dad|o m die (pl dice); **giocare ai ~i** play at dice
dalia f dahlia
dama f lady; play draughts
damasco m damask
danese m, f, adj Danish
Danimarca f Denmark
dann|are v/t damn; **~azione** f damnation; fig plague; **~eggiare** v/t damage; harm; **~o** m damage; **~o della lamiera** bodywork damage; **~oso** harmful
dantesco Dantean
Danubio m Danube
danz|a f dance; **~are** v/t, v/i dance
dappertutto everywhere
dap|prima at first; **~princi-**

pio in the beginning
dardo m dart
dare v/t give; **~ il buon giorno** say good morning; **~ del tu** address familiarly (2nd pers sg); **~rsi** v/r **a qc** devote o.s. to s.th.
dat|a f date; **~are** v/t, v/i date; **~o** adj given; **~o che** conj supposing that m **datum** (pl data); **~ore** m **di lavoro** employer
dàttero m date; date-tree
dattilograf|are v/t type (-write); **~ia** f typewriting
dattilògrafo m typist
dattiloscritto m type-script
davanti prep before; in front of; adv before; m front; fore part
davanzale m window-sill
davvero really; indeed
dazi|àbile dutiable; **~are** v/t lay duty on; **~o** m customs duty
d. C. = dopo Cristo after Christ
dea f goddess
debbo I must

9*

debilitare v/t weaken

dèbito adj due; m debt; duty

debitore m debtor

débole weak; feeble

debolezza f weakness

decad|enza f decay; **~ere** v/i decay; decline

decano m dean

decapitare v/t decapitate

decennio m decade

decen|te decent; **~za** f decency

decesso m decease

decid|ere v/t, v/i, **~ersi** v/r decide; resolve; make up one's mind

decifrare v/t decipher; decode

decim|ale: sistema m **~ale** decimal system; **~are** v/t decimate

dècimo tenth

decina: una ~ about ten

decis|ione f decision; **~ivo** decisive; **~o** decided

declam|are v/t declaim; **~azione** f declamation

declin|are v/t, v/i decline; reject; **~azione** f declination; deviation; gram declension

declivio m slope

decoll|are v/i aer take off; **~o** m take off; departure

decomporre v/t decompose; dissolve

decor|are v/t decorate; **~azione** f decoration; badge of honour; **~o** m decorum; dignity

decrescenza f decrease

decréscere v/i decrease

decr|etare v/t decree; enact; **~eto** m decree

dèdica f dedication

dedicare v/t dedicate; devote; eccl consecrate

dèdito devoted; given (to)

dedizione f devotion; surrender

ded|urre v/t deduct; infer; **~uzione** f deduction

deferente deferential

defici|ente deficient; **~enza** f deficiency

déficit m deficit

defin|ire v/t define; settle; **~itivo** conclusive; **~izione** f definition; settlement

deform|are v/t deform; disfigure; **~e** deformed; **~ità** f deformity

defraud|are v/t cheat; **~azione** f defrauding; deceit

defunto deceased

degener|are v/i degenerate; **~azione** f degeneration

degènere degenerate

degente bedridden

degli genitive pl m of the

degn|are v/t deem worthy; **~arsi** v/r deign; **~o** worthy; respectable

degradare v/t degrade

dei genitive pl m of the

deità f deity

del genitive sg m of the

delatore m spy; informer

deleg|are v/t delegate; **~ato** m delegate; deputy; **~azione** f delegation

delfino m dolphin

deliber|are v/t, v/i deliberate; resolve; **~ato** adj delib-

erate; decided; *m* resolution;
~azione *f* deliberation

delic|atezza *f* delicacy; discretion; **~ato** delicate

delimitare *v/t* delimit

deline|amento *m* delineation; **~are** *v/t* sketch; outline

delinquen|te *m* delinquent; **~za** *f* delinquency

delirio *m* delirium

delitto *m* crime

delizi|a *f* delice; delight; **~oso** delightful; delicious

dell', della, delle, dello of the

del|ùdere *v/t* delude; disappoint; **~usione** *f* delusion

demanio *m* state property

demarcare *v/t* trace the boundaries of

demen|te insane; **~za** *f* insanity

demeritare *v/t* forfeit

democràtico *adj* democratic; *m* democrat

democrazia *f* democracy

demolire *v/t* demolish; tear down

dèmone *m* demon; devil

demoralizzare *v/t* demoralize

denar|o *m* money; **~i** *pl* **contanti** ready cash

denomin|are *v/t* name; **~atore** *m* denominator; **~azione** *f* denomination

denot|are *v/t* denote; **~azione** *f* signification

dens|ità *f* density; **~o** dense; thick

dent|ario: nervo *m* **~ario**

dental nerve; **~e** *m* tooth; *mech* cog; **~e artificiale** artificial tooth; **~e cariate** dental caries; **mal** *m* **di denti** toothache; **radice** *f* **del ~e** root of a tooth; **strappare un ~e** have a tooth extracted; **~iera** *f* set of artificial teeth; toothed gearing; **acqua** *f* **~ifricia** mouth water; **~ifricio, pasta** *f* **~ifricia** *m* tooth paste; **~ista** *m, f* dentist

dentro *prep* in; within; inside

denudare *v/t* divest

denunci|a *f*, **denunzi|a** *f* denunciation; information; **~are** *v/t* denounce; report; **~are il rèddito** declare one's income; **~atore** *m* denunciator

deodorante *m* deodorant

deperire *v/i* perish; decay

depil|are *v/t* depilate; **~atorio** *m, adj* depilatory

deplor|are *v/t* deplore; **~évole** deplorable

deporre *v/t* lay (down); put (down); depose; depone

deportare *v/t* deport

depositare *v/t* deposit

depòsito *m* deposit; warehouse; depot; **~ bagagli** cloak-room; luggage-office

deposizione *f* deposition; *eccl* Descent from the Cross

depressione *f* depression, dejection

deprezzamento *m* depreciation

deprìmere *v/t* depress

depurare v/t purify; cleanse

deputato m deputy

deragli|amento m derailment; **~are** v/i run off the rails

deridere v/t deride; laugh at

deriv|are v/t, v/i derive; **~azione** f derivation; tel extension

dermatologìa f dermatology

derogare v/i derogate; disregard

derubare v/t rob

descr|ìvere v/t describe; **~izione** f description

deserto adj uninhabited; desolate; m desert

desider|àbile desirable; **~are** v/t desire; want; **~io** m desire; wish

designare v/t designate; nominate

desinare v/i have lunch; m lunch

desinenza f ending

desistere v/i desist

desol|are /t desolate; distress; **~ato** desolate; distressed

dest|are v/t awaken; stir; **~arsi** v/r wake up

destin|are v/t destine; **~atario** m addressee; **~azione** f destination; **~o** m destiny

destitu|ìre v/t remove; **~zione** f dismissal

desto awake; fig alert

destra f right (hand, side); **a ~** on the right; **tenere la ~** keep to the right; pol conservative party; naut starboard

destrezza f dexterity; skill

destro right; clever

detergente m, adj detergent

deteriorare v/t deteriorate

determin|are v/t determine; **~arsi** v/r resolve (upon); **~ativo** determinative; **~azione** f determination

detestare v/t detest; loathe

detonazione f detonation

detr|arre v/t deduct; **~azione** f deduction; slander

detronizzare v/t dethrone; depose

dettagli|ante m, f retail dealer; **~ato** detailed; **~o** m detail; particular; **véndere al ~o** sell by retail

dettare v/t dictate

detto adj said; m saying

devastare v/t devastate

deve he must

devi|amento m rail derailment; **~are** v/i deviate; depart; **~azione** f deviation

devo I must

devotìssimo very truly (yours); **~o** devout; eccl pious

devozione f devotion; piety

di of; from; **~ buon 'ora** early; **~ ferro** of iron; **io sono ~ Roma** I am from Rome; **~ giorno** by day; **soffrire ~** suffer from; **~ chi è questo libro?** whose book is this?; comp than

dì m day

diab|ete m diabetes; **~ètico** diabetic

diabòlico diabolic(al)

diàcono *m* deacon

diàfano transparent

diaframma *m* diaphragm

diàgnosi *f* diagnosis

diagnosticare *v/t* diagnose

diagonale diagonal

dialetto *m* dialect

dialogare *v/i* converse

diàlogo *m* dialogue

diamante *m* diamond

diàmetro *m* diameter

diàmine! the deuce!; the dickens!

diari|a *f* daily allowance; **~o** *m* diary

diarrea *f* diarrhoea

diàspora *f* diaspora

diàvolo *m* devil

dibàtt|ere *v/t* debate; argue; **~ersi** *v/r* struggle

dibattimento *m* debate; legal bearing

dibàttito *m* argument

diboscare *v/t* deforest

dice he says

dicembre *m* December

dicerìa *f* gossip; rumour

dichiar|are *v/t* state; declare; **~are ricevuta di** acknowledge receipt of; **~azione** *f* statement; **~azione doganale** customs declaration

diciamo we say

dico I say

didàttico didactic

diecina *f* about ten

dieta *f* diet; assembly

dietètica *f* dietetics *pl*

dietro after; behind; back

difèndere *v/t* defend

difensivo defensive

difesa *f* defence; protection; **legìttima** ~ self-defence

difett|ivo defective; **~o** *m* defect; lack; **~o di qc** defect in s.th.; **~oso** imperfect

diffamare *v/t* defame; malign

differen|te different; **~za** *f* difference; **~ziare** *v/t* differentiate

differire *v/t* put off; *v/i* differ

difficile difficult

difficoltà *f* difficulty

diffid|a *f* warning; **~are** *v/t* warn; **~are** *v/i* **di qu** mistrust s.o.; **~enza** *f* suspicion

diffónd|ere *v/t* diffuse; spread; **~ersi** *v/r* expatiate

diff|usione *f* spreading; *radio:* broadcasting; **~uso** widespread; diffuse

difterite *f med* diphteria

diga *f* dike; dam

dige|rìbile digestible; **~rire** *v/t* digest; **~stione** *f* digestion; **~stivo** digestive; **di-sturbo** *m* **~stivo** digestive trouble

digiun|are *v/i* fast; **~o** fasting; hungry

dignit|à *f* dignity; **~oso** dignified

digrad|amento *m* descent by degree; **~are** *v/i* diminish; slope (down); *paint* shade off

digrassare *v/t* scour; skim

dilagare *v/i* inundate; spread

dilat|àbile dilatable; **~are**

v/t expand; **~azione** *f* dilatation

dilett|ante *m, f* amateur; **~are** *v/t* amuse; delight; **~arsi** *v/r* take delight (**di** in); enjoy; **~évole** pleasant

dilig|ente *adj* diligent; **~enza** *f* diligence; stage-coach

diluvi|are *v/i* rain in torrents; **~o** *m* deluge

dimagr|are, ~ire *v/i* grow thin

dimenare *v/t* toss; shake

dimensione *f* dimension; size

dimentic|àggine *f* forgetfulness; **~anza** *f* inadvertence; **~are** *v/t* forget

dimétter|e *v/t* dismiss; remove; **~si** *v/r* resign; quit

dimezzare *v/t* halve

dimin|uire *v/t* diminish; (prices) reduce; **~utivo** *m, adj* diminutive

dimission|are *v/i* resign; **~e** *f* dismissal

dimor|a *f* residence; dwelling; **~are** *v/i* reside; live

dimostr|are *v/t* demonstrate; show; **~ativo** *adj* demonstrative; **~azione** *f* evidence; demonstration

dinàmica *f* dynamics

dinamite *f* dynamite

dìnamo *f* dynamo

dinanzi *prep* in front of; *adv* before; in front; *m* frontpart

dinastìa *f* dynasty

dindo *m* turkey-cock

diniego *m* denial

dinosàuro *m* dinosaur

dintorn|o *prep* around; *adv* round about; *m* outline; **~i** *pl* surroundings *pl*

Dio *m* God; Lord; *pl* **gli dei** the gods; **grazie a ~!** thank God!; **per amor di ~** for God's sake

dipanare *v/t* wind off

dipart|imento *m* department; **~ire** *v/t* divide; **~irsi** *v/r* leave; **~ita** *f* departure

dipend|ente *adj* depending; *m* dependent; subordinate; **~enza** *f* dependence; dependency

dipèndere *v/i* (**da**) depend (upon)

dipingere *v/t* paint; *fig* depict

diploma *m* diploma

diplomàtico *adj* diplomatic; *m* diplomat

diplomazìa *f* diplomacy

dire *v/t* say; tell; **vale a ~** that is (to say); **voler ~** mean; **dico sul serio** I am talking in earnest

dir|ettissimo *m* express train; **~etto** direct; straight; **treno ~etto** *m* fast train; **~ettore** *m* director; manager; editor; principal; **~ettore d'orchestra** conductor; **~ettrice** *f* directress; headmistress; **~ezione** *f* dorection; management; **~igere** *v/t* direct; manage; aim; steem; **~igersi** *v/r* direct one's steps; **~igibile** *adj* dirigible; *m* airship

dirimpetto (**a**) opposite;

facing

dir|itta f right (hand); **~itti** m/pl **d'autore** copyright; **~itto** adj straight; right; m right; law; **a ~ittura** downright; sheer

dirottamente excessively

dirup|ato steep; **~o** m precipice

disabitato uninhabited

disabituare v/t disaccustom

disaccordo m disagreement; discord

disadatto unfit (for)

disaffezionare v/t estrange

disagévole uneasy

disagi|ato uncomfortable; **~o** m discomfort

disappetenza f lack of appetite

disapprov|are v/t disapprove; **~azione** f disapproval

disarm|are v/t disarm; **~o** m disarmament

disar|monia f disharmony; **~mònico** disharmonious

disastro m disaster; debacle; **~so** disastrous

disatten|to inattentive; **~zione** f inattention

disavanzo m deficit

disavvantaggi|are v/t place at a disadvantage; **~o** m disadvantage

disavventura f mishap

disborso m disbursement

discàrico m unloading

discendenza f descent

discéndere v/i descend

discépolo m disciple; pupil

discèrnere v/t discern

discesa f descent; fall; **strada** f **in ~** downhill road

disciògliere v/t melt; dissolve

disciplina f discipline

disco m disk; discus; record; **~o microsolco** long-playing record; **~òbolo** m discus thrower

disconóscere v/t slight; repudiate

disc|ordanca f disagreement; **~òrdia** f discord

disc|órrere v/i talk; chat; **~orso** m speech; talk

discost|are v/t remove; **~o** distant

discreto discreet; moderate; fair; **~ezione** f discretion

discrimin|are v/t discriminate; **~azione** f discrimination

discussione f discussion

discùtere v/t discuss; argue

disdegn|are v/t disdain; **~ato** angry

disdegno m contempt; scorn; **~so** scornful

disdetta f notice; fig misfortune

disd|ire v/t cancel; **~irsi** v/r contradict o.s.

disegn|are v/t draw; **~o** m drawing; design; fig intention; **~atore** m designer; draftsman

diseredare v/t disinherit

diser|tare v/t, v/i desert; **~tore** m deserter; **~zione** f disertion

dis|fare v/t undo; destroy; disassemble; **~fatta** f defeat

disfida

disfida f challenge

disgrazia f bad luck; accident; **per ~** unfortunately; **~to** adj wretched; unfortunate; m wretch

disgregare v/t disintegrate; dissolve

disgust|are v/t disgust; **~o** m disgust; **~oso** disgusting

disillusione f disappointment

disimparare v/t unlearn; forget

disinf|ettante m disinfectant; **~ettare** v/t disinfect; **~ezione** f disinfection

disinteressato disinterested

disinvolt|o free and easy; **~ura** f ease (of manners)

dismisura f excess

disobbedire = **disubbidire**

disoccupa|to out of work; unemployed; **~zione** f unemployment

disonest|à f dishonesty; **~o** dishonest

dison|orare v/t dishonour; **~ore** m disgrace; shame

disopra: al ~ di above

disordinare v/t disorder; confuse

disórdine m disorder; litter

disotto under; beneath; **al ~ di** below

dispaccio m dispatch; telegram

disparere m dissension

dispari odd; uneven

disparire v/i disappear

disparte: in ~ aside; apart

dispendio m expense; **~so** costly

dispensa f distribution; exemption; pantry

dispensare v/t exempt

dispepsia f dyspepsia

disper|ar(si) v/i (v/r) di despair of; **~ato** desperate; **~azione** f despair

dis|pèrdere v/t disperse; break up; **~persione** f dispersion

dispetto m spite; vexation; **a ~ di** in spite of; despite; **~so** spiteful

dispiac|ente sorry; **~ere** v/i be sorry; mind; I regret; trouble; **mi ~e** I am sorry; **~évole** unpleasant

disponibile available

disp|orre v/t dispose (di of); arrange; **~osizione** f arrangement; disposition (a for); **méttere a ~osizione di qu.** place at s.o's disposal; **~osto** inclined (a to)

disprezz|are v/t despise; **~o** m contempt; scorn

disputa f dispute

disput|àbile questionable; **~are** v/i dispute; argue; **~arsi** v/r qc. contend for s.th.

dissenso m dissent

dissenteria f dysentery

disserrare v/t unlock

dissertazione f dissertation

disservizio m bad service

dissetare v/t quench one's thirst

dissid|ente adj dissenting; m dissident; **~io** m dissension

dissìmile unlike

dissimul|are v/t dissemble; conceal; **~azione** f dissimulation

dissip|are v/t dissipate; squander; **~azione** f dissipation

dissociare v/t dissociate

dissol|ùbile dissoluble; **~uzione** f dissolution

dissolvente: **~** m **dello smalto** nail polish remover

dissòlvere v/t dissolve; decompose

dissomigli|ante unlike; **~anza** f unlikeness

disson|ante dissonant; **~anza** f dissonance; discord; **~are** v/i be out of tune

dissuadere v/t dissuade

distacc|amento m detaching; **~are** v/t detach; separate; **~o** m separation

dist|ante distant; far; **~anza** f distance; **~are** v/i be distant

distèndere v/t extend; stretch out

distensione f stretching; relaxation

distesa f extension

distillare v/t destill

distìnguere v/t distinguish

distinguìbile distinguishable

distint|a f list; note; **con ~i saluti** yours sincerely; **~o** distinct; distinguished

distinzione f distinction

distorsione f distortion

distr|arre v/t distract; divert; **~azione** f distraction

distretto m district; **~ mili-**

tare military district

distribu|ìre v/t distribute; **~tore** m **automàtico** slot-machine; **~tore di benzina** petrol station; **~zione** f distribution; (mail) delivery

distr|ùggere v/t destroy; **~uzione** f destruction

disturb|are v/t disturb; **~o** m trouble; disturbance; **~i** m/pl **circolatori** circulatory disturbance

disubbid|iente disobedient; **~ienza** f disobedience; **~ire** v/i disobey

disugu|aglianza f inequality; **~ale** unequal

disumano inhuman

disunione f discord

dis|uso m disuse; **~ùtile** useless

dit|ale m thimble; fingerstall; **~o** m finger; **~o (del piede)** toe

ditta f firm; company

dittàfono m dictaphone

ditta|tore m dictator; **~tura** f dictatorship

diurno diurnal; daily

diva f famous singer; diva

divagare v/i ramble; digress

divano m divan; sofa

diven|ìre v/i, **~tare** v/i become

di|vergenza f divergence; disagreement; **~vèrgere** v/i diverge; branch off

diversione f diversion; deviation; **~o** different

divert|ente amusing; **~imento** m amusement; hobby; recreation; **buon ~i-**

divertirsi

mento! have a good time!; **~irsi** v/r enjoy o.s.

divezz|are v/t wean; **~o** weaned

dividere v/t divide; separate

divieto m prohibition; **~ di parcheggio** no parking; **~ di sorpasso** no overtaking; **~ di sosta** no stopping

divin|are v/t foresee; foretell; **~ità** f divinity; **~o** divine; godlike

divis|a f motto; coat of arms; (hair) parting; uniform; **~e** f/pl foreign exchange; currency; **~ibile** divisible; **~ione** f division (mil); separation

divor|are v/t devour; eat up

divorzi|arsi v/r be divorced; **~o** m divorce

dizionario m dictionary

do I give

dobbiamo we must

doccia f shower

docente m, f teacher; lecturer

dòcile docile; submissive

docum|entare v/t document; **~entario** m documentary (film); **~entazione** f documentation; **~ento** m document; **~ento** m **personale** identification (paper); **~enti** m/pl **d'automobile** car documents

dodicèsimo twelfth

dogan|a f customs pl; costom-house; **soggetto a ~a** liable to duty; **controllo** m **~ale** customs examination; **guardia** f **~ale** cus-

toms agent; **~iere** m customs officer

dogli|a f pain; ache; **~anza** f complaint

dolc|e adj sweet; soft; mild; m sweetmeat; **~i** m/pl sweets pl

dolc|ezza f sweetness; mildness; **~ificare** v/t sweeten

doll|ente aching; grieved; **èssere ~ente** be sorry; **~ere** v/i ache; regret; **~ersi** v/r complain (**di** about)

dòllaro m dollar

Dolomiti f/pl Dolomites

dolor|e m pain; grief; sorrow; **~oso** painful; grievous

domanda f question; request; application

domandare v/t ask; demand; inquire; **~ a qu.** ask s.o.; **~ di qu.** ask about s.o.; **~ un favore a qu.** ask a favour of s.o.; **~ perdono** beg pardon

domani tomorrow; **~ l'altro** day after tomorrow; **~ sera** tomorrow evening; **~ a otto** tomorrow week

domare v/t tame; subdue

domattina tomorrow morning

domènica f Sunday

do|mèstica f (house-)maid; **~mesticare** v/t tame; **animale** m **~mèstico** domestic animal

domicili|ato resident; **~o** m residence

domin|ante dominant; **~are** v/t dominate; **~io** m rule; dominion

dunque

don|are v/t give; present; **~atore** m donor; **~azione** f donation; gift

donde whence; from where

dondolare v/t, v/i rock; sway

dòndolo m pendulum

dondoloni, (a ~) idly

donna f woman; (card-playing) queen; **~ di servizio** maid

dono m gift; present

donzella f maiden

dopo prep after; adv afterwards; **~domani** day after tomorrow; **~chè** since

dopo|guerra m post-war period; **~pranzo** m afternoon

doppi|are v/t double; film: dub; **~o** double; **~one** m duplicate

dor|are v/t gild; **~ato** gilt; golden

dòrico Doric; Dorian

dorm|iente sleeping; **~icchiare** v/i slumber; **~iglione** m sleepyhead; **~ire** v/i sleep; **~itorio** m dormitory

dors|ale spina: **~ale** backbone; spinal chord; **~o** m back

dos|are v/t dose; **~e** f dose

dosso m back

dot|are v/t endow; **~azione** f endowment; outfit; **~e** f dowry

dotto adj learned; m scholar

dottor|a f bluestocking; **~grado** m **~ale** doctoral degree; **~e** (abbr dott.) m doctor; physician; **~essa** f woman doctor

dottrina f doctrine; learning; eccl catechism

dove where

dover|e v/i ought to; have to; must; should; v/t owe; m duty; **~oso** dutiful

dovizi|a f abundance; **~oso** rich

dovunque wherever; anywhere

dovuto due; owing

dozzina f dozen

draga f dredge

drago, ~ne m dragon

dramm|a m drama; **~àtico** dramatic; **~aturgo** m playwright

drappeggiare v/t drape

dràstico drastic

drog|a f spice; drug; **~are** v/t spice; drug

droghe|ria f, m drug-store; chemist's shop; **~iere** m chemist

dubbio m doubt; **mèttere qc. in ~** doubt s.th.; **~so** doubtful; uncertain

dubit|àbile open to doubt; **~are** v/i doubt; distrust

duc|a m duke; **~hessa** f duchess

duce m (Fascist) leader

due two; **a ~ a ~** two by two; **tutt'e ~** both; **~ parole** a few words

duell|are v/i fight a duel; **~o** m duel

duetto m duet

duna f dune; down

dunque then; therefore; well

duomo *m* cathedral

duplic|are *v/t* double; **~ato** *m* duplicate; **~ato** *m* duplicate

dùplice twofold; double

duplo double

dur|ante during; **~are** *v/i* last; hold out; **~ata** *f* duration; durability; **~ata di volo** flying time

durévole lasting

durezza *f* hardness; severity; **~o** hard; harsh; **~o d'orecchi** hard of hearing

E

e and; **e ... e ...** both

è he is; **(Lei) ~** *polite form* you are

èbano *m* ebony

ebbe he had

ebbene well then

èbbero they had

ebbi I had

ebr|àico Hebraic; Jewish; **~aismo** *m* Hebraism

ebre|a *f* Jewess; **~o** *m* Jew

ecc = eccètera et cetera

eccèdere *v/t* exceed; **~** *v/i* in qc. exaggerate s.th.

eccell|ente excellent; **~enza** *f* excellence; **2enza** *(title)* Excellency

eccess|ivo excessive; **~o** *m* excess; intemperance

eccètera and so forth

eccett|o except(ing); **~o te** except you; **~uare** *v/t* except

eccez|ionale exceptional; **~ione** *f* exception; **per ~ione** exceptionally

eccit|ante *adj* exciting; *m* stimulant; **~are** *v/t* excite; stimulate; stir; **~azione** *f* excitement; excitation

ecclesiàstico *adj* clerical; *m* clergyman

ècco look here; here is (are); **~mi** here I am; **~lo** here he is; **èccoti il tuo libro** here you have your book

echeggiare *v/i* echo; resound

eco *f* echo

eco|nomìa *f* economics *pl*; economy; thrift; **fare ~nomìa** save; **~nomìa polìtica** economics; **~nòmico** economic(-al); thrifty; **~nomista** *m/f* economist; **~nomizzare** *v/t* economize; save

ecònomo *m* treasurer; bursar

eczema *m* eczema

ed = e *(before vowels)*

èdera *f* ivy

edìcola *f* news-stand; kiosk

edific|are *v/t* build (up)

edifi|cio *m*, **~zio** *m* building; edifice

edit|ore *m* editor; publisher; **casa** *f* **~rice** publishing house

editto *m* edict

editoriale editorial

edizione *f* edition

educ|are *v/t* bring up; educate; **~ato** well-bred; **~a-**

zione f education; training; manners

effervescente effervescent

effett|ivo real; actual; **~o** m effect; **con ~o cambiario** bill of exchange; **fare un grande ~o** create a sensation; **mandare ad ~o, ~uare** v/t carry out

effic|ace effective; **~acia** f efficacy; effectiveness

effici|ente efficient; **~enza** f efficiency

effig|(i)e f effigy; image

effóndere v/t pour out

effusione f effusion; shedding

Egitto m Egypt

egiziano m, adj Egyptian

egli he

ego|ismo m selfishness; **~ista** m, f ego(t)ist; adj selfish

egregio distinguished; ♀ **signore!** Dear Sir!

eguagli|amento m equalization; **~anza** f equality; **~are** v/t make equal

eguale equal; alike

elabor|are v/t work out; **~atezza** f elaborateness

elasticità f elasticity

elàstico m, adj elastic

elefante m elephant

eleg|ante elegant; smart; **~anza** f elegance

elèggere v/t elect; appoint (**a** to)

element|are elementary; **scuola ~entare** elementary school; **~ento** m element; **~enti** pl principles pl

elemòsina f alms pl

elemosinare v/i beg for alms

elenco m list; catalogue; inventory; **~ degli indirizzi** address directory; **~ telefònico** telephone directory

elett|a f choice; selection; **~o** chosen; **~ore** m elector; **~rice** f electress

elettricista m electrician

elettricità f electricity

elèttrico electric(al)

elettr|izzare v/t electrify; **~izzazione** f electrization

elettro m amber; **~domèstici** m/pl electric household appliances; **~motrice** m railcar; **~tècnica** f electrical engineering; **~tècnico** m electrical engineer

elev|are v/t raise; lift; **~atezza** f loftiness; nobleness; **~ato** elevated; fig noble; **~azione** f elevation

elezione f election

èlica f screw; propeller

elicòttero m helicopter

elimin|are v/t eliminate; **~azione** f elimination; exclusion

ella she

elmo m helmet

elogi|are v/t praise; **~o** m praise; eulogy

eloqu|ente eloquent; **~enza** f eloquence

eman|are v/i emanate; **~azione** f emanation

emancip|are v/t emancipate; **~azione** f emancipation

embargo m embargo

emblema m emblem; badge

embrione m embryo

emergenza f emergency

emèrgere v/i emerge

emèrito emeritus

eméttere v/t emit; give out

emicrania f headache

emigr|ante m f emigrant;
~**are** v/i emigrate; ~**ato** m
refugee; ~**azione** f emigration

emin|ente eminent; ~**enza** f
eminence; **Sua ~enza**
(title) His (Your) Eminence

emisfero m hemisphere

emiss|ario m emissary; ~**ione** f emission; **banca** f **di**
~**ione** bank of issue

emoglobina f hemoglobin

emorragia f hemorrhage

emorròidi f/pl hemorrhoids
pl

emostàtico styptic;
staunching

emozione f emotion

émpiere, empìre v/t fill
(up)

empio impious; wicked

empírico empirical

empòrio m trade-centre

emulare v/t emulate

encefalite f encephalitis

enciclopedìa f encyclopaedia

endovenoso intravenous

energìa f energy; ~ **nucleare** nuclear energy

enèrgico energetic; vigorous

ènfasi f emphasis

enigm|a (**enimma**) m riddle; ~**àtico** enigmatic

enorme enormous; huge

ente m per il turismo tourist bureau; tourist office

entrambi both

entrare v/i enter; go in; fig
meddle

entrata f entrance; admittance; income

entro within; in

entusi|asmare v/t enrapture; ~**asmo** m enthusiasm;
rapture; ~**àstico** enthusiastic

enumer|are v/t enumerate;
~**azione** f enumeration

èpic|a f epic; ~**o** epic(al)

epidemìa f epidemic

epidèmico epidemic(al)

epidèrmide f epidermis;
skin

epìgrafe f inscription

epilessìa f epilepsy

episcop|ale episcopal; ~**ato**
m episcopate

epistola f letter; epistle

epitaffio m epitaph

època f epoch

eppure and yet; and still

equatore m equator

equi|àngolo equiangular;
~**librare** v/t balance; equilibrate; ~**librio** m equilibrium; balance; ~**nozio** m
equinox

equipaggi|amento m
equipment; ~**are** v/t equip;
naut fit out; ~**o** m crew

equità f equity

equivalente equivalent

equìvoco adj equivocal; m
misunderstanding

equo equitable; fair

era[1] f era; age

era[2] he was; she was; it was

èrano they were

erava|mo we were; **~te** you were *pl*

erb|a f grass; herb; **~accia** f weed; **~e** f/pl herbs *pl*; vegetables *pl*; **~ivéndolo** m greengrocer

erede m heir; f heiress; **~ità** f inheritance; **~itare** v/t inherit; **~itario** hereditary

erem|ita m hermit; **~itaggio** m hermitage

eresia f heresy

erètico *sdj* heretical; m heretic

erezione f erection

ergàstolo m penitentiary

eri you were (*sg*)

erig|ere v/t erect; found; **~ersi** v/r pretend to be

ermellino m ermine

ermètico hermetic; airtight

ernia f hernia; **cinto m ~ario** truss

ero I was

er|oe m hero; **~òico** heroic(al); **~oìna** f heroine; **~oismo** m heroism

érpice m harrow

err|are v/i rove; err; **~ore** m error; mistake

erta f steep ascent; **stare all'~** be on one's guard

erto steep

erud|ito *adj* learned; m scholar; **~izione** f learning

eruttare v/t eject (*lava*); v/i belch

eruzione f eruption (*volca-*

no); rash

esager|are v/t exaggerate; **~azione** f exaggeration

esal|are v/t, v/i exhale; **~azione** f exhalation

esaltato exalted; exultant

esam|e m examination; **~inare** v/t examine

esangue bloodless

esatt|ezza f exactitude; **~o** exact

esaudire v/t examine

esaurire v/t exhaust; wear out

esca f bait; *fig* allurement

esce he (she) goes out

esclam|are v/t exclaim; **~azione** f exclamation; cry; **punto d'~azione** exclamation mark

esclùdere v/t exclude

esclus|ione f exclusion; **~ivamente** exclusively; **~ivo** exclusive

esco I go out

escoriare v/t excoriate

escursione f excursion; trip

esecutore m executor; **~ (testamentario)** executor (of a will)

esecuzione f execution; *thea* performance

esegu|ibile executable; **~ire** v/t execute; perform

esempio m example; **per ~** for instance

esemplare *adj* exemplary; m pattern; copy

esente exempt; immune; **~ da dogana** duty-free

esèquie f/pl obsequies *pl*; funeral

eserc|ire v/t carry on; run; **~itare** v/t exercise; practise; **~itazione** f practise; drill

esèrcito m army

esercizio m exercise

esib|ire v/t exhibit; offer; **~zione** f exhibition; display

esig|ente exigent; **~enza** f exigence; need

esigere v/t require

esiguo scanty

esili|are v/t exile; **~o** m exile

esistenza f existence; life

esistere v/i exist

esitare v/i hesitate

èsito m issue; result

esòfago m oesophagus

esorbitante exorbitant

esortare v/t exhort

esoso odious

esòtico exotic

espàndere /t expand

espans|ibile expansible; **~ione** f expansion; **~ivo** expansive; fig effusive

espatriare v/i emigrate

espediente m expedient; device

espèllere v/t expel; eject

esper|ienza f experience; **~imentare** v/t experience; try; **~imento** m experiment

esperto adj experienced; m expert

espi|are v/t expiate; atone for; **~atore** m expiator; **~zione** f expiation

espilazione f swindling

espir|are v/i breathe out; **~azione** expiration

esplicito explicit

esplòdere v/t shoot; v/i explode

explor|are v/t explore; investigate; **~atore** m explorer; **~azione** f exploration

explosi|one f explosion; fig outburst; **~vo** explosive

esponente m exponent

esporre v/t expose; display

esport|are v/t export; **~azione** f export(ation)

esposimetro m light-meter

esposizione f exposition; show

espress|ione f expression; **~ivo** expressive; **~o** adj explicit; m special delivery; express train; (**caffè**) **~o** express coffee; **per ~o** by express

esprimere v/t express; utter

espropri|are v/t expropriate; **~azione** f expropriation

espugnare v/t conquer

espulsione f expulsion

ess|a she; **~e** f/pl they

essenz|a f essence; gasoline; **~iale** adj essential; m main point

èssere v/i be; **~ di qu.** belong to s.o.; m being

essi m/pl they

esso he; it

est m east; **all'~ di** east of

èstasi f ecstasy; rapture

estasiarsi v/r be enraptured

estate m summer

estemporàneo unprepared

estènd|ere v/t extend; **~ersi** v/r stretch

esten|sione f extension; **~si-vo** extensive

estenuare v/t extenuate; weaken

esteriore m, adj exterior

esterminare v/t exterminate

esterno adj external; m outside

èster|o adj foreign; external; **ministro m degli (affari) ~i** Foreign Secretary; Secretary of the State; m foreign country; **all'~o** abroad

estètic|a f aesthetics; **~o** aesthetic(al)

èstimo m valuation

est|inguere v/t extinguish; **~inguersi** v/r die (out)

estintore m fire-extinguisher

estivo estival; summer ...

estradizione f extraction

estràneo adj strange; m stranger

estr|arre v/t extract; draw (lots); **~atto m** extract; abstract; **~atto di conto** statement of account

estr|emità f extremity; end; **~emo** extreme

estroverso m extrovert

esuberante exuberant

èsule m exile

esultare v/i rejoice

età f age; **~ massima** maximum age

ètere m ether

etern|ità f eternity; **~o** eternal; **in ~o** for ever

ètica f ethics

etichetta f label; etiquette

èttaro m hectare (2.47 acres)

ett|o m hectogram; **~òlitro m** hectolitre

Europ|a f Europe; **~eo m**, adj European

eucalitto m eucalyptus

eunuco m eunuch

eutanasia f euthanasia

E. V. = Eccellenza (Eminenza) Vostra

evacu|are v/t evacuate; **~a-zione f** evacuation

evàdere v/t dispatch; v/i escape

evangelista m evangelist

evaporarsi v/r evaporate

evasione f evasion; escape

evento m event

eviden|te obvious; **~za f** evidence; clearness

evitare v/t avoid

evviva! hurrah! long live

extra extra

F

F = **freddo** (on water taps) cold

fa he (she) does; **3 anni ~ 3** years ago

fàbbrica f factory

fabbric|ante m manufacturer; **~are v/t** manufacture; build; **~ato m** make; building; **~atore m** manufacturer; **~azione f** manufacture

fabbro m (blacks)smith; ~

ferraio locksmith

faccenda f business; matter

facchinaggio m rail porterage; fig drudgery

facchino m porter

faccia f face; appearance; **di ~** opposite; **~mo** we do; **~ta** f facade; front

faccio I do

fac|eto witty; **~ezia** f joke; witticism

fàcile easy; **~ a crèdere** credulous

facil|ità f facility; **~itare** v/t facilitate; **~itazione** f facility

facol|tà f faculty; authority; **~tativo** optional

facond|ia f eloquence; **~o** eloquent

fascimile m fasimile

faggio m beech(-tree)

fagiano m pheasant

fagi|olini m/pl French beans; **~uolo** m bean

fagotto m bundle; mus bassoon

falcat|o hooked; **luna** f **~a** sickle moon

falce f scythe; sickle

fal|ciare v/t mow; **~ciatore** m mower; **~ciatrice** f mowing-machine

falco m hawk; **~ne** m falcon

fald|a f fold; layer; (snow) flake; (hat) brim; geog slope; **~oso** in flakes

falegn|ame m carpenter; **~ameria** f carpentry

fall|ibile fallible; **~imento** m bankruptcy; failure; **~ire** v/i fail; go bankrupt; **~ito**

unsuccessful; **~o** m fault;

senza ~o without fail

fals|a¦moneta m forger; **~are** v/t alter; forge; **~ariga** f sheet of ruled paper

falò m bonfire

falsific|are v/t adulterate; **~azione** f falsification

fals|ità f falsity; **~o** false; counterfeit

fama f fame; reputation

fame f hunger; **aver ~** be hungry

famigli|a f family; **~are** familiar; acquainted; **~arità** f familiarity

famoso famous

fanal|e m lamppost; lighthouse; auto: (head)light; **~e òttico** headlight flasher; **~e posteriore** auto: taillight; **~i** m/pl **d'arresto** stoplight

fanalino m **di posizione** auto: parking light; **~ stop** stop light

fanàtico adj fanatic(al); m fanatic

fanatizzare v/t fanaticize

fanciull|a f girl; maiden; **~ezza** f childhood; **~o** m young boy

fanfara f fanfare

fang|o m dirt; mud; **~hi** m/pl mud-bath; **~oso** muddy

fant|asia f fancy; imagination; **di ~asia** fancy; **~asma** m phantom; ghost; **~asticare** v/i fancy; day-dream; **~asticheria** f daydream; **~àstico** fantastic

fant|e m mil infantryman; **~eria** f infantry; **~ino** m

fegato

jockey
fardello m burden
far|**e** v/t make; do; **~e a meno di** go without; **~e finta di** pretend to; **~e il mèdico** be a physician; **~e il pieno** refuel; **~si** v/r become; **sul ~si del giorno** at daybreak
farfalla f butterfly
farin|**a** f flour; **~ata** f porridge
faringite f pharyngitis
farinoso floury; mealy
farmac|**ia** f pharmacy; **~ista** m, f chemist; pharmacist
faro m light; lighthouse; **~ (abbagliante)** full (headlight) beam
farsa f farce
fascetta f corset
fasci|**a** f band; swaddle; **sotto ~a** under cover; **~are** v/t wrap; bandage; swaddle; **~atura** f surg dressing
fascicolo m issue; number (of a periodical)
fascinare v/t fascinate
fàscino m charm; fascination
fascio m bundle; **andare in ~** go to pieces
fascis|**mo** m fascism; **~ta** m, f, adj fascist
fase f phase; stage
fast|**idio** m annoyance; trouble; **dare ~idio a qu.** give trouble to s.o.; **~idioso** tiresome
fasto m pomp
fat|**a** f fairy; **~ale** fatal; **~alità** f fatality; **~are** v/t bewitch

fatic|**a** f labour; trouble; **~are** v/i toil; **~arsi** v/r exert s.o.; **~oso** fatiguing; hard
fato m fate; destiny
fatto adj done; m deed; fact; act(ion); **sul ~** in the very act; **di ~** in fact
fatt|**ore** m factor; creator; **~oria** f farm; homestead; **~orino** m messenger (boy); **~ura** f invoice; bill
fàtuo fatuous; silly
fausto happy; lucky
fautore m favourer
fàvola f fable
favol|**oso** fabulous
favore m favour; kindness; **per ~** please; **fare un ~** do a favour; **prezzo di ~** special price
favor|**eggiare** v/t favour; **~évole** favourable; **~ire** v/t favour; **~ito** adj favoured; m favourite
fazzoletto m handkerchief; **~ da collo** neckerchief; **~ di carta** tissue handkerchief
febbraio m (abbr febb) February
febbr|**e** f fever; **~icitante** feverish; **~ile** febrile
fècola f starch
fecond|**ità** f fertility; **~o** fertile
fede f faith; belief; wedding-ring; **prestar ~** give credit (to); **le faithful**; **~ltà** f faithfulness; allegiance
fèdera f pillow-case
feder|**ale** federal; **~ato** federerate; **~azione** f federation
fégato m liver; fig courage

fel|ice happy; **~icità** *f* happiness

felicit|are *v/t* congratulate; **~azione** *f* congratulation

felpa *f* plush

feltro *m* felt

felza *f* gondola's cabin

fémmina *f biol* female

femmin|esco womanly; womanish; **~ile: scuola** *f* **~ile** school for girls

fémore *m* thigh

fèndere *v/t* cleave; split

fenditura *f* cleft

fènico carbolic

fenicòttero *m* flamingo

fenòmeno *m* phenomenon

feri|a *f* holiday; **~e** *f/pl* vacation; **~ale: giorno** *m* **~ale** working day

fer|ire *v/t* wound; hurt; **~ita** *f* wound; **~ita di taglio** cut; **~ito** *adj* wounded; injured; *m* wounded person

ferma! stop!

fermaglio *m* clip; brooch; **~ dentario** brace

ferm|are *v/t, v/i* stop; arrest; fix (a on); **~arsi** *v/r* stop; halt; **~ata** *f* **a richiesta, ~ata facoltativa** optional stop; **~ata obbligatoria** obligatory stop; sojourn; *mus* pause

ferment|are *v/i* ferment; **~azione** *f* fermentation

fermezza *f* firmness; steadiness

ferm|o firm; steady; still; **~ terra** *f* **~a** land; **per ~o** positively; **~o posta** poste restante

fer|oce wild; ferocious; **~o-cia** *f* ferocity

ferraio *m* blacksmith

ferr|ame *m* iron ware; **~are** *v/t* shoe; **~o** *m* iron; tool; horseshoe; **~o da stiro** flatiron; **ai ~i** *gast* grilled; roasted

ferrovia *f* railway; railroad; **~ sotterrànea** underground railway; tube

ferroviere *m* railway-man

fèrtile fertile

fertil|ità *f* fertility; **~izzare** *v/t* fertilize

fèrvere *v/i* be fervent

fèrvido fervid; ardent

fervore *m* fervour

fessura *f* fissure; crack

fest|a *f* holiday; feast; **buone ~e** *f/pl* happy holidays; **~a nazionale** public holiday; **~a religiosa** festive day

fest|eggiare *v/t* celebrate; **~ival** *m* festival; **~ivo, ~oso** festive; **giorno ~ivo** holiday

feto *m* foetus

fetta *f* slice

feudalismo *m* feudalism

fiaba *f* dairy tale

fiacc|are *v/t* break down; tire out; **~hezza** *f* lassitude

fiàccola *f* torch

fiamm|a *f* flame; blaze; *naut* pennant; **~eggiare** *v/i* flame; **~ifero** *m* match

fianc|are *v/t* support; **~o** *m* side; flank; **di ~o a** beside; abreast of

fiaschetteria *f* wine-shop

fiasco *m* bottle; *fig* fiasco;

failure

fiat|are v/i breathe; **~o** m
  breath; **senza ~o** fig
  speechless; **tutto d'un ~o**
  all in one breath

fibbia f buckle

fibr|a f fibre; **~oso** fibrious

fico m fig(-tree)

fidanz|amento m betrothal;
  engagement; **~are** v/t be-
  troth; **~arsi** v/r become
  engaged; **~ata** f fiancée;
  ~ato m fiancé

fid|are v/i confide; trust;
  ~arsi v/r di qu. rely upon
  s.o.; **~arsi di fare qc.** dare
  to do s.th.

fido adj faithful; m credit

fiducia f confidence; trust

fiele mgall; **vescica del ~**
  gall-bladder

fien|agione f hay-harvest;
  ~o m hay

fiera f wild beast; fair; **~
  campionaria** industrial
  exhibition

fier|ezza f fierceness; pride;
  ~o fierce; proud

figgere v/t fix; stick

figli|a f daughter; **~astra** f
  step-daughter; **~astro** m
  step-son; **~occia** f god-
  daughter; **~occio** m god-
  son; **~uola** f daughter;
  ~uolo m son

figura f figure; shape

figur|àbile imaginable; **~
  are** v/t represent; **~arsi** v/r
  imagine; suppose; **~ato** figurative

fila f line; row; **fare la ~**
  queue up; **in ~ indiana** in

Indian file

filanda f spinning-mill

filàntropo m philantropist

filare v/t spin; v/i run

filatelìa f philately

filetto m fillet

film m film; **~ giallo** mys-
  tery movie; **~ a colori** coloured picture; **~ muto**
  silent film; **~ sonoro**
  sound-film; **girare un ~**
  shoot a film

filo m thread; yarn; **~ conduttore** lead-in-wire; **~ da
  cucire** sewing-cotton; **~ di
  ferro** iron (or steel) wire

filobus m trolley-bus

filòlogo m philologist

filoso stringy

filosofìa f philosophy

filòsofo m philosopher

filtr|are v/t filter; strain; **~o**
  m filter

filugello m silk-worm

filza f string; file

final|e final; **~ità** f finality;
  purpose; **~mente** finally; at
  last

finanze f/pl finances; **~iare**
  v/t finance; **~iario** financial

finché until; as long as

fine adj fine; thin; m purpose; f end; **in ~** at last

finestr|a f window; **~ino** m
  small window

finezza f daintiness; polite-
  ness

fing|ere v/t, v/i pretend;
  simulate; **~ersi** v/r feign

finire v/t finish; end

fino adj fine; thin; prep
  until; **~ a** till; up to; as far

as; ~ **a quando?** how long?; ~ **da** ever since; ~ **dove?** how far?

finocchio *m* fennel

finora up to now

fint|a *f* feint; **~o** feigned; false; pretended

fiocc|are *v/i* snow; **~o** *m* knot; (snow-)flake

fiocina *f* harpoon

fioco weak

fior|aio *f* florist; **~e** *m* flower; **~entino** *m* Florentine; **~icultura** *f* floriculture; **~ire** *v/i* blossom; bloom; *fig* flourish; **~itura** *f* bloom

Firenze *f* Florence

firm|a *f* signature; **~are** *v/t* sign; **~atario** *m* signer

fisarmònica *f* accordion

fischi|are *v/i* whistle; *v/t* hoot down; **~erellare** *v/i*, *v/t* whistle softly; **~o** *m* whistle; hiss

fisco *m* exchequer

fisic|a *f* physics *pl*; **~o** *adj* physical; *m* physicist; *anat* physique

fisioterapia *f* physiotherapy

fiss|aggio *m* fixing-bath; **~are** *v/t* fix; determine; **~are qu.** stare at s.o.; *phot* fix

fisso fixed; firm; steady

fitt|a *f* stitch; **~e** *f/pl* al **fianco** stitches in the side; **~o** *adj* thick; dense; *m* rent; **~izio** fictitious

fiume *m* river; *fig* flow

fiutare *v/t* sniff; smell

flagell|are *v/t* scourge; whip; **~o** *m* scourge

flagrante flagrant; **in ~** (*be caught*) in the very act

flanella *f* flannel

flaut|ista *m*, *f* flutist; **~o** *m* flute

flemmàtico phlegmatic

fless|ìbile flexible; **~ione** *f* flexion; **~uoso** supple

flirtare *v/i* flirt

flòrido flourishing

floscio flabby

flotta *f* fleet; **~ aèrea** airfleet

flùido fluid; fluent

fluire *v/i* flow

flusso *m* flux; *naut* floodtide; *med* discharge

flutt|o *m* wave; **~uare** *v/i* fluctuate; float

fluviale fluvial

fobia *f* phobia

foca *f* seal

focaccia *f* cake

foce *f* river-mouth

fochista *m* fireman

focol|aio, **~are** *m* fire-place

focoso fiery

fòdera *f* lining; cover

foderare *v/t* line

fòdero *m* sheath (*sword*)

fogli|a *f* leaf; **~a laminata** foil; **~ame** *m* foliage; **~o** *m* sheet (*paper*)

folata *f* puff; **~ di vento** gust of wind

folclore *m* folklore

folgorare *v/t* flash

fólgore *m* thunderbolt

folla *f* crewd; throng

follare *v/t* press

foll|e *adj* mad; *m* madman; **~ìa** *f* madness

folto *adj* thick; *m* thickness

fomentare *v/t* foment; *fig* excite

fondaccio *m* dregs *pl*

fondament|ale fundamental; **~o** *m* foundation; ground; **le ~a** *pl* foundations *pl*

fond|are *v/t* found; establish; **~arsi** *v/r* rely on; **~tore** *m* founder; **~azione** *f* foundation

fóndere *v/t*, *v/i* melt; (*ore*) smelt

fond|eria *f* foundry; **~itore** *m* caster

fondo *adj* deep; *m* bottom; background; *com* fund; *naut* **dar ~** come to anchor; **a ~** thoroughly

font|ana *f* fountain; **~e** *f* source

forare *v/t* pierce; drill

foratura *f* puncture

fòrbici *f/pl* scissors *pl*; **~ per le unghie** nail scissors

forbire *v/t* polish; clean

for|ca *f* (hay-)fork; **~cella** *f* (bicycle-)fork; **~chetta** *f* fork; **~cina** *f* hairpin

forense forensic

foresta *f* forest

forestiero *adj* foreign; *m* foreigner

forma *f* form; shape; mould

formaggio *m* cheese; **~ grattugiato** grated cheese

form|ale formal; **~alità** *f* formality; **~are** *v/t* form; **~ato** *m* shape; size; **~azione** *f* formation; **~ella** *f* block; briquette

formic|a *f* ant; **~aio** *m* anthill

formidàbile dreadful

fòrmula *f* formula

formul|are *v/t* formulate; **~ario** *m* formulary

forn|aio *m* baker; **~ello** *m* kitchen stove; **~ello a spirito** spirit-stove

forn|ire *v/t* supply; **~irsi** *v/r* provide o.s. (**di** with); **~itore** *m* tradesman; **~itura** *f* supply; equipment

forno *m* oven

foro *m* hole; law-court; forum

forse perhaps

forte strong; hard; **parlare ~** speak aloud

fort|ezza *f* strenght; fortress; **~ificare** *v/t* strengthen; fortify; **~ificazione** *f* fortification

fortùito accidental

fortuna *f* fortune; luck; **~tamente** fortunately; **~to** lucky

forùncolo *m* boil; furuncle

forz|a *f* strength; force; **le ~e** *f/pl* the (armed) forces; **~are** *v/t* force; compel

fòsforo *m* phosphorus

fossa *f* pit; ditch; **~to** *m* ditch

fossetta *f* dimple

foste you were (*pl*)

fosti you were (*sg*)

fotocromìa *f* chromophotography

fotogènico photogenic

fotograf|are *v/t* photograph; **~ìa** *f* photography

fotògrafo *m* photographer

fototipìa f phototypy

fra among; between; within; **~ di noi** between ourselves; **~ poco** soon

fracasso m uprear

fradicezza f rottenness

fràdicio soaked; rotten

fràgile brittle; fragile

fràgola f strawberry

fragor|e m crashing noise; **~oso** noisy

fragr|ante fragrant; **~anza** f fragrance

fraintèndere v/t misunderstand

frammento m fragment

fran|a f landslide; **~are** v/i collapse

francare v/t stamp (letter)

francese adj French; m Frenchman

franch|ezza f frankness; **~igia** f free postage

Francia f France

franco adj free; outspoken; m franc; **~ svizzero** Swiss Franc; **~bollo** m stamp

frangenti m/pl breakers pl

fràngere v/t break; crush

frangetta f fringe

frant|oio m oil-press; **~umare** v/t shatter; smash; **~umi** m/pl splinters

frase f phrase; gram sentence

fràssino m ash-tree

frastornare v/t divert; interrupt

frastuono m noise

frate (abbr **fra**) m friar

fratell|anza f brotherhood; **~astro** m step-brother; **~o**

m brother

fratern|ità f fraternity; **~o** brotherly

frat|tanto meanwhile; **nel ~tempo** m meantime; **frata d'un osso** fracture of a bone; **~are** v/t fracture

fraudare v/t defraud

frazion|are v/t divide; split; **nùmero** m **~ario** fractional number; **~e** f fraction

freccia f arrow; **~ di direzione** auto: direction-indicator

fredd|arsi v/r become cold; **~o** adj cold; m cold; **aver ~o** be cold; **far ~o** be cold (weather); **~oloso** chilly

freg|agione f friction; **~are** v/t rub; fig cheat; **~arsene** not to care a rap

frèm|ere v/i quiver; **~ito** m shudder

frenare v/t restrain; v/i apply the brake

freno m bridle; restraint; mech brake; **~ a disco** disc brake; **~ a mano** handbrake; **~ a pedale** footbrake; **~ d'allarme** emergencybrake; **~ ad aria compressa** air brake; **~ contropedale** backpedalling brake

frequ|entare v/t frequent; **~ente** frequent; **~enza** f attendance

freschezza f freshness

fresco adj fresh; cool; m coolness

frett|a f haste; **in ~a e furia** in a hurry; **~oloso** hurried

frìggere v/t fry

frigorìfero m refrigerator

fringuello m (chaf)finch

fritt|ata f omelet; **~ella** f fritter; pancake; **~o** fried; **~ura** f fry

frìvolo frivolous

frizione f friction; rubbing; auto clutch

frod|are v/t cheat; defraud; **~atore** m swindler; **~e** f fraud; **~o** m smuggling; **~olento** fraudulent

froge f/pl nostrils pl

froll|are v/t soften; **~o** tender

fronte f forehead; m (also mil) front; **di ~** opposite; in comparison (with)

front|iera f frontier; **~one** m pediment

frugare v/t search

frull|are v/t whisk; **~ino** m whisk

frum|ento m wheat; **~entone** m corn

frust|a f whip; **~are** v/t whip

frustrazione f frustration

frutt|a f fruit; **le ~a** f/pl dessert; **~a cotta** stewed fruit; **~are** v/t, v/i bear fruit; pay; **~eto** m orchard; **àlbero ~ìfero** fruit-bearing tree; **~ivéndolo** m fruiterer; **~o** m fruit; **~i** m/pl fruits pl; **~i di mare** marine products; **~uoso** fruitful

fu he was

fucil|are v/t shoot; **~ata** f shot; **~e** m gun; rifle

fucin|a f smithy; forge; **~are** v/t forge

fuga f escape; flight

fuggévole fleeting; fugitive; **~ire** v/i flee

fui I was

fulgente shining

fulìggine f soot

fuligginoso sooty

fulminare v/i lighten

fùlmine m lightning

fum|aiuolo m chimney-pot; **~are** v/t, v/i smoke; **~atore** m smoker; **scompartimento m per (non) ~atori** (non-) smoking-compartment

fumett|o m comic strip; **giornalino a ~i** comic book

fummo we were

fum|o m smoke; **~oso** smoky

fune f rope

fùnebre funeral; **carro m ~** hearse; **messa f ~** funeral mass

funerale m funeral

fungo m mushroom; fungus

funicolare f cable-railway

funivìa f cable-railway

funzion|are v/i function; work; **~ario** m official

fuoc|o m fire; **~hi** m/pl d'artifìcio fireworks

fuori out(side); **~ di** out of; beyond; **di ~** from outside

fuoruscìto m pol exile

furbo sly

furgoncino m utility van

furgone m van; freight-car

furi|a f fury; rage; hurry; **~bondo, ~oso** furious

fùrono they were

furto m theft; robbery

fuscello m twig

fusìbile *m elec* fuse
fusione *f* melting; cast; *fig* fusion

fuso *m* spindle
fusto *m* shaft; cask
futuro *adj* coming; *m* future

G

gabardine *m* gabardine
gabbia *f* cage; *naut* top-sail
gabbiano *m* sea-gull
gabella *f* tax; duty
gabinetto *m* cabinet; closet
gaggia *f* acacia
gagliardo vigorous
gai|ezza *f* gaiety; **~o** *m* gay
galantuomo *m* gentleman
galeotto *m* galley-slave; convict
galera *f* galley; jail
galla *f* gall; **noce** *f* **di ~** oak-apple
galleggiare *v/i* float
galleria *f* gallery; tunnel; arcade
gàllico Gallic
gallin|a *f* hen; **~accio** *m* turkey-cock; **~aio** *m* vendor of cocks
gallo *m* cock
gallone *m* stripe; gallon
galoppare *v/i* gallop
galvànico galvanic
gamba *f* leg
gàmbero *m* crayfish
gambo *m* stalk; stem
gamma *f* gamut; range
gancio *m* hook
gànghero *m* hinge
gara *f* competition; match; race; **~ finale** the Cup Final
garage *m* garage
garan|te *m* guarantor; **~zìa** *f* guaranty

garb|are *v/i* please; suit; **~ato** polite; **~o** *m* politeness; grace
garbuglio *m* confusion
gareggiare *v/i* compete
gargar|ismo *m* gargle; **~izzare** *v/i* gargle
garòfano *m* carnation; **chiodi** *m/pl* **di ~** clove
garzone *m* shop-boy; apprentice
gas *m* gas; **~òmetro** *m* gasometer; **~osa** *f* sparkling drink
gastrite *f* gastritis
gastronomìa *f* gastronomy
gatt|a *f* (she-)cat; **~ino** *m* kitten; **~o** *m* (tom)cat; **~opardo** *m* leopard
gazza *f* magpie
gazzetta *f* newspaper
G. C. = Gesù Cristo
gel|are *v/i*, **~arsi** *v/r* freeze; be frozen; **~ata** *f* frost; **~atería** *f* ice-cream parlour; **~atina** *f* gelatine; jelly
gelato *adj* frozen; *m* ice-cream; **~ di fràgola** strawberry ice-cream; **~ di frutta** sundae
gèlido icy
gel|o *m* frost; cold; **~one** *m* chilblain
gel|osia *f* jealousy; Venetian blind; **~oso** jealous (**di** of)
gelso *m* mulberry(-tree)

~mino m jasmin

gemell|o m, adj twin; **~i** m/pl twins pl; (cuff-) links pl

gèm|ere v/i groan; moan; **~ito** m moaning

gemma f gem

gener|ale general; **~alità** f/pl personal data pl

gener|are v/t generate; **~atore** m generator; **~azione** f generation

gènere m gender; kind; sort; paint genre; **in ~e** generally; **~i** m/pl alimentari foodstuffs

gènero m son-in-law

gener|osità f generosity; **~oso** generous

genetlìaco m birthday

gengiva f gum

geni|ale bright; ingenious; **~o** m genius

genitivo m genitive

genitori m/pl parents

gennaio m January

Gènova f Genoa

gente f people; **c'è ~** there is s.o.

gentil|e gentle; kind; **~e (~issima) signora!** (dear) madam!; **~ezza** f kindness; **~uomo** m nobleman

genuin|ità f genuineness; **~o** genuine

genziana f gentian

geo|grafìa f geography; **carta** f **~gràfica** map

geometrìa f geometry

geràrio m geranium

ger|ente m manager; **~enza** f management

gergo m slang

gerla f basket

Germàn|ia f Germany; **2ico** Germanic; German

germ|e m germ; **~inare** v/i germinate; **~ogliare** v/i sprout; **~oglio** m sprout

gess|are v/t plaster; **~ino** m plaster figure; **~o** m chalk; plaster; sculpture: plaster cast

gesti|one f management; **~ire** v/i gesticulate; manage; **~o** m gesture

Gesù m Jesus

gesuita m Jesuit

gett|are v/t throw; **~o** m throw; (steam-)jet; **~one** m counter; token

gheriglio m (nut-)kernel

ghiacci|aia f ice-box; **~aio** m glacier; **~are** v/t freeze; **~ata** f iced drink; **~o** adj icecold; m ice

ghiaia f gravel

ghianda f acorn

ghign|are v/i grin; **~ata** f sneer

ghindare v/t hoist

ghiott|o gluttonous; fig greedy; **~oneria** f delicacy

ghirigoro m flourish frills

ghirlanda f garland

ghiro m dormouse

ghisa f cast-iron

già already; formerly

giacca f jacket; **~ a maglia** cardigan; **~ di pelle** leatherjacket

giacché since; as

giacchetta f jacket

giacere v/i lie (down)

giacinto m hyacinth

giada f jade

giaguaro m jaguar

giall|astro yellowish; **~o** yellow

giammai never

Giappone m Japan; **~se** m, f, adj Japanese

giardin|aggio m gardening; **~iera** f woman-gardener; flower-stand; **~iere** m gardener; **~o** m garden; **~o d'infanzia** kindergarten; **~o d'inverno** winter garden; **~i** m/pl pùbblici public parks

gigante m, adj giant; **~esco** gigantic

giglio m lily

gilè m waistcoat

gin m gin

ginecòlogo m gynaecologist

ginepr|a f juniper-berry; **~o** m juniper

ginestra f genista

ginn|asio m gymnasium; grammar school; **~àstica** f gymnastics pl

ginocchio m knee; **stare in ~** kneel; **~ni** kneeling

giocare v/t play; v/i gamble; **~ ai dadi** (play) dice; **~ alle carte, al biliardo** play cards, billiards; **~ d'azzardo** gamble; **~ di denaro** gamble for money

gioc|atore m player; **~àttolo** m toy

gioco m game; play

gioc|ondità f mirth; **~ondo** cheerful

giogo m yoke

gioia f joy

gioi|elliere m jeweller; **~ello** m jewel; **~elli** m/pl jewel-(le)ry

giorn|alaio m newsagent; **~ale** m newspaper; diary; **~ale radio** newscast; **~aliero** daily; **~alista** m, f journalist

giornata f day's work; day's wages

giorno m day; **~ feriale** weekday; workday; **~ festivo** holiday; **sul far del ~** at daybreak; **al ~** daily; **buon ~!** good morning!; **l'altro ~!** the other day; **di ~** by day

giostra f tournament; merry-go-round

gióvane adj young; m young man

giovan|etto m boy; **~ile** juvenile; **~otto** m young man

giovare v/i be of use

giovedì m Thursday

gioventù f youth

gioval|e jolly; **~ità** f joviality

giovinezza f youth

giràbile transferable

giradischi m record-player

giraffa f giraffe

gir|are v/t turn; v/i go about; **mi gira la testa** my head spins; **~ata** f turn; com endorsement

girell|a f revolving disk; **~are** v/i stroll about

giro m turn; tour; walk; **prendere in ~** make fun of; **~ turìstico** sightseeing trip

gita f trip; excursion

gitante m, f excursionist

giù down; below; downstairs; **in ~** downstairs

giubb|a f jacket; coat; **~etto** m di salvataggio life-jacket

giubil|are v/i exult; v/t pension off; **~azione** f retirement

giùbilo m joy

giudic|are v/t judge; **~ato** m judgement

giùdice m judge

giudizio m judgement; opinion; common sense

giugno m June

giument|a f mare; **~o** m beast of burden

giunco m rush; reed

giùngere v/i reach; v/t join; **~ a qc.** arrive at s.th.

giunt|a f surplus; addition; **per ~a** in addition; **~are** v/t join; sew together; **~o** m joint

giuoco = gioco

giuramento m oath; **~ falso** perjury

giurare v/t, v/i swear

giur|ìdico juridical; legal; **~ista** m, f jurist

giusta according to

giust|ezza f justness; **ificare** v/t justify; **~ificazione** f justification; **~izia** f justice; **~o** adj right; lawful; m just man

gl' (before vowel) **= gli**

glaciale icy; **ocèano** m **~** polar sea

gladìolo m gladiolus

glàndola f gland; **~ salivale** salivary gland

glauco sea-green; **~ma** m

glaucoma

gli article m/pl the; pron pers him; it

glicerina f glycerin(e)

globale total

globo m globe; ball; earth; **~ oculare** eyeball; **~so** globose

gloria f glory; fame

glori|are v/t praise; **~arsi** v/r pride o.s.; **~ficare** v/t glorify; **~oso** glorious

glossa f gloss

glòttide f anat glottis

glucosio m glucose

glùtine m gluten; glue

glutinoso glutinous

gnòc|co m dumpling; fig simpleton; **~chi** m/pl small dumplings

gobb|a f hunch; **~o** adj hunchbacked; m hunchback

goc|cia f drop; **~ce** f/pl **per il naso** nose drops

gòcciola f drop

gocciolare v/i drip

godere v/t enjoy

godimento m enjoyment; use (of)

goffo clumsy

gola f throat; gorge; **~ del camino** flue; **mal** m **di ~** sore throat

golf m golf; sweater

golfo m gulf; bay

goloso adj gluttonous; m glutton

gómena f cable; rope

gómito m elbow; fig bend; crank

gomìtolo m ball of a thread

gomm|a f gum; rubber; tire; **~a di scorta** spare tire; **~a lacca** shellac; **~apiuma** f foam rubber; **~a senza càmera d'aria** tubeless tire; **~ato** gummed; **~oso** gummy

góndola f gondola

gondoliere m gondolier

gonfi|are v/t inflate; swell; **~arsi** v/r swell; **~atura** f swelling; fig exaggeration; **~o** swollen; fig conceited

gonn|a f, **~ella** f skirt

gonorrea f gonorrhea

gonzo m simpleton

gorg|o m whirlpool; **~ogliare** v/i gurgle; purl

gorilla m gorilla

gòtico Gothic

gotta f gout

gotto m goblet

gottoso gouty

govern|ante f nurse; governess; **~are** v/t govern; naut steer; **~arsi** v/r control o.s.; **~ativo** governmental; **~atore** m governor; **~o** m government; administration; naut steering

gozzo m crop; med goitre

gracchi|a f crow; **~are** v/i croak

gracidare v/i croak

gràcile delicate

gradazione f gradation

grad|évole pleasant; **~evolezza** f pleasantness; **~imento** m approval

grad|ino m step; **~ire** v/t welcome; like; appreciate; **~ito** agreeable; welcome

grado m degree; rank; **di buon ~** with pleasure; **èssere in ~** di be able to; **di in ~** step by step; **mio mal ~** against my will

graduazione f graduation

graffi|are v/t scratch; **~o** m scratch

grafite f graphite

gramaglia f mourning clothes pl

gramm|a m, **~o** m gram(me)

gramm|àtica f grammar; **~àtico** grammatical; **~òfono** m grammophone

gran = **grande**

gran|a f grain; **~aio** m barn; granary; **~ata** f broom; grenade; pomegranate; **~ato** m garnet

Gran Bretagna f Great Britain

granchio m crab; cramp; fig mistake; **~lino** m small crab; fig blunder

grand|e great; big; **gran tempo** m long time; **~ezza** f greatness

grandin|are v/i hail; **~ata** f hail-storm

gràndine f hail

grandi|osità f grandiosity; **~oso** grandiose

granduc|a m Grand Duke; **~ato** m Grand Duchy

gran|ello m grain; seed; **~oso** seedy; **~o** m wheat; corn; grain

granocchia f frog

granturco m (Indian) corn; maize

guanciale

grapp|a f brandy; clamp; **~ino** m brandy

gràppolo m bunch; cluster

grass|ello m bit of fat; lime; **~o** adj fat; leshy; m fat; grease

grassoccio plump

grat|a f grate; **~ella** f grill; **~iccio** m trellis work; **~icola** f gridiron; **~icolare** v/t grate

gratificare v/t gratify

gratis free; gratis

gratitùdine f gratitude

grato grateful; agreeable

grattacielo m skyscraper

gratt|are v/t scratch; scrape; rasp **~ino** m eraser; **~ugia** f grater

gratùito gratuitous; free

gravare v/t burden; weigh (on)

grav|e heavy; serious; **~ezza** f heaviness; sadness

gràvida pregnant

grav|idanza f pregnancy; **~ità** f gravity; **~itazione** f gravitation; **~oso** irksome

grazi|a f gracefulness; grace; **~e** f/pl thanks pl; **~e!** thank you!; **~e tante** many thanks; **~oso** gracious; lovely

Greci|a f Greece; **2o** m, adj Greek

gregge m herd; flock

gregg|io raw; **materia f ~a** raw material

gremb|iale (**~iule**) m apron; **~o** m lap; bosom

grem|ire v/t fill; **~ito** crowded

greppia f crib; manger

gretto stingy; mean

grid|are v/i shout; scream; **~io** m shouting; **~o** m cry; scream

grifagno ravenous; wild

grifo m snout; **~ne** m griffin

grigio grey

griglia f grate; grill

grignolino m Piedmontese claret

grill|are v/i simmer; **~o** m cricket

grinfia f claw; talon

grinz|a f wrinkle; ripple; **~oso** wrinkled

grond|aia f gutter; **~are** v/i drip; gush

gross|a f gross; **~ezza** f size; bigness; **~ista** m wholesaler; **~o** big; thick; heavy; with child; **mare m ~o** rough sea; **~olano** coarse

grotta f grotto

groviera f Gruyere (cheese)

gru f crane (also mech); **mech** derrick

gruccia f crutch

grugn|ire v/i grunt; **~o** m snout

gruma f tartar (of wine)

gruppo m group

grùzzolo m hoard; savings pl

guadagn|are v/t earn; win; **~o** m earnings pl; gain

guadare v/t wade across

guai! woe!; **~ m/pl** troubles pl

guaio m mishap; trouble; moaning

gualcire v/t crumple

guanci|a f cheek; **~ale** m

pillow
guanto *m* glove
guarda|barriere *m* gate-keeper; **~boschi** *m* forester; woodman; **~caccia** *m* gamekeeper; **~coste** *m* coast guard; **~freni** *m* brakesman
guard|are *v/t* look at; watch; guard; look after; **~arsi** *v/r* beware
guarda|roba *f* wardrobe; **~robiera** *f* cloak-room attendant
guardia *f* guard; watchman; *mil* sentry; policeman; **~no** *m* guardian; caretaker; **~forestale** forester; **~mèdica** ambulance station; **~notturna** night watchman
guar|ìbile curable; **~igione** *f* recovery; cure; **~ire** *v/i* recover; *v/t* cure
guarn|igione *f* garrison; **~ire** *v/t* adorn; equip
guastare *v/t* spoil
guasto *adj* spoiled; out of order; **orologio** *m* **~** broken

clock; **~ al motore** motor trouble; **~ al cambio** gear-box trouble
guazz|are *v/t* ford; *v/i* wallow; **~etto** *m* stew; ragout
guercio squint-eyed
guerr|a *f* war; **~eggiare** *v/i* wage war; **~iero** *adj* warlike; *m* warrior
gufo *m* owl
guglia *f* spire
guid|a *f* guide; guidebook; directory; guidance; **~a alpina** alpine guide; **~a di conversazione** phrase-book; **~a telefònica** telephone directory; **~àbile** amenable; **~are** *v/t* lead; guide; drive
guidoslitta *f* bobsled
guisa *f* manner; way; **di ~ che** so that
guizzare *v/i* flash
guscio *m* shell; pod
gust|are *v/t* taste; relish; **~o** *m* taste; **~osità** *f* tastiness; **~oso** tasty

H

ha he (she, it) has; (**Lei**) **~** *forma di cortesia* you have; **hai** you have (*sg*); **hanno** they have
hangar *m* hanger; shed

hascisc *m* hashish
ho I have
hobby *m* hobby
hockey *m* hockey
hostess *f* stewardess

I

i *article m/pl* the
ìbrido hybrid
Iddìo *m* God
idea *f* idea; notion; **avere**

l'idea di fare qlc have the intention of doing s.th.
idèntico identical
ideologìa *f* ideology

imboscata

idìlli|co idyllic; **~o** m idyll

idiom|a m idiom; **~àtico** idiomatic

idiòta m, f idiot

idol|atrare v/t idolatrize; **~atria** f idolatry

ìdolo m idol

idoneità f fitness

idòneo fit; qualified

idrante m hydrant

idràulico adj hydraulic; m plumber

idròfobo hydrophobic; **~geno** m hydrogen

idro|motore m hydromotor; **~plano** m hydroplane; **~terapia** f hydrotherapy

ieri yesterday; **~ l'altro** day before yesterday; **~ mattina** yesterday morning

igiene f hygiene; hygienics pl

igiènico hygienic(al)

ignaro ignorant

ignavo lazy; sluggish

ignor|ante ignorant; **~anza** f ignorance; **~are** v/t ignore

ignoto unknown

il article m the

ilare cheerful

ilarità f hilarity

illécito illicit

illegale illegal

illegìbile illegible

illegìttimo illigitimate; unlawful

illimitato unlimited

illùdere v/t deceive

illumin|ante illuminant; **gas** m **~ante** illuminating gas; **~are** v/t illuminate; fig enlighten; **~azione** f illu-

mination

ill|usione f illusion; **~usorio** illusory

illustr|are v/t illustrate; elucidate; make famous; **~azione** f illustration; **~e** illustrious; famous; (letter) **~e signore, illustrìssimo signore** dear Sir

imball|aggio m wrapping; **~are** v/t pack

imbalsamare v/t enbalm; (animals) stuff

imbandierare v/t flag

imbarazz|are v/t obstruct; embarrass; **~ato** embarrassed; **~o** m embarrassment; obstacle

imbarc|adero m wharf; pier; **~are** v/t ship; **~arsi** v/r embark; **~azione** f boat; **~o** m embarkation; landing-stage

imbarilare v/t barrel

imbast|ire v/t baste; tack; **~itura** f tacking

imbàttersi v/r: **~ in qu** run across s.o.

imbecille adj foolish; m imbecile

imbell|ettare v/t paint (the face); **~ire** v/t embellish

imbianc|are v/t whiten; bleach; whitewash; v/i become white; **~hino** m whitewasher

imbitumare v/t tar

imbocc|are v/t feed; suggest; enter; **~atura** f mouthpiece; mouth (river)

imborsare v/t pocket

imboscata f ambush

10*

imbottare

imbott|are v/t put in barrels; **~igliare** v/t bottle (up); **~ire** v/t pad; stuff; **~itura** f padding

imbrodare v/t soil

imbrogli|are v/t entangle; muddle (up); swindle; **~o** m tangle; swindle; **~one** m swindler

imbronci|are, **~re** v/i pout

imbrunire v/i grow dark

imbucare v/t post (letter)

imbuto m funnel

imit|àbile imitable; **~are** v/t imitate; **~azione** f imitation

immacolato immaculate

immagin|àbile imaginable; **~are** v/t, **~arsi** v/r imagine; fancy; **~azione** f imagination

immàgine f image

immancàbile unfailing

immane huge; ruthless

immatricol|are v/t matriculate; register; **~azione** f registration

immaturo immature; early (death)

immedi|ato immediate; **~tato** unpremeditated

immens|ità f immensity; **~o** immense; huge

immèrg|ere v/t immerse; soak; **~ersi** v/r plunge

immeritato undeserved

immersione f immersion

immigr|ante m, f, adj immigrant; **~are** v/i immigrate; **~azione** f immigration

immischiarsi v/r meddle; interfere

immissione f letting in; introduction

immòbile motionless; immovable

immoderato immoderate

immodest|ia f immodesty; **~o** immodest

immondizi|a f sweepings pl; **bidone ~** delle **~e** dustbin; garbage-box

immoral|e immoral; **~ità** f immorality

immort|ale immortal; **~alità** f immortality

immoto motionless

immune immune; free

immut|àbile unchangeable; **~ato** unaltered

impaccare v/t wrap up

impacci|are v/t hinder; embarrass; **~o** m impediment; embarrassment

impacco m packing; wet compress

impadronirsi v/r get hold (of)

impagàbile invaluable

impagliare v/t cover with straw

impalcatura f ceiling; scaffold(ing)

impallidire v/i turn pale

impannare v/t line with cloth

imparagonàbile incomparable

imparare v/t learn

impareggiàbile incomparable

impari uneven; odd

imparità f imparity

imparziale impartial

impassìbile impassive
impastare v/t knead; paste
impaurire v/t frighten
impazien|te impatient;
eager; **~tirsi** v/r get impatient; **~za** f impatience
impazzire v/i go mad; go
crazy
impeccàbile faultless
imped|imento m hindrance; drawback; **~ire** v/t
prevent; obstruct
impegn|arsi v/r engage o.s.;
~o m engagement; commitment
impenetràbile impenetrable; fig inscrutable
impenn|are v/t cover with
feathers; **~arsi** v/r rear
impens|àbile unthinkable;
~ato unexpected; **~ierito**
uneasy
imperativo m, adj imperative
impera|tore m emperor;
~trice f empress
imperdonàbile unforgivable
imperf|etto adj imperfect;
m imperfect (tense); **~ezione** f imperfection
imperiale adj imperial; m
(car-)top
imperizia f lack of skill
impermeàbile adj impermeable; water-, air-tight;
water-proof; m rain-coat
impermutàbile unchangeable
impero m empire; rule
impersonale impersonal
impertin|ente impertinent;

~enza f impertinence
imperturbàbile imperturbable
impestare v/t infect
ìmpeto m vehemence
impetuoso vehement; violent
impiant|are v/t plant;
found; **~ìto** m floor; m
installation; plant; **~o d'accensione** ignition system;
~o elèttrico electric plant;
~o lavacristallo (wind)screen washer; **~o m radio**
wireless plant
impiccare v/t hang
impicci|are v/t obstruct;
embarrass
impiccinire v/t make smaller; v/i grow smaller
impiccio m hindrance
impieg|àbile employable;
~are v/t employ; **~ato** adj
employed; m employee; **~o**
m employment
impietrire v/t, v/i petrify
impiombare v/t seal;
(tooth) fill
implac|àbile unrelenting;
~abilità f implacability;
ruthlessness
implacidire v/t appease
implor|are v/t implore; **~azione** f imploration
impolver|are v/t cover with
dust; **~arsi** v/r get dusty
imponente imposing; **~enza** f impressiveness
imp|orre v/t impose; **~orsi**
v/r be overbearing
import|ante important;
~anza f importance; **~are**

v/t import; *v/i* be necessary; **non importa** it does not matter; **~atore** *m* importer; **~azione** *f* import (-ation); **~o** *m* amount

importun|are *v/t* bother; **~o** importunate; annoying

imposs|ibile impossible; **~ibilità** *f* impossibility

impost|a *f* tax; duty; (*window*) shutter; **~are** *v/t* mail (*letter*); state (*problem*)

impot|ente powerless; impotent; **~enza** *f* impotence

impoverire *v/t* impoverish

impratic|àbile impracticable; **~chirsi** *v/r* practise

imprec|are *v/i* curse; **~azione** *f* imprecation

impreciso inexact

impres|a *f* enterprise; **~ario** *m* contractor; manager

impression|àbile susceptible; **~are** *v/t* impress; **~e** *f* impression

imprèstito *m* loan

imprevisto unforeseen

imprigionare *v/t* imprison

imprimere *v/t* impress; (im-)print

improb|àbile unlikely; **~abilità** *f* improbability

impront|a *f* impression; mark; **~a digitale** fingerprint; **~are** *v/t* mark; **~o** importunate

impròprio unbecoming

improvvis|are *v/t* improvise; **~o** sudden; **all' ~o** all of a sudden

imprud|ente imprudent; rash; **~enza** *f* imprudence

impud|ente impudent; **~enza** *f* impudence

impugn|àbile impugnable; **~are** *v/t* seize; impugn

impuls|ivo impulsive; **~o** *m* impulse

impun|e, **~ito** unpunished

impunt|are *v/i* stumble; **~arsi** *v/r* be obstinate; **~ato** obstinate; **~ire** *v/t* quilt; **~uale** unpunctual; **~ualità** *f* unpunctuality; **~itura** *f* stitching

impuro impure

in in; to; **~ Italia** in (to) Italy; **~ italiano** in Italian; **andare ~ treno** go by train

in... (*prefix with often negative meaning*) un...

inàbile unable; unfit

inaccessìbile inaccessible

inaccettàbile unacceptable

inadempì|bile unrealizable; **~imento** *m* unfulfilment

inal|are *v/t* inhale; **~azione** *f* inhalation

inalterato unaltered

inamidare *v/t* starch

inammissìbile inadmissible

inappellàbile final

inappetenza *f* lack of appetite

inapprezzàbile invaluable

inappuntàbile irreproachable

inargentare *v/t* silver-plate

inaridire *v/t* dry up; wither

inarrivàbile unattainable

inaspettato unexpected

inattendìbile unreliable

inatt|ento unattentive; **~en-zione** f carelessness
inatteso unexpected
inatt|ività f inactivity; **~ivo** inactive
inatto unapt
inattuàbile impracticable
inaudito unheard of
inaugur|are v/t inaugurate; **~azione** f inauguration; opening
inavvert|enza f inadvertence; **~ito** unnoticed
incalcolàbile incalculable
incalorire v/t heat; warm
incalzare v/t pursue; fig urge
incanalare v/t canalize
incandescente incandescent
incant|are v/t charm; **~évole** enchanting; **~o** m charm; enchantment; auction; **véndere all'~o** sell by auction
incap|ace incapable (**di** of); **~acità** f incapacity
incarcerare v/t imprison
incaric|are v/t entrust (**di** with); charge; **~arsi** v/r di qc take s.th. upon o.s.
incàrico m task; charge
incarn|are v/t embody; **~a-tino** flesh-coloured; m fresh complexion
incart|are v/t wrap (in paper); **~o** m documents pl; **~occiare** v/t put in a paper-bag
incasellare v/t file
inc|assare v/t encase; (money) collect; **~asso** m

takings pl; collection
incastonare v/t set
incatenare v/t chain
incatramare v/t tar
incauto incautious
incav|are v/t hollow out; **~a-to** hollow
incendi|are v/t set fire to; **~àrio** m incendiary; **~o** m fire; conflagration
inceneri|mento m incineration; **~ire** v/t incinerate
incens|are v/t incense; **~iere** m thurible; **~o** m incense
incerato m tarpaulin
incer|tezza f uncertainty; **~erto** uncertain; insecure
incessante incessant
incettatore m forestaller
inchiesta f inquiry
inchin|are v/t incline; **~arsi** v/r bow; **~o** m bow
inchiodare v/t nail
inchiostro m ink
inciamp|are v/i stumble; **~o** m obstacle
incid|entale incidental; **~ente** m incident; **~ente stradale** road accident
incidere v/t incise; med lance; engrave; fig penetrate
incinta pregnant
incipriare v/t powder
incirca: all'~ approximately
incisione f incision; **~ in legno** wood-cut; **~ in rame** copperplate engraving
incisore m engraver
inciv|ile uncivilized; uncivil; **~ilire** v/t civilize
inclem|ente stern; severe;

~enza f severity

inclin|àbile inclinable; **~are** v/t, v/i incline; **~ato** inclined; bent; **~azione** f inclination

incl|ùdere v/t include; enclose; **~usa** f enclosure; **~usivamente**, **~usive** inclusively

incoerente inconsistent

incògnito unknown

incollare v/t glue; stick

incol|orarsi v/r (take on) colour; **~ore** colourless

incolp|are v/t accuse; inculpate; **~azione** f accusation; **~évole** innocent

incolto incultured; uncultivated

in|cómbere v/i be incumbent (on); **~combustibile** incombustible; **~combusto** unburnt

incominciare v/t, v/i begin (a with); start

incommutàbile unalterable

incomod|are v/t disturb; **~arsi** v/r trouble o.s.; **non si incòmodi!** don't trouble (yourself)!

incòmodo uncomfortable

imcomparàbile matchless

incompatibile incompatible

incompetente incompetent

incompiuto unfinished

incomprensibile incomprehensible

incon|cepìbile inconceivable; **~ciliàbile** irreconcilable

inconfortàbile inconsolable

inconsapévole unaware

inconscio m, adj unconscious

inconseguenza f inconsequence

inconsiderato inconsiderate

inconsolàbile inconsolable

inconsueto unusual

incont|entàbile insatiable; **~abilità** f insatiability

incontestato uncontested

incontrare v/t meet

incontro m encounter; match; adv towards; **all'~** on the contrary

inconveni|ente inconvenient; **~enza** f inconvenience

inconvincìbile inconvincible

incoragg|iamento m encouragement; **~iare** v/t encourage; **~iarsi** v/r take courage

incorniciare v/t frame

incoron|are v/t crown; **~azione** f coronation

incorporare v/t incorporate

incorr|eggìbile incorrigible; **~ettezza** f incorrectness; **~etto** incorrect; **~otto** incorrupt; **~utìbile** incorruptible

incosciente unconscious

incost|ante fickle; **~anza** f inconstancy; **~ituzionale** inconstitutional

incredibile incredible

incrèdulo incredulous

incremento m increase

increspare v/t ripple; frown

incrociare v/t cross; **~atore** m naut cruiser; **~o** m crossing; cross-breeding

incrollàbile unshakeable

incubo m nightmare

incùdine f anvil

incuràbile incurable

incurvare v/t bend

indagare v/t investigate

indàgine f inquiry; research

indebitàrsi v/r get into debt; **~ato** indebted

indebolire v/t weaken

indecènte indecent; **~enza** f indecency

indecisione f indecision; **~iso** undecided

indefinito indefinite

indegnità f unworthiness; **~o** unworthy; worthless

indelicato indelicate; unscrupulous

indènne unharmed; v/t indemnity; **~izzare** v/t indemnify; **~izzo** m indemnity

indescrivìbile indescribable

indeterminato vague; indetermined

India f India

indiano Indian

indicare v/t indicate; **~ativo**, m, adj indicative; **~atore** m indicator; **~azione** f indication

ìndice m index; forefinger; mech hand

indicìbile unspeakable

indietreggiare v/i withdraw; **~o** back; behind;

all'**~o** backwards

indifferènte indifferent; **~enza** f indifference

indìgeno adj indigenous; m native

indigènte needy

indigerìbile indigestible; **~estione** f indigestion

indignazione f indignation

indipendènte independent; **~enza** f independence

indire v/t announce

indirètto indirect; **~izzare** v/t address (**a** to); **~izzo** m address

indiscreto indiscreet; intrusive

indispensàbile indispensable

indispettito vexed; **~osizione** f indisposition; **~osto** indisposed; unwell

indisputàbile indisputable

indistinto indistinct

indivia f endive

individuale individual; **~alità** f individuality

individuo m individual

indiviso undivided

indizio m sign; symptom

indòcile indocile

indocilità f indocility

indolcire v/t sweeten

ìndole f temper

indolènte indolent; **~enza** f indolence

indomani m: l'**~** the next day

Indonesia f Indonesia

indorare v/t gild

indossare v/t put on; wear

indovinare v/t guess; **~ello** m

m riddle

indubbio undoubted

indugi|are *v/i* delay; **~o** *m* delay

indulg|ente indulgent; **~enza** *f* indulgence

indurare *v/t* harden

ind|urre *v/t* induce; **~ursi** *v/r* decide

industr|ia *f* industry; manufacture; *fig* diligence; **~ia pesante** heavy industry; **~iale** *adj* industrial; manufacturing; *m* industrialist; **prodotti,** *m/pl* **~iali** manufactured goods

ineducato ill-bred

ineffàbile ineffable

ineffettuàbile unpracticable

inefficace inefficient

ineguale unequal; uneven

inerte inert

inerudito unlearned

ines|atto inaccurate; **~auribile** inexhaustible

ineseguìbile inexecutable

inesoràbile unrelenting

inesp|erienza *f* inexperience; **~erto** unskilled

inesplicàbile inexplicable

inesprimìbile inexpressible

inetto inept; unqualified

inevitàbile inevitable

inezia *f* trifle

infallìbile infallible

infam|are *v/t* defame; **~e** disgraceful; vile; **~ia** *f* infamy

infant|icidio *m* child-murder; **~ile** childish

infanzia *f* childhood

infarto *m* infarct; **~ miocàrdico** myocardinal infarct

infaticàbile indefatigable

infatti in fact; really

infausto ill-omened

infecond|ità *f* barrenness; **~o** sterile

infedel|e *adj* unfaithful; *m* unbeliever; **~tà** *f* infidelity

infelice unhappy

inferior|e *adj* inferior; *m* subordinate; **~ità** *f* inferiority

inferm|erìa *f* infirmary; sick-room; **~iere** *m* hospital attendant; **~ità** *f* infirmity; **~o** *adj* sick; *m* invalid

infern|ale infernal; **~o** *m* hell

inferriata *f* grating

infestare *v/t* infest

infett|are *v/t* infect; **~ivo** *m* infectious; **malattia** *f* **~iva** infectious disease

infezione *f* infection

infiamm|àbile inflammable; **~are** *v/t* inflame; *fig* excite; **~azione** *f* inflammation; **~azione agli occhi** inflammation of the eyes

infido untrustworthy

infil|are *v/t* thread; (*beeds*) string; **~arsi** *v/r* **qc** put sth on

infiltrarsi *v/r* infiltrate; penetrate

infilzare *v/t* pierce

ìnfimo lowest; basest

infin|e finally; **~ità** *f* infinity; **~ito** *adj* infinite; *m* infinitive

infiorare *v/t* adorn with flowers

ingrosso

infless|ibile inflexible; **~io-ne** *f* inflection

influ|ente influent(ial); **~enza** *f* influence; in-fluenza; **~ire** *v/t* influence

influsso *m* influx

infoc|are *v/t* make red-hot; **~ato** red-hot; burning

infondato unfounded

infóndere *v/t* infuse

inform|arsi *v/r* inform o.s.; **~azione** *f* information; **~e** shapeless

infortun|io *m* accident; **as-sicurazione f contro gli ~i** accident insurance

inforzare *v/t* strengthen

infossato sunken; fallen in

infràngere *v/t* break; in-fringe

infrazione *f* infraction; in-fringement

infredd|are *v/i*, **~arsi** *v/r* catch cold; **~atura** *f* cold; **~olire** *v/i* shiver with cold

infruttuoso fruitless; un-successful

infuori: all'~ di except (for)

infuri|arsi *v/r* grow furious; **~ato** furious

infusione *f* infusion

ingann|are *v/t* deceive; betray; **~atore** *m* swindler; **~o** *m* deceit

ingegn|arsi *v/r* strive; **~ere** *m* engineer; **~o** *m* intelli-gence; talent; **~oso** ingen-ious.

ingènito inborn; innate

ingenu|ità *f* simple-mindedness; **~ènuo** ingen-ious; naive

ingessare *v/t* plaster

Inghilterra *f* England

inghiottire *v/t* swallow; engulf

ingiallito yellowed

inginocchi|arsi *v/r* kneel down; **~atoio** *m* kneeling-stool; **~oni** *adv* on one's knees

ingiù downwards; down

ingiuri|a *f* insult; outrage; **~are** *v/t* insult

ingiust|izia *f* injustice; **~o** unjust; unfair

inglese *adj* English; *m* Englishman

inglorioso inglorious

ingoiare *v/t* swallow

ingo|mbrare *v/t* obstruct; **~mbro** blocked

ingommare *v/t* gum; paste

ingordo greedy

ingorg|arsi *v/r* become choked, blocked; **~o** *m med* congestion

ingran|aggio *m mech* gear (-ing); **ferrovia f ad ~aggio** cog-wheel railway; **~are** *v/i* be in gear

ingrand|imento *m* enlarge-ment; **~ire** *v/t* enlarge; *v/i* become larger

ingrass|aggio *m* lubricating; **~are** *v/t* fatten; grease; *v/i* grow fat; **~o** *m* manure

ingr|atitùdine *f* ungrateful-ness; **~ato** ungrateful

ingrediente *m* ingredient

ingresso *m* entrance; admit-tance

ingross|are *v/t*, *v/i* enflate; increase; **all'~o** wholesale

inguantarsi *v/r* put on gloves

inguaribile incurable

inguinale: ernia ~ inguinal hernia

inguine *m anat* groin

inibire *v/t* inhibit

iniettare *v/t* inject

iniezione *f* injection

inim|icare *v/t* estrange (from); **~icizia** *f* hostility

inimmaginàbile unconceivable

ininterrotto uninterrupted

iniqu|ità *f* iniquity; **~o** unjust

inizi|ale *f* initial; **~are** *v/t* initiate; start; **~ativa** *f* initiative

innaffi|are *v/t* sprinkle; **~atoio** *m*, **~atrice** *f* watering-cart; watering-can

innalzare *v/t* raise

innamorarsi di fall in love with ...

innanzi before; forward

innato inborn

innaturale unnatural

innegàbile undeniable

innestare *v/t* graft; *aut* **~ la marcia** engage the gear

inno *m* hymn; **~ nazionale** national anthem

innoc|ente innocent; **~enza** *f* innocence

innòcuo innocuous

innov|are *v/t* innovate; **~azione** *f* innovation

innumerévole innumerable

inodoro odourless

inoltr|are *v/t* send; (letter) forward; **~e** besides

inond|are *v/t* flood; **~azione** *f* inundation

inoperoso idle

inopportuno inopportune

inorridire *v/t* horrify; *v/i* be horrified

inospitale inhospitable

inosservato unobserved

inquadr|are *v/t* frame; *mil* enroll

inquiet|are *v/t* worry; **~o** uneasy; **~ùdine** *f* apprehension

inquilino *m* lodger; tenant

insal|are *v/t* salt; **~ata** *f* salad; **~ata di cetrioli** cucumber salad; **~ata di lattuga** lettuce; **~ata di patate** potato-salad; **~atiera** *f* salad-bowl

insalubre unhealthy

insano insane

insaponare *v/t* soap; lather

insaputa: all'~ di without the knowledge of

insaziàbile insatiable

inscrìvere = iscrivere

insedi|amento *m* installation; accession to office; **~arsi** *v/r* enter upon office

insegna *f* colours *pl*; sign (-board); **~mento** *m* teaching; **~nte** *adj* teaching; *m,f* teacher; **~re** *v/t* teach

insegu|imento *m* pursuit; **~ire** *v/t* pursue

insens|ato *adj* rash; *m* fool; **~ìbile** insensible

inseparàbile inseparable

inser|ire *v/t* insert; put in; **~zione** *f* insertion; (news-

paper) advertisement

insetticida *m* insecticide

insetto *m* insect

insìdi|a *f* snare; **~are** *v/t* ensnare; **~oso** insidious

insième *adv* together; *m* whole

insignificante trifling

insincero insincere

insinu|àrsi *v/r* insinuate o.s.; **~azióne** *f* insinuation

insìpido insipid; tasteless

insistènte insistent

insìstere *v/i* insist (**in, su** on)

insod(d)isfatto unsatisfied

insolazióne *f* sunstroke

insolènte insolent; pert

insòlito unusual

insolùbile insoluble

insómma in short; after all

insònn|e sleepless; **~ia** *f* insomnia

insopportàbile unbearable

insòrgere *v/i* rise (in revolt)

insostenìbile untenable

install|àre *v/t* instal; **~atóre** *m* plumber; **~azióne** *f* installation

instancàbile untiring

insù up(wards); above

insuccèsso *m* failure

insudiciàre *v/t* soil

insuffici|ènte insufficient; **~ènza** *f* insufficiency

insulare insular

insulina *f* insulin

insult|àre *v/t* insult; abuse; **~o** *m* insult

insuper|àbile insuperable; **~ato** insurpassed

insurrezióne *f* insurrection

intagliatóre *m* carver;

engraver

intanto meanwhile; **~ che** while

intarlato worm-eaten

intàrsio *m* inlay-work

intascàre *v/t* pocket

intatto intact; unimpaired

intavolàre *v/t* (*conversation*) start

intavolato *m* planking

integràre *v/t* integrate; complete

intell|ètto *m* intellect; **~ettuale** intellectual; **~igènte** intelligent; **~igènza** *f* intelligence

intemperante intemperate

intèndere *v/t* hear; understand; mean; intend; **s'intènde!** of course!

intènso intense

intèn|to intent (**a** on); **~zióne** *f* intention

interamente wholly

inter|cèdere *v/i* intercede; **~cessióne** *f* intercession; **telèfono** *m* **~comunale** trunkline

interdétto prohibited

interd|ìre *v/t* prohibit; **~ìre qu** *for* disable s.o.; **~izióne** *f* interdiction; *for* disqualification

interèss|aménto *m* interest; sympathy; **~ante** interesting; **~are** *v/t* interest; concern; **~ato** *com* having a share; *m* interest; concern; **~i** *m/pl* (*money*) interest

interiezióne *f* interjection

interiore *adj* interior; *m* inside

interlocutore *m* partner in a conversation

interm|ediario *m* mediator; **~edio** intermediate

intermezzo *m* interval

intermitt|ente intermittent; **febbre** *f* **~ente** intermittent fever; **~enza** *f* intermittence

internare *v/t* intern; *med* confine

internazionale international

interno *adj* internal; inner; *m* interior; inside

intero entire; whole; **latte** *m* **~** full-cream milk

interporsi *v/r* intervene

in|terpretare *v/t* interpret; **~tèrprete** *m* interpreter; *thea* actor

interpunzione *f* punctuation

interregno *m* interregnum

interrog|are *v/t* question; **punto** *m* **~ativo** question mark; **~atorio** *m* (cross-)examination; **~azione** *f* query

interr|ómpere *v/t* interrupt; **~uttore** *m elec* switch; **~uzione** *f* interruption; *radio* jamming

inter|secare *v/t* intersect; **~sezione** *f* intersection; **~vallo** *m* interval

interv|enire *v/i* intervene; interfere; **~ento** *m* intervention; interference

intervista *f* interview

intes|a *f* agreement; *pol*

entente; **ben ~o** well understood

intest|are *v/t* head; *com* register (under a name); **~arsi** *v/r* be obstinate; **~azione** *f* heading; headline

intestino *adj* internal; *m* intestines *pl*; **~ cieco** appendix

intimare *v/t* intimate; enjoin

intimidire *v/t* intimidate

intimità *f* intimacy

intimo intimate; close

intimorire *v/t*: **~ qu** frighten s.o.

in|tìngere *v/t* dip (into); **~ìngolo** *m* ragout; **~into** *adj* soaked; *m* sauce

intirizzire *v/t* (be)numb

intitolare *v/t* entitle; name

intoller|àbile intolerable; **~ante** intolerant

intonacare *v/t* plaster

intònaco *m* plaster(ing)

intonare *v/t* intone; tune

intopp|are *v/i* come across; stumble (**in** over); **~o** *m* obstacle

intorbidare *v/t* make muddy

intormentirsi *v/r* get numb, cramped

intorno *prp* **~a** (a)round; about; *adv* around; about

intossic|are *v/t* intoxicate; **~azione** *f* intoxication; **~azione alcoolica** alcoholic poisoning; **~azione alimentare** food poisoning

intra =**tra, fra**

intralciare *v/t* hinder;

entangle

intransitivo intransitive

intrapr|**èndere** v/t undertake; **~esa** f enterprise

intrattàbile unmanageable

intratten|**ere** v/t entertain; **~ersi** v/r stop; (subject) dwell (**su** upon)

intrecci|**are** v/t interlace; **~arsi** v/r be intertwined; **~o** m interlacing; plot

intrig|**ante** adj intriguing; **~are** v/t plot; **~o** m plot

intrìnseco intrinsic; intimate

intristire v/i fig pine away

introd|**urre** v/t introduce; **~uzione** f introduction; preface; mus overture

intromèttersi v/r interfere

intruso m intruder

inturgidir|**e** v/i, **~si** v/r swell up

inumano inhuman

inumidire v/t moisten

inùtile useless

invàdere v/t invade

invalid|**are** v/t invalidate; nullify; **~ità** f invalidity

invàlido adj invalid; void; m disabled soldier

invano in vain

invariàbile invariable

invasione f invasion

invecchiare v/t make old; v/i grow old

invece on the contrary; **~ di** instead of; **~ di lui** (**in sua vece**) in his place

invelenire v/t envenom

invendìbile unsaleable

invent|**are** v/t invent; **~ario**

m inventory; stock-taking

inven|**tivo** inventive; **~tore** m inventor; **~zione** f invention

invernale wintry

invernici|**are** v/t varnish; **~atore** m varnisher

inverno m winter; **d'~** in winter time

invero truly; really

inverosìmile unlikely

invers|**ione** f inversion; **~o** inverse

investig|**are** v/t investigate; **~azione** f investigation

invest|**imento** m investment; rail collision; **~ire** v/t empower (**di** with); run over (car); (money) invest; **~irsi** v/r collide

invetri|**are** v/t glaze; **~ata** f glass window

invi|**are** v/t send; **~ato** m speciale correspondent

invìdi|**a** f envy; **~àbile** enviable; **~are** v/t envy; **~oso** envious

invigor|**ire** v/t invigorate; **~irsi** v/r get strong

invilire v/t debase; (prices) lower

invil|**uppare** v/t envelop; **~uppo** m bundle

invincìbile invincible

invio m mailing; shipment

inviolàbile inviolable

invisìbile invisible

inviso disliked

invitare v/t invite; request

invito m invitation; **~ a presentarsi** summons

invocare v/t invoke; implore

invogliare v/t raise a desire

involontario unintentional

in|voltare v/t wrap up; **~olucro** m covering; envelope

inzolfare v/t sulphurate

inzuccherare v/t sugar

inzuppare v/t soak; steep

io I

iòdi|co iodic; **~o** m iodine

ipno|si f hypnosis; **~tizzare** v/t hypnotize

ipocondria f spleen

ipocrisìa f hypocrisy

ipòcrita m hypocrite

ipoteca f mortgage

ipòtesi f supposition

ippica f horse-racing

ippòdromo m hippodrome; racecourse

ira f anger; wrath

iracond|ia f rage; **~o** hot-tempered

irato angry

iride f iris; rainbow

iris f iris

Irland|a f Ireland; **2ese** Irish

ir|onìa f irony; **~ònico** ironic(al)

irradi|are v/t (ir)radiate; **~azione** f irradiation

irragionévole unreasonable

irrancidire v/i become rancid

irrazionale irrational

irreale unreal

irreconciliàbile irreconcilable

irrefrenàbile unrestrainable

irregol|are irregular; **~arità** f irregularity

irreparàbile irreparable

irreprensìbile irreproachable

irre|quietezza f restlessness; **~quieto** restless

irresistìbile irresistible

irresolutezza f irresolution

irrespons|àbile irresponsible; **~abilità** f irresponsibility

irrevocàbile irrevocable

irrig|are v/t irrigate; **~azione** f irrigation

irrit|àbile irritable; **~abilità** f irritability; **~are** v/t irritate

irruzione f irruption

irsuto shaggy; bristly

irto bristling; standing on end

ischio m hip-joint

iscr|ìvere v/t inscribe; enroll; **~izione** f enrollment; registration

ìsola f isle

isol|amento m isolation; **~ano** m islander; **~are** v/t isolate; **~arsi** v/r live secluded; **~ato** m block of houses

isp|ettore m inspector; **~ezionare** v/t inspect; **~ezione** f inspection

ìspido shaggy

ispir|are v/t inspire; instil; **~arsi** v/r be inspired (by); **~azione** f inspiration

Israele m Israel

issare v/t hoist

istant|ànea f snapshot;

àneo instantaneous; **~e** *m* petitioner; instant, moment
istanza *f* petition
istèrico hysterical
istint|ivo instinctive; **~o** *m* instinct
istitu|ire *v/t* establish; found; **~uto** *m* institute; **~uto di bellezza** beauty shop; **~utore** *m* tutor; **~uzione** *f* institution
istmo *m* isthmus
istru|ire *v/t* instruct; teach; **~ito** educated

istruttivo instructive
istruzione *f* instruction; teaching; **~ pùbblica** public education; **~ obbligatoria** compulsory school-attendance
Italia *f* Italy
italiano *m, adj* Italian
itinerario *m* itinerary
ito gone; **bell' e ~** done for
itterizia *f* jaundice
iùta *f* jute
ivi there

K

ketchup *m* ketchup
kg = chilogramma

km = chilòmetro
kWh = chilowattora

L

L = lire (italiane)
l = litro
l' (*before vowel*) **= lo, la**
la *article f/sg* the; *pron pers* (*accusative*) she; **Ω forma di cortesia** you; *m mus* la
là there; **di ~** from there; **al di ~** beyond
labbro *m* lip; **~ leporino** hare-lip
labor|atorio *m* laboratory; work-shop; **~ioso** hard-working; toilsome
lacca *f* laquer
laccetto *m* (boot)lace
laccio *m* string; *fig* trap; **~ per le scarpe** shoe-lace
lacerare *v/t* tear; rend
làcero torn; in rags
lacuna *f* gap; blank

lacustre lacustrine; **dimora** *f* ~ lake-dwelling
laddove (there) where; whilst
ladro *m* thief; burglar; **~ne** *m* highwayman
laggiù down there; yonder
lagn|anza *f* complaint; **~arsi** *v/r* complain (**di** of); **~o** *m* lament(ation)
lago *m* lake
làgrima *f* tear
laguna *f* lagoon
làico *adj* laic; *m* layman
laidezza *f* foulness
làido ugly; filthy
lament|are *v/t* lament; **~arsi** *v/r* complain (**di** of); **~o** *m* moaning; **Ωoso** plaintive
lametta *f:* **~ da barba**

lamiera

razorblade

lamiera f plate; sheet

làmina f (metal) sheet

laminare v/t laminate

làmpada f lamp; ~ **ad arco** arc lamp; ~ **a raggi ultra-violetti** sunlight-lamp; ~ **tascàbile** torch; flash-light

lampad|ario m lustre; **~ina** f torch; electric bulb

lampeggiante m blinking light

lamp|eggiare v/i lighten; flash; **~eggiatore** m traffic-indicator; **~ione** m street-lamp

lampo m lightning; flash; **treno** m ~ express-train

lampone m raspberry

lana f wool; **~pura** pure wool; ~ **di acciaio** steel wool

lancetta f hand (of a watch)

lanci|a f lance; naut boat; **~are** v/t throw; fling; **~arsi** v/r dash; rush; **~o** m throw; jump; **~o del disco** discus-throw; **~o del giavellotto** javelin-throw; **~o della palla di ferro** shot-put

landa f heath

laneria f woollens pl

languidezza f languidness

lànguido languid; weak

languire v/i languish; be stagnant (trade)

lanoso woolly

lanterna f lantern; ~ **cieca** dark lantern

lan|ùgine f down; fluff; **~u-to** woolly

làpide f tomb-stone; me-

morial tablet

lapilli m/pl volcanic ashes

lapis m pencil; **~làzzuli** m lapis lazuli

lardo m lard; bacon

larghezza f width; breadth; fig generosity

largire v/t give liberally

largo adj wide; broad; large; m open space; **fare** ~ make room

làrice m larch-tree

laringe f larynx; **~ite** f laryngitis

larva f larva; mask; ghost

lasagn|a f big noodle; **~e** f/pl **verdi** green noodles

lasca f roach

lasciare v/t leave; desert; let

làscito m legacy

lassativo m laxative

lassù up there; there above

lastra f slab; plate; (window-)pane

lastric|are v/t pave; **~ato** m pavement

làstrico m pavement; fig misery

latente latent

laterale lateral; **porta** f ~ side door

latifondo m large estate

latino Latin

latit|ante at large; **~ùdine** f latitude; breadth

lato adj wide; m side

latore m bearer

latrare v/i bark

latrina f lavatory

latta f tin-plate; can

latt|aia f milkmaid; **~ante** m suckling; **~e** m milk; **~eria** f

milkshop; **~iera** f milk-jug;
~ivéndolo m milkman
lattoniere m plumber
lattuga f lettuce
làurea f academic degree;
doctorate
laur|eto m laurel grove; **~o** m
laurel
lava f lava
lavabiancherìa f washing
machine
lav|àbile washable; **~abo** m
wash-stand; **~aggio** m
washing
lavagna f slate; blackboard
lav|amano m wash-stand;
~anda f lavender; **~andaia**
f laundress; **~anderìa** f
laundry; **~anderìa a secco**
dry-cleaning shop; **~andi-
no** m sink; **~are** v/t wash;
~atoio m wash-house
lavina f snow-slip
lavor|are v/t, v/i work; **~a-
tore** m worker; **~o** m work;
labour
Lazio m Latium
le article f/pl the; pron pers
(dative f/sg) her; (accusative
f/pl) they; 2 forma di cortesia
(to) you
leale loyal; **~tà** f loyalty
lebbra f leprosy
leccare v/t lick
lecc|one m glutton; **~ornia** f
dainty bit
lécito allowed; lawful
lega f union; league; alloy
legàcciolo m boot-lace;
garter
leg|ale legal; **~alizzare** v/t
legalize; **~alizzazione** f

legalization
legame m bond; tie
leg|are v/t bequeath; tie; fig
join; **~ato** m legacy; **~atore**
m book-binder; **~azione** f
legation
legge f law; **studiar ~** study
(for) the law
leggend|a f legend
lèggere v/t read
legger|ezza f lightness;
frivolity; **~o** light; fig
thoughtless
leggiadrì|a f grace(fulness);
~o charming
leggìbile legible
leggiero = leggero
leggio m reading-desk; mus
music-stand
legisl|atore m legislator; **~a-
zione** f legislation
legittim|are v/t legitimate;
(**carta** f **di**) **~azione** f
identity card
legìttimo lawful; legitimate
legn|a f/pl fire-wood; **~aiuo-
lo** m carpenter; **~ame** m da
costruzione building-
timber
legno m wood
legume m vegetable
lei pron pers she; 2 forma di
cortesia sg you; **dare del** 2
address formally
lembo m edge; (dress) hem
len|imento m soothing; **~ire**
v/t soothe; **~itivo** soothing
lent|e f lens; **~e d'ingrandi-
mento** magnifying glass; **~i**
f/pl **di contatto** contact
lenses
lentezza f slowness

lenticchia f lentil
lentiggine f freckle
lento slow; tardy; loose
lenz|a f fishing-line; **~uola** f/pl sheets; bedclothes; **~uolo** m (bed-)sheet
leon|e m lion; **~essa** f lioness
leopardo m leopard
lepre f hare
lesso adj boiled; m boiled meat
lesto quick; agile
letizia f joy
lèttera f letter; **~ aèrea** air-mail letter; **~ espresso** special delivery letter; **~ per l'estero** foreign letter; **~ raccomandata** registered letter
letter|ale literal; **~ario** literary; **~ato** adj learned; m man of letters; **~atura** f literature
lett|iera f bedstead; **~iga** f litter; **~ino** m: **~ino da campeggio** camp bed; cot
letto m bed; pp read; **~ da bambino** cot; crib; **~ supplementare** additional bed
lettura f reading
leucemia f leukaemia
leva f lever; **~ di marcia** gear lever
levante m east
lev|are v/t take (off); raise; **~arsi** v/r get up; (sun) rise; take off (hat, dress); **~ata** f collection (of letters); **~atrice** f midwife
lezione f lesson; lecture
li pron pers them

lì there
libbra f pound
liber|ale liberal; **~alità** f munificence; **~are** v/t liberate
libero free
libertà f liberty; freedom
libr|aio m bookseller; **~eria** f library; book-shop; **~etto** m booklet; mus libretto; **~etto di risparmio** savings booklet; **~o** m book
licenz|a f licence; leave; degree; **esame** m **di ~a** leaving certificate examination; **~iare** v/t dismiss; graduate
liceo m grammar school
licitare v/t bid (at auction)
lido m beach
lieto glad; happy
lieve light; slight
lievitare v/t leaven; ferment
lièvito m barm; yeast
lilla m, adj lilac
lim|a f file; **~are** v/t file
limit|are v/t limit; **responsabilità** f **~ata** limited liability; **~azione** f limitation
limite m limit
limon|ata f lemonade; **~e** m lemon(-tree)
limpidezza f limpidity
limpido limpid
lince f lynx
lindo neat; tidy; trim
linea f line; **~ dell'autobus** bus line; **~ ferroviaria** railway line; **~ secondaria** branch line
line|amenti m/pl features;

~are adj linear; v/t delineate

linfa f lymph

lingua f language; tongue; **~ parlata** colloquial language; **~ scritta** literary language

lino m flax; linen

liquid|are v/t liquidate; settle; **~azione** f liquidation

liquido m, adj liquid; **~ per i freni idràulici** brake fluid

liquore m liquor

lira f lira; mus lyre

lìrica f lyrics pl; **~o** adj lyric(al); m lyric poet

lisca f (fish-)bone

lisciare v/t smooth

liscio smooth

lisciva f lye

lista f list; **~ dei prezzi** price-list; **~ dei cibi** bill of fare; menu; **~ dei vini** wine-list

lite f quarrel; law-suit

litig|are v/i quarrel; **~io** m quarrel

litografia f lithography

litro m litre

littorale m (sea-)shore; littoral

liuto m mus lute

livell|are v/t level; **~atrice** f bulldozer; **~o** m del mare sea-level; **~o d'olio** oil-level

lìvido livid

lo article m/sg the; pron pers (accusative) him; it

lòbulo m ear-lobe

loc|ale adj local; m place; room; **~ale da ballo** dance hall; **~alità** f locality; **~alità**

balneare watering-place; **~alità di confine** border town; **~anda** f inn; **~atàrio** m tenant; lodger

locomotiva f (locomotive-) engine

locomotore m electric locomotive

locusta f locust

lod|are v/t praise; **~e** f praise; **~évole** praiseworthy

lòdola f lark

loggia f loggia; open gallery

loggi|ato m covered gallery; **~one** m thea upper gallery

lògic|a f logic; **~o** logical

logorare v/t wear (out)

lomb|ata f loin-steak; undercut; **~o** m loin

lont|ananza f remoteness; **~ano** far; distant; **di (da) ~ano** from far

loquace talkative

lord|are v/t soil; dirt; **~o** dirty; com **peso m ~o** gross weight

loro pron pers they; them; ♀ (to) you pl; pron poss their; theirs; ♀ yours, yours

lott|a f struggle; wrestling; **~are** v/i fight; strive; **~atore** m wrestler

lott|erìa f lottery; **~o** m lot

lozione f: **~ da barba** aftershave lotion; **~ per capelli** hair-lotion; **~ per il viso** face-lotion

lubrific|ante m lubricant; **~are** v/t lubricate; grease; **~atore** m lubricator

lucchetto m padlock

luccicare v/i glitter

luccio m pike

lùcciola f fire-fly

luc|e f light; **~e di magnesio** flash; **~e di posizione** parking light; **~ente** shining

lucèrtola f lizard

lucherino m siskin

lucid|are v/t polish; **~ezza** f brightness

lùcido adj bright; shining; m brightness; **~ da scarpa** shoe-polish

lucignolo m wick

lucr|ativo profitable; **~o** m gain

luglio m July

lui he; him; **di ~** of his; **a ~** to him

lumaca f snail

lum|e m light; lamp; **~iera** f chandelier; **~inoso** luminous

luna f moon; fig bad mood; **~ di miele** honeymoon

lunedì m Monday

lung|hezza f length; **~i** far (off); **~o** long; along; **alla ~a** in the long run; **~omare** m seafront

luogo m place; spot; **avere ~** take place; **~ climatico** health-resort; **~ di nascita** birth-place; **in primo ~** in the first place; **in qualche ~** somewhere

lupo m wolf

lùppolo m hop

lusinga f allurement; **~are** v/t flatter

luss|are v/t sprain; dislocate; **~azione** f dislocation

luss|o m luxury; **~uoso** luxurious

lustr|are v/t polish; **~ascarpe** m, **~astivali** m shoeblack; **~o** adj shining; m polish; lustrum

lutto m mourning

M

m abbr for mare; maschile; metro; minuto; monte

ma but; yet

maccheroni m/pl macaroni

macchi|a f spot; stain; thicket; **~are** v/t stain

màcchina f machine; engine; **~ fotogràfica** camera; **~ da scrivere** typewriter; **~-roulette** trailer

macchin|ale mechanical; **~are** v/t contrive; plot;

~ista m machinist; engineer

macedonia f fruit-salad

macell|aio m butcher; **~are** v/t slaughter; **~eria** f butcher's shop

macerare v/t macerate; (hemp) ret

macerie f/pl ruins pl; rubbish

màcero macerated; fig worn out

macilento emaciated

màcina f mill-stone

macin|are v/t grind; **~ino** m coffee-mill

màdido damp; wet

Madonna f Our Lady

madre f mother; **lingua** f ~ mother tongue; **~perla** f mother of pearl; **~vite** f female screw; screw-nut

madrina f godmother

maest|à f majesty; **~oso** majestic

maestr|a f (school-) mistress; **~o** adj main; m teacher; master; **~o di cappella** choir-master; **strada** f ~a main street

maga f sorceress

magari! would to heaven!; even

magazzin|o m warehouse; store; **grandi ~i** m/pl storehouse; department store

maggio m May

maggiol|ata f May-song; **~ino** m cockchafer

maggioranza f majority

maggiore adj greater; larger; **il ~** the greatest; elder, eldest

maggior|enne of age; **~ità** f full age; majority

magìa f magic

màgico magic(al)

magist|ero m skill; mastery; teaching; **~rale** masterly

magli|a f stitch; undervest; pullover; **fare la ~a** knit; **~eria** f hosiery; **~etta** f light vest

magnano m locksmith

magn|ete m magnet; **~ètico** magnetic; **~etòfono** m tape recorder

magnific|are v/t exalt; **~enza** f magnificence

magnifico magnificent; splendid

magnolia f magnolia

mag|o m magician; **i tre re ~i** the Magi

magr|ezza f leanness; **~o** lean; thin; **giorno** m **di ~o** fast day

mai ever; **non ~** never; **~ più** never more; **come ~?** how so?; **se ~** if ever

maiale m pig; pork

maionese f mayonnaise

maiùscola f capital letter

mal|afede f bad faith; **di ~affare** ill-famed; **~agévole** difficult

mal|ànimo m ill-will; **a ~apena** hardly

malaria f malaria; marshfever

mal|aticcio sickly; **~ato** adj sick (**di** of); m sick person; **~attia** f illness; **~attia contagiosa** contagion; **~attie** f/pl **venèree** venereal diseases pl

malavita f underworld

mal|contento dissatisfied; **~destro** awkward

mal|e m evil; wrong; suffering; **~ di denti** tooth-ache; **~ di gola** sore throat; **avere ~ di mare** be seasick; **~ di testa** head-ache; adv badly; **capire ~e** misunderstand; **di ~e in peggio** from bad to worse

male|detto cursed; **~dire**

v/t curse

mal|educato ill-bred; **~efizio** *m* crime; evil spell; **~erba** *f* (noxious) weed

mal|èssere *m* discomfort; **~èvolo** malevolent; **~fido** unreliable; **~governo** *m* misgovernment; **~grado** in spite of

maligno spiteful; malignant

malinc|onìa *f* melancholy; **~ònico** melancholic

mal|inteso *adj* misunderstood; *m* misunderstanding; **~izia** *f* malice; **~izioso** malicious

mallèolo *m* ankle-bone

mallevadore *m* bail; guarantor

mal|sano unhealthy; **~sicuro** unsafe; **~tempo** *m* bad weather

malto *m* malt

maltrattare *v/t* illtreat

malumore *m* ill-humour

mal|vagio *adj* wicked; *m* rascal; **~versazione** *f* embezzlement; **~volenti** unwillingly

mamm|a *f* mother; ma(m)ma; **~ella** *f* (woman's) breast; **~elle** *f/pl* udder; **~ìfero** *m* mammal

manata *f* handful

manc|a *f* left hand; **~anza** *f* lack (**di** of); **~are** *v/i* want; be lacking; **~hévole** defective; faulty

mancia *f* tip

manc|ina *f* left hand; **a ~ina** left; **~ino** left-handed; **~o** *m* deficiency; lack

mandare *v/t* send; **~ a prèndere** send for; **~ giù** swallow

mandarino *m* tangerine

mandato *m* order; mandate; **~ bancario** cheque

mandolino *m* mandolin

màndorl|a *f* almond; **~o** *m* almond-tree

maneg|gévole handy; **~giare** *v/t* handle; **~gio** *m* handling; riding-ground

man|esco ready with one's hands; brutal; **~ette** *f/pl* handcuffs *pl*

manganare *v/t* mangle

màngano *m* mangle

mang|iàbile eatable; **~iare** *v/t, v/i* eat; corrode; consume; *m* food; **~ime** *m* fodder

mànic|a *f* sleeve; **la Mànica** the (British) Channel; **~o** *m* handle; shaft

manicomio *m* lunatic asylum

manicotto *m* muff

manicure *f* manicure

manier|a *f* manner; fashion; **di ~a che** so that; **in nessuna ~a** not at all; **~e** *f pl* manners *pl*

manieroso well-mannered

manifatt|ore *m* maker; workman; **~ura** *f* manufacture; factory; **~ure** *pl* manufactured goods *pl*

manifest|are *v/t* manifest; show; **~arsi** *v/r* appear; **~azione** *f* manifestation; **~ino** *m* handbill; **~o** *adj* clear; plain; *m* placard; poster

maniglia f handle

manipolare v/t manipulate; handle

mano f hand; **èssere di ~** lead; **cèdere la ~** give precedence; **man ~** gradually; **a ~ a ~** little by little; **dòpera** f labour; **man ower**

manòpola f gauntlet; knob

mano|scritto m manuscript; **~vella** f handle; crank

manovr|a f manoeuvre; **~are** v/t steer; work; **~atore** m (tram) driver

mans|uefare v/t appease; tame; **~ueto** meek

mant|ellina f cape; **~ello** m cloak; coat

mantenere v/t maintain; support (s.o.); keep

màntice m bellows pl; (car) hood

mantiglia f mantilla

manuale m handbook; adj: **lavoro** m **~** manual labour

manubrio m handle-bar

manzo m beef; **~ lesso** boiled beef; **arrosto** m **di ~** roastbeef

mappa f map

marasca f morello cherry

maraviglia = meraviglia

marca f mark; brand; **~ di fàbbrica** trade-mark

marcare v/t mark; score; stamp

marches|a f marchioness; **~e** m marquis

marchio m brand

marcia f march; pus; auto:

gear); **~a indietro** reverse (gear)

marci|apiede m side-walk; platform; **~are** v/i march; **~ata** f marching

marcio rotten; putrid

marco m (German) mark; **tre marchi** 3 marks

mare m sea; **bagno m di ~** sea-bath; **viaggio m per ~** sea voyage

marea f tide; **alta ~a** flood (-tide); **bassa ~a** ebb

mar|eggiata f rough sea; **~emoto** m sea-quake

marescialllo m marshal

màrgine m margin

marin|a f sea; coast; navy; paint sea-scape; **~aio**, **~aro** m sailor

marionetta f puppet

marit|àbile marriageable; **~are** v/t marry (off)

marito m husband

marittimo marine; maritime, sea ...; **commercio** m **~** maritime trade

marmellata f jam

marmo m marble

marmotta f marmot

marrone adj brown; m chestnut; gross mistake

marsina f dress-coat

martedì m Tuesday; **~ grasso** Shrove Tuesday

martell|are v/t hammer; **~o** m hammer; knocker

màrtire m martyr

martirio m martyrdom

màrtora f marten

marzapane m marzipan

marzo m March

mascalzone m scoundrel

mascell|a f: ~ **inferiore (superiore)** lower (upper) jaw; **dente** m ~**are** back-tooth

màschera f mask; usher; ~ **antigas** gas mask; **ballo** m **in** ~ masked ball

mascherare v/t mask

maschile male; **scuola** f ~ boys' school

maschio adj male; m biol male

massa f mass; heap

massacr|are v/t slaughter; **~o** m massacre

mass|aggiatore m masseur; **~aggiatrice** f masseuse; **~aggio** m massage

mass|aia f housewife; **~erìa** f farm

massiccio massive

màssima f maxim; rule

màssimo adj greatest; m maximum

masso m block; rock

masticare v/t chew

mastro m master; **libro** m ~ ledger

matemàtica f mathematics

materasso m mattress; ~ **pneumàtico** air-mattress

materi|a f matter; material; **~a prima** raw material; **~ale** m, adj material; **~ale di pronto soccorso** first-aid kit

matern|ità f maternity; **~o** motherly; maternal

matita f pencil; ~ **colorata** coloured pencil

matrice f matrix; womb

matrigna f step-mother

matrimoni|ale matrimonial; **letto** m ~**ale** double bed; **~o** m marriage; matrimony

mattina f morning; **di** ~ in the morning; **questa** ~ this morning; **domani** ~ tomorrow morning

mattin|ata f morning; matinée; **~o** m morning; **di buon** ~o early

matto adj mad; m madman

matt|onaia f brick-yard; **~onato** m brick floor; **~one** m brick

mattutino m matins pl

matur|are v/i ripen; mature; **~ità** f ripeness; maturity; **~o** ripe; fig mature

mazza f (walking-)stick; club

mazzo m bunch; pack; ~ **di fiori** bunch of flowers; ~ **di chiavi** bunch of keys; ~ **di carte** pack of cards; **~lino** m small bunch

me me; (= **mi** before **lo, la, li, le, ne**) to me; **pòvero** ~! poor me!; **come** ~ like myself; **di** ~ of mine

meccànic|a f mechanics pl; **~o** adj mechanic(al); m mechanic(ian); **~o d'automòbile** car-mechanic

meccanism|o m mechanism

mecenate m Maecenas; patron

medaglia f medal

medèsim|o same; self; **il ~o, la ~a** the same

media f average; mean;

~iano adj median; m football: half-back; **~iante** by means of; **~iatore** m mediator; com broker

medic|amento m remedy; **~are** v/t dress (wound); **~astro** m quack; **~azione** f treatment; dressing; **~ina** f medicine; **erba** f **~inale** medicinal herb

mèdico m physician; doctor

medi|o middle; average; **scuola** f **~a** secondary school; **dito** m **~o** middle finger

mediocr|e mediocre; **~ità** f mediocrity

medio|evale mediaeval; **~evo** m Middle Ages

medit|are v/t, v/i mediate; ponder; **~azione** f meditation

mediterràneo mediterranean; **~mare** m 2 = 2 m Mediterranean (Sea)

medusa f jelly-fish; medusa

meglio adj better; **~!** or **tanto ~!** so much the better!; m best

mela f apple

melagran|a f pomegranate; **~o** m pomegranate-tree

melanconìa = malinconìa

melanzana f eggplant; gast aubergine

mellone m melon

melo m apple-tree

mel|odìa melody; **~òdico** melodious

membrana f membrane

membro m anat (pl **le membra**) limb; fig (pl **i membri**) member

memor|àbile, **~ando** memorable

mèmore mindful

memoria f memory; **a ~** by heart

menadito: a ~ perfectly

menare v/t lead

mendace mendacious

mendic|ante m, f beggar; **~are** v/t, v/i beg; **~o** m beggar

mening|e f meninx; **~ite** f meningites

meno less; **fare a ~ di** do without; renounce; **per lo ~** at least

mensa f table; cafeteria; mess; **sacra ~** Holy Communion

mensile monthly

mènsola f console

menta f peppermint

mentale mental; **malattìa** f **~ mental** disorder

mente f mind; **avere in ~ di** have a mind to...; **venire in ~** come into s.o.'s mind

mentire v/i lie

mento m chin

mentre, nel ~ che while

menzion|are v/t mention; **~e** f mention

menzogna f lie

meravigli|a f wonder; astonishment; **~are** v/t amaze; **~arsi** v/r wonder; **~ato** amazed; **~oso** wonderful

mercant|e m merchant; dealer; **~ile** mercantile;

commercial; **flotta** f ~**ile** merchant fleet

mercato m market; ~ **coperto** covered market; **a buon** ~ cheap; ~ **mondiale** world market

merc|e f merchandise; **treno** m **~i** goods train

mercé f mercy

merc|ede f reward; salary; **~eria** f mercery; **~iaio** m mercer; **~iaiuolo** m pedlar; hawker

mercoledì m Wednesday

mercuri|ale adj mercurial; m market report; **~o** m mercury

merenda f afternoon-tea

meridiana f sun-dial

meridionale adj Southern; **Italia** f ~ Southern Italy

meriggio m midday; noon

meringa f meringue

merino m merino (sheep)

meritare v/t deserve

mèrito m merit; **in** ~ **a** concerning

merlett|are v/t trim with lace; **~o** m lace

merlo m battlement; blackbird

merluzzo m cod-fish

mesata f monthly pay

méscere v/t pour out; mix

meschino mean; paltry

méscita f bar; pub

mescolare v/t mix

mese m month

mess|a f eccl mass; **~a in piega** setting (*hair*); **~a in scena** thea staging; **~a solenne** High Mass; **~aggero**

m messenger; **~aggio** m message; **~ale** m missal

messe f harvest

Mèssico m Mexico

mestic|are v/t paint prime; **~heria** f oil and colour shop

mestiere m craft; profession

mest|izia f sadness; m sad

mestruazione f menstruation

meta f aim; goal

metà f half; **a** ~ half(way)

metàllico metallic

metall|o m metal; **~urgìa** f metallurgy; **~ùrgico** m metal worker

meteorològico: bollettino m ~ weather report

meticoloso meticulous

metòdic|a f methodics pl; **~o** methodic(al)

mètodo m method

mètrica f metrics pl

metro m meter; **~ quadrato** square meter; **~ cubo** cubic meter

metròpoli f metropolis

metropolitana f metropolitan railway

méttere v/t put; place; lay; **~ in fuga** put to flight; **~ in scena** stage

mezz|alana f linsey-wolsey; **~aluna** f crescent; gast chopping knife; **~anino** m mezzanine

mezzanotte f midnight

mezzo adj half; **un** ~ **litro** half a litre; **un litro e** ~ **a** litre and a half; m half; middle; means; **per** ~ **di** by means of; **in** ~ **a** among; **nel**

miopia

~ **del** in the middle of ...;
~**busto** m half-length portrait; ~**cerchio** m half-circle; ~**dì** m, ~**giorno** m noon; geog south

mi me; to me; myself

miagolare v/i mew

mica: non ... ~ not at all

microbo m microbe

micro|càmera f miniature camera; ~**film** m microfilm; ~**motore** m small motorcycle; ~**scopio** m microscope

midoll|a f crump; marrow; ~**o** m **spinale** spinal cord

miei m/pl my; mine

miele m honey

mietère v/t mow

mietitore m mower; reaper

migliaio m thousand

miglio m mile

miglior|amento m improvement; ~**are** v/t, v/i improve; ~**arsi** get better; ~**e** better; **il** ~**e** the best

mignolo m little finger; little toe

Milano f Milan

miliardo m milliard

miliare: pietra f ~ mile stone

mili|onario m millionaire; ~**one** m million

militare adj military; m soldier

milite m militiaman

mili|zia f militia; army; ~**e** pl troops pl

mille thousand

mill|enne millenary; ~**ennio** m millennium; ~**ìme-**

tro m millimetre

milza f spleen

mìmica f gestures pl; mimicry

mimosa f mimosa

mina f mine; ~ **di ricambio** refill

minacci|a f menace; threat; ~**are** v/t threaten; ~**oso** threatening

min|are v/t (under)mine; ~**atore** m miner

minchionare v/t ridicule

minerale m mineral; **acqua** f ~ mineral water

minestr|a f soup; ~**a di verdura** vegetable-soup; ~**ina** f clear soup; ~**one** m thick vegetable soup

miniatura f miniature

miniera f mine; quarry

minigolf m mini-golf

minimo smallest; least

minist|eriale ministerial; **crisi** f ~**eriale** cabinet crisis; ~**ero** m ministry; office; department; ~**ro** m minister; secretary of state

minor|anza f minority; ~**e** minor; less(er); younger; ~**enne** under age

minùscolo small (letter)

minuto adj minute; small; **al** ~ detailed; **commercio** m **al** ~ retail sale; m minute; ~ **secondo** second

minuzi|a f trifle; ~**oso** punctilious

mio my; m mine; **i miei** my family

miope short-sighted

miopia f myopy

miosòtide _f_ forget-me-not

mira _f_ aim; **avere in** ~ intend to

miràbile admirable

miràcolo _m_ miracle

miracoloso miraculous

miraggio _m_ mirage

mirare _v/t_ look at; _v/i_ aim (at)

mirino _m_ _phot_ view-finder

mirtillo _m_ crown-berry

mirto _m_ myrtle

misàntropo _m_ misanthropist

miscela _f_ mixture

mischi|a _f_ fight; **~are** _v/t_ mix; blend; **~arsi** _v/r_ meddle; **~o** _adj_ mixed; _m_ mixture

miscredenza _f_ unbelief

miscuglio _m_ mixture; medley

miser|àbile miserable; wretched; **~évole** pitiful

miseria _f_ misery

misericordi|a _f_ compassion; **~oso** merciful

misero wretched

miss|ione _f_ mission; **~iva** _f_ message

mister|ioso mysterious; **~o** _m_ mystery

mistic|a _f_ mysticism; **~o** mystical

mistificare _v/t_ hoax

misto mixed; **treno** _m_ **~** passenger- and goods-train

mistura _f_ mixture

misur|a _f_ measure; size; **su ~a** made to measure; **~are** _v/t_ measure; **~ato** measured; moderate

mit|e mild; **~ezza** _f_ gentleness

mitigare _v/t_ alleviate

mitra _f_ _eccl_ mitre

mitragliatrice _f_ machinegun

mittente _m_ sender

mòbile _adj_ movable; _m_ piece of furniture

mobiliare _v/t_ furnish

moca _m_ mocha

moda _f_ fashion; **alla ~** in fashion; **di ~** fashionable; **fuor di ~** out of fashion

modell|are _v/t_ mould; **~o** _m_ model; pattern

moder|are _v/t_ moderate; **~ato** moderate; **~azione** _f_ moderation

mod|estia _f_ modesty; **~esto** modest

modific|are _v/t_ modify; **~azione** _f_ modification

modista _f_ milliner

modo _m_ manner; way; _mus_ key; **ad ogni ~** at any rate

mòdulo _m_ blank; form; **~ per telegrammi** telegraph form

mògano _m_ mahagony

moglie _f_ wife; **prènder ~** get married

mola _f_ grindstone

molare _v/t_ grind; **dente ~** molar tooth

molest|are _v/t_ molest; **~ia** _f_ molestation; **~o** irksome

moll|a _f_ spring; **~e** soft; **~eggiare** be springy; **~eggio** _m_ springing; **~ezza** _f_ softness; **~ificare** _v/t_ soften

molo _m_ pier; wharf

moltéplice multiple

molteplic|ità f multiplicity; **~are** v/t multiply; **~arsi** v/r increase

moltitùdine f multitude; crowd

molto much; very

moment|àneo momentary; **~o** m moment

mònaca f nun

monacale: àbito m **~** monk's frock

mònaco m monk

mon|arca m monarch; **~archia** f monarchy

monastero m monastery

monco maimed; fig incomplete

mond|ano wordly

mondare v/t clean; (fruit) peel

mondiale: fama ~ world-wide renown

mondo m world; **l'altro ~** the other world

monello m urchin

moneta f coin; **carta f ~** paper money

mongolfiera f air-balloon

monile m necklace

monitore m monitor

mon|òcolo m monocle; adj one-eyed; **~opolio** m monopoly; **~osillabo** m monosyllable; **~òtono** monotonous

Monsignore m (Your) Lordship; (Your) Grace

mont|agna f mountain; **~agnoso** mountainous; **~anaro** m highlander; **~are** v/t mount; mech assemble;

~are a amount to

monte m mount(ain); fig heap; **~ di pietà** pawn-broker's shop

montone m ram

montuoso mountainous

monumento m monument

mora f mulberry; black-berry; negress; delay

moral|e adj moral; f morals pl; **~ità** f morality

morbidezza f softness

mòrbido soft; fig feeble

morbillo m measles pl

mordace biting

mòrdere v/t bite; sting; corrode

morfina f morphine

mor|ibondo dying; **~ire** v/i die

mormor|are v/i murmur; **~io** m murmur; muttering

moro adj black; m negro; mulberry-tree

moros|a f fam beloved; sweetheart; **~o** adj tardy; m lover

morsa f vice

mors|icare v/t bite; **~o** m bite; sting; (horse) bit

mortaio m mortar

mortal|e mortal; deadly; **~ità** f mortality

mort|e f death; **~ificare** v/t mortify; humiliate

morto adj dead; deceased; **stanco ~** dead tired; m dead man

mort|orio m burial; **annuncio** m **~uario** announcement of death

mosàico m mosaic

mosc|a f fly; **~aiuola** f flynet

mosc|atello m muscatel (vine); **~noce f ~ata** nutmeg

moschea f mosque

moschetto m rifle

mossa f move(ment); **~ di corpo** med stool

mostard|a f mustard; **~iera** f mustard-pot

mosto m must

mostr|a f show; display; dial-plate; **~are** v/t show; **~o** m monster; **~uoso** monstruous

mota f mud; slime

motiv|are v/t motivate; **~azione** f motivation; **~o** m motive; reason; **a ~o di** because of

moto m motion; **~cicletta** f motor-cycle; **~ciclista** m, f motor-cyclist; **~leggera** f moped; **~nave** f motor-ship; **~re** m motor; engine; **~re a due (quattro) tempi** two- (four-)cycle engine; **~re Diesel** Diesel engine; **~re fuoribordo** outboard motor; **~retta** f scooter; **~scafo** m motor-boat

motrice moving; **forza ~** driving power

motto m motto; device

mov|ente m motive; cause; **~ibile** movable; **~imento** m movement; traffic

mozz|icone m cigar stub; **~o** m cabin-boy

muca f (milk-)cow

mucchio m heap; pile

muc|o m mucus; **~osa** f mucous membrane

muff|are v/i grow mouldy; **~ato** mouldy

mugghi|are v/i (bel)low; moo; **~o** m (bel)lowing; roar(ing)

mughetto m lily of the valley

mugnaio m miller

mulin|ello m whirl; mech windlass; **~o** m mill

mulo m mule

multa f fine

multi|colore many-coloured; **~forme** multiform; **~laterale** multilateral

mùltiplo multiple

mùngere v/t milk; fig squeeze

municip|ale municipal; **consiglio** m **~** town-council; **palazzo** m **~** town-hall; **guardia** f **~** policeman

municipio m municipality; town hall

mun|ire v/t supply (**di** with); **~izione** f (am)munition

muòvere v/t move; stir

mur|aglia f wall; **~atore** m brick-layer; mason; **~atura** f masonry; **~o** m wall

muschio m musk

musco m moss

muscolatura f muscles pl

mùscolo m muscle

museo m museum; **~ archeològico** archeological museum; **~ dell'arte** arts and crafts museum; **~ etnogràfico** museum of ethnology; **~ nazionale** national museum; **~ delle**

scienze naturali museum of (natural) science
museruola f muzzle
musetto m pretty face
mùsica f music; band; ~ **da càmera** chamber music; **negozio** m **di** ~ music shop
musicale musical
musicista m, f, **mùsico** m musician
muso m snout; muzzle
mustacchi m/pl moustaches

mutàbile changeable
mut|ande f/pl drawers pl, pants pl; **~andine** f/pl panties pl; **~andine da bagno** bathing-drawers pl
mutare v/t change; alter
mutil|are v/t mutilate; **~ato** m cripple
muto adj dumb; mute; m dumb person
mùtuo adj mutual; m loan

N

nàcchere f/pl castanets pl
nafta f naphtha; petroleum
nailon m nylon
nano adj dwarfish; m dwarf
napoletano m, adj Neapolitan
Nàpoli f Naples
nappa f tassel
narciso m narcissus; daffodil
narc|osi f narcosis; **~òtico** m, adj narcotic; **~otizzare** v/t narcotize
narice f nostril
narr|are v/t tell; narrate; **~azione** f tale
nasale adj nasal; f nasal
nàsc|ere v/i be born; fig (a)rise; bot shoot (forth); **~ita** f birth
nasc|óndere v/t hide; conceal; **~ondiglio** m hiding-place
naso m nose
nassa f eel-pot
nastro m ribbon; ~ **isolante** insulating tape; ~ **magnè-**

tico recording tape
Natale m Christmas; **vigilia** f **di** ~ Christmas Eve
nat|ale native; natal; **città** f **~ale** birth-place; **giorno** m **~alizio** birthday
natante floating
nat|ività f nativity; **~ivo** native; **paese** m **~ivo** birthplace
nato born
natura f nature; ~ **morta** paint still life
natur|ale adj natural; m temper; constitution; **~alezza** f naturalness; **scienze** f/pl **~ali** (natural) science; **~alità** f citizenship; **~alizzare** v/t pol naturalize
naufrag|are v/i be shipwrecked; **~io** m shipwreck
nàufrago m shipwrecked person
nàusea f sickness; disgust
nauseare v/t make sick
nàutica f nautical science

navale naval; **cantiere** m ~ dockyard

navata f nave

nave f ship; boat; ~ **mercantile** cargo-ship; freighter; ~ **passeggeri** passenger-steamer; liner

navicella f barge; aer gondola

navig|àbile navigable; ~**atore** m navigator; ~**azione** f navigation

navone m turnip

nazional|e national; **prodotto** m ~**e** home product; ~**ità** f nationality; ~**izzare** v/t nationalize

ne of it; its; of them; of that, etc from there

né: ~ ... ~ neither ... nor

neanche not even

nebbia|a f fog; mist; ~**oso** foggy

necess|ario adj necessary; m needful; ~**ità** f necessity; need

nefrite f nephritis

neg|are v/t deny; ~**ativo** negative; ~**azione** f negation

negletto neglected

negli: prep in with article gli

neglig|ente negligent; ~**enza** f negligence

negozi|ante m merchant; ~**are** v/t, v/i negotiate; carry on business; ~**azione** f negotation

negozio m shop; store; ~ **grande** ~ store; ~ **speciale** special shop; ~ **di articoli fotogràfici** camera shop; ~ **di**

articoli musicali music-shop; ~ **di calzature** shoe-shop; ~ **di gèneri alimentari** food shop; ~ **di oggetti d'arte** fine-art dealers

negr|a f negress; ~**o** adj black; m negro

neh? isn't it?

nei, nel, nella, nelle, nello prep in with article i, il, la, le, lo

nem|ica f enmy; hostile; ~**ico** adj enemy

nemmeno not even

neo m mole; ~**nato** m new-born infant

neppure not even

nero black; **vino** m ~ red wine; ~**fumo** m lampblack

nerv|ino nervine; ~**o** m nerve; ~**osità** f nervousness; ~**oso** nervous

nèspol|a f bot medlar; ~**o** m medlar-tree

nessuno no; no one; nobody

nett|apipe m pipe cleaner; ~**are** v/t clean(se); ~**ezza** f pùbblica street-cleaning

netto clean; **guadagno** m ~ net gain

neutr|ale neutral; ~**alità** f neutrality; ~**o** neutral; gram neuter

nev|e f snow; ~**icare** v/i snow; ~**icata** f snow-fall; ~**ischio** m sleet

nevr|algia f neuralgia; ~**àlgico** neuralgic; ~**osi** f neurosis; ~**òtico** neurotic

nicchia f niche

nich|el m nickel; ~**elare** v/t nickel(-plate)

nido m nest

niente adj, adv nothing; m nothing(ness); **non ho ~ da fare** I have nothing to do; **~ affatto** not at all; **per ~** for nothing

nimbo m nimbus

ninn|a nanna f lullaby; **~are** v/t lull asleep

ninnolo m toy; **~i** pl knick-knacks

nipote m nephew; f niece; m, f grandchild

nitidezza f neatness

nitido neat; clear

nitr|ire v/i neigh; **~ito** m neigh(ing)

nitro m nitre; salpetre

no no; **se ~** if not; otherwise; **dire di ~** say no

nòbile adj noble; m noble-man

nobiltà f nobility

nocca f knuckle

nòcciolo m (fruit-)stone; kernel

nocciuol|a f hazel-nut; **~o** m hazel-tree

noce m walnut-tree; walnut-wood; f walnut; **~ moscata** nutmeg; **~ del piede** ankle; **~lla** f wrist

nocivo harmful

nodo m knot; bow

noi we; us; **~ altri** we

noi|a f tedium; annoyance; **~oso** tedious; annoying

noleggi|are v/t hire; naut charter; **~o** m hire; freight; **~o automòbili** car rental

nolo m hire; feight; **prèndere a ~** hire; **dare a ~** let

out on hire

nome m name; **~ (di battésimo)** Christian name; **~ di ragazza** maiden name

nòmina f appointment

nomin|are v/t appoint; mention; **~arsi** v/r be called

non not; **~ ancora** not yet; **già che** not that; **~ ti scordar di me** m bot forget-me-not

noncurante careless

nondimeno nevertheless

nonn|a f grandmother; **~o** m grandfather; **~i** m/pl grand-parents; ancestors

nonostante notwithstanding; in spite of

nord m north; **mare** m **del ~** North Sea; **~èst** m north-east

nòrdico northern

nord-ovest m north-west

norma f rule; regulation; standard; **a ~ di** according to

normale normal

Norvegia f Norway

nossignore no, Sir

nostalgia f home-sickness (**di** for); nostalgia

nostrano domestic; **vino** m **~** home-grown wine

nostro our; ours

nostromo m naut boatswain

nota f note; bill; list; **~ bene** nota bene

notàbile noticeable

notaio m notary

not|are v/t note; notice; **~arile** notarial; **~évole** note-worthy; remarkable; **~ifi-**

care v/t notify; **~izia** f
news; **~o** (well-)known; **far
~o** make known; **~orio**
notorious

notte f night; **di ~** at night;
buona ~! good night!

notturno nightly

nov|anta ninety; **~antenne**
ninety years old; **~azione** f
innovation

novell|a f news; (short) story

novembre m November

nov|ità f novelty; innovation; news; **~iziato** m apprenticeship; **~izio** adj inexperienced; m beginner;
eccl novice

nozione f notion

nozze f/pl wedding

nub|e f cloud; **~ifragio** m down-pour

nùbile marriageable (of girls only)

nuca f nape (of the neck)

nucleare nuclear; **centrale**
f **~** nuclear power station;
energia f **~** nuclear energy

nud|are v/t bare; **~ità** f nudity; **~o** adj naked; m paint
nude

nulla nothing; **per ~** not at all

nullo null; void

numer|àbile numerable;
~ale m numeral; **~are** v/t
number; count; **~atore** m
numerator

nùmero m number; **fare il ~**
tel dial; **~ di casa** street
number; **~ telefònico** telephone number

numeroso numerous

nunzio m eccl nuncio

nuòcere v/i harm; hurt

nuora f daughter-in-law

nuot|are v/i swim; **~atore**
m swimmer; **non ~atore**
non-swimmer; **~o** m swimming

nuov|a f news; **~o** adj new;
di ~o again; once more

nutr|ice f wet-nurse; **~imento** m nourishment;
food; **~ire** v/t nourish; feed;
~itivo nourishing

nùvola f cloud

nuvoloso cloudy

nuziale nuptial; **velo** m **~**
bridal veil

nylon m nylon

O

o or; either; else; **~ ... ~** either
... or

o! oh!; **~ signore!** oh God!

òasi f oasis

obbed|iente, ~ienza, ~ire =
ubbid—

obblig|are v/t oblige; compel; **~are a letto** confine to
one's bed; **~ato** obliged;

~atorio compulsory; **~azione** f obligation; com
bond

òbbligo m obligation; duty

obelisco m obelisk

obeso obese

obiett|are v/t object; **~ivo**
adj objective; m aim;
object-glass

obiezione f objection

oblazione f donation

obliquo oblique

oblungo oblong

òboe m oboe

oca f goose

occasion|ale occasional; **~e** f occasion

occhi|aia f eye-socket; **~ali** m/pl spectacles; **~ali da lettura** reading glasses pl; **~ali da sole** sun-glasses; **~alino** m monocle; **~ata** f glance; **~ello** m button-hole; **~o** m eye

occident|ale western; **~e** m west

occorr|ente adj necessary; m needful; **~enza** f need; occasion

occòrrere v/i be necessary; happen

occult|are v/t hide; **~o** occult

occup|are v/t occupy; employ (s.o.); **~arsi** v/r busy o.s. (**di**, in with); **~ato** (seat) taken; occupied; **~azione** f occupation

oceàno m ocean

ocra f ochre

ocul|ista m oculist; **~istica** f ophthalmology

od = o (before vowels)

ode he hears

odi|are v/t hate; **~ato** hated; **~o** m hatred; **~oso** hateful

odo I hear

odontoligìa f dentistry

odor|are v/t, v/i smell; **~ato** m smell; scent; **~e** m smell; **~oso** odorous; scented

offèndere v/t offend; hurt

offer|ente m bidder; **maggior ~** highest bidder

offerta f offer; bid

offesa f offence

offic|ina f: **~ concessionaria** authorized repairer; **~ di riparazioni** repair-shop

offrire v/t offer

offuscare v/t obscure

oftalmìa f ophthalmia

ogget|tivo adj objective; m objective; **~o** m object; **~i m/pl di valore** valuables pl

oggi today; **d'~** today's; **~ a otto** today week; **~dì, ~giorno** nowadays

ogni each; every; **~ giorno** every day; **~ tanto** now and then; **~ sei giorni** every sixth day

Ognissanti m All Saints' Day; **~uno** everybody

oh! oh!; **~ibò!** shame!

Olanda f Holland

olandese Dutch; **formaggio ~** Dutch cheese

ole|andro m oleander; **~ificio** m oil-mill

olezz|are v/i smell sweetly; **~o** m fragrance

oliera f oil-cruet

olio m oil; **~ per il cambio** transmission oil; **~ per il motore** motor oil; **~ d'oliva** olive oil; **~ di ricino** castor oil; **~ solare** sun-oil

oliv|a f olive; **~astro** olive-coloured; **~eto** m olive grove; **~o** m olive-tree

olmo m elm(-tree)

olocàusto m holocaust

oltracciò besides

oltraggiare v/t outrage

oltre beyond; besides; **~ché** besides; **~mondo** m the other world; **~passare** v/t overstep

omaggio m homage; **i miei ~i** my respects

ombr|a f shade; shadow; **~eggiare** v/t shade; **~ellaio** m umbrella-maker, -seller; **~ellino** m parasol; **~ello** m umbrella; **~ellone** m large parasol; **~oso** shady

òmero m shoulder

ométtere v/t omit

om|icida adj murderous; m, f murderer; **~icidio** m homicide; murder

omissione f omission

òmnibus m bus; **treno ~** m slow passenger-train

omosessuale m, adj homosexual

oncia f ounce

ond|a f wave; **~ata** f surge; **~ata di caldo** heat wave; **~ata di sangue** rush of blood

onde whence; from where; by which; in order to

ondeggiare v/i undulate; waver

ond|oso wavy; **~ulare** v/t wave

ònere m burden

oneroso burdensome

onest|à f honesty; **~o** honest

ònice m onyx

onnipotente almighty

onomàstico m name-day

onor|àbile honourable; **~a-**

bilità f honorability; **~ando** venerable; **~anza** f honour; **~are** v/t honour

onorario m fee; **membro ~** m honorary member

onor|e m honour; **~évole** honourable; **~ificenza** f honour; title

onta f shame; **ad ~ di** in spite of

opaco opaque

òpera f work; mus opera; **mano d'~** labour

oper|aio m worker; **~are** v/t med operate; act; work; **~ativo** operative; **~atore** m operator; **~azione** f operation; com transaction; **~etta** f operetta; **~oso** active; industrious

opinione f opinion

oppio m opium

opp|orre v/t oppose; **~orsi** v/r be opposed; **~ortuno** opportune; **~osizione** f opposition; **~osto** opposite; **all'~osto** on the contrary

oppr|essione f oppression; **~imere** v/t oppress

oppure or; or else

opulen|to opulent; **~za** f opulence

opùscolo m pamphlet

ora f hour; **~ estiva** summer time; **~ locale** local time; **~ di chiusura** closing time; **~ di partenza** time of departure; **~ d'ufficio** office-hour; **che ~ è?** what time is it?; adv now; at present; **di buon'~** early; **or ~** just now; **per ~** for the present; **d'~ in**

poi henceforth

òrafo m goldsmith

orale oral

oramai by this time

or|are v/i pray; **~azione** f oration; prayer

orario adj hourly; m timetable; **in ~** punctual(ly); **~ di volo** time-table

orat|ore m speaker; **~orio** m oratory

òrbita f orbit; socket

orchestra f orchestra

orchidèa f orchid

orcio m jar; pitcher

ordin|ale ordinal; **nùmero** m **~ale** ordinal number; **~amento** m arrangement; **~are** v/t order; direct; arrange; **~ario** ordinary; on the staff; **~atore** m organizer; **~azione** f order; eccl ordination

órdine m order; rank; thea tier; eccl holy orders pl; **~ del giorno** agenda; **fino a nuovo ~** until further orders

ordire v/t plot

orecchi|no m earring; **~o** m ear; **~oni** m/pl mumps

oréfice m goldsmith; jeweller

oreficeria f jeweller's shop

òrfano m, adj orphant

orfanotrofio m orphanage

organaio m organ-builder

orgànico organic

organ|ino m barrel-organ; **~ismo** m organism; **~ista** m, f organist; **~izzare** v/t organize; **~izzazione** f organ-

ization

òrgano m organ

orgogli|o m pride; **~oso** proud; haughty

orient|ale adj Eastern; Oriental; m Oriental; **~amento** m orientation; **~amento professionale** vocational guidance; **~are** v/t orient(ate); **~arsi** v/r find one's way; **~e** m east; Orient

originale original

origine f origin

origliare v/i eavesdrop

orina f urine

orinale m chamber-pot

orizzont|ale horizontal; **~e** m horizon

orl|are v/t hem; **~atura** f hemming; **~o** m hem; border

orma f footstep; trace

ormone m hormone

orn|amento m ornament; **~are** v/t adorn

oro m gold; **d'~** golden

orolog|eria f watchmaker's shop; **~iaio** m watchmaker; **~io** m clock; watch; **~io da polso** wrist-watch; **~io da tasca** pocket-watch

oròscopo m horoscope

orpello m tinsel (also fig)

orr|endo dreadful; **~ibile** horrible

òrrido horrid

orrore m horror

orso m bear

orsù! come on!

ortica f nettle

orticultura f horticulture

orto m kitchen-garden

orto|dosso orthodox; **~gra-fia** f orthography

ortolano m vegetable-gardener; greengrocer

ortopèdico orthopedic

orzaiuolo m sty(e) (*on the eye*)

orzo m barley; **~ perlato** pearl barley

osare v/t, v/i dare

oscur|are v/t darken; dim; **~ità** f darkness; **~o** dark

ospedale m hospital; **~mili-tare** military hospital

ospit|abile hospitable; **~alità** f hospitality; **~are** v/t shelter (*guests*)

òspite m host; guest; visitor

ospizio m hospice; convent

ossatura f osseous frame

ossequi|o m homage; respect; **~i** m/pl regards pl; **~ioso** respectful

osservanza f: **con perfetta ~** most respectfully Yours

osserv|are v/t observe; **~a-tore** m observer; **~atorio** m observatory; **~azione** f observation

ossesso adj possessed; m madman

ossia or (rather); that is to say

ossidare v/t oxidize

ossigen|are v/t peroxide (*hair*)

ossigeno m oxygen

osso m bone

ost|àcolo m obstacle

ostante: ciò non ~ nonetheless

oste m innkeeper; **~llo** m per

la gioventù youth hostel

ostensorio m monstrance

ost|eria f inn; pub; **~essa** f hostess; landlady

ostètrico adj obstetrical; m obstetrician

ostia f eccl Host; wafer

ostile hostile

ostilità f hostility

ostin|arsi v/r insist on; be obstinate; **~ato** obstinate

òstrica f oyster

ostric|aio, **~aro** m oyster-bed; oyster-seller

ostr|uire v/t obstruct; **~u-zione** f obstruction

otite f otitis

otorinolaringoiatra m ear, nose and throat specialist

otre m goat-skin bottle

ott|anta eighty; **~antenne** eighty years old

ottavo eighth; m eighth; octavo

ottenere v/t obtain; get

òttic|a f optics; **~o** adj optic(al); m optician

òttimo very good; best

otto eight; **oggi a ~** today week

ottobre m October

ottone m brass

otturatore m phot shutter

ottuso blunt

ov|aio m egg-seller; **~aiuolo** m egg-cup; **~ale** oval

ovatta f cotton-wool

ove where; whereas

ovest m west

ovile m sheepfold

ovunque wherever; everywhere

palla

òvvio obvious

oziare v/i idle; lounge

ozi|o m idleness; **~oso** adj

idle; m idler

ozòn|ico ozonic; **~o** m ozone

P

pacchetto m small parcel

pacchia f food; good living

pacco m package; parcel

pace f peace; **darsi ~** calm o.s.

paciere m peace-maker

pacific|are v/t appease; **~arsi** v/r **con qu.** get reconciled with s.o.; **~azione** f pacification

pacifico peaceful; **ocèano** ~ 2 the Pacific

padella f frying-pan; anat knee-pan

padiglione m pavilion; tent; **~ dell'orecchio** outer ear

Pàdova f Padua

padr|e m father; **~ino** m godfather

padron|a f mistress; landlady; **~ale** belonging to the master; private; **~ato** m possesssion; **~e** m master; employer; master; principal; **~e di casa** landlord

paes|aggio m landscape; **~ano** adj native; m countryman; **~e** m country; village; **~ista** m f landscape painter

pag|a f pay; salary; wages pl; **~àbile** payable

pagaia f paddle

pagamento m payment; **~ anticipato** advance payment

pagan|èsimo m paganism;

~o adj pagan; m heathen

pagare v/t pay; **~ a rate** pay by instalments

paggio m page

pàgina f page

paginare v/t paginate

paglia f straw; **cappello m di ~** straw-hat; **~ d'acciaio** steel wool

paglino m straw-work

pagliuzza f straw

paio m pair

pala f shovel

palafitta f pile-dwelling

palan|ca f plank; board; thea box; fam coin; **~chino** m sedan-chair

palàncola f plank

palato m anat palate

palazzina f country mansion

palazzo m palace; **~ comunale** (also **municipale**) City Hall; **~ di giustizia** law-court; **~ reale** Royal Palace

palchetto m shelf; thea box

palco m scaffold; stand; thea box; **~scènico** m stage

pales|amento m revelation; **~are** v/t disclose; **~e** evident

palestra f gymnasium

paletta f shovel; palette

paletto m door-bolt

palio m race

palla f ball; bullet; **~ a**

mano hand-ball; **~ di neve** snowball; **~ dell'occhio** eyeball; **fare alla ~** play ball; **~canestro** m basket-ball; **~corda** f tennis; **~maglio** m cricket; **~nuoto** m water-ball; **~ta** f blow from a ball

palliativo m palliative

pallidezza f paleness

pàllido pale

pallina f small ball; **~o** m small shot

pall|oncino m child's balloon; Chinese lantern; **~one** m football

pallore m pallor

pallòttola f bullet

pallottoliere m (child's) counting-frame

palma f palm

palm|eto m palm-grove; **~izio** m palm-branch; **~o** m hand's breadth, span

palo m post; **~ del telègrafo** telegraph-pole

palombaro m diver

palp|àbile touchable; **~are** v/t touch

pàlpebra f eyelid

palpit|are v/i throb; pant; **~azione** f, **pàlpito** m throbbing

paltò m overcoat

palud|e f marsh; moor; **~oso** marshy

palustre marshy; **febbre f ~** marsh fever

panca f bench

panchetto m (foot)stool

panci|a f belly; **~otto** m waistcoat; **~otto pneu-**

màtico life-jacket; **~uto** corpulent

pane m bread; **~ bianco** white bread; **~ bigio** grey bread; **~ nero** brown bread; **~ tostato** toast; **un ~** a bread-loaf; **~ di zùcchero** loaf of sugar; **fare il ~** bake bread

panett|erìa f bakery; **~iere** m baker

panfilo m yacht

panforte m ginger-bread

pànico adj panic; m (also **timor** m **~**) panic (terror); millet

pan|iera f basket; **~ieraio** m basket-maker; **~iere** m basket; **~ificare** v/t bake bread; **~ificio** m bakery

panino m roll; **~ imbottito** sandwich

panna f cream; auto: break-down; **~ montata** whipped cream; **essere in ~** have a break-down

pann|eggiare v/t drape; **~ello** m piece of cloth; panel; **~o** m cloth; **méttersi nei ~i di qu.** put o.s. in s.o.'s place; **~olino** m linen cloth

pannocchia f corn-cob

panorama m view

pantaloni m/pl trousers pl

pantòfola f slipper

pantomima f pantomime

paonazzo violet; purple

papà m dad; father

pap|a m pope; **~ale** papal; **~ato** m papacy

papàvero m poppy

parsimonia

pappa f pap
pappagallo m parrot
pappare v/t gulp down
pàprica f red pepper
para|brezza m windscreen; **~cadute** m parachute; **~cadutista** m,f parachutist; **~carro** m curbstone; **~cènere** m fender
paradiso m paradise
parafango m auto: mudguard; fender
parafùlmine m lightning-rod
paragon|àbile comparable; **~are** v/t compare; **~e** m comparison
paràlisi f paralysis; **~ progressiva** progressive paralysis
paralìtico paralytic
parallel|a f parallel; **~e** pl parallel bars; **~o** parallel
para|lume m lamp-shade; **~mosche** m fly-net; **~petto** m parapet
parare v/t adorn; protect (**da** against); avert
parasole m parasol
parassita m parasite
parata f parade
parato m ornament
paraurti m bumper
parcare v/t park
parcella f bill
parcheggiare v/t park
parcheggio m parking (-place); **divieto** m **di ~** no parking
parchìmetro m, **parcòmetro** parking meter
parco adj sparing; m park

parecchi|o a good deal; **~i** m/pl, **~ie** f/pl several
pareggiare v/t level; com balance; **~ qu.** be equal to s.o.
pareggio m balance
parent|ado m kinship; **~e** adj related; m,f relative; **~ela** f relatives pl
parèntesi f parenthesis; f/pl brackets pl
parere v/i seem; **che Le pare?** what do you think?; m opinion; advice
parete f wall
pari like; equal; even; **un ~ tuo** the like of you
pariment|e, ~i likewise
parità f parity
parlament|are adj parliamentary; m parliamentarian; v/i parley; **~ario** m negotiator; **~o** m parliament
parl|antino gabby; **~are** v/t, v/i speak (**a qu.** to s.o.); **lingua** f **~ata** colloquial language; **~atore** m speaker; **~atorio** m parlour
parmigiano m Parmesan cheese
parol|a f word; **~e** f/pl incrociate crossword puzzle
parrocchi|a f parish; **chiesa** f **~ale** parish church
pàrroco m parson
parr|ucca f wig; **~ucchiera** f, **~ucchiere** m hairdresser; **~ucchiere per signore** ladies' hairdresser; **~ucchiere per uomo** men's hairdresser; barber
parsimonia f parsimony

parte f part (*also* thea); side; party; **a ~** part; **da ~** aside; **da mia ~** on my behalf; **in ~** partly; **lo saluti da ~ mia** give him my regards

particip|ante m, f participant; **~are** v/i partake (in); attend; v/t inform; **~azione** f participation; announcement

parteggiare v/i side (with)

partenza f departure; starting); sailing

participio m participle

particol|are adj particular; m detail; **~areggiato** detailed; **~arità** f detail; peculiarity

partigiano m partisan

partire v/t divide; v/i leave (**per** for)

partit|a f game; com lot; **~a di calcio** football match; **~a sémplice (doppia)** single (double) entry

partitivo: articolo m ~ partitive article

partito m party; decision

partizione f partition

parto m delivery, child-birth

partoriente f woman in childbed

parvenza f appearance

parzi|ale partial; **~alità** f partiality

pàscere v/i graze

pascolare v/t, v/i pasture

pàscolo m pasture

Pasqua f Easter

passàbile tolerable

passaggio m passage; trans-

it; **di ~** in passing; **~ a livello** level crossing (**custodito** guarded, **incustodito** unguarded); **~ di confine** frontier crossing point

passante m passer-by

passaporto m passport

passare v/t, v/i pass (along); happen; elapse(time); **~ di moda** get out of style; **~ di mente** slip one's memory

pass|ata f passing; glance; shower (rain); gast mash; **~atempo** m pastime; **~ato** m, adj past; **~atoia** f stair-carpet

passegero m passenger; traveller

passeggi|are v/i walk; **~ata** f walk; **fare una ~ata in carrozza** take a drive; **~o** m promenade

passeraio m twittering

passerella f gangway

pàssero m sparrow

passion|ato passionate; **~e** f suffering; passion

passiv|ità f inactivity; com liability; **~o** adj passive; m gram passive; com liabilities pl

passo adj faded; dried; m step; pass; literary: passage; **~ falso** false step

pasta f dough; paste; pastry; **~ dentifricia** tooth-paste; **~ al brodo** noodle soup; **~ asciutta** macaroni

pastaio m macaroni seller

pastello m pastel

past|icceria f pastry-shop; **~icciere** m pastry-cook;

~iccio m pie; **~iccio di fégato d'oca** pâté de foie gras; **~ificio** m macaroni factory; **~iglia** f tablet; **~ina** f fine noodles; **~ina in brodo** noodle soup

pasto m meal; **vino m da ~** table-vine

past|orale adj pastoral; m crozier; f pastoral letter; **~ore** m shepherd; pastor

pastoso soft; mellow

past|ura f pasture; **~urare** v/t, v/i pasture

patat|a f potato; **~e** pl **fritte** fried potatoes

patent|are v/t license; **~e** adj obvious; f certificate; auto: driver's license

paterno fatherly

paternostro m Lord's Prayer

patimento m suffering

patire v/t, v/i suffer

patri|a f fatherland; **~arca** m patriarch; **~gno** m stepfather; **~monio** m patrimony

patrio native

patriot(t)a m, f, f patriot

patrizio m patrician

patr|onato m patronage; **~ono** m patron (saint); protector

patteggi|are v/t, v/i bargain; **~atore** m negotiator

pattin|aggio m skating; **~aggio artístico** figure skating; **~are** v/i skate; **~atore** m skater

pàttino m skate

patto m agreement; condi-

tion; **a ~ che** on condition that

pattuglia f patrol

patt|ume m sweepings pl; **~umiera** f dustbin

paur|a f fear; fright; **avere ~a** be afraid; **~oso** afraid

pausa f pause

pav|esare v/t deck with flags; **~ese** m flag

pàvido timid

paviment|are v/t pave; floor; **~ento** m floor

pavon|azzo purple; **~e** m peacock

pazi|entare v/i have patience; **~ente** adj enduring; m patient; **~enza** f patience

pazz|ia f insanity; madness; **~o** adj mad; insane; m madman

p. e. = per esempio for instance

pecc|àbile liable to sin; **~are** v/i. sin; **~ato** m sin; **~ato!** che **~ato!** what a pity!; **~atore** m sinner

pece f pitch

pècora f sheep; ewe

pecor|aio m shepherd; **~ile** m sheepfold; **~ino** m cheese from ewe's milk

peculiarità f peculiarity

pecuni|a f money; **~ario** pecuniary

pedaggio m toll

pedagogia f pedagogy

ped|alare v/i pedal; cycle; **~ale** m pedal; **~ale della frizione** clutch pedal; **~ana** f footboard

pedante adj pedantic; m pedant

pedata f footprint; kick

pediatra m, f paediatrician

pedicure f pedicure

pediluvio m foot-bath

pedina f man (chess)

pedone m pedestrian

pegg|io worse; **il ~o** the worst; **~oramento** m getting worse; **~orare** v/i deteriorate; v/t make worse; **~ore** worse; **il ~ore** the worst

pegno m pawn; token; **méttere qc. in ~** pawn s.th.

pégola f melted pitch

pell|ame m hair (animals); fur; **~are** v/t (fowl) pluck; fleece; (fruit) peel; **~arsi** v/r lose one's hair; **~ato** bald; stripped

pell|agra f pellagra; **~aio** m tanner; **~ame** m hides pl; skins pl

pelle f skin; hide; peel; **~ di camoscio** suède chamois-leather; **~ di bue** cow-hide

pellegr|ina f woman pilgrim; pelerine; **~inaggio** m pilgrimage; **~inare** v/i go on pilgrimage; fig wander; **~ino** m pilgrim

pellerossa m, f red-skin (American) Indian

pelletter|ia f leather shop; **~ie** f/pl leather articles

pellicc|eria f furrier's shop; **~ia** f fur (coat); **~iaio** m furrier; **~iame** m furs pl

pellicola f phot film; **~ a caricatore** cassette film; **~** cinematografica film, (moving) picture, movie; **~ a colori** colour film; **~ impressionata** exposed film; **~ a passo ridotto** cinefilm; **~ in ròtolo** roll film

pelo m hair; (animals) fur; **contro ~** against the grain; **~so** hairy

pell|uria f down; **~uzzo** m soft hair

pena f penalty; pain; trouble; **sotto ~ di** on pain of; **a mala ~** hardly

penale penal; **~lità** f penalty

pend|ente hanging; pendent; **torre ~ente** leaning tower; **~enza** f slope; fig. pending matter

pèndere v/i hang; lean; slope; (business) be pending

pendio m slope; declivity

pèndol|a f (pendulum) clock; **~o** m pendulum

penetrare v/t penetrate; enter into

penicillina f penicillin

penisola f peninsula

penit|ente adj repentant; m penitent; **~enza** f penitence; **~enziario** m penitentiary; **~enziere** m eccl penitentiary

penn|a f feather; pen; **~a a sfera** ball-pointed pen; **~a stilogràfica** fountain-pen; **~ello** m brush; **~ino** m steel pen

penoso painful; toilsome

pens|àbile thinkable; **~are** v/t, v/i think; consider; provide (a for); **~atore** m thinker; **~iero** *m* thought; trouble; **~ieroso** thoughtful

pension|are *v/t* pension (off); **~ato** *m* pensioner

pensione *f* (retiring) pension; **boarding-house**; **~ completa** room and (full) board; **mezza ~** room with breakfast and one principal meal

pensoso pensive

Pentecoste *f* Whitsuntide

pent|imento *m* repentance; **~irsi** *v/r* repent; be sorry (**di qc.** for s.th.)

pèntola *f* pot; kettle; **~ a pressione** pressure cooker

penùltimo last but one

penuria *f* penury (**di** of)

penzol|are *v/i* dangle; **~oni** dangling

pep|aiuola *f* pepper-pot; pepper-mill; **~ato** peppered; **pan** *m* **~ato** gingerbread; **~e** *m* pepper; **~erone** *m* pimento; chilli

per for; through; by; **~ mano** by hand; **~ 3 giorni** for 3 days; **~ mancanza di** for want of; **~ partire** leave for; **~ terra** by land; **~ mare** by sea; **~ esempio** for instance

pera *f* pear

per|cento *m* percent; **~centuale** *f* percentage

perce|pire *v/t* perceive; **~zione** *f* perception

perchè because; so that; **~?** why?

perciò therefore; **~occhè** because; since

perc|órrere *v/t* run through; **~orso** *m* distance; journey; **~orso di arresto** *aut* stopping distance

perc|ossa *f* blow; stroke; **~uòtere** *v/t* strike; **~ussione** *f* percussion

pèrd|ere *v/t* lose; miss; **~ersi** *v/r* get lost

perdigiorno *m* good-for-nothing

perdìo! by God!

pèrdita *f* loss

perd|itempo *m* waste of time; **~itore** *m* loser

perdon|àbile forgivable; **~are** *v/t* forgive; **~o** *m* forgiveness

perdurare *v/i* last; persist

peregr|inare *v/i* wander; **~ino** foreign; *fig.* strange

perenne everlasting

perf|etto *adj* perfect; *m gram* perfect tense; **~ezionamento** *m* completion; **~ezionare** *v/t* finish; improve; **~ezione** *f* perfection

perfidia *f* perfidy

pèrfido wicked; treacherous

perfino even

perfor|are *v/t* pierce; **~atore** *m* puncher; **~atrice** (**màcchina** *f* **~atrice**) *f* drill; borer; **~azione** *f med* perforation; rapture

pergamena *f* parchment

pèrgola *f* vine-trellis

perìcolo *m* danger; **~ di valanghe** danger of avalanches

pericoloso dangerous

periferia f periphery; ~ **della città** outskirts of the city

perifrasi f periphrasis

per|iòdico periodic(al); m magazine; ~**iodo** m period; gram sentence

peripezie f/pl vicissitudes pl

perire v/i perish

peristilio m peristyle

per|ito adj versed; m expert; ~**izia** f expert's report; skill

perla f pearl

perlomeno at least

perlustrare v/t reconnoitre

perman|ente adj permanent; f permanent wave (**a freddo** cold); ~**enza** f permanence; stay

perme|àbile permeable; ~**are** v/t permeate

perm|esso m permission; leave; ~**esso di soggiorno** residence permit; ~**èttere** v/t allow, permit; ~**issione** f permission

permut|are v/t barter; ~**atore** m elec switch

pernice f partridge

pernici|oso a f malignant fever; ~**o** pernicious

pernott|amento m stay over night; ~**are** v/i spend the night

pero m pear-tree

però but; yet

perocché because

perpend|icolare perpendicular; ~**ìcolo** m plummet

perpètuo perpetual; **for** life

perplesso perplexed

perquis|ire v/t search; ~**izione** f search

persec|utore m persecutor; ~**uzione** f persecution

persegui|re, ~**tare** v/t pursue

persever|ante persevering; ~**anza** f perseverance; ~**are** v/i persevere

persiana f shutter; Venetian blind; ~**o** Persian

pèrsico: **pesce** m ~ perch

persino even

pers|istenza f persistence; ~**sistere** v/i persist

person|a f person; ~**aggio** m thea character; personage; ~**ale** adj personal; m staff; ~**alità** f personality; ~**ificare** v/t impersonate

perspic|ace keen; ~**acia** f shrewdness; ~**icuo** perspicuous

persu|adere v/t persuade; ~**asione** f persuasion

pertanto therefore; consequently

pertin|ace stubborn; ~**enza** f pertinence

perturb|are v/t trouble; ~**azione** f perturbation

perven|ire v/i attain; ~**erso** perverse; ~**ertire** v/t pervert

pes|alèttere m letter-balance; ~**ante** heavy; ~**are** v/t weigh; far ~ consider

pesc|a f peach; fishing; ~**a all'amo** fishing; angling; ~**are** v/t, v/i fish; ~**atore** m fisher(man)

pesce m fish; ~ **pèrsico**

perch; **~ rosso** goldfish; **~cane** *m* shark; *fig* profiteer

pescheria *f* fish-market

pescivéndolo *m* fishmonger

pesco *m* peach-tree

peso *adj* heavy; *m* weight; **~ massimo** heavyweight; **~ lordo** gross weight; **~ a vuoto** dead weight

pèssimo very bad; **il ~** the worst

pestare *v/t* trample; crush

peste *f* plague; *fig* pest; **~ilenza** *f* pestilence

pest|o pounded; **carta** *f* **~a** papier mâché

pètalo *m* petal

petardo *m* fire-cracker

pet|ente *m* petitioner; **~izione** *f* petition

petr|iera *f* stone-quarry; **~ificare** *v/t* petrify; **~ificazione** *f* petrification

petrolio *m* petroleum; oil

pett|égola *f* tattler; **~egolezzo** *m* gossip; **~égolo** gossippy

pettin|are *v/t* comb; **~atura** *f* hair-do, hair-style

pèttine *m* comb

petto *m* breast; bosom; chest

petul|ante impertinent; **~anza** *f* arrogance

pezz|a *f* cloth; diaper; **~etta** *f* small rag

pezzo *m* piece; **~ di ricambio** spare part

pezzuola *f* (hand)kerchief

piac|ente pleasant; pretty; **~ere** *v/i* like; please; *m* pleasure; **mi faccia il ~ere** do me the favour; **tanto ~ere!** very pleased!; **per ~ere** please; **~évole** agreeable; pleasant

piag|a *f* sore; wound; **~are** *v/t* wound

pial|la *f* plane; **~are** *v/t* plane; **~atrice** *f* planing-machine

pian|a *f* plain; thick plank; **~are** *v/t* smooth; level; **~eròttolo** *m* landing

pianeta *m* planet; *f eccl* chasuble

piàngere *v/i*, *v/t* weep

piangévole lamentable

pianista *m*, *f* pianist

piano *adj* level: smooth; *adv* gently; slowly; quietly; *m* plain; floor; piano; **~forte** *m* piano(forte); **~forte a coda** grand piano

pianta *f* plant; plan; map; **~ della città** map of the town; **~ del piede** sole

piant|agione *f* plantation; **~are** *v/t* plant; **~are qu.** jilt s.o.

pianterreno *m* ground floor

pianto *m* weeping

pianura *f* plain

piatt|aforma *f* platform; **~ino** *m* small dish; saucer

piatto *adj* flat; dull; *m* dish; plate; (meal) course; **~ fondo** soup-plate; **~ di carne** dish of meat; **~ di uova** dish made of eggs; **~ne** *m* big plate

piazza *f* square; market (-place); **~le** *m* large square

picc|ante piquant; pungent;

gast spicy; **~ato** larded

picche _f/pl_ spades (_playing-cards_)

picchetto _m_ picket

picchi|are _v/t_ beat; knock; **~ata** _f_ blow

piccino _adj_ small; _fig_ mean; _m_ little boy

picci|onaia _f_ dovecot; _thea_ gallery; **~one** _m_ pigeon, dove

picco _m_ peak; **a ~** perpendicularly; _naut_ **andare a ~** sink

piccolezza _f_ smallness

piccolo _adj_ little; tiny; _m_ youngster

piccozza _f_ ice-axe

pie' = **piede**

pied|e _m_ foot; **a ~i** on foot; **stare in ~i** stand up; **~istallo** _m_ pedestal

pieg|a _f_ fold; pleat; _fig_ **buona ~a** a turn for the better; **~amento** _m_ bending; **~are** _v/t_ fold (up); bend; _fig_ submit; **~arsi** _v/r fig_ yield

piegh|évole pliable; _fig_ yielding; **sedia** _f_ **~évole** folding chair; **~evolezza** _f_ pliability

Piemonte _m_ Piedmont

pien|a _f_ flood; crowd; **~ezza** _f_ fullness

pien|o _adj_ full; complete; **in ~o giorno** in broad daylight; _m_ fullness; **~otto** plump

pietà _f_ pity (**di** with); mercy; **monte ~ di** _m_ pawnbroker's shop

pietoso pitiful; lamentable

pietr|a _f_ stone; **~a preziosa** precious stone; **~ificare** _v/t_ petrify; **~oso** stony

piffero _m_ fife; piper

pigiama _m_ pyjamas

pigi|are _v/t_ press; cram; **~atoio** _m_ wine cellar

pigione _f_ rent

pigli|are _v/t_ take; seize

pigna _f_ pine-cone

pignolo _m_ pine-seed; _fig_ pedant

pignorare _v/t_ distrain

pigol|are _v/i_ chirp; **~io** _m_ chirping

pigr|izia _f_ laziness; **~o** lazy; indolent

pil|a _f_ pile; _elec_ battery; _eccl_ font; **~astro** _m_ pillar

pillola _f_ pill

pilot|a _m_ pilot; steersman; **~are** _v/t_ pilot; drive; fly

pina _f_ = **pigna**

pinacoteca _f_ picture-gallery

pin|astro _m_ pinaster; **~eta** _f_ pine forest

ping-pong _m_ ping-pong

pinna _f_ fin

pinnàcolo _m_ pinnacle

pin|o _m_ pine; **~occhiata** _f_ cake with pine-seeds; **~occhio** _m_ pine-seed

pinz|a _f_ pliers _pl_; **~are** _v/t_ sting; **~ata** _f_ sting

pìo pious; charitable

piogg|erella _f_ drizzle; **~ia** _f_ rain

piomb|are _v/t_ seal; plumb; **~atura** _f_ sealing; filling (_tooth_); **~ino** _m_ plummet; **~o** _m_ lead; plumb; **a ~o** perpendicular

pioniere m pioneer

pioppo m poplar

piotare v/t sod; turf

piòvere v/i rain

piovoso rainy

pip|a f pipe; **~are** v/i smoke (pipe)

pipistrello m bat

pira f pyre

piràmide f pyramid

pirata m pirate

pir|òscafo m steamship; **~osi** f pyrosis; **~otècnica** f fireworks pl

piscina f swimming-pool; fish-pond

pis|ello m pea; **~olino** m nap

pisside f pyx

pista f track; aer runway; **~ da ballo** dance floor; **~ da sci** skiing ground; **~ di lancio** runway; landing-strip; **~ per ciclisti** cycle path

pistacchio m pistachio

pist|ola f pistol; **~ola automàtica** automatic pistol; **~olettata** f pistol-shot

pistone m piston

pitale m chamber-pot

pitonessa f fortune-teller

pitt|ore m painter; **~oresco** picturesque; **~rice** f (woman) painter; **~ura** f painting

più more (**di**, **che** than); plus; **a ~ tardi** see you later; **~ giorni** several days; **di ~** more; (**tutto**) **al ~** at the most; **i ~, le ~** most people

piuma f down; feather; **~aggio** m plumage; **~ino** m eiderdown; quilt; **~ino per la cipria** powder-puff; **~o-so** downy

piuttosto rather (**che** than)

pizza f pizza

pizzic|àgnolo m grocer; **~are** v/t pinch; v/i itch; **~herìa** f delicatessen-shop

pizzico m pinch; nip

pizzo m lace; goatee; **barba f a ~** pointed beard

placare v/t appease

placc|a f plate; **~are** v/t plate

placidezza f placidity

plàcido placid

plan|are v/i aer glide down; **volo** m volplane

plancia f naut bridge

planetario planetary

planimetrìa f planimetry

plasma m: **~ sanguino** blood plasma

plasmare v/t mould

plàstica f modelling; plastic (art)

plasticare v/t plasticize

plàstico adj plastic; m model

plàtano m plane-tree

platea f thea pit

plàtino m platinum

plaus|ibile plausible; **~so m** applause

pleb|aglia f mob, rabble; **~e** f common people

plebiscito m plebiscite

pleni|lunio m full moon; **~potenza** f full power

pleur|a f pleura; **~ite** f pleurisy

plùmbeo leaden; livid

plur|ale m plural; **~alità** f plurality

pluviòmetro m rain-gauge

pneumàtic|o m tire, tyre;

pompa f **~a** air-pump;
posta f **~a** pneumatic dispatch
po. = *primo*; *mus* piano
po' = *poco* little
pochezza f smallness; **~ino** adj (very) little; m little bit
poco little; scanty; **senti un po'** now listen; **a ~ a ~** little by little; **~ fa** a short time ago; **~ dopo** shortly afterwards; **press'a ~** nearly
poder|e m real property; **~oso** powerful
podestà m mayor; f authority
podio m podium
pod|ismo m foot-racing; **~ista** m, f runner
poema m poem
poesia f poem; poetry
poet|a m poet; **~are** v/i write poetry; **~essa** f poet(ess)
poètico poetic(al)
poggi|are v/t, v/i lean on; rest; **~o** m hillock
poi then; after(wards); **dalle 8 in ~** from 8 o'clock onwards
poiché since; as
polacc|a f polonaise; **~o** adj Polish; m Pole
polca f polka
polenta f polenta
poliambulanza f outpatients department
poliglotto polyglot
poligono m polygon
poligrafare v/t mimeograph
poligrafo m polygraph
polio f, **poliomielite** f polio,

poliomyelitis
politic|a f politics pl; policy; **~o** adj politic(al); m politician
polizia f police; **~ confinaria** border police; **~ di porto** harbour-police; **~ sanitaria** sanitary police; **~ stradale** traffic police
poliziotto m policeman; detective
pòlizza f com policy; **~ di càrico** bill of lading
poll|aio m poultry-yard; **~ame** m poultry; **~astrina** f teenage girl; **~astro** m young fowl; *fig* youngster; **~erìa** f poulterer's shop
pòllice m thumb; big-toe; inch
poll|icultura f poultryfarming; **~o** m chicken; fowl; **~o arrosto** roast fowl
polmon|e m lung; **~ite** f pneumonia
polo m pole; **~ nord** North Pole
Polonia f Poland
polpa f pulp; flesh
polp|accio m calf; **~acciuto** plump; **~etta** f meat ball; **~ettone** m gast minced meat; roasted forcemeat; **~oso** pulpy; fleshy
pols|ino m cuff; **~o** m pulse; wrist
poltr|ire v/i be lazy; **~ona** f easy-chair; *thea* stall; **~ona letto** deck chair; **~oncina** f pit stall; **~one** adj lazy; m sluggard
pólvere f dust; powder;

caffè _m_ in ~ ground coffee

polver|ificio _m_ powder-factory; ~ina _f_ med powder; ~izzare _v/t_ pulverize; ~oso dusty

pomata _f_ pomade

pomer|idiano afternoon; ~iggio _m_ afternoon

pometo _m_ (apple-) orchard

pòmice _m_ pumice(-stone)

pomicultura _f_ fruit-growing

pomo _m_ apple; apple-tree; ~doro _m_ tomato

pomp|a _f_ pomp, splendour; pump; ~a d'aria air-pump; ~a della benzina gasoline (or fuel) pump; ~a d'olio pressure-feed; ~are _v/t_ pump

pompelmo _m_ grapefruit

pompier|e _m_ fireman; ~i _pl_ fire-brigade

pomposo pompous; showy

ponce _m_ punch

ponderare _v/t_ ponder

pone he puts

ponente _m_ west

pongo I put

poniamo we put

ponte _m_ bridge; _naut_ deck; ~ di passeggiata promenade deck; ~ superiore upper deck

pont|éfice _m_ pontiff; Stato _m_ ~eficio Pontifical State

popol|are _adj_ popular; _v/t_ populate; ~arità _f_ popularity

pòpolo _m_ people

popoloso populous

popone _m_ melon

poppa _f_ naut stern

popp|ante _m_ suckling baby; ~are _v/t_, _v/i_ suck

porca _f_ sow

porcellana _f_ china; porcelain

porc|ellino _m_ sucking pig; ~ile _m_ pigsty; ~o _m_ pig; swine; pork

pòrfido _m_ porphyry

pòrgere _v/t_ hand; give

porgitore _m_ bearer

pornografia _f_ pornography

por|o _m_ pore; ~oso porous

pórpora _f_ purple

porporino _m_ purple

porre _v/t_ put; place; set

porro _m_ bot leek; _med_ wart

port|a _f_ door; gate; ~bagagli _m_ porter; carrier

portàbile portable

porta|cénere _m_ ash-tray; ~cipria _m_ compact

porta|flaschi _m_ bottle-rack; ~fogli _m_ wallet; portfolio; ~le _m_ portal; ~lèttere _m_ postman; ~mento _m_ gait; behaviour; ~monete _m_ purse; ~penne _m_ penholder

port|are _v/t_ bring; carry; ~arsi _v/r_ behave; ~asigarette _m_ cigarette-case; -holder; ~atore _m_ bearer

porta|uova _m_ egg-cup; ~voce _m_ mouthpiece; spokesman

porticato _m_ colonnade

pòrtico _m_ porch; portico

port|iera _f_ door-curtain; door-keeper; ~iere _m_ goal-keeper; ~inaio _m_ door-keeper

porto m port, harbour; postage; ~ **assegnato** cash on delivery; ~ **di mare** seaport; ~ **franco** free port

Portogallo m Portugal

portone m gate

porzione f share; portion

posa f posture; *phot* exposure

pos|are v/t lay (down); put; place; *paint* sit; ~**ata** f cutlery (*knife, fork, spoon*)

poscritto m postscript

positivo positive

posizione f position

posporre v/t postpone

possedere v/t possess; (*language*) master

poss|essione f possession; belonging; ~**essivo** possessive; ~ **esso** m possession; ~**essore** m, f owner

possiamo we can

possibile possible

possibilità f possibility

posso I can

posta f post, mail; ~ **aèrea** air mail; ~**centrale** main post-office; ~ **le** postal

postare v/t place; post

posteggi|are v/t, v/i park; ~**o** m parking(-place)

pòsteri m/pl posterity

poster|iore posterior; hind; ~**ità** f posterity

posticcio sham; false

posticipare v/t put off

posto adj put; placed; m place; room; job; ~ **al finestrino** window-seat; ~ **a sedere** seat; ~ **di primo**

soccorso first-aid post; **fa-re** ~ **a** make room for; ~ **in piedi** standing-room; ~ **di rifornimento** service-station; ~ **riservato** reserved seat; ~ **vacante** vacancy

pòstumo posthumous

potàbile drinkable; **acqua** f ~ drinking-water

potassa f potash

pot|entato m potentate; ~**ente** powerful; ~**enza** f power; might; *mech* efficiency

potere v/i can, may; be able to; m power

potuto pp of **potere**

pover|etto, ~ino m poor man; pauper

pòvero adj poor; needy; ~ **me!** poor me!; m poor (man); beggar

povertà f poverty

pozzo m well

pranz|are v/i dine; ~**o** m lunch; dinner; **dopo** ~ after lunch; ~**o m a prezzo fisso** menu at a fixed price

pràtica f practice; training

pratic|àbile practicable; ~**a-re** v/t practise; perform

pràtico practical; experienced

prato m meadow; lawn; ~ **per riposare** meadow for sun-bathing

preavviso m preliminary announcement

precauzione f (pre)caution

preced|ente adj preceding; previous; m precedent; ~**enza** f precedence; priority

precèdere v/t precede

precett|are v/t summon; cite; **~o** m precept

precipit|are v/t, v/i precipitate; **~arsi** v/r rush; **~oso** steep; rash

precipizio m precipice

precis|ione f precision; **~o** precise; exact; **alle tre ~e** at three o'clock sharp

precoce precocious

preconcetto m prejudice

preda f prey; booty; **~are** v/t prey; pillage

predella f foot-board

predestin|are v/t predestin(at)e; **~azione** f predestination

predetto aforesaid

prèdica f sermon

predic|are v/t, v/i preach; **~ato** m predicate; **~atore** m preacher

predil|etto adj favourite; m darling; **~ezione** f predilection

pred|ire v/t predict; **~izione** f prediction

predomin|are v/i prevail; **~inio** m prevalence

prefabbricato prefabricated

prefazione f preface

prefer|enza f preference; **~ire** v/t prefer

prefett|o m prefect; **~ura** f prefecture

prefiggere v/i pre-arrange; **~isso** m gram prefix

preg|are v/t pray; ask; **~évole** valuable

preghiera f prayer; request

pregi|are v/t appreciate; **~arsi** v/r have the pleasure to; **~o** m value; merit

pregiudizio m prejudice

prego please

preistoria f prehistory

prel|azione f pre-emption; **~evare** v/t withdraw (money); **~udio** m mus prelude

prèm|ere v/t press; urge; **~e** urgent!

premi|are v/t reward; **~azione** f distribution of prizes; **~nente** pre-eminent; **~o** m award; premium

prem|ura f zeal; solicitude; hurry; **~uroso** solicitous

prèndere v/t take; seize; get; v/i catch (cold); **~ersi** refuel; **andare (venire) a ~** go (come) for

prendisole m sun-suit

pre|nome m Christian name; **~notare** v/t book; reserve; **~notazione** f reservation

preoccup|arsi v/r worry; **~ato** worried

prepar|are v/t prepare; **~ativo** m preparation; **~atorio** preparatory; **~azione** f preparation

preponderare v/t prevail

prep|orre v/t place before; **~osizione** f gram preposition

prepot|ente overbearing; **~enza** f arrogance

presa f seizure; phot picture; shot; mil conquest; **~ di**

corrente wall plug; socket; **~ di terra** (electrical) earth; **~ in giro** making a fool of s.o.

presagio m prognostic
prèsbite long-sighted
prescritto m ordinance; **~ivere** v/t prescribe; **~izione** f prescription

present|are v/t present; show; offer; **~arsi** v/r introduce o.s.; (occasion) arise; **~azione** f presentation; **~e** adj present; m gift; present tense; **~imento** m premonition; **~ire** v/t have a premonition

presenza f presence
presep|e, ~io m manger, crib
preservare v/t preserve (**da** of)

presid|ente m president; chairman; **~enza** f presidency; chair; **~io** m managing committee

presièdere v/t, v/i preside (over)

preso taken
press|a f crowd; press; **~are** v/t press; urge; **~ione** f pressure; **~ione delle gomme** tyre-pressure; **~ione sanguina** blood-pressure (**troppo alta** too high; **troppo bassa** too low)

presso near; close to; by; **~a poco** approximately; **~chè** almost; nearly

prestabilire v/t arrange beforehand

prest|are v/t lend; **~azione** f

loan; tax; **~ezza** f quickness
prèstito m loan; **dare in ~** lend; **prèndere in ~** borrow

presto quickly; early; **far ~** hurry (up)

presùmere v/i presume
presun|tuoso self-conceited; **~zione** f presumption

prete m priest
pret|endente m, f pretender; claimant; **~èndere** v/t, v/i pretend; claim; **~enzioso** pretentious; **~esa** f pretence; claim

pretesto m pretext
pretore m judge
pretto pure; mere
pretura f court of first instance

prevalere v/i prevail
prevedere v/t foresee
prevenire v/t prevent
preventivo: bilancio m **~** estimate

previdente provident
prezi|osità f preciousness; **~oso** precious; **pietra** f **~osa** precious stone

prezzémolo m parsley
prezzo m price; **a buon (basso) ~** cheap; **~ di costo** cost price; **~ di favore** special price; **~ del noleggio** aut rent; **~ per una notte** overnight expenses pl

prigion|e f prison; **~iero** m prisoner; **fare ~iero** take prisoner

prima before; formerly; **~ di** before; first; **~ che** before; **da** ~ at first; **colazione** f breakfast; ~ **visione** f film: first run; premiere; ~**rio** adj primary; m head physician; **scuola** f ~**ria** primary school

primavera f spring

primitivo m primitive

primo first

primordio m beginning; origin

principi|ale adj main; chief; m principal; boss; ~**ato** m principality

principe m prince

principessa f princess

principi|ante m, f beginner; ~**are** v/t, v/i begin; start; ~**o** m start; principle

priv|are v/t qu. di qc. deprive s.o. of s.th.; ~**arsi (di)** v/r abstain from; renounce; ~**ato** private; **scuola** f ~**ata** private school; ~**azione** f (de)privation; need

privilegi|are v/t privilege; ~**o** m privilege

privo deprived; without

prò m benefit; **buon** ~! may it do you good

probàbile probable

probabilità f probability

problema m problem

procèdere v/i proceed; act

process|ione f procession; ~**o** m process; trial

procinto: èssere in ~ **di** be about to

proclam|a m proclamation; ~**are** v/t proclaim; ~**azione** f proclamation

procur|are v/t procure; get;

~**atore** m proxy; attorney

prodig|alità f extravagance; ~**io** m prodigy; ~**ioso** prodigious; wonderful

pròdigo adj prodigal; m spendthrift

prod|otto m product; produce; ~**otto nazionale** home product; ~**urre** v/t produce; ~**uttivo** productive; ~**uzione** f production; output

profan|are v/t profane; ~**o** adj profane; m fig layman

profess|are v/t profess; declare; ~**ione** f profession; calling; ~**ionista** m, f professional; practitioner; ~**o** m (professed) monk; ~**orato** m professor-ship; ~**ore** m professor; instructor; ~**oressa** f woman professor

prof|eta m prophet; ~**etizzare** v/t foretell; ~**ezìa** f prophecy

proficuo profitable

profilo m profile; side-view

profitt|are v/i profit; gain; ~**are di** benefit from; ~**o** m profit; gain

profluvio m overflowing

pro|fóndere v/t lavish; squander; ~**fondità** f depth; ~**fondo** deep

pròfugo m refugee

profum|are v/t perfume; scent; ~**erìa** f perfume-shop; ~**iera** f scent-bottle; ~**o** m scent; perfume

prog|ettare v/t plan; ~**etto** m project; plan

programma m programme; ~ **televisivo** television programme; ~ **d'escursione** excursion programme

progredire v/i progress

progress|ivo progressive; ~**o** m progress

proib|ire v/t prohibit; ~**izione** f prohibition

proiettile m projectile

proi|ettore m search-light; projector; ~**iezione** f projection

prole f offspring; issue; ~**tariato** m proletariat; ~**tario** m proletarian

prolisso long-winded

prólogo m prologue

prolung|amento m prolongation; ~**are** v/t prolong; extend

pro|messa f promise; ~**messi sposi** m/pl betrothed (couple); ~**méttere** v/t promise

prominente prominent

promontorio m headland

prom|ozione f promotion; ~**uòvere** v/t promote; (exam) pass

pronome m gram pronoun

pronosticare v/t forecast

pront|ezza f promptitude; ~**o** ready; prompt; quick; ~**o soccorso** m rescue station; tel ~**o!** or ~**i!** halloh!

pronunci|a f pronounciation; same as pronounce; ~**arsi** v/r express one's opinion

pronunzia f = **pronuncia**

propaganda f: **far** ~ advertise

propagare v/t spread; diffuse

propizio favourable

prop|orre v/t propose; ~**orsi** v/r intend

proporzion|ale proportional; ~**e** f proportion; ratio

propòsito m purpose; aim; **a** ~ **by the way; venire a** ~ come at the right time; **di** ~ on purpose

proposta f proposal

propri|amente properly; ~**età** f property; propriety; ~**etario** m owner; ~**o** own; proper; ~**o?** really?

propulsore m propeller

prora f naut prow; bow

pròroga f extension; respite

prorogare v/t put off; extend

pros|a f prose; ~**àico** prosaic

proscenio m proscenium

prosciugare v/t dry (up); drain

prosciutto m ham; ~ **cotto (crudo)** cooked (uncooked) ham

proscrivere v/t proscribe, outlaw

proseguire v/i proceed; v/t continue

prosper|are v/i thrive; prosper; ~**ità** f prosperity

pròspero thriving

prospett|iva f outlook; perspective; ~**o** m prospect(us); view

prossimità f proximity

pròssimo adj next; near; m

fellow creature

protèggere v/t protect (**da** from)

proteina f protein

protest|ante m, f, adj Protestant; **~are** v/t, v/i protest; **~o** m protest; objection

protett|o m protégé; **~orato** m protectorate; **~ore** m protector

protezione f protection; patronage

protocoll|are v/t record; file; **~o** m protocol; minutes pl

prov|a f proof; trial; **~a generale** dress rehearsal; **~are** v/t prove; test; feel; **~ato** tried; tested

proven|ienza f origin; source; **~ire** v/i come from

proverbio m proverb

provinci|a f province; **~ale** provincial

provoc|ante provocative; **~are** v/t provoke; cause; **~azione** f provocation

provv|edere v/t provide; furnish; **~edimento** m measure; step; **~editore** m purveyor; **~idente** provident; **~idenza** f providence

provv|isione f supply; **~isorio** temporary; **~ista** f supply; stock; **~isto di** supplied with

prua f naut prow; bow

prudente prudent; **~enza** f prudence; caution

prugn|a f plum; **~o** m plum-tree

pruno m thorn-bush

prur|iginoso itchy; **~ito** m itch

P.S. = Poscritto postscript

psichiatra m, f psychiatrist

psìchico psychic(al)

psic|ologia f psychology; **~òlogo** m psychologist

pubblic|are v/t publish; **~azione** f publication; **~ità** f publicity; advertising; **~ità luminosa** luminous advertising

pùbblico m, adj public

pudore m modesty; shyness

puer|ile childish; **~izia** f childhood

pugil|ato m boxing; pugilism; **~e** m pugilist

Puglia f Apulia

pugn|a f fight; **~ale** m dagger

pugno m fist; punch

puh! pooh!

pulc|e f flea; **~inella** m buffoon; **~ino** m chick

pulire v/t clean; polish

pul|ito clean; tidy; **~itura** f clean(s)ing; **~itura a secco** dry cleaning; **~izia** f cleaning; cleanliness

pullman m de luxe bus

pullover m sweater

pùlpito m pulpit

puls|are v/i pulsate; throb; **~azione** f pulsation

pùngere v/t sting; prick

pungitura f pricking

pun|ire v/t punish; **~izione** f punishment

punta f point; tip; **~ di terra** spit of land

punt|are v/t, v/i point; level;

stake; **~ata** f thrust; stake;
instalment; **~eruolo** m
punch

puntina f **da grammòfono**
gramophone needle; **~ da
disegno** drawing-pin

punto adv not at all; m
point; spot; stitch; **~ di vista** point of view; **fino a
che ~?** up to where?; **alle
dieci in ~** at ten o'clock
sharp; **~ e virgola** semicolon

punt|uale punctual; **~ualità**
f punctuality; **~ura** f puncture; injection; **~ura di
zanzara** gnat-bite

può he can

pupill|a f pupil; **~o** m pupil;

ward

purché provided (that)

pure also; too; yet

purè m purée; mash; **~ di
patate** mashed potatoes

purezza f purity

purg|a f purge; laxative;
~ante m purgative; **~are** v/t
purge; **~ativo** purga-
tive; **~atorio** m eccl purga-
tory

purific|are v/t purify;
cleanse; **~azione** f purifi-
cation

pur|ità f purity; **~o** pure

purpùreo purple; crimson

purtroppo unfortunately

puzz|are v/i stink; **~o** m
stink; **~olente** stinking

Q

qua here; **di ~** on this side; **di
~ ... di là** to and fro

quàccquero m eccl quaker

quad|ernaccio m scrap-
book; **~erno** m copy-book

quadr|agèsima f Quadra-
gesima (1st Sunday in
Lent); **~àngolo** m quadrangle; **~ante** m quadrant;
dial; **~are** v/t square; **~ato**
m, adj square; **~ello** m
arrow; tile; **~iforme**
square

quadr|o m, adj square; m
painting; **~i** m/pl playing-
cards: diamonds

quadr|ùpede adj four-
footed; m quadruped; **~ù-
plice** fourfold

quaggiù down here

quagli|a f quail; **~arsi** v/r
curdle

qualche some; any; **~ giorno** a few days; **~cosa** something; anything; **~ volta**
sometimes

**qual|cheduno = qualcu-
no**; **~cosa** something;
anything; **~cuno** some-
body; anybody

quale which; what; **il (la) ~**
he (she) who; whom; like;
as

qualific|are v/t qualify;
define; **~azione** f qualifi-
cation

qual|ità f quality; **~ora** if;
when; **~siasi** whatever;
any; **~unque** whatever;
every, each

quando when; **da ~?** since when?; **di ~ in ~** from time to time

quantità f quantity

quanto how much?; **tutto ~** all that; **tutto ~ il libro;** ~ **tempo** how long; **quanti ne abbiamo oggi?** what day is today?; ~ **a me** as for me; ~ **prima** as soon as possible; **per ~ ricco tu sia** as rich as you may be

quarant|ena f quarantine; **~enne** forty years old; **~è-simo** fortieth

quar|ésima f eccl Lent; **vit-to m ~esimale** Lenten food

quart|etto m quartet; **~iere** m lodgings pl; district (town); quarter

quarto m quarter; forth

quarzo m quartz

quasi nearly; almost

quassù up here

quattrin|o m farthing; **~i** m/pl money

quattro four; **far ~ passi** take a stroll; **~cento** m 15th century

quegli he; those

quei he; they, those

quel, ~la that; **~lo** that; that one

quercia f oak

querel|a f complaint; **~ante** m, f plaintiff; **~are** v/t lodge

a complaint (against)

quest|a this; **~i, ~e** this; these

question|are v/i argue; **~a-rio** m questionnaire; **~e** f question

questo this; **per ~** therefore; **quest'oggi** today

quest|ore m (police) super-intendent; **~ura** f police headquarters; **~urino** m police-officer

qui here; **di ~** from here; **di ~ a un mese** a month from now; **di ~ innanzi** from now on

quietanz|a f receipt; **~are** v/t receipt

quiet|are v/t quiet; **~e** f quiet(ness); **~o** quiet

quindi from there; then therefore; then

quindic|èsimo m fifteenth; **~i giorni** fortnight; **una ~ina di giorni** about two weeks

quint|a f fifth (also mus); thea wings pl; **~ale** m quintal (100 kg.); **~o** m fifth; **~úplice** fivefold

quintuplo m fivefold amount

quivi there; then

quot|a f quota; share; height; aer **prèndere ~a** climb; **~are** v/t assess; quote

quotidiano daily

R

rabàrbaro *m* rhubarb

rabbellire *v/t* embellish anew

rabbia *f* rage; *med* rabies; **fare ~ a qu.** enrage s.o.

rabbino *m* rabbi

rabbioso furious; rabid

rabbrividire *v/i* shudder

rabbuiarsi *v/r* grow dark

raccapezz|are *v/t* understand; collect; **~arsi** *v/r* make out

raccartocciare *v/t* curl up

raccattare *v/t* pick up; collect

racchetta *f* racquet, racket

racchiùdere *v/t* contain; enclose

rac|còagliere *v/t* gather; pick up; **~coglimento** *m* concentration

racc|olta *f* collection; *agr* harvest; **~olto** *m* crop

raccomand|are *v/t* recommend; (*letter*) register; **~ata** *f* registered letter; **~azione** *f* recommendation

raccomod|are *v/t* mend; repair; **~atura** *f* repairing

raccont|are *v/t* tell; narrate; **~o** *m* story

raccorciare *v/t* shorten

rada *f* *naut* roadstead

raddensare *v/t* thicken

raddolc|imento *m* softening; **~ire** *v/t* sweeten; soothe

raddoppi|amento *m* doubling; **~are** *v/t* (re)double

raddormentarsi *v/r* fall asleep again

raddrizzare *v/t* straighten

ràdere *v/t* raze; shave

radi|are *v/i* radiate; **~atore** *m* radiator

ràdica *f* root; briar-wood

radic|ale radical; **~are** *v/i* take root

radice *f* root; radish; **~ del dente** root of a tooth

radio *m* radium; *f* radio, wireless; **~ascoltatore** *m* (radio-)listener; **~attivo** radioactive; **~commedia** *f* radio play; **~comunicazione** *f* radio communication; **~diffusione** *f* broadcasting; **~fònico: apparecchio** *m* **~fònico** wireless set; **~fonògrafo** *m* wireless set with recordplayer; **~giornale** *m* newsbroadcast; **~grafia** *f* X-ray; **~grafista** *m, f* (wireless) operator; **~gramma** *m* radiotelegram; **~scopia** *f* radioscopy; **~valigia** *f* portable radio

radioso radiant

radiotele|fonia *f* radiotelephony; **~grafia** *f* radiotelegraphy; **~grafista** *m, f* wireless operator

rado scattered; rare; **di ~** seldom

radun|anza *f* gathering; **~are** *v/t*, **~arsi** *v/r*, assemble; gather

ràfano *m* radish

rafferma *f* confirmation

ràffica f squall

raffigurare v/t recognize

raffin|amento m refining; **~are** v/t refine; **~ato** refined; subtle; **~eria** f refinery

rafforzare v/t strengthen; reinforce

raffreddamento m cooling; fig abatement; **~ ad acqua** water-cooling; **~ ad aria** air-cooling

raffredd|are v/t cool; chill; **~arsi** v/r catch a cold; **~ato** cooled off; **èssere ~ato** have a cold; **~atura** f, **~ore** m cold; chill

raffresc|are v/t cool; **~arsi** v/r grow cool

ragazz|a f girl; **~o** m boy; errand-boy

raggi|ante radiant; beaming; **~are** v/i radiate; shine; **~o** m ray, beam

raggiùngere v/t overtake; (goal) reach

raggiustare v/t repair

raggruppare v/t group

ragguagli|are v/t equalize; inform; **~o** m equalization

ragion|amento m reasoning; **~are** v/i reason; argue; **~ato** logical; **~e** f reason; cause; right; **aver ~e** be right; **per ~i di** on grounds of; **a ~e** rightly; **~eria** f book-keeping; **~évole** reasonable; **~iere** m accountant

ragn|atelo m spider's web; **~o** m spider

ragù m ragout

rallegr|amento m rejoicing; **~arsi** v/r be glad; **~arsi con qu. di qc.** congratulate s.o. on s.th.

rallent|amento m slowing down; **~are** v/t, v/i slow down

rame m copper

ramificarsi v/r branch out

rammaricarsi v/r complain

rammàrico m grief; regret

rammend|are v/t mend; **~atura** f mending

ramment|are v/t remind; **~arsi** v/r recall (**di qc.** s.th.)

rammollire v/t soften

ramo m branch; (river) arm; **~ d'affari** line of business; **~laccio** m horseradish; **~scello** m twig

rampicare v/i climb

ramp|ino m hook; prong; **~ollo** m scion

rana f frog

ràncido rancid

rancio m soldier's food; ration

rancore m grudge

randagio stray

rango m rank; degree

rannicchiarsi v/r crouch; cower

ranno m lye

rannuvol|amento m clouding over; **~arsi** v/r cloud over

ranocchio m frog

rantolare v/i rattle (in one's throat)

rap|a f turnip; **~accio** m Swedish turnip

rap|ace rapacious; **~acità** f rapacity

rapidità f rapidity

ràpido adj swift; m express train

rap|ire v/t rape; kidnap; **~i-na** f plundering; **uccello m di ~ina** bird of prey

rappezz|are v/t patch up; **~o** m patch

rapport|arsi v/r a have reference to; be advised by; **~o** m report; reference; **in ~o a** in a connexion with

rappresaglia f reprisal; retaliation

rappresent|ante m, f representative; **~anza** f representation; agency; **~are** v/t represent; thea perform; **~azione** f representation; performance

rar|ità f rarity; **~o** rare

ras|are v/t shave; clip; **~ato** shaven

raschi|are v/t scrape; erase; **~no** m scraper; eraser; **~o** m roughness of the throat

rasentare v/t skim; border upon

ras|o adj shaven; fig naked; m satin; **~oio** m razor; **~oio di sicurezza** safety razor; **~oio elèttrico** electric shaver

rassegn|a f review; mil parade; **~arsi** v/r resign o.s. (**a** to); **~ato** resigned; **~azione** f resignation

rasserenare v/t cheer up

rassicurare v/t reassure

rassomigli|ante resem-

bling; like; **~anza** f likeness; **~arsi** v/r be like; resemble

rastrellare v/t rake; search

rasura f shave

rat|a f rate; instalment; **a ~e** by instalments

rateazione f spacing (of payments)

ratto m rape; zo rat

rattoppare v/t patch up

rattoppo m patch(work)

rattrappito contracted; paralysed

rattrist|are v/t sadden; **~ar-si** v/r grow sad

rauc|èdine f hoarseness; **~o** hoarse

ravanello m radish

ravioli m/pl ravioli

ravv|isare v/t recognize; **~i-vamento** m revivification; revival; **~ivare** v/t revive

ravvòlgere v/t wrap up

razion|ale rational; **~e** f ration

razza f race; fig kind

razz|o m rocket; **~olare** v/i scrape; fig rummage

re m king

reagire v/i react

reale real; royal

real|ismo m realism; **~izz-zare** v/t realize; **~izzazione** f realization; **~tà** f reality

reame m kingdom

reazione f reaction; **aèreo** m a ~ jet plane

rec|are v/t bring; cause; **~arsi** v/r go

recèdere v/i recede; give up

recensione f (book-)review

recent|e recent; new; **~is-sime** f/pl latest news

recesso m recess

recider|si v/r split up

recidiva f relapse

rec|ingere v/t surround; **~into** m enclosure; pen

recipiente m vessel; container

reciprocità f reciprocity

reciproco reciprocal

reciso sharp; decided

recita f recital; performance

recit|are v/t recite; thea act; **~azione** f recital; acting

reclam|are v/i complain; v/t claim; **~e** f advertising; **~o** m complaint

recluta f mil recruit

record m record

red|attore m editor; producer **~azione** f editing; editor's office

reddito m income

Redentore m Redeemer, Saviour

redimere v/t redeem

reduce adj returned; m veteran

refe m thread

refettorio m refectory; dining-hall

refriger|are v/t refrigerate; refresh; **~io** m refreshment

regal|are v/t make a present; give away; **~e** royal; **~o** m present, gift

regata f regatta

reggente m regent

règgere v/t bear, v/i bear; support; rule

reggilume m lampstand

reggimento m government; regiment

reggipetto m bra(ssière)

regia f (stage-)direction

regime m government; gast diet

regin|a f queen (also playing-cards); **~o** royal

regione f region

regista m director; producer

registr|are v/t register; record; **~atore** m **a nastro** tape-recorder; **~atura** f entry; **~o** m register; com books pl

regn|ante m ruler; **~are** v/i reign; **~o** m reign; kingdom

règola f rule

regol|amento m regulations pl; settlement; **~amento stradale** traffic regulations; **~are** v/t regulate; settle (accounts); adj regular; **~arità** f regularity; **~atore** m regulator

règolo m ruler; **~ calcolatore** slide-ruler

regr|essivo regressive; **~esso** m regress

relativo relative; pertinent

relazione f report; **in ~ a** in relation to

religi|one f religion; **~osa** f nun; **~osità** f religiousness; **~oso** adj religious; pious; m monk

rem|are v/i row; **~are a pagaia** paddle; **~atore** m rower; oarsman

reminiscenza f reminiscence

remissione f remission;

senza ~ without repeal

remo *m* oar

remoto remote; **passato** *m* ~ *gram* past definite

rena *f* sand

renale: calcolo *m* ~ renal calculus

rèndere *v/t* give (back); make; ~ **felice** make happy

rèndita *f* income; rent

rene *m* kidney

renit|ente recalcitrant; **~enza** *f* reluctance

renoso sandy

reo guilty; evil

reparto *m* department

repentino sudden

repertorio *m* *thea* repertory

rèplica *f* reply; repetition

replicare *v/i* reply; *v/t* repeat

repr|essione *f* repression; **~ìmere** *v/t* repress

repùbblica *f* republic

repubblicano *m*, *adj* republican

reput|are *v/t*, *v/i* deem; consider; **~azione** *f* reputation

requis|ire *v/t* requisition; **~ìto** requisite; **~izione** *f* requisition

resa *f* surrender; rendering

rescritto *m* rescript

reseda *f* mignonette

resid|ente resident; **~enza** *f* residence

resìduo *m* remainder

rèsina *f* resin

resinoso resinous

resist|ente resisting; **~enza** *f* resistence

resìstere *v/i* resist

resìstore *m* *elec* resistor

resoconto *m* account; report

respìngere *v/t* repel; reject

respir|are *v/t*, *v/i* breathe; **~atore** *m* snorkel; **~azione** *f* breathing; **~o** *m* breath

respons|àbile responsible **(di** for); **~abilità** *f* responsibility

ressa *f* crowd; throng

rest|ante remaining; **~are** *v/i* stay; be left over

restaur|are *v/t* restore; **~azione** *f* ~ *m* restoration

restitu|ire *v/t* give back; restore; **~zione** *f* restitution

resto *m* remainder; **del** ~ besides

restrìngersi *v/r* restrain o.s.; shrink

ret|e *f* net; **~e stradale** network of highways; **~icella** *f* small net; hairnet; **~icella per il bagaglio** luggage-rack

retiforme retiform

rètina *f* retina (*eye*)

retòrica *f* rhetoric

retro|attivo retroactive; **~bottega** *f* back-shop; **~cèdere** *v/i* recede; **~marcia** *f* *auto:* reverse (gear); **~visivo: specchio** ~ **~visivo** rear-view mirror

retta *f:* **dare** ~ listen (to)

rett|angolare rectangular; **~àngolo** *m* rectangle

rettificare *v/t* rectify

rettile *m* reptile

retto straight; right; correct

rèum|a *m* rheumatism; **~à-**

tico rheumatic; ~atismo m rheumatism

reverendo (abbr rev.) adj reverend; m priest; 2! Sir; Your Reverence

revisione f revision

revoc|àbile revocable; ~are v/t revoke

ri... (prefix) mostly again

rialto m ramp

rialzare v/t raise (up)

riap|ertura f reopening; ~poggiare v/t tel ring off (again); ~rire v/t reopen

riassùmere v/t sum up

riatt|amento m restoration; ~are v/t repair

riavere v/t get back

ribalta f flap; thea footlights pl; tàvola f a ~ folding table

ribaltare v/t overturn; capsize

ribass|are v/t (price) lower; ~o m discount; drop

ribell|ante rebellious; ~are v/t stir up; ~arsi v/r rebel; ~e m rebel; ~ione f rebellion

ribes m gooseberry

ribollimento m ebullition; agitation

ribrezzo m disgust

ricaduta f relapse

ricamare v/t embroider

ricambi|are v/t return; reciprocate; ~o m exchange; di ~o spare

ricamo m embroidery

ricapitolazione f summary

ricatt|are v/t blackmail; ~o m blackmail

ricav|are v/t derive; extract; ~o m proceeds pl

ricchezza f wealth

riccio adj curly; m curl

ricciolo m curl

ricco rich (di in)

ricerc|a f research; ~are v/t seek (for); investigate; ~atore m research worker

ricetta f prescription; recipe

ricévere v/t receive

ricev|imento m reception; ~itore m receiver; ~uta f receipt; accusare ~uta acknowledge receipt

ricezione f reception

richiam|are v/t call back; ~arsi v/r refer (a to); ~o m mil call-up

richiedente m applicant

richièdersi v/r be required

richiesta f request; application

ricino m: olio m di ~ castoroil

ricognizione f recognition

ricompens|a f reward; ~are v/t reward

ricompr|a f repurchase; ~are v/t buy back

riconciliare v/t reconcile

ricondurre v/t bring back

riconosc|ente grateful; ~enza f gratefulness

riconóscere v/t recognize

riconsegn|a f handing back; ~are v/t hand back; redeliver

ricord|arsi v/r remember (di qc. s.th.); ~o m recollection; ~o di viaggio souvenir

ricorrere v/i recur; appeal

ricorso m petition; claim; **fare ~ a** resort to

ricostit|uire v/t reconstitute; **~uzione** f reconstitution

ricostru|ire v/t rebuild; **~zione** f reconstruction

ricotta f buttermilk curd

ricoverare v/t shelter

ricòvero m shelter; asylum

ricrearsi v/r take recreation

ricuperare v/t recover

ricurvo bent; curved

ricusare v/t refuse

ridente smiling; bright

rid|ere v/i laugh (**di** at); **~ersi** v/r **di qu.** make fun of s.o.

ridìcolo ridiculous

ridosso m sheltering wall

ridotto adj reduced; m thea foyer

rid|urre v/t reduce (**a** to); (prices) lower; **~uzione** f reduction; discount; **~uzione sul prezzo dei biglietti** reduction on fare

riémpiere v/t fill (up)

riemp|imento m filling; **~ire** v/t (re)fill

rifacimento m remaking; compensation

rifer|ire v/t report; **~irsi** v/r refer (**a** to)

rifiatare v/i take breath

rifin|imento m finish(ing); exhaustion; **~ire** v/t finish; wear out

rifior|imento m reflourishing; **~ire** v/i reflourish; v/t retouch

rifiut|arsi v/r refuse; **~o** m refusal

rifless|ione f reflection; **~ivo** thoughtful; gram reflexive; **~o** m reflex

riflètt|ere v/t reflect; fig concern; **~ersi** v/r be reflected

riflettore m search-light

riflusso m ebb(-tide)

riform|a f reform; eccl Reformation; **~are** v/t reform; improve; **~atore** m reformer; **~azione** f reformation

rifuggire v/i flee; shrink (from)

rifug|iarsi v/r take refuge; **~iato** m refugee; **~io** m refuge; shelter; **~ugio alpino** alpine hut

riga f line; row; stripe; ruler

rig|are v/t rule; **~ato** striped

rigett|are v/t reject; **~o** m rejection

rigidezza f stiffness; austerity

rigido rigid; strict

rigir|are v/t turn about; **~o** m winding; fig trick

rigogli|o m luxuriance; **~oso** exuberant

rigor|e m rigour; **di ~e** strictly required; **~oso** strict

rigovernare v/t wash up (dishes)

riguard|are v/t look at; concern; **~arsi** v/r beware (of); **~o** m respect; **~o a** with regard to; **senza ~o** regardless; **aversi ~o** take care of o.s.

rilasciare v/t release; issue (certificate)

rileg|are v/t bind (book); refasten; **~atore** m bookbinder; **~atura** f (book-)binding

rilievo m remark; projection; relief; **alto ~** high relief; **basso ~** low (bas) relief

rilucente shining

rilùcere v/i glitter

rima f rhyme

rimandare v/t send back; postpone

rimane he stays

rimaneggiare v/t remodel

riman|ente m, **~enza** f remainder; **~ere** v/i remain; stay

rimango I stay

rimaniamo we stay

rimar|care v/t notice; **~chévole** remarkable

rimasto remained

rimbombare v/i boom; resound

rimbors|are v/t reimburse; **contro ~o** cash on delivery

rimedi|àbile remediable; **~are** v/t, v/i remedy; cure; **~o** m remedy

rimembr|anza f remembrance; **~are** v/t remember

rimenare v/t bring back; stir

rimescolare v/t blend; shuffle

rimessa f shed; com remittance; garage; aer hangar

riméttere v/t replace; put off; **~ersi** v/r recover; improve (weather)

rimodernare v/t modernize; renovate

rimorchi|are v/t tow; haul; **~atore** m tow-boat; **~o** m trailer; **autocarro** m **con ~o** trailer coupling

rimòrdere v/t bite again; prick (conscience)

rimorso m, **~ di coscienza** remorse

rimozione f removal

rimpasto m re-mixing; shuffle

rimpatri|are v/t, v/i repatriate; return to one's country; **~atrio** m repatriation

rimpiàngere v/t regret; lament s.o.; **~anto** m regret

rimpiatt|are v/t conceal; hide; **~ino** m (game of) hide-and-seek

rimpiazzare v/t replace

rimp|iccinire, ~iccolire v/t, v/i make smaller; grow smaller

rimprover|àbile reproachable; **~are** v/t rebuke (s.o.)

rimpròvero m reproach; rebuke

rinascimento m rebirth; Renaissance

rincarare v/t, v/i raise the price of; become dearer

rincaro m rise in price

rinchiùdere v/t shut up

rinc|órrere v/t run after; pursue s.o.; **~orsa** f run; spring

rincréscere v/i be sorry

rincresc|évole regrettable;

~imento *m* regret

rinculare *v/i* recoil

rinforz|amento *m* reinforcement; **~are** *v/t* strengthen; **~o** *m* support

rinfresc|amento *m* refreshment; cooling; **~are** *v/t* cool; refresh; **~arsi** *v/r* refresh o.s.; **~o** *m* refreshment

ringhiare *v/i* snarl

ringhiera *f* rail(ing)

ringiovan|imento *m* rejuvenation; **~ire** *v/t, v/i* rejuvenate; grow younger

ringrazi|amento *m* thanks *pl*; **tanti ~amenti** *pl* many thanks *pl*; **~are** *v/t* (**qu. di qc.**) thank (s.o. for s.th.)

rinnegare *v/t* disown; abjure; **~ato** *m* renegade; **~azione** *f* renegation

rinnov|amento *m* renewal; **~are** *v/t* renew; remodel; **~azione** *f* renovation

rinoceronte *m* rhinoceros

rinomato renowned

rinserrare *v/t* shut in; tighten

rintracciare *v/t* trace (out)

rintronare *v/t, v/i* resound; deafen

rinunci|a *f* renunciation; **~are** *v/t* renounce (**a qc.** s.th.)

rinvenire *v/i* come to o.s.

rinviare *v/t* send back; adjourn

rinvigorimento *m* strengthening

rinvilire *v/t* lower (*prices*)

rinvio *m* dismissal; adjournment

rione *m* district (*of city*)

riordinare *v/t* rearrange

riorganizz|are *v/t* reorganize; **~azione** *f* reorganization

ripagare *v/t* repay

ripar|àbile reparable; **~are** *v/t* repair; protect (**da** from); *v/i* remedy; **~azione** *f* repair; *fig* amends *pl*; **~o** *m* shelter; cover

ripart|ire *v/i* leave again; *v/t* distribute; **~izione** *f* distribution; **~o** *m* department

ripassare *v/i* pass again; *v/t* look over; overhaul

ripensare *v/i* think over

ripercussione *f* repercussion

ripètere *v/t* repeat

ripetizione *f* repetition

ripian|are *v/t* level; **~o** *m* landing; terrace

ripido steep

ripiegare *v/t* fold (again); *v/i mil* retreat; **~o** *m* shift; expedient

ripieno *adj* stuffed; *m* stuffing

riport|are *v/t* bring back *etc* (*cf* **portare**); report; carry off (*prize*); **~o** *m com* amount to be carried forward

ripos|are *v/i* rest; **~arsi** *v/r* lie down; **~o** *m* rest; retirement

ripresa *f* resumption; revival

riproduzione *f* reproduction; **~ vietata** all rights

reserved

riprov|a f confirmation; **~àbile** blamable; **~are** v/t try again; reject (*candidate*)

ripudiare v/t repudiate

ripugn|ante repugnant; **~anza** f repugnance; **~are** v/i be repugnant

ripulsione f repulsion

riputazione f reputation

riquadratore m (house-) decorator

risaia f rice-field

risalt|are v/i stand out; **~o** m relief

risan|àbile curable; **~are** v/t heal; cure

risarcire v/t indemnify

riscaldamento m heating; **~ centrale** central heating

riscald|are v/t heat; warm; **~arsi** v/r get hot; *fig* get excited; **~atore** m heater

riscattare v/t, **riscatto** m ransom

rischiar|amento m brightening; **~are** v/t illuminate; clarify; **~arsi** v/r clear up (*weather*)

rischi|are v/t risk; **~o** m risk; danger; **a ~o di** at the risk of; **a vostro ~o e pericolo** at your own risk; **córrere il ~o di** run the risk of; **~oso** risky

risciacqu|are v/t rinse; **~atura** f rinsing-water; washing-up water

riscontr|are v/t meet; find; check; **~o** m encounter; checking; **~o d'aria** draught

riscuòtere v/t shake; (*money*) collect

risentire v/t feel again; v/i feel the effects (**di** of)

riserbare v/t reserve; keep

riserva f reserve; reservation

riserv|are v/t reserve; **~arsi** v/r reserve (to) o.s.; **~ato** reserved; confidential

riso m laugh(ter); rice

risolare v/t resole

risol|utezza f resoluteness; **~uto** resolute; **~uzione** f resolution; solution; **~uzione d'un contratto** annulment of a contract

risòlv|ere v/t resolve; (dis-) solve; **~ersi** v/r decide

risolvìbile solvable

rison|anza f sound; resonance; echo; **~are** v/i resound; ring (again)

risòrgere v/i rise (again)

risorgimento m revival

risorsa f resource

risotto m boiled rice served in the Italian fashion

risparmiare v/t save; spare

risparmio m savings; **cassa f di ~** savings bank

rispecchiare v/t reflect

rispett|àbile respectable; **~are** v/t respect; **~ivo** respective; **~o** m respect; **~i** m/pl regards pl; **~oso** respectful

risplèndere v/i shine

risp|óndere v/t, v/i answer; reply (**a** to); **~osta** f answer; reply; **~osta pagata** reply paid

rissa f fight; affray

ristabili|mento m re-establishment; restoration; **~ire** v/t re-establish; **~irsi** v/r recover

ristampa f reprint; new impression

ristor|ante m restaurant; refreshment-room; **carozza ~ante** dining-car (train); **~are** v/t restore; refresh

restr|ettezza f narrowness; straitness; **~etto** restricted; limited; **caffè m ~etto** very strong coffee

result|are v/i result; **~ato** m result; issue

risurrezione f resurrection

risuscitare v/t, v/i resuscitate

risvegli|are v/t awaken; **~arsi** v/r wake up

ritard|are v/t delay; v/i be late; (watch) be slow; **~atario** m laggard; latecomer; **~o** m delay; **èssere in ~o** be late

ritegno m restraint; **senza ~** unrestrainedly

riten|ere v/t retain; **~ersi** v/r restrain o.s. (from)

ritir|are v/t withdraw; (money) draw; (mail) collect; **~arsi** v/r retire; **~ata** f retreat; lavatory; **~ato** secluded; **~o** m retirement; **in ~o** retired

rito m rite

ritoccare v/t retouch

ritornare v/i come back; **~ in sé** come to o.s.; return

ritorno m return; **èssere di**

~ be back

ritorsione f retort; retaliation

ritrarre v/t withdraw; draw (advantage)

ritratt|àbile retractable; **~are** v/t portray; retract; **~azione** f recantation; **~ista** m, f portrait-painter; **~o** m portrait

ritrov|are v/t find again; **~arsi** v/r meet; **~o** m meeting-place; **~o notturno** night club

ritto upright; straight; **star ~** stand (upright)

riun|ione f reunion; meeting; **~ire** v/t (re)unite; gather

riusc|ire v/i succeed; **riesco a fare** or **mi riesce di fare** I succeed in doing; **~ita** f success

rituale m, adj ritual

riva f shore

rivale m, f, adj rival

rived|ere v/t see again; review; **~erci, ~erla** good-bye

rivel|are v/t reveal; disclose; **~azione** f revelation

rivénd|ere v/t resell; **~ita** f resale

rivenditore m reseller; retailer

rivenire v/i come back

river|ente reverent; **~enza** f reverence; **~ire** v/t respect; revere; **La riverisco** letter: with kind regards

rivestire v/t cover; line

riviera f coast

rivista f review; *mil* parade; **~ della moda** fashion show; **~ settimanale** weekly (magazine)

rivo m brook; streamlet

rivòlg|ere v/t address; **~ersi** v/r apply (**a** to)

rivolgimento m upheaval; **~ di stòmaco** sickness; nausea

rivolta f revolt; mutiny

rivolt|are v/t turn (over); overthrow; **~ella** f revolver

rivoltolare v/t roll (over)

rivoluzion|ario m, adj revolutionary; **~e** f revolution

rizz|are v/t erect; (flags) hoist; **~arsi** v/r stand up; bristle

rob|a f stuff; things pl; **~accia** f rubbish; junk

robust|ezza f sturdiness; **~o** sturdy; strong

rocca f fortress; distaff; **~forte** f stronghold

rocchetto m reel; bobbin; eccl surplice

rocci|a f rock; **~oso** rocky

rococò m, adj rococo

rodaggio m auto: running-in

ród|ere v/t gnaw; **~ersi** v/r chafe (with rage)

rognone m gast kidney

rollare v/i roll ship

Roma f Rome

Romania f R(o)umania

rom|ànico Romanic; architecture: Romanesque; **~ano** m, adj Roman; **~anticismo** m Romanticism; **~àntico** adj romantic; m romanticist

romanz|a f romance; **~iere** m novelist; **~o** m novel

rombare v/i rumble; roar

rombo m turbot

romeno m, adj Roumanian

rom|ito adj solitary; m hermit; **~itorio** m hermitage

rómpere v/t break; smash

ronc|are v/t weed; **~o** m billhook; fig deadlock

ronda f patrol

róndine f swallow

rondò m rondeau

ronfare snore

ronz|are v/i buzz; hum; **~io** m buzzing

ros|a f rose; **~àceo** rosaceous; **~aio** m rose-bush; **~ario** m eccl rosary

rosbiffe m roast beef

ròseo rosy

ros|eto m rose-garden; **~etta** f rosette

rosmarino m rosemary

rosol|are v/t roast brown; **~ia** f measles pl

rospo m toad

rossetto m (**per le labbra**) lipstick

ross|iccio reddish; **~o** red; **~o chiaro** bright red; **~o cupo** dark-red; **~ore** m blush

rosticc|erìa f cook-shop; **~iere** m cook-shop keeper

rostro m rostrum

rot|àbile carriageable; **~aia** f rail; **~are** v/i rotate; **~azione** f rotation; **~ella** f small wheel; knee-cap

rotolare v/t, v/i roll (up)

ròtolo m roll

rotondo round

rotta f course; rout

rottame m fragment; **~i**
m/pl ruins pl

rotto broken

rottura f fracture

ròtula f kneecap; patella

roulotte f caravan; trailer

róvere m oak

rovèscia f facing (of sleeves
etc); **alla ~** inside out; **~are**
v/t overturn; upset; **~o** m
wrong side; reverse; **a ~o**
backhand; reversed; upside
down

rovin|a f ruin; **~are** v/t ruin;
v/i collapse; crumble

rovo m blackberry-bush

rozzo coarse; uncouth

rubare v/t steal

rubinetto m tap; faucet; **~**
d'acqua water-tap

rubino m ruby

rublo m rouble

rubrica f rubric; column

rude rough

rudimenti m/pl rudiments

ruffa f crowd; throng

ruga f wrinkle

rùggine f rust; fig grudge

ruggin|ire v/i get rusty;
~oso rusty

ruggire v/i roar; **~ito** m
roar(ing)

rugiada f dew

rugoso wrinkled

rull|are v/i roll; **~o** m roll;
drum; roller; cylinder; **~o**
compressore road roller

rum m rum

rumor|e m noise; **~eggiare**
v/i make noise; rumble; **~o-**
so noisy

ruolo m roll; list; thea part

ruota f wheel; **~ anteriore**
fore wheel; **~ di ricambio**
spare wheel; **~ posteriore**
hind wheel

rupe f rock; cliff

ruscello m brook

russare v/i snore

Russia f Russia

russo m, adj Russian

rùstico rustic

rutto m belch

ruvidezza f roughness

rùvido rough; harsh

ruzz|o m romping; **~olare**
v/i roll; tumble down

S

sa he knows

sàbato m Saturday

sàbbi|a f sand; **~oso** sandy

saccheggi|are v/t sack;
plunder; **~o** m sack(ing)

sacc|o m sacking; bag;
quantity; **~o alpino**, **~o da**
montagna rucksack; **~o a**

pelo sleeping-bag; **~one** m
straw mattress

sacerdot|ale priestly; **~e** m
priest; **sommo ~e** high
priest

sacerdozio m priesthood

sacrament|are v/t qu. ad-
minister the sacraments to

s.o.; **~arsi** v/r receive the sacraments; **~o** m sacrament

sacr|are v/t consecrate; dedicate; **~ario** m sanctuary; shrine; **~estia** f sacristy; vestry; **~ificare** v/t sacrifice; **~ificio** m, **~ifizio** f sacrifice

sacro sacred; holy

saettare v/t shoot (arrows); dart (glances)

sagace shrewd; keen

saggezza f wisdom

saggiare v/t try; test

saggio adj wise; m essay; test; sample; **~ d'interesse** com rate of interest; **~ di vino** wine-test; **numero m di ~** specimen copy

sagra f (church) festival

sagr|are v/i swear; **~ato** m curse; churchyard

sagrest|ano m sacristan; **~ia** f sacristy

sagù m sago

sala f hall; room; biol reed; mech axle-tree; **~ d'aspetto** waiting-room; **~ di biliardo** billiard-room; **~ da colazione** breakfast room; **~ da concerti** concert-hall; **~ di lettura** reading-room; **~ da pranzo** dining-room; **~ di soggiorno** lounge

salace lecherous

salame m (pork-)sausage; **~oia** f pickle; brine; **in ~oia** salted; pickled

salare v/t salt; dry-salt

salario m wages pl

salato salted; **carne** f **~a** salt

meat

salc|eto m willow-thicket; **~io** m willow(-tree)

salda f starch

sald|are v/t weld; solder; com settle; **~atoio** m soldering-iron; **~o** adj firm; m balance; settlement

sale he climbs

sal|e m salt; wit; **~gemma** m rock-salt

salgo I climb

saliamo we climb

sàlice f willow; **~ piangente** weeping willow

salicilato m salicylate

sal|iera f salt-cellar; **~ifero** saliferous; **~ina** f salt-pit

salire v/t, v/i climb; go up; rise; increase

sal|iscendi m latch; **~ita** f ascension; slope; increase

salito climbed

saliva f saliva, spittle

salma f mortal remains pl

salmiaco m sal ammoniac

salmo m psalm

salmone m salmon

salnitro m saltpetre

sal|one m hall; saloon; **~one fumatori** smoking room; **~one da parrucchiere** hairdresser's shop; **~otto** m drawing-room; sitting-room; **~otto da pranzo** dining-room

salpare v/i weigh anchor; set sail

salsa f sauce

salsicci|a f sausage; **~a di fégato** liver-sausage; **~aio**

m sausage-maker; **~otto** *m* thick sausage

salsiera *f* sauce-boat

salso *adj* salty; *m* saltiness

salt|are *v/t* jump; *fig* skip; **~erellare** *v/i* hop about; **~imbanco** *m* acrobat; mountebank

salto *m* jump; leap; **~ in alto** high jump; **~ in lungo** long jump; **~ mortale** somersault

salubr|e healthy; **~ità** *f* healthiness

salum|aio *m* pork-butcher; **~i** *m/pl* sausages; **~erìa** *f* delicatessen shop

salut|are *adj* salutary; *v/t* salute; greet; **~e** *f* health; **alla Sua ~e!** your health!

saluto *m* salute; greeting; **tanti ~i** kind regards

salva|danaio *m* money-box; **~gente** *m* life-belt; (traffic) island; **~guardia** *f* safeguard; **~mento** *m* rescue

salv|are *v/t* save; rescue; **~ataggio** *m* salvage; **barca** *f* **di ~ataggio** lifeboat; **tela** *f* **di ~ataggio** jumping-sheet

salvatore *m* rescuer; ♀ *eccl* Saviour

salvietta *f* napkin

salvo safe, secure; except; **~ che** unless

sambuco *m* elder(-tree)

San = **Santo**

san|àbile curable; **~are** *v/t* cure; heal; **~atorio** *m* sanatorium; nursing-home

sancire *v/t* sanction

sàndalo *m* sandal

sangu|e *m* blood; **fare ~e** bleed; **~igno** sanguine; bloody; **gruppo** *m* **~igno** blood group; **~inaccio** *m* black-pudding; **~inare** *v/i* bleed; **~inario** bloodthirsty; **~inoso** bloody

sanitario sanitary; **ufficio** *m* **~** health office

sano healthy; **~ e salvo** safe and sound

santificare *v/t* sanctify; canonize

sant|issimo *adj* most holy; *m* Blessed Sacrament; **~ità** *f* holiness

santo *adj* holy; *m* saint; **acqua** *f* **santa** holy water

santuario *m* sanctuary; shrine

sapere *v/t*, *v/i* know; know how to; get to know; learn; **far ~** let know; *m* knowledge

sap|iente *adj* wise; *m* learned person; **~ienza** *f* wisdom

sapon|ata *f* lather; soapsuds *pl*; **~e** *m* soap; **~e da barba** shaving soap; **~erìa** *f* soap-works *pl*; **~etta** *f* cake of toilet-soap; **~iera** *f* soapdish

sapor|e *m* flavour; taste; **~ire** *v/t* flavour; relish; **~ito** savoury

sappiamo we know

saputo known; learned

sar|à he will be; **~ai** you will be (*sg*); **~anno** they will be

sarcàstico sarcastic

sarchiare *v/t* weed

sardella *f* pilchard

Sardegna f Sardinia

sardina f sardine

sardo m, adj Sardinian

sare|mo we shall be; **~te** you will be (pl)

sarò I shall be

sart|a f dressmaker; **~o** m tailor; **~oria** f tailor's shop; dressmaking

sasso m stone; pebble; **di ~** stony

sàssone m, adj Saxon

Sassonia f Saxony

sassoso stony

satèllite m satellite

satirico adj satiric(al); m satirist

savio wise

sazi|are v/t satiate; **~o** satiated

sbacchettare v/t dust; beat

sbaciucchiare v/t cover with kisses

sbadato heedless

sbadigliare v/i yawn

sbagli|are v/i, **~arsi** v/r make a mistake; err; **~o** m mistake; error; **per ~o** by mistake

sballare v/t unpack; fig talk big

sballottare v/t toss about

sbalord|imento m bewilderment; **~ire** v/t astonish; bewilder

sbalz|are v/t overthrow; cast out; **~o** m bound

sbandare v/t disband; v/i aut skid

sbandire v/t banish

sbarazz|are v/t clear; **~arsi** v/r get rid (of)

sbarb|are v/t uproot; shave; **~ato** clean shaven

sbarc|are v/t disembark; v/i land; **~atoio** m landing-place; **~o** m landing; unloading

sbarr|a f bar; barrier; **~amento** m obstruction; **~are** v/t bar; block up; (eyes) open wide

sbàttere v/t beat; whip; (door) slam

sbeffare v/t mock

sbendare v/t remove bandages

sbiadito faded

sbiancare v/i grow pale

sbigottire v/t frighten

sbilanci|are v/t put out of balance; **~o** m derangement; deficit

sbocc|are v/i flow into; **~atura** f mouth (of river)

sbocciare v/i open; bloom

sbocco m mouth (of river); com outlet; market; **~ di sangue** blood-spitting

strada f **senza ~** blind alley

sborni|a f intoxication; **~ato** drunk

sbors|are v/t disburse; pay; **~o** m outlay

sboscare v/t deforest

sbottonare v/t unbutton

sbozz|are v/t sketch; outline; **~o** m sketch

sbrattare v/t clear; tide up

sbriciolare v/t crumble

sbrig|are v/t dispatch; finish off; **~arsi** v/r hurry up

sbrinare v/t defrost (*refrigerator*)

sbrogliare v/t disentangle

sbucciare v/t peel; skin

sbuffare v/i puff; snort

scabr|osità f roughness; **~o** so rough; rugged; uneven

scacchiera f chess-board

scacci|amosche m flywhip; **~are** v/t drive away; expel

scacc|o m square; **~hi** pl chess; **giocatore m di ~hi** chess-player; **giocare a ~hi** play chess; **~o matto** checkmate

scad|ente falling due; inferior (*quality*); **~enza** f maturity; expiration; **a breve ~enza** short-dated; **~ere** v/i expire; fall due; **~uto** expired

scaffale m shelf

scafo m hull

scagionare v/t justify

scaglia f scale; chip

scala f stairs pl; **~ (a pioli)** ladder; **~ mòbile** escalator

scalcare v/t carve (*at table*)

scalciare v/i kick (*horse*)

scalda|bagno m boiler; **~letto** m hot-water-bottle; **~piatti** m plate-warmer; **~piedi** m foot-warmer

scald|are v/t heat; warm; **~ino** m warming-pan

scal|ea f flight of steps; **~eo** m step; ladder; **~ino** m step

scalo m landing-place; port of call; **~ merci** freight station

scaloppina f cutlet; chop

scalpell|are v/t chisel; **~ino** m stone-cutter; **~o** m chisel

scalp|icciare v/i trample; **~itio** m pawing

scaltro sly; crafty

scalz|are v/t take off (*shoes and stockings*); **~o** barefoot

scambi|are v/t exchange; mistake (for); **~évole** mutual

scambio m exchange; rail switch

scampagnata f trip in the country

scampan|ata f chiming; **~ellare** v/i ring the bell

scamp|are v/t rescue; v/i escape; **~o** m escape

scàmpolo m remnant (*of tissue*)

scancellare v/t cancel

scandaglio m sounding-line

scandalizzare v/t shock

scàndalo m scandal

scansare v/t avoid; shun

scanton|are v/i turn the corner

scapato heedless

scapestrato dissolute

scàpito m loss; detriment

scàpol|a f shoulder-blade; **~o** adj single; m bachelor

scapp|amento m mech exhaust; **~are** v/i escape; flee; **~atoia** f subterfuge; pretext

scappellarsi v/r take off one's hat

scarabocchio m blot

scarcerare v/t release (*from prison*)

scàrica f discharge

scaric|are v/t discharge; un-

load; **∼arsi** v/r relieve o.s.;
(clock) run down; **∼atoio** m
wharf

scàrico adj unloaded;
empty; m unloading; mech
exhaust

scarlatt|ina f scarlet-fever;
∼o scarlet

scarno lean; meagre

scarp|a f shoe; boot; **∼e** f/pl
per bambini children's
shoes pl; **∼e da signora**
ladies' shoes pl; **∼e da
spiaggia** sand shoes pl;
∼etta f small shoe; **∼ette** f/pl
da bagno bathing slippers
pl

scarrozz|are v/t, v/i drive
around; **∼ata** f drive

scars|ità f scarcity; **∼o**
scarce; lacking

scartafaccio m waste-book

scartoccio m paper-bag

scass|are v/t unpack; agr
plough up; **∼o** m burglary

scatenare v/t unchain

scàtola f box; tin; can

scatto m release (lever); **∼
automàtico** phot auto-
matic trigger

scaturire v/i gush out

scavalcare v/t, v/i dismount

scav|are v/t dig out; ex-
cavate; **∼o** m excavation

scegliamo we choose

scéglie he chooses

scégliere v/t select

scelgo I choose

scellino m shilling

scelta f choice; selection;
fare la ∼ choose; select

scelto chosen; exquisite

scem|are v/t lessen; reduce;
∼o m fool

scena f stage; scene

scéndere v/t, v/i descend; go
down; lower

sceneggiatura f stage-
directions pl

scesa f slope; descent

scèttico adj sceptic(al); m
sceptic

scettro m sceptre

scheda f card; (piece of)
paper; label

scheggi|are v/t splinter; **∼a** f
splinter

schèletro m skeleton; fig
frame

schema m outline; plan

scherm|a f fencing; **tirare
di ∼a, ∼ire** v/i fence

schermo m (phot, movie etc)
screen; defence; **∼ giallo**
phot yellow filter; **∼ gigante**
film: wide screen

schern|ire v/t sneer (at); **∼o**
m sneer

scherz|are v/i joke; **∼évole**
jesting; **∼o** m joke; **∼oso**
playful; joking

schiacci|anoci m nut-crack-
er; **∼are** v/t crush; squash;
squeeze; **∼ata** f gast cake

schiaffo m box on the ear;
slap

schiamazzare v/i cackle;
squawk

schiant|are v/t smash; **∼o** m
crash; fig pang

schiar|imento m elucidation;
∼ire v/t fig elucidate;
∼irsi v/r become clear

schiav|itù f slavery; **∼o** m,

adj slave

schiena f back

schier|a f group; **~are** v/t
array

schietto frank; open;
genuine

schifo adj disgusting; m disgust; **~oso** loathsome

schiocco m snap; crack

schiodare v/t unnail

schiopp|ettata f shot; **~o** m
gun; rifle

schiùdere v/t open

schium|a f foam; lather;
~aiola f skimmer; **~are** v/t
skim; v/i foam; **~oso** frothy

schiv|are v/t shun; **~o**
averse; shy

schizz|are v/t squirt; **~o** m
sketch

schnorchel m snorkel

sci m ski; **nàutico** water ski

sciàbola f sabre

sciacallo m jackal

sciacquare v/t rinse

sciag|ura f disaster; **~urato**
unfortunate

scialle m shawl

scialuppa f sloop; shallop

sciam|are v/i swarm; **~e** m
swarm

sciampagna f champagne

sciampo m shampoo

sciancato adj crippled; m
cripple

sciare v/i ski

sciarpa f scarf; sash

sciàtica f sciatica

sci|atore m, **~atrice** f skier

scicche stylish; elegant

scientifico scientific

scienz|a f science; knowl-

edge; **~e** f/pl **econòmiche**
economics; **~e politiche**
politics; **~iato** m scientist

scimm|ia f ape; monkey;
~iottare v/t ape

scintill|a f spark; **~are** v/i
sparkle

sciocchezza f foolishness;
stupidity

sciocco adj stupid; m fool

sciògli|ere v/t untie; **~ersi**
v/r melt (snow)

sciolt|ezza f ease; **~o** loose

scioper|ante m striker; **~are**
v/i strike; **~atezza** f idleness; **~ato** adj lazy; m
never-do-well

sciòpero m strike; **fare ~** (go
on) strike

sciovìa f ski-lift

scirocco m sultry African
wind

sciroppo m syrup

sciupare v/t waste; spoil

scivolare v/i slip; glide

scivolo m chute

scodella f porringer

scogliera f cliff

scoglio m rock; **~so** rocky

scol|aro m, **~ara** f, **~aro**,
~àstico: anno m **~àstico**
school-year

scol|atoio m drain; gutter;
~atura f draining

scollato low-necked; décolleté

scolo m drain

scolor|are, ~ire v/t, v/i discolour; fade; **~irsi** v/r grow
pale

scolpire v/t sculpture; chisel

scombinare v/t disarrange

scommessa f bet

scomméttere v/t bet

scomodarsi v/r trouble

scomodo uncomfortable

scomparire v/i disappear

scompartimento m compartment

scompiac|ente unkind; **~enza** f unkindness

scompigliare v/t upset

scompleto incomplete

scomporre v/t decompose

scomùnica f excommunication

sconcertare v/t perturb

sconci|are v/t spoil; mar; **~o** indecent; nasty

sconcordia f discord

sconfinato boundless

sconfitta f defeat

sconfortare v/t discourage

scongiurare v/t beseech; conjure

sconn|esso disconnected; desultory; **~éttere** v/t disjoin

scon|óscere v/t underrate; **~osciuto** unknown

sconsacrare v/t desecrate

sconsiderato rash

sconsigliare v/t dissuade

sconsol|ato disconsolate; **~azione** f grief

scontare v/t deduct; discount; expiate

scontent|ezza f dissatisfaction; **~o** discontent (**di** with)

sconto m discount

scontrino m check; ticket; **~ del bagaglio** luggage-ticket

scontro m collision

sconven|iente unbecoming; **~ire** v/i be unsuitable

sconvolgimento m derangement; overturn; **~ di stòmaco** upset stomach

scooter m (motor-)scooter

scop|a f broom; **~are** v/t sweep

scopert|a f discovery; **~o** uncovered

scopo m aim; purpose

scoppiare v/i burst; explode; **~ in una risata** burst out laughing

scoppi|ettare v/i crackle; **~o** m burst; explosion

scoprire v/t discover; uncover

scoraggi|are v/t discourage; **~ato** discouraged

scorciare v/t shorten

scordare v/t mus put out of tune; forget

còrgere v/t perceive

scórrere v/i flow; elapse; v/t run through

scorretto incorrect

scorso past (year)

scorta f escort

scort|ese impolite; **~esìa** f rudeness

scorticare v/t skin

scorz|a f bark; skin; **~are** v/t peel

scossa f shake; shock; **~ di pioggia** downpour; **~ di terremoto** earthquake shock; **~ elèttrica** electric shock; **~ nervosa** nervous shock

scostarsi v/r go away; fig

wander (*from subject*)

scostumato profligate

scott|are v/t, v/i scorch; burn; **~atura** f burn; scald; **~atura del sole** sunburn

scotto m bill; score

scovare v/t dislodge

Scozia f Scotland

scozzese Scottish

screditare v/t discredit

scrédito m discredit

screpol|arsi v/r crack; split; **~atura** f crack

scricchiolare v/i creak

scrigno m jewel-box

scriminatura f parting (*hair*)

scritt|a f inscription; contract; **~o** m writing; **per iscritto** in writing; **~oio** m writing-desk; **~ore** m writer; **~ura** f (hand-)writing; com entry

scrivania f writing-desk

scrivere v/t, v/i write

scroll|are v/t shake; **~o** m shake

scrosciare v/i roar; pelt

scrùpolo m scruple

scrupol|osità f scrupulousness; **~oso** scrupulous

scrutare v/t scrutinize

scucire v/t unsew

scuderia f (racing-)stable

scudo m shield; five-lira-piece

scult|ore m sculptor; **~ura** f sculpture; **~ura in legno** wood-carving

scuola f school; **~ commerciale** commercial school; **~**

d'aviamento professionale vocational school; **~ d'equitazione** riding-school; **~ media** secondary school; **~ superiore** high school

scuòtere v/t shake; toss

scur|e f axe; hatchet; **~etto** m (window-)shutter; **~o** dark

scus|a f excuse; pretext; **~àbile** excusable; **~are** v/t excuse; **~arsi** v/r apologize

sdaziare v/t pay duty; clear

sdegn|are v/t disdain; **~ato** indignant; **~o** m indignation

sdentato toothless

sdrai|are v/t stretch (out); **~a** f **~o** deck-chair

sdrucciol|are v/i slide; slip; **~évole** slippery

se if; whether; **~ no** otherwise

se = **si** before **lo, la, li, le, ne**

sé himself; herself; itself; oneself; themselves; **da ~ (stesso)** by himself; by oneself

sebbene (al)though

secante f secant

secc|a f sand-bank; **~are** v/t, v/i dry (up); fig bother; **~arsi** v/r dry up; be bored

secchia f bucket; pail

secco adj dry; withered; m dryness

seco (= **con sé**) with him, her, them; with oneself

secol|are adj century-old; secular; m layman; **~arizzare** v/t secularize

sècolo m century; fig age

seconda: a ~ di according to

second|are v/t support; **~ario** secondary; **scuola ~aria** secondary school; **~o** prep according to; **~o me** in my opinion; m, adj second

secreto = segreto

sèdano m celery

sedare v/t appease; soothe

sede f seat; residence; office; **la Santa 2** the Holy See

sed|ere v/i sit; **~ersi** v/r sit down

sedia f chair; **~ a sdraio** lounge-chair; **~ a dòndolo** rocking-chair

sedicèsimo sixteenth

sedile m seat; bench

sedurre v/t seduce

seduta f meeting

seduzione f seduction

sega f saw

segalaio m rye-field

ségale f rye

segare v/t saw; agr mow

seggio m seat; throne

sèggiola f seat; chair

seggiol|ino m child's chair; **~one** m easy-chair

seggiovìa f chair-lift

segheria f saw-mill

segnal|are v/t signal; **~atore** m indicator; marker; **~e** m signal; sign; **~e d'allarme** alarm-signal

segn|alibro m book-mark; **~are** v/t mark; note; show; **~o** m mark; sign

seg|o m tallow; **~oso** adj tallowy

segregare v/t segregate

segr|etaria f secretary; **~eto** adj secret; private; m secret

seguace m follower

segugio m bloodhound

segu|ire v/t follow; **~itare** v/t continue; literary: **séguita** to be continued

séguito m continuation; train; di **~** continuously; **in ~a** owing to

sei you are (sg)

seicento m 17th century

selci|are v/t pave; **~ato** m pavement

selettività f selectivity

selezione f selection

sella f saddle; **cavallo m da ~** saddle-horse

sell|aio m saddler; **~are** v/t saddle

seltz m: **acqua f di ~** soda (-water)

selva f forest

selv|aggina f game; venison; **~aggio** adj wild; m savage; **~àtico** wild

semàforo m traffic lights pl

sembrare v/t, v/i seem; look like

seme m seed; **~enta** f sowing

semestre m half-year

semi|aperto half-open; **~cerchio** m half-circle

semin|are v/t sow; **~ario** m seminary; **~atore** m sower

semi|nudo half-naked; **~tondo** half-round

sémola f fine flour; bran

semolino m semolina

semovente self-propelled

sémplice simple; fig naive

semplicità f simplicity

semplific|are v/t simplify; **~azione** f simplification

sempre always; **~verde** m evergreen

sènap|a f, **~e** f mustard

senato m senate

sen|ile senile; **~iore** senior; elder

senno m sense; **è fuor di ~** he is out of his wits

seno m bosom; womb; naut bay

senonché only that; but

sensale m broker

sens|azione f sensation; **~ibile** sensitive; **~ibilità** f sensitivity; **~itivo** sensitive

sens|o m sense; feeling; **buon ~o** common sense; **strada a ~ único** one-way street; **~i** m/pl scnse-organs pl

sentenza f sentence

sentiero m path

sentimental|e sentimental; **~ità** f sentimentality

sentimento m feeling

sentinella f sentry

sent|ire v/t feel; hear; smell; **~irsi** v/r feel (o.s.)

senza without; **~ difetti** faultless; **~ di me** without me

senzatetto m homeless person

separ|àbile separable; **~are** v/t separate; sever; **~azione** f separation

sep|olcrale sepulchral; **~olcro** m tomb; **~olto** buried

seppell|imento m burial; **~ire** v/t bury

sequestr|are v/t sequester;

~o m sequestration; **~o di persona** kidnapping

sera f evening; **di ~** in the evening; **buona ~** good evening; **dare la buona ~** wish good evening; **~le:** **scuola ~le** evening-school; **~ta** f evening

serb|are v/t keep; preserve; **~atoio** m reservoir; **~atoio di benzina** petrol-tank; fuel-tank; **~atoio di riserva** reserve tank

seren|ata f serenade; **~ità** f serenity; **~o** serene; bright; clear

serie f series; set; **~ di carte** pack of cards; **~ di franco-bolli** issue of stamps

serio adj serious; m earnest; **sul ~** in earnest

sermone m sermon; lecture

serp|eggiare v/i wind; meander; **~ente** m snake

serr|are v/t lock (up); press; **~arsi** v/r close up; **~ata** f lock-out (of workers)

serratura f lock; **~ d'accensione** ignition lock; **~ della portiera** (auto) (door)lock; **~ di sicurezza** safety-lock

serv|ire v/t, v/i serve; wait upon; be of use; **~irsi** v/r help o.s.

serv|itore m servant; **~itù** f servants pl; slavery

servizio m service; duty; **di ~** on duty; **~ d'emergenza** stand-by service; **~ militare** military service; **~ ri-parazioni** road patrol; **donna** f **di mezzo ~** half-day charwoman

servo m (man-)servant

sess|o m sex; **~uale** sexual

set|a f silk; **~a da cucito** sewing-silk; **~aiuolo** m silk-merchant; **~aiuolo** m silk-manufacturer

sete f thirst; **aver ~** be thirsty

seteria f silk-factory

sétola f bristle

setolino m little brush

settantenne seventy years old

settecento m 18th century

settembre m September

settentrion|ale adj northern; m northerner; **~e** m north

settimana f week; **~ santa** Holy Week; **~le** weekly

sèttimo seventh

sever|ità f severity; **~o** severe

sezione f section

sfacciat|aggine f impudence; **~o** shameless

sfacelo m breakdown

sfarz|o m pomp; **~oso** pompous

sfasciare v/t unbind; remove the bandages

sfavor|e m disfavour; **~évole** unfavourable

sfera f sphere; globe

sférico spherical

sfiat|arsi v/r talk, shout o.s. hoarse; **~ato** out of breath

sfibbiare v/t unbuckle

sfid|a f defiance; **~are** v/t challenge; brave

sfiducia f mistrust

sfigurare v/t disfigure

sfilare v/t unthread

sfinimento m exhaustion

sfiorire v/i fade

sfogarsi v/r give vent to one's feelings

sfoggio m display; luxury

sfogli|a f foil; **pasta f ~a** puff-paste; **~are** v/t strip off (leaves); go through (a book)

sfolgorare v/i shine; flash

sfolla|gente m truncheon; **~re** v/t evacuate

sfond|ato bottomless; **~o** m background

sformare v/t deform; mech remove from the mould

sfort|una f bad luck; **~unato** unlucky

sforz|are v/t force; **~o** m effort; strain

sfracellare v/t smash; shatter

sfrattare v/t evict

sfregare v/t rub

sfrenato unbridled

sfrontato shameless

sfruttare v/t exploit

sfugg|évole fleeting; **~ire** v/i escape

sfum|are v/t tone down (colour); **~atura** f shade; nuance

sfuriata f outburst, fit

sgabello m (foot)stool

sgambettare v/i kick

sganciare v/t unhook

sgangherare v/t unhinge

sgarbato impolite; rude

sgel|are v/t, v/i thaw; **~o** m thaw; **tempo di ~o** thaw

sghembo oblique; slant (-ing)

sghiacciare v/i thaw

sgocciolare v/i drip; trickle

sgol|arsi v/r shout o.s. hoarse

sgomb(e)rare v/t, v/i clear out; remove

sgómbero m removal

sgombro m mackerel

sgomitolare v/t unwind

sgorbio m (ink-)blot

sgorgare v/i gush forth; flow (tears)

sgoverno m misgovernment

grad|évole unpleasant; **~ire** v/t, v/i displease; dislike

sgraffiare v/t scratch

sgranare v/t shell; husk

sgranchir|e v/t stretch; **~si le gambe** stretch one's legs

sgravare v/t unburden

sgraziato ungraceful

sgretolare v/t grind

sgrid|are v/t scold; **~ata** f scolding

sgualcire v/t (c)rumple

sgualdrina f strumpet

sguardo m look; glance

sguazzare v/i splash; wallow

sgusciare v/t shell; **~** v/i **di mano** slip from the hand

shampoo m shampoo

si one; people; oneself, him-, her-, itself; each other; **~ dice** they (people) say

sì yes; so; **dire di ~** say yes

siamo we are

sibilare v/i hiss

sibilo m hiss(ing); whistle

sicché so that

siccità f drought

siccome as; since

Sicili|a f Sicily; **~ano** m, adj Sicilian

sicomoro m sycamore

sicurezza f security; **pùbblica ~** police; **chiusura f di ~** safety-lock; **porta f di ~** emergency door

sicuro safe; sure; **per ~ for** certain

sidro m cider

siepe f hedge; fence

siesta f afternoon nap

siete you are (pl)

siffatto such

sifone m siphon

sigaretta f cigarette; **~ a filtro** filter cigarette

sigaro m cigar

sigill|are v/t seal; **~o** m seal

signific|ante significant; **~are** v/t mean; **~ato** m meaning

signora f lady; woman; wife; mistress; **~!** Madam!; **la ~ N. N.** Mrs. N. N.

signor|e m gentleman; master; mister; **~!** Sir!; **~ia** f mastery; **~ile** noble; refined

signorina f young lady; **~!** Miss!

signorino m young gentleman

silenziatore m silencer

silenzio m silence; **fare ~** keep silent; **~!** silence!; be quiet!; **~so** silent

sillaba f syllable

sillab|are v/t spell; **~ario** m spelling-book

silòfono m xylophone

sill|urare v/t torpedo; **~uro** m torpedo; biol silurus

simbòlico symbolic(al)

simbolo m symbol; creed

similare similar

simile adj like; m neighbour

simm|etria f symmetry; **~è-trico** symmetrical

sim|patia f liking; **~pàtico** nice; congenial; **~patizzare** v/i take a liking to; get on with

simulare v/t feign; sham

sinagoga f synagogue

sincer|arsi v/r make sure; **~ità** f sincerity; **~o** sincere

sinché until; as long as

sindac|alista m trade-unionist; **~ato** m trade-union

sìndaco m mayor

sinfonia f symphony

singhiozz|are v/i sob; **~o** m sob

singol|are adj singular; peculiar; m singular; **~arità** f singularity

singolo single

sinistr|a f left (hand); **a ~a** on, to the left; **~ato** m victim; **~o** left; sinister

sino up to; as far as

sinònimo adj synonymous; m synonym

sinora up to now

sintassi f syntax

sìntesi f synthesis

sìntomo m symptom

sinuoso sinuous

sipario m thea curtain

sirena f siren

siroppo = **sciroppo**

sism|ògrafo m seismo-graph; **~ologia** f seismology

sistem|a m system; **~are** v/t arrange; settle; **~àtico** systematic

sito m situated; m site

situ|ato situated; **~azione** f situation

slanci|are f/t hurl; **~arsi** v/r rush; **~ato** slim; **~o** m rush; impetus; élan

slargare v/t widen

slavo Slavic

sleale disloyal; unfair

slegare v/t unbind

slip(s) m(/pl) panties

slitt|a f sleigh; sled; **~are** v/i sledge; slide; skid; **~ino** m toboggan; **~pista** f per **~ini** toboggan-run

slog|amento m dislocation; **~are** v/t dislocate; **~atura** f dislocation

sloggiare v/t drive out; v/i move

smacchi|are v/t remove stains; **~atore** m cleaner

smagrire v/i grow thin

smalt|are v/t glaze; **~o** m enamel; glaze; **~o per le unghie** nail polish

smani|a f eagerness; frenzy; **~are** v/i rave; **~erato** ill-mannered

smarr|imento m loss; **~ire** v/t mislay; lose; **~irsi** v/r get lost

smemorato forgetful

smentire v/t deny; belie

smeraldo m emerald

smerci|are v/t sell (off); **~o**

m sale; market
smeriglio *m* emery
smerlo *m* scallop edging
sméttere *v/t, v/i* give up;
(*dress*) cast off; stop
smezzare *v/t* halve
smisurato immeasurable
smobiliato unfurnished
smobilit|are *v/t* demobilize; **~azione** *f* demobilization
smoderato immoderate
smontare *v/i* dismount;
alight; *v/t mech* take apart
smorfia *f* grimace
smott|amento *m* landslide;
~are *v/i* slide
snatur|are *v/t* denaturalize;
~ato *adj* monstrous
snello slender; nimble
snervare *v/t* enervate
snodare *v/t* unknot
snudare *v/t* bare
so I know
soave sweet; gentle
sobbalzare *v/i* jolt
sobborgo *m* suburb
sobri|età *f* sobriety; **~o**
moderate
socchiùdere *v/t* half-shut;
(*door*) leave ajar
soccómbere *v/i* succumb;
yield
socc|órrere *v/t* aid; help;
~orso *m* help
soci|ale social; **~età** *f*
society; company; **~età
anònima** joint-stock
company; **~età d'aviazione** airline company; **~età di
navigazione** navigation
company; **~évole** socia-

ble; **~evolezza** *f* sociability;
~o *m* associate, partner;
member; **~ologia** *f* sociology
soda *f* soda
soddisf|acente satisfactory;
~are *v/t* satisfy; **~azione** *f*
satisfaction
sodo solid; hard
sofà *m* sofa
soffer|ente suffering; **~enza**
f suffering; pain
soffermarsi *v/t* stop a little
soffi|are *v/t, v/i* blow; puff;
~etto *m* bellows *pl*; **~o** *m*
breath
soffitt|a *f* attic; garret; **~o** *m*
ceiling
soffocare *v/t, v/i* suffocate
soffriggere *v/t* fry slightly
soffrire *v/t* bear; *v/i* suffer
(**di** from)
sofisticato sophisticated
sogget|tivo subjective; **~o**
adj subject(ed); **~o a tasse**
liable to taxation; *m* subject
sogghignare *v/i* sneer
soggiogare *v/t* subdue
soggi|ornare *v/i* stay; sojourn; **~orno** *m* stay; **tassa** *f*
di ~orno visitors' tax
soggiùngere *v/t* add
soggiuntivo *m* subjunctive
sogli|a *f* threshold; **~o** *m*
throne
sògliola *f* sole
sogn|are *v/t, v/i* dream; **~o** *m*
dream
solaio *m* garret; attic
solamente only; **~ ieri** only
yesterday
solata *f* sunstroke

solatura f soling (shoe)

solc|are v/t furrow; plough;
∼o m furrow

soldato m soldier

sold|o m penny; pay; **∼i** m/pl
money

sole m sun; **c'è il ∼** the sun is
shining

soleggi|are v/t, v/i sun; **∼ato**
sunny

solenn|e solemn; **∼ità** f so-
lemnity

solere v/i be used (to)

soll|erte assiduous; **∼erzia** f
industriousness

soletta f sole (of stocking)

solfa f mus gamut

solf|anello m sulphurmatch;
∼are v/t sulphur (-ate); **∼o**
m sulphur; **∼òrico: àcido ∼**
òrico sulphuric acid

solid|ezza, **∼ità** f solidity

sòlido solid

sol|ista m, f soloist; **∼itario**
adj solitary; **∼** m hermit

sòlito usual; **al ∼** as usual

solitùdine f solitude

soll|azzare v/t amuse; **∼azzo**
m amusement

solle|citare v/t hasten; solicit;
∼cito prompt; eager;
∼citùdine f promptness

solleticare v/t tickle; (appetite) stimulate

sollevare v/t lift; alleviate

sollievo m relief; comfort

solo adj alone; only; sole;
adv only; **∼** m mus solo

solstizio m solstice

soltanto only

sol|ùbile soluble; **∼uzione** f
solution; **∼vente** solvent

somigli|ante resembling;
∼anza f resemblance

somigliare v/i (a) qu. look
like, resemble s.o.

somm|a f sum; in **∼a** after
all; **∼are** v/t add up; **∼ario**
m, adj summary

sommèrg|ere v/t sub-
merge; **∼ersi** v/r sink; dive

sommergìbile m submar-
ine

sommesso subdued

sommo adj highest; m summit

somm|ossa f riot; **∼uòvere**
v/t stir up

sonare v/t, v/i play (instrument); **∼ il campanello**
ring the bell; sound; toll

sond|a f sound; naut sound-
ing-line; **∼aggio** m sound-
ing; **∼are** v/t sound; probe

soneria f (clock) alarm;
chime; **∼ elèttrica** electric
bell

sonetto m sonnet

sonn|àmbulo m sleep-walk-
er; **∼ecchiare** v/i slumber;
∼ellino m nap; **∼ìfero** m
sleeping-draught

sonno m sleep; aver **∼** be
sleepy

sonnolento drowsy

sono I am; they are

son|orità f sonority; **∼oro**
sonorous; film m **∼oro**
sound-film

sontu|osità f luxury; **∼oso**
sumptuous

sop|ire v/t lull; **∼ore** m
slumber

soppalco m lumber-room

sopport|àbile bearable; **~a-re** v/t endure; **~o** m support

soppress|are v/t press; **~are** v/t press; **~ione** f suppression;

sopprimere v/t suppress; abolish

sopra (up)on; over; above; **~ tutto** above all

sopr|àbito m overcoat; **~acciglio** m eyebrow; **~affare** v/t overwhelm; **~affino** superfine; **~aggiùngere** v/i turn up; happen; **~ascarpa** f galosh; **~ascritto** above (written); **~attassa** f additional tax; **~attutto** above all; **~avanzare** v/t surpass; v/i be left over; **~avvenire** v/i supervene; **~avvivere** v/t **a qu.** outlive s.o.; **~intendente** m superintendent

sorb|etto m ice-cream; **~ire** v/t sip

sòrdido filthy; mean

sord|ità f deafness; **~o** deaf; **~omuto** adj deaf and dumb; m deaf-mute

sorella f sister; **~astra** f step-sister

sorgente f spring

sòrgere v/i (a)rise

sor|montare v/t overcome; **~passare** v/t surpass; overtake

sorpr|èndere v/t surprise; **~esa** f surprise

sorrèggere v/t sustain; **~ersi** v/r support o.s.

sorr|ìdere v/i smile; **~iso** m smile

sors|eggiare v/t sip; **~o** m sip; draught

sort|a (also **~e**) f sort; kind; **~e** f lot; destiny; **~eggiare** v/t draw by lot; **~eggio** m drawing of lots; **~ire** v/i go out; v/t obtain (by lot)

sorvegliare v/t supervise

sorvolare v/t fly over; fig skip over

sosp|èndere v/t hang up; interrupt; suspend; **~ensione** f suspension; **~eso** suspended

sosp|ettare v/t suspect; **~etto** adj suspicious; m suspicion; **~ettoso** suspicious

sosp|irare v/i sigh; **~iro** m sigh

sosta f stop; pause; **divieto m di ~** no parking

sost|antivo m gram noun; **~anza** f substance; **in ~anza** essentially; **~anzioso** substantial; aut park; **~egno** m support; prop; **~enere** v/t sustain; support; **~entare** v/t support (s.o.)

sostit|uire v/t replace; **~uto** m substitute; deputy

sott|acqua underwater; **~ana** f petticoat; **di ~ecchi** stealthily

sotterra adv underground; **~àneo** adj underground; m cave; **~are** v/t bury; hide

sottile thin; subtle

sotto under; below; beneath; **~ aceto** in vinegar; **~ pena** on penalty

sotto|braccio arm in arm; **~esposto** phot under-exposed; **~lineare** v/t underline; **battello** m **~marino** submarine; **~méttere** v/t subdue; submit; **~minare** v/t undermine; **~passaggio** m underground passage; **~porre** v/t subject; **~posto** adj exposed; m subordinate; **~scrivere** v/t (under-)sign; **~scrizione** f subscription; signature; **~sopra** topsy-turvy; **~tenente** m second lieutenant; **~vaso** m saucer; **~veste** f slip; **~voce** in a low voice

sottrarre v/t withdraw; mat subtract; deduct; **~azione** f subtraction; theft

sottufficiale m non-commissioned officer

sovente often

soverchiare v/t overcome; **~o** adj excessive; m surplus

Soviet m Soviet

soviètico Soviet

sovrabbondante superabundant

sovrano adj sovereign; fig supreme; m sovereign

sovrappeso m overweight; **~pressione** f overpressure

sovreposto phot over-exposed

sovvenzionare v/t subsidize; **~ne** f subsidy

spaccapietre m stonebreaker; **~are** v/t split; cleave; **~atura** f cleft; **spaccare** v/t sell (off); **~o** m sale; shop; **~o di tabacchi** tobacco shop

spacco m cleft; split; **~one** m braggart

spada f sword

spaghetti m/pl spaghetti

Spagna f Spain

spago m string; packthread

spalancare v/t throw open

spalla f shoulder; **stringersi nelle ~e** shrug one's shoulders; **~iera** f (chair) back; bot espalier

spalmare v/t smear

spàndere v/t spread; shed

spàrago = aspàrago

sparare v/t shoot; **~ato** m shirt-front

sparecchiare v/t clear the table

spàrgere v/t spread

sparire v/i disappear; **~o** m shot

spartiacque m watershed; **~ire** v/t divide; distribute; **~ito** m mus score; **~itoio** m water-tower; **~izione** f distribution

spasimare v/i agonize

spàsimo m agony; spasm

spassare v/t amuse

spasso m fun; pastime; **andare a ~** go for a walk; fig **èssere a ~** be unemployed

spauracchio m bugbear; scarecrow; **~ire** v/t frighten

spaventarsi v/r be scared; **~ento** m fright; **~entoso** dreadful

spaziale: nave f ~ spaceship; **~are** v/i rove

spazio m space; **~o di tempo** period; **~o vitale** living space; **~oso** spacious

spazz|acamino m chimney-sweep(er); **~aneve** m snow-plough; **~are** v/t sweep; **~atura** f sweepings pl; **~ino** m dustman

spàzzola f brush

spazzol|are v/t, **dare una ~ata (a)** brush; **~ino** m da denti tooth-brush; **~ino per le unghie** nail-brush

specchi|arsi v/r be reflected; look at o.s. in a mirror; **~era** f looking-glass; **~etto** m hand-mirror; **~etto retrovisivo** rear-view mirror; **~o** m mirror; fig example; **~o retroscòpico** aut driving mirror

speciale special; **treno m ~e** extra train; **~ista** m, f specialist; **~ità** f speciality; **~izzare** v/t specialize

specie f species; kind

specifico m, adj specific

specul|are v/t, v/i meditate; com speculate (**in** in); **~azione** f speculation

sped|ire v/t send; ship; **~ito** speedy; prompt; **~itore** m sender; **~izione** f shipping; **~izione bagagli** dispatch of luggage; **~izioniere** m forwarding agent

spegnare v/t redeem

spègn|ere v/t extinguish; turn out (light); **~ersi** v/r die (out)

spelarsi v/r lose one's hair

spell|are v/t skin; **~arsi** v/r peel

spèndere v/t spend; fig employ

spennacchiare v/t pluck

spensierato thoughtless

spenzolare v/i dangle

sper|anza f hope; **~are** v/i hope (**in** for)

spèrdere v/t disperse; **~si** v/r get lost

spergiuro adj perjured; m perjury; perjurer

sperimentare v/t experiment

spes|a f expense; **~e** pl expenses pl; **fare le ~e** go shopping; **~are** v/t pay s.o.'s expenses

spesso adj thick; dense; adv often

spett|àcolo m spectacle; thea performance; **~are** v/i concern; be due; **~atore** m spectator

spettr|ale ghostly; **~o** m ghost

spezie f/pl, **~rie** f/pl spices pl

spezz|are v/t break; **~atino** m ragout; **~ato** chopped

spia f spy

spiac|ente sorry; **~ere** v/i displease; be sorry; **~évole** unpleasant

spiaggia f shore; beach

spian|are v/t level; (dough) roll out; **~ata** f esplanade; **~atoio** m rolling-pin

spiant|are v/t uproot; fig demolish; **~ato** fig penniless

spiare v/t spy (upon)

spiccare v/t detach

spicci|are v/t dispatch; **~arsi** v/r hurry up; **~o** quick

spìccioli m/pl change

spiedo *m* broach; spit; **allo ~ gast** roasted (*on a spit*)

spiegar|e *v/t* unfold; explain; **~arsi** *v/r* make o.s. clear; **~azione** *f* explanation

spig|a *f* ear (*of corn*); **~are** *v/t* form ears

spigliato easy; free

spigo *m* lavender

spigol|are *v/t* glean; **~atura** *f* gleaning(s)

spigolo *m* corner-edge

spill|a *f* tie-pin; brooch; **~o** *m* pin; **~o di sicurezza** safety-pin

spina *f* thorn; sting; (fish-) bone; *elec* plug; **~ doppia** two-pin plug; *anat* **~ (dorsale)** spine

spinaci *m/pl* spinach

spìng|ere *v/t* push; shove; **~ersi** *v/r* push forward

spin|o *m* thorn (-tree); **~oso** thorny

spinta *f* push; shove

spinterògeno *m auto:* ignition distributor

spion|aggio *m* espionage; **~are** *v/t* spy; **~e** *m* spy

spir|a *f* coil; spire; **~ale** *m, adj* spiral; **~are** *v/t, v/i* breathe (out); expire

spirito *m* spirit; humour

spirit|oso witty; **~uale** spiritual

splènd|ere *v/i* shine; **~ido** splendid

splendore *m* splendour

spogli|are *v/t* deprive; **~arsi** *v/r* undress o.s.; divest o.s.;

~o (di) bare; deprived; free of

spola *f* shuttle

spolver|are *v/t* dust; **~ino** *m* featherwhisk; **~izzare** *v/t* pulverize

sponda *f* bank; edge

spontàneo spontaneous

spora *f* spore

sporc|are *v/t* soil; **~o** dirty

spòrg|ere *v/t* stretch out; **~ersi** *v/r* lean out; stand out

sport *m* sport; **~ invernale** winter sports *pl*; **~ motociclìstico** motoring; **~ nàutico** aquatic sports *pl*; **~ sciìstico** skiing; **~ della vela** yachting

sport|a *f* bag; basket; **~ello** *m* shutter; small door; **~ello per biglietti** ticket-window

sportivo *adj* sporting; *m* sportsman

spos|a *f* bride; (young) wife; **~alizio** *m* wedding; **~are** *v/t* marry; **~arsi** *v/r* get married; **~o** *m* bride-groom; (young) husband; **~i** *m/pl* bride and groom; young couple; **promessi ~i** betrothed couple

spossare *v/t* exhaust

spost|amento *m* displacement; **~are** *v/t* displace; shift

spregévole despicable; **~iare** *v/t* despise

sprèmere *v/t* squeeze

spremilimoni *m* lemon-squeezer

spremuta f squash

sprigion|**are** v/t set free; **~arsi** v/r exhale; rise

sprizzare v/t, v/i sprinkle; gush out

sprofond|**are** v/t sink; **~arsi** v/r sink in

spron|**are** v/t spur; **~e** m spur

sproposito: a ~ unopportunely

spruzz|**aglia** f drizzle; **~are** v/t (be)sprinkle; **~atore** m sprayer; **~atore per i capelli** hair spray

spugn|**a** f sponge; **~olo** m morel

spum|**a** f foam; froth; **spumante** m, **vino** m **~ante** sparkling wine; **~are**, **~eggiare** v/i foam

spunt|**are** v/t break the point of; v/i sprout forth; (sun) rise; (day) break; **~ino** m snack

sput|**acchiera** f spittoon; **~are** v/t, v/i spit; **~o** m spittle

squadra f square; mil squad(ron); sport: team; **~ volante** flying squad

squagliare v/t melt

squàllido squalid; dreary

squam|**a** f scale; **~are** v/t scale

squarcio m rent; tear; literary: passage

squart|**are** v/t quarter; **~atoio** m chopper

squisito exquisite

sradicare v/t eradicate; fig extirpate

sregolato disorderly; licentious

SS. ¹ **Santi** pl Saints; **Sua Santità** His Holiness; **Santa Sede** Holy See

sta he stays

stàbile stable; durable; **bene** m real estate

stabilimento m establishment; factory; **~ balneare**, **~ termale** (public swimming) baths pl

stabil|**ire** v/t establish; **~irsi** v/r settle down; **~izzare** v/t stabilize

stacc|**are** v/t detach; tel unhook; rail slip; **~arsi** v/r **da qu.** part from s.o.

stacci|**are** v/t sieve; sift; **~o** m sieve

stadera f steelyard

stadio m stadium; (time) stage

staffa f stirrup

stagione f season; **~ estiva** summer season; **~ invernale** winter season; **alta ~** height of season; **fuor di ~** out of season

stagn|**aio** m tinker; **~are** v/t tin; (blood) stanch; v/i stagnate; **~o** m tin; pond; **~ola** f tin-foil

stall|**a** f stable; **~o** m stall

sta|**mane**, **~mani**, **~mattina** this morning

stambugio m dark hole; den

stamp|**a** f print(ing); press; (mostly pl **~e**) printed matter; **libertà** f **di ~a** freedom of the press; **~are** v/t print; publish; impress; **~ati** m/pl printed matter; **~atore** m printer; **~erìa** f printing-house; **~igliare** v/t stamp; **~ino** m stencil

stanc|are v/t tire; **~hezza** f weariness; **~o** tired

stang|a f bar; shaft; pole; **~are** v/t bar

stanotte tonight

stantuffo m mech piston

stanza f room; **~ da bagno** bathroom; **~ da letto** bedroom

stare v/i be; stay; **~ in piedi** stand; **~ seduto** sit; **~ bene (male)** be well (ill) (clothing) suit; **~ per** be about to; **~ a vedere** wait and see; **stia bene!** keep well!; **come sta?** how are you?

starnut|are, ~ire v/i sneeze

stasera this evening

statale (of the) state

stàtica f statics

statista m statesman

stato pp been; stayed; m state; status; condition; **~ civile** marital status; registrar's office; **~ maggiore** (general) staff; **èssere in ~ di** be able to

stàtua f statue

statura f stature

statuto m statute; constitution

stazionare v/i stop; stay

stazione f station; **~ balneare** watering-place; **~ climàtica** helath resort; **~ d'autobus** bus-station; **~ di tassì** taxi rank; cab stand; **~ trasmittente**

(broadcasting) station

stearina f stearin

stecc|a f slat; billiard-cue; **~are** v/t fence in; **~hino** m toothpick; **~o** m stick; twig

stella f star; rowel; **~ alpina** edelweiss; **~cadente** shooting star

stemma m coat of arms; crest

stendardo m standard

stèndere v/t spread (out); (document) draw up

stenditoio m drying-place

stenodattilògrafa f shorthand-typist

sten|ografare v/t write (in) shorthand; **~ògrafo** m stenographer

stent|are v/i a fare qc. have difficulty in doing s.th.; **~ato** stunted; weak; **~o** m: **a ~o** with difficulty

stèrile barren

sterilizzare v/t sterilize

sterlina f pound sterling

sterm|inare v/t exterminate; destroy; **~inato** boundless; **~inio** m extermination

sterz|are v/t steer; **~o** m auto: steering gear

stesso self; same; **lo ~** the same; **oggi ~** this very day

stetoscopio m stethoscope

stiamo we stay

stigmatizzare v/t stigmatize

stil|e m style; dagger; **~ettare** v/t stab; **~ìstica** f stylistics

stilogràfica f, **penna** f **~**

fountain-pen

stima *f* esteem; respect; **con profonda ~** Yours respectfully

stim|àbile respectable; **~are** *v/t* esteem; appraise; consider

stimmatizzare = stigmatizzare

stimolare *v/t* stimulate; incite

stinco *m* shin

stipendi|are *v/t* pay a salary (to); **~o** *m* salary; stipend

stipulare *v/t* (contract) draw up

stiramento *m*: **~ di tèndine** pulled tendon

stir|are *v/t* iron; **~atrice** *f* ironer; presser; **~atura** *f* ironing; **senza ~atura** non-iron; drip-dry

stirpe *f* descent; race

stitico constipated

stivale *m* boot

stizzito cross

sto I stay

stoccafisso *m* stockfish

stoffa *f* material; cloth

stoia *f* (straw-)mat

stolt|ezza *f* foolishness; **~o** *adj* silly; *m* fool

stòmaco *m* stomach

stomàtico *adj* stomatic; *m* stomachic

stoppa *f* tow; oakum

stoppia *f* stubble

stòrcere *v/t* twist; distort

stord|ire *v/t* stun; daze; **~ito** stunned

stòri|a *f* history; **~a dell'arte** history of art; **~co** *adj*

historical; *m* historian

storione *m* sturgeon

storm|ire *v/i* rustle; **~o** *m* flock; swarm

storpi|ato crippled; **~o** *m* cripple

stort|a *f* sprain; bend; retort; **~o** crooked

stoviglie *f/pl* pottery

stra- *prefix* extra-

stracàrico overloaded

stracchino *m* spread cheese

stracci|are *v/t* tear; rend; **~o** *m* rag; *adj*: **carta** *f* **~a** waste paper

stra|contento overjoyed; **~cotto** *adj* overdone; *m* stew

strada *f* road; street; way; **~ costiera** coastal street; **~ ferrata** railway; **~ maestra** main road; highway; **~ nazionale** arterial road; **~ strucciolévole** slippery road; **~ facendo** on the way; **~ con precedenza** major road; **~ a senso unico** one-way street

stradone *m* large road

strage *f* massacre

stralunare *v/t* roll the eyes

stramazzare *v/i* fall heavily

strangol|are *v/t* strangle; **~azione** *f* strangling

stran|iare *v/t* estrange; **~iero** *adj* foreign; *m* stranger; alien; foreigner; **lingua** *f* **~iera** foreign language; **~o** strange

straordinario extraordinary

strapazz|are *v/t* ill-treat; **~ato: uova** *f/pl* **~ate**

scrambled eggs; **~oso** wearisome

strappare v/t tear (out); snatch; **~o** m tear; wrench

straricco extremely rich

strasciccare v/t drag; drawl

stràscico m train (of a dress)

strascinare v/t drag along

strato m layer; coating

stravagante extravagant

stra|vecchio very old; **~vòlgere** v/t roll; twist

straziante heart-rending; **~are** v/t torture; distress; **~o** m torment

strega f witch; **~are** v/t bewitch

stremato exhausted

strenna f gift; present

strepitare v/i make noise

strèpito m noise

strepitoso noisy

stretta f grip; grasp; **~a di mano** handshake; **~ezza** f narrowness; straits pl; **~o** adj narrow; tight; m strait

strid|ere v/i screech; creak; **~o** m shriek

strigliare v/t curry

strill|are v/i scream; **~o** m shriek; **~one** m news-boy

strimpellare v/t, v/i strum

string|a f (shoe-)lace; **~ente** urgent

stringere v/t press; tie; **~la mano a qu.** shake hands with s.o.

strisc|ia f strip(e); **~ia di carta** paper-strip; **~ia di terra** strip of land; **~e** f/pl **pedonali** zebra crossing; **a ~e** striped

strisci|are v/t drag; graze; v/i crawl; **~o** m grazing; touching

strizzare v/t squeeze; wring

strofa, **~e** f strophe; stanza

strofin|accio m duster; **~are** v/t scour

strombettare v/i trumpet

stroncare v/t break off

stronfiare v/i snort

stropicciare v/t rub; shuffle

strozz|a f throat; **~are** v/t choke; **~ino** m fig usurer

strügg|ere v/t melt; **~ersi** v/r long for

strumento m instrument; mech tool; **~ ad arco** string-instrument; **~ a percussione** percussion instruments pl

strutto m lard

struzzo m ostrich

stucc|are v/t plaster; coat with stucco; **~atore** m plasterer; **~hino** m plaster figure; **~o** m stucco

stud|ente m student; **~entessa** f student (female); **~iare** v/t, v/i study; **~io** m study; studio; office

stuf|a f stove; oven; **~are** m stew; **~ato** m stew; **~o di** fed up with

stuoia f (straw-)mat

stupefatto amazed

stupendo wonderful

stupidàggine f foolishness

stùpido adj stupid; m fool

stup|irsi v/r be amazed; **~ore** m astonishment

sturare v/t uncork; (cask) tap

stuzzicadenti m toothpick

stuzzicare v/t stir; tease

su on; upon; over; above; about; **~!** come on!; **~ e giù** up and down; **~ per giù** approximately

sub|affittare v/t sublet; **~alterno** m subordinate

subire v/t endure; **~ un esame** go in for an exam

sùbito adj sudden; adv at once

sublime sublime

subordin|are v/t subordinate; **~azione** f subordination

suburbano suburban

succ|èdere v/i succeed; happen; **~essione** f succession; **~essivo** following; **~esso** m success; **~essore** m successor

succhiare v/t suck; absorb

succo m sap; juice; **~ d'arancia** orange juice; **~ di frutta** fruit juice; **~ di mele** cider; **~ di pomodori** tomato juice; **~ d'uva** grape juice

succ|oso, ~ulento juicy

succursale f branch office

sud m south; **~est** southeast; **al ~** southward

sudare v/i perspire; sweat

suddetto (afore)said

sùdicio dirty

sudiciume m filth

sudore m sweat

sufficien|te sufficient; **~za** f sufficiency; **a ~za** enough

suffragio m suffrage; vote

suffumigio m fumigation

sugante: carta f **~** blotting paper

sugare v/t absorb; agr manure

suggellare v/t seal; **~ello** m seal

sùggere v/t suck

sugger|ire v/t suggest; **~itore** m thea prompter

sùghero m cork(-tree)

sugli = **su gli**

sugna f lard

sug|o m juice; gravy; **~oso** juicy

sui on the

suic|idarsi v/i commit suicide; **~idio** m suicide

suino adj of swine; m swine

sulfùreo sulphureous

sulla on the

sultano m sultan

summenzionato, sunnominato above-mentioned

sunteggiare v/t summarize

sunto m summary

suo his, her, its

suòcer|a f mother-in-law; **~i** m/pl in-laws pl; **~o** m father-in-law

suola f sole

suolo m soil

suono m sound; **~stereofònico** stereophonic sound

suora f nun; sister

super m super

superàbile surmountable

superare v/t overcome; outdo; (exam) pass

super|bia f pride; **~erbo** proud

super|ficiale superficial; **~ficie** f surface

superfluità f superfluity

supèrfluo superfluous

superi|ora f Mother Superior; **~iore** superior; upper; labbro m **~iore** upper lip; scuola f **~iore** secondary school; **~iore a** above, beyond; m superior; **~iorità** f superiority

supermercato m supermarket

supèrstite m survivor

superstizi|one f superstition; **~oso** superstitious

superuomo m superman

supino lying on one's back

suppellèttile f household goods pl

suppergiù approximately

suppl|emento m supplement; addition; rail extra fare; **~ente** m substitute; **~enza** f substitution; **~etorio** supplementary

supplì m rice with hashed meat

sùpplica f petition; supplication

supplic|are v/t implore; **~azione** f supplication

supplichévole imploring

supplire v/t substitute

supplizio m torture; capital punishment

supp|orre v/t, v/i suppose; presume; **~osizione** f supposition; **~osta** f med suppository; **~osto** supposed

suppur|are v/i suppurate; **~azione** f suppuration

supremo supreme

surriferito above-mentioned

surrog|are v/t replace; **~ato** m substitute; **~azione** f substitution

suscettì|bile susceptible; **~bilità** f, **~ività** f susceptibility; touchiness

suscitare v/t provoke; rouse

susin|a f plum; **~o** m plumtree

susseguire v/i follow

sussidiare v/t subsidize

sussidio m subsidy

suss|istenza f livelihood; **~istere** v/i subsist

sussult|are v/i start; jump; **~o** m start

suss|urrare v/t, v/i whisper; rustle; **~urro** m murmur

sutura f suture

svag|are v/t entertain; **~o** m recreation

svalut|are v/t depreciate; **~azione** f devaluation

svanire v/i vanish

svantaggi|o m disadvantage; **~oso** detrimental

svaporare v/i evaporate

svariato varied

svedese adj Swedish; m, f Swede

svegli|a f alarm-clock; **~are** v/t awaken; **~arsi** v/r wake up; **~o** awake

svelare v/t fig reveal

svèllere v/t uproot

svelto nimble

svéndere v/t sell out

svéndita f sale

sven|imento m swoon; **~ire** v/i faint

sventolare v/t, v/i fan; wave; fly

sventura f misfortune; **~urato** unfortunate

svenuto unconscious

svergognare v/t disgrace

svergognato shameless

svernamento m wintering; **~are** v/i hibernate

sverza f splinter

svestire v/t undress

Svezia f Sweden

svezzare v/t wean

sviamento m deviation; rail derailment; **~arsi** v/r go astray

svignarsela v/r sneak away

sviluppare v/t develop; **~atore** m developer; **~o** m development

svisare v/t distort

svista f: **per ~** erroneously

svitare v/t unscrew

Svizzera f Switzerland

svizzero m, adj Swiss

svogliatezza f listlessness

svolazzare v/i flutter

svolgere v/t unroll; fig explain

svolgimento m unfolding; fig development

svolta f turn; bend; **~are** v/i turn

svuotare v/t empty

T

tabaccaio m tobacconist; **~heria** f tobacconist's shop; **~o** m tobacco

tabe f tabes; **~ polmonare** pulmonary consumption; **~ dorsale** spinal disease

tabella f table

tabernàcolo m tabernacle

tacchino m turkey

tacco m heel

taccuino m note-book

tacere v/t, v/i keep silent (about)

tachìmetro m speedometer

tàcito tacit; silent

taciturno taciturn

tafano m ox-fly

taffetà m taffeta

taglia f ransom; size; **di mezza ~** middlesized; **~borse** ~ pickpocket;

~boschi m wood-cutter; **~re** v/t cut; **~telli** m/pl noodles pl

taglio m cut; edge

tailleur m ladies' suit

tale such; **quale ... ~ such ... as**; **un ~** a certain man; **il signor ~** il signor tal dei **tali** Mr So and So

talento m talent

tallone m heel

talmente in such a way

talora sometimes

talpa f mole

talvolta sometimes

tamburare v/i drum; **~o** m drum; drummer

tampoco even; either

tamponamento m congestion (traffic)

tampone m tampon; plug

tana *f* den; hole

tanagli|a *f* (mostly **.e** *f/pl*) pincers *pl*

tangibile tangible

tànnico: àcido *m* ~ tannic acid

tant|o so (much); so long; **.i saluti** best regards; **.e grazie** many thanks; **ogni** ~**o** every now and then; **di** ~**o in** ~**o** from time to time; ~ **meglio** so much the better

tapioca *f* tapioca

tappare *v/t* cork; plug

tappeto *m* carpet; rug

tappezz|are *v/t* paper (wall); ~**erìa** *f* tapestry; upholsterer's shop; ~**iere** *m* decorator; upholsterer

tappo *m* stopper; cork

tara *f* tare

tarchiato square-built

tard|are *v/t* delay; *v/i* be late; ~**i** late; **al più** ~**i** at the latest

tardivo late; backward

targa *f* (name-)plate; tablet; *auto*: license-plate; ~ **della nazionalità** country's identification sign

tariffa *f* tariff; rate

tarlato worm-eaten

tarm|a *f* moth; ~**are** *v/i* be moth-eaten

tarsia *f* marquetry

tartagli|are *v/i* stutter; ~**one** *m* stutterer

tàrtaro *m* tartar (from wine, teeth)

tartaruga *f* tortoise; turtle

tartassare *v/t* harass

tartina *f* sandwich

tartufo *m* truffle

tasc|a *f* pocket; ~**àbile: edizione** *f* ~**àbile** pocket-(-book) edition

tass|a *f* tax; duty; ~**a mìnima** minimum price; ~**a d'aeroporto** airport tax; ~**a di noleggio** price for the hire; ~**a di soggiorno** visitor's tax; ~**a di utilizzazione** fee for the use of s.th.; ~**are** tax; charge (with duty); ~**ì** *m* taxi; cab; ~**ista** *m*, *f* taxi-driver

tasso *m* rate (of interest, discount); zoology; badger; *bot* yew-tree

tast|are *v/t* touch; feel; ~**iera** *f* keyboard; ~**o** *m* key; touch; ~**oni** gropingly

tàttic|a *f* tactics *pl*; ~**o** tactical

tatto *m* touch; tact

tatu|aggio *m* tattoo(ing); ~**are** *v/t* tattoo

taumaturgo *m* wonder-worker

tavern|a *f* tavern; pub; ~**iere** *m* inn-keeper

tàvola *f* table; ~ **da allungarsi** pull-out table

tavolino *m* small table; ~ **da giuoco** gaming table

tàvolo *m* table

tavolozza *f* palette

tazza *f* cup

te you; **come** ~ like you; **di** ~ your(s)

tè *m* tea; ~ **di camomilla** camomile tea

teatro *m* theatre; *fig* scene; ~ **all'aperto** open-air stage; ~

tecnica 390

dei burattini Punch and Judy show

tècnic|a f technics pl; technique; **~o** adj technical; **tèrmine ~o** technical term; **~o** m technician

teco with you

tedesco m, adj German

tegame m pan; **uova** f/pl **al ~** fried eggs

teglia f pan

tegolaia f tile-works pl

tégola f tile

teiera f tea-pot

tela f linen; thea curtain; **~ cerata** oil-cloth; **~ di ragno** cobweb; **~ a quadri (a righe)** check (cloth); **~io** m loom; frame

telecomando m tele-starter

tele|fèrica f cable-way; **~fonare** v/t (tele)phone; **~fonata** f (tele)phone-call; **~fonata interurbana** long-distance call; **~fonata urbana** local phone-call; **~fonìa** f (senza fili wireless) telephony; **~fònico** telephonic; **~fonista** m, f telephone operator

telèfono m telephone; **~ di càmera** telephone in one's room; **~ pùbblico** public telephone

tele|fotografìa f telephotography; **~giornale** m daily news; **~grafare** v/t telegraph; wire; **~grafìa** f (senza fili wireless) telegraphy; **~gràfico** telegraphic; **~grafista** m, f telegraphist

telègrafo m telegraph; wire; cable; **~ lampo** lightning telegram; **~ lèttera** letter telegram

telègramma m telegram; wire; cable; **~ lampo** lightning telegram; **~ lèttera** letter telegram

telèmetro m telemeter

telerìa f linen-drapery

tele|scòpio m telescope; **~scrivente** f teleprinter; **~spettatore** m (tele)spectator; **~visione** f television (abbr TV); **~visione a colori** colour television; **~visore** m television set

tellina f clam

telo m arrow

telone m thea curtain

tema f fear; m theme; composition; gram stem

tem|eràrio reckless; **~ere** v/t fear; dread; **~erità** f temerity

temperalapis m pencil-sharpener

temper|amento m temper (-ament); mitigation; **~are** v/t mitigate; moderate; (pencil) sharpen; **~ato** temperate; **~atura** f temperature

tempèrie f climate

temperino m penknife

tempest|a f storm; **~a di neve** snow-storm; blizzard; **~oso** stormy

tempia f anat temple

tempio m temple

templare m Templar

tempo m weather; time; gram tense; **a ~, in ~** in time; **di ~ in ~** from time to time; **per ~** early; **~ di volo**

flying time

tempor|ale *adj* secular; *m* storm; **~àneo** temporary

tenac|e tenacious; **~ità** *f* tenacity

tenda *f* curtain; tent; awning

tendenza *f* tendency

tèndere *v/t* stretch (out); (hand) hold out; *v/i* aim (**a** at)

tendina *f* (window-)curtain

tèndine *m* tendon

tendinoso sinewy

tènebr|a *f* (*mostly pl* **~e**) darkness

tenebroso dark

tenente *m* lieutenant

tenere *v/t* keep; hold; contain; think

tenerezza *f* tenderness

tènero tender; soft

tengo I hold

teniamo we hold

tennis *m* tennis; **~ da tàvolo** ping-pong

tenore *m* terms *pl*; *mus* tenor

tensione *f* tension; strain; **alta** (**bassa**) **~** high (low) voltage

tent|are *v/t* try; attempt; **~ativo** *m* attempt; **~azione** *f* temptation

tentennare *v/t* shake; *v/i* waver; stagger

tenton|e, **~i** gropingly

tenuità *f* smallness

tenuto held; bound

teologia *f* theology

teòlogo *m* theologian

teor|ètico theoretic(al); **~ìa** *f* theory

tepidezza *f* tepidity

teppista *m, f* ruffian

tèrgere *v/t* wipe (off)

tergicristallo *m* windscreenwiper

tergo *m* back; rear

termale thermal; **stabilimento ~** *m* thermal spa

terme *f/pl* hot springs *pl*

termin|are *v/t* terminate; **~azione** *f* termination; *gram* ending

tèrmine *m* term; limit

termòforo *m* thermophore

termòmetro *m* thermometer

term|os *m* thermos (flask); **~osifone** *m* radiator; **~òstato** *m* thermostat

terr|a *f* earth; land; **~e** *pl* estates *pl*; **di ~a** earthen; **di questa ~a** earthly; **a ~a** to, on the ground; **per ~a** by land; **prèndere ~a** land; **~acotta** *f* terracotta

terraglia *f* pottery

terrapieno *m* embankment

terrazz|a *f* terrace; **~o** *m* balcony

terr|emoto *m* earthquake; **~eno** *adj* earthly; *m* ground; soil; **~estre** terrestrial

terrìbile terrible

terrina *f* tureen

territorio *m* territory

terr|ore *m* terror; **~orista** *m, f* terrorist

terroso earthy

terzo third

tesa *f* brim (*of hat*)

teschio *m* skull

tesor|eggiare v/t hoard; **~e-ria** f treasury; **~iere** m treasurer; **~o** m treasure

tèssera f card; ticket; **~ d'ostello per la gioventù** youth hostel card

tesserato m member (of a party)

tèss|ere v/t weave; **~ile: industria f ~ile** textile industry; **~ili** m/pl textile goods pl

tess|itore m weaver; **~uto** m cloth; fabric; anat tissue

testa f head; **alla ~ di** at the head of ...; **mal di ~** headache

testamento m will, testament

test|ardàggine f stubbornness; **~ardo** headstrong

testare v/i make one's will

testata f head(ing); top; **~ del cilindro** mech cylinder head

teste m, f witness

testìcolo m testicle

testimon|e m witness; **~e oculare** eyewitness; **~ianza** f evidence; **~iare** v/t testify; **~io** m witness

testo m text

testuale textual

testùggine f tortoise

tètano m tetanus

tetro gloomy

tett|o m roof; **~oia** f shed; glass roof (of station)

Tèvere m Tiber

ti you; to you

tibia f shin-bone; tibia

tic tac: fare ~ ~ tick

ticchio m whim

tièpido lukewarm

tifo m typhus

tiglio m lime(-tree); fibre; **~so** fibrous

tigre f tiger

timballo m kettle-drum

timbr|are v/t stamp; **~o** m (rubber-)stamps; mus timbre

timid|ezza, ~ità f bashfulness

timido bashful, shy

timon|e m pole; naut rudder; **~eggiare** v/t steer; **~iere** m helmsman

tim|ore m fear; awe; **~oroso** timorous

tìmpano m mus kettledrum; anat ear-drum

tinca f tench

tingere v/t dye

tino m vat; tub; **~zza** f (bathing-)tub

tinta f dye; colour

tinteggiare v/t tint

tintinnare v/i tinkle

tint|oria f dye-works; **~ura** f dye; med tincture; **~ura di iodio** tincture of iodine

tìp|ico typical; **~o** m type

tipografìa f printing-office

tipògrafo m printer

tirann|eggiare v/t tyrannize; **~ia** f tyranny; **~o** adj tyrannical; m tyrant

tir|are v/t draw; pull; shoot; **~arsi** v/r **da parte** stand aside; **~arsi indietro** draw back; **~astivali** m bootjack; **in una ~ata** in one pull; **~ato** strained; **~atore** m

marksman; *sport :* shooter
tirchio stingy
tiretto m drawer
tiro m draught; throw; shot; fig **brutto** ~ bad trick; **arma** f **da** ~ firearm; **campo** m **del** ~ shooting-range
tirocinio m apprenticeship
tirolese m, adj Tyrolese
Tirolo m Tyrol
Tirreno: **mare** m ~ Tyrrhenian Sea
tisi f phtysis
tisico consumptive
titolare adj titular; regular; m owner
titolo m title; com security
to' (= **togli**) look!; hold!
toast m toast
toccare v/t touch; hit; concern; ~**a me** it is my turn; ~**o** m touch; stroke (bell); **al** ~**o** at one o'clock
toeletta f = **toletta**
tògliere v/t take (away); (dress) take off; ~ **la corrente** cut off the electricity supply; ~ **il gas** aut release the accelerator
tolda f bridge deck
toletta f toilet(-table)
tollerante tolerant; ~**anza** f tolerance; ~**are** v/t tolerate; bear
tomba f grave
tómbola f raffle
tómbolo m lace-pillow
tomo m tome; volume
tònaca f frock
tonalità f tonality
tonare v/i thunder

tondo round; **chiaro e** ~ frankly
tonfare v/i plop
tonfo m thump; splash
tònico m tonic
tonnellata f ton; ~ **di registro** gross register ton
tonno m tuna(-fish)
tonno m tunny
tono m tone; tune
tonsille f/pl tonsils pl; ~**ite** f tonsilitis
tonto silly
topaia f rats' nest
topo m mouse; rat; ~**lino** m Mickey Mouse
toppa f (door-)lock; patch
toppo m log, block
torba f peat
tórbido turbid
tòrcere v/t twist; wring; distort
torchio m press
torcia f torch
tordo m thrush; fig simpleton
Torino f Turin
torlo m (egg-)yolk
torma f swarm
tormentare v/t torment; ~**o** m torment
tornaconto m profit
tornare v/i come back; return; ~ **a fare qc.** go back to do s.th.; **ben tornato!** welcome!
tornire m lathe; ~**ire** v/t mech turn
toro m bull
torpèdine f torpedo
torpedone m motorcoach
torpore m torpor; lethargy

torre f tower

torrefare v/t roast

torrente m torrent

tòrrido torrid

torrone m nougat

torsione f torsion

torso m trunk; torso

torta f tart; pie; ~ **alla cioccolata** chocolate-cake; ~ **alla crema** cream-cake; ~ **di ciliege** cherry-tart; ~ **di frutta** fruit pie; ~ **di mele** appletart; ~ **di noci** cake with nuts in it

torto m wrong

tórtora f turtle-dove

tortur|a f torture; ~**are** v/t torture

tosare v/t shear; clip

toss|e f cough; ~**e canina** whooping-cough; ~**ire** v/i cough

tostapane m toaster

tost|are v/t toast (bread); roast (coffee); ~**ino** m coffee-roaster

tosto soon; ~**o tardi** sooner or later; ~**che** as soon as

tot|ale adj total; whole; m total; ~**alità** f totality

tovagli|a f table-cloth; ~**olo** m napkin

tozzo adj stumpy; m morsel

tra = fra

traballare v/i stagger; rock

trabocchetto m pitfall; thea trap-door

traccia f trace; outline

trachea f windpipe

tracoma m trachoma

trad|imento m betrayal; **alto ~imento** high treason; ~**ire** v/t betray; ~**itore** adj treacherous; m traitor; ~**izione** f tradition

trad|otto translated; ~**urre** v/t translate; ~**uzione** f translation

trae he pulls

trafficare v/i traffic; trade

tràffico m traffic; trade; ~ **circolare** roundabout traffic

trafor|are v/t perforate; pierce; ~**oro** m tunnel; ~ **stoffa** f a ~**oro** open-work material

tragèdia f tragedy

traggiamo we pull

traggo I pull

traghetto m ferry(-boat)

tràgico tragic(al)

tragicommèdia f tragicomedy

trag|ittare v/t cross; ~**itto** m trip; passage

traguardo m sport: finishing-line

train|are v/t drag; haul; ~**o** m sledge; truck

tralasciare v/t omit

tralùcere v/i shine through

tram, tranvai m tram(way)

tramandare v/t hand down

trambusto m bustle

tramenìo m fuss

tramestìo m muddle

tramezz|a f second sole (shoe); ~**are** v/t partition; insert; ~**o** adv between; among; m partition wall

tràmite m path; course

tramont|ana f north wind; north; ~**are** v/i set; fade;

m sunset

tramortimento *m* swoon

tramortito unconscious

trampolino *m* spring-board; diving-board

tramutare *v/t* change; alter

trancia *f* slice

tranello *m* trap

tranne except; save

tranquillo calm

transatlàntico *m* Ocean-liner

transigere *v/i* yield

trànsito *m* transit; passage

transitorio transitory

tranvai *m* tram(-car)

trapanare *v/t* drill; *med* trepan

tràpano *m* drill

trapassare *v/t* pierce through; trespas

trapasso *m* transfer; decease

trapelare *v/i* leak out

trapiantare *v/t* transplant

tràppola *f* trap, snare

trappolare *v/t* entrap

trap|unta *f* quilt; **~untare** *v/t* quilt; **~unto** *m* quilting

trarre *v/t* pull; draw

trasalire *v/i* start

trasand|amento *m* negligence; **~are** *v/t* neglect; **~ato** neglected

trasb|ordare *v/t* tranship; **~ordo** *m* transhipment

trascinare *v/t* drag; *fig* carry away

trascórrere *v/t* spend; (*script*) go through

trascr|ivere *v/t* transcribe; **~izione** *f* transcription

trascur|are *v/t* neglect; **~a-**

tezza *f* carelessness; **~ato** negligent

trasfer|ibile transferable; **~imento** *m* transfer; **~ire** *v/t* transfer; (re)move; **~irsi** *v/r* move

trasform|are *v/t* transform; **~atore** *m* transformer; **~azione** *f* transformation; change

trasfusione *f* transfusion

trasgr|edire *v/t, v/i* transgress; violate; **~essione** *f* transgression

traslato metaphorical; figurative

trasloc|are *v/t, v/i* move; **~o** *m* removal; move

trasméttere *v/t* transmit; send; (*radio*) broadcast

trasmissione *f* transmission; **~ radiofonica** broadcast; **~ delle ruote posteriori** backwheel drive

trasognato dreamy

traspar|ente transparent; **~enza** *f* transparence; **~ire** *v/i* be transparent

traspirare *v/i* perspire

trasport|are *v/t* carry; transport; **~o** *m* transport (-ation); conveyance

trastullo *m* toy; pastime

trasversale *adj* transversal; *f* side-street

trasvolare *v/t* fly across; fly over

tratta *f* tug; pull; *com* draft; **~ in bianco** blank bill; **~ postale** postal collection order

tratt|amento *m* treatment;

~**are** v/t, v/i treat; handle; deal (with); **si tratta di** it is a matter of; ~**ato** m treaty; treatise

tratten|ere v/t detain; entertain; ~**ersi** v/r stay; refrain (from)

tratto adj drawn; m tract; stroke; **a un** ~ all of a sudden; **di** ~ **in** ~ from time to time; ~ **d'unione** hyphen

trattore m tractor

trattoria f restaurant; inn

travagli|are v/t torment; ~**o** m **di stòmaco** sickness

travas|are v/t decant; ~**o** m decanting; med effusion

trave f beam

travedere v/i catch a glimpse (of)

travers|a f cross-bar; -road; ~**are** v/t cross; ~**ata** f crossing; ~**o** cross; **di** ~**o** awry; **vie** f/pl ~**e** shady methods pl

travestimento m disguise

travestire v/t disguise

travòlgere v/t overthrow

trebbi|a f flail; ~**are** v/t thresh

treccia f tress; plait

trecento m 14th century

tredicèsimo thirteenth

trégua f truce; fig rest

tremare v/i tremble (**da** with)

trementina f turpentine

tremolare v/i quiver

trèmulo quivering

treno m train; ~ **accelerato** fast local train; ~ **autocucette** car sleeper train; ~ **diretto** fast train; ~ **locale**

suburban train; ~ **merci** goods train

Trento f Trent

trèpido m trembling

treppiedi m tripod

triangolare triangular

triàngolo m triangle; ~ **di avvertimento** warning triangle

tribolare v/t torment

tribordo m starboard

tribù f tribe

tribun|ale m tribune; ~**unale** m law-court; tribunal

tribut|ario tributary; ~**o** m tribute; tax

tricheco m zoology: walrus

tri|ciclo m tricycle; ~**colore** adj three-coloured; m tricolour (flag)

Trieste f Trieste

trifoglio m clover

triglia f mullet

trill|are v/i trill; ~**o** m trill

trimestr|ale quarterly; ~**e** m quarter (of year)

trin|a f lace; ~**aia** f lacemaker

trincare v/t swill

trincea f trench

trinchetto m foremast; foresail

trinci|apolli m poultry shears pl; ~**are** v/t carve; cut up

trinità f trinity

trionf|ale: **arco** m ~**ale** triumphal arch; ~**are** v/i triumph (over); ~**o** m triumph

trìplice threefold

trippa f tripe; paunch

trist|e sad; **~ezza** f sadness; **~o** wicked

trit|are v/t mince; chop; **~o: carne** f **~a** hashed meat

triv|ellare v/t drill; **~ello** m borer

triviale trivial

trògolo m trough

troia f sow

tromba f trumpet; (auto) horn; biol trunk

tronc|are v/t cut off; **~o** m trunk; rail trunk-line

troneggiare v/i sit on a throne

tronfio conceited

trono m throne

tropicale tropical

troppo too; too much

trota f trout

trott|are v/i trot; **~o** m trot

tròttola f spinning-top; games: top

trov|are v/t find; meet; think; **andare a ~are qu.** call on s.o.; **~arsi** v/r be; feel; **~atello** m foundling

trucco m trick; fig makeup

truce grim; fierce

trucidare v/t massacre

truff|a f cheat; **~are** v/t cheat; **~atore** m swindler

truppa f troop

tu you (sg); **dare del ~** address familiarly

tuba f trumpet; fam tophat; **~zione** f pipe

tubercolosi f tuberculosis

tùbero m bot tuber

tuber|osa f tuberose; **~oso** tuberous

tubetto m small tube

tubo m tube; pipe; **~ d'aria** snorkel; **~ di scàrico** exhaust pipe

tuff|are v/t plunge; **~arsi** v/r dive; **~atore** m diver

tuffo m plunge; dive; **~ in avanti** header

tulipano m tulip

tulle m tulle

tumefa|re v/t, v/i swell; **~zione** f swelling

tùmido swollen

tumore m tumour

tumulare v/t bury

tùmulo m tomb

tumult|o m riot; **~uante** m, f rioter

tumultu|are v/i riot; **~oso** tumultuous

tuo your; yours

tuono m thunder

tuppè m touppee

tuorlo m egg-yolk

turabuchi m stop-gap

turàcciolo m cork; stopper

turb|a f crowd; **le ~e** f/pl mob; **~amento** m disturbance; confusion; **~are** v/t trouble; disturb; **~arsi** v/r become upset; grow murky

turbinare v/i whirl

tùrbine m whirlwind; hurricane

turbol|ento turbulent; **~enza** f turbulence

turchese f turquoise

Turchia f Turkey

turchinetto m washerwoman's blue

turchino adj Turkish; m Turk

tùrgido turgid

tur|ismo m tourist business;

∼ista m, f tourist
turno m turn
turpe vile; indecent
tuta f overalls pl; **∼ d'allenamento** training overall
tut∣ela f guardianship; pol trusteeship; **∼ore** m guardian

tuttavia yet; nevertheless
tutt∣o all; whole; everything; **∼i, ∼e** everybody; **∼ il libro** the whole book; **innanzi ∼o** first of all; **∼i e tre** all three; **∼o** or **del ∼** wholly; entirely
tuttora still

U

ubbia f superstition; whim
ubbid∣iente obedient; **∼ienza** f obedience; **∼ire** v/t, v/i obey
ubriac∣arsi v/r get drunk; **∼o** drunk; tipsy; **∼one** m drunkard
uccell∣agione f fowling; **∼o** m bird; **∼o di rapina** bird of prey
uccidere v/t kill
udiamo we hear
udibile audible
ud∣ienza f audience; hearing; **∼ire** v/t hear; listen; **∼ito** m hearing; **∼itore** m hearer; **∼itorio** m audience
ufficiale adj official; m officer
ufficio m office; **∼ cambi** exchange office; **∼ doganale** customhouse; **∼ informazioni** information bureau; inquiry office; **∼ oggetti smarriti** lost-property office; **∼ postale** post office; **∼ di turismo** tourist office
ugu∣aglianza f equality; **∼agliare** v/t equalize; **∼ale**

equal; level
ùlcera f ulcer; **∼ gàstrica** gastric ulcer
uliva f = **oliva** f olive
ulteriore further; ulterior
ùltimo last; ultimate; **in ∼, da ∼** finally
ulul∣are v/i howl; **∼ato** m howling
uman∣ità f humanity; **∼o** human
Umbria f Umbria
umidità f humidity
ùmido damp; wet
ùmile humble
umili∣are v/t humiliate; **∼tà** f humility
umor∣e m humour; **∼ìstico** humorous
un, una a, before vowel an; **∼ànime** unanimous
uncin∣etto m crochet-hook; **lavorare all'∼etto** crochet; **∼o** m hook
ùngere v/t anoint; grease
Ungheria f Hungary
unghia f nail; claw
unguento m ointment; salve; **∼ per ferite** healing ointment; **∼ per le scotta-**

ture anti-burn ointment

ùnico unique

unicolore unicoloured

unifica|re v/t unify; **~zione** f unification

uniforme adj uniform; f uniform

unione f union; **~ire** v/t unite

unit|à f unity; **~o** united

univers|ale universal; **storia ~** f ale world history; **~ità** f university; **~o** m universe

uno m one; **a ~ a ~** one by one; **l'un l'altro** each other

unto adj greasy; m fat

unzione f ointment; **estrema ~** extreme unction

uomo m man

uovo m egg; **~ affogato** poached egg; **~ alla coque** soft boiled egg; **~ al tegame** fried egg; **~ sodo** hard boiled egg; **~ strapazzato** scrambled eggs pl

uragano m hurricane

uranio m uranium

urbano urban; civil

urètra f urethra

urgente urgent

url|are v/i howl; yell; **~o** m yell

urna f urn

urt|are v/t push; **~o** m collisione; push

us|àbile usable; **~anza** f custom; **~are** v/t use; v/i be used

usciamo we go out

usci|ere m usher; **~o** m door

usc|ire v/i go out; (book) come out; **~ita** f exit; **~ita di sicurezza** emergency exit; **~ito** gone out

usignuolo m nightingale

uso m use; custom; **in ~** in use; **avere l'~ di** be in the habit of; med **per ~ esterno** for external application

ustione f burn; scald

usuale usual

usufrutto m usufruct; **~uario** m usufructuary

usur|a f usury; **~aio** m usurer

usurp|are v/t usurp; **~azione** f usurpation

utensile m tool; implement

utente m user; tel subscriber

ùtero m womb; uterus

ùtile adj useful; **in tempo ~** at the right time; m profit; gain; **~ netto** net profit

util|ità f usefulness; **~izzare** v/t utilize; **~izzazione** f utilization

utopia f utopia

uva f grape; **~ secca** raisin; **~ spina** f gooseberry

V

va he goes

vacan|te vacant; **~za** f vacancy; **~ze** f/pl holidays pl

vacc|a f cow; **~hetta** f cowhide

vaccin|are v/t vaccinate; **~azione** f vaccination; **~azio-**

ne antivaiolosa vaccination against smallpox

vacillare v/i reel

vacuità f vacuity

vàcuo vacuous

vademecum m hand-book

vado I go

vagabond|are v/i rove; ~o m tramp

vagare v/i wander

vagina f sheath; vagina

vag|ire v/i wail; ~ito m whimper

vaglia f worth; ability; m money-order; cheque; ~ postale postal order

vagliare v/t sift; fig weigh

vaglio m sieve

vago vague

vagone m wagon; car; ~ letto sleeping-car; ~ ristorante dining-car

vainiglia f vanilla

vaiuolo m smallpox

valanga f avalanche

vale it is worth

val|ente able; clever; ~ere v/i be worth; be valid; ~ersi v/r avail o.s.; make use (di qc. of s.th.)

valeriana f valerian

valévole valid

valgo I am worth

valicare v/t pass; cross

vàlico m pass; passage; ~ alpino mountain pass

validità f validity; force

vàlido valid

valig|eria f shop for leather goods; ~ia f suit-case

vall|e f valley; ~igiano m dalesman; ~o m rampart;

wall

vallone m large valley

valor|e m value; courage; ~e dichiarato declared value; ~i m/pl securities pl; valuables pl; ~i postali stamps pl; ~izzare v/t utilize; ~izzazione f revaluation; ~oso brave

valso pp was worth

valut|a f value; currency; ~a nazionale national currency; ~are v/t value; ~azione f valuation

vàlvola f valve; (radio) tube; ~ di sicurezza safetyvalve

valzer m waltz

vampiro m vampire

vang|a f spade; ~are v/t dig

Vangelo m Gospel

vaniglia f vanilla

vano adj vain; useless; empty; m room

vantaggi|o m advantage; ~oso profitable

vantare v/t praise

vanto m pride; glory; boast

vapor|are v/i evaporate; ~azione f evaporation; ~e m steam; steamer; ~izzare v/t vaporize; spray; ~oso vaporous

varare v/t launch

varc|are v/t cross; ~o m passage; aprirsi il ~o push one's way through

vari|àbile variable; ~are v/t, v/i vary; change; ~ato varied; ~azione f variation

varice f varicose vein

varicella f chicken-pox

vari|egato variegated; ~età f

variety; **teatro m di ~età** music-hall; **~o** various; different; changeable; **~opinto** manycoloured

varo m launching

vasaio m potter

vasca f basin; tub; **~ da bagno** bath-tub

vascello m ship

vaselina f vaseline

vas|ellame m pottery; **~o** m pot; vase; vessel; **~o da fiori** flower-vase; **~o da notte** chamber-pot

vassoio m tray

vastità f vastness; immensity

vasto vast; huge

ve = vi (before **lo, la, li, le, ne**)

vecchi|aia, ~ezza f old age; **~o** adj old; m old man

vec|e: in ~ sua in his place; **fare le ~i di qu.** act as substitute for s.o.

vede he sees

vedere v/t see; **andare a ~ qu.** call on s.o.; **stare a ~** wait and see

vediamo we see; let us see

vedo I see

védova f widow

vedovile f widow's dower

védovo adj widowed; m widower

veduta f view; sight

veem|ente vehement; **~enza** f vehemence

veget|are v/i vegetate; **~ariano** m, adj vegetarian; **~azione** f vegetation

veglia f watch; wake

vegliare v/t watch over; v/i sit up

veglione m masked ball

veicolo m vehicle

vel|a f sail; **a gonfie ~e** with full sails set

vel|ame m naut sails pl; **~are** v/t veil; **~eggiare** v/i sail; **~eggiata** f sail(ing); **~eggiatore** m glider

veleno m poison; **~enoso** poisonous

velina: carta ~ tissue paper

velluto m velvet

velo m veil; gauze

veloce swift; rapid; **~ista** m, f sprinter

velocità f speed; **~ màssima** maximum speed; **merce f a grande ~** express goods pl

velòdromo m cycling-ground

veltro m greyhound

ven|a f vein; **~ale** mercenary; **~alità** f venality; **~ato** veined; **~atura** f veining

vend|émmia f vintage; **~emmiatore** m vintager

véndere v/t sell

vendetta f revenge

vendibile saleable

vendicare v/t avenge

vendicat|ivo revengeful; **~ore** m avenger

véndita f sale

vendit|ore m, **~rice** f seller

vener|ando venerable; **~are** v/t venerate; worship; **~atore** m worshipper; **~azione** f veneration

venerdì m Friday; **~ santo**

Good Friday

Vènere f Venus

Venezia f Venice

vengo I come

veniamo we come

venire v/i come; arrive; happen

ventaglio m fan

ventil|are v/t air; fan; **~ato**re m fan; **~azione** f ventilation

vento m wind; **~ di levante** east wind; **~ di ponente** west wind

véntola f (fire-)fan

ventoso windy

ventre m belly

vent|ura f luck; **~uro** next; future

venut|a f arrival; **~o** pp come; **ben ~o** welcome; m comer; **il primo ~o** the first comer

ver|ace truthful; **~acità** f truthfulness; **~amente** really; indeed

veranda f porch

verbale adj verbal; **~ m** or **processo ~** minutes pl

verbo m verb

verd|astro greenish; **~e** green; **~ chiaro** light green; **~eggiare** v/i grow green; **~erame** m verdigris

verd|ógnolo greenish; **~ura** f vegetables pl; greens pl

verg|a f rod; **~ato** striped

vergine, **verginale** adj virgin(al); **~e** f virgin

vergogn|a f shame; disgrace; **~arsi** v/r be ashamed; **~oso** ashamed;

disgraceful

veridico truthful

verifica f verification

verific|are v/t verify; check; **~arsi** v/r happen; come true

verità f truth

verme m worm; **~ solitario** tapeworm

vermicell|o m small worm; **~i** m/pl thin noodles pl

vermiglio vermilion

vermut m vermouth

vern|ice f varnish; polish; **scarpe** f/pl **di ~ice** patent-leather shoes; **~iciare** v/t varnish

vero adj true; real; m truth; **~simile** likely

verruca f wart

vers|amento m payment; **~are** v/t pour (out); spill; (money) deposit; **~ione** f version; translation; **~o** prep towards; about; m verse

vèrtebra f vertebra

vertebr|ale: **colonna** f **~ale** spinal column; **~ato** m vertebrate

verticale vertical

vèrtice m vertex; summit

vert|ìgine f vertigo; **ho le ~ìgini** f/pl I am feeling giddy; **~iginoso** giddy

verz|a f, **~otto** m green cabbage

vescica f bladder; blister

vescov|ado m bishopric; **~ile** episcopal

vèscovo m bishop

vespa f wasp; motor scooter

vest|aglia f dressing-gown; **~e** f dress; robe; **~iario** m garments pl

vestibolo m entrance-hall

vest|ire v/t dress; wear; **~ito** m dress; suit; **~ito da sera** evening dress

Vesuvio m Vesuvius

veterano m veteran

veterinario m veterinary

veto m veto

vetr|aio m glazier; **~ami** m/pl glassware; **~eria** f glass-works pl; **~erie** f/pl glassware; **~ina** f shopwindow; **~o** m glass; window

vetta f summit

vettovagli|are v/t supply; **~e** f/pl victuals pl

vett|ura f carriage; car; **rail in ~ura!** take your seats!; **~urino** m cabman; driver

vezzeggi|are v/t fondle; **~ativo** m pet-name

vezzoso charming

vi pron pers (to) you (pl); adv there; to it; at it

via f road; street; **~ Mazzini** Mazzini Street; adv away; **andar ~** go away; **e così ~** and so on

viadotto m viaduct

viaggi|are v/i travel; **~atore** m traveler; **~o** m journey; **~o aèreo** air travel; **~o d'affari** business trip; **~o in comitiva** conducted tour; **~o in màcchina** trip by car

vi|ale m avenue; **~avai** m coming and going

vibr|are v/i vibrate; **~azione** f vibration

vicecònsole m vice-consul

vicenda f vicissitude; event; **a ~** one another; in turn

viceversa vice versa

vicin|anza f vicinity; surroundings pl; **~ato** m neighbourhood; **~o** adj near; m neighbour

vicissitùdine f vicissitude

vicolo m lane; **~ cieco** blind alley

vidim|are v/t authenticate; visa; **~azione** f visé; visa

viene he comes

vie(p)più more and more

vietare v/t forbid

vigil|ante watchful; **~anza** f vigilance; **~are** v/t watch over; guard

vigile m policeman; **~ del fuoco** fireman

vigilia f eve; **~ di Natale** Christmas Eve

vign|a f vineyard; **~aiolo** m wine-grower; **~eto** m vineyard

vig|ore m vigor; force; **~oroso** vigorous; forceful

vile adj cowardly; vile; m coward

vill|a f country-house; **~aggio** m village; **~ano** rude; **~eggiante** m summer visitor; **~eggiatura** f healthresort

villino m cottage

viltà f lowness; cowardice

vimine m osier

vinaio m vintner

vincere v/t, v/i win; conquer

vincibile conquerable

vincita f winnings pl

vincitore m winner; victor

vincolo m bond; tie

vino m wine; ~ **bianco** white wine; ~ **caldo** mulled claret; ~ **dolce** sweet wine; ~ **rosso** red wine; ~ **secco** dry wine; ~ **da tàvola** table wine; ~ **di Xeres** Sherry

viola f mus viola; violet; ~ **del pensiero** pansy; **~cciocca** f wallflower

viol|are v/t violate; **~entare** v/t force; rape; **~ento** violent; **~enza** f violence

violetto a violet; **~o** violet

viol|inista m, f violinist; **~ino** m violin; fiddle

viòttola f foot-path

vìrgola f comma

virile manly; masculine

vir|tù f virtue; **~tuoso** virtuous

viscer|e f/pl, **~i** m/pl entrails pl; bowels pl

vischio m mistletoe

visciola f wild cherry

viscoso sticky

vis|ìbile visible; **~iera** f visor; **~ione** f vision

vìsita f visit; inspection; (med) examination

visit|are v/t visit; examine; inspect; **~atore** m visitor

viso m face

vista f sight; vision; view; **avere buona ~** have good sight; **a prima ~** at first sight; mus at sight; **pèrdere qu. di ~** lose sight of s.o.

visto pp seen; m visa; ~ **di entrata** entry visa; ~ **di trànsito** transit visa

vit|a f life; waist; **a ~** for life; **~ale** vital; **~amina** f vitamin

vite f screw; vine

vitello m calf; veal

viticultura f vine-growing

vìtreo glassy

vìttima f victim

vitto m food; board

vittori|a f victory; **~oso** victorious

viva! long live!

viv|ace lively; **~acità** f vivacity; **~anda** f food

vìv|ere v/i live; **~eri** m/pl victuals pl

vivo alive; lively

vizi|are v/t spoil; **~o** m vice; **~o cardìaco** cardiac defect; bad habit; **~oso** vicious

vizzo withered

vocabolario m dictionary

vocàbolo m word

vocale adj vocal; f vowel

voce f voice; fig rumour; **a viva ~** orally

vodka f vodka

voga f rowing; fashion; **èssere in ~** be in fashion

vog|are v/i row; **~atore** m rower

voglia f desire; **di buona ~** willingly

vogliamo we want

voglio I want

voi you (pl)

voll|ano m shuttlecock; **~ante** m (steering-)wheel; **squadra f ~ante** flying squad; **~àtili** m/pl poultry; fowls pl

volent|eroso willingly; **~ieri**

with pleasure

volere v/t want; wish; ~ **dire** mean (to say); ~ **bene a qu.** love s.o.; ~ m will

volgare vulgar; **lingua** f ~ vernacular

vòlgere v/t, v/i turn

volgo m populace; mob

volo m flight; ~ **diurno** day flight; ~ **notturno** night flight; ~ **sémplice** outward flight; ~ **andata e ritorno** outward and homeward flight

volontà f will; **a** ~ at will; at pleasure

volon|tario adj voluntary; m volunteer; **~tieri = volentieri**

volpe f fox

volta f turn; architecture: vault; time **a ~ di corriere** by return of mail; **questa ~** this time; **una ~ per sempre** once and for all; **una ~** once upon a time; **molte volte** many times; **alle volte** sometimes; **due volte tre** twice three; **tre volte cinque** three times five

voltaggio m elec voltage

volt|are v/t, v/i turn; **~ata** f turn; bend

volto m face

voltolare v/t roll

vol|ume m bulk; volume; **~uminoso** bulky

voluto wanted

volutt|à f voluptuousness; **~uoso** voluptuous

vomit|are v/t vomit; belch out; **~atorio** m vomitive

vòmito m vomiting

vòngola f gast mussel; clam; sallap

vorace voracious

vorà|gine f gulf; gorge

vòrtice m vortex; whirl (-pool)

vostro your

votare v/t, v/i consecrate; vote

vot|azione f voting; **~o** m vow; pol vote

vulc|ànico volcanic; **~anizzare** v/t vulcanize; **~ano** m volcano

vuole he wants

vuot|are v/t empty; **~o** adj empty; blank; m emptiness; vacuum

Z

zabaione m hot egg-punch with Marsala wine

zafferano m saffron

zaffiro m sapphire

zaffo m stopper; bung

zàino m knapsack

zampa f paw; claw

zampogna f bagpipe

zampone m pork knuckle

zàngola f churn

zanzar|a f mosquito; **~iera** f mosquito-net

zapp|a f hoe; **~are** v/t hoe; till

zàttera f raft

zavorra f ballast

zebra f zebra

zecca f mint; zo tick

zell|ante zealous; ⸰o m zeal

zènzero m ginger

zepp|a f wedge; ⸰are v/t cram in; ⸰o crammed; **pieno** ⸰o chock-full

zerbino m scraper

zero m zero; nought; cipher

zia f aunt

zibíbbo m raisin

zigzag m zig zag

zimb|ellare v/t decoy; ⸰ello m decoy-bird; fig laughing-stock

zinc|are v/t zinc; ⸰o m zinc

zíngaro m gipsy

zio m uncle

zirlare v/i chirp

zit(t)ella f spinster; f old maid

zitto silent; **sta** ⸰! keep quiet!

zoccol|aio m clog-maker; ⸰ante m Franciscan friar

zòccolo m wooden shoe; clog

zolf|anello m sulphur match; ⸰are v/t sulphur; ⸰atara f sulphur-mine; ⸰ino m match; ⸰o m sulphur

zolla f clod

zona f zone; belt

zoo|logia f zoology; ⸰lògico zoological

zopp|icare v/i limp; ⸰o lame

zòtico boorish

zoticone m boor

zucca f pumpkin; fig pate

zucchèr|iera f sugar-basin; ⸰ino sugary

zùcchero m sugar

zufolare v/i whistle

zùfolo m whistle

zuppa f soup; ⸰ **di fagioli** bean-soup; ⸰ **alla marinara** fish-soup; ⸰ **di verdura** vegetable soup

zuppiera f soup-tureen

Lista dei verbi irregolari inglesi

Irregular English Verbs

abide (*dimorare*) – abode* – abode*

arise (*sorgere*) – arose – arisen

awake (*svegliare*) – awoke – awoke

be (*essere*) – was – been

bear (*portare; sopportare; partorire*) – bore – portato: borne – partorito: born

beat (*battere*) – beat – beaten

become (*divenire*) – became – become

begin (*cominciare*) – began – begun

bend (*curvare*) – bent – bent

bet (*scommettere*) – bet* – bet*

bid (*ordinare*) – bade – bidden

bind (*legare*) – bound – bound

bite (*mordere*) – bit – bitten

bleed (*sanguinare*) – bled – bled

blow (*soffiare*) – blew – blown

break (*rompere*) – broke – broken

breed (*generare, allevare*) – bred – bred

bring (*portare*) – brought – brought

build (*costruire*) – built – built

burn (*bruciare*) – burnt* – burnt*

burst (*scoppiare*) – burst – burst

buy (*comprare*) – bought – bought

cast (*gettare*) – cast – cast

catch (*acchiappare*) – caught – caught

choose (*scegliere*) – chose – chosen

cling (*aderire a*) – clung – clung

come (*venire*) – came – come

cost (*costare*) – cost – cost

creep (*strisciare*) – crept – crept

cut (*tagliare*) – cut – cut

deal (*trattare*) – dealt – dealt

dig (*vangare*) – dug – dug

do (*fare*) – did – done

draw (*tirare; disegnare*) – drew – drawn

dream (*sognare*) – dreamt* – dreamt*

drink (*bere*) – drank – drunk

drive (*guidare*) – drove –

driven

dwell (*dimorare*) – dwelt – dwelt

eat (*mangiare*) – ate – eaten

fall (*cadere*) – fell – fallen

feed (*imboccare*) – fed – fed

feel (*sentire*) – felt – felt

fight (*combattere*) – fought – fought

find (*trovare*) – found – found

flee (*fuggire*) – fled – fled

fly (*volare*) – flew – flown

forbid (*vietare*) – forbade – forbidden

forget (*dimenticare*) – forgot – forgotten

forgive (*perdonare*) – forgave – forgiven

forsake (*abbandonare*) – forsook – forsaken

freeze (*gelare*) – froze – frozen

get (*ottenere*) – got – got, *Am* gotten

gild (*dorare*) – gilt – gilt

give (*dare*) – gave – given

go (*andare*) – went – gone

grind (*macinare*) – ground – ground

grow (*crescere*) – grew – grown

hang (*pendere*) – hung – hung

have (*avere*) – had – had

hear (*udire*) – heard – heard

heave (*sollevare*) – hove* – hove*

hide (*nascondere*) – hid – hidden

hit (*colpire nel segno*) – hit – hit

hold (*tenere*) – held – held

hurt (*far male*) – hurt – hurt

keep (*mantenere*) – kept – kept

kneel (*inginocchiarsi*) – knelt* – knelt*

knit (*fare a maglia*) – knit* – knit*

know (*conoscere; sapere*) – knew – known

lay (*porre; stendere*) – laid – laid

lead (*condurre*) – led – led

learn (*imparare*) – learnt* – learnt*

leave (*lasciare*) – left – left

lend (*prestare*) – lent – lent

let (*lasciare*) – let – let

lie (*giacere*) – lay – lain

light (*accendere*) – lit* – lit*

loose (*perdere*) – lost – lost

make (*fare*) – made – made

mean (*significare*) – meant – meant

meet (*incontrare*) – met – met

mow (*falciare*) – mowed – mown*

pay (*pagare*) – paid – paid

put (*mettere*) – put – put

read (*leggere*) – read – read

rid (*liberare*) – rid* – rid

ride (*cavalcare*) – rode – ridden

ring (*suonare*) – rang – rung

rise (*alzarsi*) – rose – risen

run (*correre*) – ran – run

saw (*segare*) – sawed – sawn*

say (*dire*) – said – said

see (*vedere*) – saw – seen

seek (*cercare*) – sought – sought

sell (*vendere*) – sold – sold

send (*mandare*) – sent – sent

set (*porre*) – set – set

sew (*cucire*) – sewed – sewn*

shake (*scuotere*) – shook – shaken

shave (*far la barba*) – shaved – shaven*

shear (*tosare*) – sheared – shorn

shed (*spargere*) – shed – shed

shine (*splendere*) – shone – shone

shoot (*sparare*) – shot – shot

show (*mostrare*) – showed – shown

shred (*tagliuzzare*) – shred* – shred*

shrink (*restringersi*) – shrank – shrunk

shut (*chiudere*) – shut – shut

sing (*cantare*) – sang – sung

sink (*affondare*) – sank – sunk

sit (*sedere*) – sat – sat

slay (*ammazzare*) – slew – slain

sleep (*dormire*) – slept – slept

slide (*scivolare*) – slid – slid

sling (*lanciare*) – slung – slung

slit (*tagliare*) – slit – slit

smell (*odorare*) – smelt* – smelt*

sow (*seminare*) – sowed – sown

speak (*parlare*) – spoke – spoken

speed (*sfrecciare*) – sped* – sped

spell (*compitare*) – spelt* – spelt*

spend (*spendere*) – spent – spent

spill (*rovesciare*) – spilt* – spilt*

spin (*girare*) – spun, span – spun

spit (*sputare*) – spat – spat

split (*spaccare*) – split – split

spoil (*guastare*) – spoilt* – spoilt*

spread (*spargere*) – spread – spread

spring (*balzare*) – sprang – sprung

stand (*stare*) – stood – stood

steal (*rubare*) – stole – stolen

stick (*appiccicare*) – stuck – stuck

sting (*pungere*) – stung – stung

stink (*puzzare*) – stank, stunk – stunk

strew (*cospargere*) – strewed – strewn*

stride (*andare a passi grandi*) – strode – stridden

strike (*percuotere*) – struck, stricken

string (*infilare*) – strung – strung

strive (*sforzarsi*) – strove – striven

swear (*giurare; bestemmiare*) – swore – sworn

sweat (*sudare*) – sweat* – sweat*

sweep (*spazzare*) – swept – swept

swell (*gonfiare*) – swelled – swollen

swim (*nuotare*) – swam – swum

swing (*dondolare*) – swang –

swung

take (*prendere*) – took – taken

teach (*insegnare*) – taught – taught

tear (*strappare*) – tore – torn

tell (*dire*) – told – told

think (*pensare*) – thought – thought

thrive (*prosperare*) – throve* – thriven*

throw (*gettare*) – threw – thrown

thrust (*cacciare*) – thrust – thrust

tread (*camminare*) – trod – trodden

wake (*svegliare*) – woke* – woke(n)*

wear (*indossare*) – wore – worn

weave (*tessere*) – wove – woven

weep (*piangere*) – wept – wept

wet (*bagnare*) – wet – wet

win (*vincere*) – won – won

wind (*girare*) – wound – wound

wring (*torcere*) – wrung – wrung

write (*scrivere*) – wrote – written

* oppure forma regolare

Numerals

Numerali

Cardinal Numbers – Numerali Cardinali

0 zero *naught, zero, cipher*	28 ventotto *twenty-eight*
1 uno; una, *one*	29 ventinove *twenty-nine*
2 due *two*	30 trenta *thirty*
3 tre *three*	40 quaranta *forty*
4 quattro *four*	50 cinquanta *fifty*
5 cinque *five*	60 sessanta *sixty*
6 sei *six*	70 settanta *seventy*
7 sette *seven*	80 ottanta *eighty*
8 otto *eight*	90 novanta *ninety*
9 nove *nine*	100 cento *a* opp *one hundred*
10 dieci *ten*	200 duecento *two hundred*
11 undici *eleven*	300 trecento *three hundred*
12 dodici *twelve*	400 quattrocento *four hundred*
13 tredici *thirteen*	
14 quattordici *fourteen*	500 cinquecento *five hundred*
15 quindici *fifteen*	
16 sedici *sixteen*	1000 mille *a* opp *one thousand*
17 diciassette *seventeen*	
18 diciotto *eighteen*	1001 mille uno *a* opp *one thousand and one*
19 diciannove *nineteen*	
20 venti *twenty*	1002 mille due *a* opp *one thousand and two*
21 ventuno *twenty-one*	
22 ventidue *twenty-two*	2000 duemila *two thousand*
23 ventitré *twenty-three*	10000 diecimila *ten thousand*
24 ventiquattro *twenty-four*	100000 centomila *a* opp *one hundred thousand*
25 venticinque *twenty-five*	
26 ventisei *twenty-six*	1000000 un milione *a* opp *one million*
27 ventisette *twenty-seven*	

Ordinal Numbers – Numerali Ordinali

1º il primo, la prima *1st, the first*

2º il secondo, la seconda *2nd, the second*

3º il terzo, ecc *3rd, the third*

4º il quarto, ecc *4th, the fourth*

5º il quinto *5th, the fifth*

6º il sesto *6th, the sixth*

7º il settimo *7th, the seventh*

8º l'ottavo *8th, the eight*

9º il nono *9th, the ninth*

10º il decimo *10th, the tenth*

11º l'undicesimo[1] *11th, the eleventh*

12º il dodicesimo[2] *12th, the twelfth*

13º il tredicesimo[3] *13th, the thirteenth*

14º il quattordicesimo[4] *14th, the fourteenth*

15º il quindicesimo[5] *15th, the fifteenth*

16º il sedicesimo[6] *16th, the sixteenth*

17º il diciassettesimo[7] *17th, the seventeenth*

18º il diciottesimo[8] *18th, the eighteenth*

19º il diciannovesimo[9] *19th, nineteenth*

20º il ventesimo *20th, the twentieth*

21º il ventunesimo[10] *21st, the twenty-first*

22º il ventiduesimo[11] *22nd, the twenty-second*

23º il ventitreesimo[12] *23rd, the twenty-third*

24º il ventiquattresimo[13] *24th, the twenty-fourth*

25º il venticinquesimo[14] *25th, the twenty-fifth*

26º il ventiseesimo[15] *26th, the twenty-sixth*

27º il ventisettesimo[16] *27th, twenty-seventh*

28º il ventottesimo[17] *28th, the twenty-eight*

29º il ventinovesimo[18] *29th, the twenty-ninth*

30º il trentesimo *30th, the thirtieth*

40º il quarantesimo *40th, the fortieth*

50º il cinquantesimo *50th, the fiftieth*

60º il sessantesimo *60th, the sixtieth*

70º il settantesimo *70th, the seventieth*

---

opp [1]undecimo, decimo primo, [2]decimosecondo, [3]decimoterzo, [4]decimoquarto, [5]decimoquinto, [6]decimosesto, [7]decimosettimo, [8]decimoottavo, [9]decimonono, [10]ventesimo primo, [11]ventesimo secondo, [12]ventesimo terzo, [13]ventesimo quarto, [14]ventesimo quinto, [15]ventesimo sesto, [16]ventesimo settimo, [17]ventesimo ottavo, [18]ventesimo nono.

80°	l'ottantesimo *80th, the eightieth*
90°	il novantesimo *90th, the ninetieth*
100°	il centesimo *100th, the (one) hundredth*
200°	il du(e)centesimo *200th, the two hundredth*
300°	il trecentesimo *300th, the three hundredth*
400°	il quattrocentesimo *400th, the four hundredth*
500°	il cinquecentesimo *500th, the five hundredth*
1000°	il millesimo *1000th, the one thousandth*
1001°	il millesimo primo *1001st, the one thousand and first*
1002°	il millesimo secondo *1002nd, the one thousand and second*
2000°	il duemillesimo *2000th, the two thousandth*
10000°	il diecimillesimo *10000th, the ten thousandth*
penultimo	*last but one*
ultimo	*last*
ultimissimo	*very last*

Fractions and other numerals
Frazioni ed altri numerali

$^1/_2$ (un) mezzo *(one) half*
$^1/_3$ un terzo *one third*
$^1/_4$ un quarto *one fourth*
$^2/_3$ due terzi *two thirds*
$^3/_4$ tre quarti *three fourths*
$^4/_5$ quattro quinti *four fifths*
mezzo miglio *half a mile*
un quarto d'ora *a quarter of an hour*
tre quarti di libbra *three quarters of a pound*
$2 \times 3 = 6$ due per tre uguale sei *twice three are six*
$3 \times 4 = 12$ tre per quattro uguale dodici *three times four are twelve*
$7 + 8 = 15$ sette più otto uguale quindici *seven and eight are fifteen*
$10 - 3 = 7$ dieci meno tre uguale sette *ten less three are seven*
$20 : 5 = 4$ venti diviso cinque uguale quattro *twenty divided by five make four*

Phrases
Frasi

Enquiring one's way – Indicazioni di strada

È questa la strada giusta per ...?	Is this the right way to ...?
Sì è sbagliato.	You are going the wrong way.
Lei va bene.	You are going the right way.
Qual'è la strada per ...?	Which is the way to ...?
È ... distante da qui?	Is ... far from here?
Quanto tempo occorre per ...?	How long will it take to get to ...?
Sempre diritto fino a ...	Straight on as far as ...
Gira a sinistra (a destra).	Turn left (right).
Giri all'angolo.	Go round the corner.
La prima strada a sinistra.	The first street to the left.
In fondo alla strada.	At the end of the street.
Ho smarrito la via.	I have lost my way.

The motorcar – L'automobile

Tenere la destra (la sinistra).	Keep to the right (left).
Rallentare nelle curve.	Slow down in the curves.
Sorpassare a sinistra.	Overtake on the left.
Veicoli al passo (d'uomo).	Vehicles at a slow pace.
Andare adagio (più adagio).	Drive slowly (more slowly).
Con la massima velocità.	At top speed.
Moderare la velocità.	Lessen your speed.
Proseguire diritto.	Go straight ahead.
Dare la precedenza.	Give way.
Vada avanti (indietro).	Drive forward (backward).
Che velocità è ammessa?	What is the speed limit here?
Dall'altra parte.	On the other side.
Ci vogliono circa 8 minuti.	It takes about 8 minutes.
Quanto dista? È vicino.	How far is it? It is quite near.
Dov'è il più vicino garage?	Where is the nearest garage?

Un'officina di riparazioni.	A repair shop.
Venga con me, prego.	Please come with me.
C'è una locanda qui vicino?	Is there an inn near here?

Lodgings – Alloggio

Ha camere da affittare?	Have you any rooms to let?
Per il giorno? Per la notte?	For the day? For the night?
Ne ho parecchie; eccone una.	There are several. This is one of them.
Quali altre camere ha?	What other rooms have you?
Quanto chiede per questa?	What do you charge for this one?
Mi sembra troppo caro.	That seems rather dear.
Mi deciderò in seguito.	I will decide afterwards.
Dov'è il gabinetto?	Where is the W.C.?
Dov'è la cabina telefonica?	Where is the call box?

Railway – Ferrovia

A che ora arriva il treno?	When does the train arrive?
A che ora parte il treno?	When does the train leave?
Il treno è in ritardo.	The train is late.
Il treno è in orario.	The train is on time.
Il treno sta per partire.	The train is about to leave.
Faccia presto! Quale treno?	Be quick! Which train?
Biglietto semplice.	Single ticket.
Andata e ritorno.	Return ticket.
Prima (seconda) classe.	First (second) class.
La biglietteria è chiusa.	The booking office is closed.
La biglietteria apre alle ...	The booking office opens at ...
Si cambia treno per ...	Change trains for ...
Dov'è il deposito bagagli?	Where is the left luggage office?
Mi procuri un facchino?	Will you get me a porter?
Porti il mio bagaglio:	Take my luggage:
alla stazione (all'albergo).	to the station (hotel).
al deposito (al piroscafo).	to the left luggage office (steamer).
a questo indirizzo.	to this address.
Ha spiccioli?	Have you got any change?
Ritiri il bagaglio dal deposito; ecco lo scontrino.	Fetch my luggage from the left luggage office; here's the ticket.

Telegraph – Telegrafo

Quanto si paga per un telegramma di ... parole?	What does a message of ... words cost?
Si pagano ... per ogni parola.	You pay ... for every word.
Ecco il vostro denaro.	Here is your money.
Posso avere la ricevuta?	May I have a receipt?

Mail – Posta

È arrivata la posta?	Has the postman been yet?
Ci sono lettere per me?	Are there any letters for me?
Imposti questa lettera.	Post this letter for me.
Posso vedere la Sua carta d'identità?	May I see your identity card?
Mi favorisca Suo passaporto.	Show me your passport, please.
Ecco per farmi riconoscere.	This proves my identity.
Riempisca questo modulo.	Please fill in this form.
Alcune cartoline illustrate.	Some picture postcards.
Quanto costa una lettera per ...?	How much is a letter to ...?

Restaurant – Ristorante

Cameriere, la carta?	Waiter, the menu.
Birra scura (chiara).	Dark (light) beer.
Acqua minerale.	Mineral water.
La carne ben cotta.	Well-done meat.
La carne poco cotta.	Underdone meat.
Cameriere, il conto!	Waiter, the bill!
È compreso il servizio?	Is the service included?